W9-AQU-447

KENNIKAT PRESS SCHOLARLY REPRINTS

Dr. Ralph Adams Brown, Senior Editor

Series in
AMERICAN HISTORY AND CULTURE
IN THE NINETEENTH CENTURY

Under the General Editorial Supervision of
Dr. Martin L. Fausold
Professor of History, State University of New York

For Mrs Frothingham from
With the kindest regards

Edward Everett.

EDWARD EVERETT

Orator and Statesman

BY

PAUL REVERE FROTHINGHAM

KENNIKAT PRESS
Port Washington, N. Y./London

Wingate College Library

EDWARD EVERETT

First published in 1925
Reissued in 1971 by Kennikat Press
Library of Congress Catalog Card No: 76-137910
ISBN 0-8046-1478-4

Manufactured by Taylor Publishing Company   Dallas, Texas

KENNIKAT SERIES ON AMERICAN HISTORY AND
CULTURE IN THE NINETEENTH CENTURY

TO
CHARLOTTE EVERETT HOPKINS
A GRANDDAUGHTER OF
EDWARD EVERETT
LOYAL TO HIS MEMORY, JEALOUS FOR HIS FAME
BY CONSTANT PUBLIC SERVICE
CARRYING ON HIS TEACHINGS
AND THE HIGH EXAMPLE
OF HIS LIFE

075441

Themistocles said that a man's discourse was like to a rich Persian carpet, the beautiful figures and patterns of which can be shown only by spreading and extending it out; when it is contracted and folded up, they are obscured and lost.

PLUTARCH

PREFACE

THE Life of Edward Everett never has been written. About three years after his death his two surviving sons, H. Sidney Everett and William Everett, published a fourth and final volume of the 'Orations and Speeches.' In the preface to that posthumous volume they made this statement: 'The republication of other writings of Mr. Everett's, and a memoir of his life, are in contemplation.'

This promise never was fulfilled. The private papers, letters, and journal all passed into the possession of William Everett, who apparently made one or two beginnings on a Life, but never carried the undertaking far. With all his brilliant mental gifts William Everett lacked the precious quality of perseverance. Year by year, therefore, as he became absorbed in other lines of work, he postponed the filial task, until at length all reference to the subject caused him pain.

Dr. Andrew P. Peabody wrote as late as 1888, 'The public still awaits, with an impatience diminishing as the years roll on, the Memoir of Mr. Everett which his sons undoubtedly will furnish, it is to be hoped, before the desire for it dies away.' Whether that desire can be rekindled, after all these years, remains to be seen. But at least it has seemed worth attempting. John Bright said of himself when some one referred to a possible biography, 'My life is in my speeches.' But as the younger Trevelyan remarked in his admirable Life of that great orator, 'After two generations have gone by not even the greatest speeches can be widely read or completely understood except by the help of historical comment.'

The same might be said of Edward Everett. He died sixty years ago, and the younger generations hardly know of his existence. But he was a great American, and one of the greatest of all American orators. He achieved distinction in many lines, and his brilliant career deserves to be rescued from oblivion. If the present volume does no more than redirect attention to his 'Orations and Speeches,' it will at least accomplish something. It is perhaps too much to hope that it will do tardy justice to the memory of a great and brilliant man.

Mr. Everett was not as voluminous a diarist as John Wesley, but for forty years he kept a journal which is not without many passages of interest. It is almost wholly lacking, however, in the spice of careless gossip and malicious references to people and events. Such passages of the kind as here and there occur, have been passed over by the author partly on general principles, but also in order to keep faith with the diarist himself. For Mr. Everett prefaced nearly every volume of his journal with this explicit note, copying it off year after year with meticulous precision before beginning the record of another twelvemonth:

I have kept this journal since 1825, partly for the convenience and utility of having a record of many of the things contained in it, and partly for the amusement of my old age should I live to be old. I have at all times foreborne to set down much of that which would be most curious, in order not to run the risk, in the event of any undesigned publicity, of injuring the feelings of others; altho' I fear this rule has not been so strictly observed as it might have been. It is my intention if my life is spared, to revise it and omit much of the insignificant detail which it now contains and every thing of which any person could have a right to complain. Should I die before this is done, I earnestly entreat those into whose hands any portion of it may fall, to make none but a prudent and sparing use of it. It is altogether unfit for publication in its present state, and the greater part of what is not positively unfit for the public eye, would be at best wholly uninteresting.

I have endeavored faithfully to heed this warning, although it has to be confessed that temptations to err upon the side of indiscretion have been neither numerous nor great. Whether in life or in death it was a cardinal principle with Mr. Everett not to wound other people's feelings. He was above all else a Christian gentleman whose charity never failed, and with whom courtesy reigned supreme.

March, 1925   P. R. F.

CONTENTS

I. BACKGROUND AND BEGINNING   1

II. PEGASUS IN THE PULPIT   19

III. WANDER YEARS   36

IV. THE GREEK PROFESSOR   61

V. APOLLO IN POLITICS   93

VI. GOVERNOR OF MASSACHUSETTS   127

VII. PORT AFTER STORMY SEAS   157

VIII. AT THE COURT OF SAINT JAMES'   188

IX. A DIPLOMAT IN LONDON   220

X. PRESIDENT OF HARVARD   265

XI. AN INTERLUDE   302

XII. SECRETARY OF STATE AND SENATOR   329

XIII. THE ORATOR   373

XIV. WITH THE GOD OF BATTLES   414

INDEX   473

EDWARD EVERETT

I

BACKGROUND AND BEGINNING

E DWARD EVERETT wrote in a fragment of autobiography: 'I am proud of my descent, my forefathers were very humble men and devoted themselves to a most unambitious career. They left nothing to their descendants either of fame, or fortune, but a good name.' The progenitor of the family in America was a certain Richard Everett, or Everad, as the name was sometimes written, who reached these shores in young manhood as early as 1634, or 1635. The precise date of his arrival has never been discovered, nor even the part of England that he came from, although it is thought that the Everetts were a Wiltshire family. He seems to have wandered around in a rather aimless fashion for a time, settling temporarily in Watertown, and receiving somewhat later a grant of land in Springfield, or Agawam, as it was then called. After his marriage, however, which occurred in 1642, Richard Everett established himself in Dedham, Massachusetts. There his children were born, and there his descendants continued to live, being farmers for the most part, or mechanics. None of them apparently acquired wealth, nor became in any way distinguished. It may be that Edward had in mind the history of the Everett family when he wrote as a young man in some Phi Beta Kappa verses:

'Our thriftiest man but crowns a life of pains
With decent harvest of his moderate gains,
Then to his numerous sons divides his store,
And thus their life begins as his before.'

Certain it is, at least, that the sons in the Everett family were numerous, and the gains but few. 'John Everett, in the next generation to Richard, served with the rank of Captain in the colonial wars. . . . In 1684 he was one of the four commissioners who received a confirmatory grant of the town of Dedham from the grandson of Chickatawbut, of whom it was originally purchased.' The family homestead stood in what was known as South Dedham. Edward Everett looked it up in 1863 and described it in his journal as 'an old wooden house, apparently never painted: no large trees near it: a well of the old construction at one corner: no surrounding fence.'

Such was the place where Oliver Everett, the father of Edward, was born. He was the youngest of nine children, of whom eight were sons. As was still the case two centuries ago in most New England families, they all had Bible names except one, and his — Oliver — stood in the next degree of veneration as that of the great Protector. He was born on the 11th of June, 1752. Of his childhood and youth scarce any traditions remain. The humble circumstances of Ebenezer Everett forbade his giving more than one son what was called a 'public,' that is, a college education. This privilege generally fell to the son, if there was one, who, on account of a slender constitution and feeble health, seemed least qualified for the rude labors of a New England farm. 'The narrow-chested, hectic Benjamin of the domestic flock was usually selected to enjoy the dangerous boon of a sedentary life and pulmonary exertion.' This privilege devolved upon Moses, who was the youngest but one of the sons. Oliver was apprenticed to his older brother Aaron to learn the trade of a carpenter. He also, however, was of a slender constitution. The odor of pitch in the pine boards affected him disagreeably, and he early determined to get, if possible, a college education as soon as he became of age, and to prepare himself for a professional career. Almost the only anecdote preserved of his early years relates to his love of music. He contrived somehow to earn money enough to buy a violin. It must have been a poor one, and no doubt the tones that he drew from it were not altogether harmonious, and far from a delight to the

Dedham household. But it was not this alone that aroused the wrath of Ebenezer Everett. The old man distrusted music of all kinds, sharing in this respect the general prejudice of his generation; and of all musical instruments the violin was looked upon as a particular abomination. One day, therefore, when Oliver came back from the carpenter's bench he found that his violin had been consigned to the flames.

But the youth's desire for an education could not be disposed of thus easily. Being deprived of his violin, he bent with greater eagerness above his scanty supply of books. He was aided in his studies by his older brother Moses, who was by this time a settled minister in Dorchester. His face was set toward Harvard, and in 1775 he was admitted to the freshman class. He was twenty-four years of age — older by five years than his famous son was to be at graduation — and he was probably the oldest member of his class.

So far as we know he gained no distinction in the college course. Indeed, distinction, or anything else, must have been difficult to give as well as to gain at just that period; for the college buildings were occupied by the Revolutionary army, and the college itself was closed for a time. The library was moved to Andover; the pupils were transferred to Concord, where they were most uncomfortable and much dissatisfied. Confusion still continued, even after the college proper was reopened, and in 1779, when Oliver Everett received his Bachelor's Degree, there were no Commencement Exercises.

To the man, however, now twenty-eight, and older for the struggle he had made, this must have mattered little. The main thing was that his desired end was reached. He had gained admission to the ranks of 'educated men,' and he was ready now to carve for himself a career with other tools than those of saw and hammer, plane and chisel. After studying Divinity for a space of about two years — his teacher still being his older brother Moses — he received a 'call' to the New South Church in Boston, which was situated at that

time on Church Green, at the corner of Bedford and Summer
Streets. It was a post of honor and distinction, calling for a
man of training and ability; and the Reverend Oliver Everett
met these requirements, giving entire satisfaction to the parish, and making a marked position for himself in the community. He belonged to the liberal wing of the Congregational
body, and was a close and particular friend of Dr. James
Freeman, of King's Chapel, who carried his congregation
over to Unitarianism in 1787. As a preacher Oliver Everett
was 'serious and practical, unadorned in matter and unim-
passioned in manner'; in which respects, as we shall later see,
his famous son was most unlike him. He had marked metaphysical acumen, and it was said of him by the Reverend
Mr. Bradford, of the Boston Association, that 'if the talents
of all the Boston ministers were put together in a crucible and
reduced to one they would not equal Oliver Everett's.'

But his career, which began so well, and grew in usefulness
and power, was soon cut short. Ill-health beset him. He
never had been strong, and after ten years in the ministry he
resigned his charge, and the church reluctantly 'dismissed'
him in 1792. In the meantime he had married, his wife being
Lucy Hill, a daughter of Alexander Hill, of Boston. Three
children already had been born, and, with a growing family to
provide for, Oliver Everett removed to Dorchester, where he
bought a large colonial house at the 'Five Corners,' which had
been built a score of years before by a Royalist of some distinction, Colonel Robert Oliver. In this house, which stood
on what now is known as Edward Everett Square, and which
was destroyed about a hundred years later to make room for
'improvements,' Edward Everett was born on April 11, 1794.
He was the fourth child in a family of eight, six of them being
sons and only two of them daughters, Edward himself coming
in between the two girls. They followed one another at regular and somewhat rapid intervals, the youngest being born
nearly seven months after the father's death, which occurred
in 1802. Oliver Everett had been ceaselessly besieged by

somewhat uncertain health, and he seems to have grown no stronger in the country air of Dorchester. He was not a man weakly to succumb, however, and after retiring from the pulpit he was made a Judge of the Court of Common Pleas. It was an indication of his prominence and public activity, also, that after removing to Dorchester he was nominated for Congress by the Federal Party, and that he was suggested for the Presidency of Bowdoin College. One of his last public appearances of importance was in the Dorchester Church on February 22, 1800, when he gave the oration at a meeting held in memory of Washington. It was an occasion of mourning, the great man having died but two months previous, and the pulpit was hung with black. In lieu of a fee, it is related that when the hangings were taken down the orator was 'complimented with a suit of clothes from them.' Oliver Everett went about, therefore, for the last two years of his life clothed, as it were, in the mantle of his own eloquence. He died of paralysis on December 19, 1802, in the fifty-seventh year of his age. The date was indelibly stamped upon the memory of Edward, then a boy of eight. Perhaps it was because of a certain similarity of taste and talent between the two that Edward Everett in his maturer years never was so busy, nor so burdened with cares that he let the anniversary of his father's death occur without a reference to it in his diary; and the reference was generally a lament. He could say that the first event in life that he clearly remembered was being called to his father's knee and told to repeat the Lord's Prayer. The following entry is typical:

Dec. 19: 1850: Forty-eight years ago this day since the decease of my father. He was fifty-six years old the 11th of June preceding. I have but a general recollection of his appearance and of a few of his habits. Nothing could well be imagined in greater contrast with my own, although my father was a man of literary tastes. But his means were quite frugal. His books, perhaps one hundred and fifty in number, were in a book case, resting upon a desk with drawers underneath, which stood in the room which was at once parlor, dining-room, nursery, and for him to some extent dressing-room;

for in the drawers was kept the linen of the male members of the family. He had no study, and when he was employed in writing the Eulogy on Washington in 1800, he passed his time in his bedchamber, where I also slept in a trundle-bed. Here he shut himself up with Sheridan's Dictionary in two quarto volumes, the only English dictionary in his possession. On one occasion, after I had been put to bed, I was made uneasy by the faint crackling of the embers, which had been raked up under the ashes. I alarmed the family once or twice; and the third time received a decided intimation that no fourth alarm would be tolerated. This Eulogy was the only composition of my father's ever published.

Lucy Hill Everett, the mother, was only thirty-four when left a widow with a large and growing family to support. The oldest, named after his father, was fourteen, and the youngest was yet to be born. Edward, as we have seen, was nearly nine, and he had made rapid progress on the road of letters where he was destined to achieve such marked distinction. He had begun his schooling at the early age of three, being taken by his sister to the village school. In the bit of autobiography, already referred to, he recorded the event as follows:

When I first went to a village school — I remember it as yesterday — I seem still to hold, by one hand, for protection (I was of the valiant age of three years) to an older sister's apron: with the other I grasped my primer, a volume of about two and a half inches in length, which formed then the sum total of my library, and which had lost the blue paper cover from one corner — my first misfortune in life. It was the practice then, as we were trudging along to school, to draw up by the road-side if a traveller, a stranger, or a person in years passed along, and 'make our manners,' as it was called. The little girls curtsied; the boy made a bow. It was not done with much grace, I suppose — but there was a civility and decency about it which did the children good, and produced a pleasing impression on those who witnessed it.

Soon after her husband's death, Mrs. Everett broke up the Dorchester home and moved with her family back to Boston. She wished to be near her grandfather, the only parent she had ever known, Mr. Alexander Hill, a Boston merchant of the day, and a man of no small worth as well as wealth. With this object in view she took a house at the North End of the city on what was known as Procter's Lane. The eldest brother by that time had been placed in a counting-room, and the second son, Alexander, had entered Harvard at the early age of twelve and one half years.

On arriving in Boston, Edward was placed in the reading and writing schools in North Bennett Street — the former kept by Mr. Ezekiel Little, the latter by old Master Tilestone.

According to the system which then prevailed in the Boston schools, Reading and grammar were taught on one floor by one master, and writing and arithmetic on another floor by another master — the two sexes attending in each room alternately.

Mr. Little was a giant in stature and stout in proportion. More than thirty years after this time he assured Governor Everett by way of compliment, that he had always been 'an accommodating boy.' The same, however, hardly could be said of Mr. Little as a teacher. He had the most objectionable habit of 'mingling pleasantry with the infliction of punishment.' He had, with his pen-knife, rounded off the edges of his ferule — a heavy box-wood implement — on one side; the other face was carved with a kind of herring-bone figure. When a boy was called to receive punishment, he was asked whether he would have a biscuit or gingerbread. If he elected 'biscuit,' he was struck with the rounded edge; if gingerbread, with the other. And in either case the dolorous tone in which the word was generally pronounced raised a laugh in the school.

Master Tilestone was not much better, and had outgrown his usefulness by this time, being deaf and nearly blind, and was very irascible. The distinctest thing remembered of him was that he had a misshapen right hand which was unfitted for almost every purpose except writing. Fortunately the fingers were so fixed that a pen could just be slipped in between them and held firm. But the misfortune was also turned to another use. The fingers of the hand were very hard and callous, and if a boy brought up a copy-book blotted, or ill-written, Master Tilestone would strike him 'a kind of pouncing blow with his bony fingers which, without causing pain to himself, acted upon the culprit like the beak of a gamecock.'

At the annual exhibition in 1804, Edward took a Franklin Medal for reading, and we find him studying Latin out of school hours with Mr. Little. The next step would normally have been to the Public Latin School. That famous institution, however, was just then 'disorganized under Master Hunt,' and the boy was sent for a time to a private school in Short Street, that was kept by Ezekiel Webster. His stay there was a brief one, but it was memorable on one account. Ezekiel Webster was taken ill, and sought the temporary assistance of a younger brother who had recently completed his law studies. Into the little schoolroom, therefore, where young Everett sat, there strode one day a youth with heavy brows, dark hair, and deep black eyes. As he took his place at the master's desk, he must have made a profound impression on the lads before him, for Daniel Webster even then was a person to attract attention.

Thus began a friendship for young Everett which lasted nearly half a century, and left its mark upon the literature and politics of America. Three months before his death, Webster's mind went back to those early days and he wrote to his lifelong friend and former pupil these words of touching reminiscence: 'We now and then see, stretching across the heavens, a long streak of clear, blue, cerulean sky, without cloud, or mist, or haze, and such appears to me our acquaintance, from the time when I heard you for a week recite your lessons in the little schoolhouse on Short Street to the date hereof.'

There in the Webster School we may almost say that Everett's career began. Then and there at least he established one of the deepest influences of his life, and from that time on he was to give an account of himself in little ways that widened slowly into large ones! In 1805, when eleven years old, we find him in the Latin school where he took another Franklin Medal and delivered an English oration of his own composition. Indeed, it is interesting to discover that he belonged at this time to a society for declamation which met at the different boys' houses, and where 'pieces' were regularly spoken. If his own memory is to be trusted, however, and his judgment on the matter taken, he 'was among the poorest speakers and made little or no improvement' at this time. Moreover, he added in his fragment of autobiography: 'Neither did I derive any advantage from the exercises in speaking which were had once a week at School. I wanted courage to make the first essay at improvement: and as our Master did not possess the art of speaking well himself, he could not impart it to others.'

Whether for this reason, or for others, the Latin School did not content him. Even at this early age we begin to see some signs of a restless eagerness for change of scene and occupation which in later years was strongly marked. It would have been natural, especially for one so young, to proceed to Harvard, when the time came, through the customary doorway of the Latin School. But his older brother Alexander had just graduated from Harvard, and was serving as assistant instructor at the Phillips Academy at Exeter, New Hampshire. The boy persuaded his mother, therefore, to send him to Exeter, and he made the journey alone in the month of February by stage-coach. The trip was nothing, however, with a dearly loved brother at the other end, and for a short two terms of three months each the brothers were together in the Academy — the one as teacher, the other as pupil. And the pupil as usual gave a good account of himself, being greatly inspired no doubt by Alexander's brilliant presence. [1] Although a new boy, when it came to the closing exhibition he had the honor of delivering a Valedictory Latin Address of his own composition. He was thirteen years old, and in August, 1807, he joined the freshman class at Harvard.

Everett was the youngest member in a class which num-

[1] Alexander Hill Everett graduated from Harvard in 1806, the youngest member of the class and with highest honors.

bered forty-nine. Among his classmates were Samuel Gilman, destined to sing his way along the college generations as the author of 'Fair Harvard'; Nathaniel Langdon Frothingham, a lifelong friend, and with whom, by his marriage, he was later to become allied; and John White Webster who was destined to awful notoriety and a tragic fate. Other familiar names that appear on the college rolls with his were John Chipman Gray, Edward Reynolds, and Harrison Gray Otis. The college itself — or the University, as even then it was proudly called — was a somewhat small affair. Its total enrolment fell short of two hundred. Massachusetts, Hollis, and Stoughton Halls were the only dormitories. Holworthy was not built until two years after his graduation, the money for it being raised by means of a public lottery. In Massachusetts Hall the hooks were still to be seen 'from which had swung the hammocks of Burgoyne's famous red-coats.'[1] The centre of the college life was Harvard Hall. 'There the Professors met the pupils; there the pupils met each other; and there was the library.'[2] Everett, at a later time, described the Yard as it became impressed upon his freshman mind. He said: 'A low, unpainted board fence ran along the South of Massachusetts, and East of Hollis and Stoughton, at a distance of two or three rods, forming an enclosure of the shabbiest kind. The college wood-yard was advantageously posted on the site of University Hall, and farther to the Northeast stretched an indefinite extent of wild pasture and whortleberry swamp, the depths of which were seldom penetrated by the most adventurous freshman.'[3] Those were the days when 'Boston was not yet a city, and Cambridge was still a country village, with its own habits and traditions, not yet feeling too strongly the force of suburban gravitation.'[4] A single stage-coach supplied sufficient facilities of transportation between the two places. It ran through Cambridgeport which 'was then (in the native dialect) a huckleberry

[1] Lowell: *Works*, 1, 56.   [2] O. B. Frothingham: *Boston Unitarianism*, p. 20.
[3] A. S. Pier: *The Story of Harvard*, p. 110.   [4] Lowell: *Works*, 1, 53.

pasture,' and so bare of houses and trees that one could see
Beacon Hill from the upper windows of the college buildings.
The President of the college, when this lad of thirteen
entered, was Samuel Webber. In Everett's junior year, however, Dr. Webber died, and a successor was chosen who was
destined to have no little influence upon the youth's career.
The Reverend John T. Kirkland was elected President in
1810, and Dr. Kirkland up to that time had been minister of
the New South Church in Boston where he had succeeded
Everett's father. The attention of the new President would
naturally have been drawn to so good a scholar and so industrious a student as young Everett had already proved himself; but here was an added tie, and a cause for special interest, which soon began to show itself. The Hollis Professor of
Divinity, another of his teachers most likely to exert an influence, was the Reverend Henry Ware. He had been appointed in 1805 because of his liberal, or Unitarian tendencies,
and in the teeth of somewhat bitter opposition. Perhaps for
this reason his ministrations in the college chapel were freely
criticised and commented upon with some disfavor. It was
said among other things that he had a carefully arranged
series of sermons, one for each Sunday in the college year.
These he preached over and over in rotation with a four-year
interval between — the result being that no student heard
any sermon twice, and none missed any in the repertory. But
youths are proverbially irreverent, and college rumor may
have been the sole and insufficient basis for the accuracy of
such a tale. The Reverend Henry Ware, at any rate, was a
man of forceful intellect, and he exercised considerable influence in directing students toward the ministry.

Of young Everett's college life but little now is known, and
not much can be discovered. He roomed with Charles P.
Curtis, a classmate, during the freshman year. They lived in
a wooden building standing on the corner of Main and Church
Streets. It was officially known as 'College House,' but the
students called it 'Wiswall's Den,' or just 'The Den' for

short. It was a poor place at the best, and according to tradition it had been the scene of an ugly domestic tragedy, and was haunted by the ghosts of the Wiswalls. The room of Curtis and Everett was a small one, about fourteen feet square, containing two beds under which they kept the fuel, which was wood. The furnishing was of the scantiest. There was no carpet nor window curtains; no sofa nor easy-chair. The students in those days lived in 'commons,' the four classes coming together daily for their meals in the Commons Hall, where the tutors and other parietal officers occupied an upper table.

The practice of permitting students from Boston and the neighborhood to pass Sunday at home had not yet been introduced. The only weekly holiday was on Saturday after the morning recitation. On Saturdays, therefore, when the roads were passable, young Everett used to walk to Boston carrying home the week's soiled clothes in a bundle, and bringing back the parcel of clean clothes in the evening. There were no express wagons in those days, and the single stage, which made but two trips daily, was generally crowded.

In 1808, upon entering his sophomore year, Everett moved into the Yard, and shared Hollis 20 with a freshman, Joseph S. Hixon, who had been an intimate school friend. He kept diligently at work, avoided temptation, and with the excellent example of his brother Alexander to guide him he took high rank among the best scholars of the class. There was no branch in which he stood preëminent, unless perhaps metaphysics. But he was an all-round scholar — good at everything. He said of himself in later years, 'Story, a brother of Mr. Justice Story, excelled me in Greek, but he neglected everything else; Fuller, Gray, and Hunt were my superiors in mathematics, but made no pretensions to general scholarship. Gilman was a more practised writer than I, and Frothingham greatly excelled me in speaking, and was in everything an accomplished scholar. If I had any strong point, it was that of neglecting no branch and doing about equally well in all.'

He had a particular fondness, however, for metaphysics, and it was in connection with the study of Locke's 'Essay on the Human Understanding' that he gave one of the earliest evidences of remarkable memory.

We recited from it [he says] three times a day, the four first days of the week, the recitation of Thursday afternoon being a review of the rest. We were expected to give the substance of the author's remarks: but were at liberty to condense them and to use our own words. . . . I had at that time a memory which recoiled from nothing, and I soon found that the shortest process was to learn the text by heart nearly verbatim. I recollect particularly on one occasion of the review on Thursday afternoon that I was called upon to recite early and I went on repeating word for word, and paragraph after paragraph, and finally, not being stopped by our pleased tutor, page after page, till I finally went through in that way the greater part of the eleven recitations of the week.

Another trait that displayed itself in college was that of editorial ability. In connection with a handful of his classmates, among them being John C. Gray with whom he roomed in his junior year, he started a literary venture. It was called the 'Harvard Lyceum,' and he assumed the post of editor and contributor in chief. It was published twice a month, but died of inanition and general neglect before the year was out. As the burden was heavy, the editors were not unduly downcast when their efforts failed. They gathered strength, however, to fire a well-directed shot at the proverbial spirit of Harvard indifference as the little vessel, with the freight of so much promise, sank beneath the waves of college life. 'The legacy,' they wrote in the final issue, 'which we leave to our college posterity is our advice that they enjoy all those exquisite pleasures which literary seclusion affords, but that they do not strive to communicate them to others.'

In the meantime, as if college studies and editorial duties were not enough to occupy his active brain, the lad must try his hand at teaching. For the winter vacation, which lasted ten weeks, he went to East Bridgewater and imparted of his store of learning in a country school. It was a mixed class of

Wingate College Library

boys and girls that he had to handle, many of them older than himself; and he confessed in after years that the experiment was not much of a success. We can easily imagine that the bright-cheeked boy with auburn hair must often have felt his cheeks grow redder and distinctly hot when he sought to discipline his pretty and engaging country pupils.

Thus the weeks and years sped by till graduation came. Commencement at the college then as now was a day of great importance. Friends and family came out from Boston and the exercises were held in the First Parish Church. The local newspapers gave an account of the proceedings on that August day in 1811, from which it appears that the Valedictory English Oration was delivered by Edward Everett, while among other features on the programme was an oration by N. L. Frothingham, 'On the Cultivation of the Taste and Imagination.' These two young men, moreover, divided the poetical honors of the day between them. Frothingham wrote a hymn for the occasion which was set to the tune of 'Ye Mariners of England.' Everett in his turn composed a song which was sung by the class to the time of 'Adams and Liberty.' The first stanza was as follows:

> 'Ye offspring of Science who quit these loved walls
> To launch on the world where your sires have preceded,
> March fearlessly on where your destiny calls —
> By no perils dismayed, by no labours imperilled,
>   By your country stand fast
>   Till the danger be past,
> And the moment of Slavery — may that be your last:
> For the sons of old Harvard their rights shall maintain,
> While its strength nerves an arm, or the blood swells a vein.'

Everett, as we have seen, was the youngest member of the class, and he graduated with the highest honors. He was now a Bachelor of Arts at the age of seventeen, and the question was, What next? It was evident enough that he had talents in a great abundance. Among them was that greatest talent of all — capacity for hard work — and he seems to have hesitated for a time as to how and where those talents best might be employed. His eärliest inclination was for the law, and perhaps, had he been permitted to follow his natural inclination, the law would have been selected. But such freedom was not his. Persuasion and well-meant pressure were exerted. His father had been a minister, and his father's successor in the pulpit was now, as we have seen, the President of the college. Dr. Kirkland, therefore, as a matter of course, advised the ministry. To the President's advice was added the strong appeal of the brilliant, gifted, and famous Buckminster who was known as the 'Chrysostom of America' and was generally reputed to be 'the best read and most accomplished theological scholar in the country.' The Everett family, for some years past, had been parishioners of Dr. Buckminster at the Brattle Street Church. The minister kept his eye on the brilliant young member of his flock. He had him come to his house each week. They talked things over, and the manifest success and influence of the gifted pulpit orator did not tend to fasten the youth's attention on the least attractive side of the ministerial profession. Moreover, Dr. Buckminster had recently been appointed the first lecturer on the new Dexter Foundation in the Divinity course at Cambridge. Altogether, the claims were irresistible, even if the choice had not been natural. Everett decided to continue at the college as a resident graduate and study for the ministry. President Kirkland at that time was unmarried, and the young man went to live at his house. His studies were for the most part theological. But his interest in general literature and history was keen. He was busy also with his pen. Like most young men of literary gifts he tried his hand at verse. He was successful and promising enough in this direction to be chosen one year after graduation as Poet of the Phi Beta Kappa. At the age of eighteen, therefore, he came before the public with some rather elaborate and carefully prepared verses which were read at the annual meeting of the Harvard Chapter on August 27, 1812. The poem which he recited before the scholars of that day was naturally not

of much account, although the newspapers commended it
in the highest terms. It was entitled 'American Poets,' and
the young author thought well enough of it to send an autograph copy printed on heavy paper with wide margins to the
Boston Athenæum. The theme of the youthful bard was a
lament for the lack of poets in America. He pursues his point
through many stanzas, seeking out the causes why New
England failed of being 'a nest of singing birds.'

. . . .

> 'Since too the simple strain of earlier lays
> Has lost its charm for these degenerate days,
> Our plain Republicks, with their homely modes
> Yield to the dizened muse no fit abodes.'

Courts and Kings, apparently, with their rewards of rank
and titles, were necessary for the nurture of poets: but in
America —

> 'No stars, but what on heaven's fair breast you see,
> No garters sacred to a knighted knee,
> Where ribbons mark the fashion, not the rank
> And e'en our nation's chief is Mister — blank.'

The young orator, moreover, had a telling fling in verse at
the ugliness of American life and its dominant commercial
note, while he deplored the absence of ivy-mantled turrets,
with only towers for trade to take their place. The following
is not bad, and must at least have called out from his hearers
vociferous applause.

> 'And if the poet seek throughout our land
> Where our famed turrets, towers and castles stand,
> Show him each brick-kiln pile, whose aspect meets
> The admiring gaze, in Boston's pompous streets.
> To Faneuil's dome! Where freedom's infant days
> Learned the first notes of liberty to raise:
>
> . . . .
>
> To the fond traveller's eager notice show
> The hall above, the market-house below.
> *There* came our Sires to feed the patriot hearts
> And *here* they came to feed a different part.
> From each to each, at proper times they move,
> And bought their meat below, and gave their vote above.'

Withal, however, the youth was not despondent. There was inspiration and to spare in American scenery and life for those who had the eyes to see and the hearts to understand. The time would come, he felt, when a new and noble race of singers would arise, finding their theme in the Nation's fight for liberty and a setting in the majesty of familiar mountains and the Great Lakes.

> 'Yet do our native scenes some themes display
> Which oft have filled, and yet shall fill a lay:
> Yes! he shall touch the lyre with feeling hand
> Who loves, how rude soe'r, his native land.
> And sees kind Nature round its borders throw
> All boons that man can love, or heaven bestow.
>
> . . . .
>
> Here all the gifts of valley, plain, and hill,
> Of mighty stream, calm lake and fertile rill.
>
> . . . .
>
> Like leaves the laureats of July appear,
> And the Phi Beta makes a bard a year.
>
> ———————
>
> 'But yet, in soberer mood, the time shall rise
> When bards will spring beneath our native skies;
> Then Homer's arms shall ring in Bunker's shock,
> And Virgil's wanderer land on Plymouth Rock,
>
> . . . .
>
> Fitz James's horn Niagara's echoes wake,
> And Katrine's lady skim o'er Erie's Lake.'

This Phi Beta Poem has deserved some mention for it marked the beginning of Everett's career in the world of letters. Moreover, we detect through the youthful lines a throb of intense patriotism which is a quality we shall see declaring itself continually throughout his long and brilliant career. He might wander, as he often did, in European lands, and drink deep of the inspiration which the older civilization of the world could give; but this note of excessive patriotism, which some people criticised as overstrained, was characteristic of him to the last.

The poetic instinct burned on fitfully for many years. Nearly thirty years after this early effort we shall find him writing verses which he thought worthy of putting into print even at the height of his success. His strength, however, lay along other lines, and few people now remember that his verses, not his orations, first found their way into American schoolbooks. Soon after the Phi Beta Kappa occasion he received an appointment at the college as Latin tutor. The duties were light, as his pupils were confined to the freshman class, and his studies in theology were eagerly pursued. Continuing to live as a member of the President's household, he took the degree of Master of Arts at Commencement in the summer of 1813. The day was described as 'uncommonly pleasant,' and, in the newspaper language of the time 'a large and respectable auditory was early assembled to witness the exhibition of the children of our Alma Mater.' Among those taking the Master's degree only two had parts. Everett spoke 'an English oration,' his subject — a prophetic one, and not suggestive of a ministerial career — being 'On the Restoration of Greece,' while his friend Frothingham delivered a 'Valedictory in Latin.' The excellence of the whole occasion was commented on most favorably at the time. Invidious particularization was deprecated; but the oration by Everett was said to have 'impressed a numerous audience with the talents and profound learning of the candidate.' [1]

Thus with an appeal for the restoration of Greece on his lips young Everett left the classic shades of Harvard to enter the profession of the Christian ministry.

[1] *Columbian Centinel.* At this same Commencement James Walker took his A.B. Degree and had an oration on 'Decision of Character' — a quality for which he became so marked in later years. William Hickling Prescott read a Latin poem.

II

PEGASUS IN THE PULPIT

IN 1813 the Christian ministry was still at its height in New England. It was the calling preëminently of scholars — the 'chosen profession.' It offered a splendid field for earnest, active, consecrated men of literary tastes and high ideals. It was honored in the community and adorned by men of culture and influence. In the words of Lowell: 'The New England clergy were still an establishment and an aristocracy, and when office was almost always for life and often hereditary.' It left ample leisure for study and literary pursuits. It supplied one with a wide and intelligent hearing. There was at that time no social problem in the country to absorb a minister's time, nor to claim his constant attention. The 'institutional' church was unknown. The community contained no poor people — at least, none in sufficient numbers to constitute a problem. Parish activities were few, and organizations, whether for fighting vice, or diminishing intemperance, or establishing social justice, were unknown. The minister was preëminently a preacher. The sermon was supreme.

Moreover, the doctrinal tests at just that time were not severe. The Liberal Movement was well upon its way, although the unfortunate breach which later came in the ranks of Congregationalism had not yet taken place. When Everett came forward to begin his life-work, Channing was already firmly established, with his liberal influence visibly spreading. He had been preaching for eight years in the church in Federal Street, where large and eager congregations hung upon his words and were thrilled by his rapt devotion and ethereal presence.

It was natural, therefore, even without the pressure and persuasion which came from Buckminster and Kirkland, that Everett should have chosen as he did, seeing in the pulpit a

sphere of influence which fitted well his powers and inclination. We behold him, then, at the age of nineteen equipped
and ready to begin his career as a minister of Christ. Brilliant, handsome, eloquent — the son of a Boston minister
whose faithful service was well remembered, he was certain
to be sought by several churches, and his only problem would
be one of elimination. But even this was spared him. For a
door was dramatically and suddenly opened to admit him to
a sphere of splendid opportunity. The brilliant Buckminster,
the idolized minister of the church in Brattle Square where
the Everett family were worshippers, suddenly died. He
was only twenty-eight. The fatal disease was epilepsy. The
mourning was universal. His parishioners were left desolate.
The loss occurred in June of 1812. Everett in his Phi Beta
Kappa Poem had paid a tribute to his friend and pastor in
the following lines:

> 'But Heaven's dread hand has quenched each generous flame —
> The beam of friendship and the light of fame.
> Faith yields the Priest, with sorrow and complaint,
> And weeping virtue envies heaven the saint.
> Farewell, thou blest! too dark thy lot appears;
> Yet faith looks up, though sight is dim with tears.
> Serve thine own Master through the eternal hours,
> In nearer presence and with nobler powers.'

The people at Brattle Square were too stunned at first to
think of a successor. Then it was decided to wait. The eyes
of the parish were probably fixed on Everett from the first.
He was one of themselves, and shared their grief. No sooner,
therefore, was his course at Cambridge finished than he was
asked to 'supply' the pulpit for a series of Sundays. The
period of 'supply' being ended, he was next invited to preach
'four Sabbaths on probation.' At the close of this second
period the Pew Proprietors were called together and after
due deliberation took action as follows:

At a meeting of the Society of the Church in Brattle Square
Nov. 28th, 1813 — by adjournment —
Mr. Edward Everett having compleated the term for which he

was requested to preach to the Society on probation and having exhibited satisfactory proofs of his talents learning and piety and other ministerial endowments: — the Society being likewise impressed with the belief that his settlement with us as a Gospel Teacher would promote the happiness of this Church and would serve the interests of our holy religion — therefore

Voted — that Mr. Edward Everett be invited to settle with us as the Pastor of this Church — that the Standing Committee be requested to communicate to him this Vote and to cause his answer, when received, to be made known to the Society.

Voted — That on his settlement with the Society we will provide and keep in repair a house for his residence — will procure and have sawed and housed the wood he may want and will pay him Twenty-five dollars a week as his salary.

Voted — That Mr. Everett be requested to supply the Pulpit until he shall give his answer

Attest. —

RD. SULLIVAN *Clerk*

A copy of this vote was entrusted to the Honorable Samuel Dexter and Joseph Hall, Esq. — two of the leading members of the Society — who took it out to Cambridge and delivered it to young Everett in person.

That was on November 28th. There followed a period of waiting, and doubtless of suspense. The young man evidently hesitated; and there was every reason why he should. It was not so much a matter of his youth. To be sure he was only nineteen at the time; but his predecessor had been settled at the age of twenty-one, and Channing was only twenty-three when he was ordained at Federal Street. It was the custom in those days for churches to settle men in their youth — and keep them. The great obstacle which loomed up in young Everett's eyes was probably the size and standing of the church. Channing had declined a call to Brattle Square in 1803, pleading his lack of physical strength, and adding in his letter, 'Do not the very circumstances of your influence and numbers attach high responsibility to the office of your minister, and render experience, improved talents and insight of character peculiarly necessary?'[1] Everett must have

[1] *Life of Channing*, p. 91.

been aware that he lacked all the qualities that Channing named. He declared in later years that 'nothing but the blind indiscretion of youth could excuse the undertaking of such a task.' For the church was unquestionably the largest and most fashionable in Boston at the time; and that meant the most critical and exacting. The élite of old Boston occupied the pews, among them being the Otises, the Derbys, Hammonds, Russells, Lawrences, Amorys, Palfreys, Ticknors, Salisburys, Wainwrights, Langdons, Minots, and Boylstons.

The building itself, though not beautiful, was imposing and possessed of a certain dignity. It was box-like in proportions, square and plain, and must have been capable of seating at least one thousand people. It was constructed of brick, and wore a coat of dull brown paint. But it had historical associations.

During the Revolutionary War, when Boston was held by the British troops, services were discontinued. The church was occupied October 27, 1775, as barracks for the British soldiery. The night before the evacuation of Boston the building was struck by a cannon ball, which fell to the ground after knocking out a few bricks. The ball was carefully preserved, and somewhat later, when the church was undergoing repairs, it was inserted in the spot where it struck. From that time on until it was taken down, the church, in the words of Oliver Wendell Holmes —

'Wore on its bosom, as a bride might do,
The iron breastpin that the British threw.'

In every sense, therefore, it was a marked church. John Adams spoke of it as having the 'politest congregation in Boston.' Its ministers had been men of eminence. All this was enough to make the heart of youth stand still, except that youth is always bold and calmly dares the utmost.

But there was another and still greater reason for hesitation. Everett had already formed the desire to continue his education in Europe. This thought and hope had been awakened in him by Mr. Buckminster himself. He was disposed, therefore, to make it a condition of accepting the invitation to Brattle Square that he should be allowed to spend a year or two abroad. Messrs. Dexter and Hall, however, advised against such a stipulation. They expressed at the same time the confident opinion that after a reasonable length of service there would be no difficulty in effecting the much desired object. This was vague enough as a promise, and hardly a safe suggestion on which to build much hope; but probably it had some influence. None the less the young man weighed the matter for a month, drawing back instinctively when on the point of yielding his consent. His letter of acceptance was not dated till the day before Christmas, and then it read as follows:

CAMBRIDGE, *Decr 24th*, 1813

To the Society in Brattle Square.

My Christian Friends, — Having made the call to be your Pastor the subject of my most serious deliberations and prayers, I now signify to you my acceptance of it. I am encouraged to this decision, less by a reliance on my own strength, than on your kindness and candor and the hope, I feel, that in all my duties and trials, I shall be supported by your councils and prayers. Deeply as I am affected with the experience I have had of your indulgence and especially with this last mark of your confidence, I will not profess to look forward to the arduous office to which you have called me without a deep anxiety. I regard with great diffidence of myself the various and extensive duties, which it devolves upon me, and the solemn responsibility with which I must discharge them. And when I recall the illustrious gifts and graces of him in whose place I am called to stand, I am oppressed with the sense of my weakness. Yet I know that your indulgence which has brought me to this station, will not desert me there, and I humbly trust that the good providence of God will not first fail me, at the season when I need it most. While I rest therefore in him, for the grace which is sufficient for me, suffer me to look to you for that liberal reception of my services, and that generous interpretation of my conduct, on which all the outward comfort and happiness of my life depend.

The happy circumstances under which you have given me this invitation, have not been lost upon my gratitude. I have felt and shall feel it my duty to preserve by every effort, that Christian unity of which you have made so grateful an exercise and it is my heart's desire to God, that the connexion which has thus commenced in harmony, may be continued in the unity of the Spirit in the bond of peace; and that God would bless this connexion to the promotion of Christian Truth, and make it subservient to our common and eternal good, is the fervent and humble prayer of your faithful

And Affectionate Servant
And Friend
EDWARD EVERETT

The ordination and installation took place on February 9, 1814. The public exercises were preceded, as was usual in those days, by a meeting of an ecclesiastical council. It was necessary, in Congregational fashion, to pass upon the theological fitness of the candidate, and this meeting was far from peaceful. Debate was warm. The theological storm was brewing which in a few years' time was destined to divide the Congregational body into Unitarian and Trinitarian believers. Brattle Square was a leader on the liberal side. Some of the more conservative ministers at the council desired a profession of faith from the candidate. The suggestion was resisted, and it was finally moved to 'proceed to Ordination upon the candidate professing his belief in the (commonly called) Apostles' creed.' The motion was carried unanimously. Two of the visiting ministers, however — Dr. Holmes, of Cambridge, and the Reverend Mr. Huntington, of the Old South Church — refrained from voting, and one of the visiting deacons withdrew in disgust.[1] No further inconvenience was experienced, however, and the meeting adjourned to the church where the public service was held. Dr. Lathrop, of the Second Church, offered the opening prayer, and the prayer of ordination was by Dr. Osgood. Dr. Kirkland, the President of the college, who had stood so close to the young man and befriended him in many ways, preached the sermon.

Then began the brief but brilliant ministry of Edward

[1] *Records of the Church in Brattle Square*, p. 58.

Everett. He threw himself into the work with extraordinary ardor. He left nothing to chance, but prepared himself for the pulpit with the greatest care, committing his sermons to memory. The result was that the church, which had been crowded by people who listened to the golden eloquence of Buckminster, was now thronged by those who found delight in the greater and more vivid eloquence of his successor. He gave full rein to a 'florid and affluent fancy.' It is recorded [1] of him that he abounded 'in splendid allusions, in quotations impossible to forget, in daring imagery, in parable, and even in a sort of defying experiment of his own wit and skill in giving an oracular weight to Hebrew or Rabbinical words: — feats which no man could better accomplish, such was his self-command and the security of his manner. All his speech was music, and with such variety and invention that the ear was never tired.' Hardly more than a boy himself, he exercised an extraordinary power over young men and boys. To one youth, destined afterwards to greatness, Everett became a demigod in these pulpit days. Ralph Waldo Emerson was a student at the time in the public Latin School. He was at the most impressionable age, and the young minister at Brattle Square became his hero. He and his brother Edward 'used to go on Sunday and peep into the church where their favorite was expected to preach, to make sure that he was in the pulpit.' [2] He made notes of the preacher's impressive passages, and learned by heart certain of his striking sayings. It was an era of rhetoric when schoolboys caught at brilliant figures of speech and 'went into ecstasies over a happy turn of expression.' Writing much later of this pulpit period in his hero's life, Emerson could record that 'he who was heard with such throbbing hearts and sparkling eyes in the lighted and crowded churches, did not let go his hearers when the church was dismissed, but the bright image of that eloquent form followed the boy home to his bed-chamber.' [3]

[1] O. B. Frothingham: *Recollections and Impressions.*
[2] Cabot: *A Memoir of Ralph Waldo Emerson*, I, 62, note I.
[3] Emerson's *Works*, x, 315.

The young preacher was evidently in great demand. It
was natural that he should be wanted at Exeter, New Hampshire, where he had been a student at the Academy so short
a time before. Thither he went, therefore, for a Sunday in
April, 1814, entrancing old and young by the power of his
speech. In the morning he apparently touched the deep
emotions of his hearers, and dealt with the pathetic side of
life; but at the service in the afternoon he turned his magic
instrument around and touching the iron string of the heroic
led his hearers 'as one man on a crusade.'

It is interesting to find, however, that even at this time
there were those who criticised and were conscious of a certain aloofness and lack of deep reality in the speaker's whole
performance. Young Henry Ware, Jr., who was just then a
teacher at the Academy, wrote his father enthusiastically of
Everett's eloquent performance; but he felt bound to add
that all did not agree with him, and he quoted a friend 'as
complaining that Everett spoke like some superior intelligence, discoursing to mortals of what they ought to feel and
know, but as if [he] himself were too far exalted to require
such feelings, or such knowledge himself.'[1] Others spoke of
him as 'too rich for common use'; by which I take it was
meant that his very wealth of rhetoric and the ornateness of
his speech kept him from being practical enough to take hold
of the deep and hard realities of daily life. Such a tendency
is natural with youthful prophets. Not having lived, they
must learn from books; and what they have not felt, they
imagine with excessive fervor! Add to this the scholar's
temperament and a somewhat cold and stately bearing, and
we can hardly wonder that he seemed to speak like 'some
superior intelligence.'

It is exceedingly difficult to frame a definite picture of
Everett at this time in his career, or to get a clear understanding of the nature of his hold on people. Some idea,

---

[1] *Life of Henry Ware, Jr.*, by his brother, John Ware, p. 72. I have assumed that
the reference here is to Everett. He is spoken of as 'E.'

however, of his pulpit methods, as well, indeed, as the style
and models of his oratory, may perhaps be gained from the
sermon which he preached at the funeral of the Reverend
John L. Abbot, pastor of the First Church. The sermon was
published by request, and it is the only sermon belonging to
the time of his active ministry which passed into print. It
was delivered on October 14, 1814, and bears upon the title-
page a motto from Cicero's Orations. The motto was well
chosen: for the whole discourse was thoroughly Ciceronian,
and betrays the model which the youthful orator kept before
his mind. After dealing with the events of Mr. Abbot's life,
we find the preacher addressing the mourners thus:

Friends, brethren, Christians, why have you assembled in this
house of mourning? Is it to witness unaffected these funeral rites,
to gaze without emotion on these lifeless remains, to spend a barren
hour in useless observations, and to depart with a cold, unsanctified
heart? . . . Canst thou not, my brother [addressing the deceased],
approach nearer this sacred place! Must thou rest in that dark and
narrow house: art thou going to a darker, narrower yet! Hast thou
not a word, a look to give; no truth, no warning to impart!

'Hark! from the tombs a doleful sound.' Sons of the earth, he
calls to you: daughters of pleasure, he calls to you: slaves of the
world, he calls to you! Awful eloquence, persuasion of the grave!
Shut not your hearts, your consciences to the sound. Redeem a
transient feeling to the welfare of your souls.

Friends, Christians, all is not lost! Death, indeed, has gained
another victim to his dominion, and reduced another frame to its
original dust. Death has conquered a mortal body, but heaven has
gained an immortal soul. While these walls are resounding with
the accents of grief, another voice has joined the chorus of angelick
praises! Christians, why grieve at this happy change? Mourners,
why weep at this blessed consummation? Farewell, dear brother,
thy Saviour calls. . . . Already thou hast past the portals of death;
already thou hast mounted on seraph's wings; already thou hast
caught the vision of God! Ages of happiness are bursting on thy
soul! Thy march of Eternity has begun!

The taste of those days was not that of these. A wholly
different standard of oratory prevailed, and much was admired then which would now be put aside as artificial and

exaggerated. But even making such allowances, one can hardly believe that flights of rhetoric and borrowed methods such as these did not strike many listeners as a trifle strained, to say the least. The youth who could indulge in such extravagance had much to learn in regard to the power of restraint, and the dignity of simple, unaffected speech. It did not come at once, and was only acquired with difficulty. His besetting sin was magniloquence. He fought against it to the very end. Six years later in the Capitol at Washington, after one of the last and greatest sermons that he ever preached, and when all were praising his eloquence and rhetoric, Henry Clay could complain of him as 'too theatrical.'

But Everett did not confine himself to preaching. At this busy, overcrowded period, when he had two sermons nearly every Sunday to prepare, and many parish calls to make, together with all the ordinary demands upon his time and strength which the ministry implies, he found it possible to produce and publish a volume of nearly five hundred pages entitled 'A Defence of Christianity.' The circumstances which led up to the achievement are significant and interesting. They give evidence of Everett's zeal, and of his prodigious power for hard work. A certain George Bethune English, a Harvard graduate of 1807, had written a book entitled 'The Grounds of Christianity Examined.' The book was published in 1813, and it attracted widespread and excited attention, not only for the reason that the 'grounds' were found to be unstable, but because the author was a minister who had only lately, after studying law, obtained a license to preach from the Boston Association of Ministers. Not making much of a success in the pulpit, however, and leaving the profession, he published, partly perhaps in pique, an attack upon the Christian claims. As the author was supposed to be a person of 'profound Biblical knowledge,' the book created a furor and awakened a kind of consternation. Henry Ware, Jr., wrote to his father, from Exeter, on October 20, 1813:

You seem not to have heard of the *book* which engages all the attention here at present: — Mr. English's apology for leaving his profession. You will have heard of it, however, before you receive this — for it will pass like wild-fire through the country; and like that, too, it will flash, and crackle, and sparkle, and dazzle, and amaze for a moment, and then go out, or be put out, and all will be as quiet as before: and as soon as the first meteoric effect is over, our eyes will recover themselves, and we shall see things as clearly, and in the same light, as if nothing had taken place.[1]

There was one young man, however, who was not so sure that the fire, after spreading and flashing and sparkling, would 'go out,' and he determined that if it lay in his power it should be 'put out.' Everett had not yet been settled or ordained, when in October of 1813, just as young Ware was writing the above, he made up his mind to answer and refute 'the book' which was engaging all attention. Fresh from his studies in Divinity, he set about his task with vigor and enthusiasm. While others talked, he wrote; while others deplored the influence of such a book, this youthful preacher sat up late at night arranging that its influence should end. It was a ten months' task. Begun in October, his 'Defence' was finished in August, and dedicated to President Kirkland in graceful terms expressing 'respect, affection, and gratitude.' The young author, now twenty years old, informed the public in a preface that he had not prepared the pages with a view to his own reputation, since he was conscious of many defects which were due in part to the disadvantages under which he wrote. 'I commenced the pages,' he could add, 'about a fortnight after I began to preach as a candidate for the Christian ministry. They have accordingly been written while my hands were filled with other duties and my heart with other cares.'

But from whatever point of view it is considered the achievement was remarkable. The book was the production of a scholar. The first two chapters were submitted to Dr. Channing for criticism and advice. The whole thing was

[1] *Life of Henry Ware, Jr.*, p. 57.

carefully and thoroughly done. Whether the book was necessary, or not, is another question. Probably it was not. For
while Everett was at work, the interest in Mr. English's attack seems to have subsided, and the young author acknowledged in his preface that he might be charged with prolong-
ing a fruitless controversy. None the less, the undertaking
gives evidence of an ardent spirit and proves the young man
to have been a kind of David in his day, giving battle to one
who seemed at first a giant of infidelity endangering the
safety of the faithful. 'As the composition of a mere youth,'
the book has well been called, 'one of the most remarkable
productions of the human mind.' There is no need at the
present time, however, to consider it in detail. Written long
before the day of the Higher Criticism, it ceased long since
to have any value except as a monument to the author's zeal
and industry. Perhaps it was at this time that Everett received the nickname of 'Ever-at-it,' which the satirical and
envious were fond of making use of in the days that followed.
However that may be, the epithet both in his youth and
later life was well deserved, and it did him honor in a way
that those who first applied it little intended that it should.

The penalty, however, of such hard and persistent work
was almost instantly inflicted. It was more than even youth
could stand, and a nervous breakdown was the consequence.
For close upon a year he had given himself no respite from
writing, preaching, making calls, and attending to the many
exactions of a large and influential parish. He had been ever-
at-it from early morning until late at night, and in the autumn he tried what a period of rest would do. With a friend
he went to Maine and made a trip along the Kennebec. It was
a delightful experience, and gave the youth some new and
interesting vistas. On returning to his work, however, he was
not much better, and again he was forced to seek a change of
scene. This time he went in the opposite direction, and with
prophetic impulse planned a trip to Washington. He armed
himself with letters of introduction to the people of political

and social influence. Harrison Gray Otis, a prominent member of his parish and a figurehead of social Boston at the time, whose 'low-hung carriage, with splendid horses and livery, were the glory of Beacon Street,' gave him letters to Gouverneur Morris and Robert S. Harper, both of them members of the Senate. The most interesting letter that he took, however, was one from John Adams to Thomas Jefferson. It was so characteristic as to be worth preserving. Mr. Adams wrote:

QUINCY, *Oct.* 28, 14.

DEAR SIR

I have great pleasure in giving this letter to the gentleman who requests it. The Revd Edward Everett, the successor of Mr. Buckminster and Thatcher and Cooper in the politest congregation in Boston, and probably the first literary character of his age and State, is very desirous of seeing Mr Jefferson. I hope he will arrive before your Library is translated to Washington.

By the way I envy you that immortal honour: but I cannot enter into competition with you for my books are not half the number of yours; and moreover, I have Shaftesbury, Bolingbroke, Hume, Gibbon and Raynal, as well as Voltaire.

Mr Everet is respectable in every Vein; in Family fortune Station Genius Learning and Character. What more ought to be said to Thomas Jefferson by

JOHN ADAMS

PRESIDENT JEFFERSON

Those were high words of commendation to live up to, especially as coming from an Adams. But unfortunately the youth did not get as far as Monticello, and so failed to make the personal acquaintance of the great Democratic leader; with whom, however, he was destined a few years later to have some correspondence on the subject of Slavery.

He started off early on Monday morning, October 31st, by stage-coach for Hartford — a weary journey of twenty-three hours. The best stage-coaches in those days contained three seats inside, intended for nine persons. The middle seat had no support of any kind for the back. In addition to the nine adults as many children were taken inside as could be accommodated on the knees of willing or reluctant passengers. Small trunks and boxes placed on the floor added to the general discomfort of long-legged passengers. Everett made the journey to Hartford without particular discomfort, leaving Boston at 1 A.M., and arriving just before midnight. The next day, however, on the way to New Haven, though his knees were bent to an acute angle by reason of the baggage on the floor of the coach, he was obliged to carry a fellow traveller of about ten years on his lap all the way. He was ready to drop with fatigue on arrival; but he had the pleasure in New Haven of meeting Professor Silliman and President Dwight, among other celebrities. As he took leave of President Dwight, after a call at his house, the great man stood before his gate with his head bare. The air being keen, Everett warned him against catching cold. But the President expressed no fear, and remarked with a smile, that he could stand in the open as safely as if he wore 'that triple hat which you Boston folk say I wear.'

Arriving in New York, Everett delivered his letter of introduction to Gouverneur Morris, and had the satisfaction of being received by the great man at his residence 'Morrisania,' where, 'like the Barons of the Middle Ages he was entrenched in stone, every building on his estate being of that material.' Mr. Morris's appearance struck him as one of the finest he had ever seen, notwithstanding the loss of a leg. He was sixty-two at the time, but had 'married only about five years before a relative of John Randolph of Roanoke, and their infant child was almost constantly in the father's arms.'

After passing a day at 'Morrisania,' the young traveller moved on by way of Philadelphia to Baltimore, where he met Charles Carroll of Carrollton and his brother the venerable Archbishop Carroll, and attended service at the Cathedral. He was 'not offended by the tapers and the flowers on the altar; nor by the incense and the paintings on the walls.' In spite of his New England Puritan training, he could see their value. The next day he started at five in the morning for Washington. The greater part of the way there appeared to be no 'made road.' Beyond Bladensburg was the high ground from which the chief resistance was offered to the advance of the British in the War of 1812. Traces of the battle were still to be seen. There was a line of graves along the roadside, and in one place, where the road had been washed away, he saw a projecting hand. Entering Washington, they passed 'the blackened ruins of the Capitol and the President's house,' and reached Crawford's hotel in Georgetown at 5 P.M., it having taken twelve hours to make the journey of thirty-six miles from Baltimore to Washington.

The accommodations at Washington were so scanty at that period that several members of Congress boarded out in Georgetown; a large coach, called 'the Royal George,' plying forward and back between the two places two or three times a day. Among other people of distinction whom the young minister met at Crawford's were Rufus King, Jeremiah Mason, and Christopher Gore of the Senate, Webster and Gaston of the House.

The capture of Washington and the wanton destruction of the public buildings by a small hostile British force had taken place only about three months before Everett's visit. It was still the general topic of conversation. The vandalism of the act was thoroughly discreditable, and the wonder is that the young man's mind was not permanently poisoned against England as he looked upon the shapeless ruins of the Capitol and the charred walls of the White House.

But Everett's consuming interest even then was in people. He enjoyed the brilliant and sprightly talk at the table of his hotel, and was taken to see President Madison, who 'treated him with great kindness.' It was far from an idle time, and it is hardly any wonder that after the fatigue of the long journeys he returned to Boston no more rested than he went away. The strain he had put upon himself was excessive, and the burden of the big and fashionable parish was proving too much for a constitution never very robust. What to do was now the question? Happily just then an unexpected offer came which was destined to affect his whole career, and suddenly to lead him away from service of the Church to service of the State. In the latter part of 1814 a gift was made to Harvard College for the establishment of a chair of Greek Literature. The donor's name was at first kept secret. After his death in 1820, the Corporation learned for the first time that the generous benefactor of the College was Samuel Eliot.

Everett was invited to assume the new professorship. The offer meant a critical decision — nothing less than a change in his entire life-work. He naturally hesitated. There was a heavy obligation to his church, which had suffered a very serious loss in the early death of his predecessor. But the opportunity was great. It might never come again. Moreover, the offer carried with it permission to spend two years for study in Europe. That seemed to settle the matter. He decided to accept the flattering invitation of the college. At his earnest request the church sorrowfully 'dismissed' him, entering on the records the regret that was felt at 'the dissolution of a connection, which, though of short continuance, had been attended with mutual harmony, and with great advantage and happiness to the Church.' That was on the 5th of March; and a little more than a month later, on April 12th, fourteen months after his ordination to the ministry, and on the day after his twenty-first birthday, Edward Everett was inaugurated as Professor of Greek Literature at Harvard University. The exercises took place in the new Chapel of University Hall, which is now the Faculty Room; and a large audience was on hand to witness the interesting scene. President Kirkland offered prayer, and then delivered an address in Latin setting forth the nature and advantages of the new professorship. The Professor-elect then made an address of acceptance in the same language, which he followed with an inaugural discourse in English. It was agreed at the time that it would be difficult to speak of the latter performance in terms of too much praise. 'In a manner at once convincing and eloquent,' we are told that the new professor 'explained the benefits to be derived from the culture of the Greek language and literature: more especially from their connection with the true understanding of the Sacred Scriptures.' [1] Four days later, on April 16, 1815, he sailed from Boston for Liverpool, leaving behind him general regret that the pulpit should have lost so brilliant a scholar and so matchless an orator.

As we look back now, however, we cannot help believing that the young minister's decision was a wise one. In taste and temperament he was essentially a scholar — a Greek in the wide acceptance of the term, as defined by Matthew Arnold, and not in the same sense Christian. Classic models were the ones he had set before himself, and he lacked both the missionary spirit of the apostle and the organizing genius of the pastor. He knew himself better than Buckminster had known him, and he was wise in being willing to make a change in his career before it was too late. There were evidences, however, that the break was not made without resentment and hard feeling on the part of the church. In this connection the following entries from the 'Diary of William Bentley' are interesting and significant.

Sunday, Feb. 26, 1815 Mr. Everett was in the North pulpit [2] this day. He is appointed Professor of the Greek language at Cambridge and it is expected he will resign his charge in the Brattle Street Church in Boston. He stands among our first in New England. He tells me he intends a tour of Europe immediately.... We have never sent a man of greater learning than Mr. Everett since Norton.

Sunday, March 12, 1815 Mr. Everett, lately of Brattle Street Church, has accepted the Professorship.... He left his charge without any consultation with them and this has been construed into a great offense. His establishment is to connect Greek literature with Biblical Criticism. Thus Genius has given a disposition to humble him and he is blamed only because there is nothing else to blame, but what he thought his prudence. [3]

[1] *Columbian Centinel* for April 15, 1815. [2] Salem, Massachusetts.
[3] *Diary of William Bentley, D.D.*, vol. IV, 317–19.

III

WANDER YEARS

THE packet ship in which Everett sailed away was a large one for the time, being of three hundred and fifty tons burden. It was the second vessel to leave port after the conclusion of peace. With him, as fellow-passengers, and forming a most congenial company, were George Ticknor, a young lawyer and graduate of Dartmouth College who was to go with Everett to Göttingen and study literature; Mr. and Mrs. Samuel G. Perkins and their son whom Everett was to take charge of; Mr. Haven, of Portsmouth, New Hampshire; and two sons of John Quincy Adams, who were going out to join their father, who was the United States Minister at St. Petersburg.

The voyage was a quiet one occupying a little over a month. They were not to make port, however, without some exciting experiences. All went well till they neared the English coast, and were running through St. George's Channel. The weather was thick, the wind was blowing a gale, and no observations had been secured for the past two days. The captain was uncertain as to his exact position, but thought himself on the Irish side of the Channel. Suddenly what was taken to be a ship loomed up through the mist, not two miles distant. A moment later, however, the man on the lookout at the masthead cried out with a frightful voice — 'A lighthouse — breakers!' The captain thought it was Waterford Light, and the helm was jammed to port. But the next instant he discovered his error and whipping out a mighty oath the ship was put about in the nick of time. They had been sailing straight for the boiling breakers on the Welsh coast. Forty years afterwards Everett could say that he had never forgotten the captain's oath, nor the roar of the awful breakers which they just escaped.

But excitements were not over. News travelled slowly in those days, and when the vessel had left port it was supposed that Napoleon was safely secured in his island realm of Elba. The first news to greet them, therefore, was that of the mighty conqueror's escape and triumphal march on Paris. The weather-beaten pilot, who scrambled on board at the mouth of the Mersey, startled all hands with the announcement, 'Boney has broken loose again.' The Americans could not believe their ears, and were filled with dismay and apprehension. The air was electrical with the coming conflict. Little else was talked of when they got to London. They met Byron among others, who expressed it as his opinion that Napoleon would 'drive the Duke of Wellington.' Years afterwards Mr. Everett wrote out this account of the interview with Byron:

Being in London in June, 1815, and having a great desire to see Lord Byron, I sent him a copy of a little poem delivered by me in 1812 before the Phi Beta Kappa in which honorable mention is made of him, and expressed a wish to make his acquaintance. He returned me a very kind answer, asked me to come to see him the next day, and sent me a copy of his poems — all the volumes then published — with some autograph corrections. When I called upon him, he received me with great kindness, talked freely, and without restraint or affectation, expressed satisfaction at his transAtlantic fame: spoke warmly of Greece, and said that but for domestic circumstances he should like to end his days there; promised me letters to the consul at Athens, and especially to Ali Pasha. On one topic only his conversation was such as to leave a painful impression and to show the violence of his passions. The armies of the Duke of Wellington and Napoleon were then near each other; it was but a few days before the battle of Waterloo. He alluded to the probability of a conflict; said he had no doubt 'Wellington would be driven': he should be sorry to have his countryman worsted, but should rejoice in the effect which such an event would have on the state of domestic politics, and wound up by expressing the hope that he should 'live to see Lord Castlereagh's head carried on a pike under his window.'

A few days later, when the news of Waterloo arrived, brought by a clerk of the Rothschilds who arrived in advance of Wellington's courier, young Ticknor was calling upon Byron. Some one came into the room while they were talking and said: 'My Lord, my Lord, a great battle has been fought and Bonaparte is entirely defeated.' The poet, however, was incredulous and asked, 'But is it true, is it true?' And being assured that it was, he exclaimed, after a moment's hesitation, 'I am d——d sorry for it.'

Their stay in London was brief. It was long enough, however, for them to meet other people of distinction — among them Zachary Macaulay and Hallam, who were probably more of their own way of thinking on the all-absorbing subject. Being assured that there would be no difficulty in travelling on the Continent the little party sailed from Harwich on June 30th. Landing at Hellevoetsluis, they secured the only two conveyances which the village appeared to possess — the one 'a coach which seemed to be without springs,' and the other 'a wagon which did not even pretend to have any.' In this slow and lumbering fashion they were driven into Rotterdam. From Rotterdam they went to The Hague, and thence to Leyden, Haarlem, Amsterdam, and Utrecht. At Utrecht the young men said good-bye to Mr. and Mrs. Perkins, and Everett, Ticknor, and young Perkins went on to Göttingen where they arrived on August 4th. After securing lodgings, they at once betook themselves to the famous university.

And then began for Everett a life of constant and the closest study. His industry was boundless, impressing even the German professors. Six hours only were set aside for sleep. The rest of the time was devoted to his work, broken only by a daily walk with Ticknor. Later on, finding added relaxation necessary, the young men took fencing lessons together three times a week. Everett at first paid some attention to Oriental languages, but confined himself afterwards almost wholly to philosophy. His special instructor was Dissen, the editor of Pindar; but he also came into friendly touch and cordial relations with Eichhorn, Heeren, and the venerable Blumenbach. His chief courses were, as he called them, 'pri-

vatissima.' He said of himself afterwards that he was 'not a
very neat note-taker,' and that his notebooks would be of
little use to any one else, since he 'wrote in English, German,
French, or Latin as the whim seized him, often changing in
the same sentence from one to another.' Sunday evenings
were generally passed at the house of some professor, all of
whom were hospitable, and evidently took to the young
Americans, who were the first of their countrymen to study at
a German university, thus leading a long line of students who
were destined to follow in the years to come. Before long they
both were taken into the only club at Göttingen. Of course it
was a literary club. Like all literary clubs, however, that
'ever survived the frosts of the first winter, its chief occupation was to eat suppers.' The total membership was only
twenty-four, more than one third of the number being professors. The student members were selected, indeed, by the
professors, so that the honor of membership was considerable. The Americans did not allow themselves, however, to
be unduly flattered. It occurred to them that they had been
taken in 'as a kind of raree show, with much the same curiosity that a tame monkey or a dancing bear would be.' Indeed, it was confided to them later that, coming from such a
distance, they were looked upon as hardly civilized, and
some of the members appeared surprised to find them white.
Perhaps their popularity was due in part to the violence of
the reaction that was sustained in finding men of so much
culture and such charming manners. Everett was known
as 'the Professor,' and Ticknor was accorded the title of
'Doctor.' Ticknor appears to have been the more popular
with the ladies, but Everett was universally respected for his
scholarship and general knowledge.

The arduous and confining work at the University was
broken, however, from time to time, with periods of rest and
travel. During the early part of his Göttingen career, Everett
went to Hanover where he met Count Münster, Minister of
State, and Professor Martens, who had written a book on the

law of nations which was widely read in the United States. Later on he wisely found his way to Weimar where he had the privilege and great good fortune of an interview with Goethe. He described the meeting in a letter to his brother Alexander:

GÖTTINGEN, *Nov.* 16, 1816

... I hardly know whether to try to tell you any more of my experiences, as in the multitude of them, it is hard to choose. However, at Weimar we saw Goethe. As I gave Ma a high-flown account of the interview, I will state to you the facts as they were. We had letters to him from particular friends of his here, Mr. and Mrs. Sartorius, and one from Wolff. There was also a letter from Mrs. S. to one Professor Riemer, author of the best Manual Greek Lexicon, who had lived nine years in Goethe's house, and who was to conduct us to him, in one of his mollissima tempora fandi. He informed us that he had used, indeed, to sacrifice much time to Mr. G., but was now obliged to live for himself and wife, and that this had produced a coldness between G. and him. This I thought was rather stumbling on the threshold. The next morning we sent our letters and asked at what time we should wait upon him, and were told at eleven. At the appointed time, we went. He was very stiff and cold, not to say gauche and awkward. His head was grey, some of his front teeth gone, and his eyes watery with age.[1] He was oppressed at feeling that we were gazing at him, looked restlessly out of the window, at which he sat, and talked low and anxiously. He spoke of Byron, and admired 'The Corsair,' he ascribed the English eloquence to the influence of parliamentary speaking, and asked a few questions about America. He spoke, however, with no interest, on anything. When we went, he did not ask us to call again, but offered us some letters to Jena. These he did not send that day, nor the two next, though the day after our call he sent his servant with his card, by way of returning it, at half-past eight. This I suppose he thought was English manners, but he is mistaken. The evening of the third day we called on him again. His servant brought us down word that the Minister was sorry he could not see us, giving no reason and not saying when he should be disengaged. At Jena we found, by the merest accident in the world, that he had written to the Professor of Mineralogy a note of recommendation telling him to present us each with a diploma of membership of the Jena Mineralogical Society, of which Goethe is president. As not one word had been said in our interview with him, and as I do not know a flint from a marble, till I see it in a tinder box, I thought

[1] Goethe was sixty-seven at the time, and lived to be eighty-three.

it a very modest way of asking us to send them a box of American minerals. I forgot to say that the day after our call on G., George sent him Byron's 'Siege of Corinth,' which had been mentioned in the interview, of which he did not even acknowledge the receipt. And thus ended our introduction to Goethe. . . .

Dresden was visited with its Madonnas to be seen, Leipsic also, and Berlin. Then there was a tramping-trip through the Hartz Mountains. Joy of joys, too, was a trip he made and a visit that he had in Holland. Soon after he had left home, his brother Alexander was appointed Secretary of the Legation to the United Kingdom of the Netherlands. He was living at The Hague, and there Edward joined him for a time, the two brothers having much in common. Thus the weeks and months and even years sped by, being crowded not alone with studies, but with rich experiences which were destined to abide and yield rich fruit throughout a long and busy lifetime. On the morning of September 17, 1817, the Göttingen experience came to an end. Ticknor's studies had been concluded in March, but Everett remained to receive his diploma as Doctor of Philosophy — 'the first American,' he wrote, 'and, so far as I know, the first Englishman [sic] on whom it has ever been conferred.'[1]

He had already written home and obtained an extension of his leave of absence. Two years had originally been granted him. This period had been allowed that he might travel for his health. As he had spent the time in study, he felt free to ask the College for two years more, which somewhat reluctantly was granted.

It had been Everett's first intention to go at once from Göttingen to Oxford, and there to pass the winter. He changed his mind, however, and went instead to Paris, setting forth his reasons for doing so in the following interesting words:

You will perhaps have heard that it was my intention to have passed from this University to that of Oxford, and to have spent the

winter there. . . . I have altered this determination for the sake of
joining forces with Theodore Lyman at Paris this winter: and as he
proposes to pass the ensuing summer in travelling in the South of
France, I shall take that opportunity of going to England. It is
true I should have liked to have kept the thread, as it were, unbroken and gone on with my studies without interruption. But I
find even at Paris that I have no object there but study: and Professor Gaisford, at Oxford, writes me that it is in every way better
that I should be there in summer, as the library is open a greater
part of the day. Meanwhile, I try to feel duly grateful to Providence and my friends at home to whom I owe the opportunity of
resorting to the famous fountains of European wisdom.[1]

After two years of German university life, therefore, the
winter of 1817–18 was passed in Paris. And there a new
world of men and women was opened to him, with new and
wonderful opportunities for seeing life. Study was his first
object. Many hours a day were passed accordingly in the
King's Library, to which he was freely admitted. He special-
ized in Italian and modern Greek, as he hoped to use both
languages in further travel he was planning. He was to learn
much else, however, that never could be gained from books.
He was wise enough wherever he went to seek out the most
interesting people and to make the acquaintance of the great.
In Paris, therefore, we find him 'passing many happy and
instructive hours at the Institute' with Alexander von Humboldt. He had several meetings with Lafayette, who was
destined, six years later, to be the occasion of his most
spectacular triumph as an orator. Then there was Benjamin
Constant, Madame de Staël, and others.

His most interesting experience in this line, however, was a
visit to the Tuileries where he was presented to Louis XVIII,
who had come to the throne two years previously on the final
abdication of Napoleon. Mr. Gallatin at that time was the
United States Minister to the Court of France and high in
kingly favor. He graciously offered to present Everett and
his companion Theodore Lyman, and the invitation was

[1] *Harvard Graduates' Magazine*, VI, 14.

greedily accepted. Court-dress was required, and the various paraphernalia that this included put a tax upon the young professor's purse and personal belongings which neither was equipped to bear. Several of his friends accordingly came to his assistance, and their joint contributions furnished 'a very tolerable, though not entirely homogeneous costume for the occasion.' Thus arrayed, he drove in Mr. Gallatin's carriage to the Palace where the representatives of the various European Governments soon assembled for the stately ceremonial. When he reached the Royal Presence, after some delay, he found His Majesty 'in sad contrast with what Burke had said the restored King of France must be: "An energetic prince, always on horseback."' He was presented instead to a corpulent individual, somewhat under six feet in height, who walked with considerable difficulty, 'his round and somewhat unmeaning face indicating an amiable disposition, but no strength of character. He was dressed in a blue coat and small-clothes: a white Marseilles vest, which would have fitted a much larger man, and stout hussar boots. He wore the English order of the garter, and supported himself with a cane, being stiff in one knee, and a great sufferer from gout.'[1]

A much more impressive and interesting person to whom he paid his respects afterwards, being conducted to her reception room through the State apartments of the Tuileries, was the Duchess d'Angoulême, the daughter of Louis XVI and Marie Antoinette. Her tragic history made her romantically interesting to the young American, for she had been imprisoned with her parents at the time of the Revolution and had seen them both led out to lay their heads beneath the guillotine. At this time she was about forty years old, and Everett described her as having a face which was 'neither beautiful nor pleasant; the lines were hard; the eyes indescribably sad; the expression austere.' None the less she inspired a respect which was wanting in the King, and she talked with

[1] See Mount Vernon Papers, for an interesting account of this whole episode.

the young professor pleasantly in French. Not even this was all, however; for under the wing of Mr. Gallatin he was taken the whole length of the Palace, visiting in turn the Count d'Artois, afterwards to be known as Charles X, and the Duke de Berri and his wife. He found the Count a man of 'fair appearance,' but with a 'countenance that was ordinary and meaningless,' while the wife of the Duke de Berri, who was the daughter of the Prince Royal of Naples, and was about twenty years old, 'looked embarrassed and terrified, and rather crept than walked around the circle.' Altogether, French Royalty did not impress him favorably, and the whole experience tended to deepen in him that ardent love for republican principles and institutions which came to be among his most distinctive characteristics.

Much more to his liking were the *literati* whom he was next to meet in England. For in April he set out from Paris and made his way to London. He had letters to many people of importance, among others one from Alexander von Humboldt to his brother William, who was at that time Prussian Minister to England, and with whom he soon became 'intimately acquainted.' Altogether, the next five months were destined to be among the most memorable and rewarding of his entire trip. The time was divided between London, Cambridge, Oxford, the Lake Region, and Scotland. But it will be best, perhaps, to let him tell his own story as we find it in his journal.

Saturday, March 14, 1818. This day, at six o'clock A.M. I left Paris, in the boot of the diligence. My companion in it, a man dressed in English fashion, announced himself to me, in the first salutation, as from the wrong side of St. George's Channel, by remarking that 'we'd be as snug as a pig in a bed.' I had avoided going to Calais, with a private party of countrymen, principally to have one more long lesson of French, before I left the land; and riding in the diligence, with a French party is the best lesson. But I found myself, in a coach filled with Irish. . . .

I was often amazed, in the course of the ride, by the boldness with which Monsieur the Conductor of the diligence, who sat next

me, expressed himself on political subjects. He not only sang, at
my request, the somewhat suspicious songs of 'Ca ira,' the 'Mar-
seillaise,' and the 'Reveille du Peuple,' but he lamented over the
absence 'of the brave boy,[1] who used to keep the roads in order,'
and execrated very liberally the payment of the contributions to the
Allies, particularly the English. He repeatedly said, that if there
were but six hundred thousand men in France, as faithful friends
of their country as he, they would pay off the score at one coup: at
which the postilion would look up and nod assent. The opinion,
among all the French I have conversed with, is universal that there
was great treachery at Waterloo.

Our ride — or drive as they call it in England — was of two days
and one night. . . . At four P.M. of the second day's journey, we
reached Boulogne where Napoleon collected his famous camp, and
menaced England. The camp was upon a small hill, separated
from the town, by an inlet of the sea, which like the harbour of the
town was filled with barges; now rotting in the mud, and furnishing fuel to all who will go and steal it. This camp enriched the
town of Boulogne to such a degree that gold rolled in its streets,
said our informant, like pebbles. . . . The country about Boulogne
is occupied by English troops, though there are none in the city
itself. We saw a great many of the young officers riding out un-
armed, at which my Irish friend, who was himself of the army, and
had been in the expedition to New Orleans, could not sufficiently
express his surprise. One sees about Boulogne some remnants, I
think, of the former possession of this part of the country by the
English, in the small fields into which it is divided, and the haw-
thorn hedges by which they are separated, the only ones I have
seen on the Continent. . . .

Let all those who embark from Calais and who do not like to
crop high breakers in rowboats, wait for a tide which will allow the
packet to come up to the quai. Ours was lying in the stream, near
two miles off, and as the wind was fresh we had no small sea to encounter. One or two heavy waves passed over the board, and
drenched us well. The captain of the packet went out in the boat
I did, and I kept my eye fixed on him, to see whether he flinched.
Once I thought he did, and then it was time for my poor lands-
man's heart to flutter. All at once the boatmen threw down their
oars, and left us weltering, without support, on the waves. 'What
are you at!' roared out our captain, half starting from his seat.
'Setting the sail' was the answer, in French; and after the sail was
set, we did better. After reaching the packet we had still to get
into it. For this there was no kind of provision made: neither of

[1] Napoleon.

ladder to assist one up, nor of gate or door in the bulwarks, to
shorten the distance to be climbed. And as in that tempestuous
sea it was impossible to lay peaceably alongside the ship, we could
only wait till a wave wafted us up to it, when the ladies were thrown
on board like trunks, and the gentlemen scrambled in, as well as
they could, in imminent danger of falling down and serving as a
fender between the packet and the boat.

These little troubles surmounted — which every traveller
fancies greater in his own case than in any former, though we all
have about the same story to tell — the ship was put before the
wind, and we began our way — shooting and rolling over the waves.
The faces of the company began to gather blackness, with each
higher swell. There was a Lord, in the company, whose title
afforded him so little protection that he was much the sickest on
board. There was soon, however, little room for invidious com-
parisons. I succeeded, by dint of peppermint lozenges, in sustaining my stomach some time. . . .

And thus passed away our voyage. The wind shifted and became unfavourable — hour after hour we beat our way — and it
was after seven in the evening, when we arrived off Dover harbour.
Here we were boarded by a boat from town, and informed that the
harbour had been choked up in the late storms, and that it was impossible to enter. Not Cæsar, when, from the very spot where we
were now tossing on the waves, he beheld the fierce Britons drawn
up to oppose his landing, could have been more disconcerted than
we at this condemnation to new delays in getting by boat to shore.
It was now a grand sight that was presented to us: the precipitous
cliffs of Dover rendered still more magestick by the obscurity of the
evening — their dusky chalkiness just seen, as it were grey marble,
by the lights from the town beneath — and the broad flare of
the lighthouse to which we seemed approaching as often as we re-
ceded.

We were at length transferred from the packet to a boat and from
that put on shore; and here it was that a merry scene ensued. The
emissaries of all the taverns in town, to the number of some twenty
or thirty, had gathered round the spot where we were to land; and
each poor seasick creature, as he sprung on shore, fell into the
hands of these remorseless wretches, who, with deafening cries of
the 'Angel,' the 'Shakespeare,' the 'City of London,' the 'Ship,'
and a dozen other names, would seize upon him, as if each meant
to carry a limb of him to his respective lair. This confusion was
not a little heightened by the fainting of some of the ladies, and the
calls for salts and water, which ensued. We decided for the 'Ship,'
one of the best inns at Dover and thither were led by the guide. . . .

Wednesday the 18. Having thus reposed ourselves a day at Dover, we started at six o'clock this morning for London. . . .

We arrived to breakfast at Canterbury. The velocity of the coaches — the fineness of the roads — and the neatness of the country and villages, through which we passed, formed a most striking contrast with the journeyings I have for near three years made on the Continent. It was not without some sentiment of veneration, that I traversed this first of the Saxon States in England, the Kingdom of Kent — and on arriving at Canterbury, the thought that I was at the capital of Hengist and the See of Saint Augustine furnished me with matter of reflection. At four o'clock P.M. we reached London, and at five I was established at the Petersburg Hotel, Dover Street, whither I advise no man to go who would not be cheated. On leaving it, three days after — though I had dined but twice — I was charged five pounds: — I had been in the house just seventy-two hours. . . .

Thursday 19. I presented to Murray, the bookseller, my letters from Mr. Dudgate and Miss Williams. . . . While I was with Murray, Lord Erskine came in, a very plain-looking man — poorly dressed in black, having lately lost, I think, a son, and apparently sixty-four years old. He, like so many distinguished persons in England, was very free in the use of language not thought seemly among us from respectable lips. . . .

Tuesday March 31. Called upon Mr. Rose in the Palace Yard, but did not find him. Who could pass the open door of Westminster Abbey, and see 'Poets' Corner' written up, without going, at least for a moment, in? Not I. I looked round upon the monuments of Shakespeare, Gay, Goldsmith, Addison, etc., mingled there with dust high-titled, indeed, but unworthy to partake even this monumental immortality. — What right hath John, the great Duke of Argyle, by the side of Shakespeare? — The door of this part of the Abbey is constantly open, and no guard is placed at it. This gives a sort of appearance of a thoroughfare to it — something dirty and at the same time irreverent. It were idle to repeat the exclamations which every traveller has made against the scrawls and names with which every monument is defaced and the still greater barbarity which has been exercised upon fingers, arms, noses, etc., and all the projecting members of the statues. The only consolation is that most of them are in so bad a taste that no mutilation can make them look worse than they do. . . .

Monday 20. I set out, at one o'clock to-day, upon an expedition to Sydenham, a village near London, to visit Mr. Campbell. It is in reality not more than seven miles from town, but by the perfidy of the stage-driver, I made it twelve. Not finding a stage to

Sydenham on the stand, I was beguiled into one for Deptford, and told that from Deptford to Sydenham was but a mile and a half. Arrived at the former place, my first care was to put myself under the conduct of an urchin, who promised to guide me in safety, and that by a short cut across the fields. He led me, it is true, o'er hedge and bridge, o'er gate and stile, but it was a good five miles' walk: and ever, as we crossed a field, he would caution me not to tread upon the springing grain, under the agreeable penalty of being shot at by the gamekeepers.

At last we reached Sydenham Common where not a poet, but the genius of desolation might have fixed his abode. I was on the top of a high and dreary hill, which bore nothing — not even heath or furze. I accosted some gravel diggers, and they referred me to the next pit for information. There I luckily got it, and was pointed to a house yet a mile off, but in sight, as that where the poet lived. For this then I resumed my march, and reached his door at half-past four, having left London at one.

An ominous clank of plates announced me that I had unluckily come at the hour of dinner: — how unfavourable that is for making acquaintances is known to any one, who has ever tried to caress a dog with a bone. Gifford, moreover, had told me that C. was cynical, and his gate was bolted without any external means to open it. The poetical feelings, with which I came down, chilled under all these unpromising realities. I rung the gate-bell, gave Murray's letter to the servant who appeared, and was soon bid to walk in. All my fears subsided, as I saw Mr. C., who met me at his door, a man of beautiful countenance — rather small figure — bright black eyes, and fine open manner. He apologized for the smell of the dinner in the next room, and said I had done wrong not to come half an hour sooner. He observed that he had a brother in America, who left England so early that he had hardly seen him and was very curious to know — on my saying I had met his brother — if they resembled each other. By this time, the folding doors opened, and Mrs. C. appeared to usher us into the other room. Mr. C.'s only son, a youth of about thirteen, and a fine pet pointer made up the rest of the family.

C. discovered himself to be a great enthusiast for America: he said he had long talked of going to it to see his brother. He said there was a beautiful American poem called the 'Copper-Coloured Boy' which he wished much to get. He spoke of his Works — extracts from the English poets, now printing at Murray's in six volumes, and brought me down the sheets which had appeared to look at. He read some of the passages with great spirit; though a bad Scotch voice, which he did not discover in conversation.

Mrs. C. spoke pretty broadly. She is apparently thirty-seven, with rather a virago expression, but as her husband appealed to her, once or twice, I think she must be amiable. The dog too appeared fond of her. C. spoke of Walter Scott, said he supposed he was the most popular poet in America, and called him by his Christian name Walter. He spoke with great regard of Washington Irving and Brevoort. He was full in the faith of a revolution's taking place in England, in the event of another Continental War.

Mrs. C. insisted upon having me a luncheon gotten, and when I went, C. walked a mile with me toward town. He said he was independent two thirds of the year, but must support himself by his wits the other third. He said the greatest hope for American literature was the theatre: that we must try to form a national theatre; that were he twenty years younger he would go out, and try to be a dramatick poet; that here there was not freedom enough. He said, when he wrote poetry, he wrote it at once, but could not command himself, at all times, to write. He gave me at parting the freedom of the house, in so cordial a manner that I could not think he did not mean it. . . .

Tuesday 28. I dined at Murray's, in company with Tom Moore the poet; Hobhouse, Lord B.'s friend; — Milman,[1] author of 'Fazio,' 'Shee's Rhymes of Art'; Hugo Forcolo, a learned Italian born in Zante, author of the article on Dante in the 'Edinboro Review,' and others. The conversation wanted decency and wit, but there was much laughter. . . . Tom Moore is a very short, thick little man, with red, bloated cheeks, vulgar, tippy looks, and coarse, ordinary manners. He made me some civilities, but we had little talk. His 'Fudge' is pronounced to be a failure by all. Milman is a tall, most dark-complexioned man — grave and pensive as a poet should be — and dressed in solemn black; — he said little and when he laughed, it was like a flower springing up on a tomb. . . .

Tuesday 5. I walked out to Kensington to breakfast with Mr. Wilberforce. Thinking to have a pleasanter walk, I took my way through Hyde Park, not being aware that this would take me into the road beyond Mr. Wilberforce's, so that it was eleven before I got back to his house. Late as it was, he was not up: having been kept up in the House till three o'clock, in expectation of something relative to the slave-trade, which however did not come on. He did not appear at breakfast. There was Mr. Stephen, author of 'War in Disguise.' As everyone joined to paint the horrors of the crowd at the meeting of the Church Missionary Society to-day, I hastened back to attend it. Mr. Macaulay had sent me a ticket for

---

[1] H. H. Milman, author of *The History of Latin Christianity*, etc.

the platform, or stage reserved for the officers and speakers. Not knowing precisely what was meant by the platform, I proceeded to the common floor of the hall, already crowded to overflowing; and, as nothing was to be seen or heard there, was upon the point of quitting in disgust. I luckily fell in with a gentleman, who said something about going upon the platform, and I determined to follow him; which brought me in safety to the stage where were the best accommodations for seeing and hearing. . . .

Wilberforce spoke to great effect. His manner, as far as respects movement and gesture are bad — his figure quite diminutive and unprepossessing, and his air much hurt by his extreme nearsightedness. But his fluency — happy use of metaphor — affectionate and cordial manner of allusion to the persons or topicks in question — make him one of the happiest speakers I ever heard: nothing can be imagined more hearty than the welcome given him: and to one, who has seen him only in private, nothing can be more unexpected than his power as an orator. In private, he is distracted — flies from topick to topick — seems whirled round in a vortex of affairs: nervous and restless. When he gets up, all this subsides — he rises above himself, and his immediate personality, and reminds one of that image in Goldsmith,

'To them his hopes, his fears, his cares were given, —
But all his serious tho'ts found rest in heaven.'

It is a curious reverse of what happens in most men, who, though they be calm and tranquil in private, are thrown into trepidation whenever they address the publick, or rise to do it. Mr. Wilberforce has the consolation of having done more good than any man living. I bear him this testimony the more readily, because I differ from him myself on most of his religious opinions; and the more pointedly because the miserable infection of party spirit goes so far here that it is getting to be quite fashionable to abuse him in the papers, and even such men as Dr. Rees, who think themselves and really are rather candid, speak contemptuously of him. . . .

Thursday 14. This morning at Mr. Belsham's, I met Lant Carpenter to breakfast. He was not a little pleased at hearing that his geography had been reprinted, and was thought highly of, in America. I have been surprised to find how often it happens that authors are ignorant of the republication of their works in America. Dr. Gillies had not heard of the American edition of his history, nor Miss Porter of that of her novels, nor Dr. Carpenter of that of his geography of the New Testament. Dr. Carpenter, Mr. Belsham, and myself discussed the German theology; and I must say that I find them just as intolerant to those, who go a little farther than themselves, as the Orthodox are to them. But why do I remark on this; is it not always so? . . .

After London came Cambridge, and the young man was impressed by the beauties and the academic quiet of the place. He pictured in contrast his own Cambridge far across the sea. The journal says:

My eyes filled with tears, as I thought of the day of small things at home. I envied not the sublime turrets of King's College Chapel rising in simple majesty so high and gracefully, nor the imposing fronts of the Senate-House or the Halls, which I passed. But when I entered the gates of Peterhouse, and saw the calm seclusion — court within court — the quadrangles filled with fine shaven grass plats of most perfect neatness — all quiet and still, with here and there a student in his black gown stealing out under the trees, and contrasted this with our noisy flaring exposure, open to the four winds of heaven, the spaces between our halls worn down to a burning sand by the infinite intersection of the paths of idlers, a rattling stage-coach dashing four times a day through our Yard, and that sometimes when all college is assembled in the Chapel — when I thought of this I was grieved too much, for the first moment, to give up my heart to the lovely scene.

From Cambridge, naturally enough, he made his way to Oxford, where again he entered into university life, met many of the professors, and laid the foundation for precious friendships which he was to build upon twenty-five years later when he became minister at the Court of Saint James'. He was fortunate enough to be there for Commemoration, and witnessed the conferring of honorary degrees in the Sheldonian Theatre. Little did he think when he heard the Vice-Chancellor ask for the 'non placets' in connection with some gentlemen who were recommended for the degree of Doctor in Civil Law — 'no objection was of course made' — that a few years later the theatre would ring with 'non placets' when he himself was presented for the same degree, the objection being raised that he had formerly been a Unitarian minister.

From Oxford he went across to Bath, visited Bristol, took the famous trip on the Wye, made his way to Chester, spent several days in the Lake Region, where he took most of the excursions, and finally found himself in Edinburgh. Here, too, he was well provided with letters, and he proceeded at once to make good use of them.

July 6. My first call this morning was on 'Mr. Walter Scott, Advocate,' as it stands engraved on brass, on the door of No. 39 Castle Street. I found him in his study, at his books. His room was lined with books, and hung around various ancient guns, pieces of armour, shields, and other relicks; and the portentous mastiff — which one sees in Wilkie's picture — reclined on the floor. Mr. Scott is six feet high, and passed the middle period of life; his hair is now and was probably always a dusky white; his face is plain like that of a sensible country farmer; his person not corpulent, but bony: his right leg deformed and shorter than the other. He is the first clerk of the Sessions. He received me with great courtesy and said Mr. Gifford had prepared him to expect me. He said Edinburgh was better than London, in the respect of 'having less of the literary trade'; and that the classes of society were better mixed; 'the literary giving dignity to the fashionable, and they grace to the literary,' or something like this more simply expressed. He spoke very affectionately of W. Irving, who he said made himself beloved to a Scotchman, by the attachment he formed for the Tweed.

Willing to see how he would notice an allusion to one of the novels ascribed to him, I quoted the remark in 'Rob Roy,' and asked him whether 'he got to lift his hat, as the Scotch did when they name their great rivers.' I thought he looked queer, said, 'Yes, the Scotch really do name their great rivers with veneration'; and then turned the subject. I told him I had ridden through a part of the country, which he had made classic ground, Tariotdale and Branksome: he laughed, and said, 'Branksome was a good deal changed since the border days.' He said he had seen the American edition of his poems, on my telling him I would give him the 'Lady of the Lake' — that Mr. Irving had given his daughter Sophia a set: — that they were very pretty.

He showed me a sword, which had belonged to the Marquis of Montrose, and was given to him by King James. It had formerly been the sword of James's son, Prince Henry, but was made for his father. On the blade were some Latin lines beginning, 'Jacolec pacis alumne.' Mr. S. asked me to come and spend a day or two with him at Abbotsford, near Melrose, and to dine with him to-day. I spent the morning with calling on sundry people to whom I had letters. None of whom except Mr. Morehead, I found at home. This gentleman spoke in the highest terms of T. Lyman who had been a year with him, and also of J. Gray.

At a quarter before five I repaired to dinner at Mr. Scott's. It was *en famille*. There were his mother, an aged, cheerful old lady, one lady visitor, Mrs. Scott, the two sons and two daughters, and a gentleman. Every one likes to know the secret history of the families of such persons as Walter Scott, and as my journal shall never be in the way of ministering to scandal I make no scruple in this speaking of his family.

Mrs. Scott is a short little woman and was probably a handsome one in her youth. I think I have heard that she was a Swiss; she has the appearance of a foreigner and the French accent. I should think she was forty-eight years old. The eldest son is about nineteen or twenty, and named Walter, a good-looking and well-behaved young man. He asked his father's permission to go to the theatre, after dinner, which his father withheld. The asking, I thought, very creditable to the boy's dutifulness, the refusing to the father's discipline. Miss Sophia Scott, the eldest daughter, appears to be seventeen or eighteen. Very pretty, without being regularly beautiful, with bright, laughing eyes. She is quite easy and ladylike in her manners. Her sister is younger, apparently by two years, than herself, less pretty, has full black eyes, and when I rose and gave her a chair, her father said, 'Don't mind her. She's a fine buxom lassie able to take care of herself.' The other boy, named Charles, seemed about twelve, and did not dine at table.

We had much pleasant talk, but none perhaps journalable. An original oil-painting of Rob Roy, junior, was handed round the table. It was about a foot and a half high. Mr. Scott had borrowed it to get it copied. Nothing was said in the way of allusion to the book, except Mr. Scott's saying that Helen McGregor composed a piece of musick. I considered this as a sign that Scott wrote it. For had it been by anybody else, it would have been mentioned, on occasion of handing round the picture. The father of the lady present had been threatened to have his house plundered by Rob Roy, the son.

All the persons present, Mr. S. among the rest, spoke in the peculiar Scottish tone, but made use of no Scottish word, as I remember, but 'ye' for 'you' and 'mind' for 'remember,' which Mr. Scott frequently used.

There were present three dogs, at dinner — all of them of great merit and treated with attention. The hairs on my blue pantaloons will testify that I did my share of civility to them. The cat came in to the dessert; and took post upon a side-table. After the ladies retired, she came upon our table. . . .

But Scott, though the most conspicuous, was not the only

man of letters in Scotland whom he wished to meet, and the young man pushed up north to Aberdeen in search of others.

With Sir William Hamilton he took a long walk out of town, and had 'much pleasant conversation of men and things; finding his learning equalled only by his modesty.' Best of all, however, he passed a day and night with Dugald Stewart at Kinniel on the Firth of Forth. Stewart was Emeritus Professor of Moral Philosophy, having been professor in the University of Edinburgh for forty-four years, ever since he was eighteen. Kinniel House belonged to Lord Douglas, son of the Duke of Hamilton — a castle of considerable extent and apparent age, approached by a long and straight avenue of fine old trees. Everett 'rejoiced to find that Mr. Stewart lived in a spot so worthy of his character, and for this retirement so favorable to his pursuits.' Stewart had recently been very sick with typhus, which he thought he took from shaking hands with an old servant who had just recovered. He seemed languid and exhausted, though cheerful. He took the young man to walk in his garden and they talked of Adams and Franklin and Jefferson and Jay, all of whom the great philosopher had met in connection with his various visits to Paris. When Everett told him that Kant's philosophy was now nearly exploded in Germany, Stewart replied that it was still much in vogue with eminent persons in England. He repeated many anecdotes of Campbell, Scott, and Byron, and read aloud to him Campbell's 'Soldier's Dream.' The reading was done with feeling and expression, but with *moderate* emphasis. 'This, I suspect,' wrote Everett, 'is considered the true way of reading in Edinburgh, for twice in the novels, the opposite practice is condemned. I think a theatrical manner best and most impressive; but it requires great judgment. Mr. S. expressed the highest admiration of Campbell.'

The visit was in all respects a memorable one, and Everett congratulated himself on leaving that he had 'been the guest of the greatest philosopher since Plato.' Mr. Stewart's breadth of spirit, tolerance of opinion, and charity of judgment impressed him deeply. In connection with this Scotch visit Everett expressed his opinion of political prejudices and narrow-mindedness, saying: 'In England as in America, it were just as wise to take a blind man's deposition on the merits of a color, as a politician's on the character of his opponent. It is not that there is always an intention to vilify, but the prejudice is positively insurmountable! Candor, charity, and justice sink beneath it like grubs under an elephant's tread.'

Withal, however, the most interesting of all the Scotch experiences was the visit that he paid to Abbotsford. Scott, as we have seen, had cordially extended the invitation at their first meeting, and it was accepted with alacrity! After a hurried trip through Perthshire, therefore, Everett took the coach at Edinburgh for Melrose on the first of August. Good fortune attended him, and he was destined to renew his acquaintanceship with Scott in a most favorable fashion. For as the coach drove out of Edinburgh, on the way to Abbotsford, they passed a bookstall where the quick eyes of the American caught sight of an advertisement of 'The Heart of Mid-Lothian' which was just out. Everett persuaded the coachman to pull up for a moment, while he sprang down and bought the book. Scott, as we have seen, was not yet the avowed, although the generally suspected, author of the Waverley Novels, and Everett put into his host's hands the first copy of 'Mid-Lothian' that reached Abbotsford.

Thus began a most delightful visit which lasted several days, in the course of which the guest apparently made himself a welcome presence in the house. Scott's two daughters were at home, and Everett found a pleasant companion in Sophia, who later married Lockhart. They went on a mushroom hunt together and she took him over the park and grounds, discussing with him the probability of her father being the author of the famous novels, of which she was convinced. Scott himself took the young man to the lovely and romantic ruins of Melrose Abbey — a visit which twenty years later he was to describe with feeling on a public occasion in Boston.[1] Altogether he was a very privileged and highly honored guest, and young Charles Scott begged his father to let him go with Everett on the trip to Greece and Constantinople which was being planned. The friendships thus established were to last through many years, and Everett in later periods sent several of his countrymen with letters of introduction to the 'Wizard of the North' which were duly honored. In 1820, introducing a New England friend, he wrote to Sir Walter: 'Tell Miss Scott that the sugar almonds are in my desk before me, and Lady Anne that I still retain, as faithfully as did ever knight his lady's favour, a bit of her sash which I had the audacity to cut off.'[2]

The visit to Abbotsford was the last event of importance in the English trip. Toward the end of August he set out for the Continent, avoiding the beaten track by Dover and Calais and going by coach to Southampton. There he met Colonel Thomas H. Perkins, who beguiled him into a little side-trip for seeing Stonehenge, Salisbury, and Wilton. They then crossed to Havre, and Everett was struck at once with the difference made then as now by a little strip of salt water. Instead of 'the neat, tasteful stage-coach,' which had been so characteristic of England, 'with the nicely caparisoned horses and driven four-in-hand by the bluff coachman,' he found himself in a 'lumbering diligence, half baggage-wagon and half stage-coach, drawn by five, fiery Norman steeds, loosely tied together by rope harness, and straggling over the road, guided by postilions sunk to the thighs in gigantic trunk boots.' In this kind of a conveyance, he made the trip back to Paris stopping at Rouen long enough to see the sights and to moralize over the tragic fate of Joan of Arc.

His destination was Rome where he was to pass his fourth

[1] Address before the Scots Charitable Society in Boston, November 30, 1839.
[2] See *Sir Walter Scott's Letters*, II, 24, and Allibone, *Dictionary of English Literature*, p. 1966.

winter abroad. But he wisely gave some weeks to Switzerland on the way. That was one hundred years ago, but he saw most of the sights which thrill Americans, and indeed the people of all nationalities, to-day. He went to Chamonix, crossed the Mer de Glace, and made the other trips in that romantic neighborhood, which are safe enough to-day, but were somewhat hazardous in those times. Geneva, Vevey, Freiburg, Berne, Lucerne — he saw them all, going over the Brünig and even the famous Furca Pass, and finally descending into Italy by the winding wonders of the Simplon Road, which had been built under Napoleon's direction a few short years before. Although impatient to reach Rome, where he was planning to carry on another arduous course of study, he took the time to visit Venice, and lingered in Florence for a fortnight. The late autumn, however, found him in the Eternal City where he plunged into a study of Roman antiquities. Nearly every day saw him at the libraries of the Vatican. Here again he enjoyed the company of George Ticknor and of Joseph G. Cogswell, a fourth member of the party being Edward Brooks, of Boston. Rome, then as now, was thronged with strangers every winter from all parts of Christendom. People of learning and of culture found their way to the former mistress of the world, and in those days, as in these, the foreigners settled down into 'colonies of their own, generally determined by their nationality.' Thus there were the English, the German, and the French contingents — each preserving a good deal of the ways of life which distinguished them at home. Nevertheless, there was not a little general intercourse, and among the distinguished people whom Everett met and came to know were Bunsen and his family, Niebuhr the Prussian Minister, the Crown Prince of Bavaria, and the artists Schadow and Thorwaldsen. There were, however, no people in Rome at that time, whose acquaintance was so generally sought after, or whose society was so pleasant, as that of the Bonaparte family. They were there in force, including Lucien, Louis the ex-King of Hol-

land, their sister the beautiful Pauline Borghese, and noblest
of them all the mother of the mighty exile at St. Helena!
Madame Lætitia, or 'Madame Mère,' to use the title which
her imperial son had proudly and fondly decreed that she
should bear, was about sixty-eight at the time, and still preserved much of her dignity and beauty. She was living with
her brother, Cardinal Fesch, in the Palazzo Falconniere, in
apartments that were large and beautifully appointed, but
'private and unostentatious.' She received people in the
evening, and a distinguished company did her frequent
honor. Everett was duly introduced and paid his courtly respects. It is doubtful, however — his Napoleonic prejudice
was such — if he duly appreciated her force of character and
unique position, or did her the honor that was rightfully her
due.

Pauline Borghese also received the Americans in the palace
where she lived in Eastern splendor and great luxury. While
confessing her beauty, the thing that most impressed the
Americans was her coquetry. On one occasion she showed
the four young men her jewels, and they could think of nothing but her arch manœuvres and flirtatious manner, and
went away with but one opinion of her character. The member of the famous family whom they oftenest saw was Lucien,
who lived in more retirement than any of the others, spending
most of his days in his favorite study of mathematics, and
particularly astronomy. He was always at home to personal
friends in the evening, and many of them went there night
after night, finding his company the pleasantest in Rome.
The evening was always a somewhat dreary time in Rome for
strangers, and to Lucien's quiet family circle Everett went
again and again.

But other fields remained to be explored. Byron had inspired him with a desire to see Athens, Delphi, and the other
spots of classic Greece, and had supplied him with needful
letters. Ticknor was inflamed with the same desire, but his
cautious father at home dissuaded him, writing curtly, 'To

see Athens my son is not worth exposing your life.' As a companion, however, Everett had Theodore Lyman. The second of February, therefore, he set out from Rome and bent his steps toward Naples. Nearly a month was passed in visiting the surrounding country — Vesuvius, Baiæ, and Pompeii, and then he turned his face toward Greece! He had to travel on horseback, through a dangerous bandit country, as far as Otranto before he could get a vessel that took him to Corfu. At Corfu he was cordially received by Sir Thomas Maitland, the British Lord High Commissioner. The next step was across to the rocky coast of Albania, not far away, and he made the trip in a rowboat. Albania is anything but a safe place for travel in these days, and a hundred years ago it was vastly less so. Everett, however, had a letter from Lord Byron to Ali Pasha, and he made his way at once to the capital of the country, where Ali took him under his courteous and hospitable protection. From one Turkish dignitary and governor he was handed on to another, till he had passed through Thessaly to Thermopylæ. Taking the rough road over Mount Parnassus he made his way — and it must have been a perilous one — to Delphi, Thebes, and Athens. There are many travellers nowadays who think the trip to Sparta not worth while because of the discomforts that have to be encountered; but Everett was undaunted. Down across the Isthmus of Corinth he went to the site of the warlike city, back over Parnassus again into the north of Greece to the Gulf of Volos. There he took ship and crossed to Troy, before proceeding through the Dardanelles to Constantinople. In the famous city on the Golden Horn he was under the guidance of the English Ambassador, through whose influence the imperial mosques, including Saint Sophia, were open to his wondering inspection. That was in June, and toward the end of the month he set out for Adrianople, crossed the Balkan Mountains, and made his way to Bucharest. After being held in quarantine for a week on the Austrian frontier, he passed through Transylvania and Hungary to Vienna.

He gave a few weeks to that gay imperial city, then saw something of the Tyrol, made his way to Bavaria, then back to Paris, crossed to London, and took passage for America early in September. On the seventh of October he landed in New York, having been absent four years and seven months, and went at once to Cambridge to begin his work as Greek Professor.

It is interesting and significant to note that the first person to call upon him and to welcome him home to America was Daniel Webster, who had recently removed his residence from Portsmouth to Boston. Mr. Webster had already served a term in Congress. And thus for Everett began in earnest the closest and most influential friendship of his life.

IV

THE GREEK PROFESSOR

THE Harvard to which Everett returned as Greek Professor in 1819 did not differ greatly from the institution which he had left as Latin tutor six years previously. It was somewhat larger, that was all: but still in most respects a school, with the aims and ideals of schools at that particular period. It was distinctly difficult, no doubt, for the young professor to settle down after nearly five long 'wander years' abroad. The little college, with its scanty library, contrasted strongly with the famous institutions he had come to be familiar with in England, Italy, Germany, and France. After being presented to kings, and having freely conversed with monarchs in the world of art and letters, he suddenly found himself face to face with a group of boys in a recitation-room whom he was expected to instruct in the rudiments of an ancient language. But whatever may have been his sensations, he entered on his task with his usual industry and with no apparent lack of enthusiasm. He introduced his youthful pupils to Wolff's theory of the Homeric writings. He made a translation, for use in the classroom, of Buttmann's Greek grammar, which was considered of sufficient importance to be reprinted in England. Curiously enough, however, when the English edition appeared, 'Massachusetts' was omitted after 'Cambridge' at the end of the preface, lest a knowledge of its American origin might militate against its use in England.[1]

A young man still himself, Everett had a singular attraction at this time, and for long years afterwards, for the youthful mind. His grace of manner and skill of presentation, no doubt contributed to the effect; and 'the modest undergraduate,' we are told, 'found a new morning opening to him in

[1] Lowell: *Works*, VI, 156.

the lecture-room of Harvard Hall.' Goethe had said to him at Weimar, 'Eloquence is out of place in the lecture-room — eloquence does not teach.' The saying seems to have made a deep impression, and the young professor, known already as an eloquent pulpit orator, carefully refrained from all ornaments of rhetoric in his classes, talking instead with the utmost directness and simplicity.

Among the young men who came under his influence at this time, and who were later to achieve distinction, and some of them to remain his lifelong and devoted friends, were William Henry Furness, Ezra Stiles Gannett, Frederic Henry Hedge, Robert C. Winthrop, Charles F. Adams, Andrew Preston Peabody, George S. Hillard, William Parsons Lunt, and C. C. Felton, who was destined to succeed him in the Greek professorship. Dr. Peabody recalled in after years the young professor's kindness and considerate helpfulness, when he came before him as a lad to be examined for admission to the college. Everett, he wrote, 'received us so kindly, gave us such an encouraging view of the ordeal before us, and dismissed us with such well-framed advice as to the self-possession and quietness of spirit required for our success, that I have always ascribed my entrance without condition in great part to my having started for that day's work under his auspices.' [1] The pupil, however, who was destined to attain by far the greatest measure of distinction and success was one who also entertained for Professor Everett the greatest admiration. We have seen how young Ralph Emerson as a schoolboy had worshipped at the shrine of Everett in the pulpit, peeping in at church doors where he was to preach. And now, when a junior in the college, he was privileged to sit almost daily in the presence of his idol. And very devoutly he did so, making copious notes of the lectures that were given, and deriving inspiration and example from the ways of the careful scholar and the words of the graceful speaker. Emerson's admiration was so marked, and went to

[1] A. P. Peabody: *Harvard Reminiscences*, p. 93.

such extremes, as to cause him to be laughed at by his class-mates, who, though to a large extent sharing his sentiments, were more careful not to make them manifest. The best picture which remains to us of Everett at this time, and indeed at any time in his career, was drawn for us by this fond disciple who saw him at short range. Writing in later years, when admiration had long since given way to critical dis-agreement upon public matters, and disappointment that the career of politics had crowded out the claims of scholarship, Emerson recalled the Everett of those Harvard days.

His radiant beauty of person, of a classic style, his heavy large eyes, marble lids, which gave the impression of mass which the slightness of form needed; sculptured lips; a voice of such rich tones, such precise and perfect utterance, that, although slightly nasal, it was the most mellow and beautiful and correct of all the instruments of the time.

Moreover, he could say of him:

There was an influence on the young people from the genius of Everett which was almost comparable to that of Pericles in Athens. He had an inspiration which did not go beyond his head, but which made him the master of elegance. . . . The word that he spoke, and the manner in which he spoke it, became current and classical in New England. He had a great talent for collecting facts, and for bringing those he had to bear with ingenious felicity on the topic of the moment. Let him rise to speak on what occasion soever, a fact had always just transpired which composed, with some other fact well known to the audience, the most pregnant and happy co-incidence. It was remarked that for a man who threw out so many facts he was seldom convicted of a blunder. He had a good deal of special learning, and all his learning was available for purposes of the hour. It was all new learning, that wonderfully took and stimu-lated the young men. It was so coldly and weightily communicated from so commanding a platform, as if in the consciousness and con-sideration of all history and all learning — adorned with so many simple and austere beauties of expression, and enriched with so many excellent digressions and significant quotations, that, though nothing could be conceived beforehand less attractive or indeed less fit for green boys from Connecticut, New Hampshire, and Massa-chusetts, with their unripe Latin and Greek reading, than exegeti-cal discourses in the style of Voss and Wolff and Ruhnken, on the

Orphic and Ante-Homeric remains — yet this learning instantly took the highest place to our imagination in our unoccupied American Parnassus. All his auditors felt the extreme beauty and dignity of the manner, and even the coarsest were contented to go punctually to listen, for the manner, when they had found out that the subject-matter was not for them. In the lecture-room, he abstained from all ornament, and pleased himself with the play of detailing erudition in a style of perfect simplicity. In the pulpit (for he was then a clergyman) he made amends to himself and his auditor for the self-denial of the professor's chair, and, with an infantine simplicity still of manner, he gave the reins to his florid, quaint, and affluent fancy.[1]

Such an influence had probably never before been exerted at the College. The fame of his foreign training, at that time something wholly new in America, and the magic of his long residence abroad at Old-World seats of learning, made him a marked and alluring figure. A new lustre was conferred on the University, and students were drawn to Cambridge from the South and West, some of them coming from points as remote as Louisiana, Georgia, and Tennessee.

It was not to be expected, however, that Everett could confine himself to the classroom, nor even to the scholarly seclusion which Cambridge then afforded its professors. He continued in great demand as a preacher. He stood again in his old pulpit at Brattle Square, and reawakened in the congregation the great regret which was felt at losing such a preacher. A Unitarian church was organized in New York, and he was persuaded to deliver the Dedication Sermon. His discourse on this occasion was printed, and bears clear witness to his own conservative cast of mind, and to the generally conservative position of Unitarians at this period. He could say: 'We dedicate it (this church) to the glorious cause of the Gospel. It is sacred henceforth to that alone. Let no other message be heard within its walls, no human science, no learning or art of this world, no cause or interest which begins or ends with man: but the holy faith of the Son of God, and the truth as it is in Jesus.'

[1] Emerson's *Works*, x, 312–16.

More significant than this, however, and much more widely heralded abroad was the sermon that he preached in Washington. Services in those days were held at the Capitol in the Chamber of the House of Representatives, preachers of different denominations, and from various parts of the country being heard. Everett preached on Sunday, February 13, 1820, and took the city by storm. The effect was magical. Cabinet members, Justices, Senators, and Congressmen were loud in their praises, covering the young man with their commendations, and writing to their friends about the wonderful discourse.

It is interesting to read Everett's own account of these experiences. We have it in the following letter which he wrote to his sister, Mrs. Nathan Hale,[1] and it foreshadows the step that he was soon to take, leading from the pulpit to the platform:

BALTIMORE, *February* 5, 1820

DEAR SARY — I received your letter of the 29th the day before yesterday. It was very pleasant also for me to get one yesterday from Mr. Pickman, partly superscribed by your husband's hand, from which I infer that his eyes are really on the mending hand.

You see me thus far advanced on my mission. After I wrote you from New York, I preached a lecture Thursday evening and another Sunday. For the lecture I preached my Thanksgiving sermon, and for Sunday my New Year's. Sunday evening was the greatest crowd I ever saw; and multitudes had to go away. I came straight on to Baltimore, not stopping at all in Philadelphia, much to the discomposure of the Unitarians there, who are almost famished under the lay preaching. I arrived here on Wednesday, and preached to a very full house last evening. The church here is the finest building I have seen in America, I think the finest church of its size in the world. It is not, of course, to be compared with the great Gothic cathedrals or Italian temples, but it is very grand and beautiful; and, with one or two defects, in good taste. It resembles closely, in general plan, the imperial mosques of Constantinople. The Society here under Mr. Sparks is mostly an Eastern colony, at least the most respectable part are natives of New England. This is in some respects an unfortunate circumstance. It increases the

---

[1] In 1816, his sister Sarah had married Nathan Hale, editor of the *Boston Daily Advertiser*.

public prejudice, already very strong, against it; and gives the Orthodox an occasion of enlisting the local and geographical prejudices of the Baltimoreans, in opposition to the Unitarian Church.

Did Unitarianism, or any other ism rest where it begins, in mere critical, theological questions, they would have little of my aid; whether I thought their cause just or not. But as the cause of learning, refinement, and free enquiry is most intimately connected with it; and as the ignorance, necessary to keep up Orthodoxy, is so gross as to darken everything else, I resist the natural disdain I feel for the narrow controversial arena. But I am almost sick of it, and if things do not in a few years take a different turn, I shall quit the field, and confine my efforts and studies to subjects where there is a reasonable chance of a fair hearing; and where your adversary will not be listened to, in inverse ratio to his learning and sense.

I preached to a very full house last evening, my Thanksgiving sermon. This, too, I despise; hawking round two or three holiday discourses; but my old stock is insufferable to me, for the puerility of style: and the affectation of literary correctness, caught from the example of Mr. Buckminster and Thacher, whose sermons are calculated to do least good to those who most need it. I am to preach here to-morrow, and then go to Washington. Whether I shall preach or not, I cannot yet say. If I were a Member of Congress, after hearing all the debates of the week, it would seem to me but a poor day of rest, hearing a sermon of an hour and a half: as I shall certainly preach, if I do at all.

Everett returned to Cambridge in a blaze of glory; nor was the impression that he left behind in Washington soon forgotten. Statesmen and politicians wanted more of him. He was suggested for the chaplaincy of Congress. The movement took definite shape, and had he wished the position he could undoubtedly have been elected. But other plans were taking shape in his fertile mind.

In the first place, he had undertaken a course of lectures in Boston on 'Antiquities.' They proved a great success, and attracted crowds of hearers. So far as their value was concerned, we must turn again to the testimony of Emerson, who wrote in his Journal:

I have been attending Professor Everett's lectures which he has begun to deliver in this city, upon Antiquities. I am as much enamored as ever with the incomparable manner of my old idol, though much of his matter is easily acquired from common books. We think strong sense to be his distinguishing feature; he never commits himself, never makes a mistake.[1] . . .

Another entry reads:

I have heard this evening and shall elsewhere record Professor Everett's lecture on the Eleusinian Mysteries, Dordona, and Saint Sophia's Temple. Though the lecture contained nothing original, and no very remarkable view, yet it was an account of antiquities bearing everywhere that 'fine Roman hand,' and presented in the inimitable style of *our Cicero*.[2]

More important, however, and much more burdensome than a course of lectures was the fact that the young professor was appointed at this time the editor of the 'North American Review.' It was a very responsible position; and one for which he was eminently fitted. He was a ready, easy writer, a confident critic, and a man of most painstaking method. In 1820, therefore, when he accepted the editorship, he threw himself into the task with characteristic ardor. He often sat down, as he said of himself, 'with tired fingers, aching head, and a bad heart, and wrote for his life.' But he had the reward that he deserved. The magazine when he took hold of it had a languishing circulation among five hundred subscribers. He gave it life, made it interesting, edited it with skill, and the circulation soon increased fivefold. He wrote to Henry Clay at about this time, asking for information on a matter connected with the tariff, and he said in the course of his letter: 'You do not perhaps know the importance of the "North American Review" as a means of influencing public opinion. Thirty-five hundred copies of it are printed, and about thirty-two hundred copies of it circulate throughout the country, particularly to the South and West. I believe I may say there is not a social library, reading-room, literary club, mess-room, or public institution in any degree connected with politics or learning which it does not reach.' The articles, in those days, and for many years afterward, were unsigned,

[1] Cabot: *Memoir*, I, 95.   [2] Emerson: *Journal*, I, 207.

and the overworked editor more than once had to make good the deficiencies of contributors who disappointed him. Indeed, his own articles exceeded in number those of any other editor, and there can be no doubt that he gave the magazine 'a standing in literature that it hardly had before.' When the centennial of the famous periodical was celebrated in 1915, the historian of the event could write: 'Mr. Everett closed his labors as editor with a contribution of a remarkable article on European politics which not another man in America, unless it were Thomas Jefferson, could have written.' Later on we shall have to call attention to other contributions from his pen, but he certainly had good reason to be proud that at the age of twenty-five he raised the magazine to the standard of a first-class review. Moreover, the editorship gave him a public standing in this country and abroad. It brought him also into interesting touch with statesmen and men of letters.

We have seen how he visited Campbell in 1818, finding him at his home at Sydenham. The poet since then had become the editor of the 'New Monthly Magazine,' and Everett wrote him August 7, 1822, as one editor to another, the following interesting letter:

I ought on many accounts some time ago to have written you a letter of thanks for your polite notice of me in the preface to the 'New Monthly Magazine' at the end of the last year. When I left Europe with a mind crowded with what I had seen of men and things, I resolved to keep up my familiarity with them beyond the sea; but I have found that each hour has had its duties more urgent than that of a friendly letter and I have now nearly completed the third year of my return to America without having written as many letters except on business to England or the Continent.

One of my chief occupations has been the editorship of the 'North American Review,' a journal which had had a languishing circulation among five hundred subscribers for several years. By good industry on the part of myself and my friends it has now reached an edition of twenty-five hundred copies, a circumstance without example in this country, and we are at this moment printing the third edition of the first numbers of the new series. The most gratifying circumstance to me about it has been that by putting the publishing of it into the hands of a brother who with ten children was wholly without resource I have been enabled to relieve a great amount of domestic misery. I am sure you are too kind-hearted a man not to sympathize with me in the pleasure this gives me.

All editors, conscious like myself of being pretty stupid people, hold their heads up the higher for being able to count you in the fraternity. You are doubtless aware that the 'New Monthly Magazine' has since your editorship of it been reprinted in this country. My brother to whom I just alluded informs me that he intends to propose to Messrs. Colburn & Co. as exchange for the 'North American,' but I doubt whether our humble trans-Atlantic literature find sufficient favor in your dainty country to make such arrangement eligible to your booksellers. You have been nobly encouraging my friend and countryman Irving. His 'Bracebridge' is not wholly to my taste, and yet it is hard to say to a man who has done well, 'You ought to have done better.'

When I was in England three or four years ago and you laughed at me for coming to see the greatest poet in Sydenham, I gave you a copy of a youthful production of my own which you were pleased to praise far beyond its merits. Since my return to this country, I have nearly forsworn the Muse, which it was high time to do if I would be even with that delicate lady. I find, however, one or two pieces in my desk which may pass tolerable muster as Yankee poetry. If they are good enough, I should like to have you put them in your magazine: if not, you have few would-be contributors from whom you are more effectually screened than from a man from the other side of the Atlantic. Whatever you do with my poetry, a line of your own prose in the form of a letter would renew many pleasant recollections and be highly gratifying.

Among the 'pieces of Yankee poetry' referred to in this letter, and sent to the English editor, was evidently the 'Dirge of Alaric.' At any rate, early in 1823 the 'New Monthly' contained the following note, and a poem of thirteen stanzas of which these that follow are characteristic.

POETRY

The editor, though unauthorized to name the author of the following lines, ventures to announce their having been written by Professor Everitt [*sic*] of America, and conceives that they do no discredit to that gentleman's respectable name.

Dirge of Alaric, the Visigoth

Who stormed and spoiled the city of Rome, and was afterwards buried in the channel of the river Busentius, the water of which had been diverted from its course that the body might be interred.

When I am dead no pageant train
Shall waste their sorrows at my bier,
Nor worthless pomp of homage vain
Stain it with hypocritic tear;
For I will die as I did live
Nor take the boon I cannot give.

Ye shall not raise a marble bust
Upon the spot where I repose;
Ye shall not fawn before my dust,
In hollow circumstance of woes,
Nor sculptured clay with lying breath
Insult the clay that moulds beneath.

But ye the mountain stream shall turn
And lay its secret channel bare,
And hollow, for your Sovereign's urn,
A resting-place forever there:
Then bid its everlasting springs
Flow back upon the king of kings,
And never be the secret said
Until the deep give up his dead.

.   .   .   .

My course is run, my errand done,
I go to Him from whence I came
But never yet shall set the sun,
Of glory that adorns my name,
And Roman hearts shall long be sick
When men shall think of Alaric.

My course is run, my errand done —
But darker ministers of fate
Impatient round the Eternal throne
And in the caves of vengeance wait;
And soon mankind shall blench away
Before the name of Attila.

The verses, naturally enough, soon found their way back to America, where they attracted considerable attention. Twenty years later they were reprinted in the Boston Book, but almost at once they were given place in the school readers. Boys for many years used them for declamatory purposes and spoke them on school platforms. They have a definite dramatic value, and call attention anew to Everett's love of the theatrical and spectacular.

And yet, in spite of all this, and much besides, young Everett was still restless and discontented. As a brief year of experience in the ministry had convinced him that the pulpit was not what he wanted, so a brief period in the professor's chair was sufficient to persuade him that an academic life was just as little to his liking. Pegasus was not to be confined to the classroom. A consciousness of great ability contributed to what must have seemed to his friends conspicuous instability.

The wings of ambition were now beating fiercely, and he was battling with the bars of fate that he had forged for himself with too great haste. The following letters to Judge Story reveal his state of mind, and tell a somewhat surprising tale of restlessness and pride.

CAMBRIDGE, *April* 13, 1821

Private.

DEAR JUDGE:

You have occasionally, though undesignedly, planted a thorn in my side, by remarks which you have dropped, that you thought I would have been a good lawyer; — the rather as I find I am a poor professor. From the first week of my return hither, I saw that our university — as good I doubt not as the state of society admits — would furnish me little scope for the communications of the higher parts of ancient literature, and that a good grammatical driller, which I cannot consent to be, is wanted. But I find besides that the whole pursuit, and the duties it brings with it, are not respectable enough in the estimation they bring with them, and lead one too much into contact with some little men and many little things.

In short, I die daily of a cramped spirit, fluttering and beating from side to side of a cage. I am not quite sure that I cannot break through its sides. I was twenty-seven years old two days ago, which, though something ancient to take a new start, is not, in our simple state of society where the servitude to forms is moderate, a period wholly desperate. My studies for some years past and my observations abroad have not been wholly foreign from topics connected with your profession, and I have some facility of acquisition. I have mentioned this subject to our good friend Webster, who expressed little surprise at my state of mind, and no apprehension of the result of a change. I have also consulted the President, to know especially what effect the thing would have on the College. He agrees with me that the first *announce* of it would produce no pleasant impression; but as I should take no steps without providing for the repayment of the sums advanced me by the College for my travel, he thought no solid permanent objection would be, in the minds of the candid, and seemed inclined to think it a case where one might encounter a passing evil for a greater permanent object. My brother Hale expresses nearly the same opinions and feelings, and these three persons are the only ones I have consulted, and these all in the course of yesterday. During my period of law study, I should live on the 'North American Review,' which, if it do not fall off, will furnish me an ample support; — and I shall probably be able to make it a good deal better than it has been, without undue encroachment on time devoted to law studies.

I would only add that I am actuated now by no motive of political ambition. I regard the high offices of our country as splendid burdens — hardly splendid; — and I am desirous of embracing the profession of the law, with a view of supporting myself by the laborious practice of it. I am fully aware that it is laborious, in all its ways, but labor has no terrors to me. I work *now* all my time, and for seventeen hundred dollars a year, quod nullo modo, duitius perferre prosum. Tu igitur, pidex ammasime, dic mihi, quæro, quid tibi di his rebus videtur. Pray mention not the subject to any one, for it is yet only a vision. I wish to proceed with deliberation, which the importance of the thing demands, consult those whose wisdom I can trust, and for whom I feel respect and affection, and then make up my mind, and meet the shock at once. Pray be careful what you say to me, for I shall put a good share of the responsibility on your shoulders.

P.S. Please to honor this letter with a warm place under your fore *stick*.

In those days Cambridge was a town apart; the professors naturally enough lived near the College. Everett, himself, on returning from Europe, had established himself in 'the brick house with a bow window' which stood on Cambridge Common. But he did not enjoy the seclusion of the college town. He had grown up in Boston, had been settled there during his brief ministry, and he liked it. His friends were there, and he was unusually fond of human companionship. The thought occurred to him, therefore, that, if he could live in town and go to Cambridge for his classes, life might become a little more endurable. There had been a few instances in which professors had been given this privilege of residing away from Cambridge. If others had been permitted to do so, why might not he? Here, therefore, seemed a solution for his restlessness. The Greek Professor would continue to teach, not giving up his chair for a study of the law, *provided* he were given permission to live in Boston. The Corporation approved of the arrangement, and, without waiting for the consent of the Overseers, Everett moved into Boston and established himself on Beacon Street, in a house that was owned by Jonathan Phillips. But the Overseers disapproved of non-residence on general principles, and their consent was necessary. Judge Story was an Overseer, and Everett wrote him thus:

DEAREST JUDGE:
Our vacation is up next Friday, and I am overwhelmed with business of all sorts. I shall not be able to accept your kind invitation. You will perhaps have heard the turn my affairs have taken. I am to be a non-resident professor on twelve hundred dollars. You are opposed to non-residence, so am I; but I thought it better than residence; and there were so many hearts to be grieved by the other movement that I gave it up.

On the eve of the Overseers' meeting he wrote again, directly asking for support.

DEAR JUDGE:
The Overseers to-morrow are to take my non-residence into consideration. Pray come up, if possible and make them *concur* with the Corporation. You shall put it on grounds you will not object to: the hardness of making me the first to suffer; of forcing me to reside where half the professors are dispensed; and on the *safe* nature of the vote of the Corporation which allows me non-residence *only for so long as it be found unprejudicial* to College. Do, if possible, come; for with me it is the cast of the die. If I cannot live in town, I resign; and then a train of consequences (God knows what) succeeds. I was taken by surprise, or I would have spoken to you sooner. I have spoken to no one else of the Overseers.

But the Judge was obdurate. His friendship for the brilliant and restless young professor was not strong enough to overcome his settled convictions. At a meeting of the Overseers held on November 6, 1821, 'After ample discussion of the vote of the Corporation presented for concurrence to this Board respecting Professor Everett's exemption from residence at Cambridge, it was voted that the subject be referred to the next semi-annual meeting, and in the meantime committed to the Honorable Joseph Story, Honorable Judge Jackson, and the Honorable John Pickering to report at said meeting.'

There was still some room for hope, therefore, and Everett sent off one more letter of expostulation and resentment, which was written in some heat, and not without clear evidence of pride. It did not seem to occur to him that his long period of travel abroad had already put him under considerable obligation to the College.

November 8, 1821

DEAR JUDGE:

I have just received your kind letter of the 6th. I was, as you justly state, aware of your objection to non-residence; and I had no hope of your assistance but on the ground that you might think I had as good a right to live in Boston as so many others. I could not of course complain of being forced to share the common fate (for a *fate* and that a hard one it is), but I trusted, and do still trust that I shall convince you, the community, and the Overseers that they cannot in justice begin with me: and apart from all other consideration, the necessity of submitting to a disability from which any colleague was exempted, would be a thing I could not for a moment endure. This is no affected pride, put as for the sake of making your task more difficult, by evidencing several other cases. But I really could not hold up my head, under the shame of having been formally denied an indulgence, which (to say the least) three others, precisely in my situation, enjoy.

I heard of your kind expressions and those of other gentlemen. Yours I know were sincere, and I thank you kindly for them. I will take no rash step you may depend. I think I am engaged to Judge Putnam's when I come to preach, but I will contrive to have some time with you.

But the fates were against him. Six months later, at an Overseers' meeting held on May 7, 1822, the report of the committee was made, and it was adverse. But to have the blow appear less personal and direct, the whole question of the non-residence of professors was considered, and it was voted, 'that it would be highly detrimental to the interests of the University to depart from the ancient usage of requiring the constant residence of those professors, whose offices, from the nature of them, are essentially connected with the necessary studies of the undergraduates.'

'The cage' was therefore locked, and Everett submitted with such grace as he could summon up. Henceforth, however, his lot was to be less lonely, and for a time at least the confines of Cambridge were less uncongenial than they had been hitherto. On May 8, 1822, Professor Everett was married to Charlotte Gray Brooks, a daughter of Peter Chardon Brooks, of Medford and Boston. The marriage took place at Mr. Brooks's residence on Atkinson Street in Boston, the ceremony being performed by the Reverend N. L. Frothingham, minister of the First Church in Boston. Mr. Frothingham had been married but a short time previously to Ann Gorham Brooks, a sister of the bride, and on May 11th the two young men with their wives 'set out on a short journey.'

The connection was a fortunate one for Everett. Mr. Brooks was a man of wealth and of conspicuous public spirit, highly honored and universally respected in the community. He was a man who had the cardinal virtues. Like Ruskin's father he was 'an entirely honest merchant.' He had made his own way, and had amassed a large fortune. His ancestors landed in this city about 1630, and belonged to the yeoman class. His father was a clergyman, and he himself, when he came to Boston in 1782, was without a dollar; but he was industrious and sagacious, had many friends, and made money steadily. Having acquired a fortune before he was forty, he gave himself to public service, serving as Representative and State Senator, and also as a member of the Governor's

Council. But he much preferred private life, especially in the country. He passed his summers in Medford, where he built a large and comfortable house for himself and his family. He was in all respects a most estimable citizen — scrupulously upright, influential, and highly respected, the father of a large family of sons and daughters. The day after the wedding he wrote Mr. and Mrs. Everett saying that, besides paying for the furniture for their future house, he would send them quarterly the interest at five per cent on $20,000, which was the arrangement he had made with Mr. and Mrs. Frothingham when they were married. Mr. Brooks that year, in 1822, estimated his income at $61,695.36, and considered the value of his estate to be $1,187,698.22 — which was a very considerable fortune for those days. The young couple, therefore, had no financial fears as regarded the future. None the less they did not furnish for themselves at once a home. The youthful professor, as we have seen, had no desire to establish himself permanently in Cambridge. He took his bride, therefore, to the Craigie House, which just then was the most fashionable and expensive boarding-place in Cambridge. Mr. Craigie, who had been a man of means and much importance, had lost his money, and the family became so reduced that Mrs. Craigie grudgingly let rooms to people. Her name was Miriam, and her charges were considered so exorbitant that she came to be known as 'Miriam the Profitess.'

But the arrangement was only temporary, which was true also of his college post. Matrimony did not lessen the young man's craving for a wider field. It soon looked as though an opening had come which would enable him to go abroad again. In 1821, the Greeks revolted against the unbearable atrocities and cruelties of Turkish rule. In due course they appealed to the United States, the one real Republic in the world, to help them in the frantic struggle for freedom, and to recognize their independence. Everett was stirred at once. He had been in Greece. He knew the country, the people, and many of the leading men. His information was first-hand, and he was able to write and speak with distinct authority. He contributed an article on the subject to the 'North American Review' in the October number for 1823. Webster read it, became persuaded, and decided to champion the cause of the Greeks. He turned to Everett for counsel and assistance, receiving in return minute information on many points of interest, and being posted at the same time in all details of the war itself. In acknowledging the handsome and ungrudging service Webster wrote: 'I have gone over your two manuscripts with the map before me, and think I have mastered the campaign of 1821–22, historically and topographically. My wonder is when and how your most extraordinary industry has been able to find all the materials for so interesting and detailed a narrative.'

But Everett did not stop at this. He thought he saw a way of being of still wider use. At the same time that he was supplying Webster with ammunition for a speech to Congress, he wrote to John Quincy Adams, then Secretary of State, asked him to use his influence to have the President appoint a commission to go out to Greece and make enquiries into the progress of the Revolution, and suggested himself as a member of such a commission. There was a cordial friendship between the younger man and the older one, destined to grow deeper and closer in the years to come, and there seemed for a time some likelihood that the suggestion would bear fruit. Calhoun became his champion, and Webster lent his influence. It was even proposed that he should go out as special commissioner to represent the Government and report. In this connection he became for the first time closely associated in a political way with Mr. Webster — a relationship which was to continue and grow steadily deeper and more intimate through a period of thirty years, and only to be terminated by Webster's death in 1853. We have seen that Everett had supplied his friend with materials, and the following letters indicate how valuable they had proved.

December 6, 1823

There was, as I believe, a meeting of the members of Administration yesterday, at which interview they talked of Greece. The *pinch* is, that in the message the President has taken, as it happened, pretty high ground as to *this continent*, and is afraid of the appearance of interfering in the concerns of the other continent also. This does not weigh greatly with me. I think we have as much community with the Greeks as with the inhabitants of the Andes and the dwellers on the border of the Vermillion Sea. It was, or I am not well informed, stated, yesterday, that there ought to be a commission, and that you ought to be persuaded to go. Go you will and go you shall — if you choose so to do. Yours most sincerely.

Sunday evening, December 21, 1823

Two days ago I received your Greek statistics, and to-day your letter of the 15th. I pray you not to think that my engagements are such as to make your correspondence inconvenient. . . . I find your communications of the utmost utility. In regard to the history of the campaign I could have done nothing without your aid.

My intention is to justify the resolutions against two classes of objections — those that suppose it not to go far enough, and those that suppose it to go too far. — Then to give some little history of the Greek Revolution — express a pretty strong conviction of its ultimate success, and persuade the House, if I can, to the merit of being the first Government among all the civilized Nations who have publicly rejoiced in the emancipation of Greece. There will be Speeches enough — some of them no doubt tolerably good. Whatever occurs to you — if it be but a *scrap* — in season to be sent here, pray forward it. Mr. C. is greatly obliged to you for your *map* — I hope to hear from you a short word, at least, every day or two.

I feel now as if I could make a pretty good speech for my friends the Greeks — but I shall get *cool*, in *fourteen days*, unless you keep up my temperature.

But Everett was not the man to let his friend get cool. His heart was in this matter. He was thoroughly aroused. Letters were not enough. He would go to Washington, supply Webster with new material, and hear his contemplated speech. The new year, therefore, saw him leaving Cambridge suddenly, and posting with all haste to the seat of government. I have found no record of his stay in Washington; but these letters from his wife which he carefully preserved give a picture of love and loneliness that his absence caused at home, and they also hint at some of his social diversions at the Capital.

BOSTON, *Saturday, January 10, 1824*

When I read your letter from New York last Tuesday, I felt discouraged, and was sure you would not reach Washington in time for the speech; but when I saw by the paper that Mr. Webster's speech was deferred, I made up my mind never to feel discouraged about you again; for somehow or other you always seem to hear the very thing you set out to. I hope, when the famous speech does come, that it will fully answer your expectations, and that after you have heard it you will send me a faithful account of it. The letter of Mr. Adams in the paper of Wednesday, in answer to that of the Greek gentleman in London, showed such a want of feeling toward the poor Greeks, that I fear Mr. Webster's eloquence will hardly soften his hard heart, but I suppose I know too little about it to give any opinion and I will give the Greeks up to you, knowing that you will do your best for them. . . .

I think of you all the time, and miss you more and more every day. Every time the bell rings, I hope there is a letter for me, though I ought not to expect you will write by every mail. For my own part I find but very little time to write, and as to writing by myself I cannot, for the chamber is always full, and the little room never has a fire in it, but I am resolved to write to my dear husband as often as once a week, and trust to his love to excuse all the blunders of his affectionate

LOTTY

P.S. If you think it is unpleasant to Mr. W. to have me direct your letters to him, I beg you will send me word and I will pay postage.

BOSTON, *Thursday, January 15, 1824*

I had yesterday resigned myself to despair concluding that you, whom I thought my best and indeed my only friend, had forgotten me, when Abby came running upstairs and asked me what I would give her for what she had in her hand. I knew that she must have letters from you, and as soon as I had *snatched* them from her hand I was obliged to run into my own chamber that I might cry for joy. Only think, dear husband, I did not receive your letters of the 6th

and 7th till yesterday — and this delay they tell me is occasioned
by the bad roads. If ever I hailed a good brisk northwester with
any pleasure, it was yesterday — for I thought it might improve
the riding and thereby enable me to get your letters more punctually. . . .

I want very much to get your account of Mrs. Adams's party,
and to hear how you made out among 'The Belles and Matrons,
Maids and Matrons.' I hope you did not lose your heart for the
'Belles and Maids,' and that your being there did not break their
hearts. I am sorry, very sorry that you should feel yourself so
humbled by being among the great folks — great only in name,
though, in my opinion. *My* pride was touched that you should
have descended so low as to have called on Mrs. A. the day before
her party, that you might get an invitation to it. Why could you
not have waited till you were invited? — or not have gone at all.
We have as famous parties here as you have in Washington, though
we don't publish them in the daily papers. . . .

Friday evening

I got your letter from Washington to-day, and as I had not sealed
this when it came, I thought it would be best just to tell you that I
had received it, and to say, as you were coming home so soon, I may
not write again. It was good news to me, I assure you, to hear that
I should see you in a week or two; but you must not hurry home on
my account, for I am comfortable. We were quite amused with
your account of Mrs. A.'s party — and Mother thought your joke
with General Jackson excellent. I think, however, that you stand
but a poor chance of being President unless you make better jokes.
You had much better content yourself to come home and buy Mr.
Farrer's house, for I begin to think I shall like it. But of that hereafter. For the present, dear husband, good-night. Dream if you
can of your affectionate

LOTTY

The young wife's intuition was right. Webster's eloquence
could not soften the hard heart of Mr. Adams; the Secretary
of State was not to be persuaded. He considered Everett too
distinct and pronounced a partisan, and claimed that with
such an agent in the field it would be impossible for the
United States to accomplish anything at Constantinople.
And so the suggestion finally fell through — Mr. Adams apparently not having any great amount of sympathy with the

Greeks, and believing that a lot of feeble sentiment was entering into the entire matter.

The young professor, therefore, was once more disappointed. Instead of being sent on a romantic mission into revolutionary Greece he was obliged to content himself with continuing to teach Greek roots to a handful of college boys in Harvard Hall. Again he swallowed his chagrin, and plunged with added fierceness into editorial work on the 'North American Review.'

The entire Greek episode, however, gives evidence among other things of the restless and ambitious nature of the man. He had been teaching for less than five years at Harvard, after being allowed five years' preparation. He had only recently been married; had a child a few months old, and suddenly we find him eager to relinquish everything and go off on a Byronic expedition to Greece. Nothing daunted him unless it were monotony. Moreover, the experience at Washington throws further light on his career. It is evident that during this visit the possibility of a political life first took shape. Why should he not go to Congress? Might he not continue as professor meeting his classes between the sessions? It is obvious that he and Webster talked the matter over.

The following letter would indicate that a change in the Middlesex District was near at hand, and that a vacancy would soon occur. Apparently the friends took counsel with leading men in Concord and the neighborhood. All that was needed was something that would call Everett before the public mind; and the opportunity suddenly presented itself in one of the most dramatic occasions on which he ever came forward as an orator.

SANDWICH, *August* 15, 1824

Mr. Knowles suggested to me the same idea that Mr. Marshall whispered to you — and I believe he was quite sincere in the wish he expressed. I am afraid it is too good a thing to be hoped for; nevertheless, there is no occasion to discourage any suggestions of that sort. To be thought of a little, and talked of a little, in that connexion [*sic*] would do ultimate good. Mr. Fuller, I believe, means to decline, at least I think such has been his intention. His preference, I imagine, as to a successor, is likely to fall on Mr. *Keyes*, of Concord, unless he should happen to like the present suggestion. I think he is not favorable to Mr. Knowles's election. I shall make it matter of duty to be at Commencement, principally on account of the φ B.K., and I will find out how Mr. F. feels. The *public* of Middlesex would like it well, I have no doubt. The difficulty will lie with the *politicians*.

Mrs. W. sends her remembrances, such as may be thought most proper and affectionate. She sets her heart on the φ B. Oration.

Edward Everett was chosen the Harvard Phi Beta Kappa Orator for 1824. The meeting of the Chapter was appointed for August 25th, the College Commencement exercises coming the day before! Everett prepared himself with the greatest care, choosing for his theme 'The Circumstances Favorable to the Progress of Literature in America.' It was a subject that gave him freedom to speak on public affairs and patriotic duties from the point of view of literature and scholarship. Not long before the day arrived, however, it became apparent that the meeting was to be one of no ordinary interest and significance.

On the eighteenth of August, just a week before Commencement, Lafayette, the hero of two continents, arrived in New York for his memorable visit — the first that he had paid since serving as a youth in the Revolutionary War. The whole country opened wide its arms to embrace with gratitude and fervor the friend and companion of Washington. New York went wild with enthusiasm when the old man stepped ashore from the ship that had brought him across from Havre. Processions, receptions, balls, and functions of every kind were arranged in his honor.

The ardor of New York was somewhat chilled, however, when the hero announced his intention of proceeding almost at once to Boston in order to be present at the Harvard Commencement, Harvard having conferred upon him the honorary degree of LL.D. in 1784. His progress in a coach and four through Connecticut and Rhode Island was a triumphal procession. In order to redeem his pledge to be in Boston at a stated time, he was obliged to ride his last forty miles at night. Reaching Roxbury, he was received by Governor Eustis, who had fought side by side with him in the Revolution, and who now proceeded with him to the city limits. Met here by a military escort, he continued to the head of the mall on Tremont Street where the children of the public schools were drawn up to receive him. All accounts of the period agree that never before, on any occasion, had there been so many people in Boston.

And now, having paid his respects to the Governor and the Council in the Senate Chamber, the General was conveyed to his lodgings. Standing at the corner of Park and Beacon Streets was the mansion which had been erected by Thomas Amory some years prior to 1800. Since Mr. Amory's time the house had been variously occupied. During the term of his governorship Christopher Gore had used it as an Executive Mansion. At the time of Lafayette's visit the house was being used as a club. This club-house Mayor Quincy rented and turned over to the uses of the city's guest. Under its windows, day and night, throughout the stay of the visitor, crowds gathered who cheered him to the echo whenever he went abroad. Men pressed forward to shake his hand, and women and children to be kissed. 'If Lafayette had kissed me,' declared one enthusiastic lady, 'depend upon it I would never have washed my face again as long as I lived.' On the twenty-fourth of August the great man attended the Harvard Commencement. The next day he drove again to Cambridge to be present at the Phi Beta Kappa meeting. He had entertained young Everett when, a few years previous, he had been a student in France; and was eager, doubtless, to hear him now. The 'Public Exhibition,' as it was called, began at twelve o'clock and was held in the old meeting-house which stood on Harvard Square. The place was packed. As an eye-witness described the scene:

The remotest parts of the old church were crowded to their utmost capacity with eager and expectant throngs. The old-fashioned square pews were filled, and every inch of space on the top of the narrow railing which encloses them was occupied by persons who, unable to find seats or standing-places, remained perched upon these sharp edges, hour after hour, wholly unconscious of the discomfort of their uncertain elevation.[1]

The speakers faced a solid mass of humanity, and the atmosphere was charged with excitement. The Reverend Henry Ware was poet of the day, and the press described his verses as 'a delicious morsel.' Then the orator arose — the picture of radiant grace, an embodiment of youthful beauty, and in quiet, even, deliciously modulated tones began one of the greatest orations of his life. Never did his manner seem more charming, never did his art appear so perfect. There was no element of affectation, no evidence of anything but exquisite spontaneity and ease of diction, both in matter and address. He had chosen well his theme, for it gave him an opportunity not only to display his learning, and to draw upon his personal experiences in foreign travel, but it supplied as well an outlet for the expression of patriotic feelings! Everett had come back from Europe, as many a young man since then has returned, with a deepened love of his own country, and a quickened confidence in political liberty and democratic institutions. He set himself to prove, therefore, that a republican form of government is the very form which is best calculated to develop and encourage learning. He said with prophetic vision:

Should our happy Union continue, in no remote futurity this great continent will be filled up with the mightiest kindred people known in history; our language will acquire an extension which no other ever possessed; and the empire of the mind, with nothing to resist its sway, will attain an expansion, of which, as yet, we can but partly conceive. . . . Divisions may spring up, ill blood may burn, parties may be formed, and interests may seem to clash; but the great bonds of the Nation are linked to what is past. The deeds of the great men, to whom this country owes its origin and growth,

[1] James Spear Loring: *The Hundred Boston Orators*, p. 536.

are a patrimony . . . of which its children will never deprive themselves. As long as the Mississippi and the Missouri shall flow, those
men and those deeds, will be remembered on their banks. The
sceptre of government may go where it will; but that of patriotic
feeling can never depart from Judah. In all that mighty region
which is drained by the Missouri and its tributary streams . . . will
there be, as long as the name of American shall last, a father that
will not take his children on his knee, and recount to them the
events of the twenty-second of December, the nineteenth of April,
the seventeenth of June, and the fourth of July?

This, then [he could add, as the audience quivered beneath the
glowing fervor of his periods], this, then, is the theatre on which
the intellect of America is to appear, and such the motives to its
exertion; such the mass to be influenced by its energies; such the
glory to crown its success. If I err in this happy vision of my
country's fortunes, I thank Heaven for an error so animating. If
this be false, may I never know the truth. Never may you, my
friends, be under any other feeling, than that a great, a growing, an
immeasurably expanding country is calling upon you for your best
services. . . . As I have wandered over the spots once the scene of
their labors, and mused among the prostrate columns of their senate houses and forums, I have seemed almost to hear a voice from
the tombs of departed ages; from the sepulchres of the nations
which died before the sight. They exhort us, they adjure us, to be
faithful to our trust. They implore us by the long trials of struggling humanity; by the blessed memory of the departed; by the
dear faith which has been plighted, by pure hands, to the holy
cause of truth and man; by the awful secrets of the prison houses,
where the sons of freedom have been immured; by the noble heads
which have been brought to the block; by the wrecks of time, by
the eloquent ruins of nations, they conjure us not to quench the
light which is rising on the world. Greece cries to us by the convulsed lips of her poisoned, dying Demosthenes; and Rome pleads
with us in the mute persuasion of her mangled Tully.

Then came the climax of the great oration. The speaker
paused for a moment, looked to where Lafayette was sitting,
and, stepping forward, said:

Welcome, friend of our fathers, to our shores! Happy are our
eyes, that behold those venerable features! Enjoy a triumph such
as never conqueror nor monarch enjoyed — the assurance that,
throughout America, there is not a bosom which does not beat with
joy and gratitude at the sound of your name! You have already

met and saluted, or will soon meet, the few that remain of the ardent patriots, prudent counsellors, and brave warriors, with whom you were associated in achieving our liberty. But you have looked round in vain for the faces of many, who would have lived years of pleasure, on a day like this, with their old companion in arms and brother in peril. Lincoln, and Greene, and Knox, and Hamilton, are gone; the heroes of Saratoga and Yorktown have fallen before the enemy that conquers all. Above all, the first of heroes and of men, the friend of your youth, the more than friend of his country, rests in the bosom of the soil he redeemed. On the banks of his Potomac he lies in glory and in peace. You will revisit the hospitable shades of Mount Vernon, but him, whom you venerated as we did, you will not meet at its door. His voice of consolation, which reached you in the dungeons of Olmütz, cannot now break its silence to bid you welcome to his own roof. But the grateful children of America will bid you welcome in his name. Welcome! thrice welcome to our shores! and whithersoever your course shall take you, throughout the limits of the continent, the ear that hears you shall bless you, the eye that sees you shall give witness to you, and every tongue exclaim, with heartfelt joy, Welcome! welcome, La Fayette!

With the name of the French hero the last word upon his lips the orator took his seat, and a period of absolute silence followed! Not a sound was heard — save of suppressed sobs; not a movement seen, except the wiping of eyes, for nearly every face was bathed in tears. The spell was so supreme that the entire audience seemed hypnotized. But the response came at length, and it was overwhelming. Cheers were given; handkerchiefs were waved, and it seemed as though the clapping of hands would never cease.

But whatever may have been the momentary effect of the oration on others, its influence on the speaker's own career was lasting. So far as he himself was concerned, it marked the termination of a purely scholarly career, and saw him launched on the stormy waters of political existence. Little did he think, little did his hearers dream, that he was destined in his own person to disprove his eloquent contention and was to find for himself, at least, conditions in America unfavorable for devotion to literary pursuits.

The patriotic tone of that Phi Beta Kappa Address suggested the fitness of Professor Everett for public office. Always a power with young men, his name was now brought forward by the young voters in the Middlesex District as a candidate for Congress. A regular nominee already had been named; but less than two months after the delivery of the great oration, a volunteer convention was held in Lexington on October 14th, made up of independent voters, which placed him in nomination, and put forth an earnest appeal for his election. He was commended as 'national in his feelings, acute and penetrating, unwearied in application, intimately versed in foreign politics and intimately acquainted with the interests of every section of our country.' A committee was appointed to wait upon him immediately, and the next day Everett accepted the nomination in the following letter:

CAMBRIDGE, *October* 15, 1824

GENTLEMEN:

Permit me to express my thanks for the honor done me by the gentlemen whom you represent in placing me in nomination for Congress. The circumstances that my name had already been mentioned in other quarters, and the state of the public mind on the subject of the approaching presidential election, call upon me in frankness to say that, in consenting to be a candidate, I would not be understood in any degree to enter into opposition, on the subject of that election, with another gentleman who has been already nominated. It is known to my friends, that, some time since, I was applied to by leading Republican friends of Mr. Adams, to consent to be put in nomination for Middlesex District, and that my consent was given. I have been informed, indeed, that at the former convention at Lexington the suggestion was made that my nomination had been originally brought forward by the opposers of Mr. Adams; but this suggestion was wholly unfounded.

Candor has seemed to demand of me this explanation, although the presidential question, in a few weeks to be decided, has really no connection with a nomination to the nineteenth Congress; and although I presume it would not be expected of any candidate to give pledges beforehand either to support or to oppose the measures of any administration which is yet to be formed.

I have the honor to be, gentlemen, your faithful humble servant

EDWARD EVERETT

Messrs. Wm. Ward, Jun., Marshall B. Spring, C. Stetson, John Clark, and James M. Whittemore, Committee.

The above letter was written in reply to a personal interview, held at once after the convention on October 14th at Lexington.

The campaign was a brief one, lasting less than three weeks, and his friends were active in his behalf. Three days before the election a meeting of his fellow-townsmen was held at Willard's Hotel, Cambridge, and resolutions were passed commending the candidate, and declaring that his election would be 'a triumph of Virtue, Talent, and Learning over party feeling and sectional influence.' The citizens of Charlestown were particularly strong in his behalf. He had won favor in that locality because of his connection with the project for a monument at Bunker Hill. He had been a prime mover in the Association which had been formed to promote the scheme, and had served with great acceptability and activity, writing to the newspapers and arousing public sentiment. Charlestown people, therefore, knew his qualifications for office, and they were unsparing in their public praise. In a broadside published in the 'Columbian Centinel' he was described as having abilities of the highest order, 'with a mind eminently gifted by Nature, enriched by learning, enlightened and liberalized by travel, having visited and examined other countries and other systems, and having returned an ardent admirer and able defender of our National Rights, feelings, principles, and institutions.'

There was, of course, opposition. He was accused of being too academic for public life, and, curiously enough, it was charged against him that he was 'tinctured with radicalism.' This latter defect, however, it was acknowledged that 'a few years' experience was likely to cure.' It was a presidential year. There were no recognized parties, and what was known as 'the scrub race for the presidency' took place, the principal candidates being Henry Clay, John Quincy Adams, William H. Crawford, and Andrew Jackson. Daniel Webster was the congressional candidate from the Suffolk District, running without opposition, and being elected unanimously

— people of all classes and parties voting for him. Everett's chief opponent was the Honorable John Keyes. Election day was the first Monday in November, and Everett was an easy victor, receiving 1529 votes to 603 for Mr. Keyes.

The immediate fruits of victory were not destined, however, to be altogether to his taste. He still had the college authorities to reckon with. In deciding to enter public life, he had had no thought of severing his connection with Harvard. He expected to continue as Professor of Greek Literature while serving as member of Congress, returning to the task of teaching between sessions. The double duty would have been signally acceptable to one of his restless energy and exceptional industry. Indeed, he thought he had taken pains to satisfy himself on this point, and to make his position sure, before accepting the congressional nomination. In answer to his direct enquiry, President Kirkland had given him to understand that there was no necessary inconsistency in the double function. John Quincy Adams had continued as Professor of Rhetoric while holding office as a United States Senator. Under the circumstances, therefore, Professor Everett was taken suddenly aback at receiving a communication from the President and Fellows of the College early in March asking whether he had 'accepted the office of member of Congress to which he had been elected.' Everett answered this by saying that he 'had not accepted the office in any other way than by consenting to be a candidate for election'; but that he 'considered his acceptance to be implied in the consent given to stand as a candidate.'

Thereupon the Corporation passed the following Resolution:

Whereas, it appears from the foregoing answer of Professor Everett that he has accepted the office of member of Congress, and thereby vacated his Professorship, therefore Voted, that he be requested to perform the duties of said Professorship during the present college year, and in the event of his compliance with this request that his salary be paid him for that period.

Everett was naturally not a little nettled by this somewhat brusque and wholly unexpected action. Young as he was, he was not the kind of man to be treated cavalierly by committees or corporations, especially when precedent was clearly on his side, and when he was acting in the line of public service. His letter to President Kirkland was dignified, but not without a sting:

CAMBRIDGE, *March* 14, 1825

I have received your letter of the 8th, enclosing a vote of the Corporation of the 7th to the following effect: 'Whereas, it appears from a communication from Professor Everett that he has accepted the office of a member of Congress, and thereby vacated his Professorship, therefore Voted, that he be requested to perform the duties of said Professorship during the present college year, and in the event of his compliance with this request that his salary be paid to him for that time.'

In answer to this communication, I beg leave respectfully to object to the form of the preamble of the vote just cited.

At the time the vote was communicated, I did not know even on what grounds the Corporation stated it to appear that I had vacated my office. I have been informed since that it is [in] virtue of a law passed in 1781 [?] omitted on the revised edition of the Laws, and not enforced in the cases of Mr. Adams, Chief Justice Parker, Mr. Stearns, and Judge Story. I do not think that it can in virtue of such a law be said 'to appear' that I have vacated my office; that is, to be a matter of course.

I do not question the right of the Corporation to remove me; but I do not think it ought to be said that I have vacated the office, that is, taken a step previously known to be incompatible with holding it.

In compliance with the request contained in the vote of the Corporation cited, I shall be happy to continue in the discharge of the duties of my office till the close of the academic year.

President Kirkland answered him the next day, saying that 'the law alluded to was passed in April, 1787. It was first published in the edition of the College Laws of 1790, and it was continued in the editions of 1798 and 1807.' There the matter ended, except that Everett, in order wholly to square himself with the authorities, paid over to the College the sum of $5300, which represented, with certain deductions, the amount which had been advanced him for travel and study abroad. The little controversy had been conducted with due dignity and restraint on both sides. It is evident enough, however, from a study of the college records, that the Corporation was not wholly satisfied with the way in which the Greek Professorship had been conducted. The brilliant Everett had been too much of a public character, with too many irons in the fire, to please the staid members of the teaching staff. They wished a drillmaster in the chair who would school a classroom of boys in the roots and rudiments of the Greek language; whereas Everett had always contended that he was, according to the title of the foundation, the Professor of 'Greek *Literature*.' In addition to this distinction, it is probable, too, that professional jealousy entered somewhat into the dispute. Envy is not unknown to scholars. His older colleagues could not look with altogether kindly eyes on one who occupied so brilliant and conspicuous a public position. Moreover, it must be remembered that the College was still under clerical control. The President and many of the governing board and teaching staff were ministers of religion. The feeling for the Profession was very strong, and they had not yet wholly forgiven Everett for giving up the pulpit. It seemed a fall from grace, and the new Congressman was soon to have it flung in his face in Washington that he had committed almost an act of sacrilege in ceasing to be a minister of the Gospel in order to enter the arena of politics.

At any rate, the first incumbent of the Eliot Professorship of Greek Literature was released without apparent regret, and the Corporation proceeded to lay down rules for the conduct of the Department which his successor was expected to follow. In due season John Snelling Popkin was appointed to the vacant chair — an able man, in the active ministry — but about as different from Everett in most respects as one man could possibly be unlike another.

Thus Edward Everett for a second time had changed the course of his career in life. Having turned from the exacting calling of a preacher to the cloistered, studious pursuit of teaching, he was now to embark on the boisterous, troubled sea of politics, with what a mingling of pain and pleasure, of failure and success will soon become apparent.

V

APOLLO IN POLITICS

DURING the first thirty years and more of our Government the House rather than the Senate held the centre of the congressional stage. The sessions of the Senate, in the early days of the Republic, were generally secret. Debates took place behind closed doors. Senators harangued one another, but did not have the ear of the country. And even after this was changed, and the public came to be admitted to the galleries of the Upper House, the Senate was too small a body to encourage eloquence or stimulate debate. There were only twenty-two Senators when the Government was first organized, and in 1825 there were barely twice that number. Eloquent contests and dramatic appeals, such as we long since became accustomed to, were hardly likely to be indulged in under such conditions. The sessions were sessions of a committee rather than of heated parliamentary debate.[1]

In the House, however, things were wholly different. The House, when Everett became a member, still challenged public attention and was the chief force in the education of public opinion. The chamber itself in those days was not the enormous extinguisher of telling and persuasive speech that it is in these. Its size was well adapted for discussion and debate. The good speaker had things in his favor. It was in the House that the Jay Treaty aroused the eloquence of Gallatin and Fisher Ames. It was in the House that Clay and Webster and Calhoun established their reputations for eloquent address and passionate appeal that kindled the country into flame. Indeed, in 1811, when Henry Clay was elected to the House, after serving for a time in the Senate, he looked upon the transfer as a welcome change, and considered that he had obtained a larger field of opportunity.

[1] Rhodes: *History of the United States*, I, 33.

Such was the relative importance of the two branches of Congress up to 1825. Everett might well consider, therefore, that in leaving Harvard Hall for the Hall of Representatives he was stepping from a school-room into a National arena! Henceforth, he might naturally feel that, instead of teaching Greek to a handful of students in a classroom, he was to speak to the heart and conscience of the entire country! There was, however, one great difference, which he was soon to feel. He had been carefully prepared for a scholar's career. He was counted the best Greek scholar of his day. But when it came to politics he had little but the 'gift of tongues' to recommend him. Up to the time of his election to Congress, we have his own word for it that he had never even cast a vote whether at a National or State election. From the shades of learning he was now to pass suddenly into the fierce glare of political publicity, and he was soon to experience the difference between a Phi Beta Kappa Oration and a speech in opposition to an amendment to the Constitution.

The member-elect to the nineteenth Congress from the Middlesex District in Massachusetts left Boston for the new scene of his labors on December 19, 1825. He went by stage-coach to Providence and New London, and thence by steamboat to New York. The trip from Boston to Washington was no simple matter in those days. The roads were bad — at certain seasons so deep in mud as to be almost impassable — and the steamboat accommodations were none too comfortable or safe. When children were of the party, which was the case with the Everetts — for they now had a small but growing family — the journey was a serious if not a hazardous undertaking.

He wrote in his journal many years afterward by way of reminiscence:

When I first began to go to Washington it was an affair of a week. The first night brought us to Providence. The old Connecticut steamer was about thirty hours on the Sound. Two days were required from New York to Philadelphia, a day and a half from

Philadelphia to Baltimore, and a day from Baltimore to Washington. The consumption of time was but a part of the evil. There was much inconvenience in the numerous changes of conveyances, and you arrived at your destination weary and travel-sore.

Nor were conditions wholly comfortable or congenial when the Capital was reached. Washington, in those days, was a very different place from the city that we now admire. The public buildings were few and magnificent, but the hotels and private residences were also few, and very far from magnificent or even comfortable. Negro shanties predominated. The long, wide streets were unpaved — deep with mud in winter, and almost as deep with dust when the early spring arrived. Cattle were left to wander at will in the public squares, and cows were often milked by their owners on what passed for sidewalks. Altogether, the Capital was a cross between a village and a city, and life there had its primitive and unpleasant features. Few members of either branch of Congress had their private houses. Some of them lived at the hotels; but for the most part they made headquarters at some boarding-house. Members and their families clubbed together, took over some boarding establishment which they controlled, and formed congenial centres which were known as 'messes.' Social life under such conditions was extremely difficult, and entertaining on any large scale was out of the question. There were periodic receptions and stated gatherings at the 'Palace,' as the White House was colloquially called, and sometimes such functions took place at the houses of Cabinet members, and the residences of foreign ministers; but all such affairs were few in number and simple in character.

The Everetts, however, were unusually fortunate when it came to matters such as these. In the first place, the new Congressman was a particular and intimate friend of Daniel Webster, who at this time was a fellow-Congressman, but destined soon to be promoted to the Senate. Mr. and Mrs. Webster took the Everetts under their wing. They became members of the same 'mess.' Professor Everett was introduced to all Mr. Webster's friends. And Mrs. Webster posted Mrs. Everett in regard to Washington etiquette.

But a second and even greater advantage lay in Mr. Everett's personal relations with President Adams. John Quincy Adams was serving his first year in the White House in 1825. There had been no choice by the people at the 1824 election. The contest had been carried, therefore, to the floor of the House, where Adams had finally triumphed. There had been charges, however, of a corrupt bargain when Henry Clay became Secretary of State, and the President's asperity had been rather accentuated than decreased by the ugly rumors that were spread abroad. Everett had known President Adams for a number of years, and the relationship between the two was very cordial. The President had once served as Professor of Rhetoric at Harvard, and he was very naturally interested in the career of the young orator, if not wholly captivated by his eloquence. The new Congressman was therefore a welcome as well as frequent visitor at the White House. These ties, too, were soon to be immeasurably strengthened by the engagement of Mr. Adams's son to Abigail Brooks, a younger sister of Mrs. Everett. Charles Francis Adams was serving as the President's private secretary, and the attachment was formed when Abby Brooks came to visit her sister Charlotte Everett in Washington. Everett was serving *in loco parentis* to the young lady, and he was soon sent by Mr. Brooks to interview President Adams on other than political matters. Thus the intimacy between the two men grew, and the young professor was soon to become the President's particular champion on the floor of the House. But the budding statesman seems never to have abused these privileges. He was able to say in after years that he had never asked of Mr. Adams 'any favor for himself, for any relative, or any friend.'

Everett's arrival in Washington had been awaited with not a little interest, for he was already well known for his brilliant and scholarly attainments, his wide learning and his captivating powers of speech. His long residence in Europe and wide range of travel marked him out at once for certain spheres of influence. He was appointed to membership upon the important Committee on Foreign Affairs, and also became a member of the Committee on the Library and Public Buildings.

With his usual ardor, industry, and careful attention to details, Everett entered quickly into the full and faithful discharge of his new duties. There were many brilliant men among his colleagues in the House — Cambreling, of New York, McDuffie, of South Carolina, Forsyth, of Georgia, and, leading all the rest, Daniel Webster. Even in such a company of acute and educated men, Everett held from the first a unique position and stood out conspicuous for his broad scholarship and extensive fund of learning. He was soon to make friends, and also enemies; but even his opponents speedily recognized his fairness, sound judgment and ability, and soon formed the habit of consulting him when in search of information. A fellow-member of the opposite political party, who was later promoted to the Supreme Bench, stated in after years that whenever, in those days, he wanted any information upon a matter of public importance, he always went to Everett, political opponent though he was, and added that he always got the information he sought. Everett himself, however — in his latter years — did not entertain so high a regard for the learning and intellectual equipment of his fellow-Congressmen as to be unduly flattered by their attention. There were many of them, he discovered, who did not know their way into the library, or once there were ignorant of how to secure the information they desired.

The maiden effort of this brilliant young member of the House was naturally awaited with considerable interest. He himself looked forward to the event with not a little trepidation. It became his wish that he might make his début in some informal way, rather than in a set or elaborate speech.

And his wish was unexpectedly granted — so much so that he took himself as well as other members wholly by surprise. The question of the Congress of Panama was before the House. A reference was made to the Committee on Foreign Affairs — a reference which did not seem to Everett correct, and before he knew it he was on his feet to say so. 'I have, Sir,' he said, addressing the Speaker — 'I have, I believe, attended every meeting of the Committee on Foreign Affairs and been present at nearly every moment when business has been transacted in that committee. I feel, therefore, able to say that this call for papers on the Panama Mission has never been before that committee, and that the Honorable Chairman has never been instructed to have any special communication with the Department of State. . . . I therefore respectfully protest against its being understood that any such information on this subject is in possession of the House, or of any member of it.' He spoke with diffidence and simplicity, referring to himself as 'a very humble and subordinate member of that committee, who felt himself called upon to explain a certain matter in order that the House might be properly possessed of the facts.' Then, being on his feet, and feeling secure, he passed on to another matter, saying as he did so: 'Before I sit down, allow me a word in reply to the gentleman from South Carolina — a remark I should have made the other day, could I have conquered my diffidence at taking the floor.'

That the diffidence was very genuine there can be no doubt. Moreover, the relief that he actually felt at having broken through the congressional ice appears from the following letter that he wrote to his sister:

WASHINGTON, 13 *February*, 1826

. . . You perceive, I made a sort of *coup d'essai* in the House, on the Panama question. I succeeded in doing what I always hoped I might get courage to, that is, in making my début in some other way than a set speech previously prepared. What I said was extorted from me, on the spur of the moment, and, as I succeeded without stumbling, I hope I shall find no difficulty hereafter. But

when I see almost every member, who speaks at all, injuring himself by speaking too often, I feel the more fixed in my determination
to take the floor very rarely. . . .

Moreover, his friends at home soon learned that the
impression he had made was favorable in the extreme.
J. Hamilton, Jr., wrote to George Bancroft on February 6:

I send you the debate on the resolution calling on the President
for information in relation to the Congress of Panama in which our
friend Mr. Everett made his début. It was fresh as it ought to have
been, because it was entirely extemporaneous, and therefore took
the House by surprise, the members of which did not entertain any
expectation of hearing Mr. E. except on some topic of elaborate
preparation. His manner is mild, prepossessing, and urbane in the
extreme, his fluency uninterrupted, and with practice I have little
doubt of his becoming a first-rate offhand debater, the only de-
bating talent that is worth a farthing in a House constituted like
ours.

But the good beginning, which was in part so excellent
because it was impromptu, and gave promise of better things
to come, was soon followed by an elaborate effort, carefully
studied, but not carefully enough considered, and which was
destined to be remembered and referred to till his dying day.
It was a full month after his diffident and unpremeditated
beginning that he made his first set speech. It will be well to
study it with care; for it reveals both the strength and weakness of the man — but more especially the weakness. We
shall find in this first formal utterance in his political career a
declaration of principles and a statement of faith which will
supply us with a standard for measuring his entire life as a
public man in the service of his country.

The question before the House was a proposed amendment
to the Constitution, which was being considered 'in Committee of the Whole.' The failure of the people to choose a President at the election of 1824, whereby the contest had been
carried into the House of Representatives, led Mr. McDuffie,
of South Carolina, to propose an amendment to the Constitution. This amendment was intended to prevent such an

event happening again. It took the form of certain resolutions, which were as follows:

Resolved: That, for the purpose of electing the President and
Vice-President of the United States, the Constitution ought to be
amended in such manner as will prevent the election of the afore-
said officers from devolving on Congress.

Resolved: That a uniform system of voting by Districts ought to
be established in all the States, the number of Districts in each
State to equal the number of Senators and Representatives to
which each State may be entitled in Congress, and each District
having one vote.

The debate was long and spirited. It lasted many weeks
and the matter was not settled until April 4th, when the first
resolution was carried, and the second lost by a very narrow
margin. Everett and Webster voted in the negative on both
propositions. Everett rose in his place on March 9th. His
speech was a long one, and lasted nearly three hours. He was
in poor physical condition for making a great mental effort.
He had passed a sleepless night, due, no doubt, to extreme
nervous excitement — awoke with a splitting headache, and
ate no breakfast. In writing his sister, Mrs. Hale, the next
day, he said:

DEAR SARY — ... I did not sleep any the night before; awoke
with such a headache as I never felt; and went to the House and
implored McDuffie to put off the debate for a day. This he declined, and I then thought I must give up speaking from physical
inability. Knowing, however, the insidious interpretation that
would be put on this, and not choosing to enter again into the disgraceful scramble, with twenty competitors, for the floor, and
trusting to the good Providence which has never yet failed me in
the hour of trial, I got up, and after a slight ringing in my ears and
dimness before my eyes had passed off, I felt wholly revived and
never spoke with more ease to myself. I was about three hours, and
when I got through, felt so exhausted as to come home and go to bed.

He began, therefore, with a word of apology, saying: 'I
rise to address the committee in a state of indisposition, under
which I ought in prudence to be at home rather than on this
floor.'

It soon became apparent to himself and others, however, that apologies were altogether out of place. He quickly got himself in hand, and went on to say:

I am opposed to the resolutions of the gentleman from South Carolina. It is with me a matter of some question whether the alterations in the Constitution for which they provide are not, in their spirit and tendency, unconstitutional. To amend is one thing, essentially to change another.... I am in the fullest persuasion, I am under the most perfect conviction, that every proposed alteration, which avowedly goes to change the essential features of this instrument, is neither more nor less than unconstitutional. We have accordingly no right even to consider it, which is all we can do at best — we have no right to propose it; it is not within our competence.... In setting my face against all alterations of the essential provisions of this frame of government, I am in no degree influenced by a belief or feeling that it is a perfect system. Far otherwise; perfect! how can it be? was it not a compromise between parties evenly balanced?... But the Constitution — the Constitution — the only thing permanent which we have; the only thing which the people of the United States have taken out of this daily changeful legislature, the thing which is to stand us instead of all the perpetuities of the Old World, ecclesiastical, political, social, and personal. Sir, I do not think it perfect; but it is good enough for me. I have lived under other political institutions. Nearly a third of my life, since I came to years of discretion, has been passed under other forms of government; and I have learned enough of the state of foreign societies to be well contented with what Providence has given us in the Constitution of the United States. I am contented to live by it; contented to die by it. Contented when I die to leave my children in its safeguard; and I would sooner lay down this right hand to be cut off than I would hold it up to vote for any essential change in this form of government.

And then he reached this climax of rather redundant and elaborate rhetoric, but which had the ring of passionate patriotism, and drew forth loud applause:

Let the States that now compose this happy Union ... contract the habit of tampering with the Constitution; let them, in the excitement of an election passed, or of an election to come, disturb that curious, that happy adjustment of powers, which is now our life and our peace, and all will be lost for them. Sir, let the people of this country believe what the gentleman has so earnestly told them of the corruptibility of this House, of their Representatives, and I say not all *will* be lost, but all is lost, irretrievably, totally, forever. But such, I thank Heaven, is not my opinion — all is not lost — all is safe — very safe. The country stands at this moment in that position firm and erect, in which Providence intended that it should stand; at home, a model of a wise and prosperous administration of domestic affairs; abroad, an examplar to the discouraged nations of that long-desired union of liberty and law. Sir, if I held the opinion to which I allude — which, I hope, on mature deliberation, the gentleman from South Carolina himself will revise — I say sincerely, I would not come here to proclaim them! Here they can do no good; the hour is gone by; the battle is fought and lost. But I would go with them to England, and I would there sound them in the ears of the reformers, so called; that poor deluded company, who, without leaders, without counsel, are following the phantom of reform through the dark paths of treason and assassination to the scaffold. I would fly with them to the continent of Europe — and see if I could there do nothing to repress the movements of revolution, ready to break out in that fair quarter of the globe, in pursuit of the same delusive good, proved, by the failure of our experiment in this favored land, to be thus delusive. I would go with my doctrines to Turkey, and there strive to nerve the arm of the Sultan, that he might drive the steel still deeper into the bleeding heart of mangled Greece, fighting for the same insulting mockery of freedom for which we fought, and, at best, for the same treacherous and short-lived success! Then, Sir, if I could find on the face of the earth one mild, parental, beneficent despot, who loves his people as his children, I would go and lay my forehead on his footstool, and beg him to set his foot on my head, as a recreant citizen of a recreant Republic. If I could find such a living monarch, in weeds of deepest sable I would join that mournful procession, that spectacle perhaps never before witnessed on earth, the funeral convoy of the nations, which even now, while I utter the words, is following the kind and departed arbiters of life and death of fifty millions, from province to province — from mourning Asia to mourning Europe.

Taken as a whole the speech was that of an extreme conservative. It was the florid utterance of a patriot who was passionately devoted to things as they were, and who dreaded any kind of change. And no objection to this could fairly be taken. He had travelled extensively abroad, as very few men in those days had done, and his comparison of the happy condition of things in America with what he had seen in Europe was well calculated to fall upon approving ears. Washington rang with praises of his eloquence. Mrs. Everett could write home to her family and friends in Boston that her husband had spoken with the most perfect success. Indeed, she thought him as eloquent in parts of his speech as she had ever heard him, and added that 'once or twice, he produced an effect on the House that I suspect was never before equalled.' The address continued for some time to be the talk of the town, and two weeks after its delivery Mrs. Everett wrote her sister-in-law this rather amusing letter:

WASHINGTON, *March 25*, 1826

Husband's speech has produced a great sensation here, particularly among the ladies who are quite inspired by it. Several of them wrote impromptus on the occasion. Two of them I have seen which were very pretty. One was an acrostic by Mrs. Van Rennsselaer, and another was a piece of poetry written by Mrs. Adams praising husband in the most extravagant terms. Mrs. A. was not in the House to hear him, but she had a very animated description of his performance from Miss Maise, of Philadelphia, who is passing the winter with Mrs. Adams. I begin almost to be jealous — husband is so admired by the girls, and I keep hearing from all quarters that they wish he was not married, and they wonder who the *second* Mrs. Everett will be. I beg he may not make another speech — if it is only to spare my feelings. . . .

But the talk was not all of it by way of praise, and the exuberant flamboyant orator soon had cause for serious qualms, if not for painful regrets. Young ladies might write impromptus in the excess of their ardor, complimenting him on his periods and gestures; but there were men who wrote him down permanently from that time onward as a time-server and coward because of what he said in regard to slavery. He committed in this connection a ghastly error of judgment, and exposed himself to grave misunderstanding. Moreover, what he said was as unnecessary as it was unwise, and the stain of his words was destined to cling to him thereafter until all was finally washed away in the blood of the Civil

War. It was, too, a bad beginning, especially for one who had been a Christian minister, and he never wholly recovered from it. There is the more reason to lay emphasis upon it at this point, for the slavery question came to prove for him a veritable Nemesis, and for nearly forty years his somewhat hesitating, compromising policy in regard to it was to throw a sinister shadow over many of his public acts.

The subject of the debate, as we have seen, was the question of amending the Constitution, and every one knew that the Constitution never would have been adopted except for the compromise with slavery. All that Mr. Everett needed to do was to declare that he did not believe in anything likely to disturb this historic compromise; and that it would be dangerous, if a beginning should be made in making changes. Not content with this, however, or something like it, Everett proceeded to rush headlong upon his fate. He launched out suddenly into a gratuitous consideration of what would be the duty of Northern citizens in the event of a slave insurrection at the South, which was nothing more than the remotest kind of possibility. The subject had not entered into the debate, and it does not appear that there was any need of referring to it. The uprising of the blacks in Hayti, however, was still fresh in people's minds, and a member of Congress had recently gone so far as to suggest in published form that in the event of an insurrection among the Southern slaves there were people at the North who would think it both immoral and irreligious to join in suppressing such a revolt. The young Congressman, for some reason best known to himself, considered it advisable to answer the unimportant charge. He may have thought to propitiate the South; he may have hoped to silence unwise talk at the North; he may have had, as he distinctly and passionately had throughout his life, the interests of the Union foremost in his mind; but at any rate, whatever were his motives, this is what he said:

I ought perhaps to add, that if there are any members of this House of that class of politicians to whom the gentleman from

North Carolina (Mr. Sanders) alluded, as having the disposition, though not the power, to disturb the compromise contained in the Constitution on this point, I am not of the number. Neither am I one of those citizens of the North, to whom another honorable gentleman lately referred, in a publication to which his name was subscribed, who would think it immoral and irreligious to join in putting down a servile insurrection at the South. I am no soldier, Sir; my habits and education are very unmilitary; but there is no cause in which I would sooner buckle a knapsack to my back, and put a musket on my shoulder than that. I would cede the whole continent to any one who would take it — to England, to France, to Spain; I would see it sunk in the bottom of the ocean, before I would see any part of this fair America converted into a continental Hayti, by that awful process of bloodshed and desolation by which alone such a catastrophe could be brought on. The great relation of servitude, in some form or other, with greater or less departures from the theoretic equality of man, is inseparable from our nature. I know of no way by which the form of this servitude shall be fixed but political institution. Domestic slavery, though I confess not that form of servitude which seems to be most beneficent to the master — certainly not that which is most beneficent to the servant — is not, in my judgment, to be set down as an immoral and irreligious institution. I cannot admit that religion has but one voice to the slave, and that this voice is, 'Rise against your master.' No, Sir, the New Testament says, 'Slaves obey your masters': and though I know full well that, in the benignant operation of Christianity which gathered master and slave around the same communion table, this unfortunate institution disappeared in Europe, yet I cannot admit that, while it subsists, and where it subsists, its duties are not presupposed and sanctified by religion — I certainly am not called upon to meet the charges brought against this institution, yet truth obliges me to say a word more on the subject. I know the condition of the working classes in other countries; I am intimately acquainted with it in some other countries, and I have no hesitation in saying that I believe the slaves in this country are better clothed and fed and less hardly worked than the peasantry of some of the most prosperous states on the Continent of Europe. These are opinions which I have long entertained, and long since publicly professed on this subject, and which I here repeat in answer to the intimations to which I have already alluded. But, Sir, when slavery comes to enter into the Constitution as a political element, when it comes to affect the distribution of power amongst the States of the Union, that is a matter of agreement. If I make an agreement on this subject, I will adhere to it like a man: but I will protest against . . . popularity as well as votes being increased by the ratio of three-fifths of the slaves.

It was a rhetorical outburst, ringing with dramatic fervor, and graphic in the picture that it drew. It made an instant and profound impression, and it stuck. Other parts of the speech were soon forgotten; but this portion was called up against him till his dying day, and even afterwards. The last echo to be heard was fifty-five years later, and it lost nothing in coming from another famous orator. In 1881, in his memorable Phi Beta Kappa Address at Harvard on 'The Scholar in a Republic,' Wendell Phillips referred to 'that un-rivalled scholar, the first and greatest New England ever sent to Congress, who signalled his advent by quoting the original Greek of the New Testament in support of slavery, and offer-ing to shoulder a musket in its defence.'

The trouble began almost instantly. Two weeks after the delivery of the speech, while many were still voicing their praises, Horace Binney wrote to a friend:

Professor Everett has made a speech in Congress, which has made more noise than from the printed sketch it deserves. He has uttered a sort of confession of faith on the subject of slavery that was gratuitous, not at all called for by the occasion, and will make him infinitely odious to many people who wished him well.[1]

The prophecy was all too true. Mr. Whipple was the first to sound the note of censure. He said in the course of the debate on March 26th:

As the gentleman from Massachusetts has taken occasion to sub-mit his confession of faith on this subject, I must be permitted to utter mine also. I cannot agree with that gentleman, that involun-tary servitude is either founded in, or sanctioned by the laws of nature. . . . Sir, I ask the gentleman to point out any mandate of the law of nature which has consecrated human beings upon the altar of slavery. . . . The evil was entailed upon us. It is a disease which has 'grown with our growth and strengthened with our strength,' and should not be irritated and aggravated by the rash hands and nostrums of political charlatans.

[1] Charles C. Binney: *Life of Horace Binney*, p. 82.

Three days later, Michael Hoffman of New York, attacked him much more savagely, saying:

As the doctrine which he [Mr. Everett] has enunciated may be applied to my children, I will repeat to deny it. . . . What a doctrine has the gentleman adopted! . . . It is a terrible doctrine! . . . It has enslaved Asia, and depopulated the fairest parts of the earth. Desolation marks its progress, and if insular Hayti be odious, is continental Barbary less so; when he, who on one side of the Mediterranean is a master, on the other side is a slave, doomed to servitude?

The climax of rebuke was reached, however, on April 20th, when Mr. Cambreling, of New York, but a North Carolinian by birth, in the course of a speech upon another subject lashed the young orator with stinging and sarcastic words that must have cut to the quick. ´

I cannot [he said] concur with the gentleman from Massachusetts. . . . I was astonished to hear him declare that 'slavery, domestic slavery, is a condition of life as well as any other to be justified by morality.' If, Sir, amidst the wild visions of German philosophy I had ever reached a conclusion like this — if in the Aulæ of Göttingen, I had persuaded myself to adopt a political maxim so hostile to liberal institutions and the rights of mankind — I would have locked it up forever in the darkened chamber of my mind. Or, if my zeal had been too ardent for my discretion, this, at least, should never have been the theatre of my eloquence. No, Sir; . . . this was not the proper theatre for declaring such opinions, nor was it the quarter from whence we might have expected them. Had they been expressed by gentlemen from the South or West, it might not have excited so much surprise. . . . But coming from another quarter, and from a mind rich with intelligence, I heard them with astonishment.

This was more than Everett could endure, and he sprang up at once to defend himself, and to make such explanation as was possible. He called attention to the fact that he was referring to a slave *insurrection*. As to slavery being sanctioned by religion, morality, and law, he meant, he said:

Slavery as it exists under the circumstances of the case supposed (that of a revolt to be suppressed in this country) and on the basis of long-standing political institutions. I said nothing [he added] of reducing men to slavery, as the gentleman insinuates. I did not justify kidnapping and the slave trade, as I have been accused of doing.... The charge does not deserve to be contradicted by me. I spoke of the relation of slavery as existing with us; where nearly two millions of individuals already stand in that relation; where the safety and lives of half the citizens of the United States are involved in it; where a general emancipation is allowed to be attainable, if at all, by an exceedingly gradual process; and in reference to the question of a war of horror and extermination between these two portions of the population.

But it was not in Washington alone that defence was needed. People at home were censorious and hostile. His brother-in-law came to his assistance in the 'Boston Advertiser,' calling attention to the fact that it was the possibility or eventuality of a slave insurrection that had been referred to, and not slavery itself. Everett was appreciative, but professed himself callous and indifferent — as of course he was not. He wrote somewhat significantly to his sister:

Your husband is very kind in defending my speech; but I hope he will not give himself much trouble about it. I anticipated the consequences of what I said, and am willing to meet them. Had I not made the remarks I did on slavery, something else would have been found to cavil at, by the coterie in Boston and Salem, who think everything good, done by one who does not belong to them, is a personal insult. I never heeded them; — though I do not wish to provoke, I am not afraid of them.

It was long, however, as we have seen, before he heard the last of the matter. It was reported years afterward that John Randolph, standing up in his place, pointed to him with his long finger and said that 'he envied not the head or the heart of the Northern man who could utter such sentiments.' The statement was made over and again, and Everett was kept busy denying the story, and proving it a fabrication for the reason that Randolph was not a member of the House at that time.

But if Everett was wrong on the subject of slavery, and

drew down upon himself a great deal of abuse that was undeserved, he did a good deal to redeem himself when it came to
the question of another downtrodden and long-suffering race.
He came forward nobly and whole-heartedly as the chivalrous
champion for the just and honorable treatment of the
Indians. When a bill was introduced into Congress for removing the Creek and Cherokee tribes from the east to the
west side of the Mississippi, depriving them of their lands and
driving them into the wilderness, his righteous anger was
aroused, and he spoke with no uncertain tones. His speeches
on the matter glowed with noble sentiments and human feeling, and he denounced the scheme with impassioned energy
and ardor, insisting on the execution of the laws and treaties
which the United States had entered into with the various
tribes. He presented petitions from 'Sundry citizens of
Massachusetts, praying that the Indian Tribes may be
protected in the rights secured to them by the laws.' Over
and over again we find him returning to the subject, holding
up to Congress a vivid picture of the cruelty of the proposed
action, and portraying the Red Men, more especially the
Cherokees, not as barbarians, but as

people, living as we do, by husbandry, and the mechanic arts, and
the industrious trades; and so much the more interesting, as they
present the experiment of a people rising from barbarity, into
civilization. . . . Whoever heard of such a thing before? [he cried]
Whoever read of such a project? Ten or fifteen thousand families,
to be rooted up, and carried hundreds, aye, a thousand miles into
the wilderness! There is not such a thing in the annals of mankind. . . . [To remove] unoffending communities, subject to our
sovereignty, indeed, but possessing rights guaranteed to them, by
more than one hundred treaties — to remove them, against their
will, by thousands, to a distant and a different country, where they
must lead a new life, and form other habits, and encounter the
perils and hardships of a wilderness: Sir, I never heard of such a
thing. . . . They are not barbarians; they are essentially a civilized
people. . . . They are planters and farmers, they are tradespeople
and mechanics, they have cornfields and orchards, looms and work-
shops, schools and churches, and orderly institutions. . . . I am not
without hopes [he concluded] that Congress will yet throw its broad

shield over these, our fellow-beings, who look to us for protection; being perfectly satisfied that, if the question could be presented free from all extraneous considerations to the decision of the House, it would be for the preservation of the treaties.

In much the same spirit, too, this scholar in politics came forward fervently in favor of pensioning the surviving officers of the Revolutionary War. As the time drew near for celebrating the semi-centennial of the signing of the Declaration of Independence, a bill was introduced into Congress looking toward the relief of the surviving veterans of the Revolution. The cause was one which appealed to Everett's patriotism — always easily aroused. His arguments in favor of the measure resemble those that were heard in Congress at a much later day and after a much greater war.

I want [he cried] to do something. I want a substantial tribute to be paid. Praise is sweet music to old and young; but I honestly confess that my mind relucts and revolts, by anticipation, at the thought of the compliments with which we are going to fill the ears of these poor veterans while we leave their pockets empty and their backs cold. If we cast out this bill, I do hope that some member of the House, possessing an influence to which I cannot aspire, will introduce another, to make it penal to say a word, on the Fourth of July, about the debt of gratitude which we owe to the heroes of the Revolution. Let the day and the topic pass in decent silence. I hate all gag-laws; but there is one thing I am willing to gag — the vaporing tongue of a bankrupt, who has grown rich, and talks sentiment, about the obligation he feels to his needy creditors, whom he has paid off at 2s. 6d. in the pound.

In the meantime Mr. Everett continued in close and somewhat intimate, if not wholly confidential, relations with the occupant of the White House. Indeed, he was soon to act as Mr. Adams's champion in Congress, defending him against absurd and unjust attacks on the part of the Jackson men, and warning him against cabals that were being formed against the Administration. Letters passed between the two when Congress was out of session and Everett had returned to Boston. Before his first term in Congress was completed, he sought the President's advice on a matter of great personal importance. In 1827 Mr. E. H. Mills decided not to be a candidate for reëlection to the Senate. Everett was suggested as a possible successor — and so, even more forcibly, was Mr. Webster. The former sought to sound out the President, and he wrote a letter dated Boston, April 23, 1827, in which, as often happens, the postscript was the important part and ran as follows:

There is difficulty here in knowing how to fill the vacancy in the Senate of the United States occasioned by Mr. Mills's withdrawal as a candidate, which will be announced in due time. . . . I am, however, disabled from saying a word on the subject here from the circumstances that I have myself been named for the Senate, a suggestion which — however flattering — I strongly discountenanced last winter, as likely to do the cause no good and hurt me should I be supposed to encourage it.

But if the immature Congressman hoped to secure the support of the veteran statesman, he was doomed to disappointment. Mr. Adams took refuge in generalities and astutely wrote in reply:

WASHINGTON, 29 *April*, 1827

. . . I take it for granted Mr. Webster or yourself would have an easy transition from the House to the Senate. I know not how your services [of both] could be spared from the House for the *next session*. The session after will be comparatively unimportant. I write all this confidentially, and with the hope that you will not take it as undue interference with the elections. . . .

Mr. Everett was deliberate in making answer to this cryptic utterance. He gave the matter careful thought, and, after taking counsel of his friends at home, he wrote:

BOSTON, 21 *May*, 1827

I was duly favored with yours of the 29th April. Shortly after I received it I had a long conversation with Mr. Webster, on the subject of his becoming a candidate for the place of Senator. He expressed decidedly the opinion that the Governor had better go, and a disinclination to go himself except to avoid the evil of having either an inefficient or a doubtful friend chosen. . . . He requested me to write to you on the subject, which, however, feeling myself in some degree possessed of your views and unwilling to importune you by frequently writing, I forbore to do.

The Governor [Governor Lincoln] since has positively declined, in terms that seem to preclude the idea of his yielding to any urgency, even were it proper to urge him. . . . The opinion is, so far as I know, universal here, that Mr. Webster ought not to leave the House of Representatives. It is also, however, a prevalent impression, that he wishes to go into the Senate. His competency to judge where he can best serve the cause is so undoubted, and his right to be gratified, in whatever his friends here can bestow, so strong, that I apprehend he will be put and chosen.

And so it turned out. Indeed, the matter was a foregone conclusion. Mr. Webster hesitated, for many of his friends felt that he could be of greater usefulness, just at that present time, in the lower branch. But the destiny seemed manifest. In June, 1827, the Massachusetts Legislature conferred the office of Senator on Mr. Webster, and in due season Everett was reëlected to the House. His time had not yet come for the higher post. Indeed, it was to be many years, and only after having served in several other fields of public life, that he was to find his way into the Senate. The matter was of importance to Everett, however, not so much because he was not promoted to the Senate as because the transition of Mr. Webster left Everett to be the champion of the Administration in the House. He became at this time Chairman of the Committee on Foreign Affairs, and defender in particular of affairs at home.

Mr. Adams just then became the object of venomous and scurrilous attacks in the newspapers and on the floor of the House. The Jackson men were highly elated and encouraged by the returns at the recent congressional election, and marshalled their forces at Washington, doing everything in their power to discredit the Administration and to advance the interests of their candidate. The session was a long one, and as disgraceful as it was long. The meanest subterfuges were resorted to, and the pettiest and most personal tactics were pursued. The Adams supporters fell into line and fought with vigor. Everett bore more than his share in the fighting, and must many times have sighed for the peaceful shadows of the College at Cambridge. He could not claim to be Browning's ideal of 'Ever a fighter: So one fight more, the best and the last.' He was constitutionally peaceful; yet in this instance he was literally thrust by peculiar and personal circumstances into the forefront of the struggle. It was proposed, for instance, early in the session, by Hamilton, of South Carolina, a Jackson man, that a picture of the battle of New Orleans should be painted to fill one of the vacant 'pannels [*sic*] of the Rotundo' at the Capitol, and the resolution called for the engagement of Washington Allston, of Massachusetts 'to design and finish the work of art.' In speaking for the scheme Mr. Hamilton said that he 'felt entire gratification in confiding his resolution to the judgment and patriotism of his honorable friend from Massachusetts (Mr. Everett), who was well acquainted with the merits of the great artist to whom he had referred.' Everett was Chairman of the Library Committee, and he was placed in a most awkward position. He had little wish to further the interests of the hero of the battle of New Orleans, but the compliment of selecting a Massachusetts artist for the task added to his embarrassment. Very wisely, however, he did not combat the proposition, but suggested that the plan ought to be made much wider.

The battle of New Orleans [he said] ought not to be omitted; but it was only one of a series of significant actions, and other events should also be depicted. He moved, therefore, to amend the resolution and to have it read as follows: 'That the Committee of the House of Representatives on the library be instructed to enquire into the expediency of taking measures, at this time, to procure a suitable *series* of historical paintings for the empty "pannels of the Rotundo."'

The move was a shrewd and skilful one. It opened the door for other amendments, leading for instance to the suggestion that Commodore Perry's exploits should also be depicted. After much discussion, therefore, the resolution for the aggrandizement of General Jackson failed by a close vote of 103 to 98.

The bitterest attack, however — leading to a long and fierce debate — centred around the subject of retrenchment. Resolutions were offered by the Jackson men proposing an enquiry into the expenditures of the Government, which were said to be excessive and extravagant. Particular attention was directed against the Executive, and a special committee was appointed to report in detail upon expenditures. Mr. Everett was a member of the committee, the other minority member being John Sergeant, of Pennsylvania. The majority report was a disgraceful document. Silly charges were trumped up against the President; but they were charges of a kind to do him much harm with the narrow-minded and puritanical. In setting up his household at Washington it appeared that he had bought a billiard-table costing fifty dollars, together with a set of chess-men. This led to the charge that he was making a gambling-den of the White House, corrupting youth, and all the rest. These and other insinuations, dealing with petty items of expenditure which he had incurred while abroad, were, as Adams himself set down not very elegantly in his 'Diary,' 'squirted about the floor of the House by the skunks of party slander.' When it came to the debate, Mr. Sergeant was ill, and Everett was left to bear the brunt of it alone. He did so with dignity and forcefulness. In February, 1828, in the course of a long and careful speech, marked by courtesy and self-restraint, he defended the Administration and the President. In words that have a very modern ring he showed how parsimonious the Government was in its payment of its various officials, especially those whom it sent abroad. He took up the matter of the billiard-table at the White House, calling attention to the many great and good men who had patronized the game. With particular insistence he dealt with Mr. Adams's expenditures when Minister to Russia, and when appointed one of the Commissioners to go to Ghent and arrange for the famous treaty of peace with England.

Altogether, Everett's defence was an admirable piece of work, in splendid contrast to the sordid tactics that were being pursued by the opposition. Judge Story wrote George Ticknor on the subject, saying:

Mr. Everett has made a speech which is thought by all who heard it to be a good one. Our New England friends think it very well done. Mr. Randolph replied with a good deal of tartness, but I am told his javelin was harmless.

During all this period, at intervals between sessions, Everett was busily employed at home. After leaving Cambridge he had established a home at Winter Hill in Charlestown. Thither, after escaping from the boarding-house at Washington, he returned to his studies and his books. He had come to be in constant demand as a speaker on public and patriotic occasions, and we owe some of his greatest orations to this congressional period in his life. He spoke at Charlestown his Adams and Jefferson oration; at Cambridge, on the Fourth of July, his address on the 'Principle of the American Constitution.' College affairs still claimed a certain amount of his attention, as he had been elected to the Board of Overseers in 1827. Moreover, his old friend Dr. Kirkland had retired from the presidency of the College in 1828, and both he and his brother Alexander were suggested and a good deal talked of for the position. He himself apparently had no ambition in that direction, and withdrew his name almost at once, but he was eager that his brother, who by this time had made a good deal of a reputation for himself, both in diplomacy and literature, should be elected. He did what he could to promote the matter, but had to act with considerable caution. None the less, he did not hesitate to express his chagrin when his brother's cause was lost, and Josiah Quincy chosen.

But before he had been called upon to suffer this family

disappointment, the political reverse of 1828 had tested his powers of cheerful endurance in disaster. When the presidential election came on, he had exerted himself in every way to stem the tide that was running against the Administration. Mr. Adams had made many enemies, and the editorials and speeches of his supporters availed but little. Everett foresaw defeat, as many others did, and in a letter marked 'private,' and dated October 30, 1828, he wrote the President:

Before this reaches you, the great question will have been decided, and so far as I can judge against you, or rather against your friends and the people. I make this sinister prediction with less reserve, as men bet heavily with good-will in favor of an event they deprecate; they are willing to lose their money and gain their end. I shall rejoice to be shown a false prophet by your reëlection. In this respect, however, I have taken care to lay an anchor to windward, for though I have been led singularly enough to prophesy your defeat to you, I have performed the office of cheerer and encourager among our friends. So that, in the event of success, I shall have a great many witnesses to my skill in augury, which, in the event of failure, will be attested by you alone. . . . Should you fail of it, after the momentary mortification of defeat is over, I think you will find as many sources of happiness within your reach as if you had been reëlected. But I may as well stop myself here, in the somewhat laughable attempt to inoculate the lessons of philosophy upon you. . . .

President Adams needed, however, no such trite reflections as the youthful friend and Congressman was competent to offer. He had long foreseen defeat at the polls, and had read no other omens in the political sky. With such self-command as he possessed, he bowed before disaster, and nursed his disappointment sullenly in silence. The advent of General Jackson was awaited gloomily by New-Englanders in Washington.

The change of administration meant a more serious difference to Mr. Everett than it made to many, for his relations with the White House had been exceptionally close. Unlike others, too, he seems to have scented its significance. A new day was dawning. The country was growing. The centre of power was no longer on the seaboard. The East must take henceforth a fuller account of the West and Southwest. With this thought in view, and seeking to extend his knowledge and widen his mental horizon, Everett determined to learn more of his own land. He had an irresistible desire to see for himself 'the stupendous work of human advancement which was going on in the remotest parts of the country,' and of which he believed the history of mankind afforded no other example. With his acquisitive mind he had had his fill in Europe 'of crumbling towers, of prostrate columns, of cities once renowned and powerful reduced to miserable ruins,' and now he felt a wish to look upon the opposite scene, 'not of decay, but of teeming life,' and 'of improvement almost too rapid to seem the result of human means.' Leaving Andrew Jackson, therefore, in the White House with his feet upon the fender, Everett determined to see something of the country that had given birth to Jackson. He took his family home to Charlestown, and then started out alone. In the journal of Peter C. Brooks occurs the entry, 'April 1, 1829, Monday. Mr. Everett set out for the western country.' It was as much of an event as if he had been starting for Europe or the Orient. Making his tedious way back to Philadelphia, he took the route to Pittsburgh, thence down the Ohio and the Mississippi Rivers to New Orleans. Returning he ascended the Mississippi and the Cumberland as far as Eddyville, whence he made the trip by land to Nashville, visiting Louisville, Lexington, Cincinnati, and Dayton.

He was sixteen days in reaching New Orleans, and the trip was an extremely hard one. Once there, however, he was dined and wined in the hospitable city with characteristic generosity. He visited the lines that were dug at the battle of New Orleans, and studied the city within and without. He was taken to Lake Pontchartrain where he saw 'two live chameleons on the shore and a dead alligator in the water.' Mr. Montgomery gave him 'a famous dinner' which was

served in a room which was General Jackson's lodging-
chamber during the siege. A large pile of cannon balls and
grapeshot lent interest to the garden. He visited Mr. Mil-
ligan's plantation where he studied the quarters occupied
by the slaves, finding them 'neat and clean, the beds furnished with mosquito nets.' Such was the hospitality of the
New Orleans people that during his stay of a full fortnight he
dined at home only once, and that was on the last day of his
visit when he had expected to leave early on his homeward
trip. He met all the important people, among them a Mrs.
Henderson, who told him that she had heard him deliver his
Phi Beta Kappa Oration.

On the trip North, one of the passengers on the steamer
was discovered to have smallpox, and a small riot took
place. The captain was finally forced to put the sick man
ashore to take his chances near a woodyard, where a little
cabin was hastily put together for him. At Vicksburg — so
new a place that it was not down on Everett's map — a
company of strolling players came on board. They were a
motley throng of the lowest order, among them 'a female to
whom the description of the woman of Samaria might be very
likely applied — "thou hast had five husbands, and he whom
thou hast now is not thy husband." She seemed to be not
exactly wife, widow, or maid, but something of each.'

There were a number of Scott's novels in the limited library of the boat, and Everett read them all, noticing with
interest that Scott's characters supplied the names for steam-
boats, canal barges, and even stage-coaches in the South —
Rob Roy being the particular favorite. After the roughest
kind of journey, part of the time on horseback when the
steamer was held up by low water, he reached Nashville
where he was welcomed by many friends. On one of the
stage-coach journeys he met a French captain who had made
the retreat from Moscow. Reaching Lexington, Kentucky,
on June 10th, he went to the inn. But Mr. Clay soon 'drove
up in his barouche,' and carried him off to Ashland, his hos-

pitable home, about a mile from the city, where he gave a dinner in his honor, and kept him for eight days as his guest. He spoke eloquently at a banquet given in his honor at Nashville, June 2d, where among many others who were present was his congressional colleague, John Bell, destined at a much later date to be his running-mate on the presidential ticket. At a great dinner, two weeks later, at Lexington, Kentucky, he spoke glowingly of the great West, and the astounding progress it was making, giving as a toast: 'The Eastern and the Western States: one in origin; one in interests; united in government; may they be still more united by mutual good-will.' In a similar vein he spoke at a public dinner in Yellow Springs, Ohio, saying: 'The ties of interest which connect all the States of this Union are innumerable; and those of mutual good-will are destined, I trust, to add all their strength to the compact. It ought to be the desire and the effort of every true patriot to merge in one comprehensive feeling all discordant sectional prejudice. In the leading characteristics here,' he added, 'we recognize the qualities to which we have been familiarized at home. While we witness your auspicious progress, we take pride in reflecting that it is the extension of our own immediate kindred — the ripening of a fruit which our fathers planted.' It is evident from these words what his fears were, and what his hopes, even in those early days. The thought of the 'irrepressible conflict' never left him, and always in connection with it he extolled the glories of the Union. He reached his home at Winter Hill on July 9th, after an absence of more than three months, but not without being overturned in the stage twenty miles west of Baltimore, when he sustained a considerable scalp wound.

The late autumn found him back in Washington, the wiser and more fervently patriotic for his trip, but no more reconciled than before to the Jacksonian dispensation. Democracy of the kind that came with the hero of New Orleans was hardly to his liking. He was, however, more tolerant since this visit to the South, and more disposed to view the country as a whole. On the last day of November, Van Buren took him to the White House and introduced him to General Jackson, whom, up to this time, he had never met. The General's reception of him was very civil, and when Mr. Van Buren took his leave the conversation centred on Everett's journey to the South, and the people whom he had met, particularly those whom he had seen in Nashville.

The young Congressman frankly remarked to the President that he was not among those who had wished his election, but that, being elected, he wished the Government to prosper under his administration. Jackson applauded the sentiment, and assured Everett that some of his best friends were opposed to him. Before long an invitation came for dinner at the White House. But things were very different, as of course they could not help but be. With the change of administration his position in the House was affected. He was removed from the head of the Committee on Foreign Affairs on the ground that the chairman of that important committee ought to be a political friend of the Secretary of State. He continued his activities, however, in connection with Indian affairs, and assumed a certain prominence in the work of the Colonization Society. The great questions of the day found him a staunch supporter of the Bank of the United States, and a consistent advocate of the Tariff.

It gradually began to dawn upon him, none the less, that he was not altogether happy in the life. Great things were freely prophesied for him; but he found himself wondering more and more whether those things were likely to be obtained in the atmosphere of Washington. A particular friend of his was John McLean, Postmaster-General under Mr. Adams, and later to be made a Justice of the Supreme Court. Mr. McLean wrote him in 1828:

Your position is an important one, and if rightly improved may become highly advantageous to yourself and your country. After the termination of Mr. Adams's service, I know of no man in New England who is now above the political horizon that can come in competition with you in a career of extensive influence. I apprehend the general popularity of Mr. Webster is greatly overrated in Massachusetts and perhaps in some others of the Northern States. With his acknowledged talents he will never be able to rise in the public estimation beyond the boundaries of New England. His course during the late war will always prove the grave of his prospects. Indeed, his prominency in the present contest for the presidency has been of great injury to Mr. Adams. Against you there can be no such objections of any weight. The ungenerous and contemptible taunts against your late profession could only proceed from vulgar minds and will be of no disservice. They have heightened in my feelings an interest in your future welfare. With your spotless character, fine talents and acquirements, clear of political inconsistencies, I cannot see anything to impede your future career.

But Mr. Everett knew himself, and what is more he knew Daniel Webster and his widespread popularity much better than others knew them. He was not to be deluded, therefore, by the praises or the prophecies of Mr. McLean or any one else. In these early days, as indeed continuously throughout his career, he was singularly sensitive to criticism, censure, and attack. He had an inborn dislike for controversy, and the hurly-burly of the House was not to his taste. His early training had not been for the bar where disputation is expected; but for the pulpit where the expression of opinion generally goes unanswered. He was stung to the quick when political opponents flung it at him in debate that he had resigned his sacred calling in order to gratify a vulgar ambition. The foregoing letter from Mr. McLean was called out by one in which Everett had bewailed his fate.

You have not been obliged, in Congress [he wrote], to take part in the debates of the day, nor found yourself pursued by a pack of unkennelled hounds let loose upon you for no other provocation than having defended slandered conscience. I am for mild measures, although daily insulted and vilified in the coarsest and bitterest terms.

Five years later, he wrote in much the same terms to his friend Dr. Joseph E. Worcester:

You, I think, who have known something of my tastes, will find it easy to credit me, when I declare that it would be the happiest day of my life — the day in which I could see and feel it my duty to retire altogether from politics. I besought my friends last December to tell me they thought so then. What do I reap but care, obloquy, and ingratitude for labors, which in any private pursuit would give me wealth, agreeable occupation, and the consciousness, in my humble measure, of doing good in the world? The mere work I have done for my constituents, in pursuing their private claims, would give me a decent livelihood at wood-sawing, or making shoes; and yet I am held up to scorn as a deserter of them because I express the opinion that Masonry is not ante-diluvian, and disapprove of taking extra-judicial oaths.

But a different and perhaps deeper reason for his discontent lay in the conditions under which it was necessary for him to live. Mr. Everett, who was generally thought and spoken of as the proverbial 'block of ice,' was really a man of very deep affections. He was now the father of several children. He could not very well continue taking them and his wife on to Washington for the sessions. Generally, therefore, during the latter part of his congressional career, he left them with his wife's father, Mr. Brooks, either at the house in Medford or Boston. But he missed them acutely. Moreover, he felt that he was needed in the education of the children. Altogether he was lonely in the Washington life. People who have only known about the stately, dignified, and formal Mr. Everett will find a new and very tender side to his character revealed in the letters that he wrote at this period to his little girls. They give evidence of playfulness and wit, as well as deep affection.

WASHINGTON, *March* 28, 1830

MY DEAR LITTLE DAUGHTER,

I hope I shall not trouble you by printing too frequently. But have lately witnessed an occurrence, so important, that I think you ought to know it immediately. I was walking down the avenue, and I saw a black woman walking along, with a nice tidy little girl. The black woman, I believe, was named Phillis. And they came to a pump; and Phillis stopped and pumped some water, and drank it, as it ran out of the pump. And the little girl was very thirsty and said, 'I want to drink too.' And Phillis told her to step close up to the pump, and she would pump her some water. And the little girl stepped up to the pump, and Phillis pumped pretty hard, and the water not only ran into the little girl's mouth, but over her face and down her frock. And when the little girl had got enough, she walked on, with the black woman, and said very prettily, 'I got enough, did you, Phillis?' And here you see little girl.

[Picture]

P.S. Give my love to Mama, to Grandpapa, to sisters, and to all the folks. Good-bye, dearest; your affectionate

FATHER

But if he was an affectionate father and missed his children, he was likewise a devoted husband and deplored the constant separation from his wife. They wrote each other nearly every day during his periods of absence, and he was careful to preserve the letters. They record illnesses and births and deaths in the family while the two were separated; but they tell in every page of affection, mutual confidence, and devotion. She tells him of the children and their doings, of her father and brothers — and of the life at Medford and Boston and Charlestown. And he writes her of the doings in Congress, of the debates, and at times of the social gatherings in which he had but little heart to mingle. The most constant refrain, however, tells of his loneliness and his longing to be at home.

WASHINGTON, *January 29, 1831*

... I dined yesterday with Judge Smith's wife, as I told you I was to. Mrs. Wayne was the lady patroness of the party, the only lady present. She is a lady of considerable *pretension*, soft, whispering, and a little blue. I did not, however (which I mention for your satisfaction), sit near her: in fact, the idea of a flirtation to a man with a cold in his head is, as Mrs. Sheafe used to say, perfectly pragmatical. I have not had such a thing since that evening that Mary passed with us in Charlestown. We had of the party Mr. Webster, two Mr. Ogdens of New York, a Colonel Hunt of South Carolina, Mr. Johnston, and myself. The room where we dined was as cold as Spitzbergen, aye, as the northwest corner of Melville's Island. I, as usual (hang my diffidence), crawled into the room last, like a dog caught stealing and coming up to be thrashed, and sat in the wake of a door. The door would open; a blast would rush in from the entry; and I could feel the incarnate demon of rheumatism draw his cold paws over my body. My right shoulder stiffened when the venison was brought in; and the canvasback ducks gave me a twinge in the left arm. But to-day I do not feel much the worse, which I ascribe to my having taken scarce any poison.

I suppose you keep the children pretty much within doors this very cold weather. Grace's French will be a little retarded, but *qu'importe?* My love to them all; and to all the family. I am happy to hear that Horatio feels himself well enough to think of a journey, but if he comes here, he must be quick about it, or I shall give him the slip. Adieu, my dearest wife; pray take care of your health. . . .

WASHINGTON, February 1, 1831

This may certify, that the health of Mrs. Charlotte G. Everett is such as to require her to pass her winters in a Southern climate. It is also the opinion of the subscriber, that the health of Mr. Everett, Jr., and the three Miss Everetts, would not seriously suffer, by a visit also to the seat of government.

EDWARD EVERETT
Husband of the said Charlotte

At length he can stand it no longer. His mind is made up. He will retire and devote himself to his family. Mrs. Everett will have to content herself with being the wife henceforth of a plain private citizen.

I thank you for the kind expressions in your letter and note. Mine may seem to you more cold than you could expect, in return; but I write, under the supposition that your father wishes to see my letters. . . .

I have firmly made up my mind not again to be a candidate for reëlection. I do no good here; I sacrifice my happiness; neglect my duty to my family, and get not even thanks for my reward. The lowest and worst influences direct everything, and I am determined to have no more to do with it. Shall you be willing, my dearest wife, to settle down with me a plain private citizen? Farewell: I would to Heaven you were here, to comfort me through this cheerless storm.

In much the same vein he wrote to his sister, Mrs. Hale, saying:

It is enough to make a man who has a wife and three children and a comfortable home — hang himself to go and live as I do in a boarding-house. At the same time I ought to acknowledge that I am as pleasantly situated in that respect as any of my brother members of Congress, and more so than most of them.

With forces like these tugging at his heartstrings it was only a question of time when affection would triumph over ambition. He had had enough — or he thought he had — of political existence. In the summer of 1834 he expressed to his constituents his determination not to be a candidate for reëlection. At the same time he asked to be allowed to resign for the remainder of his term. He was dissuaded, however, from taking the latter step, and filled out his term. One of his last acts was to furnish the Minority Report of the Committee on Foreign Affairs dealing with the French controversy in 1834.[1] His speech on the subject was called to the attention of Louis Philippe, who gave it cordial commendation.

The politician was now almost as eager to make his escape from Washington as the professor had been to step outside the limits of the college at Cambridge. He was still restless, and in search of something that was unattained. He wrote to his sister during the closing days of his last session: 'You have no idea how happy I feel at the approach of my retiracy from Congress. There was a moment when I thought it barely possible that I might be chosen Senator, and the idea, flattering as it was, gave me real pain.' He had devoted the ten best years of his life to Congress, and he was still dissatisfied, and uncertain as to where his conspicuous talents best could be employed. And yet the years were far from lost or wasted years. His congressional career had been useful if not brilliant. What is of more account he had become identified with National affairs. He was in touch with leading men all over the country, and was in more or less constant correspondence with Clay, Calhoun, Van Buren, Madi-

---

[1] The dispute related to the question of an indemnity to be paid by France for Napoleon's spoliations of American shipping.

son, Jefferson, Adams. He had become a National character, if not a leader, and, though still a statesman in the making, he had unquestionably made good.

He had faced the possibility, as we have seen, of complete retirement from public life on leaving Washington. But it was not so to be. The signs began to be quite unmistakable. By the end of January, 1835, the future course of things seemed fairly clear. His wife wrote him on the twenty-ninth of January:

The barbarous treatment you have met with in the House is enough to make you sick. I rejoice that you are so soon to turn your back on such ill-bred and ungrateful wretches. What do you think of Governor Davis's election to the Senate? Dr. Thompson says it has decided your fate at once. How does your *Excellency* like the prospect?

A month later, in a letter dated February 22d, she returned to the alluring topic:

You must lay aside your modesty, dear, and consent to be Governor, for all our political friends here are sending me word that you are the only candidate named, and all the ladies say they are ready to make their courtesy to me. I feel pretty much as Sally Hale did when her husband was chosen to the State Legislature — that 'I am ready to do everything that is expected of me as wife of the Governor.'

VI

GOVERNOR OF MASSACHUSETTS

IT is highly probable that the possibility of becoming
Governor had more or less to do with Everett's definite
decision to withdraw from Congress. It gave him something at least to which he could reasonably look forward.
He had been talked about as a candidate for some time past,
and political influence had been exerted in his favor. John
Quincy Adams seemed at first to stand in his way. The ex-
President was not yet clear about remaining in Washington
as a Congressman. He was still considering where he could be
of greatest public service. The governorship of Massachusetts was suggested to him, and he had no intention to let
younger men push him from the stage. An attempt on Everett's part to hasten his decision roused the old man's ire. He
recorded in his 'Diary' under date of November 26, 1833:

After dinner Mr. Edward Everett called, and we had some conversation upon the state of politics in Massachusetts. . . . I saw his
object was to prevail upon me to decline in favor of Davis; but I
was not disposed to let him know what my intentions are. He and
his brother Alexander are both reeds shaken with the wind.[1]

A year later, in 1834, almost immediately, in fact, after announcing his intention of withdrawing from Congress, Everett was strongly urged to accept a nomination for Governor
at the hands of the Anti-Masonic Party. The anti-Masonic
agitation was then at its height. It was one of those sudden
popular movements that afflict at times all countries, but to
which America appears particularly subject. In 1826, William Morgan, of Batavia, New York, was kidnapped and
disappeared from view. He had recently advertised a book
which purported to expose the secrets of Freemasonry. The
crime of putting him out of the way was charged upon the

[1] John Quincy Adams: *Memoirs*, IX, 39.

Society. It was alleged also that an investigation of the matter was resisted by leading Masons. The whole episode stirred up an immense amount of feeling. A party soon grew into being in western New York which was based upon a binding pledge to oppose the election to public office of any Freemason. The movement gathered momentum with extraordinary rapidity. It spread into other States, and began to attract attention as a National political party. In 1832 it even nominated a presidential ticket of its own, although for the most part its politics were those of the National Republicans, or Whigs. Many men of distinction and great ability shared these views and supported the party, among them being Chief Justice Marshall, Judge Story, J. Q. Adams, Calhoun, and Richard Rush. Everett for some years had been strong and open in his opposition to secret societies of all kinds. He was wise enough to see, however, that a party having no firmer basis, and no better guiding principle than opposition to all secret orders in a Republic, was not destined to exert a continuous or constructive influence. He wrote a long letter, therefore, declining the Anti-Masonic nomination, urging the support of Governor Davis, and adding that he could not become a candidate unless assured of the hearty support of his Whig associates and friends as well as anti-Masons.

In the space of another year this was precisely what happened. In January, 1835, Governor Davis was elected to the United States Senate. After that, action was quickly taken. On Wednesday, March 4th, just as he was packing up and preparing to leave Washington, Mr. Everett received word that he had been nominated by the Anti-Masonic Party for Governor, and that the Whig Convention had also nominated him. Two days later, on March 6th, he accepted both nominations, and on Tuesday, March 10th, he took his place in the Baltimore stage *en route* for Boston. In order to bring about these nominations there had been a little careful manipulation. Not every one was satisfied, and it was not to be expected that they would be. An adjustment had been brought about by which the Lieutenant-Governor, Samuel F. Armstrong, was to perform the duties of the Executive for the remainder of the term. But Lieutenant-Governors as little then as now enjoyed being casually thrust aside. John Quincy Adams, perhaps not without some personal feelings in the matter, confided this fact to his 'Diary' on June 15, 1835:

> Mr. Armstrong is much dissatisfied [he wrote] with the arrangements of the triumvirate, Webster, Edward Everett, and John Davis, in disposing of the Government of the Commonwealth as they did to Edward Everett. He thinks the people of the Commonwealth will not ratify the bargain. But the people of the Commonwealth have been so managed for the last six years that I know not how long they will be kept in leading-strings.[1]

And in this opinion the ex-President was right. Whatever quiet understanding there may have been, the arrangement in due course was heartily ratified by the people. The election took place on Monday, November 9, 1835. The Whig candidate carried Boston nearly two to one over his opponent. The returns in those days were very slow in coming in, and it was not until Saturday, November 14th, that the newspapers announced that Mr. Everett had been elected 'by a handsome majority — probably from 8000 to 10,000!' This was later increased to 12,000; but the total vote was a small one, and fell far below that of the year before. Thus the former minister of the Brattle Square Church, the brilliant but restless Professor of Greek Literature in Harvard College, and the ex-Representative to Congress from the Middlesex District, was now the Governor-elect of the Commonwealth of Massachusetts. It was a position for which he was admirably fitted. Dignified, courteous, able, upright, fond of ceremony, tireless in attention to detail, a conscientious public servant, and with no rival as an orator except Daniel Webster and possibly Rufus Choate, he seemed to

[1] John Quincy Adams: *Memoirs*, IX, 242-43.

have everything in his favor. But there were rocks ahead, and the stately Governor Everett, with all sails set, and with winds that seemed to favor, was destined soon to know the difficulties and the sorrows that beset the course not only of political life, but of human life itself. He was to take office on January 7th, and on the sixth of January his oldest child, a girl, Grace Fletcher, named for the wife of Daniel Webster, died after a lingering illness of nearly three weeks. The hearts of the parents were nearly broken. It was their first real sorrow, although other and even greater losses were to follow. 'A dear, beautiful, innocent child' the father wrote in his journal; and the next day occurs this entry:

Thursday, 7th. The last three weeks seem to me a dark, painful dream. My lovely babe sleeps in peace, and but for her sisters and brothers and their mother, I could well envy her.

This day commences my term of office as Governor. Providence has kindly shielded my heart against all elation of spirits. God's will be done.

Friends were kind and helpful, and offered all the comfort that they could. Mr. Webster wrote him with feeling and affection:

I assure you, I feel, in her death, something more than sympathy for you and her mother, indeed much more. The name she bore, owing to the kindness and friendship of her parents, the recollection which her presence always renewed in my heart, and her own most sweet and lovely temper and manners, made her an object of great interest, peculiar interest, to me. She died at the same age within a few months with our little Grace Fletcher Webster. She, too, was a very premature child, though I think not so remarkable as your daughter.

But the shaft had sunk too deep for words to give much comfort. Mr. Everett kept his equanimity, but he also kept his aching grief. A year later, January 1, 1837, occurs this entry in the journal:

I attended church all day. Dr. Walker preached and administered communion. Deep thought of the variety of life came over

me. There are times when I feel as if we should all turn hermits, if
we really believed what we think we do. What interest could men
take in the pursuits and pleasures of life, if they had an ever-
present sense of eternity?

Eternity bewilders me. Is all this beautiful organization of nature created but to perish? The question of questions is, if a man
die shall he live again? Shall his conscience continue? Shall he
know his friends? Shall I meet again my little daughter?

At the moment, however, there was no time for the indulgence of his grief. He returned from the grave-side at Mount
Auburn to find a pressure of duties at the State House.

On Tuesday, January 12th, a joint committee of the two
Houses waited on him formally, and it was arranged that he
should put in an appearance to be qualified the next day at
twelve. The Honorable J. C. Gray, a classmate and chum
in college, was the chairman of the joint committee. Three
days later the committee waited on him again, and signified
the readiness of the House to receive a communication from
him! The Governor's address was awaited with more than
ordinary interest. Again, however, as was the case with his
maiden speech in Congress, Edward Everett went out of his
way to deliver himself on the subject of slavery, and he made
almost as serious a mistake, and stirred up almost as much
ill-will in doing so, as had fallen to his lot in Washington ten
years before.

Abolitionists in those days were rapidly gaining strength
in Massachusetts. They were nearly always noisy and ir-
ritating, and were constantly stirring up discussion of the
hated subject. With every outbreak of violent opinion at
the North there was a direct increase of ugly sentiment at
the South. Those who had eyes to see could not fail to perceive that if things were allowed to go on, without charity
and forbearance being used, the end could only be an end of
violence and disastrous strife. It was for the purpose, therefore, of encouraging patience and securing mutual restraint
that the new Governor spoke these words at the beginning of
his term. He said:

The country has been greatly agitated during the past year in relation to slavery, and acts of illegal violence and outrage have grown out of the excitement kindled on this subject, in different parts of the Union, which cannot be too strongly deplored, nor too severely censured. In this State, and several of our sister States, slavery has long been held in public estimation as an evil of the first magnitude. It was fully abolished in this Commonwealth by the year 1783 by decisions of the Court of Justice, and by the interpretation placed on the declaration of equality in the Bill of Rights. But it existed in several of the States at the time of the adoption of the Constitution, and in a greater ratio to the free population of the country than at the present day. It was, however, deemed a point of the highest public policy of the non-slave-holding States, notwithstanding the existence of slavery in these sister States, to enter with them into the present Union on the basis of the constitutional compact. That no union could have been formed on any other basis is a fact of historical notoriety. The compact expressly recognizes the existence of slavery, and concedes to the States where it prevails the most important rights and privileges connected with it. Everything that tends to disturb the relations created by this compact is at war with its spirit, and whatever by direct and necessary operation is calculated to excite an insurrection among the slaves has been held by highly respectable legal authority an offence against the peace of this Commonwealth. Although opinions may differ on this point, it would seem the safer course, under the peculiar circumstances of the case, to imitate the example of the Fathers — the Adamses, the Hancocks, and other eminent patriots of the Revolution — who, although fresh from the battles of liberty, and approaching the question as essentially an open one, deemed it nevertheless expedient to enter into a union with our brothers of the slave-holding States on the principle of forbearance and toleration on this subject. . . . The patriotism of all classes of citizens must be invoked to abstain from a discussion, which, by exasperating the master, can have no other effect than to render more oppressive the condition of the slave, and which, if not abandoned, there is great reason to fear, will prove the rock on which the Union will split. Such a disastrous consummation . . . could scarcely fail sooner or later to bring on a war of extermination in the slave-holding States. On the contrary, a conciliatory forbearance . . . would leave this painful subject where the Constitution leaves it, with the States where it exists; and in the hands of an all-wise Providence, who, in his own good time, is able to cause it to disappear like the slavery of the ancient world under the gradual operation of the gentle spirit of Christianity.

Those were the words of a wise and cautious conservatism. They represented what was without doubt the majority opinion in Boston and in Massachusetts at that time. The substantial, thoughtful, law-abiding, patriotic people of the city and the State recognized the evils of slavery; but they also recognized the dangers of a sectional dispute. Everett's contention was — and he spoke as a student of history — that the time had not yet come for agitation on the subject. The Fathers had established the Union and perfected the Constitution by means of a compromise with what they recognized as undoubtedly an evil, and the thing for the children to do was to follow their example, and make the Union their first consideration. James Russell Lowell, among others, came to vent his sarcasm at a later day, in regard to this conservative point of view. 'To be told,' he said, 'that we ought not to agitate the question of slavery, when it is that which is forever agitating us, is like telling a man with fever and ague on him to stop shaking and he will be cured.' But that was a clever utterance rather than a sound one. There is a time for all things — a time to speak and a time to hold one's peace; a time to agitate and a time to bide one's opportunity.

Everett in 1836 had much upon his side. The Union was still young. It might easily be disrupted by violence and incautious agitation. The word of the hour was 'wait.' Of more importance than hatred of slavery was love of the Union and reverence for the Constitution. Judgment was called for, and not hatred; reason, not invective; patience, and not passion! But it was the great mistake of Everett in this connection to suggest that legal authority might properly be used to suppress discussion. That meant a denial of free speech. Liberty-loving America had no use for such restriction. The Governor's suggestion called forth vigorous objection. Such reactionary advice was not soon forgotten. In later years, patriots and reformers like Whittier and Curtis and a score of others were calling Everett's words to mind, and bitterly inveighing against the man who uttered them.

In 1857, George William Curtis, speaking in Plymouth Church, Brooklyn, held Governor Everett up to scorn, and referred to what he called 'that fatal inaugural address.' 'It was,' he said,[1] 'as if some kindly Pharisee had said to Christ, "Don't try to cast out the evil spirit; it may rend the body on departing." Was it not as if some timid citizen had said, "Don't say hard things of intemperance, lest the dram-shops, to spite us, should give away the rum?"' Even the gentle Whittier,[2] aroused to righteous if not poetic wrath, could speak at a later day of 'pompous Governor Everett, who had in his inaugural address endeavored to smooth his own path by choking off discussion on slavery.' But such an imputation was both ungenerous and unjust. Everett had nothing to gain, and he spoke from a sense of duty. He was enough of a statesman to be fearful of political consequences, and surely now in looking back it is impossible to deny that his fears were well founded.

Moreover, it should not be forgotten that most of the solid men of Boston and Massachusetts were with him in this matter. He had not spoken without taking careful counsel, and the great majority of the people did not censure, but approve. He had learned by this time to confide greatly to the sound judgment of his father-in-law. Indeed, he and Mr. Brooks had become firm and confidential friends, and they talked over important matters with the greatest freedom. The manuscript of the inaugural address went, therefore, to Peter C. Brooks, for criticism and advice, and the candid opinion was expressed — 'I send back your manuscript, having read it with some care. Like everything of yours, I think it very good, I could see nothing for a practical man to object to, and much to commend.'

Mr. Webster wrote to the same effect afterwards: 'I thought very well of your inaugural, and hear with much pleasure that it was well spoken of by the Legislature.'

[1] Curtis: *Orations and Addresses*, I, 81.
[2] Carpenter: *Life of Whittier*, p. 163.

But other difficulties of a more normal kind began to present themselves. One most important part of a Governor's duties consists in the making of appointments. Mr. Everett was a good judge of men; he had a very wide acquaintanceship throughout the State; his ideals of office, too, were high; and he wanted none for State positions but men of the highest character. He suddenly discovered, however, that here likewise there were reefs ahead. He had been the nominee, as we have seen, of the Anti-Masonic Party; and Anti-Masons had been, of course, in large part responsible for his election. When it came to selecting men for office, therefore, if the person appointed turned out to be a Mason, the Governor soon found himself with a full pack of fanatics barking at his heels. He was accused of going back upon his pledges, and was told that no Mason must be appointed to responsible position. The Governor protested. He denied with emphasis that he had made any pre-election pledges. He pointed out how difficult it was oftentimes to ascertain whether a man was a member or not of the famous order; and in any event, he insisted that the men best fitted for the positions by reason of education, character, and training were the ones to whose services the Commonwealth was entitled.

From considerations such as these it is pleasant to turn to a department in which the influence of the Governor had constructive value, and served to put the Commonwealth of Massachusetts in the lead of all the other States! There were those who had objected to having a scholar — one who had been a minister of religion and a college professor — elected to the post of chief executive. And yet, it was just because he was a scholar, and had finished his education at a German university, that he came, in a signal way, to serve the State in the cause of education.

The normal school at the present time is an accepted institution. We act as though it had always existed. The reason for it is perfectly obvious. As a matter of fact, however, it was introduced into our educational system only after a considerable struggle, and it was largely due to Edward Everett, the scholar in politics, that the first normal schools in the country and the first State Board of Education were established in Massachusetts. The condition of the public schools in 1835 was unquestionably bad. Professor Francis Bowen, writing on the common school system in New England in the early thirties, could declare that it had degenerated into routine, and that it was starved by parsimony. 'Any hovel,' he said, 'would answer for a school-house, any primer would do for a textbook, any farmer's apprentice was competent to keep a school.'

In his second inaugural of January, 1837, the Governor brought the entire subject to the attention of the Legislature. He said:

While nothing can be farther from my purpose than to disparage the common schools as they are, and while a deep sense of personal obligation to them will ever be cherished by me, it must yet be candidly admitted that they are susceptible of great improvement. The school-houses might in many cases be rendered more commodious. . . . Teachers well qualified to give elementary instruction in all branches of useful knowledge should be employed, and small school libraries, maps, globes, and requisite scientific apparatus should be furnished. I submit to the Legislature whether the creation of a Board of Commissioners of Schools, to serve without salary, with authority to appoint a secretary, on a reasonable compensation, to be paid from the school fund, would not be of great utility. Should the Legislature take advantage of the ample means[1] now thrown into their hands, greatly to increase the efficiency of the school fund, I cannot but think that they would entitle themselves to the gratitude of the whole people. The wealth of Massachusetts always has been, and always will be, the mind of her children: and good schools are a treasure a thousand fold more precious than all the gold and silver of Mexico and Peru.

In all of this, it was the destiny of Everett to be of enormous service. It was his great privilege to be in a position to champion effectively a cause which a less intelligent or

[1] This refers to a sum of $1,784,231 which was to be received by Massachusetts from the United States Treasury in a distribution of a portion of public revenue among the various States.

scholarly executive might have left to languish and decline.

The crusade for better schools and a more intelligent school system attracted many champions — among them, the Reverend Charles T. Brooks, a Unitarian minister settled in Hingham, Massachusetts. In 1834, Dr. H. Julius was sent over to the United States by the Prussian Government to make a study of our prison system. While making his investigations, he had occasion, more than once, to speak of the many advantages of the Prussian school system. When he returned to Germany, Mr. Brooks went with him to make a study of the Prussian schools. He came home enthusiastic in regard to what he had seen. He was on fire with missionary zeal, and set to work to preach the gospel of the better way of education as practised in Germany. The thing became a hobby with him, and he rode it so hard as to prove somewhat of an embarrassment to the Governor and to seem likely at one time to do the cause almost as much harm as good. It has been carelessly assumed, and frequently stated, that Mr. Brooks was the chief force in bringing about the normal school, and he boldly claimed that distinction for himself. In all such matters it is generally difficult to bestow the credit where it properly belongs. In this connection the following entries from Mr. Everett's journal, written many years later, are significant:

July 13, 1864. A most absurd document appears in the 'Transcript' this afternoon, being a pretended account by Reverend Charles Brooks of the introduction of normal schools into Massachusetts, of which he takes the entire credit to himself. My agency is as much ignored as possible. Whoever knows Mr. Brooks knows that he is a person wholly destitute of influence, and few things retarded the introduction of the normal schools more than the circumstances that he was riding them as a hobby.

December 20, 1864. Met President Sparks in State Street. He fully concurs with me in the opinion of Brooks's ridiculous pretensions about normal schools; one of the greatest pieces of charlatanism ever attempted.

But credit to whom credit is due, and honor to whom honor. No one ever serves the world successfully who is careful about recognition. It is a Jesuit saying that 'the only way to get things done is not to mind who gets the credit for doing them.' Edward Everett knew all about university standards in Prussia, and the idea of a seminary or preparatory school to teach teachers especially appealed to him.

As a result of the campaign that had been carried on, a bill was introduced into the Legislature calling for the creation by law of a Board of Education in accordance with the recommendation of the Governor. After weathering a storm of opposition, the bill was finally passed by both Houses and signed by the Governor. It called for 'A Board of eight members, to be appointed by the Governor and Council, one member to retire annually, the Governor and Lieutenant-Governor to be members *ex-officiis*.' That first historic Board of Education as created by Everett, consisted of such eminent men as Professor afterward President Sparks of Harvard, Dr. Putnam, James G. Carter, Robert Rantoul, Jr., and Edmund Dwight. Everett, as long as he remained Governor of the Commonwealth, wrote all the annual reports and gave the whole matter his careful and constant attention. At the first meeting of the Board, on June 29, 1837, Horace Mann was chosen secretary. 'The choice was a surprise and a disappointment to many of those who had been most active in promoting the new movement. They wanted James G. Carter.'[1] But the wisdom of the choice was quickly proved, and from that time on the great reform made steady progress.

The Board made its first report on February 1, 1838, and it contained the following suggestion by the Governor with regard to the advisability of inaugurating a system of normal schools, then practically unknown in America:

In those foreign countries where the greatest attention has been paid to the work of education, schools for teachers have formed an important feature in their systems, and with happiest results.

[1] George H. Martin: *Evolution of the Massachusetts Public School System*, p. 156.

The art of instruction has been found, like every other art, to improve by cultivation in institutions established by that specific object. . . . The Board cannot but express the sanguine hope that the time is not far distant when the resources of public or private liberality will be applied in Massachusetts for the foundation of an institution for the education of teachers.

The suggestion at once bore fruit. The Honorable Edmund Dwight immediately came forward and offered ten thousand dollars to be spent by the Board for the education of teachers on condition that the Commonwealth would appropriate the same amount. On April 19th — a day for patriotic acts — the Legislature accepted the gift, and the ball was thus set rolling. The first normal school, appropriately enough, was established at Lexington. It was for women only. In September, 1839, a second school for both sexes was opened at Barre, and finally a third school was set on foot at Bridgewater. The Lexington school was subsequently removed, first to West Newton and later to Framingham. The Barre school was transferred to Westfield, the one at Bridgewater remaining where it was first established. The Governor attended the opening of the school in Barre, and made one of his matchless addresses — carefully prepared, perfect in form, and covering the whole growth of education. It was included in a volume of his collected addresses, and is still worth thoughtful reading and study. With masterly clearness and accuracy the great orator unfolded the programme of normal schools, which, according to a biographer of Horace Mann, 'with a single exception is the programme to which our normal schools conform to-day.'[1]

The subjects of slavery and education, however, were not the only ones to claim the Governor's attention. The times were those of terrible financial stress. The disastrous panic of 1837 caused widespread confusion. Bank failures were numerous. Public confidence was badly shaken. The ad-

[1] B. A. Hinsdale: *Horace Mann and the Common School Revival in the United States*, p. 158.

dress of 1838, therefore, was devoted almost entirely to banking schemes and matters of finance. Indeed, three full fourths of the message was given up to a discussion of banks and currency. The former minister of religion and professor of Greek was apparently equal to the emergency, and he had, moreover, the invaluable counsel of Mr. Brooks. Acting under good advice, therefore, the Governor recommended the 'creation of a board of commissioners with authority to investigate the affairs of the banks of the Commonwealth, and to obtain an injunction against their proceedings in cases in which they shall consider the security of the public to make such action necessary.' He wrote Mr. Adams somewhat fully in the matter, beginning his letter by paying a compliment to Charles F. Adams, who was destined in due season to become the famous American Ambassador at the Court of Saint James'.

COUNCIL CHAMBER, *January* 27, 1838

You will find in a paper which I send you to-day a well-deserved compliment to a highly interesting lecture delivered last Thursday evening by your son. . . . As one of a large and exceedingly attentive audience I listened to the lecture with great satisfaction. I believe it gave unqualified pleasure, increasing the reputation of the lecturer and throwing new light on the characters of those commemorated by him. . . .

We think, talk, and debate of nothing here but banks. One or two a week is the average number that fail. The Legislature is obliged to keep its most active members at work on committees of investigation. The affairs of the deposite [*sic*] banks are said to be in the worst possible state. In one of them [the Franklin] things were done for which the grand jury is the only suitable committee of investigation, and the old-fashioned penalties of fine and imprisonment the only appropriate recompense. The Legislature will probably create a commission with summary powers, though this is vehemently resisted on constitutional and other grounds. A law will probably pass forbidding dividends during the suspension, and a few other small things will perhaps be done, all of which are of the nature — according to the homely adage — of shutting the barn door after a certain useful animal has been abstracted.

It was a fortunate thing that before the financial crash

came, Everett had lent his influence to promote the schemes of the 'Western Railroad Corporation.' He was always an optimist in regard to the development and progress of the country, particularly toward the West. His confidence in the future greatness of the Nation was unbounded. He saw, almost with a prophet's vision, the great things that were in the hand of destiny. He was thoroughly in accord, therefore, with the step which was taken by the Boston and Worcester Railroad Company when it became incorporated as the Western Railroad Corporation 'with authority to construct a railway from Worcester to the Connecticut River in Springfield, and thence across it to the western boundary of the State, in a direction toward the Hudson River,' whenever a certain amount of money was subscribed. But capital was timid. Money came in slowly. Individual enterprise was unequal to so great a task. State aid seemed necessary, and the Governor recommended it as a safe and profitable venture. A bill was drawn up, introduced, and finally passed by the Legislature, receiving in due course the Governor's signature, which directed 'the State Treasurer to subscribe one million dollars to the stock of the Western Railroad Corporation, and providing that three of the nine directors of the road should be chosen by the Legislature.'

When a great meeting was held in Faneuil Hall to promote the cause and impress the public with the real importance of what was contemplated, it was Abbott Lawrence who presided; but a moving spirit was Everett. Mr. Lawrence became enthusiastic as he spoke. He suggested that the Hudson River would be crossed, and the Mississippi reached. 'Mr. Everett,' he said, 'we shall live to see the banks of the upper Mississippi connected by iron bands with State Street.' And Everett agreed; only he said, by way of a reply: 'Don't talk, Sir, of Buffalo: talk of the Falls of St. Anthony and the Council Bluffs.'

Not all of this public life as chief Executive was joy, however. The duties of the governorship were not as wearing as those of a Congressman had been; but they were very burdensome at times and Everett longed for escape into his library. He wrote in his journal:

March 30, 1836. In the evening a party of young men gave Mr. Webster a dinner, at which, with a few other gentlemen, I was present — toasts, speeches, etc.; did not get home till near twelve. I cannot much longer abide these festivals. They are too unnatural, exaggerated, out of taste. People sit and swallow fulsome compliments to themselves, and get up and make as fulsome ones to others, 'O, for a lodge in some vast wilderness,' etc.

Again, a year or two later occurs this entry:

March 3, 1838. Returned an answer to the committee of the convention who nominated me a fourth time as Governor. It would have been more agreeable to me to retire from office and go into the country and devote myself to literary pursuits and the care of my family, but I want strength of purpose enough to take such an important step without stronger direct motives to prompt and justify it.

There was one part of his duties, however, that he did enjoy, and that to the utmost. He had a passion for travelling, and he was always at his best upon the platform. He went with almost boyish eagerness, therefore, to the various sections of the Commonwealth, and we owe to this period many of his best addresses and orations. The following letters telling of a visit to New Bedford, Naushon, and Nantucket are not without interest to those who are familiar with that neighborhood, and are worth preserving:

NEW BEDFORD, *July* 26, 1836

MY DEAREST WIFE,

I seize a brief interval, between dinner at Mr. Rodman's and an evening party at Colonel Clifford's,[1] to let you know that I am in the land of the living. I got here safely yesterday. . . . As far as natural scenery is concerned, the ride is not particularly interesting. Sixteen miles before you reach New Bedford, you pass Middlebury Pond, which is a very large and beautiful sheet of water; like Jamaica Pond; but six or eight times as large.

---

[1] A member of Everett's staff, and, at a later time, Governor of the Commonwealth.

I found my friend Upham, of Salem, at Mr. Warren's. Immediately on my arrival we took a walk along the street that overlooks the bay: a street of palaces — there is nothing like it in any place I have seen. After all my fatigue — waking at four in the morning, riding sixty miles, and walking two hours — I sat up till half-past twelve! and rose at half-past six this morning!

This forenoon I had a kind of levée at Mr. Warren's: many gentlemen called; among others old Captain Crocker, who has crossed the Atlantic one hundred and sixty-four times, and never lost a man! I dined at Mr. Rodman's and am to pass the evening at Clifford's. To-morrow I dine at Mr. Grinnell's — attend a meeting and make a speech in the evening, and afterwards go to a party. Thursday to Nantucket; but of that I will write you again. . . .

NANTUCKET, *July* 29, 1836

MY DEAR WIFE, . . . I wrote you, I think, Tuesday afternoon. We had had a great reception at Mr. Warren's in the morning and I had dined at Mr. Rodman's. In the evening I went to Clifford's where there was a large party of gentlemen, and a very elegant entertainment. Wednesday morning, I stole an hour to make a few notes for a speech in the evening. By half-past ten, people began to call. At half-past eleven, I went by invitation of Captain Howard on board the revenue cutter in the harbor. He gave me a salute of seventeen guns. Got back at one o'clock, and went to take a ride with Mr. Rodman in his gig to view the neighborhood. Got home, and at three o'clock went to dine at Mr. Joseph Grinnell's, a splendid mansion, as finely situated as any house I ever saw. He has a marble statue of a little child of five years old — his adopted daughter — by Greenough, and some valuable pictures brought from Italy. Mr. and Mrs. Grinnell were at Medford a year or two ago. Mrs. Henry Dalton is Mr. G.'s sister and was on a visit to us. I saw a great deal of Mrs. H. D. when poor Ward was sick. After dinner went home to Mr. Warren's where there were a good many ladies and gentlemen to tea.

At half-past eight, a committee waited on me, to invite me to attend the meeting, which was on the subject of taking measures to complete the monument on Bunker Hill. I went, and, being invited to speak, did so for about three quarters of an hour. After this went to William Rodman's to a party. This is the most magnificent establishment I ever saw in America. There was a small party and a most beautiful entertainment: — no ladies, but the sisters and sisters-in-law of Mr. R., all very superior women. Miss Rodman, the daughter of Mr. R., is also a beautiful and accomplished girl. I think you will allow that this was not an idle day.

Yesterday morning, we took the steamboat for this place —
Warren, Clifford, and I. As you leave the harbor of New Bedford
— Naushon and the other Elizabeth islands are directly before you,
a beautiful prospect. You touch at Wood's Hole, where the passage [1]
greatly resembles Hell Gate. You then cross over to Holmes's Hole,
which is in Martha's Vineyard, and then stretch across to Nantucket. A glance at the map of Massachusetts, in any of my atlases,
will make all plain. Nantucket is sixty miles from New Bedford.
We arrived at half-past two. Our passage had been a little delayed
by towing a whale ship out of harbor. Our arrival was expected at
Nantucket, and a good many persons gathered on the wharf to see
us. After an introduction to several on deck, we went up to the
hotel. I passed the afternoon in walking round the place, and the
evening in receiving a considerable number of gentlemen who called.

This morning (Friday) I went at eight to see the silk factory; at
nine to visit Admiral Coffin's school, where I had to make a speech;
at eleven drove out to the asylum for the poor, and so continued on
to Siasconset, a very singular village on the brink of the ocean. The
principal families of Nantucket come here to pass the summer,
somewhat like Nahant and yet very different. Whiled away two
or three hours in visiting and then sat down to a sort of public
dinner given by the gentlemen of Nantucket to me — where, of
course, there were toasts and speeches. About half-past six I got
back. I am spending the evening at Mr. Upton's. I thought to
have been called to go there before now, but I have had time for a
much longer letter than I expected. To-morrow morning I take the
steamboat for Naushon, where I am to spend Saturday afternoon
and perhaps Sunday. On Monday, if wind and weather permit,
they talk of an excursion by water to Gay Head. On Tuesday we
shall return to New Bedford, and on Wednesday I hope to be back
to Charlestown.

New Bedford, August 1, 1836

My dearest Wife, — Here I am, safe back from Nantucket. . . .
When I wrote you on Friday evening, I was about going to a party
at Mr. Upton's. I found there all the respectability and fashion of
Nantucket; and I assure you it was a most genteel party.

Saturday morning we left Nantucket at nine o'clock. It was at
first foggy and then for a short time rained hard; the first adverse
circumstance which has befallen us. But it cleared up by the time
we got to Wood's Hole, a little port in the town of Falmouth. Here
we found Mr. Swain and Mr. Bowdoin waiting, to take us over to
Naushon, in Mr. Swain's yacht, the Fawn. Mr. Swain is a gentle-

----

[1] The old name for Vineyard Haven.

man of wealth and respectability, and acts as Mr. Bowdoin's agent on the island of Naushon. He lives there in the mansion house in the summer, with Mrs. Swain and their only child, a boy of fourteen, in an unostentatious hospitality toward their friends, some of whom are almost always there. After crossing the strait between Wood's Hole and the island — which, as I wrote you, is much like Hell Gate — we entered the winding bay leading up to the landing. The wind was ahead and we had to beat up — but it was now lovely weather, the distance not great, and we enjoyed the prospect extremely.

Once arrived at the house, I was made as much at home as if it had been my own; which to a modest man is a great comfort. It was now about three o'clock, and we soon sat down to a most generous dinner, of which I confined myself to the prominent article, a splendid baked bass. After dinner, I took a ride with Mr. Swain and Mr. Bowdoin, to see the island. By bedtime I was pretty tired.

Sunday morning I rose at half-past four. The birds waked me, and I was glad of it; for it enabled me to see the sun rise over Falmouth. I never saw a more beautiful scene than the landscape it presented. At a very short distance from the house is the little bay in which we landed, completely landlocked, and looking like a lake. The Fawn and two or three smaller boats belonging to Mr. Swain lay at anchor in this little bay. (Beyond at a little distance was Buzzard's Bay on one side and the Vineyard Sound on the other.) The groves on its banks were repeated in the water. It was so delicious that I wondered I ever slept after daybreak. At half-past eight, Mr. Warren, Colonel Clifford, and myself took the Fawn, and a couple of men to navigate her; beat down the bay — dashed through the roaring passage with the speed of lightning — and landed at Wood's Hole. Here we took a carryall and went down to Falmouth to attend church. This is a very pleasant village four miles down the Cape.

We were three quarters of an hour before church, which we employed by a visit to Captain Swift, the principal man of the place. He took us to church, introducing me as we went to the principal men of the village. The services were exceedingly well conducted by Mr. Bent, the minister, and the music very good. After church we went back to Captain Swift's, and took a piece of cake and glass of wine. We then returned in our carryall to Wood's Hole to our yacht, and on the way over to Naushon the captain (or skipper as he is called) handed me your letter. The rest of the day was passed in dining, reading, writing, conversing, as each one pleased.

This morning (Monday) I rose later than yesterday. It was

foggy and I could not see the sun rise; but I did not sleep after half-past four. The windows and bed were furnished with mosquito nets of a very superior construction to those at Hopkinton, where, by the way, Mrs. Swain was last summer. She knows Dr. Thompson and Mrs. Hurd, and spoke very kindly of them.

After breakfast this morning, we went out to hunt the deer; four of us; there was but one shot fired and that killed a young buck. It was fired by a nephew of Mr. Swain's. I had two admirable chances, but my gun snapped both times. The deer was but twenty feet from me, and I could not well have missed him. The island abounds in deer; and in the course of our excursion, we passed through the most delightful groves you can imagine. At eleven we came home and lunched; at twelve took the beautiful Fawn again and all hands dashed over to Wood's Hole, and there in a few minutes the steamboat from Nantucket came up and took us on board. Martha Dana with her lover came on board at Wood's Hole. We had a fine run up to New Bedford, and here I am. My wish was to come home to-morrow, but I have not visited Fair Haven (which is connected with New Bedford by a bridge) and I have not called at the houses where I have been entertained.

It would not do, however, to dismiss an account of Everett's career as Governor without saying something on a larger question which was destined to absorb his thoughts for several years after his advancement into wider fields of service.

The most puzzling and perhaps the most important matter in the course of his four administrations that Governor Everett had to deal with was one of international significance and involved our relations with Great Britain. I refer to the northeastern boundary question. The line between Maine and New Brunswick had never been definitely settled. The British interpretation of the Treaty of 1783, which was based upon the mistaken proposition that the St. John is not a river flowing into the Atlantic, was not acceptable to the people of Maine, nor, indeed, to Massachusetts, which had large territorial interests at stake. The award that was reported by the King of the Netherlands had no better success. The result was that people on both sides of the disputed line were openly at odds. Encroachment took place

and claims were put forth by Maine which were distinctly
distasteful to the Canadian Government. Maine refused to
be quiet. Her Legislature made an appropriation to continue
the Aroostook road to the St. John (every inch of the way
through the disputed territory) and asked Massachusetts
to do likewise. The Government of New Brunswick protested, and Sir Charles Vaughan, former British Minister
to the United States, appealed to Mr. McLane, Secretary of
State, to have the enterprise stopped. The question, however, soon came to be one of local politics in Maine. Each
political party was afraid that the other one would get some
advantage over it in the handling of the question. In the
meantime, the dispute was taken up in England, where the
same political game was played. In 1838, in connection with
the Speech from the Throne, the matter was debated in
Parliament by the adherents of the Duke of Wellington and
Sir Robert Peel on the one side and those of Lord Melbourne
and Lord John Russell on the other. It appeared likely that
there would be a rivalry of patriotic ostentation between the
'outs' and the 'ins.' It was thought that Lord Melbourne
was heartily in favor of peace, but Everett did not feel so
sure about the conqueror of Napoleon. He became much
concerned in regard to the matter and very apprehensive.
He was fearful that a brush on the frontier might prove the
match that would start a conflagration. Another war with
England seemed very possible unless something was done to
allay the irritation. He wrote to President Van Buren very
strongly on the matter, suggesting that a special mission
should be appointed by the Government to go to England
and seek to effect an adjustment.

The Governor of Massachusetts had other reasons, moreover, than the fear of war in general, to be justly and duly
apprehensive. In case of actual hostilities breaking out,
Boston, with the Navy Yard at Charlestown, would be an
early objective for attack, and the harbor was in a wholly
defenceless condition. He wrote to the Mayor of Boston,

Mr. Samuel A. Eliot, who likewise was alert, expressing his alarm:

> I cannot [he said] disguise to you my fears that, against the sober judgment of all right thinking men on either side of the Atlantic, the two countries are in imminent danger of plunging into a most disastrous war; which Heaven avert, for if it comes the first blow will be struck at the Navy Yard at Charlestown, as your memorial justly intimates.

On this subject he wrote again with the greatest urgency to the President in a letter dated March 4, 1839, and marked 'Confidential.' He gave full expression to his fears, and urged that the State should be encouraged to coöperate with the Federal Government in providing fit defences for Boston.

President Van Buren agreed in substance with Governor Everett. He discouraged the road project and wished to appoint a commission for the study and settlement of the affair. In the meantime, a bill was introduced into the Massachusetts Legislature providing for money whereby to push forward with vigor the equipment of the forts in Boston Harbor. The bill failed to pass the Senate in the last stages, but it did not matter, for the immediate danger passed away. By the latter part of May, Everett could write with a great sense of relief:

> Our boundary troubles for the present are over. Lord Palmerston has sent me the draft of a convention, the provisions of which have not leaked out. The plan appears to be to institute a new survey, but this cannot possibly lead to any settlement of the controversy which all grows out of the pretensions of Great Britain that the St. John is not one of the rivers that empty themselves into the Atlantic. ... If the British acknowledge it, they abandon their whole case.

Two months later he could write to Webster telling him in confidence what the Palmerston plan was, and announcing that a new experimental survey on the part of the commissioners who were to be appointed was not to be hampered with the conditions heretofore insisted on by the British Government. And there for a time the entire matter rested.

Governor Everett as usual had gone into the question with great thoroughness, consulting the history of the whole controversy, and making himself familiar with all the maps that were available, and with others that were shown to him in confidence; and the careful labor was not thrown away. Before many months were past, he was destined to be of incalculable assistance to the Government in smoothing the pathway for the execution and afterwards the acceptance of the Webster-Ashburton Treaty which settled finally the knotty question of the northeastern boundary line.

His administration, however, was now rapidly approaching a dramatic end.

Everett held the office of Governor for four successive years. He was reëlected by substantial pluralities in 1836, 1837, and in 1838. His Democratic opponent at all four elections was the Honorable Marcus Morton, of Taunton. He was nominated for a fifth term in 1839, Mr. Morton being once again put up by the opposition. Notes of alarm and warning began to be sounded in the early autumn. Charges of extravagance — which it is always easy to make with considerable effect — were brought against Everett's administration. But a more serious factor in the situation was the lethargy of the Whigs. They seemed to think themselves secure. They were spoken of as asleep, and doing nothing; whereas the Van Buren people were full of energy and enthusiasm. An editorial writer in the 'Boston Advertiser' asserted that 'many years have passed since the Whigs have been so supine and inactive as now.'

There was, however, one feature in the campaign that worked in Everett's favor, and that tended to set him right with the radical element in the population. He had begun his career as Governor with an unfortunate word in regard to slavery; he was to close it with a right one. On October 18, 1839, Nathaniel B. Borden wrote him an open letter, which appeared in the press, asking him bluntly these two questions:

1st. Are you in favor of the immediate abolition by law, of slavery in the District of Columbia, and of the slave traffic between the States of the Union?

2nd. Are you opposed to the admission into the Union of any new State the constitution and government of which tolerate domestic slavery?

A week later, in a letter dated October 24, 1839, Mr. Everett publicly replied, 'I respond to both of *your enquiries in the affirmative.*'

This declaration helped; and he could note with satisfaction in his journal on November 8: 'The "Liberator" of this day announces its purpose to support me as Governor in consequence of my letter to Mr. Borden.'

In spite, however, of this unexpected accession of strength, Mr. Everett himself was apparently prepared for defeat — or *thought* he was! There were signs that he could not fail to read, and he gave definite expression to his doubts. During his years at the State House he had come into close and very intimate relations with Robert C. Winthrop, who was at that time Speaker of the Massachusetts House, and who was giving evidence of what was to prove his brilliant and notable career. The two men were very sympathetic in their points of view — both of them scholars and historians, both of them also conservative by temperament and training, and representative of the finest culture of the time. Winthrop had an almost unbounded admiration for Everett, and the latter had utter confidence in the loyalty of the younger man. From this time on, therefore, we find letters of a very confidential nature passing between the two, and there came no break in their political friendship until Everett took the bolder and the better course in connection with the Civil War, and became the champion of Abraham Lincoln and a passionate upholder of the Union at all costs! The ties between the two were particularly close in 1839 and Everett wrote his friend on October 28th:

I comfort myself with the conclusion that if I am defeated, it is the best thing that could befall me. Whether a change in the State Administration and the introduction of the Custom House dynasty will be best for the Commonwealth is a question for the ten thousand good, lazy Whigs, who will stay at home on the 11th November, one at his farm and one at his merchandise, and allow the battle to go against us.

There were weak points apparently in the patriotism of the citizens of 1840. The stay-at-home vote was no less considerable in those days than it is in these! The candidate was made to suffer because of the indifference of his friends. The election day was Monday, November 11th. The returns were very slow in coming in. The first indications were that Everett had again been successfully reëlected. But the Boston vote was disconcerting. The Governor had carried the city by less than one thousand, whereas in 1835 he had received nearly two votes to every one for his opponent. On Wednesday morning, November 14th, Everett had only one hundred votes more than Morton, with two hundred and fifty-one towns yet to be heard from. On Friday the fifteenth, it appeared that Morton had a majority of one hundred and ninety-five. On Saturday morning there began to be talk of certain 'irregularities.' It appeared that the votes of the town of Easton had not been formally 'sealed up in town meeting,' and the return from the town of Winchendon was dated November 11, 1809, instead of 1839, etc., etc. A few extracts from Mr. Everett's journal at this trying time are interesting:

November 11, 1839. To-day the general election throughout the Commonwealth. The party opposed to me have made the most incredible effort: the Whigs are divided and apathetic: the result doubtful.

Tuesday, November 12. The returns of the election thus far received make it nearly certain that Judge Morton is chosen Governor by a small majority.

Thursday, November 14. The election is probably lost. The Secretary of State did not vote. At his request, General Dearborn came to explain the omission and assure me of his continued personal and political attachment. A better mode of showing it would have been to vote: but I accept the apology, which was that on the way to the polls he was met by one of 'the Atlas Clique' who told him that he was coming to get him to vote and that they were watching him. Thus taunted, he told the person that he should vote in the afternoon, but did not do so. Tempus docebit.

Everett practically gave up hope on the 14th. On that day he wrote to Winthrop:

> I adhere to the conclusion to which I came when I heard of the Boston vote — that is, that all was gone! For my ease, comfort, and character, this is greatly the best. Should I go out now the feeling so handsomely expressed in your letter, that I had been sacrificed, would have some prevalence, and next to the credit of uniform success is that of unmerited failure. . . . However, there is no use of moralizing. If, when the smoke blows off to-day, or to-morrow, anything is left to take care of, I will get you and Mr. Fearing to come and talk it over with me.

But it was to be no question 'of to-day or to-morrow.' It soon became evident that the votes were so close that it would be necessary to wait until a report to the Legislature could be made on the basis of official returns.

The Legislature met on Wednesday, January 1st. The Secretary of State laid before the Senate the returns of the votes for Governor and Lieutenant-Governor. The matter was referred to a joint committee, consisting of thirteen members from both Houses. This committee made a careful study of the returns and investigated all the so-called 'irregularities.' Again we may wisely let the journal tell the story:

> *Wednesday, January* 8, 1840. Employed in the evening on notes for a message to the Legislature *in case* I should be called upon (which is very doubtful) to make one.
>
> *Thursday, January* 9. Colonel Winthrop called on me at ten to let me know that it was understood that Judge Morton is elected by two votes. He made the communication with evident pain.
>
> *Monday, January* 13. Council at eleven. The committee of the two Houses on the gubernatorial returns report to-day, in substance, as follows:

The whole number of votes legally returned for
    Governor was.............................. 102,066
Necessary for a choice.....................   51,034
Marcus Morton has........................   51,034
Edward Everett...........................   50,725
All others................................   307

Several illegal returns were counted, and, as I think, one unconstitutional one (the Westfield return), which was not attested by
the Town Clerk. The Chairman of the joint committee and two of
the members joined in a minority report on the ground of the un-
constitutionality of that return. Still, as the votes were unquestionably given in Westfield, and as Judge Morton has a majority of
all the votes, I think it decidedly best that this return should not
be rejected, although its admission costs my election. Principle is
no longer sufficiently powerful even in Massachusetts to warrant
an adherence to the strict provisions of the Constitution on a question of this kind.

The minority report, which dissents from the decision to
count the Westfield ballot as unconstitutional, was signed
by James Savage, Jeffrey Richardson, and James C. Starkweather.

January 17, 1840. Having received information that the Governor-elect would probably take the oath to-morrow, I stated to the
Council that when I left the Chair to-day I should request the
Lieutenant-Governor to occupy it till my successor should be
qualified. The Lieutenant-Governor and Council then rose, and he
delivered to me a short and very affectionate address on their behalf; to which I made a few words by way of reply. I then shook
hands with each member of the Council and retired. Poor old
Manning followed me into my private room and was much affected
in bidding me good-bye. He said it was a great comfort to him I
had not lost my election by want of his vote, and he wished all who
had professed friendship to me had shown it by voting for me, a
pretty severe thrust at the Secretary of State.

January 18. I sent to the Governor-elect this morning fourteen
official reports and communications of the various boards and
officers of the Commonwealth. At twelve o'clock the cannons
(fired by order of the Adjutant-General who came to take my directions about it) announced that he was sworn in. I am *now for the
first time for more than fifteen years a private citizen!*

Everett had acted wisely in the matter, and on the whole with sound judgment and restraint. It would have been possible for him to continue the contest and push the charge of various technical errors in the returns. He was urged by many of his adherents to take this step. The excitement ran high. Public opinion was on tiptoe. Charges and counter-charges were made by both parties. But Everett was sensible in deciding to take no further steps. Although the House was strongly Whig, it was also a fact that the House had voted by a large majority to accept the report of the joint committee. It was generally felt that the committee did wisely in accepting all votes and having them counted, waiving all such technicalities as errors in the form of entry and slips in regard to the date. Moreover, the fact stood out above all else that Judge Morton had received the larger number of votes. But Winthrop, among others, was for pushing the matter. He had many plans to offer. When all else had failed, he wished to print a fulsome tribute which he had prepared, and he sent the sheets to Everett. But Everett dissuaded him: 'You had better not publish it,' he wrote. 'It is far beyond my merit, and even friends would say that you have allowed your kind feelings to blind your judgment. It provokes Nemesis to put such things on record till "the last end has subdued envy."' In another connection he wrote: 'I wish no struggle made on my account. I have quite made up my mind not to be continued in office. . . . I am quite willing to let the election go.'

There the matter rested. Many of his friends, who had carelessly failed to vote, were poignantly contrite. The Secretary of State, who had neglected to cast a ballot, was heartbroken, and tried with tears to explain away his negligence. Everett himself tried his best to be philosophical; but it cannot be doubted that the strong man's pride had been greatly humbled. He felt the defeat most bitterly, and attributed it to the failure of his friends to stand by him.

The most stinging blow of all had been dealt him by his own brother. The brilliant but unstable Alexander H. Everett had been of the opposite political party for a number of years. When Edward Everett made his first campaign for Governor in 1835 and was elected, his brother ran for the State Senate on the opposition ticket, and was defeated. And this year, when Everett needed but one vote to prevent the election of Marcus Morton, Alexander Everett had presided over the Democratic Convention and had signed a public declaration in opposition to his brother's election. The act was one which Everett bore with Christian forbearance; but the experience was very far from pleasant. A diversion of some kind was desirable if not absolutely necessary. Before the political excitement had fairly died away, it became known that Governor Everett was 'planning a trip abroad for his wife's health.' The physicians had been advising for some time that a warmer climate would be of great advantage to Mrs. Everett. More than two years before the fatal election, Everett had written Webster on the subject and had expressed the fear that a winter in the South of France or Italy was necessary unless his wife's consumption was to be 'fixed.'

But Everett himself was no doubt eager for both change and complete rest. The thought of getting away and of returning for a period to the older world was most alluring. He was not allowed to leave the country, however, without having glowing tribute paid to his genius and attainments. He had held public office for fifteen years, and it seemed but a poor reward at the end of such a term of service to have the people render a verdict of 'not wanted.' His old friend Judge Story appreciated keenly the soreness of heart that the situation had caused and wrote him words that had a steadying effect.

A public dinner was suggested, and Everett finally gave his consent to the arrangement. The hall was engaged, the speakers agreed upon, and the details all carefully planned out, when Everett came down with so severe a cold and felt himself so burdened by the making of his final plans for sailing, that he begged to be excused. A few less formal meetings were held, however, at which various of his friends bade him Godspeed, mingling with their sentiments of good-will the prophecy of future high accomplishments. It is related that Judge Story gave as a toast: 'Learning, genius, and eloquence are sure to be welcome where Ever-ett goes.' Thereupon the guest of honor promptly offered this sentiment in reply: 'Law, Equity, and Jurisprudence: all their efforts to rise will never be able to get above one Story.' [1]

With such breezy sentiments to waft them on their way, and with financial assistance from Mr. Brooks, Mr. Everett and family sailed from New York for Havre on June 9th in the packet Iowa, Captain Pell.

[1] *Hundred Boston Orators*, p. 543.

VII
PORT AFTER STORMY SEAS

IT was no simple undertaking in those days to go abroad, particularly when a stay of many months, if not a year or more, was contemplated. Florence was the objective of the party, and linen and plate had to be sent in advance for keeping house in Italy, as these articles were not included by Italians when they rented their houses or apartments. In addition to such articles as these, a rocking-chair was taken along for the faithful nurse, or attendant, Ruah. It was thought that this special type of chair, which was a thing unknown in Europe, would help to preserve the equilibrium of the maid and keep her from being homesick. The chair, however, proved a little too much for the French diligence, and it got no farther than Paris. The party, too, was a large one. They were eight in all including five children. The youngest member of the group was William, who was to distinguish himself in later years as preacher, professor, poet, politician, and conspicuous public character generally, but then a child of eight months. Moreover, they narrowly escaped having their party added to most unpleasantly. When it became publicly known that Mr. Everett and his family were going abroad, the notorious Mrs. Holley, of Washington, wrote and suggested that she would like, with her son, to become their travelling companion. This was more than even the courteous Everett could stand, and the letter which he wrote to Mrs. Holley in reply gave ample proof — if any proof were needed — that he was well fitted for the important diplomatic post that he was soon to be called upon to fill.

The family were supplied with three good staterooms on the thousand-ton packet, 'each with two berths and as much accommodation as could be expected on shipboard.' For these quarters the price paid was six hundred and seventy dollars, which included everything except wine on a voyage

which was expected to extend over three weeks at least.
Among other passengers on board were several people who
had been rescued from the ill-fated Poland which had recently been lost at sea by fire. Each morning after breakfast
Mr. Everett conducted family prayers in his cabin. He wrote
in his journal:

> On leaving home for a considerable time to be passed in foreign
> countries where the accustomed means of religious instruction do
> not exist, I have thought it best to read a chapter in the Bible and a
> prayer from Mr. Furness's recent collection with the family every
> morning in my stateroom.

Just why Mr. Everett chose to go by a sailing vessel cannot be said, for steamers by this time were successfully crossing the Atlantic, and the Cunard liner Britannia was already
making passages of twelve or fourteen days. Probably, however, it was thought desirable to make port on the Continent,
and that meant going by a packet. The voyage was comfortable enough, but a long one of twenty-two days, and
Havre was reached on July 2d.

Their first objective was Rouen, and they made the trip by
steamer up the river, having 'a tremendous fuss' with the
baggage. Two crowded days were given to Rouen — nearly
everything being seen; and on July 6th, the start was made
by diligence for Paris. They accomplished the journey
quickly, for, although the diligence was big and heavy, they
had 'five stout and fiery Norman horses for the usual force,
and when a hill was to be ascended two span more.' The
speed was good — nine or ten miles an hour. 'There was not
the slightest delay in changing horses, a good deal less in fact
than could be wished.' They stopped but once, at Fouchette,
for about half an hour, to take *déjeuner*. Paris was reached
at about six, and they drove directly to the Hôtel Mont-
morency, where they found 'but indifferent accommodations.
The dinner, however, was good and sweetened by hunger,
and the beds softened by fatigue.' The search for lodgings
then began, and the family soon moved into convenient

quarters at 24 (bis), rue de Rivoli. Before long they were comfortably settled, and a normal sort of life began. The oldest of the boys, to his huge disgust, was sent to a French boarding-school, and teachers were engaged for the other children. Everett himself found his way into the great libraries, where he delved into the archives, having promised Prescott to look up some Spanish documents that he needed in the preparation of his History.

He was now a family man, however, and with ladies in Paris his time was not altogether his own. The ex-Governor of Massachusetts was soon called upon to head shopping expeditions, as this paragraph from a letter to his brother-in-law makes clear:

... Never did I fully feel to what destinies I was reserved, till I marched through the splendid apartments at Alexandre & Baudraut's at the head of a *cortège* consisting of my wife, daughters, and a Philadelphia lady, each possessed with a fancy for a Parisian hat, and I to act as interpreter and bargainer for all; to say nothing of being cashier to the three first-named. I assure you I sighed as I cast my eyes upon the *armoires* of rosewood and the gilded ceilings and recollected that we were to pay our quota of the expense of these princely splendors. But I will not enlarge. I'll warrant you know the feeling. And then to act as dragoman to four ladies shopping. Fanny will easily believe that I repeated my classical exclamation, which she remembers of yore. ...

There were intervals to be found, however, for less exhausting work, and he used them in renewing old friendships made more than twenty years before, and in forming new ones. Lafayette, of course, was no longer living; but members of his family were attentive and polite. There was an insistent invitation to go to Lagrange, and Everett took his two girls and went for a visit from a Wednesday to Saturday.

A graphic account of this visit, with interesting personal details, may be taken from the journal.[1]

Wednesday, August 26. On arriving at Lagrange we sat down on

[1] Lagrange is about twenty miles from Paris, near the little town of Rozoy-en-Brie. It is still in the possession of the Lafayette family, the present owner and occupant being M. le Comte de Lasteyrie, a great-grandson of Lafayette.

the lawn, in seats and chairs placed under the trees, till a little luncheon of fruit was prepared in the dining-room. . . . At half-past four I retired to my room to dress and we had dinner at six, a most liberal meal elegantly served.

The family which sat down consisted of Mr. and Mrs. Lafayette, and a sister (I suppose) of Mrs. L., Madame Perier, Mr. and Mrs. Pusey, and Mr. and Mrs. Beaumont; these three ladies being daughters of Mr. Lafayette; of two girls, daughters of Madame Perier, of a son and daughter of Madame Pusey, and a child of two years of age, the son of Monsieur and Madame Beaumont — in all with ourselves eighteen persons.

After dinner we walked into the garden and farmyard. We saw several articles sent to the General from America, among others a rowboat which gained the prize in a match at New York.

After the walk we repaired to the hall upstairs, where we saw the counterpart of the great picture of Lafayette which hangs in the hall of the House of Representatives at Washington. . . . The portraits of all the Presidents hung round the walls. . . . I passed most of the time in conversing with Monsieur Lafayette on the subject of his (the General's) residence at Mount Vernon (in 1792). While he was there, the present King of the French, then on a visit to General Washington, and himself passed their time one day in pasting the paper upon a wall in the house.

Thursday, 27. . . . In the course of the day, I was shown the bedroom and library of the General. They are both left in the condition in which they were at his death. . . . There were a great many American books on the shelves, and a series of drawers filled with articles presented to him in the United States.

Monsieur Lafayette observed that it was Washington's custom when he returned from his ride to dress himself completely for dinner: and that on the fatal occasion on which he contracted his last malady, he neglected to do so, and left the hair on his neck wet. . . . Among the articles in the drawers was a little bound volume containing the three or four of my orations which were first bound, which I collected and sent him in 1825.

Governor Cass was the United States Minister to France at the time, and he offered all civilities, suggesting among other things to secure Everett's presentation at Court. The following letter to Winthrop tells the story:

PARIS, *July* 27, 1840

Gov. Cass has been very kind to me. He was to have presented me to the King this week, but after permission had been informally asked the thought occurred to me that I had no Court-dress, never having put on a costume at my own Court, I had not thought of such a thing at the Court of the Citizen-King. . . . I am hesitating whether to pay the modest sum of one hundred francs, which is demanded for the hire of a dress, or get one made, which could be done for twice that sum and would serve on other occasions, or deny myself the pleasure of a presentation. The tailor, by way of encouraging me to borrow a dress of him, assures me that he fitted out Mr. Webster for the same purpose. There are, however, occasions when one would not like to wear Mr. Webster's mantle — that is, if it is to be put literally upon the shoulders of a person about half his stature.

But, as it happened, the presentation had to be postponed because of a threatened insurrection on the part of Paris workmen, and something much more interesting and memorable was eventually suggested. Everett was invited to dine with His Majesty at Saint-Cloud, and 'as a mark of greater friendliness was asked to appear in citizen's dress.'

The journal contains an interesting account of the affair, but the fullest description of the whole episode is found in this letter to Mr. Brooks, dated September 21, 1840:

When I last wrote you, I spoke of the riotous gatherings of workmen. A few days afterwards they assumed a threatening aspect. Attempts were made to barricade the streets. This is always the first step taken in a popular outbreak at Paris. It is done by overturning carriages, omnibuses and wagons. The spaces are filled up with casks and boxes, and the whole rendered compact by the stones of the pavement torn up for this purpose. This constitutes a very effective bulwark against the advance of troops, if time is given to construct it substantially.

In the present case the alarm was spread very soon. The attempts to barricade took place about noon on the seventh and by three o'clock in the afternoon from forty thousand to fifty thousand troops of the line and the entire National Guard of Paris, amounting to as many more, were in movement, according to a plan of operations already conceived for such an occasion. All this was done with so much system and quiet that we heard nothing of it beyond a drum of the National Guard which passed up and down our street beating the summons to arms at intervals during an hour. The troops stationed in the neighborhood were all marched into Paris. It is not possible that the Government could have thought that this overwhelming force was necessary, but they were probably willing to show with what ease they could flood the city with troops.

As soon as the alarm reached Saint-Cloud, the King, the Queen, and Madame Adelaide, the King's sister (who is said to possess the entire confidence of the King and to be a person of much sagacity) drove into the city to the Tuileries and took up their abode for the night. At dusk every room at the palace was lighted. This was a politic measure, showing the readiness of the King to draw near the supposed field of danger, and serving to animate the headquarters which were established at the Tuileries. A council of the Ministers was called at which the King presided. The guards at every post in Paris were doubled and the night passed with some anxiety; but the peace was nowhere broken.

The King had informed General Cass that he would receive me at Saint-Cloud on Tuesday evening the 8th, but as soon as I found that the King had thought the movement of the rioters important enough to keep him in town, I gave up the expectation of being presented at the time appointed. About noon of Tuesday, as I had foreseen, a communication was received from the aide-de-camp on duty, stating that His Majesty could not receive me that night, and that due notice would be given of the day that might be fixed for my presentation. The 8th passed over in perfect quiet, which has remained unbroken to the present day. The next day, I was dining at General Cass's when invitations came to him, the secretary, and myself to dine at Saint-Cloud the next day. These invitations are given at short notice and require no answer unless some unavoidable cause of absence exists. It is expected that all engagements will yield to the royal invitation, which is in French in the following form: 'Saint-Cloud, 9 Septr. 1840. The aide-de-camp in attendance on the King has the honor to inform Mr. E. that he is invited to dine at the palace of Saint-Cloud on Thursday the 10th at six o'clock.' At the bottom of the invitation is a notice that you are expected to come in citizen's dress.

General Cass, though he gave us a dinner in Paris, in a new house to which he is about removing, is still at Versailles. His secretary, Mr. Ledyard, had come into town and I made an appointment to go with him to Saint-Cloud and meet General Cass at the palace door, that I might enter under his protection. We happened, however, to miss each other, as people sometimes do when they are very desirous of meeting. Mr. L. and I went up into the antechamber till the Minister should arrive. I had the satisfaction of hearing the clock strike six, as I set foot in it. At the same moment, looking out of window, I saw the King drive up in his carriage with eight horses in a foam, from Paris. The aide-de-camp in attendance presently joined us, and, as the royal family were assembling in the drawing-room, he took us along with him. As our Minister had not come, I regretted this circumstance, but there seemed to be no help for it.

When we entered the drawing-room, there were only some of the ladies and gentlemen in immediate attendance on the King and Queen present. I was introduced to some of them. The Queen soon came in, and Colonel de Chabaunes, the aide above mentioned, presented me. She began to speak English to me with which she is not very perfectly acquainted. Madame de Dolomieu (her first lady of honor — a person of the Queen's age and who has always been in immediate attendance upon her), to whom I had been introduced, told the Queen I could speak French, in which language she then addressed me, asking me a few civil questions about my arrival and residence in Paris, etc. General Cass came in about this time, and soon after the other members of the royal family, that is, the King, his two oldest sons (the Duke of Orleans and the Duke of Nemours), the Duchess of Orleans, and the Princess Clementine, the unmarried daughter. The King, as soon as he saw General Cass, came up to him, saying, 'Ah, my dear General Cass, I am glad to see you.' The General then presented me. The King said he was sorry he could not see me on Thursday evening; the little affair we had in Paris prevented. 'I am very happy to see you now.'

Dinner was presently announced. The King took in his daughter the Duchess of Orleans; the Duke of Orleans took in his sister Clementine; the Queen called to General Cass and gave him her arm; the Duke of Nemours took in one of the ladies; and the Marchioness de Dolomieu offered me her arm. How the rest of the company got in, I did not, of course, see. We went through a magnificent hall and gallery on the way to the dining-room. In the gallery a full band of music was stationed, playing a march as the company passed. The table held about twenty-two and the King and Queen sat opposite to each other, in the middle of the long sides. The service was of silver; — except the plateau and its appendages which were of silver gilt. The dinner was not particularly elaborate; not better than I have partaken at private tables in Boston. It lasted about an hour and a quarter. The King's sister came in, when it was half over. The attendance of servants was prodigious, more than one, I should think, to each guest, but owing to the size of the room there was no jostling with each other. The conversation was mostly in a low tone with your next neighbor.

After dinner we got back to the drawing-room in the same manner that we left it, and coffee was served. I had now a conversation with the King in English (which he speaks perfectly well) of half an hour's length. He spoke of his travels in America, a topic of which he is very fond. He named Mr. Amory, Colonel Pickering, whom he said they used to call Tim Pickering, and Mr. Otis. He spoke of his daughter, lately deceased, the accomplished Princess who produced the statue of the Maid of Orleans. He inquired about the probable event of the presidential election, spoke of our present controversy with England; of affairs in the East; and of the domestic politics of France. You will think some of these singular topics of conversation with a perfect stranger, but I suppose he felt safe in saying what he pleased to me. On my making some remark to him in an unreserved manner, I apologized for my freedom; he said he wished me to speak in that strain, and he was sure he might do so himself without fear. He then spoke of his own position with entire openness, and seemed to take a pleasure in bursting the reserve which it is almost necessary to wear on any such topic in conversing with Europeans.

The King is sixty-seven or sixty-eight, in fine health; rather corpulent, not over the middle height, a profusion of hair,[1] which is now iron-grey; a full, pleasant face; fine teeth. He wore a plain blue coat with the royal star on his breast; a white waistcoat, his watch-chain, with at least twenty seals and rings, attached to one of the buttonholes of his vest, grey pants, white stockings and shoes. The Queen is sixty — tall, well-looking, and graceful.

After coffee the Queen and her ladies at two tables sat down to their rug work. I then had some conversation with the Queen, Madame Adelaide, and the Duke of Orleans. Presently the King's musicians came in, a company of about thirty instrumental performers, all first-rate in their way, and they gave us a concert in the library, a splendid apartment adjoining the drawing-room. Before long some company began to come in; among others a brother of Don Carlos, the would-be King of Spain, his wife and daughters. We staid till about half-past nine and then stole off.

Everett was not a man to make light of opportunities, and he took advantage of the attractions that Paris had to offer. He went to the opera and enjoyed it: he found his way into churches, libraries, and galleries, refreshing his memory of earlier days: but he took particular delight in the acting of Rachel. His diary contains this entry:

September 15, 1840. Went out in the morning to engage tickets for the evening at the Français, where Mademoiselle Rachel was to play in Cinna.... The parents of Mademoiselle Rachel are Jews,

---

[1] The journal says 'a wig.'

and were porters in some ordinary dwelling where actors boarded. Rachel caught some notions of declamation from attending the theatre with the boarders, and used to go round the streets singing and declaiming for a few sous. Some one heard her who was struck with her voice and made provision for her instruction, either for the sake of patronizing talent, or, as I think I have heard, some less creditable motive. She was soon able to take the leading parts in French tragedy. On her appearance on the stage, she immediately rose to fame and influence. The theatre was filled, and her engagements were in the highest degree lucrative, negotiated, of course, by her father, and during her minority for his benefit. She is now said to be nineteen years, but this may be a little underrated.

I got four seats in the *stalles du balcon*, very near the stage. There was no orchestra, and the decorations and furniture of the scene were excessively ordinary. The part of Cinna was well performed and Augustus not ill: but the entire interest of the piece rested with Emilie. Mademoiselle Rachel is not beautiful: her eyes are small and deep-set: her nose Jewish (not aquiline, but full at the insertion): the lower part of her face pleasing, her figure good. She looks rather delicate and her health is said to be feeble. Nothing could surpass the clearness of her enunciation, her dignity and grace. She recited the heroics of Corneille with very little attention to rhythm, thereby divesting them of the monotony which haunts the French tragedy. She gave a few passages with great effect and power, but none with the extreme of passion.

As the autumn deepened, the faces of the party were turned toward Florence where they planned to pass the winter. It was decided to make the trip by way of Marseilles and the Mediterranean, instead of crossing the Alps. But the perils of Æneas were nothing to those that they were soon to experience. Storms, floods, disease, and an accident at sea, one by one awaited them, and they must frequently have regretted that they had not chosen instead one of the Alpine passes. At the easiest, the trip by the South of France was long and tedious, but in their case it came to be a nightmare of troubles.

AVIGNON, *October 26, 1840*

MY DEAR SIDNEY, . . . We left Paris on the 13th. I hired a carriage to take us to Châlons and took post-horses to that place. We stopped the first day at Fontainebleau (making a short day's work

that we might see the castle), the second at Auxerre, the third at
Sanlieu, and arrived in good season at Châlons the fourth day.
We took the steamboat for Lyons the next morning at six o'clock.
Just before starting, my servant had occasion to run back to the
hotel which is just on the quay, and a minute before he got back,
the boat started leaving me *minus* courier just when I needed his
services most, to take care of the baggage on landing at Lyons!
I soon found, however, that a second boat was to start in an hour,
and, as it was of lighter draught, Carlo overtook us before we got
to Lyons and jumped on board our boat. Although the Rhone has
lately been so high as to overflow banks and carry away bridges,
as there has been no rain for three weeks we found it too low for
the large boats which commonly run, and no boat whatever was
despatched the day after our arrival at Lyons. This gave us opportunity to look round a little. The next day a small boat excessively overloaded was despatched — an iron steamboat of light
draught. We grounded, however, just below the confluence of the
Saone and the Rhone, but got off with ease. We were constantly
scraping the shoals in the course of the day; and, as it was impossible to steer after dark, we came to for the night, at a wretched
little town called Bourg Saint-Androt. There were no berths in
the steamboat, and it was necessary to go up into the town for
the night. Our situation was rendered not a little distressing
by our daughter Charley's health, who had complained all the day
before at Lyons, and had been in a high fever all the day in the
steamboat. . . .

A drearier, dirtier house than we passed the night in, I never
wish to see, and this with one child in a high fever, another convalescent, a third an infant in arms, is no joke, I assure you. We had
been summoned at half-past three at Lyons — a good hour earlier
than was necessary — and had to rouse ourselves at four at Bourg
Saint-Androt. By half-past nine we were at Avignon, where we
found a good hotel and the most friendly sympathy and attention
from the landlady. We have been kept here a week to-morrow and
do not expect to start for three or four days. Charley has been
quite sick, but will doubtless be ready to proceed, as she is mending
rapidly. We have found her a very practical, judicious physician
and have had as little to aggravate our unpleasant condition as possible. In fact, Avignon is a place of no little interest. I went one
day with Nanny and Mr. Edward Webster [1] (who is with us) to
Vaucluse, and he has gone to-day to the Pont du Gard and Nîmes.

---

[1] Younger son of Daniel Webster, who had been studying abroad, and whom
Everett had offered to take under his care.

I should gladly have made the same excursion, but did not care to leave my flock without a shepherd long enough to do so. . . .

But Avignon did not see the end of their troubles. The little girl's illness looked amazingly like smallpox, but finally proved nothing worse than a violent form of varioloid. But other complications now set in, and he wrote of them in much detail to Mr. Brooks.

MARSEILLES, *October* 31, 1840

You will be happy to hear, my dear Sir, of our safe arrival at this place after the letter from me written at Avignon, which I suppose Sidney must have received. We were detained at that place ten days by poor Charley's varioloid; but had the consolation at last of her happy recovery. The eight first days which we passed at Avignon, we were annoyed by the strong dry north wind which is the leading feature of the climate. At length the wind came round to the south and it began to rain. Violent thunder and lightning followed, and for two days we were in a deluge.

Friday at 6 P.M. was fixed for our departure in the diligence for Marseilles, which, all things considered, was the best mode of conveyance for us. On getting up on Friday morning, I perceived the waters of the little river Sorgue, which enters the Rhone at Avignon, rapidly rising in the streets. The Rhone was already so full that the Sorgue could not run off, and both streams were fast swelling. Before midday the courtyard of our hotel was two feet deep in water, and the lower floor of the house, of course, abandoned. There was no communication with the city but in hand carts, on rafts, and pretty soon in boats. They soon sent me word from the diligence office that they did not dare to drive through the town to the Marseilles gate with their load, but that if we would meet them at that gate they would take us in. I could find no one who would engage to take us through the city. Some of the streets were six or eight feet deep; but not uniformly so, so that it was not possible to go all the way either by land or water, especially as many of the streets had holes in them, the town being old and dilapidated. I sent word to the office that we would start if they would transport us safely to the diligence, which they promised to do if possible. All this time it continued to rain, and it was expected every moment that the waters of the Rhone would begin to pour over its banks into the basin in which the lower parts of the city lie. The day was passed in no small anxiety.

At length about two we received a summons to be ready to start in a small flat-bottomed boat made simply of a single pine board for the bottom. It was necessary to have the lightest possible draft because some of the streets over which we were to pass lay high. Our frail bark came up to the stairs of the hotel and our party with a few others started. We sailed into another hotel and took up some other passengers, and finally started, about fifteen or sixteen persons. We passed along through several streets within the city wall and at length through a breach in the wall into the public promenade which surrounds the city. Just as we passed out of the city through the breach, the Rhone was pouring into the city in a strong flood-tide and the country as far as we could see was under water. The trees of the promenade served, however, as landmarks; and we coasted along, sometimes striking the gravel, often floating over places where the water was many feet deep. Instead of merely going round to the opposite gate of the city, we had, after arriving there, to proceed near a mile on the Marseilles road. We were an hour and a half in the boat, and by great good fortune the rain held up and the sun shone out pleasantly. The whole scene as we cruised along (the latter part of the way towed by a horse and light car by which our baggage had been conveyed) was curious and picturesque. The uncertainty whether we should succeed or run upon shoals, from which we could neither advance nor retreat, kept me not a little anxious. Finally we reached the diligence in safety, and though it soon came on to rain again and rained all night, we reached Marseilles without accident, though somewhat fatigued. . . .

But even then their troubles were very far from being ended. There was yet the trip by sea from Marseilles to Leghorn. The steamer was a wretched affair. A boiler burst in the engine room, and the vessel limped back to port to make repairs. Head winds and high seas were encountered with all that they usually entail. Then a second child developed varioloid. Altogether Mr. Everett found that it was not as easy to make a European tour with a delicate wife to care for and five small children, as it had been *en garçon*, as a student. It was a pretty dilapidated party that arrived at Pisa, and more than one of them must have sighed for quiet Summer Street in Boston. They had come abroad for rest and relaxation!

Reaching Florence, they soon were sufficiently settled to be able to appreciate their quarters. Mr. Urquhart, of New Orleans, with his family occupied the *rez de chaussée*, under

them, while Prince Trubetskoi, of Russia, was *au premier.*
There was a large and beautiful garden behind the house
opening upon the rampart by a private gate. The landlady,
Baroness Lagersnärd, was the widow of the former Swedish
Minister to Tuscany — herself French. Their friends the
Horatio Greenoughs were not far away, 'charmingly situated
amidst pictures of the ancient masters, books and music.'
Mr. Greenough at the time was occupied with his great
statue of Washington, the likeness being founded on Hou-
don's famous bust. Everett thought the likeness excellent,
and was impressed with the fact that 'the benignity, firmness, and tranquillity of Washington's character were well
expressed.'

Through Greenough he soon became acquainted with
Powers, with whom he passed many quiet hours gradually
forming an intimate friendship and finally sitting to the great
sculptor for his bust. Hardly more than a fortnight after his
arrival in Florence, he was taken to the Pitti Palace to be
presented to the Grand Duke who had appointed an hour at
which to give him a private audience. He found the Grand
Duke wholly alone.

He was dressed in very plain citizen's dress, with nothing that
indicated rank but the decorations of two or three orders at his
buttonhole, and several rich seal rings on his fingers. He is forty-
three years old, but his hair and whiskers being quite grey he looks
perhaps somewhat older. His air is quiet and somewhat downcast
and reminded me of Mr. Allston.[1] His conversation was intelligent
and showed considerable reading. He made judicious enquiries
about the state of things in America . . . and was very much amused
at the account I gave him of Governor Morton's election last fall
by one vote.

What was more important, however, than all else, the
Grand Duke offered the *free use of his library,* which turned
out to be no inconsiderable boon, and supplied a convenient
place for study. A few days later a ducal footman appeared
at the Casa Lagersnärd with an invitation to dine at the

[1] Washington Allston.

Palace at five-forty-five, it being stipulated that the guest should appear 'in citizen's dress with white cravat and shoes.' This was in accordance with Italian custom, all such invitations being given and answered '*orally*.'

The dinner itself proved a princely affair. 'There was more than a servant to each guest, and the service was equal to that of the Palace of Saint-Cloud.' When Everett expressed his compliments on the matter to the Grand Chamberlain, he was told that what they were using was only 'the ordinary service,' but that the Grand Duke owned a great deal of carved plate, some of it the work of Benvenuto Cellini.

It was characteristic of this busy worker and indefatigable student that, finding himself in a famous art centre, he began at once to take lessons in drawing. He worked faithfully, but soon convinced himself that he had no talent in that direction worth speaking of. He was tempted after a little to give up the lessons; but on account of setting a bad example to his children, he did not like to lend the appearance of beginning a thing and not seeing it through. The opera, too, which he sometimes attended, made slight appeal. 'However it may be with drawing,' he confessed to himself, 'I am pretty sure I have not the organ of opera. The music I like. But the diabolisms, extravaganzas, and the ballet are disgusting.' The Court balls bored him, and left him convinced that he 'was not made for a man of pleasure.' His greatest satisfaction as always was found in books and people, and Florence supplied him with both.

A few letters to members of the family and friends give glimpses of the life.

To the Honorable P. C. Brooks

FLORENCE, *February* 18, 1841

... My wife had a pretty bad time with ague three weeks ago, but has got quite well and been able to pass one or two evenings abroad, one of them at a ball at the palace. Nanny has also been presented and attended two balls at Court. These parties in the latter part of the Carnival are given every Wednesday evening.

There are usually a great many strangers presented; sometimes so many that the Grand Duchess does not get wholly round the circle. This happened to be the case when my wife was presented; but in the course of the evening, as we were standing together, the Grand Duke and Duchess came up to us and he introduced my wife to her himself. A short time before he presented me a magnificent work on the subject of the operations in progress for draining the unhealthy region on the seacoast of Tuscany, an object which he has pursued with great zeal, at vast expense, and with considerable success; a folio of the largest size in a most splendid binding. The day before yesterday he sent us a pair of pheasants from the Cascine. This bird is of the size of a large fowl — the taste much like our partridge, though not so dry a meat. . . .

I have been indebted to the Grand Duke, since I wrote you last, for a rich mental repast, viz., permission to explore the public archives. Florence is particularly rich in this respect. Besides the great public libraries, some of which contain invaluable manuscripts (among them that of Justinian's Pandects), there are three great collections of historical documents. One is composed of the contents of the libraries of the convents which were suppressed in the time of the French; the size of this collection is, I understand, vast, but I have not seen it. Although it must contain a great deal of local interest, I suppose it is not of much importance for general history. These collections are not open to the public. I requested Prince Corsini, the Minister of the Interior, to obtain me permission to examine the contents of the archives, and at the next ball the Grand Duke told me that he had given orders for my free access.

The night before last we were at a great ball at the Marquis of Mazares. This is a Spanish title. He is a native, Dane Coesvelt by name, and is said to be the original of the character of Oswald in Madame de Stael's 'Corinne.' He was for some time the active partner in the house of Hope and Company at Amsterdam. He incurred the enmity of Napoleon by remonstrating against the opening and detention of letters in the post-offices, and removed to England. He afterwards resided in Guiana and Spain, where he married his wife, thereby adding a large fortune to his own. They now live in great style at Florence. A few years ago he purchased the Spinelli Palace, one of the largest and finest in the city, and fitted it up in a style of comfort and magnificence rarely seen out of England. The passages and staircases were lined with exotics, principally camellias in bloom; and every lady, on entering the anteroom, was presented with a bouquet which contained a camellia. Ten or twelve rooms were opened. The company went principally at eleven o'clock and stayed till four. *We* came home (good simple souls) at one. Last night our little Charley — who does not go to the great balls — was at a children's fancy ball at Prince Poniatoffsky's.

FLORENCE, *January* 1, 1841

DEAR SISTER,— ... The very aspect of the streets of Florence is a feast to my eyes; not for what are called beauties in new towns, for the streets are mostly narrow, winding, and not very clean. But there are few of them which do not contain palaces, from three to six hundred years old, of the most massy structure — looking often more like fortresses than dwellings — bearing historical names — presenting a kind of history of the turbulent liberty and wild party spirit of the Middle Ages, in their dark and battered fronts. Then, too, all the ideas (many of them false) which we bring from college of the Medicean Age and the revival of letters, come back with startling freshness, as you explore the palaces, halls, cabinets, and villas, where the varied drama of the dynasty of the Medici was acted.

The magnificence of other days, of which such permanent monuments remain, is in strong contrast with the impoverishment of present times. The old families, with very few exceptions, are reduced to indigence. The greater number of the fine old palaces have passed into other families, or have been purchased by bankers and foreigners, and at very reduced prices. I visit in a palace, which was purchased last year for thirty-six thousand dollars. It is, at least, twice as large as the President's house in Washington — beautifully built — and enclosing a large garden, in the best part of Florence. At the prices of building and materials in Boston, I am sure it could not be erected there for less than a million dollars. A friend of mine here from America hires a palace of a descendant of the family of Cardinal Ximenes. It is truly a princely residence, and was occupied by Napoleon on occasion of some visit to Florence. It has a garden of several acres, and is furnished, the whole for a rent of one thousand dollars a year, on a lease of seven years. . . .

Most of the Americans here share in the rejoicing of all good Whigs at the glorious result of the elections. You speak of my not being at home to get an office. I am well content to be without one, and certainly would not come home for such an object. Having, at all times, taken as little pains as can well be (and that little I wish less) to get office, I shall leave those who have the bestowal of it to find out my address if they wish my services. . . . Adieu.

But he was not really so indifferent to political office as he would have his sister understand. His letters to Winthrop tell a different story. We find him, as early as November, 1840, stating frankly, 'My wish would be, if my friends at home desire my continuance in public life, to find employment abroad. I am now in Europe, and those domestic considerations which brought me here continue to operate. If I am fit for anything, it is a diplomatic employment.' Then, going into more particulars, he could confess to Winthrop that he would be gratified with the mission to London, having 'made a particular study of the questions between us and Great Britain.'

For the most part, none the less, Everett was disposed to enjoy the Italian present to the utmost and to let the political future take care of itself. There were many interesting people in Florence that winter, among them Mrs. Trollope, the mother of the famous and prolific novelist, as well as an authoress of considerable repute herself, and Lady Bulwer, who was living there apart from her husband. The allusion to the latter is only a passing one; but somewhat amusing, and with descriptions of Florentine life.

> FLORENCE, *March* 18, 1841
>
> MY DEAR SISTER, . . . We were at a small party the other night, where Lady Bulwer was present. The palace in one of the best situations in Florence contains over sixty rooms, the lower story thirty feet high, and the others in proportion; most of the rooms as big as my parlor in Summer Street, and the whole, with some furniture, let for seven hundred and fifty dollars a year. I had considerable conversation with Lady Bulwer, from which I gathered that she is writing a novel,[1] on some topic drawn from Venetian history. She lives here wholly alone: — is a great deal in society; but leads, I believe, an entirely irreproachable life; on a maintenance paid by her husband. Her only attendant at the parties is a lap-dog. At a masked ball in Carnival, where she was present, some one, to show her he knew her, enquired how her dog was. She answered, 'Je n'ai point de chien qu'un chien de mari.' I won't vouch for the nicety of the French; but I suppose it is as good as her ladyship used. Neither will I guaranty the truth of the story. 'I tell the tale as 'twas told me.'
>
> There is opera in Lent, but no ballet. I took a box for our ladies

[1] *Bianca Cappello:* An Historical Romance. 3 vols. London, 1843.

twice a week, but I am very apt, when the evenings come, to have some engagement which prevents me individually from going. I like music; but four hours on a stretch — you understand, Mr. Hale. Set a bee down to a cup of honey, and you poison him. There are concerts and card parties every Saturday night at Court, but no dancing. They begin next Saturday. All persons who have been presented are in the habit of going, without invitation; but the Grand Duke has favored us with an invitation. Men are obliged to wear a Court uniform to these concerts; nothing more than a common full dress is expected of ladies.

We have not quite decided what to do this summer, whether to go to Switzerland or the Rhine; or bury ourselves in the dark corridors of one of these vast stone palaces and stay in Florence.

With Mrs. Trollope he came to be rather pleasantly acquainted. She expressed a wish to meet him, and a small party was arranged for the purpose. The American found her 'a sprightly old lady, of very ordinary appearance, lively manners and conversation. She was particularly civil and complimentary.'

Mrs. Trollope was then engaged in preparing her book of Italian sketches, and Everett was persuaded to show her some verses which he had just written for a friend's album. It had happened again, as nearly always, that with a little leisure had come the impulse to express himself in verse. Mrs. Trollope, having read the lines, was sincerely enthusiastic, and begged for permission to use the poem, bestowing on it many high compliments. Everett was not eager to have it published, but eventually gave his consent. It was printed in the first volume of 'A Visit to Italy' with a complimentary note by the authoress who had not been so complimentary to Americans in general in a previous book of travels. Later on, the poem was printed in the fourth volume of the Boston Book. It had the distinction, too — which was something of an honor — of being rendered into Italian by Guido Sorelli, an Italian poet who had made a reputation by his own poetry, and also by his translation of Shakespeare into his native language.

A few stanzas are enough to indicate the character of the poem:

SANTA CROCE

Not chiefly for thy storied towers, and halls,
Nor the bright wonders of thy pictured walls;
Not for the olive's wealth, the vineyard's pride,
That crown thy hills, and teem on Arno's side,
Dost thou delight me, Florence! I can meet
Elsewhere with halls as rich, and vales as sweet;
I prize thy charms of nature and of art,
But yield them not the homage of my heart.

Rather to Santa Croce I repair,
To breathe her peaceful monumental air;
The age, the deeds, the honours to explore
Of those who sleep beneath her marble floor —
The stern old tribunes of the early time,
The merchant lords of freedom's stormy prime,
And each great name in every after age,
The praised, the wise; the artist, bard, and sage.

I feel their awful presence; Lo! thy bust,
Thy urn, O Dante! — not alas! thy dust.
Florence that drove thee living from her gate
Waits for that dust in vain, and long shall wait. . . .

Next, in an urn not void, though cold as thine,
Moulders a god-like spirit's mortal shrine.
Oh, Michael! Look not down so cold and hard,
Speak to me, Painter, Builder, Sculptor, Bard.
And shall those cunning fingers, stiff and cold,
Crumble to meaner earth than they did mould? . . .

Hosts yet unnamed, the obscure, the known, I leave;
What throngs would rise, could each his marble heave!
But we, who muse above the famous dead,
Shall soon be silent as the dust we tread.
Yet not for me, when I shall fall asleep,
Shall Santa Croce's lamps their vigils keep!
Far o'er the sea, in Auburn's quiet shade,
With those I loved, and love, my couch be made,
Spring's pendent branches o'er the hillock wave,
And morning's dew-drops sparkle on my grave;
While Heaven's great arch shall rise above my bed,
When Santa Croce crumbles o'er its dead;
Unknown to erring, or to suffering fame,
So I may leave a pure, though humble name.

Poetry, however, was not destined to hold him long. He was soon to step back, if not into politics at least into public life. We have seen some references in his confidential letters to the possibility of a diplomatic appointment. Mr. Webster, who was now Secretary of State, sounded him on the subject, and also wrote at this time to Mr. Brooks, asking what he thought Mr. Everett's preference would be. Such enquiries called forth the following:

...As you have mentioned to me the subject of appointment and intimated the purpose of submitting my name to the President for a foreign mission, you will pardon me, perhaps, for saying a few words to you on this subject, although it is a topic on which I wish to say very little. I could not with safety take my wife to Berlin or St. Petersburg. If at this critical juncture in the East the commercial and political interests of the country should be thought to warrant a full mission to Constantinople, the Minister to be also accredited to Greece, that place would be acceptable to me. Should the President deem it expedient to send a full Minister to two or more of the Italian Governments jointly (a common practice), that also would be an eligible appointment. You will find our relations with Sardinia in a very sad state requiring immediate attention, and a commercial treaty with Tuscany is much wanted. There may, however, be reasons against consolidating the accustomed missions of the second class. I am told by friends at home that I have been sometimes thought of for the mission to London. If the contingency should not arise, in which you would think it necessary to assume that station yourself, and should not Mr. Sergeant be selected, whom I see talked of and whose qualifications are by no one more highly estimated than by me, I should prefer that place on some accounts to any other, and it might not be undesirable to you to have it in the hands of a confidential friend. Next to London if there were a vacancy I should prefer to go to Paris, but I do not wish any vacancy made for me. Provision I see was made at the late session for a new minister to Vienna, where, in consequence of my long residence in Germany in former days, I should, as far as the language goes, feel in some degree at home.

To whatever post you may assign me, as I am here at Florence, should no provision be made for direct diplomatic relations with Tuscany, it might be in my power — if authorized for the purpose — before repairing to my station, to conclude a commercial treaty with this Government. The extraordinary personal kindness which the Grand Duke has shown me this winter would give me some facilities.

I need not say, my dear Sir, that I have written to you as I write to no one else on this subject; and the more unreservedly, as I shall probably, in no event, name it again. Neither you nor the President will ever by me, or with my knowledge on my account, be troubled with any solicitation for office; and what I have now said has seemed to me not wholly uninvited by your own observations.

There the matter rested for a time, and life with the Everetts went on quietly in Florence. As the spring approached, they were loath to go North and leave the lovely neighborhood. After careful thought and continued search, they decided to move out into the Italian countryside. They visited a score of villas, and finally engaged the Villa Careggi, a few miles out of Florence, one of the villas of Lorenzo de Medici. On the first day of June they took possession of their ducal summer quarters. They were near enough to Florence to drive in nearly every day, and to keep in touch with their many friends. The following letter of Everett to his sister describes the villa in detail:

FLORENCE, *June* 3, 1841

MY DEAR SISTER, ... The villa I have taken is built in the most massive style; the walls three or four feet thick; and the rooms immensely large and high. Having the whole house, we can move from side to side, and keep out of the sun. It was one of the country seats built by Cosmo de' Medici — usually known by the honorable title of 'Father of his Country,' which was given him by a decree of Magistracy; and is, of course, at least four hundred years old. It remained in the possession of the family of the Medici and of their successors in the Government till 1780, when it was sold by the Emperor Leopold, then Grand Duke of Tuscany, to the father of the present proprietor. Cosmo, his son Piero, and his grandson Lorenzo de' Medici, died here. Lorenzo and several of his children, among others Leo the Tenth, were born here. The chamber occupied by my wife and myself is said to be that where Lorenzo died. There is a deep well in the courtyard, into which, it is said, the servants precipitated the poor physician for allowing his illustrious patient to die at the age of forty-four. Another tradition states that the doctor, in despair, threw himself into a well, on his way back to

Florence. Adjoining the chamber alluded to is a small room opening upon a covered terrace or gallery; and in these two apartments,
it is said, the Platonic Academy held its sessions. So that you see
we are domesticated with the most interesting recollections. We
have passed but one night here; the sunset seemed sent on purpose
to exhibit the beauty of the scene to the greatest advantage. A
heavy rain was falling at the time, the sun set without a cloud, so
so that there was a glorious double rainbow — a clear brilliant west
— a rolling world of clouds on the mountains, a dense shower between us and Florence, and all nature in the brightest green: no
mean spectacle from the gallery of Lorenzo de' Medici's Villa! . . .

Soon after the Everett family had become comfortably
settled at Careggi, two interesting people, Louis and Joseph
Bonaparte, established themselves in Florence, and Mr.
Everett went to town to pay his respects. The latter had
only lately received permission from the Emperor of Austria,
the King of Naples, and the Grand Duke of Tuscany to come
to Italy, although his wife had been living at the Palazzo
Territori in Florence for several years. Mr. Everett was to
see Louis first, and apparently appeared somewhat earlier in
the morning than expected. At any rate, when he arrived,
Louis Napoleon 'was in his library, and his chirurgien, as he
called him, who was, however, at the best but a chiropodist,
was cutting his toe-nails. He was dressed in light morning
clothes. His appearance is a good deal as that of Napoleon is
described in the latter part of his life. He received me with
great ease and even cordiality. He expressed a wish to be useful . . . and apologized once or twice for receiving me while in
the hands of a chiropodist.'

Joseph, who was called on the next day, he had not seen
for twelve years, and he found him much changed, 'reclining
on a sofa in a darkened room having been attacked by palsy.
He placed me,' the journal says, 'on a sofa by his side and
spoke with great kindness of his pleasure in seeing me again,
recalling the visit I made at his house twelve years ago. I
told him that he had left none but friends in America. The
remark produced a strong effect on his mind (weakened by

disease); he took my hand which was nearest to him in both of his, drew me up to him and kissed me on the cheek.'

But now, in the course of July, there began again to be talk of a diplomatic appointment. Mr. Winthrop wrote him that Webster gave the information in confidence that, 'Tyler volente,' 'he [Everett] should have the mission to Paris.' But the journal says, 'I have no belief that General Cass will resign, nor that he will be removed.'

A month later, more definite as well as more acceptable news was received. The diary contains these entries:

August 18, 1841. The papers to-day from America contain a report that sundry diplomatic nominations have been sent by the President to the Senate. Among them I find my own name as Minister to England. The channel through which the report comes is not unexceptionable: but I have some reason to think it correct. Whether my nomination will be confirmed by the Senate is not so certain.

August 19. I find the report of my nomination as Minister to England in another paper, and there is, I presume, no doubt of its truth; *but I should not be surprised if some opposition — perhaps successful — should be made to it from the South. Although this is the place which above all others under the Government I thought I desired and of which I had even expressed a preference, I have been strangely depressed in spirits since I heard of the nomination.*

August 28. I received a letter from the Secretary of State containing the official information *of my nomination to London.*

The letter itself, giving definite and personal information of the nomination was cordial in tone and well calculated to give entire satisfaction:

Private
                                    WASHINGTON, *July* 24, 1841

MY DEAR SIR: I have the pleasure to inform you that you are nominated to the Senate, as Minister to England; an announcement, which you will not doubt, it gives me great pleasure to make. I am in hopes the nomination will be confirmed, so as that I may notify it to you by the same conveyance which takes this, but the Senate is much engaged to-day (Saturday), and will probably be so on Monday, so that it may not before Tuesday go into executive session, which would be too late, I fear, for this opportunity. No kind of opposition, however, is expected. So far as I hear, the nomination satisfies everybody but a few violent partisans, like the conductors of the 'Globe.'

Mr. Stevenson will leave London about the first of September, with Mr. Rush. As nobody but the consul will be left in London, it will be desirable that you repair to your post (if you accept it) as soon as may be; although it is hardly to be expected that you should be in England by the time of Mr. Stevenson's departure. I trust Mrs. Everett will not be afraid of this march to the North on her health. If I could have afforded it, I should have put myself in competition with you for this place; but, as I wrote to Mr. Brooks the other day, I am too poor even to stay here, and much less am I able to go abroad. You may hear of me soon, for aught I know, at Marshfield, with my friend Peterson.

We are in the midst of the session; and I may say in the crisis of our affairs. If we get along with the Bank Bill, Bankrupt Bill, Land Bill, and Revenue Bill, all which are on the tapis, we shall stand strong with the public. But some of these measures are of doubtful result. The great difficulty consists in producing and maintaining harmony of action among the Whigs.

I ought to mention, perhaps, while thus writing privately, that the president is of opinion that persons now appointed to missions abroad will not be expected to remain very long in their situations. Various considerations lead him to this, in regard to which I can communicate with you hereafter. I give the hint now, only to the end that you may understand that if you accept the mission, you will not be required to fill it longer than might perhaps be agreeable to you.

To this letter Everett replied as follows:

FLORENCE, *August* 24, 1841

My DEAR SIR, Your kind favors of the 24th and 28th July reached me this day. I am sure I need not tell you, how sensible I am to the distinguished proof of your regard and confidence which these letters announce to me. Should the nomination be confirmed, if I can promise you nothing else, I can at least assure you that I shall carry to the duties of the Nation the most untiring industry and a cordial attachment to the interests of your administration. I shall not probably receive information as to the action of the Senate before the 9th or 10th of September, by which time I may expect news by the packet of the 15th August. Should the nomination be confirmed, I shall immediately proceed with my family to Paris, and, leaving my wife there to pass a little time with her friends, I shall myself cross immediately to London, where I shall probably find Mr. Stevenson, for he writes me that he thinks he shall not get off till October. Should the nomination not be confirmed, I shall execute the plan, for which my arrangements had been already made, of passing the winter at Naples and Rome. ...

In spite of the guarded reflections in this letter, with its three references to the question of confirmation, it is needless to say that Everett was greatly gratified by the London appointment. The sting of his defeat at the Massachusetts polls still rankled, and this distinction served as balm and soothed the wounded pride. But with ambition gratified, there came at once the inevitable doubts and fears. In spite of Webster's assurances he scented instantly the possibility of senatorial opposition, and the bolt fell almost at once. The journal contains this entry:

August 30. To-day I received a letter from Mr. Fletcher Webster, the chief clerk in the Department of State, informing me on behalf of his father that great difficulties have arisen in confirming my nomination owing to a letter written by me in reply to one from a committee of Abolitionists prior to the last election.[1] I infer from the letter of Mr. F. Webster that the nomination will certainly be rejected, perhaps even withdrawn, for Mr. Tyler, not to say Mr. Webster himself, may wish to purge himself from the iniquity. Three days ago, considering such an event as the non-confirmation of my nomination not unlikely, I wrote down the following reasons which ought to reconcile me to it: and though the mortification is severe, they will go far to produce that effect. Some of them, it is true, resemble the reasons given by the fox for not wishing the grapes which were out of his reach.

1. I shall escape the envy which such a distinguished appointment would bring on me; and, on the contrary, become the object of some sympathy as a person ill-used.

2. I avoid the responsibility of an arduous station at a very critical period, at which much will be expected of me, with very little power to accomplish it.

3. I shall be saved the mortification of a conspicuous place, where there are constant calls and temptations to expense, which would far exceed my means.

[1] This was the letter in answer to one from Mr. Borden referred to in the last chapter.

4. I shall be spared certain other cares and trials of a very afflicting and distressing character, which would beset me in London.

5. I shall retain my personal independence and the command of my time for literary pursuits, which are more congenial perhaps to my character and more favorable to happiness. As the immediate pledge of this, I shall be able to take my family this winter to Rome and Naples, which they much desire.

All this was a brave but somewhat unsuccessful attempt to be philosophical. It is easy to read between the lines acute and bitter disappointment. It began to appear to him that perhaps a turn had come in what hitherto had been a career of phenomenal success. He wrote Webster, saying that, before the matter was finally disposed of in the Senate, he would like to be given time to send in a statement in regard to the letter which was objected to, and indeed to state his attitude in general.

The conviction was so deeply planted in Everett's mind that he had nothing to hope from the Senate that he kept to his plans to leave the neighborhood of Florence in the late autumn, and decided to take his family south to Naples. During the anxious days of waiting, he accepted Powers's invitation to sit for a bust. He had gone through the tedious process more than once with others: and looked forward to it with no exhilaration, although he had a very high opinion of Mr. Powers's art. But he found the sculptor unusually interesting to talk to.

September 11. The usual sitting to Mr. Powers. He expressed a wish to execute a statue of a Grecian slave girl carried captive to Constantinople, the hands folded before her, and a chain round her neck with a cross.

How nobly and impressively this idea was eventually given form is well remembered.

On September 23d, he gave Powers a final sitting, and on the 30th he left the villa for the visit to Naples and Rome. There was at least an even chance that the appointment would fail of confirmation, and, even if it did not, in Naples he would be but little farther away from England than in Florence. At five-thirty, therefore, on the morning of the first of October, 1841, he and his family crossed the Ponte di Trinità to the diligence office *en route* to Leghorn. The next day they boarded a new steam packet which was making her maiden trip from Marseilles to the southeast. After a rough voyage and a narrow escape from catching fire, the vessel came to anchor in the Bay of Naples at about eleven o'clock on Monday, October 4th.

Then began the usual sight-seeing. He took the family to all the points of interest. They visited the Museum, attended the opera, went to Herculaneum and Pompeii, and ascended Vesuvius. 'Francesco, who was General Lyman's servant twenty-two years ago,' and travelled with the two young men in France, Germany, Italy, and Greece, called to see him. He was found to have greatly increased in size and *auctus opibus*, being a housekeeper in Naples and a landed proprietor. He recalled to Everett's mind several minute incidents of their movements more than twenty years before.

But there was not to be much time for reminiscences or sight-seeing. Although Everett was unaware of it, things at home were moving in his favor.

It may seem strange, in looking back, that there should have been this bitter opposition in the Senate to Everett's confirmation as Minister to England. He had always done his best to conciliate his Southern friends. Indeed, he had aroused no little inconvenience and misunderstanding at the North by doing so. He was accused, and justly so, by the Abolitionists, of holding a weak and conservative position in regard to slavery. He had, however, by this time travelled far from his position in 1825 when, 'as a brown-haired boy,' as he described himself, he had volunteered to 'shoulder a musket' to help put down a possible servile insurrection. He was by this period an openly proclaimed opponent of the whole abominable system — although constantly opposing needless agitation of the dangerous subject — and had given his vote for the abolition of slavery in the District of Columbia. The simple fact was, however, that the attitude of the United States Minister at the Court of Saint James' was a crucial matter with the Southern slaveholders. England was using every effort at the time to suppress the slave-trade. She was seizing American vessels off the coast of Africa which were engaged in the nefarious traffic. The American Minister was expected to protest against the practice and to get damages for the owners. It was thought necessary, in order to have this done ardently and successfully, that there should be a Southerner, or, at least, a Southern sympathizer in London to represent America. Moreover, there can be no doubt that the South at this time was already plotting secession, and had begun her campaign to build up a party of political sympathizers in England. Altogether, the fight which was organized in the Senate against confirming the Everett appointment was a bitter sectional fight. As Webster explained it in a letter to Everett, later on, 'All spoke well of your talents and qualifications, but the objection was that we were in danger of constant controversion with England upon the subject of slaves, and that on that point your views were not such as these Southern gentlemen approved. To your appointment to France or Spain, there would have been no objection. A strong desire was expressed that the nomination should be withdrawn, and that you should be appointed to some other place. But it appeared to me that that would be worse for you than rejection.'

Webster's decision was wise. The North soon became aroused. The issue became one of national importance, and the excitement was intense. The senatorial attack was fierce and heated. Everett's cause was championed by Rufus Choate and Henry Clay. Mr. King, of Alabama, apparently had grounds to hope that if Everett was not confirmed he himself might receive the nomination. He was bitter in his denunciations, and concluded an abusive attack by saying that if any man holding such views in regard to slavery were confirmed, the Union itself would be dissolved. Whereupon Clay, springing to his feet, extended his long arm toward King, and, pointing to him with trembling index-finger, cried, 'And I tell you, Mr. President, that if a gentleman so pre-eminently qualified for the position of Minister should be rejected by this Senate, and for the reason given by the Senator from Alabama, the Union is dissolved already.' [1] Choate's speech in favor of the nomination was said to have been 'one of the most brilliant and eloquent ever delivered within the walls of the Senate Chamber.' Senator Preston, of South Carolina, was so stirred by this appeal that he said to a friend: 'I shall have to vote "No"; but by G—— he shall not be rejected.' The debate was long and angry. Letters poured in from the North demanding that the nomination be confirmed. The matter finally came to a vote on September 13th, and Everett's confirmation was carried by 23 to 19. 'Every Democrat who voted, and two Southern Whigs, voted against him, and several Northern Democrats dodged.'

That was before the day of trans-Atlantic cables. The 'Galignani' of October 4th contained the news, but the paper did not reach Naples until October 12th. Even then, when Everett saw it, he was not altogether ready to accept the report as accurate. Four days later, however, a letter from Francis C. Gray, who was in London at the time, also announced the fact and strongly expressed the opinion that Everett ought to make his way to England with all possible haste. The London papers when they arrived gave some details of the appointment, stating the figures of the vote, and W. H. Prescott wrote of the great excitement which had been aroused at the North by the attempt to defeat the confirmation. Altogether, although still without any official information, Everett decided that it was his duty to wait no longer, but to set out at once for England.

At seven o'clock on the morning of October 17th, the

[1] *Perley's Reminiscences*, I, 274–75.

family left Naples in a *vetturino*. Making all haste they entered Rome by the gate of San Giovanni at four o'clock on the afternoon of the 19th. Five days were allowed for the Eternal City, which permitted visits to Saint Peter's, the Coliseum, the Forum, the Pantheon, the Vatican Galleries, the Fountain of Trevi, and a few other of the principal sights. On the 25th they were off for Civitá Vecchia. At four o'clock the next day they boarded a Neapolitan steamer, which put in at Leghorn, where there was a tedious wait. On the 29th, they were in Genoa, having narrowly escaped running into a sailing vessel during the night. The 30th saw them in Marseilles, and, after bargaining for a carriage and making other troublesome arrangements, a start was made two days later at half-past six in the morning on the long, exhausting journey to Paris. Pushing on with all the rapidity possible, one of the party becoming ill, they passed successfully the scene of the floods a year before; but it was Wednesday, November 10th, before they drove into Paris. A miserably tired and jaded party they tumbled into the Hôtel Terrasse; and there Everett was handed his official commission, which bore the date of Washington, September 13th, the day his nomination was confirmed.

Although the worst of the journey was over, there was no time yet to rest. Arrangements had to be made for placing two of the children at school, whom it was planned to leave behind in Paris for the winter. Mr. Thorndike gave a magnificent dinner in honor of the new Minister to the Court of St. James' at which General Cass and fourteen or fifteen other gentlemen were present. In the late afternoon Everett took the Malle Poste for Calais, travelled all night, the horses being driven at a canter the entire way; got on board a French Government packet soon after noon the next day, and was landed at Dover from a rowboat in heavy surf after dark — passengers, baggage, and mail bags being tumbled down the side of the vessel into the little boat. 'No one who has been through the operation needs to have it described:

no one who has not can understand it.' He passed a comfortable night, but an impatient morning, at the Ship Inn at Dover. The early coaches were filled, and he had to wait till one o'clock, when he started for London in a tallyho — 'an accommodation coach, accommodating everybody at some risk of accommodating nobody.' It was half-past ten at night when the Bricklayers Arms in London was reached: but the impatient traveller got into a cab and drove at once to 32, Upper Grosvenor Street, which had been rented for his temporary occupancy. 'A good fire and attentive servants awaited his arrival.'

VIII

AT THE COURT OF SAINT JAMES'

MOST travellers feel themselves none too eager for work after crossing the Channel; but the new Minister at eleven o'clock at night began his official duties. His predecessor, Mr. Stevenson, had sailed for home a month before. In the interval an immense amount of correspondence had accumulated. It was piled high on the ministerial desk. But Everett in characteristic fashion set to work on it at once! With the aid of a strong cup of tea which he found waiting, he opened and read every letter and despatch that night. 'When I went to bed,' he wrote, 'I threw myself on my knees, and prayed for strength to support the great burden.' At six o'clock the next morning he was in the office again, and by twelve o'clock everything was filed away, and in order.

It was no light responsibility that he had undertaken. Without having had any experience in the subordinate posts of a diplomatic career, and with no Chargé, or First Secretary, to acquaint him with the customs and traditions of the office, he was thrown entirely upon his own resources. Acting with discretion, however, he sent a note next day to Lord Aberdeen, Her Majesty's Secretary of State for Foreign Affairs, and asked for an interview when he might present his 'Letter of Credence.' Lord Aberdeen received him 'with great kindness'; but, owing to the state of the Queen's health, his audience with Her Majesty for presenting his credentials was delayed for a month.

November 20. At half-past two, I drove to the Foreign Office where the Earl of Aberdeen had appointed to meet me. He received me with great ease and courtesy and placed me at once at my own ease. He is, I should think, about fifty-three years of age, of middle stature, slightly — very slightly — lame with one leg. He expressed great satisfaction at McLeod's acquittal. . . . On my going away, he invited me to dine on Thursday.

The next afternoon Sir Robert Peel, the Prime Minister, left his card with an invitation to dinner on Wednesday. In due season he reported to his chief at Washington telling of his arrival, outlining conditions, and asking for instructions.

It was a critical period in which to represent the United States in England. There was much irritation between the two Governments. Constant misunderstandings arose from the fact that England was seizing American vessels off the coast of Africa on the ground that they were engaged in the slave trade. War at times seemed imminent, and feeling ran very high. Three days before going out of office in the summer of 1841, Lord Palmerston 'had addressed a note to Mr. Stevenson, in a very lofty and uncompromising strain, on the "right of search," and Mr. Stevenson had sent in reply a note to Lord Aberdeen, which did not reach the Foreign Office till Mr. Stevenson had actually left London on his return home.' The outgoing Minister on reaching America referred to the note as 'a bombshell which he had thrown behind him into the enemy's camp.' It was Everett's lot, therefore, to inherit at once from his predecessor 'an angry discussion' which it was not wholly easy to allay. He had no instructions from home in regard to this or other important matters, and it was frequently difficult to decide upon the wise and proper line of action.

Moreover, negotiations of a very delicate nature were about to be opened in regard to the Northeastern Boundary question. This was a subject with which Everett long had been familiar, and was, in fact, uncommonly well posted. It was at first planned that the negotiations should be carried on in London, and it was for this reason that Mr. Webster, as Secretary of State, particularly wished to have Everett as the United States' representative in England. Curtis says, in his 'Life of Webster,' that Mr. Everett was selected for the London post, 'because, in addition to the great fitness of that gentleman for the place, their personal relations had for more than thirty years been of the most intimate and confidential character. As he [Webster] was himself to preside over the delicate negotiations that were to be undertaken with England, and as it could not be known at this time whether those negotiations would be principally conducted there or here, it was of great consequence to Mr. Webster to have in London a minister who was one of his most valued and trusted friends.' [1]

Political or diplomatic questions aside, however, it was a most interesting period for a man of letters and a scholar of distinction to take up an official residence in London. When Everett first had planned another trip abroad, and before there was any serious thought of a diplomatic appointment, Mr. Webster, who had been in England the previous summer, had given him a letter of introduction to the poet Samuel Rogers. But Samuel Rogers was only one among the many great men who were living at the time. The star of Macaulay was high in the ascendant, and was shining with a brilliancy that dazzled and amazed. Among others in the famous London coterie were Sydney Smith, Henry Hallam, Peel, Disraeli, the Duke of Wellington, Carlyle, Monckton Milnes, Dr. Holland. Whewell often came down from Cambridge and Wordsworth from his retreat in the Lake District.

Mr. Rogers at once called upon Everett, and was soon to prove one of his closest and staunchest friends. At their first interview he spoke in high eulogy of Boston, putting it above all American cities and certainly 'to the wrong' of New York, Philadelphia, and Baltimore. Everett described him as about eighty, 'with a bright, quick look, stooping a little, and very much wrapped up in a blue surtout.' He told Everett that his father had dedicated him to the love of New England from the time of the battle of Lexington. The elder Rogers, it appeared, was recorder of London, and when he received the news of the battle of Lexington he sent for his tailor and ordered a suit of mourning. When the tailor asked him if he had lost a relative, he answered, 'Several' — meaning the

---

[1] Curtis: *Life of Daniel Webster*, II, 83.

Americans killed at Lexington. This fact alone was enough to endear the aged poet to the patriotic American, and Everett came to be a constant visitor at Mr. Rogers's house, which he described as 'a perfect bijou, filled with pictures of the old masters, vases, drawings, and books.'

Everett's letters during his London stay were so numerous and full, that, together with occasional passages from his journal, they enable him to tell his own story. We have seen that he settled down at first at 32, Upper Grosvenor Street. The house, however, proved impossible, and after the arrival of his wife from Paris, they decided, after a long and discouraging search, to settle themselves at 46, Grosvenor Place. The house is a tall and narrow one, just behind the Buckingham Palace Mews, and commanding pleasant views of the Palace Gardens. It was on the corner of the street, with a little park space to the southeast which insured light, and whatever sun there was. There the American Minister dispensed a liberal hospitality, giving constant breakfasts and always being at home to his countrymen on Sunday evenings. It was from this house that most of his letters home were written. We may well enough begin, however, with a letter to Mr. Brooks, dated Windsor Castle, where he went in mid-December to be presented. .

WINDSOR CASTLE, *December* 17, 1841

MY DEAR SIR, — You will be pleased to hear that I have at length had my audience of the Queen, just two months since I started from Naples. You are acquainted in general with the circumstances which have delayed it till now. I certainly cannot complain of any tardiness on the part of Her Majesty. I arrived in London on the evening of the 13th. The next day I addressed a note to Lord Aberdeen to let him know that I had come back and to ask an interview at which I intended to ask an audience of the Queen. He appointed a meeting for the next day, but I received a second note from him late in the evening informing me that he had been commanded by the Queen to invite me to Windsor on Thursday the 16th, to have an audience to present my credentials; to dine with Her Majesty; and sleep at the Castle.

Accordingly, at four o'clock yesterday afternoon, I took the rail-

road car for Slough, a place three miles from Windsor, well known as
the residence of the great astronomer Dr. Herschel. It takes about
three quarters of an hour to go to Slough, and it was already dark
when I arrived there. I was not sorry for this, for the suddenness of
my summons had made it impossible for me to go down to Windsor
precisely in the manner in which I should otherwise have liked. I
took a modest post-chaise at Slough and drove to the castle with
great rapidity, and was as promptly admitted as if I had come in a
coach and four. I was directed by the porter to the entrance of the
apartment destined for me in the York Tower and there found
a most comfortable room ready for my reception, warmed and
lighted, and as homelike as possible, to which I was conducted by
the ladylike housekeeper of that tower. I immediately dressed myself in full black, the Court, as I had been informed by the Belgian
Minister, being in mourning for the dowager Queen of Bavaria. The
most important part of my suit of clothes had been made between
the hours of eleven and half-past two o'clock; for it was almost the
last hour that I received information as to the costume that might
be expected.

There is an immense corridor or gallery that runs round two sides
of the quadrangle of which the castle consists, giving access to the
principal rooms and filled, itself, with pictures and statues. A
portion of this gallery serves as a place of rendezvous before dinner.
On entering it, I was a little struck to see the Neapolitan Ambassador, the Prince Castelcicala, who was at the castle on the same
errand as myself, with a white vest and white gloves, for which he
gave as a reason that the Court that day was passing from full to
half mourning. I looked at my gloves, unredeemed even by a white
stitch, with dismay.

Lord Aberdeen soon came in and conducted us to a portion of the
corridor, where the gentlemen and ladies of the household were
assembled. The ladies were in white; the men in their scarlet
uniforms, while I stood among them as inky as Hamlet. Presently
it came out that, though the mourning was not over, it was suspended that day, which was the birthday of the King of the Belgians;
whose Minister had very obligingly sent me there in full black!
This was too good to be kept to myself, and I disclosed the matter
without reserve to the Earl of Warwick, one of the Lords in waiting.
He said it was of no consequence whatever — I was dressed just
right, and I soon saw that every one perceived the cause of my
dusky uniform and seemed at some pains to put me at ease by
being at ease themselves.

Soon after Lord Aberdeen conducted Prince Castelcicala to the
Queen's closet; he took precedence of me as a special ambassador.

In a few moments my turn came. I had prepared a few sentences according to custom, but when the Queen appeared, entering one corner of a very small room as I came in at the other, she approached me with so much ease and simplicity of manner, that I discarded most of my phrases and spoke to her nearly as I would to any other lady, whom it was my duty to treat with marked respect. The Queen answered me in the same unceremonial way, without formality or stateliness. The whole affair lasted perhaps five minutes. To save me from moving backward out of the room, she turned and left it as I did. (The room was about as wide and half as long as your little library in Summer Street.) Prince Castelcicala was then introduced to Prince Albert in the same room; and after he retired, I too was presented to His Royal Highness. With him I had a conversation of perhaps ten minutes principally about my residence in Germany.

After the presentations we rejoined the company in the corridor and Lord Aberdeen requested me to take the Countess of Gainsborough, the lady-in-waiting, in to dinner, and informed me that I was to sit on the Queen's right hand. We then proceeded to the drawing-room. The Queen, Prince Albert, and the Duchess of Kent came in, and I was presented to the latter. It was now a little after eight in the evening, the doors of the dining-room were opened, and a band of select musicians struck up. The Prince led in the Queen. Prince Castelcicala led in the Duchess of Kent, and I gave my arm to Lady Gainsborough whom I left at the table to take my seat as directed by the Queen. Miss Cavendish, one of the maids of honor, sat on my right hand.

There were sixteen or eighteen persons at the table, all of them belonging to the household, except Lord Aberdeen, the Neapolitan Minister, and myself. Young Mr. Murray, the master of the Household, sat at the head of the table. I met him often at Sir Charles Vaughan's in Washington; he showed me much kindness. We had a topic of conversation you would hardly have anticipated. He owns twenty thousand acres in Wisconsin, poor man! The table service, as may well be supposed, was of great magnificence; the movable parts of the service were of silver, the fixed ornaments of the table silver-gilt of great size, costliness, and beauty. The Queen did me the honor to address a great deal of conversation to me. She spoke to Prince Albert who sat at her left hand in German and asked me if I understood that language.

The dinner may have lasted from three quarters of an hour to an hour, the band playing at intervals. There were, I suppose, twenty-five servants of all sorts in the room, but not an audible movement from any or all together. Toward the close of the dinner the health of the Queen, of the Prince, and of the King of the Belgians was drank, the company standing. After the Queen and ladies had retired, Prince Albert took her place, which brought me next to him and gave me an opportunity of conversing a good deal with him, principally of Germany and Italy. I found him an exceedingly modest, intelligent, well-educated person, greatly above the average, I should think, of those of his rank in Europe. In about twenty minutes he led the way to the drawing-room where coffee was served. Here about three quarters of an hour was passed in general conversation among the ladies and gentlemen, all standing except the Queen and her mother.

In a short time they rose and were followed by the company into an adjoining room where the card tables were laid. Here Lord Aberdeen soon brought the Neapolitan minister and myself the agreeable information that the Duchess of Kent invited us to form a party of whist with her. The Prince touched my elbow and told me he knew nothing of the game. I told him I had not played a game of whist for thirty-five years and but one game of cards of any kind in the interval. We concluded, however, that Her Royal Highness's invitation was a command, and could only hope that we might be partners to each other. So by great good luck it turned out. The Duchess and Lord Aberdeen, the Prince of Castelcicala and myself, were mated. Lord A., I soon saw, was a very good player. Her Royal Highness had Mr. Murray at her elbow to sort her cards and tell her how to play them; and the Prince and I did better, I assure you, than might have been expected. Not so well, however, but that we had to pay six shillings sterling each at the end of the game, he to Lord Aberdeen and I to the Duchess of Kent. I took out a half sovereign and Mr. Murray kindly made the change. Meantime the Queen and the rest of the company were engaged in a round game at another table.

At eleven o'clock precisely the Queen left the room, and this was the signal for the breaking-up of the party. Before we separated, Mr. Murray invited me to stay the next morning and visit the State rooms of the castle. He was obliged himself to attend Prince Albert who was going out to hunt; but he promised me a guide, who should have orders to show me everything. Before the heavy clock of the castle struck twelve, I was in bed.

The next morning I employed a leisure moment before breakfast in commencing this letter and in gazing out of my Gothic window at the beautiful expanse of lawn which surrounds the castle. The day was bright and for December warm, so much so that I was able to throw up the window. At ten o'clock I proceeded through the grand corridor above mentioned to the Oak-Room, so called, to breakfast. Here the ladies and gentlemen of the household drop in one after another as they like. Nobody is waited for. The Baroness Lehzen, Secretary to the Duchess of Kent, and I sat down together, before any one else came in. The servants bring you from the sideboard tea, coffee, and whatever else you like. After breakfast I took occasion to request Lady Gainsborough and Miss Cavendish to tell me exactly what the Queen wore, for the information of my wife, it having been impossible for me to fix my eyes on anything but Her Majesty's face. This request was kindly complied with by these ladies, who informed me that the Queen wore a white satin robe, the blue ribbon of the garter across her breast, rich pearl ornaments, flowers in her hair, and a miniature of Prince Albert set in brilliants on her right arm.

Taking my leave of the ladies, I commenced the tour of the castle. It is impossible to describe the succession of rooms or do more than name the objects of interest, such as Saint George's Hall; the guard-room where there are about ten feet of the mainmast of the Victory, Lord Nelson's flagship at Trafalgar, with a hole produced by a cannonball through and through it, and Nelson's bust on the top; the Waterloo room containing splendid portraits by Sir T. Lawrence of the great men of the day; the library of thirty thousand volumes, only a beginning; the splendid Van Dyke and Rubens rooms; the ballroom gorgeously gilded; the plate-rooms where there is a complete service of silver-gilt for one hundred and twenty persons, the richest, no doubt, in the world, each of the plates being worth in gold and silver, independent of the work, twenty-six guineas. Flaxman's Shield of Achilles is one of the ornamental articles in the service. I saw here, too, the pedestal of Tippu Saib's throne taken at Seringapatam, a lion's head in gold with rock crystal teeth. There are a few carved articles ascribed to Benvenuto Cellini, but their authenticity may be doubted. I went also into the royal kitchens, where food for about three hundred is daily cooked.

Having finished a hasty circuit of the castle, which it would take a week to explore fully, I drove back to Slough and in an hour or two was at home. . . .

March 24, 1842. Breakfasted at Mr. Macaulay's. Mr. Hallam, Lord Mahon, Mr. Trevelyan, a brother-in-law of Mr. Macaulay, his wife, another gentleman and lady formed the company. Mr. Macaulay as usual with Mr. Hallam nearly engrossed the conversation. They talk so well, and so instructively that I always listen to them with pleasure, but it is agreeable sometimes to be able to say a word. It is only by extreme vigilance in watching an opportunity, not of a pause, but of a partial relaxation when you can, by boldly striking in, interrupt the speaker, that you can ever say a word. This does not apply more to Macaulay than to Hallam. They are both, however, very good-natured and bear interruption with great equanimity.

This disposition of Macaulay to do all the talking is, of course, well known, and is often referred to by Mr. Everett, who was not the kind of man to burst in and force a hearing for himself. Sydney Smith, who carried his wit even to his deathbed, predicted that Macaulay would be sorry that he had never heard him talk.

To the Honorable P. C. Brooks

LONDON, *May* 17, 1842

MY DEAR SIR.... I breakfasted to-day with Mr. Marshall. He is the father of Lady Monteagle and of the wife of Dr. Whewell, Master of Trinity College, Cambridge. Mr. Marshall is very rich. He lost £50,000 by the Bank of the United States and be hanged to 'em; but he treats it as you would, snaps his fingers at them. We had Rogers, Wordsworth, and Milnes all as gay as larks. Dr. Whewell asked us to Cambridge to attend the installation of the Duke of Northumberland next month, and Mrs. M. invited us to visit them at their country seat on the bank of one of the lakes of Cumberland.....

On the 15th we dined at the Baron Leonil de Rothschild's. He is the oldest son of the late N. M. Rothschild; lives next door to the Duke of Wellington. His wife is his own cousin, daughter of the brother who is established at Naples. She is a very pleasing person. His mother was there. She possessed, you know, the entire confidence of her late husband. He did nothing without her advice. I had a good deal of conversation with her about her family. The Rothschilds are in the best society and most of them have patents of nobility from the Emperor of Austria. The 14th I had also to refuse an invitation to the Archbishop of Canterbury, in consequence of a previous engagement at Lord Stanley's: the French Ambassador and wife, Russian Minister, Lord Aberdeen, and a most distinguished circle. I had a great deal of talk with Lord Aberdeen after dinner; and I find much may be done at these social meetings. I sat between Lady Canning and Lady Mahon, two of the most pleasing ladies here: wife sat between Lord Clanwilliam and Lord Malmesbury. After dinner Mr. Irving [1] and wife went to

---

[1] Washington Irving was at this time United States Minister to Spain.

Mr. Bates (11 P.M.) and I to the Marquis of Northampton's second *soirée* as President of the Royal Society. . . .

Breakfasted the 11th at Bingham Baring's, oldest son of Lord Ashburton, one of the Secretaries of the India Board — modest, intelligent, and amiable. Had there Henry Taylor, Captain Eliot, of Canton fame, and other pleasant lads. Dined at the Literary Fund Society, Prince Albert in the chair. My place was between Sir R. Peel and the Bishop of Gloucester, a grand-nephew, or something like it, of Monk who was wounded in State Street, March 5, 1770. I knew the Bishop at Cambridge in 1818 and had since gained a place in his regard by reviewing his 'Life' of Dr. Richard Bentley. He, the Marquis of Northampton, and one or two other speakers paid me some undeserved compliments, but I was too much out of health to speak. W. Irving was received rapturously. Tom Moore and Sergeant Talfourd spoke beautifully. Poor Campbell tried to speak, but —

Tuesday the 10th I dined with the Marquis of Lansdowne. Madame de Flahaut, whose husband is the French Ambassador at Vienna — formerly aide to 'Bony' — was there. She is herself in her own right a Scotch and an English peeress and immensely rich. Miss Elphinstone, her daughter, was also there, one of the greatest beauties and heiresses of England. Lady Morgan was also of the party. Finished the evening at the Archbishop of York's — a little concert given to the Duchess of Gloucester. Saw there Miss Burdett-Coutts, said to be the richest heiress in the country. She did me the honor to be introduced to me. Her father, Sir Francis, lives on the estate given to his ancestor by William the Conqueror and never out of the family. I saw a son of the Archbishop of York in Boston, which is the cause of their attentions.

Dined on the 9th at Lady Holland's; and afterwards went to two parties, one at Dr. Holland's and one at Mr. Murchison's, President of the Geological Society. At Lady Holland's met the Ashburtons and Sydney Smiths. Sunday evening, our American friends look in quietly upon us without invitation; they have a cup of tea.

Breakfasted on the 7th with Henry Taylor. Wordsworth was there, a fine old man. In the evening at Mr. Babbage's, an eminent man of science, inventor of a calculating machine, toward the construction of which the Government has given large sums, it is said £25,000. He is at present at a stand. They have got a little tired at an old-fashioned calculating machine called 'the Treasury.' These people have no patience. Finished at the Marquis of Northampton's first levée.

Friday, 6th, dined with Lord and Lady Francis Egerton. He is the brother of the Duke of Sutherland: she the daughter of the

Duke of Portland. The Duke and Duchess of Sutherland and their beautiful and amiable daughter, who has just come out, were of the party. I knew the Duke of Sutherland, then Lord Gower (pronounce Gore), at Rome in 1819. Lord Francis Egerton inherited the pictures of the Duke of Bridgewater, the most valuable private collection in England. There were three Raphaels in the room where we dined! Went from this to a large party at the Countess of Jersey's. The house was considered for many years as the headquarters of fashion and is perhaps so still. She has lately married a daughter to young Prince Esterhazy (the man whose father owned as many shepherds as Mr. Thomas Coke did sheep), and a son to Sir R. Peel's daughter. This party was in honor of the birthday of Lady Clementina Villiers, the second daughter.

Thursday, 5th, Mrs. Sydney Smith's party in the evening. The dowager Countess of Essex was there, formerly the much admired singer Miss Stephens. On Wednesday the 6th, a levée at the Palace, at which I presented Mr. W. Irving. In the evening we had a little dinner ourselves for Mr. Irving. The notice he gave us was so short that I could get none of the greater lions to meet him but Mr. Rogers and Henry Taylor. We had besides Dr. Booth, Mr. Bates, and some young men, among them Sidney's friend Mr. Lee. Tuesday, for a wonder, there was nothing.

Monday I dined at the Count de Sainte-Aulaire's, the French Ambassador's, a full-dress dinner in honor of the birthday of the King of the French. All the Diplomatic Corps, most of the Cabinet Ministers, and the leading officers of the Household were there, the hour named as usual half-past seven. At seven I went up to dress. My uniform coat was not at home! The tailor had taken it to do something with it and forgot when it was wanted back — a whelp; and I — a blunderbuss did not know he had got it. What was to be done. He lives a mile and a half off, and none of us knew exactly where. I knew the street, but not the number; and my menservants, contrary to the fundamental law and for the first time, were both out together! Pleasant this. Unknown to me, my wife's maid starts off in a cab to get the coat, but when she drove to the place where she thought she could learn the tailor's address, they did not know. Meantime the footman comes home; but I cannot start myself in search of the coat till the maid gets back, because I do not know but she will have found it and we may cross by the way. Time very precious just now, and a quarter of an hour lost in this way! She at length gets back without the coat, and I, dressed all but my coat, start for the tailor's, and meet him just going out, a narrow escape! Go into his shop and find my coat *with the cuffs off*; clock striking eight. Offers to sew on the cuffs, but there would be a good half-hour's work; the dinner the most ceremonious and important, next to a dinner at the Palace — what is to be done? He happened to have at his shop a modest little uniform coat which I wore at Florence, at Court, such as is worn by Secretaries of Legation and Attachés, and this I put on and drove to the Ambassador's. I was forty minutes behind my time — the company all there — and I in my secretary's coat had the satisfaction of passing through a double row of dukes, ambassadors, and grandees blazing with gold lace and glittering with orders, to make my bow to Madame de Sainte-Aulaire. For the coat I cared nothing; the other is but a trifle more ornamental. But I make it a matter of conscience to be punctual; and this was precisely the occasion, when I could have least wished to fail in that respect. But happily every one had something more important than I, my coat, or my coming to think of, and Madame de Sainte-Aulaire gave me a good-humored smile, which would have turned fustian into broadcloth. . . .

P.S. You might think that with this dissipation I can do no work. But I rather think poor Lord Aberdeen wishes there were more foundation for such an idea.

LONDON, *July* 18, 1842

I have your letter of the 2d instant by the Britannia, transmitting a check for £28.12 in payment for the Annual Register. We are all exceedingly gratified to hear that you have fully recovered your health. Since I last wrote you we have been, all hands, to the University of Cambridge to attend the installation of the Duke of Northumberland as Chancellor. We passed five days, being the guests of the Master of Trinity College, the leading college of the University. The Bishop of London and family, the Duke of Wellington, Marquis of Northampton, Mr. Goulburn, Chancellor of the Exchequer, Mr. Bunsen, the Prussian Minister, and several other distinguished persons were also entertained at Trinity, the whole or part of the time. A good many persons received honorary degrees, myself among the rest that of Doctor of Laws. The statutes of the University forbidding an honorary degree to be conferred directly upon a foreign minister below the rank of an ambassador, the Duke of Northumberland of his own accord requested the Archbishop of Armagh, who is Chancellor of the University of Trinity College, Dublin, to give me that degree there in order to my receiving it *ad eundem* at Cambridge, which was accordingly done. I should have had it at Oxford, but they were in vacation. These three universities recognize each other as equals to the exclusion of all others at home or abroad. The Duke of Northumberland took a great deal of pains in the business, and both he

and the Duchess from first to last distinguished us by their attentions. We had a dinner at Emmanuel College where our Harvard
was educated. I alluded to that fact in a few remarks at the table,
and it seemed to be new to all the company. The circumstance
appeared to afford great pleasure. . . .

I saw the great iron steamship building at Bristol. She is to be
propelled by the screw of Archimedes; 1000 horse power, 3800 tons,
330 feet long, draft of water only 16 feet; — not more than half
what it would be of wood.

LONDON, *July* 30, 1842

Saturday, July 9th, I dined with Sir Robert Peel. I sat on
his right hand at dinner and had a great deal of conversation with
him. Dwarkananth Tagore, the East Indian Zinsindar, was on
the other side — a very pleasant person who speaks good English.
He has a great deal to say about the Americans sending ice to Calcutta. He says it has saved the lives of hundreds in bilious fever.
Sir A. McNab was of the party. I asked Sir Robert whether
he was not afraid to invite us together. But he answered in the
negative. As it was only eleven o'clock at night when I got through
at dinner, we had time for an early evening visit at Mr. Bates's to
meet the Prescott Halls of New York. . . .

Saturday, 16th, we dined at the Bishop of London's at the
Episcopal Palace at Fulham; a grand mansion on the bank of the
Thames, a part of which is as old as Henry VII, but the modern
residence was built by the present Archbishop of Canterbury while
Bishop of London. The present Bishop (Dr. Blomfield) and family
staid at the Lodge at Trinity College, Cambridge, at the installation
which, of course, brought our two families a good deal together.
No party after this for two or three days.

On Wednesday, the 20th, I dined with the Archbishop of Canterbury at Lambeth Palace, a most splendid residence of which a part
is old, but the greater portion built by the present incumbent at an
expense of £50,000. I took Mrs. Howley (pronounce Hooly) into
dinner and sat between her and the archbishop. Nothing can be
imagined more unpretending and affable than this most respectable
prelate, filling as he does, with the exception of the Pope, the station
of the greatest influence of an ecclesiastical character in the world.

The next day there was a grand breakfast at Syon House, the
seat of the Duke of Northumberland, about ten miles from London.
This was formerly an abbey given by Henry VIII to one of the
Percies. The young Lord Loraine, son of the Earl of Beverley, was
speaking about it to me and said it was 'one of the religious houses
which Henry VIII *stole*, for *theft* it was.'

Five hundred were invited, and after strolling through the beautiful grounds, where there are a great many American plants brought by the Duke's father from America, where, you know, as Earl Percy he commanded the regiment which on the 19th April, 1775, saved the British force from annihilation, we sat down at half-past six P.M. to breakfast. I took in Mrs. Howley, and all our party sat at the upper table. The tables were set under an immense and beautiful tent, and if the table at which I sat was a specimen the entertainment was as sumptuous and well served as if it had been a party of twenty. We were served entirely on plate, but I can scarce think that was the case at all the tables. After dinner (for dinner it was in every thing but name) there was walking in the grounds, coffee in the state apartments, dancing in the tent, which was cleared as if by magic, and then most splendid fireworks on the lawn. The like of this altogether I have not seen.

Saturday we dined at Lord Ripon's on Putney Heath. Sir Robert and Lady Peel were of the party. After the cloth was removed, Sir Robert told a number of amusing anecdotes of Walter Scott, repeated some of the Latin translations of Mother Goose, and was in fact the life of the party. Lord Ripon traces his descent in part from Cromwell, and Lady Ripon hers from Hampden, and original portraits of both those famous personages hang in the dining-room. Lord Ripon is perhaps better known to you as Mr. Robinson, afterwards Lord Goderich, for a short time Prime Minister. He is President of the Board of Trade.

Next day (Sunday, 24th) we went down to Eton College, all hands, by invitation from Dr. Hawtrey, the Headmaster of the institution. Here we met the Bishop of Gloucester and Bristol (Dr. Monk) and his wife — a friend of mine — that is, the Bishop — of a quarter of a century's standing. Mrs. Monk took wife and Nanny to Saint George's Chapel at Windsor, where the Queen was present. I preferred going to church in the College Chapel, a fine old building of the time of Henry VI. Dr. Hawtrey had a large dinner in the evening.

Next day was an academic exhibition such as we have at Cambridge. Dinner for the men in the College Hall, long Latin grace (two or three prayers) changed before and after dinner. Retiring to the provosts' hall, we had the dessert, toasts, and speeches. When my health was drank, all the company rose, and the 'few remarks' made by me — wholly unpremeditated — by way of acknowledgment were cheered in a way that made me ashamed of myself. Lovely walk in the evening in the playgrounds immortalized by Gray: Canning's seat and the Marquis of Wellesley's willow. Next day we drove to the castle, and, though it was not a public day, our good friend Mr. Murray took us all over the palace — from the Queen's private luncheon room to the kitchen. The day was lovely and the gardens and park, seen from the castle windows, exceed in beauty any landscape where art is apparent which I have ever seen.

From the castle we drove to Stoke Park, the seat of the Penn family. This was formerly the property and residence of Sir Edward Coke, but of the old manor house in which he entertained Queen Elizabeth little is now standing. The son of William Penn bought the estate, and his son, brother of the present incumbent, built the mansion house in which we were received, a grand Doric structure of imposing dimensions and fine appearance. The library is a hall one hundred and twenty feet long. Mr. John Penn, who built this house, was an eccentric and not very popular person, and hence called 'a Penn which everybody cut and nobody mended.' The present proprietor, an aged and infirm gentleman, is respected and beloved, but not, I fear, long for this world. I saw him in his chamber, and as I left him he said, 'I hope, Sir, you will come and see Stoke again, although you probably will not see me in it.' He has employed his time of late years in an improved translation of the New Testament. From what I have seen of it, I should think him a man of no common literary attainments and most excellent principles. He seemed much gratified with our visit.

I had been led into a little previous correspondence with the family in consequence of having been directed by the Government to obtain if possible the original of one of the royal grants to William Penn to be used in evidence in a case of title pending before the Supreme Court, but I had not met any of them. Mr. Graville Penn, junior, was at the exhibition at Eton College, and kindly proposed to us to come to luncheon the next day, which was the occasion of our visit. The house contains some valuable family pictures, particularly a lovely family group by Sir Joshua Reynolds and a portrait of Mrs. Fermor, the original, I believe, of Belinda in the 'Rape of the Lock,' and an ancestress of the present family. They showed me an original letter or petition of William Penn to James II, but I did not see the mass of the Penn papers. They have promised me to let me see them at my leisure whenever I will come to Stoke for that purpose, and it would have been idle merely to look at the outside of the drawers. They sent out to the family from Philadelphia some years ago a large branch of the plane tree under which William Penn concluded his treaty with the Indians and which was blown over in a gale. It stands in an alcove with a suitable inscription. The grounds at Stoke Park are very beautiful. The flower garden, instead of being enclosed in walls of any kind, is contrived to represent a natural spot of garden in the midst of a forest: a patch of carnations encountered you here, a trained rose-bush there, a bed of gillyflowers, a scarlet verbena, a little farther along, like a natural prairie in an opening in a wood. I have never seen this before. At some distance from the house on one side the prospect terminates in a column erected in honor of Sir Edward Coke, and on another front you behold at a distance of a short quarter of a mile a monumental urn erected like Coke's column by the late Mr. Penn in honor of Gray the poet. Close by you see peeping through the woods the spire of the church of the village of Stoke.

In the churchyard Gray buried his aunt and mother who lived in Stoke, and he himself lies in the same tomb. In consequence of this the churchyard is supposed to be that which was present in his mind when he composed his Elegy, although some persons think, on what grounds I do not know, that the churchyard of Upton, a village in the neighborhood, is the scene of the poem. The locality is certainly not indicated with distinctness in the Elegy, but it seems scarcely possible that the churchyard where his mother was buried should not have been that to which his feelings were turned in composing his Elegy. There is nothing inconsistent with the supposition. The old manor house in the park still exhibits an 'ivy mantled tower'; the church is surrounded by 'rugged elms' (that epithet, by the way, applies to the English elm better than to ours). A very large 'yew tree' shades the yard, and, of course, the 'heaving turf' in its 'mouldering heaps' applies to this as to all other similar places. But it is of no great moment; Gray himself is buried there, and his ashes — if not his poem — must render it sacred ground. The church is a fine old, very old, country church almost half underground.

LONDON, *August 29,* 1842

MY DEAR SISTER, . . . I will give you an account of some of our recent experiences. The London Season, which tapers off gradually as the summer advances, comes fully to a close with the session of Parliament, which this year ended on the 10th of August. Every one then who has a country house goes to it. Those who have not go to the various watering places, particularly on the seaside. Grouse-shooting begins on the 12th of August, and vast numbers go to the principal resorts of that kind of sport; and those who pass their time in neither of these ways accept invitations, at this season, to visit their friends in the country.

We had for some time been contemplating a visit to Oxford to Dr. Buckland, the celebrated geologist. I had known him when at Oxford, in 1818, and had met him at nearly all the public occasions which I have recently attended. He was good enough to ask us to spend two or three days with him in Christ Church College, of which he is a canon. Accordingly, on the morning of the 15th, we took the railroad cars to Steventon, the nearest station to Oxford, on the Great Western Railway. We travelled the distance, fifty-eight miles, in two hours. An hour and a quarter more took us to Oxford, in a very indifferent and crowded stage-coach; the day was intensely hot, as must have been felt by our eight fellow-passengers, on the top of the coach, in a basking sun. Dr. Buckland's house is in one side of the great quadrangle of Christ Church College — and a singular abode it is.

I feel a great repugnance to describe particularly what I see within any door which has been opened to me in hospitality; and especially in this case; for a traveller from Cincinnati, who was kindly received by Dr. Buckland, published in a paper an account of all he saw in his house, which, of course, in a few weeks, got back to Dr. Buckland. But as I know all I write home, in this way, is safe and sacred, I will venture. His house, then, from the very threshold, is a perfect geological museum, with this exception, that it is in the most 'admired confusion.' There is none of that species of stratification, commonly called *order;* heaps of stones of all sizes and shapes; of bones recent and fossil; of books and of boxes lie about on the sofas, tables, chairs, floors, and staircases. Most of the apartments in the house are so encumbered in this way that it is difficult to move about in them. An open space in the middle of the dining-room barely suffices to spread the table. When a large party is invited, the stones on the inner edges are piled up a little. Some specimens of animated nature inhabit the chaos. A small serpent has for some time past lurked in the recess of one side of the room; Mrs. Buckland's little boy, in rummaging in a box of drawings while we were there, had his finger bitten by a mouse; and my wife in going up-stairs trod upon a small hedgehog. With all this confusion, however, sovereign good-nature appears to reign among all the members of the family, and they live as pleasantly as possible amidst this 'wreck of matter.'

We took a hasty luncheon — sent for an open carriage and a pair of post-horses, and galloped away to Blenheim Castle, ten miles off. You know what Blenheim is — magnificent, but tasteless and heavy; at present encumbered with the repairs going on to restore the dilapidations and neglect of the last twenty years. The family, both in the present and late incumbent, has no respectability of standing. The castle contains some very fine pictures — Rubens, Vandykes, and Titians — and a magnificent library. The private gardens occupy the site of the old park of Woodstock and Fair

Rosamond's bower. The trunks of some trees are shown which, according to tradition, are one thousand years old. The weather was too warm to allow us to walk round as much as we could have liked; but it rendered a cool draft from Rosamond's Well doubly refreshing. We got back to Oxford at five o'clock, and after dinner had a delightful walk in the cool of the evening in Christ Church meadows, and in the cloisters of some of the old conventual colleges. The Great Bell of Christ Church is the largest in England, and when it sounded filled the ear with a grand though rather melancholy tone. A full moon added the last beauty to an uncommonly pleasing scene.

To the Honorable P. C. Brooks

DRAYTON MANOR, *December* 19, 1842

MY DEAR SIR, . . . Sir Robert Peel was good enough to invite me to join a few friends, as he expressed himself, at Drayton Manor, near Tamworth, to come on Saturday the 17th and stay a few days. It is not unusual in invitations of this kind to be asked to come on such a day and go on such another, in order to be able to make definite appointments with a succession of visitors. . . .

Sir Robert received us in the library which appeared the chief place of rendezvous, a most beautiful room sixty-seven feet by twenty-seven, with three large bay windows descending to the floor and looking upon the lawn; the ceiling of oak divided into compartments by gilded rafters, and the shelves filled with about five thousand or six thousand volumes selected by Sir Robert. He has another library in his town house in Whitehall, London. Thorwaldsen's Shepherd, one of his most beautiful works, is at one end of the library, and a group by Wyatt at the other. The area of the room is completely filled up with cabinet and other tables, sofas and chairs of every description (except rocking-chairs which are rarely seen in English houses), a telescope, and one or two flower stands. I am not sure that I have seen anything in England which united more of the luxurious, substantial, tasteful, and comfortable. . . .

Lord Aberdeen joined the party on Sunday afternoon, which I was very glad of. Most of my public business is with him, and though people do not resort to the country to transact business, yet there are great opportunities in a morning's walk, or in a quiet corner of the library in the evening, to talk over matters to very good purpose. He is, besides, though of somewhat cold exterior and rather taciturn in a large circle, a person of most extensive information, straight-forward character, and goodness of heart. My intercourse with him, both official and personal, has been as agreeable as possible. After tea in the evening, Sir Robert read a short sermon and a prayer to the visitors, family, and household assembled in the dining-room. . . .

Our evenings are all spent in the library. The ladies disappear about eleven: but Sir Robert has kept his guests together by his interesting conversation till twelve or one. . . .

We were asked to stay at the end of the week, but, as I was engaged with wife and Nanny to go to Lord Ashburton's on Thursday to pass Christmas, I left Drayton on Wednesday morning, with my colleague Bunsen, and found myself in less than seven hours at my own fireside. . . .

BELVOIR CASTLE, *September* 24, 1842

We left home on the 21st for this magnificent residence of the Duke of Rutland. The name is pronounced *Beever*. It is in Leicestershire, just on the boundary of Lincolnshire. The hill on which the castle stands is supposed to have been a military station in the time of the Romans. The fortress and estate around it were granted by William the Conqueror to the ancestors of the Rutland family in which the property has remained (not always descending in a right line) to the present day. . . .

After breakfast the day after our arrival the Duke went to Grantham, the central town and seat of the Union for the Relief of the Poor, to which his parish belongs and in the management of which he takes a great interest. Deeming their business private, I did not propose to go with him, which I was afterwards sorry for. He, thinking I was an eager sportsman, did not ask me to go with him, supposing I would rather stay to shoot with Lord Granby. You doubtless are aware that almost every gentleman in England, from the time he is old enough to be trusted with a gun, follows the sport. Men of all ages, pursuits, and character agree in this. For myself, I had never, I think, fired a gun at a bird since I was nine years old. Then if the bird was at rest and I could get a fair rest for my gun, provided the bird was not above ten paces off, I was no bad shot, considering. The Duke (Lord bless him!) had got it into his head that I was a sportsman of the first order. However, I was not sorry *to see* some sport, and off I started with Lord Granby on one of the Duke's horses. We had about two and one half miles to ride before reaching the field, where three or four gamekeepers with the dogs awaited us. I had no gun of my own (everybody here travels with a gun as much as he does with a shirt) and hoped to get off with that excuse, but Lord Granby would send a keeper to get one for me. Meantime he himself went to work and I watched him as closely as I could; but, alas, there is little that can be learned in a day. But it was beautiful to see the instinct and training of the dogs and the skill of Lord Granby. At length my double-barrelled gun arrived, was duly loaded, and handed to me, and I placed it on my shoulder with the feelings with which a newly epauletted militia captain takes the field on his first review. We are close to a hedge, the dogs stop and point, Lord Granby steals round the other side, the keepers beat the bush, whirr, whirr, whirr, up flies a covey of partridges right under my nose, Lord Granby's gun, first one barrel and then another, blazes away, and two partridges fall before I had got my gun cocked. The keepers exchange a knowing look, not unperceived by me, at my greenness. Lord Granby loads again and we proceed. Dogs again point — whirr, whirr, whirr — this time I fired; partridge does all but turn round and laugh at me; Lord Granby follows suit and down he drops. And so it went on; glorious sporting, partridges and hares thick as blackberries, dogs and keepers crazy with excitement and sport, Lord Granby bringing down the game as fast as he could load and fire, and I still guiltless of the blood of hare or partridge. So we went on. About two and one half hours, when it began to rain. Lord Granby said he never minded the weather, and so I thought would not I. In a quarter of an hour I was wet to the skin. At this stage of the sport we went into a potato field, fresh and vigorous in full leaf, halfway up a man's thigh. Dogs hop up and down like imps, and at length point. 'Now's your chance, Mr. Everett,' says Lord Granby. 'A hare, Sir, a hare!' cries the head keeper; 'move forward, Sir; now Frolic (the dog's name), draw, draw — mark, Sir'; and sure enough a hare springs out. I could have hit him with my hat. I fired. 'Dead,' cried the keeper. Dead quotha! Never did I see a hare scramble out of a potato field at such a rate. As the novelists say, 'fear lent wings to his speed.' That he is stopped yet is more than I should like, in the absence of all testimony, to aver. After wasting a little more powder and shot and getting a little more drenched, I gave up the sport and rode back to the castle, leaving Lord Granby to finish the day in the field. He killed nine hares and sixteen brace of partridges. As a principal topic of conversation at dinner is always the sport of the day, you may judge what an agreeable account I had to give of myself. All, however, were too well bred to indulge in any raillery. . . .

But if Everett did not shine as a sportsman, he appeared to great advantage in the library and drawing-room, particularly when any games were in order that called for intellectual acumen and readiness. Here is an account taken from the journal of the way the evening was passed at Wentworth when he was the guest of Lord Fitzwilliam:

Sunday, October 2, 1842. After dinner the company assembled in the library, and after evening prayers composed themselves to the game of poetry, which has been played once before since we have been here. One of the company takes the chair under the name of High Priest. Pieces of paper and pencils are distributed to each of the company, on which each one first writes a question. The papers are then all handed back to the High Priest, who shuffles them and gives them out again. You now (without looking at the question) write some word under it: fold the top of the paper again so as to cover the word, and then hand all the papers back to the Priest, who gives them out again. Each one now unfolds his paper and is required to furnish a poetical answer to his question bringing in the word. The amusement consists in putting out-of-the-way questions and odd words, and then in the shifts to bring the latter into an appropriate answer. The following were the questions that fell to my lot.

Question: Does not green tea affect the nerves?
Word: Nonsense.
Answer: You ask me, 'Does green tea affect the nerves?'
    Why should I seek for wit when nonsense serves.
Question: What is your name?
Word: Wolf.
Answer: So soft thy voice, so mild thine air,
    A lamb, not wolf, art thou my fair,
    And I, though meek, to fight for thee
    A very wolf, fair maid, would be.
Question: Ought stays to be laced loose, or tight?
Word: Frog.
Answer: Approach, ye heavenly muses, and inspire
    Your timid bard with true poetic fire.
    Descend, Apollo, warn my teeming brain,
    And bid all Helicon flow thro' my strain.
    Be hushed, ye breezes, let my pensive note
    On zephyr's downy wing melodious float,
    Let no hoarse frog from marsh or reeking fen
    With murmurs harsh disturb my gentle strain.
    Attend, mankind! and thou, O Betty, say,
    For thou dost lace thy mistress every day,
    Whether is tight, or loose the better way.

In January, 1843, he paid a memorable visit to Trentham Hall, the seat of the Duke of Sutherland. It was a gay party that gathered there, and they had a gay and pleasant time.

Bad weather outside caused the party to devise many indoor games. The journal says:

> After luncheon the family collected in the billiard-room, old and young. Some played billiards, others battledore and shuttlecock. I kept it up with the Duchess thirty-four times. In my youth, I kept it up on one occasion twenty-eight hundred times. . . . We then played 'ball' and French blindman's bluff.
>
> *January* 6. A bright pleasant morning. All walked out after breakfast. Gave the Duchess a camellia which I had picked up on the floor of the conservatory, which she wore for the rest of the day in her bosom.
>
> *January* 9. I had ordered a chaise from the inn the evening before; but the Duchess chose to send Mr. Leveson and myself in a chariot to the station. Leveson disait qu'il y avait quelque soupçons contre le caractère de Mlle. Rachel. Entre autres choses pretendait-on que le Prince de Joinville lui envoyait un billet avec ces mots seulement, combien, quand, et où? Signé de son nom. La reponse fut, Rien, ce soir, chez moi.

Later in the same month he went to Woburn Abbey to visit the Duke and Duchess of Bedford. He arrived there the first of a party of thirty-five invited to meet the Duke of Sussex and Duchess of Inverness. He was taken to the library, where the Duke soon came in and received him 'with the cordiality of a brother, taking him down after a few minutes into his librarian's room and showing him some of the family manuscript. The Duke of Sussex, it appeared, had been a student at Göttingen in his youth, and Everett was surprised to find that after fifty years the Duke's recollection of the streets was more accurate than his own. 'Perhaps, however,' he adds in his diary, 'he used them more than I did, for I led almost a hermit's life. The next day the Duke sent to me to come to see him. He was dressed in white flannel pantys and a roundabout: smoking his pipe. Talked more about Göttingen: was at the meeting of the Princes of Coblenz in 1792: thinks the real object of the assembling of the Prussian army was to enforce the partition of Poland. Intimated that there was an intention on the part of the

Polish patriots to establish a separate kingdom and make him (the Duke) king; so at least I understood him.'

Woburn Abbey among other wonders contained a charming little theatre, and during Everett's stay a play was given in which several of the guests took the principal parts.

After these visits he again took up the London life.

May 25, 1843. Mr. Smith *badinant* told Mrs. Howe [Julia Ward, in London at that time with her husband] she must take an English master, that there were some twenty false pronunciations she must cure. He had had me in hand, and I had greatly profited by it. He instanced in her case a wrong pronunciation of the word 'Lords' which he said she called 'Luords.' This was not apparent to me. I told him the Lords themselves said 'Luds.' He never objected to any pronunciation of mine, but to my using 'Good Evening' as a salutation.

London, June 3, 1843 . . . I received an intimation from Lord Aberdeen that he wished to see me at twelve o'clock to-day, probably to communicate something that he wishes me to write about by the steamer. At two o'clock we are to lunch at the Duchess of Sutherland's with the Howes, who are in good favor here, in consequence of the interest taken in Laura Bridgman's case. I showed some of Dr. Howe's reports (in which she is mentioned) to the Duchess last year; but Dickens's book has made the case quite notorious; not, however, I think, that the book itself — Dickens's — is much liked. The Archbishop of Dublin (Dr. Whateley) is greatly satisfied with Dr. Howe's experiments in the education of Laura Bridgman, because they confirm his philosophical notions as to the controversy of the nominalists and realists. The other evening at Mr. Babbage's, the Archbishop was in conversation with Mr. Borrow, the author of 'The Bible and Gipsies in Spain,' who is one of the principal lions of the day. A gentleman in the company, of a quiet cast of character, was spurred up by his daughter to go and accost the chief object of attraction. In the haste of the moment, he mistook the personages; and addressing himself to the Archbishop said, 'Well, Sir, you seem to have led quite a roaming gipsy kind of life, yourself.'

December 21, 1843. Dined with Dr. Holland. Miss Edgeworth came in the evening — a diminutive, exceedingly plain, but intelligent and sprightly looking person. She talked with great freedom of O'Connell.

March 12, 1844. Miss Edgeworth, if I mistake not, is not very much liked in London. I have heard this ascribed to her having in former years brought her younger sisters with her on her visits to London and made efforts to get them married. She was supposed also to keep a journal and write down everything she heard.

To his daughter

HEWELL, BROMSGROVE, *September* 20, 1843

I reached Birmingham at the appointed hour, two o'clock Tuesday, and found Mr. Clive's servant waiting to conduct me to the town hall, where the oratorio was going on. It was three fourths executed when I reached the hall: a most spacious apartment admirably adapted for music, with an organ said to be equal to any in the world. When I went in, they were performing Handel's 'Deborah.' After it was over, I was requested to wait upon Lady Harriet Clive to one of the doors of exit, and *faire la quête*. Did you ever? When the music was over, Mr. Clive's party went to a friend's house in Birmingham, where a splendid lunch was prepared; and then we all went in carriages to Hewell, about ten miles off. And now comes the beauty. I took James with me, at the last moment, in order that, while I was waiting at Birmingham to hear the music, he might proceed to Hewell, by the way of Bromsgrove, with my trunk. There was no second-class car by the train of a quarter before nine which took me. I told Jemmy it was no matter; he might take his place in the first class; it would cost a few shillings more, but it was not material. He said he could do just as well to wait and go by the eleven o'clock train, which takes second-class passengers, and he would be sure to be at Hewell in season. I consented! I had previously told him that I should stop at Birmingham, but he was to proceed straight to Bromsgrove, and then take a fly to Hewell, four miles. Some one (I presume Mr. Carter) had informed him that these four miles were four miles backward again toward Birmingham, and that he could get to Hewell by some stagecoach more directly.[1] The consequence, as you foresee, was, that when I got to Hewell at six, there was no James: when I wanted to dress at half-past six for dinner, no James; no trunk, no black pantys, no silk stockings, no white cravat, no nothing — but desolation and despair — not even a comb and brush to snake out my hair with. Can I do anything for you? says Mr. Clive. Can I do anything says his valet? Yes! thought I (but I did not say so), build me a gallows forty cubits high, with two arms, and hang Jemmy on one and Carter on the other, and do it quick, while I go and drown myself in the horsepond. But you will observe I uttered no such nonsense, but walked down into the library, in my morning

[1] Not the case.

dress, made my excuse to Mr. Clive and Lady Harriet, and thought no more of it. Regular P.G. is your papa, n'est-ce pas?

Much, however, as he might enjoy the visits to magnificent country houses and great castles, his chief interest lay in London and the literary circle. Letters and journal are filled with allusions to famous authors, historians, poets, and essayists, chief among whom came to be Macaulay, Rogers, and Sydney Smith.

November 29, 1842. Breakfasted with Mr. Macaulay at his lodgings in the Albany. Mr. Macaulay thought Washington Irving the best imitator of Addison. Rogers called him 'Addison and Water.'

December 7. We had to-day to breakfast Mr. Rogers, Mr. Macaulay, Mr. Rives, and the Brookes. Macaulay was in high spirits, and poured out his marvellous store of thought and fact on many subjects. I differed with him on many points, but wanted courage and fluency to maintain my views. . . . Willy [1] was produced before breakfast and cited some lines from the 'Prophecy of Capys,' much to Mr. Macaulay's amusement; the dear little fellow has a memory equal to Macaulay's own — which is perfectly miraculous.

Mr. Mackintosh, rather inclined to Carlyleism, told me that Mr. Emerson did not like the patronizing strain of Carlyle's preface to his volume of essays. I read some of these essays at the Grange (Lord Ashburton's place): either because there is no meaning in them, or no perception in me, they are for the most part unintelligible to me. Some gleams, however, of thought I can trace.

To Mrs. Nathan Hale

LONDON, *January* 2, 1843

. . . I rejoice to hear of Edward's [Edward Everett Hale] *début*, of which I hear from various quarters. It is certainly not more than I expected: but the first entrance on an arduous profession is always matter of anxiety. The worst of that which he has chosen is, that there are no degrees in entering upon its labors and cares. There is, however, generally a great degree of indulgence shown to well-conducted young men. I hope Edward will keep out of transcendentalism, at least if the volume of Mr. Emerson's essays, published here by Carlyle, is a specimen of that article. I could not have believed that such a clear thinker and beautiful writer, as I knew him but a few years since, could have been betrayed into printing such conceited laborious nonsense. . . .

[1] William Everett, three years old at the time.

LONDON, *March* 2, 1843

I am much obliged to you for your letter of the 30th January, and the budget of family news which it contains. I have a little of what may be called family news to send you in return; that is, if whatever concerns the name of *Everett* is to be considered as a family matter. A short time since, I was asked to write a letter to the Collector of the port of Charleston (South Carolina), in favor of two ladies, who were going out as instructresses in a college in Georgia: one of them named Miss Cassan. I knew nothing of either of them but that they were respectable persons, engaged for the purpose mentioned, by Bishop Elliott, and on this ground I wrote the letter desired. A few days afterwards I received a note of thanks from Mrs. Cassan, the mother of Miss Cassan, in which she informed me that her mother was an Everett, and that she was staying with the Miss Everetts in Bedford Square; and Mrs. Cassan's note was left at my door with the card of Mr. William Everett who is 'receiver general' in the Board of Stamps and Taxes, and lives in Queen Anne Street.

So here seemed to be two flocks of relations, as one may say, starting up at once like two covies of partridges, on opposite sides of the field. I determined, however, to take them in succession, and drove first to Queen Anne Street. Mr. Everett was not at home; but as there is no use in standing on ceremony between first cousins, as the servant told me Mrs. Everett was at home, I thought I would e'en pay my respects to her. The stupid fellow announced me as 'Mr. Everett'; though I had taken care (as a man likes to appear to advantage among his blood kin) to add my title to my name. However, in I went as plain Mr. Everett; and as I am now upon the third winter of my surtout and the second year of my hat, there was not, I admit, much of the glare of office about me. As conversation lagged, I hinted that I had some curiosity to know 'whether I had the good fortune to be nearly related in so respectable a quarter; it was, I believe, a numerous family, etc., etc.' 'Yes,' said Mrs. Everett, 'and then there's the American Ambassador thinks he is of our family, and, what I don't think quite fair, has put our arms on his carriage.' Hurrah, boys, thought I, now we are in hot water, in good earnest. Thinking it better to stop my worthy kinswoman, before matters got worse, I owned the soft impeachment as to being myself the American Minister; and then proceeded to make as good an apology as I could for letting the coachmaker paint a coat of arms on my hired carriage door, to which my right was no doubt as good as my amiable cousin's. But the apology was useless, for as soon as she found that the real living Minister and no mistake was before her, she so far changed her view of the matter as to con-

sider my using the arms as an honor; and by this time I was ready
to go.

... We have seen a good deal this winter of the Miss Berrys,
maiden ladies — the oldest eighty — who, with very moderate
fortune, living in a very snug way, have for fifteen or twenty years
had at their house a sort of resort for the highest and best society
in London. They go out but little; one is consequently almost sure
of seeing them at home; and from ten to twelve o'clock every
evening, from eight to twelve or fourteen people whom you most
like to see — men and women of sense — are sure to be there.
Horace Walpole wished to marry Miss B., but in consequence of
the disparity of years she declined.

LONDON, *August* 4, 1843

... The day before yesterday we dined at the Palace. It was an
entertainment of great splendor, and, what is not apt to be the case
with state dinners of any kind, was remarkably pleasant. The
Crown Prince of Württemberg was the principal guest and took in
the Queen. Then Princess Clementine, daughter of Louis Philippe,
who is here as a bride, was also present with some travelling princes
of the Coburg family. Of foreign ministers, besides ourselves, there
was only the Württemberg Minister in attendance on the Crown
Prince. Sir Robert and Lady Peel, Lord Aberdeen, the Duke and
Duchess of Sutherland, Lord and Lady Seymour (the Queen of
Beauty at Lord Eglinton's tournament), Duchess of Buccleugh,
and a few others composed the party.

On these occasions every one is punctual. The hour named on the
cards (which are issued in the name of the Lord Steward) was eight.
By the time the clock had struck, every one was in the picture-
gallery except the Royal family. Mr. Murray, the master of the
household, then goes round and tells the gentlemen what ladies they
are to take in and where to place them. I was directed to take in
the Duchess of Sutherland,[1] who is often spoken of as the head of
the female aristocracy of the Court; and a lady as exemplary in her
character and amiable in her manners as she is distinguished for
rank and fortune. Under the Whig Ministry, she filled the office of
Mistress of the Robes, in which, when the Conservatives came into
power, she was succeeded by the Duchess of Buccleugh. After the
party are all assembled — which, as I observed, is always at the
hour named — the Queen and Prince Albert with their Royal
visitors and suite come in. The Queen goes up and nods to the lady
guests, and all then move off to the dining-room, a band of music
playing 'God save the Queen.' The guests go to the places assigned

[1] Lord Aberdeen took in my wife.

them, and the dinner proceeds as any other great dinner, except
that there is more elbow room, more attendance, surpassing splendor of plate and table service, and a band of music of the most
exquisite description. But there is no restraint on eating, drinking,
and conversation, beyond what good breeding ever impose. You
talk in a low tone to your right and left hand neighbor; but this is
the case at all state parties. Toward the close of the dinner, the
Master of the Household proposes 'the Queen' as a toast; and
afterwards, 'His Royal Highness Prince Albert.' At these toasts
the guests rise, but do not repeat the words. Presently the Queen
and ladies retire; the men reseat themselves; the Prince going over
to the Queen's place. I was now brought next to one of the Coburg
princes — Prince Albert's uncle — and here my German was of
use to me, as often before at this Court, which is quite German in its
interior. In about twenty minutes, the men arise, cluster about the
side-tables, where they wash their fingers if they like, and then go
back to the picture-gallery, to which the Queen and ladies have
already retired. Here coffee and tea are served; and the Queen and
Prince Albert then go round in different directions talking to every
gentleman. She has already gone the rounds with the ladies. The
Queen generally shakes hands with each lady. She was very affable
this evening, and conversed several minutes with my wife and
myself. Her conversation, at such times, is precisely that of any
high-bred person, without any assumption of condescension. She
speaks first and starts new topics of remark; but it is not considered
improper to pursue a conversation with her, as you would with any
other lady who has claims to be treated with marked deference.
You do not, in speaking to her, keep saying 'Your Majesty.' That
perhaps may be used *once;* but the ordinary style of address to her
is 'Madam'; to the Prince 'Sir.' (By the way, the English in speaking to each other never use 'Sir'; unless a son speaking to a father, or
any one addressing a person venerable for age or very high dignity.)
    After the tea and coffee are over, the Queen led the way to a
concert-room opening from the picture-gallery, where the company
broke up into three or four sections, in different parts of the room.
The Duchess of Kent formed a whist party, in which happily I was
not included, as I had formerly been at Windsor. The Queen and
Princess Clementine, with their suite, went to a sofa on one side of
the room; the other ladies opposite. The Duke of Sutherland and
myself were standing in the doorway, and the Queen sent one of the
equerries in waiting to ask us 'to take a seat at her table.' At these
words my heart leapt to my mouth. I thought of some probably
high-flown game at cards, unknown to me even by name, with the
possible loss of two or three pounds, and the recollection of having

but a poor half-sovereign in my purse. But an American Minister gets pretty callous on the point of paying state debts, and I marched up boldly to Her Majesty's table. Men march boldly to a breach in a city wall, with a battery playing upon it. However, my alarm was groundless. There was no game of cards, no money to pay; I found a vacant seat next to the Duchess of Buccleugh; and she expressed her satisfaction at having heard that my family sprung from the same county as hers! It must be admitted that it does not take much to satisfy a polite person. The Duchess of Kent's game of whist lasted about three quarters of an hour; by this time it was eleven; the Queen rose, shook hands with the ladies all round, bowed to the gentlemen, and retired. The company immediately broke up; and in a half an hour every member of it was at the Duke of Wellington's Concert. . . .

LONDON, *March* 4, 1844

. . . I made a visit to Mr. Smith last month at his rectory in Somersetshire — a visit not of a month, as the papers stated it, but of four days. It was in the middle of January; and but for the leafless trees might have passed for May. My visit extended over Sunday, and I heard Mr. Smith preach to his uninstructed village flock, in a plain sensible style adapted to their comprehension, and afterwards catechise the children. In one room of his house he has an apothecary's shop well provided with medicines, which he keeps for gratuitous distribution among his poor pensioners: and in early life he attended lectures on *Materia Medica* to enable him to do this with safety.

I dined on Saturday with Sir Edward Codrington, who commanded the British fleet at Navarino. Among the company was Lady Bunbury, a sister of the Sir C. Napier, the conqueror of Scinde, with whom I had a good deal of conversation on her brother's exploits. We had also Lady Dacre, a remarkable person, seventy-eight years old, but with all the animation of youth. She was known as Miss Barbarina Wilmot for her beautiful translations of Petrarch. She has written, I believe, a tragedy; and is a very skilful sculptress of horses. Sir Edward has a group of Phaëton's horses plunging down the sky, made by Lady Dacre which seems to me of extraordinary beauty. She was in her earlier days a great horsewoman.

To Mr. Nathan Hale

LONDON, *October* 18, 1844

I closed our recent little excursion to the North with a visit to York, during the late meeting of the British Association for the

Promotion of Science. I was the guest of the venerable Archbishop of York at his palace of Bishopthorpe, about two miles from the city. I have mentioned this most respectable old gentleman before in my letters home. He was eighty-seven on the 10th of this month and one of the finest specimens of humanity I ever saw. . . .

He had about twenty of the savants in attendance on the meeting of the Association at his house; among them Professor Liebig, Sir David Brewster, Marquis of Northampton, Mr. Murchison, Mr. Fox Talbot, Dr. Peacock, Dean of Ely and President last year of the Association, and other persons of eminence. In addition to the persons staying in the house, about as many more were invited every day to dinner. Being under a kind of compulsion to return to London two or three days before the sailing of the steamer, I staid but two days, having declined a good deal of obliging importunity to remain till the close, and take a part in the farewell speeches. A good deal of sensation was produced before I arrived, by the reading of a paper by the Dean of York, in which the modern geological theories, especially as set forth in the works of Dr. Buckland, were vehemently assailed as unscriptural and irreligious. Dr. Buckland, being unfortunately kept away by the death of a child, the task of replying to the Dean devolved upon Professor Sedgwick, which I am told he did with great power and effect. He is one of the best extemporaneous orators I ever heard, and being at the same time thoroughly versed in the science — of which I am told the Dean of York knows nothing beyond the nomenclature — the triumph was complete. The Dean, however, nothing daunted, published his essay in a pamphlet form (in fact, it was printed in London before it was delivered in York) under the rather offensive title of the 'Bible defended against the British Association,' and followed up the blow by a sermon on the following Sunday against the foolishness of worldly wisdom. The whole effect of the Dean's sally was precisely what it would have been if he had chosen the Copernican System for the object of his attack.

Wordsworth was not often in London in those days. He came to town on occasion, however, and Everett met him more than once at breakfast, and it was a great regret to him that he could not accept the poet's invitation to pay him a visit at Grasmere. The following description of Wordsworth at Court is amusing.

To Mrs. Nathan Hale

LONDON, *May* 2, 1845

... I think I have not written you much about Mr. Wordsworth, of whom in fact, as he does not live in London, I have not seen a great deal; although I have met him once or more in society, I believe, every year since I have been here. The other night there was a ball at the Palace, and shortly after the Queen entered the room, I saw an old gentleman approach her, accompanied by the Lord Chamberlain, and make the usual salutation. In a moment the Lord Chamberlain whispered to him and the Queen smiled, and he then, with some difficulty, kneeled in the usual manner in which British subjects do homage to the Sovereign, after receiving an appointment. He had not been at Court (for it was Mr. Wordsworth) since he was made laureate. I saw this scene distinctly, but being nearsighted did not recognize him in his Court dress, which, as Mr. Rogers afterwards told my wife, he borrowed of him. Mr. Rogers told him, at the same time, there was no kneeling to be done, which was the reason of his omitting that part of the ceremony; a part which sometimes produces rather ludicrous scenes, when the party is aged, stiff, and corpulent — qualities not infrequently combined. When a person of this description, with a sword by his side and spurs upon his heels, takes the Queen's hand and kneels to kiss it, it is not always that his position is as firm as could be wished. He sometimes goes near to fall, with the additional awkwardness of pulling the Queen down with him.

In the course of the evening he came up and spoke to me; and a day or two afterwards I met him at breakfast at Henry Taylor's — the author of 'Philip Van Artevelde.' He talked a great deal more than I ever heard him before and with warmth and spirit. In the decline of his life, and towards the close of his career, he is enjoying a popularity which was denied him in all the earlier part of his life, and he seems greatly to enjoy it. He has rather peculiar opinions of classical poetry; maintained that it was inaccurate in reference to the character and habits of birds and other animals. He said the note of the nightingale was not plaintive, nor that of the owl 'boding,' nor the raven's cheerless; but all of them the reverse, and that the modern poets heedlessly followed the ancients in these things without observing nature for themselves. He objected to the last line in the monody on Sir John Moore, 'we left him alone with his glory,' as ridiculous. It does not, however, strike me so, nor did he particularly state in what the ridicule consisted. He said that Campbell printed and published as his own a short piece of his (Wordsworth's), and even insisted on being the author after the plagiarism was pointed out. If there is no mistake in the facts, he was of course at the time demented. Poor Campbell's habits were very bad the last part of his life. Mr. Wordsworth has latterly made war in prose and poetry against the construction of a railroad in the Lake country. He might as well recommend a petition against the attraction of gravitation.

IX

A DIPLOMAT IN LONDON

IT should not be inferred that Mr. Everett's lot in London was a wholly happy one, or that his path was uniformly smooth. He was subjected to the customary criticisms which are passed on Americans who live at foreign Courts, and sharp eyes from home were always on the lookout for ways of living that did not seem to accord well with democratic simplicity. If he went to pass two days in the country with his friend Sydney Smith, it was reported in the American newspapers that he had stayed a month, neglecting his official duties. Because he had his private carriage, instead of depending upon the street cabs, it was reported of him that he was living in undue style.

In connection with the first charge Sydney Smith wrote an interesting letter to the London 'Chronicle,' April 18, 1844, as follows:

THE AMERICAN PRESS AND THE REVEREND SYDNEY SMITH

To the Editor of the Morning Chronicle.

SIR — The Locofoco papers in America are, I observe, full of abuse of Mr. Everett, their Minister, for spending a month with me at Christmas in Somersetshire. The month was neither lunar nor calendar, but consisted of forty-eight hours — a few minutes more or less.

I never heard a wiser or more judicious defence than he made to me, and others, of the American insolvency; not denying the injustice of it, speaking of it, on the contrary, with the deepest feeling, but urging with great argumentative eloquence every topic that could be pleaded in extenuation. He made upon us the same impression he appears to make universally in this country: we thought him (a character which the English always receive with affectionate regard) an amiable American, republican without rudeness, and accomplished without ostentation. 'If I had known *that* gentleman five years ago' (said one of my guests), 'I should have been deep in the American funds: and, as it is, I think at times that I see nineteen or twenty shillings in the pound in his face.' However this may be, I am sure we owe to the Americans a debt of gratitude for sending to us such an excellent specimen of their productions. In diplomacy, a far more important object than falsehood is, to keep two nations in friendship. In this point, no nation has ever been better served than America has been served by Mr. Edward Everett.

I am, Sir, your obedient servant,

SYDNEY SMITH

The second charge of undue display and extravagance was not, however, so easily disposed of, and it caused him considerable annoyance. Thurlow Weed, who was travelling in Europe, found himself in London when Parliament was prorogued. Because of some real or fancied slight, he hesitated to ask Everett to secure a place for him in the House of Lords where he could witness the pageant. Hiring a seat for himself, therefore, in a balcony on the line of approach, he watched the procession pass to Westminster. He wrote home of the affair, and the following paragraph appeared in his paper, the 'Albany Journal':

I observed our Minister, Hon. Mr. Everett, with his daughter, in a bright yellow coach, with coachmen and outriders in rich livery, and Mr. Everett himself (instead of the plain republican garb with which Benjamin Franklin, John Adams, and John Jay used to appear on such occasions) in full Court dress, with gold and embroidery. I don't half like this departure from the simplicity which distinguishes our form of government, though it is certain that the American Minister has acquired great popularity here, and perhaps augments his influence by his conformity in matters of displays and etiquette.

Mr. Weed confessed in his autobiography that the paragraph was written in revenge for what he thought a slight and coldness on Mr. Everett's part. That the dart with its poisoned point was deftly aimed appears from the following letter that the American plenipotentiary wrote to his friend Robert C. Winthrop:

LONDON, *November* 18, 1843

...I am sorry to trouble you about any matter of my own, especially a paltry one; but I know not to whom else to have recourse. The matter is this. Mr. Thurlow Weed is, or has been lately, in Europe; and of course has written home a series of letters giving an account of what he has seen. In describing the prorogation of Parliament, he alludes to my appearance in the manner you perceive in the enclosed slip. He makes no invidious comment, and I should have no reason to think he wished to furnish matter for any, were not his account greatly exaggerated. If you should see, or hear any such comments, of a kind or in a quarter to merit notice, the following statement will enable you to make any correction that you may think advisable. My carriage is certainly yellow; whether there is anything objectionable in that color, I do not know. It is an old carriage which I hire: as it was already yellow (rather a favorite color here for carriages) it was suggested to me that, in painting it anew, it would take the same color better than a different one; that yellow was the color that stood best; and that my predecessor's carriage was yellow. On these grounds I decided, and if, as Mr. Weed says, it is 'bright yellow' after having been used more than eighteen months — summer and winter, day and night — one of the grounds of the choice seems to be justified. He says that I had 'outriders.' This is wholly imaginary. There are, I believe, no outriders to any but Royal carriages. My coachman and outriders (he says) in 'rich livery.' My coachman and footman were in a very plain dress livery; as plain a one as was to be seen in the procession. 'Mr. Everett himself in a full Court dress.' How this could be known, by a person seeing me in a close carriage with the windows up, does not appear. I was not in what is called 'Court dress,' full or otherwise, but in my ordinary diplomatic uniform (not even the full uniform, which is worn at the Queen's Drawing-Rooms): my coat was rather less ornamented than that of my secretary, and was certainly the very plainest dress in the diplomatic box. That any gentleman, after seeing the really splendid equipages and uniforms of many of the foreign ministers and officers of the Household and of State, should describe mine as Mr. Weed has done, is, I own, matter of surprise to me. Such is the precise state of the facts, which I leave wholly to your discretion: begging you not to stir *first* in the matter.

Everett took with better philosophy another more unpleasant episode which caused him considerable annoyance, and brought him into somewhat disagreeable notoriety. It occurred when he was given the Degree of D.C.L. at Oxford in June, 1843. On this matter also he wrote to Mr. Winthrop:

LONDON, *July* 3, 1843

... I wish I had time to write you a full account of the 'row' at Oxford the other day. I use this low word, because no better one adequately describes the scene. If you will ask Mr. Brooks to show you my letter, I have no doubt he will do so. The whole affair was the more astounding to me, as I have been treated with the most distinguished attention, by the heads of the Church, both the Archbishop, the Bishop of London, and several other members of the Episcopal bench, and of the higher clergy. But Oxford is, at present, in a perfect whirl of controversial excitement, and my poor little skiff has been drawn, greatly to my annoyance, into the vortex.

I am as ever most

Sincerely yours,

EDWARD EVERETT

The so-called 'row' was precipitated by the Puseyites — the Tractarian or High-Church party — in the University. They were disturbed by the fact that the American Minister had formerly been a Unitarian preacher in the United States and still belonged to that 'dissenting' body. Having heard the evening before the Convocation that Mr. Everett was to be honored with a D.C.L., a group of objectors got together and decided to take action. When the Vice-Chancellor called Mr. Everett's name and the latter marched up the steps to the 'Seats of the Doctors,' there was a sudden uproar in the crowded theatre. Men rose in their places and shouted, '*Non placet.*' The general hubbub was increased by the undergraduates who began at the same time by a storm of groans and hisses to show their disapproval of an unpopular 'proctor.' The complimentary Latin speech of the Vice-Chancellor was drowned out by the '*non-placets*' which became louder and constantly more numerous; and the degree was conferred in the face of shouts and 'unmistakable signs' of disapproval. Among those who objected were such famous men and distinguished clergymen as Frederic A. Faber, J. B. Mozeley, R. W. Church, and W. G. Ward. These gentlemen and others, having failed to check the pro-ceedings, left the theatre and drew up at once a formal protest, which was signed by thirty-six members of the University. It was claimed that the degree was illegally granted, the ground being taken that no Oxford degree could be conferred on one who had not signed the Thirty-Nine Articles. But these narrow-minded churchmen did not fail in a certain courtesy as gentlemen. They sent, at the same time, a letter to the American Minister in which they assured him that no affront was intended either to him personally, or to the great 'country which he represented with such distinguished ability.' They took care to add, however, 'While we shrink from arbitrarily scrutinizing the opinions of individuals, we are sure that you will generously allow to members of a great University, immediately bound up with the Church of Christ, the right and the duty of scrupulously guarding against any act which may be interpreted by others as indifference on their part to divine truth and to the welfare of that Church to whose service they have been devoted.'

There the matter ended, except for some newspaper discussion; but it was not soon forgotten by Mr. Everett himself. Indeed, it was a rather trying affair altogether. The 'Times' referred to it as 'a remarkable scene which has rarely been equalled in the annals of the University'; and added in an editorial the next day: 'the degree will certainly be disputed on the point of law.'

The following letter, written to Mr. Brooks, gives a full account of the matter, and shows how Everett put the best face on what was really a somewhat unpleasant situation.

LONDON, *July* 3, 1843

...Oxford is, at present, the centre of a religious agitation by which the whole Church of England is convulsed. The contest is between a party called 'Puseyites,' from Dr. Pusey, a canon of Christ Church, and Professor of Divinity, and the body of the Church generally who oppose their views. The Pusey party is accused, by their opponents, of leaning towards Romanism, and a wish to reunite themselves with the Catholic Church. *They* maintain that they wish only to restore the Church of England — or rather the Church — to its ancient purity. I really do not feel able to judge of the merits of this controversy. It is now brought to a point of extreme bitterness, in consequence of Dr. Pusey having been suspended from his functions for two years for having preached a sermon alleged to contain expressions favoring the doctrine of transubstantiation. The following day — Wednesday — was the Commemoration, at which the heads of the Colleges had voted me the degree of Doctor of Civil Law, and as the day was pleasant, a great company assembled in the theatre. As the ceremonial of admission is quite imposing, we promised ourselves an interesting time. The event proved otherwise — at least the interest was of a very unpleasant character. You will probably see the accounts in the newspapers, some of which, in the main, are correct. In some of them it is stated, wholly without foundation, that the rising of the students was connected with my degree. This is entirely erroneous. It was altogether an affair of the undergraduates, intended to drive from the house an unpopular proctor; and so deafening was the uproar of calling on him to go out, all the time that the ceremony of conferring the degrees was going on, that no person more than three feet from the Public Orator could hear a word he said. I could not, though I stood by his side, and a part of the time held his hand. The noise continued after the degrees were conferred, and while the Professor of Poetry was delivering the Commemoration Speech; and finding it impossible to hear a word that was said, the Vice-Chancellor broke up the assembly. It would not be possible to describe the tumult, without using language which would sound like exaggeration. It seems that in the uproar, when my degree was proposed (very much as our President at Cambridge proposes the degrees to the Overseers on the stage, Commencement Day), some of the Puseyite gentlemen cried out, 'Non placet' or 'Nay,' and, as they say, demanded a 'Scrutiny,' that is, a counting of the votes. The Vice-Chancellor did not hear this call, nor, in fact, the 'non-placets,' all around him having voted 'placets,' that is, 'yea'; and he sent the beadles of the University to bring in me and my brother candidate for the degree. As soon as the assembly was broken up, those who voted 'non-placets,' met together, and calling in all of their way of thinking in the University, signed a protest against the degree, in Latin, on the technical ground that after the vote was doubted, a division was refused. They then sent a deputation to call on me, and assure me that no personal disrespect was intended, which they did in very handsome terms. They have since addressed a letter to me to the same effect, which they have published.

The objection to my degree was my having been a Unitarian minister; but it was the opinion of my friends at Oxford that the movement was made to annoy the Vice-Chancellor and others who concurred in the degree, out of revenge for the recent suspension of Dr. Pusey. It is certainly unlucky that I, who, as far as *hot water* is concerned, have a perfect hydrophobia, should be plunged up to the ears in this boiling and bitter cauldron. The matter makes no small stir. The Liberal papers rather do harm, by giving it a political aspect; and the name of 'Unitarian' is so odious, with a considerable number of people in England, that some who feel grieved and ashamed at the affair, are afraid to say so. The Vice-Chancellor, the principal heads of Colleges, and Dr. Buckland, treated me throughout with the greatest tenderness and consideration.

There was really a good deal more in the Oxford row than Everett was disposed at first to acknowledge. His friends made light of it, and assured him that the objectors, though noisy and insistent, were very few comparatively in numbers. They persuaded him to withhold a vigorous letter of protest that he had prepared.

Everett, therefore, lapsed into dignified silence. But the Puseyites were eager for warfare. Their next step was an appeal to the ecclesiastical lawyers that the degree might be pronounced illegal. Six months, therefore, after the noisy scene in the Sheldonian Theatre, the 'Times,' on December 11, 1843, published a long article announcing that eminent Church counsel had been consulted and that the degree had been pronounced 'invalid and a nullity.' But by this time the interest in the subject had waned away and the controversy was allowed at last to die a natural death.

Another matter which did a good deal to upset the equanimity of the American Minister was an official communication from President Tyler asking him to head a diplomatic mission which the American Government was planning to send to China. It was thought desirable at this time for our Government to enter into more definite and friendly relations with the Chinese Empire. Mr. Tyler had sent a message to Congress on the subject, and Congress, acting on the suggestion, had passed an act providing for the mission and appropriating money for the purpose. It was essential that the mission should be undertaken wisely and under the best auspices. The first and most important matter was to secure the right man to head it. Indeed, this was looked upon as a point of 'transcendent importance.'

The first inkling of the possibility that he might be sought out for the post reached Everett in connection with a letter which he received from the Secretary of State. It was dated January 29, 1843, and in it Mr. Webster said: 'You will see that the President has recommended to Congress to make provision for some sort of a mission to China. If the provision should be ample, and you were in the country, I think I should advise the President to send you to the Celestial Empire. It would be a mission full of interest, and with your powers of application and attainments you would make great additions to your stock of ideas.'

The suggestion did not strike Everett altogether pleasantly. He was not sure that he wanted to go to China; indeed, he was quite sure that he did not. He was very happy where he was, and he had only just got hold of things in England in a way that gave him satisfaction. He had ample time, however, to meditate upon the matter before news of the actual appointment came. But when it did come, it was accompanied by sinister rumors to the effect that the underlying reason for his nomination was to get him out of the London position in order that Webster might succeed him. If such were the case, he was in a quandary, indeed; for, while he had no desire to go to China, he had every wish to consider Mr. Webster's wishes. Before he had been a year in London the question of making room for Webster had come up. Webster had let him know that his position in Tyler's Cabinet was far from comfortable, and he suggested to Everett in a tentative way that an easy method of escape might be by accepting a post abroad. The natural one for him to take would, of course, be London, and this might be effected by Everett's transfer to Paris. Everett's response to the suggestion was firm as well as candid.

LONDON, *September* 16, 1842

. . . I have read your confidential letter of the 25th August with the deepest interest. The difficulties of your position have, of course, long been apparent to me. I have witnessed them with sympathy as well as with admiration of the skill with which you have thus far extricated yourself from them. The most unscrupulous partisan (who has a drop of Whig blood in him), unless he prefers a desolating war to an honorable peace, must now see the propriety of your having remained in the Cabinet. Your continuance there, if consistent with your principles and character, would no doubt be greatly beneficial to the country, though possibly no occasion of service so distinct and brilliant as the treaty might arise. But there is great justice in what you say as to the difficulty of your remaining. It will, however, require your consideration whether the difficulty is in your being in the Cabinet or in your general political position. Does it not consist mainly in your relations with Mr. Clay or the relations of both to the country? Can you get along better in this respect out of the Government than in it? If, as you intimate in consequence of your inability to give strength to the President's Administration on its present basis, his Cabinet is likely to be constructed on a democratic basis, could you come here and act under the instructions of the new Secretary of State, Mr. Stevenson, for instance?

Still, however, in reference to your future movements and what you say of coming abroad, you may depend on my giving you every practicable facility. I shall with all my heart accede to any arrangement agreeable to you and creditable to me, and none other would occur to you. You seem to intimate the idea of my transfer to Paris which I have also seen mentioned in the papers. Though General Cass told me a few days ago he should go home next summer, I think he will not unless he is nominated as a Presidential candidate, which does not seem to me a very likely event. You best know whether the President would recall him. I think not. Should there be a vacancy there, and you wish me transferred to it, though I should prefer a usual term of service at this Court, I should readily consent to anything desired by you, both on account of personal attachment and because — now if possible more than ever — I feel that you are entitled to anything you can wish to have and which it is in the power of the Government or people to bestow.

Having said this with entire sincerity, do not misapprehend the feelings with which I add that it is important to both of us — to you in the magnitude, to me in the modicum of consequence before the country which we have at stake — that no abrupt step be taken. I am, as you remark, 'hardly warm in my seat,' and unless displaced on public grounds, my removal so soon after my appointment to be succeeded by you would wear the appearance of a disposal of the highest places under the Government, for considerations of personal convenience, which in the present state of parties would run some risk of not being sanctioned by the Senate and would certainly offend public sentiment.

As soon as you have made up your mind as to the course to be pursued by you, if it connects itself with what concerns me, pray let me know it. For you may easily conceive that a state of uncertainty about a matter like this is not very friendly to the calm and steady action of one's faculties.

P.S. I beg you to adhere to your purpose of parting friends with the President, if you part at all. He, too, has had his trials; has been hardly dealt with; and deserves well of the country for sustaining you through this great negotiation.

In a different vein he wrote to Mr. Brooks, expressing his suspicion that Mr. Webster wished to supplant him. An incident which intensified his suspicion was the fact that his wishes in regard to a secretary had been disregarded. The individual whom he had selected for the post, and had asked for, was passed over, and a different appointment made.

LONDON, *November* 3, 1842

For Yourself alone

It was not my wish that you should speak about my Secretary. It would have done no good — but I was very *shamefully* treated in that matter. I have some reason to think there is an intention to disgust and drive me from my place. Our great men are terribly selfish; and notwithstanding the complimentary manner in which I am alluded to in the Faneuil Hall speech (in Mr. Hale's report of it, for in the 'Courier's' report, which happened to be the one selected by the London press, that allusion was stripped of everything complimentary), I am fearful not only that Mr. W. has thoughts of supplanting me, but of discrediting me in the meantime by withholding all instructions upon matters of consequence, and thus putting it out of my power to show even a willingness to do my duty. Things have already been done, or rather left undone, which I would not have believed possible on any ground but my own personal knowledge.

In the matter of the Secretary, if I am rightly informed the President did all I could wish. He repeatedly said that I should have who I pleased; and though I wrote over and over again, asking Mr. V. R.'s appointment, I presume my wish was never mentioned to the President. I may in this be mistaken, but I think not.

All these things, however, were now matters of the past, being more than a year old. So far as the Chinese Mission was concerned, he received definite and explicit assurances from Webster himself, who wrote him on March 10, 1843:

> The appointment gives, I think, universal pleasure. The President is sincerely desirous that you should accept the appointment, because he thinks you eminently fitted to fulfil its duties. . . . You will see it said in the newspapers that the object in nominating you to China is to make way for your humble servant to go to London. I will tell you the whole truth about this without reserve. . . . To succeed you in England for the mere purpose of carrying on for a year or two the general business of the mission is what I could not think of. I do not mean only that I would not be the occasion of transferring you elsewhere for any such purpose; but I mean that, if the place were vacant, I would not accept an appointment to fill it, unless I knew that something might be done beyond the ordinary routine of duties. At present I see little or no prospect of accomplishing any great objects. . . .
>
> I wish you, therefore, to feel that, as far as I am concerned, your appointment to China had not its origin in any degree in a desire that your present place should be vacated. If it were vacant now, or should be vacated by you, there is not one chance in a thousand that I shall fill it.

These assurances were explicit enough. They appeared to leave Everett wholly free to decide the question on its merits — that is to say, without reference to any obligation due his chief, or to considerations of personal friendship. But, unfortunately for his peace of mind, the same post brought him a long and urgent letter from John Quincy Adams. The communication is worth printing entire. It is much more than a purely formal or political document. It is a frank and glowing tribute to Everett's conspicuous abilities and unrivalled position in the country. Indeed, the circumspect Mr. Adams did not hesitate to say that in his opinion no other American then living was so well fitted as Everett to undertake the Mission. Such a tribute from such a man is worthy of preservation.

WASHINGTON, *March* 13, 1843

EDWARD EVERETT, ESQ.,
   Envoy Extraordinary and Minister Plenipotentiary of the
   United States at the Court of Great Britain, London.
MY DEAR SIR.

At the recent session of Congress an act was passed with an appropriation of forty thousand dollars for the establishment of a diplomatic Mission to China. This act was reported by me as Chairman of the Committee of Foreign Affairs, on a message from the President of the United States, and was a measure in which I took a deep and anxious interest. It was, therefore, with great satisfaction that I learnt your appointment to the Mission, though I was not consulted at the making of the selection, and knew not of it until the day after the close of the Session. I know not how far it may be acceptable to you, and am well aware that for personal comforts and perhaps domestic convenience your present station would be preferable to a long and tedious voyage and a strange and barbarous land. But you have learned to make sacrifices for the service of your country, and without meaning to flatter you, or to disparage any other man, I believe you and the service required so peculiarly fitted for each other, that there is not another man in the Union upon whose successful issue from it I should place equal confidence.

You will appretiate [*sic*] even if you should not share the *hopes* with which are associated my estimate of the possible results of this Mission, and my deep sense of the dangers by which those hopes may be blasted and scattered to the winds. In my own opinion, consummate abilities are but one and the least vitally essential of the qualities indispensable for the conduct of a negotiation like that now to be instituted with China. Temper, self-possession, candor, fair-dealing, firmness and conciliation, an utter detestation of all trickery and indirection, with patience and discretion, are of a stronger prevailment in a diplomatic bargaining than all the subtleties of the Old Serpent himself. I entreat you, therefore, to accept and undertake this Mission, carrying with you the good-will and good offices of those between whom and us you have so richly contributed to restore good-feeling and good-humour. I have staked much personal responsibility on the opinion that Great Britain was justifiable in her recent war with China, and now in the triumph of her success, I want the crown of my argument in the power to point the observation of my countrymen to the disinterestedness and magnanimity of her peace. And if you go to China will you find time to let me hear from you directly of your passage and success. . . .

The Mission really was a good deal of an affair. President Tyler, in his personal letter offering Everett the position, named nine thousand dollars per annum as the salary and an equal amount in addition for an 'outfit.' He added, 'A Frigate of the first class, probably a seventy-four, will be employed to convey you and be placed in other respects at your disposal. But these will be with you but inducements of a secondary character. The leading and controlling consideration with you will doubtless be that your name will be identified with a most interesting epoch in our history, and associated, should success, however partial, crown your mission, with the prominent benefactors of your country.'

But the affair never tempted Everett for a single moment. He did not like the 'trade' aspect of the expedition for one thing, and in the second place, he was very happy where he was. His position in England fitted him to perfection, and he could not but be conscious that he fitted it. He felt what he described as 'an irresistible and almost mysterious repugnance' to the Mission. A controlling consideration in his mind was the comfort and welfare of his family, whom it would have been necessary to leave behind. At this time his elder daughter Anne was seriously ill. Her condition weighed heavily on his mind. He could not think of leaving her in a foreign country, or even anywhere else, in such a precarious state of health. Altogether, the news of his appointment made him 'perfectly sick at heart.' Lord Aberdeen, to whom he spoke on the subject, said that 'he should as soon have thought of his going to the moon.'

He took a fortnight to consider the matter and then:

April 15, 1843: Wrote a private letter to President Tyler declining the appointment to China, chiefly on the grounds that there was no certainty the Mission would be received, and secondly, that the appropriation was inadequate.

The subject, however, was not finally disposed of without affecting unpleasantly Mr. Webster's mind. He resented the constant implications that he was not treating Everett fairly and was plotting to supplant him. Altogether there was serious danger of a breach between the two friends. Everett wrote a letter to Winthrop complaining of Mr. Webster, and suggesting duplicity and unfair treatment. He thought better of it, however, and tore it up. None the less, it was copied into his letter-book where it bears the words 'not sent,' giving witness of Everett's restraint and generous feelings and unfailing loyalty. Nor did Webster ever impute to his friend any hostile feelings in the matter.

It was a relief to learn, in due course of time, that those who were near to him at home were sympathetic with his wish to remain in London. The thought, however, of Mr. Webster still lurked in the background of his mind. He accepted Webster's personal assurances to the contrary, and yet he could not bear to think that he had possibly stood in the way of his friend's perhaps unconscious wishes. He wrote to Robert C. Winthrop:

LONDON, *June* 2, 1843 ·

I am glad to find my family and friends at home approve of my not going to China. In fact I do not know that anybody disapproves it. I imagine it was quite convenient to the President to have the place at his disposal, and I feel confident the public will not suffer by the change that has been made. The appointment was tendered me in the handsomest manner, both by Mr. Webster and the President. With respect to Mr. Webster, if I thought by remaining here I prevented his coming, I should, in declining the appointment to China, have tendered the President an unconditional resignation of my place here. For, though I should not have been pleased to think the Chinese appointment made for that purpose, yet I should not have felt justified in keeping Mr. Webster out of this office, and depriving the public of the benefit of his services. But not only was no intimation made to me that the two events had any connection with each other,[1] but, besides submitting the

[1] Whether or not there was any connection of the kind is a point which it is perhaps impossible now to decide. Mr. Adams firmly believed that there was. In his diary he called the appointment 'the back door by which Webster skilfully secures

Chinese Mission to my choice, Mr. Webster has assured me over and over again, that, if this place were vacated, he could not accept it. . . .

Moreover, it was still more satisfactory for Everett to know that his friends in *England* approved of his decision. I have no means of telling whether Everett himself ever saw the letter, but Lord Ashburton wrote to Mr. Webster on April 28, 1843: 'I can give you no information of what passes in the Old World, that you will not have better from your friend, Mr. Everett, who understands us thoroughly, and who is, as you may suppose, a marvellous favorite with us. I am frequently asked whether America furnishes many such men. We were in some anxiety that he might leave us for the Celestial Empire, but I find, as I anticipated, that he will remain with the Terrestrials. He would be much too fine an instrument for such a purpose; it would be like cutting blocks with a razor.'[1]

Although the perplexity of the Chinese Mission was finally settled to his own satisfaction, Everett was still left with a series of questions and disputes which were far from pleasant. A large part of the American Minister's duty in

---

for himself a safe retreat from the Tyler Cabinet. If Everett declines the Chinese mission, Webster can take it himself.' (See *Memoirs of J. Q. Adams*, XI, 335.) Inasmuch, however, as Webster did *not* 'take it himself,' but appointed Caleb Cushing, who accepted the post, this supposition seems to be groundless. A more plausible explanation is offered by Schouler, who suggests that the whole thing was a desire on the part of President Tyler to be rid of Webster. Mr. Webster was the only member of Harrison's Cabinet who had not resigned. (See Schouler, IV, 436: McMaster's *Webster*, p. 282.) Against all these rumors, suspicions, and suggestions, we have Mr. Webster's repeated statements that he did not wish the English post, and would not accept it. Nor can we think of that great man as plotting in any way to supplant one of his most intimate friends. Under all the circumstances it seems only fair and right to assume that Everett was offered the Chinese Mission for the good and sufficient reason that of all Americans he was thought best fitted to discharge it. So far as Webster's part in it is concerned, it is not impossible that a few chance remarks that the great man made, like that in the letter to Mr. Brooks, in which he said that if he could afford it he should be tempted to put himself in competition with Mr. Everett for the post in England, may have been the cause of all the gossip. It appears from more than one of Webster's letters that he rather envied Everett, in a friendly way, the good times he was having in London. By way of contrast his post in Tyler's Cabinet was far less pleasant.

[1] *The Writings and Speeches of Daniel Webster*, XVIII, 191.

England at that particular period consisted in presenting claims against Great Britain on account of vessels that were seized and sometimes held because of suspected participation in the African slave-trade. It was a most unwelcome, not to say distasteful, task. In many instances these vessels, some of them hailing from New England ports, had slave-traders on board, and apparently were provisioned and fitted out for the purpose of engaging in the disgraceful traffic. In more numerous instances there was no guilty connection whatever, and the claims of the owners against England were good. In these cases the American Minister was able to collect payment for damages. But the task was even then distinctly disagreeable. It put the American people and their representative in an unfortunate and unfavorable light. For whatever else might, or might not, be true of England, she was honestly and actively trying to suppress a most shameful practice. Moreover, there can be no doubt that Americans were directly, but more often indirectly, connected with the trade. In December, 1843, Everett wrote Mr. Upshur, who had succeeded Mr. Webster as Secretary of State, a somewhat vigorous letter on the subject. He said in the course of a despatch:

I also forward a note from Lord Aberdeen accompanied with several letters from the commanding officers of the British Cruizers [sic] in the African Sea and the British Consul at Bahia, relative to the indirect participation of American citizens in the slave-trade. *The evil undoubtedly exists*, and might probably be remedied to some extent by the application of existing laws. I presume, however, that in order to its entire suppression further legislative measures are necessary. The President, I am aware, has already asked the attention of Congress to the subject. It is greatly to be wished that some law might be passed which would put an effectual stop to the employment of American capital and the participation of American citizens in a traffic condemned by religion and humanity and revolting to the public feeling of the American people. The strenuous resistance of the United States to the methods by which Great Britain has been so long endeavoring to suppress the trade in slaves, and the great expense to which our Government is put in sustaining a squadron on the coast of Africa, make it equally our duty and our interest to resort to every measure within our competence to put an effective stop to the nefarious traffic.[1]

In much the same vein, in letters marked 'private' and 'confidential,' he wrote to Winthrop [2] on the subject, and gave free utterance to his feelings.

I earnestly hope you will have passed the law recommended by the President. . . . Another such case will cause a war. I do not say this from anything intimated to me in any official quarter, but from what I see of public opinion and public feeling. . . . You say Mr. Webster's letter of instructions to me on the 'Creole' is deemed an 'ultra slave paper'; but is not the ultra vision in the relation of slavery itself. If it is recognized at all, it must be recognized in all its incidents. . . . God grant that the millstone may be taken from the neck of the country in some peaceful and constitutional way.

In the meantime, England's attitude on the whole matter was firm, open, and decisive. Lord Aberdeen said to Mr. Everett on one occasion, as reported in one of Everett's despatches,[3] 'That it was impossible for Her Majesty's Government to make the slightest compromise on the subject of slavery; and that when slaves were found within the British jurisdiction, by whatever means, or from whatever quarters, they were *ipso facto* free.'

A typical case in point, and one of the first which Everett had to deal with, was the famous Creole case. It may be briefly related as follows:

The brig Creole sailed from Hampton Roads to New Orleans with a cargo of slaves on board; the slaves rose upon the master and crew, killed one man, overpowered the others, and steered for the British Bahamas. The Governor at Nassau treated the captors as freemen, as human beings who had conquered their enslavers. This natural view the Queen's Ministry sustained against the paradoxical demand of Tyler's Secretary of State for the negroes 'as

[1] Official Despatches.
[2] None of the letters to Winthrop marked 'private' and 'confidential' bear any signature. See Winthrop Papers, Massachusetts Historical Society.
[3] Despatch No. 90, London, February 27, 1844.

mutineers and murderers, and the recognized property of citizens of the United States.'[1]

Such was the kind of case that the American Minister had upon his hands. It was a bad sort of cause to have to argue before the bar of humanity. It made a 'special pleader' of a Christian gentleman and diplomat. It gave clear evidence that English standards were higher than those of the great Republic of the West.

Mr. Everett would have liked, and had hoped, to have an important part in settling the knotty question of the Northeastern boundary, which, as we have seen, was a subject on which he was thoroughly and well informed. Webster had written him in some detail soon after he had reached London, suggesting the possibility of this. In a letter marked 'private' and dated Washington, December 28, 1841, Mr. Webster had said:

You are called to your present post, my dear Sir, at a very important crisis, and it will require all that you can do, as well as all that we can do here, to get honorably and peacefully through the subjects now pending between us and England.

On the boundary question you are well informed. You know that a negotiation is pending for a joint commission with an umpire. It has made little progress for a twelvemonth; but it is intended to hasten it. There is much difficulty, however, in stating the proposition. It is my intention to send some confidential person to you in March (perhaps Mr. F. Webster), that the views of the Queen's Government may be informally sounded as to what would be their notion of a compromise line. But this is not to retard the negotiation of the convention for a commission.

Then there is the African question, and the Caroline question, in regard to both of which I shall write you as soon as possible, and there is another of slaves set free at Nassau, which is likely to give us new and great trouble. I know your ability and diligence will enable you soon to master these questions.

It soon turned out, however, that the matter of the Northeastern boundary was to be settled in a different way than Webster had planned. It seemed best to the British Government that the parley and preliminary discussion should be

[1] Schouler, *History of the United States*, IV, 398.

carried on at Washington, not in London, it being a boundary question on the American continent. To this end, the Queen's Government sent Lord Ashburton to Washington as a special High Commissioner. He and Mr. Webster arranged the famous treaty, and Everett was left to keep things running smoothly in London and to protest against the seizures by British vessels of American ships that were suspected of being engaged in the African slave-trade. He was obliged to appear in the unfortunate light of seeming to oppose a Christian nation in her efforts to suppress a hideous traffic. But perhaps it was all for the best, and it may be that his courteous, considerate, and friendly ways did more than ever will be known to keep a good understanding between the two Governments. But the matter was not easy. The Minister's heart was heavy and his hands were full. He stood at what he called 'the letter-mill,' wearing his fingers to the bone writing despatches, sometimes from eight in the morning until six at night with only the briefest possible break for luncheon.

Moreover, a heavy private sorrow was now to bear him almost to the ground. His eldest daughter Anne Gorham, named for her aunt, Mrs. Frothingham, became in the autumn of 1843 seriously ill. She had not been well for many months, and the trouble was at first attributed to the exposure all the family had undergone in crossing the Pontine Marshes after sunset in the hurried trip from Naples to Paris in 1840. The physicians were baffled. They sent her first to Brighton for the air, and later on to Tunbridge Wells where she took the waters. But nothing served to arrest the insidious disease or to abate the racking cough. Although the doctors pronounced her lungs free from disease, it gradually became more and more clear that the disease was consumption and the end inevitable.

October 18, 1843. About seven in the evening our beloved daughter underwent a change: great shortness of breathing followed with difficulty of swallowing. . . . About a quarter before ten she seemed to awake, but it was in the act of dying. In a few moments more calmly and without a struggle, with less apparent suffering than her fits of coughing never failed to produce, she gently moaned away her pure and lovely spirit. How many pleasant, delighted hours have I passed in that dear child's society, who, young as she was, had grown up to be my companion, my friend, sometimes my adviser, often my exemplar. Her departure seems to make a void in my being.

October 19. Unable to read the morning prayer, which I am sure the Good Being to whom it is addressed will pardon. My dear blessed child wears to-day a calmer aspect than for weeks, but so cold, so destitute of that expression of affection without which she never looked upon me while living that it almost breaks my heart. ... What a mystery is death, if possible greater than that of life. ... Will it ever be given us to penetrate this veil. ... I think in my life I have never known a person in whom the love of order, an attachment to system, and a reverence for principle were so strongly developed.

October 21. I went up to the chamber of death, but the face of my darling child is hidden from me forever. I shall go to her, but she will not come to me. Oh, God, when we have suffered all thy good pleasure on earth, receive us to thy presence and to the conscious renewal of that tender society now broken by death. So be it.

In the dark days that followed his loss, when he withdrew from all social functions, and had more time in his library, he turned over in his mind some piece of literary work, and he conceived the idea of writing a life of Julius Cæsar.

It will be an interesting theme. The topics are great, the crisis of the Roman affairs and the effectual foundation of the Empire, the conquest of Gaul, the invasion of Germany and England, the Civil Wars, Pharsalia, and the perpetual dictatorship. The characters contemporary with himself, Cicero, Cato, Pompey, Brutus, Catiline — these are brilliant topics; and as the great aim of history should be to inculcate moral lessons, what better opportunity could be desired in regard to some of the characteristic principles of the American Democracy! 1. The founder of the Roman Empire was of the Popular party. 2. He found his most efficient arms in the corruption of the Optimates. Two great lessons.

More than once the diary records beginnings made, the ground cleared, the chapters outlined. The original entry occurred on January 20, 1844, and five days later we read: 'Made a few notes on the Life of Cæsar to-day. If I could devote two or three hours daily to it for three years, I could easily complete it.' Again: 'Gave two hours of the evening to Cæsar. Oh, that I could persevere, turning neither to the right hand, nor the left, till I have given to the world a laborious, conscientious, instructive history of the foundation of the Roman Empire!'

But it was not so to be. The days of mourning could not go on forever. Slowly and sadly he took up social life again, and began to go about. But the death of his daughter hung heavy on him through the winter, and indeed for the rest of his stay in England. He visits Cambridge and its neighborhood and writes, December 8: 'Went to Emmanuel (Harvard's College) to pay my respects to Dr. Archdall. . . . On my way home stopped in at King's College Chapel, and then took a walk alone in the Gardens of Trinity. My last walk there had been with my dear lamented Nanny.' The next day at the invitation of Dr. Peacock, the Dean, he drove to Ely to see the Cathedral. Arriving there a little before ten, he was in season to attend the morning Cathedral service. 'The Bishop was present, and one or two canons; but this, with the exception of the choristers, was the whole company. The music was exquisite and some parts of it drew from me a tribute of tears to the memory of my blessed daughter.'

On September 29, 1844, a year after her death, he found himself at Bishopstowe, the guest of the Archbishop of York in the room of the palace which had been occupied by Nanny two years previously. The emotions and the memories found expression in these verses, which he wrote down in his journal:

> 'This was thy room, dear daughter, that the Tower,
> Sketched by thy youthful hand, with simple art
> Whose dial measures out the fleeting hour
> Of which thou did'st misspend how small a part!
> No more its warning voice shall bid thee start.
> Forever closed thy blameless, brief career:

Child, friend, companion, pride of my fond heart,
Whose gentle voice was music to my ear,
For whom I never shed but o'er thy grave a tear.

'Be still, my murmuring heart, God's will is best;
Oh, let me not against that will repine.
But trust that in the mansions of the blest
The cherished one that only here was mine,
Shall in her Father's presence live the life divine.'

And so the busy round began again. But he had not quite the heart for it that he had had before.

February 22, 1844. Sydney Smith said he had lately been reading Dr. Channing's works — especially his sermons on War and the Character of Christ; that he said nothing about his Unitarianism, but that there was nothing equal to these discourses by the divines of the Church of England; that he meant to preach the sermon on War at Saint Paul's,[1] and if he was called to account for it say that the Church of England had nothing so good.

March 2, 1844. Had General Tom Thumb to lunch with us to the great amusement of the whole family and household. A most curious little man. Should he live and his mind become improved, he will be a very wonderful personage.

March 8, 1844. We had to breakfast Mr. Macaulay, Mr. C. A. Murray, Master of the Household, Mr. Milman, Mr. Lyell, Mr. Hayward, Mr. Senior. At a quarter before eleven, General Tom Thumb was brought in. My particular object in this visit was to exhibit the General to Mr. Murray with a view to his being seen by the Queen.

April 7, 1844. General Tom Thumb and Mr. Barnum took luncheon with us. Mr. Barnum exhibited the Queen's present; — quite costly and valuable enough, but far less so than described by the reporters.

June 1, 1844. It must be confessed that to be the American Minister at present is not the most enviable thing in the world; a conspicuous station with nothing to support it; the representative of a country little respected and a Government not at all; faithfully and laboriously serving an Administration who so far from thanking and encouraging me are vexed at my very fidelity and assiduity which leave them no decent reason to recall me.

---

[1] He did this. See *Life and Letters*, II, 528, by his daughter, Lady Holland: 'I preached in Saint Paul's the identical Sermon. . . . I thought I could not write anything half so good, so I preached Channing.'

Everett was a great admirer of England, but there were times when he reacted against much that he saw and heard. When the Order of the Garter was given to the King of the French in 1844, he burst out in his diary thus:

Although I am decidedly of the opinion that a rational adherence to the past and an intelligent reverence of antiquity is all-important in England, yet I must confess that these orders of knighthood seem to me the silliest of things. The Order of the Garter — what does it mean? According to Hume the vulgar story of its origin is not unsuitable to the spirit of the times; a standing memorial of the adultery of Edward III and the Countess of Salisbury. Such antiquity as this is, I think, not to be reverenced, nor such legends cherished.

The social life, too, when the glamour began to wear off, was less alluring. Of a dinner at Dr. Holland's he wrote:

A very pleasant party, but most of the pleasantry consisted in ridiculing absent friends. Macaulay and Hallam were severely lashed for engrossing the conversation, and preventing all others from taking part in it.

January 22, 1845. From the theatre we went to Miss Berry's. These venerable ladies have receptions every night, but more especially Wednesdays. We found Lord and Lady Mahon, Lady Hyslop, Macaulay, etc. The last news, the last book, the last review, the last comer, is discussed at these meetings. Not wholly casual, nor yet regularly invited, they give me the idea, I suppose, of French society under the Old Régime.

February 18, 1845. Breakfasted at Mr. Hallam's. The company consisted of Lord Northampton, Mr. Macaulay, Mr. Milnes, Mr. C. Buller, and myself. Mr. Macaulay begged me to tell him the name of the person who painted him the other day, which he had forgotten (Mr. Inman). Milnes said he rejoiced to find there was anything he could forget.

February 21, 1845. Breakfasted with Mr. Rogers: no one else but Lord Northampton and Mr. Hallam. I was asked at a quarter before ten. Went punctually as I always do, but found no one, not even our host. Mr. Rogers told several anecdotes, but no one which I had not heard before.

February 23. Called on Mr. Grenville, where I heard the painful intelligence of Sydney Smith's death which took place last night. All concede to him the place of the first wit of the age. Had he been less of a wit, he would have been deemed a man of first-rate capacity, and would no doubt have risen to one of the highest places in the Church. For his profession he had no fondness, a fact which he did not conceal. He, however, discharged its duties in an exemplary manner and published two volumes of sermons. From my first arrival in England, he treated me with distinguished kindness and conversed with me more confidentially than any other person.

March 1, 1845. In the evening went to Lady Palmerston's. . . . In Boston I should have thought that the opportunity of attending such a reception and seeing some of the distinguished persons and the most historical names of Europe was an inestimable privilege. Here I find, as the hour for going out approaches, that I regard it as a burden, seize an excuse with readiness, and pass through the rooms comparatively indifferent. In fact, there is but little interest or enjoyment in a crowd even of celebrated names. Dukes and Ambassadors jostled in the crowd are but men and women in a throng, with conversation no more lively or better manners than the mass of good society everywhere.

July 6, 1845. Called on Mr. Rhett, the member of Congress from Charleston, South Carolina. Told me if I would take the Presidency of Harvard College, he would send his son there. Of late years the South has almost ceased to send students to Cambridge.

July 13, 1845. Took Willie to lunch at Lady Zetland's. Colonel Arder also came in. Willie acquitted himself with great success, having recited one or two odes of Horace; a passage in Aristophanes; the names of all the railway stations on the road to Cambridge and from London to Birmingham. Stood a very good examination in the counties of England: the geography of Italy and the Mediterranean, and the lengths of the principal rivers throughout the world.

Everett was soon in the full social rush of things again, although ever and again little touches of weariness appear, which whisper of unspoken sadness at the heart.

To the Honorable P. C. Brooks

LONDON, *January* 2, 1844

. . . While I was at Cambridge, I made a very interesting acquisition of a correspondence between Roger Williams and Mrs. Sadler, a daughter of Lord Chief Justice Coke. Roger Williams, it seems, had been patronized and educated by the Chief Justice. This fact was known by tradition, but I believe in no other way; but it is stated in a note which Mrs. Sadler has appended to one of the letters. The correspondence throws some light on the present history of Roger Williams; it took place on occasion of one of the visits which he made to England, and is quite characteristic of both the parties. I have sent it to Mr. Bancroft, thinking it might be of some value to him in his historical researches. I think it would amuse you to read it, as it is not long; and I am sure he would be gratified to send it to you. Although the Master of Trinity had been often struck with the bold spirit evinced in Mrs. Sadler's letters, he was not aware of the fact that she was Lord Chief Justice Coke's daughter, till I discovered it to be so, by more carefully comparing some things, alluded to in the correspondence. . . .

While I was at Cambridge, I dined once in the hall at Corpus Christi and once in the hall of Trinity. At the former a curious horn of spiced beer was handed round the fellows' table, after the cloth was removed. In order to drink, it was curiously attached to your right arm and brought to the lips by turning the elbow outwards. It was given to the College by one of the founders in the fifteenth century. I dined at the Vice-Chancellor's table, where we drank from a silver flagon presented by the famous Earl of Essex, who was Chancellor. In all these old bodies, there is a kind of formal symposium after dinner. Two or three stand up together, and pass the goblet with a kind of solemnity. It obtains in greatest form at the Lord Mayor's dinner under the name of 'the Loving Cup.'

To Mrs. Nathan Hale

LONDON, *April 3*, 1844

I am fearful that I shall not have it in my power to write separate letters to your husband and Edward, in return for those which I received from them by the last steamer. The shocking intelligence of the disaster on board the Princeton excited great sensation and sympathy here, and made me at first heartsick at the frailty of the tenure by which life and its most important concerns are held. I received, by the steamer of the 1st, a private letter from poor Mr. Upshur,[1] written by his own hand two or three days before his decease, and in better spirits than any he had ever written me.

The principal topic of conversation here for the last few days is General Tom Thumb. He has been twice sent for by the Queen and once by the Queen dowager, and his exhibition room is thronged with a row of carriages, blazing with coronets, as far as you can see. He is really a very curious specimen of humanity. It is to be hoped

[1] Mr. A. P. Upshur, Secretary of State succeeding Webster, was killed by the explosion of a gun on the man-of-war, Princeton.

that his parents, who are with him, will spare his strength; and give him a good education out of the golden harvest he is reaping for them. The forthcoming or rather just published number of the 'Quarterly Review' contains an able article in reply to Custine's famous book of letters from Russia. The article is by Lockhart, and the criticisms on Custine, though fair enough, are bitter in the extreme. There are one or two flings at America which might have been spared; and I wonder it did not occur to Lockhart (who in his private capacity is an amiable man) that most of what has been written about the United States is of the same quality as Custine's letters on Russia — a grain of truth in a bushel of exaggeration and falsehoods. The next number of the 'Edinburgh Review' is to contain an article on the French Revolution by Mr. Macaulay, who, all things considered, is, I think, the ablest writer of the day, and one of the most extraordinary men. His conversation is as remarkable as his writing, pouring out in a full tide, upon every subject that comes up, as if he had read everything that ever was written, and remembered everything he had read. He is also a very able speaker and made the other day in the House of Commons, one of the most masterly speeches that was made, in the debate on the state of Ireland; although it is objected to his speeches (there must always be an objection to everything) that they are too much like essays. If there is any foundation for this criticism, it arises mainly from his not speaking on the current business of the House; and reserving himself for subjects which admit this mode of treatment. His manner is far from wearing the appearance of over-preparation, being like his conversation fervid, prompt, and familiar. His company, you may suppose, is much sought; he said in my hearing last year that he had eleven invitations to dinner for one day. . . .

To the Honorable P. C. Brooks

LONDON, *May* 3, 1844

. . . The incidents of any one of the public days here would be quite curious, if set down at length; but it is out of the question to crowd into a hasty letter anything that would give an adequate idea of the reality. Take for instance the 25th April, observed by anticipation as the Queen's Birthday, the real day being a month later. The day happened to be very bright and clear — the sky absolutely without a cloud. At ten o'clock there was a military parade on the open ground between Saint James's Park (the most beautiful of the London parks) and the Horse Guards, one of the finest parade grounds that can be imagined. Four battalions of foot guards and a few companies of horse were under review. The Duke of Wellington, with the King of the Belgians on the right and Prince Albert on the left, supported by a large and brilliant staff, reviewed the troops. We had a pass into the lines and stood directly behind the Duke. His son, the Marquis of Douro, moved his horse on one side to make room for us. Three splendid military bands, consisting together of one hundred and seventy pieces, played the finest airs in a most superior manner. This lasted an hour.

At two o'clock the Queen held a Drawing-Room at St. James's Palace, fully attended by all the high officers of State, the Archbishops and Bishops, who on that day have precedence over the diplomatic body — but on no other — all the foreign ministers and their suites, and the nobility and gentry generally of both sexes, who have before been presented to the Queen; for no presentations take place on that day, except in a few exceptional cases. No mourning is allowed on this occasion. The Court, though in full mourning for Prince Albert's father, is in white. For this reason my wife and daughter, not being willing to lay aside their mourning for our poor Nanny, did not attend. The splendor of dress and jewelry on these occasions is probably beyond anything elsewhere to be seen. All official personages go in full uniform; and the ladies all wear trains of two or three yards in length. The men wear white small-clothes, silk stockings, and buckles in their shoes; the coats mostly covered with gold lace and those who are entitled to them blazing with orders of knighthood. The Bishops, on this occasion, and Cabinet ministers on all occasions enter the throne room first, and have a private audience of the Queen. . . .

The spectacle of the equipages abroad is, in its way, quite equal to that within doors. The parks, streets, windows, and house-tops are filled with people who come to look; and some hundreds of well-dressed people obtain tickets from the Lord Chamberlain's office to stand in the passages and see the company come in. The foreign ministers and those having the *entrée* have great facilities in getting away; but it is two hours after the reception is over before all the company get to their carriages. An hour or two passes, by way of breathing spell, and then the streets are alive with carriages driving to dinner. All the world dines out on the Queen's Birthday, except those who stay at home to receive the rest. The diplomatic corps dine with the Secretary of State for Foreign Affairs (Lord Aberdeen) to the number of twenty-five or thirty. These entertainments are most generous; everything in and out of season, in elegant variety, is served. Two toasts (and no speeches) are always given in French, one by the French Ambassador to the Queen: the other by Lord Aberdeen to the Sovereigns and Powers in alliance or friendship with Great Britain. After the dinner, the streets begin to ring again about half-past ten with the carriages going to the evening parties. . . .

To Mrs. Nathan Hale

LONDON, *July* 3, 1844

. . . While I write these lines, the funeral of Campbell the poet is going on in Westminster Abbey. I would gladly have attended it, but am always tied to my desk the last day or two before the sailing of a steamer. When I was in England before, I made a pilgrimage to the village of Sydenham, where he was living in an humble way, and spent the day with him. Since I have been here I have seen him but once, and then in public. He did not call upon me on my arrival, as my old friends generally did. I should not have waited for this from a person of his eminence, especially as the rule of convenience here is, that the newcomer makes the first call. But I soon found that he had withdrawn himself from all society, probably in consequence of the growth of that bad habit which too often finds its victims among men of genius. The only time I have seen him, since I have been here, was at the anniversary of the Literary Fund Society, at which he officiated as one of the Stewards, but on attempting to make a speech exhibited himself before the company in a most painful manner. But he is to be laid at the foot of Shakespeare's Monument; and if any where on earth, the ashes of a poet may rest in peace there. . . .

LONDON, *July* 18, 1844

. . . The Season, as it is called in London, is drawing to a close; but its dying efforts, like those of a speared whale, are among the most convulsive and energetic. We go to but few of the parties — especially I; for I find it beyond my strength to stand at a desk all day and in a crowded and heated room all night, and if a man can't stand he is lost; from which I suppose the proverbial mode of saying a thing is intolerable is taken. One of my brother diplomats says he has made a study of the mode of standing on one leg at a time; not absolutely drawing up the other under him like a heron, but throwing the whole weight of the body on each alternately. I believe the best way is, however, to stand bolt upright on both. . . .

Carlyle was not one of the Englishmen with whom Everett became intimate. He met the famous philosopher more than once, however, and naturally enough he met him, among

other places under the hospitable roof of Lady Harriet
Baring. Everett before meeting him never pretended to any
admiration of the great Scotchman. In this respect he was
unlike his brother-in-law, N. L. Frothingham, who had done
much to introduce Carlyle to American readers through a
brilliant critique of 'Sartor Resartus' which appeared in the
'Christian Examiner' for 1836. Everett could confess in his
journal for 1839, 'I have read nothing of Carlyle.' Nevertheless, we find an interesting and complacent entry in his
journal for August 30, 1838. Speaking of an address he had
made at the Phi Beta Kappa dinner he says: 'I compared
Carlyle's style to the composition of the *thunderbolt* which
consisted of twelve parts: three were the *twisted hail-storm*
and three *glittering fire:* three *watery cloud* and three *empty
wind.*

> Tris imbris torti radios, tris nubis aquosæ,
> Addiderant rutuli tris ignis et alitis Austri.'[1]

Did he think of this, we wonder, when he met the great man
at dinner?

May 7, 1844. In the evening, we had a small party at Mr. Coleman's to meet Mr. and Mrs. Carlyle and some other friends. I was
agreeably disappointed in Carlyle. I found him a plain, ordinary-
looking Scotsman resembling a ploughman in appearance more
than a philosopher. He spoke very highly of R. W. Emerson, but
disparagingly of the other writers on the 'Dial.' Apropos of Lynch
Law, he did not think so badly of Lynch. He was the product of
the demand for justice.

The following letter tells of another meeting — this time
at the Ashburtons' country seat. It seems to have been one
of those occasions when Mrs. Carlyle either was not invited
or found it pleasanter to stay at home.

To Mrs. Nathan Hale

LONDON, *August* 2, 1845

. . . Last Saturday I passed in the country at the seat of Mr.
Bingham Baring, the oldest son of Lord Ashburton. The Bible

[1] Virgil's *Æneid*, VIII, 430.

says that to him that hath shall be given. A certain Mr. Adair, having quarrelled with his heir, left Lord Ashburton, already one of the richest men in England, the whole of his property (about £180,000), and with it a pretty cottage on the skirt of a noble park near Croyden. He, Lord Ashburton, gave the estate to his oldest son, and here I passed Saturday and Sunday with him. We had Mr. Carlyle of the party, who appears to be a great favorite with Lady Harriet, Mr. Baring's wife. I have seen but little of Carlyle. He is somewhat plain, not to say rustic in appearance, and speaks with a broad Scotch accent. He talks very much as he writes; and as he is voluble and ready with his opinions on all subjects, it is quite amusing to hear him. His views, I think, are rather paradoxical and not very clearly fixed in his own mind. There is a strong tendency to radicalism, but I doubt if it is accompanied with any specific notions of reform. He thinks very highly of Mr. Emerson, but did not appear to be an admirer of any other of the American Transcendentalists. His last literary occupation has been the preparation of an edition of all the letters, speeches, and proclamations of Oliver Cromwell which are extant, with an introduction and notes. It is nearly ready to appear, and will, I imagine, be a curious work. He thinks Cromwell the greatest man who ever lived. He appeared to entertain a very high opinion of General Jackson, whom he called 'Old Hickory': and he does not think very unfavorably of Lynch Law, regarding it as a necessary substitute, among a frontier population, for the regular administration of justice. 'Lynch,' he said, 'was far from being the worst of magistrates. As I told you, we go down at noon to the Archbishop of York's, near Oxford. There is a congress of Seniors there — Mr. Grenville and Mr. Rogers, Miss Coutts and Mrs. Murchison (wife of the geologist and one of our intimate friends) are of the party; but we shall only be able to stay two days.

By this time, however, Mr. Everett's term of service was nearing its end. Great changes had occurred at home. The Tyler Administration became thoroughly discredited before it finally came to a close. Mr. Webster retired from the Cabinet in May, 1843. The Whig Party was now badly disorganized. When the time drew near for the nomination of Presidential candidates, Everett's name was freely suggested for the second place on the ticket. Winthrop wrote him urgently on the subject. But his time had not yet come, and he expressed the wish that he should not be considered.

Governor Davis seemed, he declared, 'to have prior claim. I could not well consent to come in competition with him for a place for which he has been so distinctly designated by our political friends in Massachusetts. It is not affected modesty which leads me to say that I do not possess so extensive a popularity as he does, particularly since his late tour in the West. . . . Finally, I think there is rather an inconvenience in a foreign minister being a candidate at home. . . . If the option were given me of being elected to that place, in the present state of affairs, or remaining abroad, I should decide for the latter, for various considerations, most of which will occur to you. . . . These, in brief, are the views I take of the subject, all stated in confidence and *bona fide* to you; and they lead me to hope that I shall not be thought of as a candidate.'

The decision was a wise one. The Whig candidates put in nomination were Henry Clay and Theodore Freling-huysen, and they went down in defeat before Polk and Dallas. In March, 1845, James K. Polk took up his residence in the White House, with James Buchanan as his Secretary of State. That meant the end of Mr. Everett's diplomatic career. His days in England were numbered. And yet he felt a curious hesitancy about asking for his recall. Apparently he thought that there was a bare possibility of his being continued in office, and he had a great desire to carry through certain important negotiations that he had begun. The following letter to Mr. Winthrop tells of his dilemma, and also refers to a diplomatic success that he had secured in connection with certain rights that had been obtained for our fishermen in the Bay of Fundy:

LONDON, *March* 29, 1845

. . . I have been much embarrassed as to what I ought to do about asking for my recall. The clear opinion of yourself, Evans, and General Scott that I ought to, has great weight with me. The opinion of all my other friends, which has reached me, is the other way. My mind being thus brought to an equilibrium, as far as the judgment of my friends is concerned, I have decided (but with great hesitation) not to ask my recall. I expect, however, to receive it, and that without delay — very likely my successor is named. When I return, I will mention one reason for my decision, which is of too confidential a nature to be put on paper. Another is that if by not asking my recall I can prolong my stay here for even a few weeks, it is my duty to do so, in order to bring some long-standing claims to a favorable result.

One matter of this kind I have within a few days succeeded in settling; that is, in procuring for our fishermen a right to fish within the Bay of Fundy. You may remember having sent some documents to Washington pertaining to a case of seizure for being found within the limits of that bay. Lord Aberdeen and Lord Stanley have at last agreed to yield it, not as a matter of right, but as an amicable concession to the United States. They do this against the opinion of the Crown lawyers. . . . It is a matter of very considerable interest to our fishermen.

In spite, however, of not formally resigning his office, Mr. Everett at once entered into a correspondence with the new Secretary of State requesting to be informed of the President's wishes in the matter. When Washington remained characteristically silent, and no information on the subject was vouchsafed him, he wrote again, saying that if a successor were to be appointed he would like to be informed of the matter since, in that case, he should wish to leave London not later than September 1st, as the lease of his house, which also served as the office of the Legation, expired on September 4th.

To Mrs. Nathan Hale

LONDON, *April* 10, 1845

. . . With respect to my own movements I am still without information from headquarters, which indeed there is hardly time to expect. It seems to be understood that my place was offered to Mr. Calhoun, from which it may be inferred that the President has determined, at all events, to recall me. If this is the case, I trust he will do it, so as to let me return before the season is too far advanced for a pleasant and safe voyage. Many friends besides yourself write to me about the Presidency of the College, but no one by authority. I think it doubtful whether the place would be offered to me, even if it were known that I would accept; and if it is awkward to deny before you are asked, it is still more so to accept when you are not likely to be. If Judge Story is about, as you say, to retire from the bench, unless his health is the cause, which I trust is not the case, I should think it quite likely he would take the Presidency. His present connection with the Law School and the Corporation, his long residence at Cambridge, and intimate acquaintance with College affairs, point directly to this, and I do not see how a better choice could be made.

To Mr. Nathan Hale

LONDON, *June* 2, 1845

. . . I get nothing from the Government, as to my own return, although they give me in other ways pretty significant indications of their design to recall me. There is no truth in the reports that I have asked my recall or expressed a wish to come home. I have written to the Secretary of State that if the President proposed to recall me, I wished my successor to be here by August at farthest. Unless I hear from him that the President wishes me to stay, I shall return in September, whether my successor is here or not.

Mr. Powers's statue of the Slave excites much sensation. Although most of the newspaper critics accord it but qualified and reluctant praise, its success is most triumphant. Everybody from the Prince down has been to see it, and the most enthusiastic, in some cases the most extravagant, compliments are continually paid to the artist. Lord Francis Egerton, the proprietor of the famous Stafford Gallery of pictures, told me he had rather have it than all the works of Canova, and has just sent Powers an order through me, for anything he chooses to execute. There was a short notice of it in the 'Times' of the 28th, in which it was said that Powers studied under Thorwaldsen. I corrected this in an article in the 'Times' the next day, in which I did an act of justice to the other American sculptors. As the two articles together will not fill the eighth of a column, I should like to have you copy them into the 'Advertiser.' . . .

In the meantime, efforts had been made both in England and at home to have him continued at his post. For himself he devoutly hoped for such an outcome, and yet he could do nothing to promote so natural a desire.

May 30, 1844. Mr. Ryan, the Illinois Commissioner, called upon me to say that in consequence of the rumors from America that I was to be removed, a number of gentlemen without distinction of party (Americans) were desirous of taking some steps, by way of expressing their opinion of the importance of my being here, to prevent it. He asks me if I had any objection. I told him it was a thing I felt it improper to give an opinion about one way or the other; that I certainly had no objection to it; that the only thing I asked was that they would take care to have it distinctly understood that the measure was not prompted by me.

We had at dinner, Mr. and Mrs. Paris, Sir H. and Lady Duckinfield, Mr. and Mrs. Mansfield, Mrs. Macready, Mr. Rogers. General Tom Thumb came and walked round the dinner table (upon it) to general satisfaction.

At length in July, official word arrived saying that Louis McLane had been appointed to succeed him, and would reach London early in August, the request at the same time being made that Mr. Everett would continue to discharge the duties of the Mission pending the arrival of his successor. The announcement relieved his mind, and left him free to make arrangements for returning home. He was not to do so, however, without some interesting events which served to show the affection and respect in which he was held.

To Mrs. Nathan Hale

LONDON, *June* 18, 1845

... I regret that I have not time to write you more full and entertaining accounts of what is passing around us. But though Mr. Calhoun's paper, the 'Charleston Mercury,' says 'Mr. Everett is idling away his time,' I assure you there is not a clerk in a counting-room that works harder than I do at the public business. Then the calls of society are *exigeant*, though we turn a deaf ear to many of them; but business and society together reduce my friendly correspondence almost to nothing. These, however, and all the other troubles connected with my station will no doubt soon be over. Yesterday was a very busy day. Just as I was sitting down to my own breakfast, I received a note from Lord Morpeth, my near neighbor, asking me to come and breakfast with him, in company with Judge Kent, of New York. Although excessively inconvenient to me to do so, I could not well refuse. Our little party consisted of Lady Mary Howard (Lord Morpeth's youngest sister), Baron Parke, one of the Judges, and Mr. D. Dundas, a lawyer and member of Parliament of eminence, and the hour went off very pleasantly. In the afternoon we went to Ealing Park to a *déjeuner*, nominally at four, but not served till half-past five. This is one of the most charming villas in the neighborhood of London, belonging to Mr. Lawrence, an eminent surgeon. Mrs. Lawrence is a very distinguished amateur florist. For the first hour and a half the weather was perfect, and the company passed the time on the lawn and in the conservatories. Then a thunder-shower set all scampering. We were already *à l'abri* in the house. Dined at the Archbishop of York's at seven. He is eighty-eight in October; Mr. Granville, ninety in December, sat by his side, and Lord Harrowby, eighty-three in December, by his; but for a little deafness they are all in full possession of their faculties. After dinner we went to two evening parties. That I call a busy day. But we were home by midnight. A quarter of an hour makes a very good visit. This evening there is a dinner and five parties, but how much of it we do remains to be seen. To-morrow I go to Cambridge to attend the meeting of the British Association, where I shall stay four or five days, as the guest of the Master of Trinity College. You will think perhaps that I am going, at the last, to justify the charge of idling: and if I were really to take the rest of my time in visiting and sight-seeing throughout the country, my conscience would not — provided I left no specific duty unperformed — reproach me. I have confined myself hitherto more than any of my colleagues on the Continent, by a great deal. Mr. Wheaton passes a good quarter of his time in Paris.

Our spring was cold and backward till about ten days since. Summer has latterly advanced with great rapidity; and the face of the country is lovely. The patches of roses and rhododendrons at Mrs. Lawrence's yesterday were in perfection; the latter perhaps a little passing off. I have often wondered, considering that the rhododendron is indigenous in the vicinity of Boston, that we see so little of it in our country seats. The same may be said of our other beautiful flowering shrubs, kalmas, magnolia glauca, and azalea.

To Mr. Nathan Hale

LONDON, *July* 3, 1845

... You will easily believe that I am well pleased to be delivered from the state of uncertainty in which I have been kept so long, not as to the fact that I should be recalled (for of that I never felt any doubt), but as to the time when I should be released, and I may add the character of my successor. What Mr. McLane's opinions as to the prominent questions of the day may be, I know nothing. The Administration, I suppose, regard him as their partisan, or he would not be sent here in my place. But he is a man of education and sense; moderate in his character, and gentlemanly in his manners. He is well recollected from his former mission, and greatly liked. For my personal reputation, I might have gained by having a successor of a different cast. But the interests at stake are too important and I hope I am too much of a patriot to admit such a reflection. I really know no selection which the President could have made so judicious.

I send you a Cambridge newspaper which will give you an account of a portion of the doings of the British Association for the Promotion of Science. You can, if you think proper, insert my speech in the 'Advertiser.' If you do so, please make the division into paragraphs, which I have indicated by the usual mark ¶. My speech was really, which I state it to be, without the slightest premeditation. I took the darkest corner on the platform, but Mr. Murchison dragged me forward, and insisted I should move the vote of thanks to Sir John Herschell. I told him if he would let me off that evening, give me time to attend the sections a day or two (I was then but a couple of hours in town), and work my way a little into the spirit of the meeting, I would, some subsequent evening, address the Association and do my best. But he insisted on my doing it then. And what little I had to say was well received; as complimentary speeches are very apt to be at public meetings. A few of the ideas had been expressed by me three years before at Cambridge, but before a small, and, with the exception of half a dozen individuals, entirely different audience. Their repetition was hardly to be avoided. But I have said a great deal more about it than it is worth. Do as you please about republishing it.

It might appear that there was ground for the charge that Everett had been rather too friendly to England to make a wholly successful representative of his country. But such was not the case. He admired England: he made a host of friends while in London: and yet he never was deceived in regard to the traditional diplomatic policy of England. He did not agree with Sir Henry Wotton's witticism that it was an Ambassador's duty 'to lie abroad for his country.' He was always courteous; always honest and straightforward; and he knew how to be firm. The following extract from a letter addressed several years later to a friend shows clearly that he was no such worshipper of the English as not to detect failings and weaknesses on England's part.

To W. B. Reed

BOSTON, *February* 20, 1859

... I congratulate you cordially on the success of your negotiations. I was confirmed in my opinion that your conduct had been wise and discreet, as well as successful, by the violence with which it was censured in the London Press. John Bull is very amia^ble in private life, and many of my best friends inhabit the 'fast anchored Isle'; but in his foreign politics he is selfish and grasping; and, where he dares, insolent. I saw him under favorable circumstances, as represented by Lord Aberdeen, who was a conciliatory and good-tempered man. He would at times put his name, in the press of business, to notes written by some of the underlings. I could detect the changed manner at a glance, and I made it a rule to reply precisely in the tone in which I was addressed. We got on extremely well together. ...

The rumors that Mr. Everett would probably be recalled began to be spread abroad in mid-winter. They led to an invitation from the Queen to visit Windsor, and the interesting experience is described as usual to Mr. Brooks.

WINDSOR CASTLE, EDWARD III's TOWER, *February* 2, 1845

Late in the evening of the 31st January I received a note from Lord Aberdeen from Windsor, saying that the Queen desired us (wife, daughter, and myself) to come to the Castle the following day and stay till Monday. I had reason to know and to regret that Lord Aberdeen was at Windsor, for I had got him, a fortnight before, to appoint a day to dine with me, and asked a party of the Cabinet and diplomatic corps to meet him; and two or three days before that which we had fixed on the Queen sent for him to Windsor. The invitations of the Sovereign are always considered as paramount to others. Subjects regard them as commands; and foreign ministers excuse themselves from any previous engagement. This we were obliged to do at the French Ambassador's, where we were engaged for yesterday to a great diplomatic dinner. It is usual, however, for the Queen to give some little notice beforehand, in order not unnecessarily to interfere with other engagements. This, however, was not done on this occasion; the reason being, I imagine, that Lord Aberdeen had intimated to her that it was not unlikely we should return home before the Court comes to Windsor next summer, and as it removes to London to-morrow, there was no time for delay. Be this as it may, it was not particularly convenient to me to leave home just before the sailing of the packet.

We reached Slough, the nearest station to Windsor, a little before five, and were soon taken by post-horses to the Castle. One arrives there just as you would at any great house in the country, or rather with still less of ceremony, for you are more completely master of your own apartments and time. The porter, on your being announced at the outer gate, directs you to which tower to drive. Ours is commonly called the Devil's Tower, but its politer name is Edward III's. We have a complete suite of rooms to ourselves, consisting of a large drawing-room, two bedrooms, and a separate dressing-room for me. Each room has a fire kept up all day, and is furnished with writing apparatus, which may be considered as an almost invariable appendage of an English room of whatever description. The dinner hour being quite late, we were offered tea, which is brought up to your own room. We bring a manservant and maid with us. The Castle is built round the four sides of a very large square; and the communication between its various parts is effected by a corridor which passes round two sides — on the first floor — and which is at the same time a gallery of pictures. This is a modern improvement and a very great convenience. I believe I described it in my letter from Windsor three years ago.

At a little after eight, the company began to assemble in the green drawing-room for dinner. We found the party consisted of the Duke and Duchess of Buccleugh, Lord and Lady Lincoln (he is the son of the Duke of Newcastle and a member of the Cabinet, she a daughter of the Duke of Hamilton), Sir Robert Peel, and Lord Aberdeen. This, with the Royal family and household, made sixteen at the table. (The ladies say twenty-two.) After the company was assembled in the drawing-room, the Queen, the Prince and Duchess of Kent came in; the Queen spoke to and shook hands with the ladies, the Prince the same to the gentlemen; the band then struck up 'God Save the Queen,' and then all move forward to the dining-room. The gentlemen are previously told what ladies they are to take in. This is done from a list made out by the Queen and given to the Master of the Household. The Prince leads the way, of course, with the Queen. The Duke of Buccleugh followed with the Duchess of Kent; I with the Duchess of Buccleugh; Lord Lincoln with wife; Lord Aberdeen with Lady Lincoln; one of the gentlemen of the household with your granddaughter, etc. After arriving in the dining-room, I was directed to leave the Duchess of Buccleugh (who sat on the Prince's left hand), and to sit myself on the Queen's right hand, which is the place I occupied on my former visit. The Prince always sits on the Queen's left hand. I had Lady Gainsborough on my right hand, one of the Ladies of the Bed-chamber and a very beautiful person. The table service was silver gilt, of great richness and elegance. Nothing particular in the serv-ing of the dinner; except that a fine band of music in the adjoining room was playing most of the time.

The Queen divided her conversation between the Prince and my-self about equally, conversing with ease on usual topics. It is not strictly proper to address any remark to a Royal personage and still less to ask a question. I have, however, found the Queen dis-posed to converse on the usual footing, and evidently not dis-pleased to break the stiffness of etiquette on this point. She talked to me about our dinner party of the day before; about our travels in Scotland and her own; about her recent visits to Stowe and Strathfield Saye; about the beautiful improvements in the manu-facture of pianos contrived by young Mr. Coleman, for whom I had procured an opportunity of exhibiting it at Windsor; about Tom Thumb, who had evidently amused her very much; about Catlin's prints of Indian life and manners and the Indians who were in England last summer; and about the King of the French and his visit to Windsor last October. You will easily see from this range of topics that there is no undue stiffness or reserve on her part. What I have mentioned are only a portion of the subjects to which she alluded.

I should think we were about an hour and twenty minutes at table. The Queen and ladies then retired and the Prince took the Queen's seat and conversed principally about shooting, across the table, with Sir Robert Peel. He, however, addressed several re-marks to me. In the course of the dinner he leaned toward me, and told across the Queen a laughable anecdote of a surgeon in the suite of Louis-Philippe, at which both the Queen and the Prince laughed heartily. In about a quarter of an hour the gentlemen followed the ladies, and coffee was served. When this was over, the Queen went round and addressed a few words to the gentlemen to whom she had not spoken before. In about half an hour she led the way to another drawing-room, where a game of whist is usually played in the even-ing. It had now, however, got to be nearly eleven, which is always the hour of retiring; and after several fine pieces from the band, the Queen retired, and this was the signal for breaking up the party.

This morning (Sunday) the usual morning prayers were dispensed with, which on week-days are at nine o'clock in the domestic chapel. At ten breakfast is served in the Oak Chamber. The Queen and Prince never breakfast with their visitors. At twelve we all assembled in the corridor, where in a few moments the Queen,

Prince, and Duchess of Kent appeared, and all proceeded to the Chapel. Wife and I with six or eight of the principal guests sat in the Queen's pew; nothing particular in the service; prayers were read by Mr. Courtenay (son of Lord Devon), the Queen's chaplain, and sermon preached by Lord Wriothesley Russell. Luncheon at two in the Oak Chamber; but not attended by the Queen and Prince. At half-past two, the Queen and Prince came into the corridor with the little Prince of Wales, a child of about three years old, and the company was invited from the Oak-room to meet them. The ladies went first; the little man shook hands with them all round, and said he wanted to see some more ladies. When I came, the Queen whispered to him to come and shake hands with me, which he did very prettily. He is a delicate-looking child, but said to be healthy and quite bright. The other children are at Brighton, where the Queen herself is going in a few days. The Queen now invited the party to go and see a very large picture of the meeting of herself and family with the King of the French and his party, which is painting for Versailles; the artist is Winterhalter, who has painted the Queen many times, and it is thought with greater success than any other artist. It will be a painting of considerable effect and no doubt hereafter of some historical interest. After this, the Queen retired, and the company dispersed.

I walked out with Colonel Wylde, one of the Prince's household, and passed a good hour and a half in making the circuit of the park, the Queen's kennel, where her pets are kept, the farm and dairy. On the walk I encountered the Duke of Buccleugh and his oldest son, Lord Dalkeith, a boy of thirteen whom they have just put at Eton. He had been there but two days, but the father could not help going down to the school to church, and getting the boy up to the Palace, to pass the day with his mother, to say nothing of the father. There is a good deal of human nature in man, duke or duchess though he may be! Turned and walked with the Duke, or rather he with me, for I was in search of wife and daughter, who had gone out with one of the ladies. After enjoying a most beautiful sunset — clear, bright, cold weather for England — we came in. Saw the Queen and the Prince at a distance taking their walk wholly alone. It is the Queen's custom on Sundays to walk on the terrace of the Castle, on which occasion the public are admitted; but for some cause or other she did not do it to-day.

Dinner to-day went off much as yesterday, except that Sir R. Peel was not of the party and Mr. Courtenay, the chaplain, was. I took in the Duchess of Buccleugh, but sat next to the Duchess of Kent and opposite the Queen. Wife sat next to Lord Aberdeen. The Duchess of Kent addressed me in German, and I had a great

deal of conversation with her on several interesting topics. Among
other things I asked her at what age the Queen first came to
the knowledge that she probably was to succeed to the throne.
She said, 'Eleven'; that she always took great pains to prevent
her learning it. After the (then) Princess had become aware
of her prospects, it was always a 'painful' subject of conversation
to her. The Bishop of Peterboro, however, who was the governor
of the Princess Victoria, told me, two years ago, that she became
aware of her prospect of succeeding to the throne when she was
but eight. After the ladies had retired, the Prince talked across the
table to me about the Order of Cincinnatus, the decimal currency,
and some other American topics. The first subject was suggested
by an eagle on a French bon-bon which he had noticed in a plate
before him: he said it looked like the badge of the Order of Cincinnatus, which he had seen in the possession of a German officer who
held a commission in our Revolutionary army. He tossed the bon-
bon over to me, which, with His Royal Highness's permission, I
pocketed for Willy.

After we joined the ladies in the first drawing-room, I had a long
conversation with the Prince about our recent elections and American field sports. He had purchased last year a brace of living can-
vas ducks, which, however, soon died. He was much amused with
my account of the habits of that animal. After coffee had been
served, we followed the ladies to the next room, in which the company sat down to two round tables. We were at the Queen's, where
several quiet games — not cards — were played. Wife and the
Duchess of Kent had a board to themselves, but I did not understand the nature of the game. The Prince and I played a couple of
games, also new to me, about halfway between chequers and chess.
The Queen gave out ivory letters to put together into words. This
lasted about three-quarters of an hour, and then all broke up: the
Queen shaking hands with the principal ladies and the Prince with
the gentlemen. . . .

And now, while he was busy making preparations to sail
for home, a piece of intelligence came which was to influence
his future career in a very decided way. Josiah Quincy, after
serving for sixteen years as President of Harvard University,
sent in his resignation to take effect in August.

The resignation was accepted, and in seeking for a successor the attention of the Governing Boards, and indeed
of the public generally, was directed almost at once to Mr.

Everett. He appeared the logical candidate. He was coming home, after serving with signal distinction at the most important diplomatic post in the gift of the Government, and there was no Harvard graduate anywhere in sight who appeared to combine so many qualifications for the office. Old friends and staunch supporters wrote him on the subject. Mr. Everett, as we shall see a little later, wrote despondingly to Peter C. Brooks about the prospect, expressing his disinclination to accept the position. But he put the matter as much as possible out of his mind, determined to finish well one piece of work before he concerned himself about taking up another.

He closed his diplomatic efforts by securing, after persistent and delicate negotiations, the right of our fishermen to fish in the Bay of Fundy, which was a very substantial and valuable concession. Ten years later he could refer to this as an achievement which entitled him to appreciable credit. Writing to a friend in 1855, he could say:

> With reference to my diplomatic labors ... the most important result obtained by me in London was the opening of the Bay of Fundy to our fishermen. This has been pronounced by a writer well acquainted with the subject 'the only advantage ever gained by our diplomacy in reference to the fisheries.' I was in a fair way to have carried our point in reference to all the other outer bays. Sir Robert Peel's Ministry had determined to make the concession. Just as they communicated that purpose to the Colonial authorities, I was recalled.

The last days in London were burdensome and sad. He took his successor to Lord Aberdeen's office and introduced him, and the two went together to Buckingham Palace. The saying good-bye to friends was hard. He drove to the Miss Berry's, 'where there was a very painful leave-taking.'

To Lord Aberdeen and Sir Robert Peel he sent 'a dozen each of old wine and requested in return a print of each of them.' Peel said that he accepted with great pleasure the proposal; that he should value the wine so much that he feared he would never want to drink it, and that he would 'send a copy of the best print of himself that had been en-

graved.' The Duke of Wellington sent his portrait. Macaulay was at work when he went to see him, but Everett 'did
not ask on what.' The great man said that this was 'his only
time to do a little study, but he could not go into the country
because he wanted books.'

Perhaps the saddest and tenderest message of farewell was
one that he received from old Mr. Rogers. One can read
between the lines a record of many kindnesses and much
courtesy and consideration on the part of Everett to the
octogenarian.

July 31, 1845

My dear Mr. Everett,

What can I say to you, what can I do, in return for all your
kindness? I can only thank you from the bottom of my heart.
Yesterday was my eighty-second birthday, and when we part, I
cannot expect that we shall meet again on this side of the grave.
But so long as I live, I shall pray for the happiness of you and all
who belong to you.

I am very, very sorry that I cannot breakfast with you at the
Deanery on Saturday.

Entirely yours
Samuel Rogers

On Monday, August 25th, the Everetts left London for
Liverpool where they had a look at the new Cunard steamship Britannia, on which passage had been taken. They then
went out to pass a few days — their last English visit — with
the Davenports at 'Capisthorne.' A final batch of letters was
received from home, among them an invitation to attend a
public dinner to be given in his honor by Boston friends on
arrival, and what was of 'vastly greater consequence a semi-
official offer from Chief Justice Shaw of the Presidency of the
University at Cambridge,' and he 'foresaw much anxiety on
that subject.'

They sailed on Thursday, September 4th, 'a crowd of
friends accompanying the wayfarers' to the dock. The voyage was uneventful. About sunrise on the morning of the
19th they passed Cape Ann and by nine-thirty steamed into
Boston Harbor. Edward Everett Hale was on the dock

waiting for him with carriages, and he got up to the house by eleven. At five-thirty he went to Faneuil Hall for the Horticultural Festival, where he was toasted by Mr. Webster. He had been absent from home for five years and three months — four of these years having been spent in hard and anxious work as Minister at the Court of Saint James'.

The Britannia on her return voyage carried these two letters to friends in England. The one to Lord Aberdeen is a model of friendly courtesy with which is mixed a drop of wit: the other was a heartbeat of affectionate greeting from the stately orator whom his contemporaries never ceased to consider cold.

BOSTON, *September 29, 1845*

MY DEAR LORD ABERDEEN,

I think you will not be displeased at receiving a few lines from me to let you know that we are safely arrived home. I remember a character in some modern farce pays his friend's tailor's bill with readiness because when first handed to him he thought it a challenge. I promise myself you will open a note from me with some satisfaction now that you are sure it is not about 'Rough Rice' nor the 'Jones' and quite free from 'distinguished consideration.'

We reached Boston on the 19th after a pretty rough and uncomfortable voyage, which (as landsmen are apt to) we thought at times dangerous. Our good ship, the Britannia, weathered two stout gales, with a gallantry beseeming her name.

We have not yet had time to hear of your return from Germany. It took place, I doubt not, at the appointed time with the good fortune or rather the kind Providence habitually attendant on the Queen. I fancy you at this time enjoying a few days of seclusion and repose at the North, and following the otter hounds up to your elbows in some Highland stream. I hope there is no proclivity in a Secretary of State for Foreign Affairs to be fishing in troubled waters.

I had the pleasure of Dr. Holland's company at dinner yesterday. He has been to Washington and seen the President and other good folks. He will be able to tell you what everybody in the United States whom you know is doing; although if he can give you that information about me, he can do more than I can just now myself. I send you a scrap from a newspaper which will show you one thing that I am not doing; i.e., making a dinner speech about matters and things in general. . . .

BOSTON, *September* 30, 1845

DEAR MR. ROGERS,

I will not allow the vessel which brought us to America to return to England without a line to let you know that we have arrived in safety; and that, even in the midst of the excitement and tumult of reaching home, we all retain the most affectionate remembrance of the second home which through the kindness of our friends we had gained in the Land of our Fathers. It is true that with the pleasing remembrance of the happy hours passed in their society is mingled the sadness of feeling we may never enjoy it again and self-reproach that we did not more assiduously cultivate it. I am now discontented with myself that I left you any peace. I assure you it was not insensibility to the worth of the moments I passed in your society, but real diffidence and desire not to be obtrusive. Will you not make me some little *dédommagement* by now giving me a few moments of your time? Let me see your exquisitely neat handwriting telling me you have not entirely forgotten us; and believe me that if it is any satisfaction to a man to know that he is remembered with affection and gratitude in another hemisphere, there is no one entitled to a greater share of it than yourself.

X

PRESIDENT OF HARVARD

MR. EVERETT'S natural joy at getting home was nearly all dispelled by the puzzling question which now presented itself directly in regard to Harvard College. He knew, of course, what to expect, because of the letters that had reached him abroad, but he was hardly prepared for such instant action as took place. He was left no time at all to settle down and look about him. He landed on a Friday, and the very next day, Saturday, September 20th, he 'received a letter from Mr. Eliot, the Treasurer of the College, transmitting one signed by all the members of the Corporation, including Judge Story, requesting him to accept the Presidency and promising unanimous support in the office.'

At the same time another letter came, signed by a group of leading citizens of Boston, saying that his friends and admirers wished to give him a public dinner in recognition of his signal services abroad in representing the country so ably and acceptably and with such distinction. After considerable hesitation, he declined the proposition for a public reception and dinner, and as for the Harvard matter he asked that he might have 'time to consider.'

That he should be wanted for President of the College was natural enough. He was conspicuously a scholar — perhaps better known both at home and abroad for brilliant intellectual attainments than any other living Harvard graduate, if not any other American. Moreover, many years before, and on more than one occasion, he had been suggested for the high and honorable post. As far back as 1814, he was given to understand, 'from a first-rate source,' probably by President Kirkland, when he accepted the Eliot Professorship of Greek, that he was looked on as 'heir-apparent.' In 1828, before the election of Josiah Quincy, he was spoken of to the Corporation, as 'a man made to your hands.' On that occasion, Dr. Bowditch had replied, 'That may do twenty years hence: but it will not do now. The eagle must take his flight into the skies.' With the flight now taken, and nearly a score of years gone by, there was every reason for the selection to be made.

But if it was natural and inevitable almost for Everett to be wanted, it was likewise natural for him to shrink from the post. He had never desired it. And his reason for not wanting it was that he shrank from the immense amount of detail connected with the office, and also that he had a positive dislike for its disciplinary features. In 1828, during his term in Congress, when he might perhaps have been elected, he withdrew his name as a candidate partly because his brother Alexander was also being considered and desired the position, but in part also because he discerned clearly the nature of the task. When his friend George Bancroft expostulated with him for withdrawing from the race, he gave him to understand in no uncertain terms what his feelings were. 'No love of letters or desire of promoting their cultivation or influence,' he wrote, 'could carry any man into the Presidency of the College. The office would give him no leisure and no liberty. A man would be in a hornet's nest. Having contemplated the subject in every possible light, I have not been able to reconcile myself to the office.' At the same time he wrote even more strongly to another friend: 'I assure you that my share in the government of the College as a Professor often gave me more anxiety than I ever encountered as a member of Congress. In the latter capacity I have never lost a quarter of an hour's sleep. In the former I have had my digestion destroyed for a week together by intense anxiety. I am therefore inclined against the Presidency of the College. The academic life presents fewer attractions to a man of letters than you probably think. President Kirkland's time was frittered away, his spirits exhausted, and his faculties scattered by a procession of petty cares and business details, which ended in breaking up the finest constitution ever given to man.'

If those were his feelings at the age of thirty-four while a member of Congress, it was natural to find them still more deeply planted when he was fifty-two, and fresh from enjoying a period of unprecedented popularity at the English Court. After all, Harvard College was hardly more than a high school in 1846, and very different in all respects from what it is to-day.

As he was preparing to leave London, and was in the throes of packing up, he had written Mr. Brooks on the subject, and had outlined the situation fully and with great frankness. The letter, particularly in the light of events that were afterwards to develop, is worth printing in full.

LONDON, *July* 18, 1845

Private and confidential

You allude to the subject of the Presidency of Cambridge, which continues also to be mentioned by other friends. I am desirous of keeping my mind open on this important matter, till I can, on my return, thoroughly consider it, in conference with those — particularly yourself — whose counsel I need. When it was first mentioned to me, I did not — as I suppose you inferred from my letter to John Gray — incline much to undertake the office. I afterwards received a letter from Mr. Ticknor, which removed some of the grounds of hesitation, by leading me to think that it was wished by himself and others, having great influence in the Corporation, that I should take the place; which I did not before suppose was the case. I wrote to Mr. Ticknor under the influence of these feelings the letter which he showed you, and which I suppose led you to think I had come to a more favorable leaning. On farther consideration my misgivings return. I think I see a theological storm brewing, more violent than that which arose forty years ago when Dr. Ware was chosen Professor of Divinity. Mr. Ticknor himself writes me that they want me to defend the College against the united attacks of the Orthodox and the radicals. If I am to put myself at the head of a battle of this kind — and I really think that whoever is President he will have to do it — farewell for the rest of my life to anything like peace. Controversy of all kinds — religious or political — I have ever disliked; the older I grow the less

I like it; and my wish now is to devote myself to the education and care of my family and literary pursuits for the rest of my days. I am sensible that I ought to do something toward the support of my family, and it would be very painful to continue for any length of time to subsist wholly on your liberality. But I am quite confident of being able, by the use of my pen, to place myself in that respect, and in a very short time, in as eligible a situation as if I took the office in question, which in point of income is far from brilliant.

I know college life well. The reality is very different from the outside. So far from being an eligible retreat for a man of literary tastes, it is a laborious and, what I think more of, a very anxious place. Mr. Quincy, in his published speech, gives you an idea of it. No parent who has children of his own needs be told what it must be to be the head of a family of two hundred boys, all at the most troublesome and anxious age. You cannot deal with them as you do with men. It is in the power of a thoughtless youth — his head perhaps inflamed with an extra glass of wine — to do deeds that plunge the whole institution into disorder. I saw but a few weeks ago, and while I was thinking most favorable of this proposal, that a row of buildings, including that in which the beautiful panorama of Athens was preserved (bought at my instance by General Lyman), had been set on fire by an incendiary. Cambridge incendiaries, in my day, were generally students. Such an occurrence, were I President, would make me sick for a week. Still, however, I will, as far as possible, keep myself free and undecided, till I am able to talk with you face to face.

It is quite impossible to say whether such feelings as were given expression to in this letter were weakened or intensified after getting home. The probability is that for a time, at least, he was given no chance for careful thought. There was a great succession of visitors at first, constantly calling; 'among others his excellent friend from London, Dr. Holland, who dropped in upon him almost from the clouds.' He had been travelling in the country for about a month, having 'covered some three thousand miles without accident,' and was preparing to sail for home in a few days. Everett took him to the First Church, 'where Dr. Frothingham preached an excellent sermon on "The well is deep," on which the famous Englishman bestowed the highest praise both as to manner and matter.' He was to give a dinner in Dr. Holland's honor the same evening, and it was somewhat disconcerting on coming home from church to find his servant drunk. The man 'had found his way into Mr. Brooks's wine cellar and abstracted ten or a dozen bottles of the best wine, with which he had regaled himself and a comrade.' But notwithstanding the unpleasant auspices, the dinner went off very well, 'the menservants of Dr. Frothingham and Mr. Hale assisting.'

But neither festivities nor functions could drive from his mind the question of the College. Something told him to decline the post. Most of his friends, however, urged him strongly to accept. Webster called to see him, and said he thought there was a destiny in affairs, and that it probably was his destiny to be President of the University, but at the same time warning him against the mass of details. Webster recommended, also, that if he did accept the post he should plan to give lectures in the Law School on International Law. This thought had occurred to Everett himself, and the more he dwelt upon it, the more he liked it. He began to think that with the Presidency he might come to unite a Professorship of Public Law in the Law School. But his brother-in-law, Nathan Hale, advised him strongly against the entire project, saying that the Presidency would occupy all his time and thoughts with petty cares and details of business and vexations of discipline. The Law Professorship might, he thought, give the office 'efficiency and dignity,' but without that he could not act 'largely and reputably in the community.'

The many, however, carried the day at last against the few. Everett was swept along against his will. He could find no good grounds for refusing the position; and five days after listening to the vehement warning of Mr. Hale, he sent for Mr. Eliot, the Treasurer, and informed him that he was willing to accept the offer of the Corporation. He added, however, that with a view to strengthen his position in the College, and to have an occupation not connected with the discipline of the institution, he was disposed to deliver a course of lectures in the Law School on the Public Law. This seemed to appeal strongly to Mr. Eliot, who evinced surprise, however, that nothing had been said by Everett in regard to financial matters, and he suggested that he thought the salary of President 'might be raised as well as not to $2500'; and that the Corporation had been disposed in two or three years to build a new house for the President. Such matters, however, were left to be settled later, only Everett then and there suggested that he wished Mr. Brooks might be persuaded to build a new house and give it to the College 'multaque alia plura.' The diary of that day, November 18, 1845, closes with this entry: 'I feel that I have made an experiment of a most perilous nature to my reputation and happiness.'

A considerable period was to elapse before the Overseers were to meet who would have to confirm his election. He almost wished at times that they would withhold their consent, so heavily did the matter weigh upon his mind. As the year closed, he confided his misgivings in his journal thus:

I am somewhat reluctantly, and with great misgivings, called to take charge of the University at Cambridge. God grant me strength to meet the expectation under which I approach this new sphere of duty. I perceive in my health some signs of advancing years. I find that even a small quantity of wine gives me a headache the rest of the day and prevents my sleeping. Under Dr. Warren's advice I have renounced it altogether. . . . I do not know that I can record any moral or spiritual progress, nor is my heavy burden in any degree lightened. God give me grace to grow more patient under it. I have much, very much, to be grateful for; let me not for one or two trials however sharp murmur or repine; but search my heart to see whether I am not myself in some degree to blame.

On February 5, 1846, his nomination as President was unanimously confirmed by the Overseers, sixty-four votes being given, the entire number present. Dr. Walker and the Chief Justice, for the Corporation, and Mr. Hoar, Dr. Codman, and Mr. J. C. Gray, for the Overseers, called on him as a committee to communicate the result.

A few weeks later, on March 16th, he began the dismal process of moving to Cambridge — 'the house in a forlorn condition.' This was Wadsworth House, and he was to be the last of the Harvard Presidents to occupy it. In the midst of general confusion, with carpets half-laid, and with bookcases standing around in considerable disorder, he confessed to himself, 'I fear I have made a great mistake in undertaking the Presidency. I will, however, give it a fair trial.'

He was cheered and encouraged at this time, however, by a cordial letter, promising support, which came from the members of the Faculty, among whom were James Walker, Henry W. Longfellow, C. C. Felton, Benjamin Peirce, and Joseph Lovering.

The inauguration exercises were postponed for a time, and did not take place until April 30th, six weeks and more after he had entered on his duties. They were held in the old First Church where Everett had scored his wonderful triumph, twenty years before, in speaking his welcome to Lafayette. Prayer was offered by the Reverend Dr. Walker, a warm friend and loyal supporter. Governor Briggs inducted the President-elect into office, and made a fitting address. President Everett replied. There followed a Latin oration by George Martin Lane of the Senior class. A hymn was sung, after which there came the new President's inaugural address. A dinner ensued at which Oliver Wendell Holmes, then a young man of thirty-seven, read a poem, 'The Modest Request,' which was received with shout after shout of laughter. Ex-President Quincy spoke; Webster offered his congratulations; and Robert C. Winthrop gave as a sentiment, 'The occasion which witnesses the consecration of the highest genius of the country to the noblest service of the country.'

Among others present at the ceremony was Ralph Waldo Emerson who came to see his former idol placed on the highest pedestal of office that his Alma Mater had to offer. Emerson went home and set down in his Journal the following account of what he saw and heard and felt that day. It is worth quoting entire, for the prophet outdid himself in prophecy in this connection, and seemingly perceived the undercurrents on an occasion when most people saw but what was on the surface.

May 1, 1846. I was at Cambridge yesterday to see Everett inaugurated. His political brothers came as if to bring him to the convent door, and to grace with a sort of bitter courtesy his taking of the cowl. It is like the marriage of a girl; not until the wedding and the departure with her husband does it appear that she has actually and finally changed homes and connections and social caste. Webster I could so willingly have spared on this occasion. Everett was entitled to the entire field: and Webster came, who is his evil genius, and has done him incalculable harm by Everett's too much admiration of his iron nature; warped him from his true bias all these twenty years, and sent him cloud-hunting at Washington and London, to the ruin of all solid scholarship, and fatal diversion from the pursuit of his right prizes. It is in vain that Everett makes all these allusions to his public employments: he would fain deceive me and himself: he has never done anything therein, but has been, with whatever praises and titles and votes, a mere dangler and ornamental person. It is in vain for sugar to try to be salt. Well, this Webster must needs come into that house just at the moment when Everett was rising to make his inaugural speech. Of course, the whole genial current of feeling flowing toward him was arrested, and the old Titanic Earth-Son was alone seen. The house shook with new and prolonged applause, and Everett sat down, to give free course to the sentiment. He saved himself by immediately saying, 'I wish it were in my power to use the authority vested in me and to say, "*Expectatur oratio in lingua vernacula,*" from my illustrious friend who had just taken his seat.'

Everett's grace and propriety were admirable through the day. Nature finished this man. He seems perfectly built, perfectly sound and whole; his eye, voice, hand exactly obey his thought. His quotations are a little trite, but saved by the beautiful modulation and falls of the recitation.

The satisfaction of men in this appointment is complete. Boston is contented because he is so creditable, safe and prudent, and the scholars because he is a scholar, and understands the business. Old Quincy, with all his worth and a sort of violent service he did the College, was a lubber and a grenadier among our clerks.

Quincy made an excellent speech, so stupid good, now running his head against a post, now making a capital point; he has mother wit, and great fund of honor and faithful serving, and the faults of his speech increased my respect for his character.

The Latin illusions flew all day:

'*Sol occubuit, nulla nox sequitur,*' [1] said Webster.

'*Uno avulso, non deficit aureus alter,*' [2] said Winthrop.

It is so old a fault that we have now acquiesced in it, that the complexion of these Cambridge feasts is not literary, but somewhat bronzed by the colors of Washington and Boston. The aspect is political, the speakers are political, and Cambridge plays a very pale and permitted part in its own halls. A man of letters — who was purely that — would not feel attracted, and would be as much out of place there as at the Brokers' Board. Holmes's poem was a bright sparkle; but Frothingham, Prescott, Longfellow, old Dana, Ward, Parker, Hedge, Clarke, Judd, the author of 'Margaret' and whoever else is a lover of letters, were absent or silent; and Everett himself, richly entitled on grounds of scholarship to the chair, used his scholarship only complimentarily.

The close of Everett's inaugural discourse was chilling and melancholy. With a coolness indicating absolute scepticism and despair, he deliberately gave himself over to the corpse-cold Unitarianism and Immortality of Brattle Street and Boston.

Everett's genius is Persian. The poetry of his sermons in his youth, his delight in Destiny, the elements, the colors and forms of things, and the mixture he made of physical and metaphysical, strongly recalls the genius of Hafiz.[3]

In speaking of Everett's address as 'chilling and melancholy, with a coolness indicating absolute scepticism and despair,' Emerson was describing the new President's state of mind much more accurately than he could possibly have known. His diagnosis of the situation was perfect. It had not needed a month in the discharge of his college duties to convince Everett that he had made a tragic mistake in yielding to the urgency of his friends. He had thought to 'escape from the turmoil of public life into a position of honorable and perhaps useful permanent literary retirement,' and he soon found the post of College President 'by far the most

[1] The sun has set, yet no night follows.
[2] When one has been torn away another golden one is not lacking.
[3] Emerson: *Journal*, VII, 166–70.

laborious and harassing office' that he had yet filled, and the only one that really wore upon him. In his inaugural address he laid emphasis on the moral side of education, saying that 'purity of spirit and the noblest religious elevation are really the great essential objects of university training.' This contention was a sound one, and in developing the thought he declared, among other things: 'We have thus far considered a liberal education as designed, in the first place, to furnish an ample store of useful knowledge by way of preparation for the duties of life; and secondly, as intended to unfold and exercise the mental powers. But these objects, important as they certainly are, and fitting in their attainment too often the highest ambition of parents and children, are in reality of but little worth if unaccompanied by the most precious endowment of our fallen nature, a pure and generous spirit, warmed by kind affections, governed by moral principle, and habitually influenced by motives and hopes that look forward into eternity.'

All this, I repeat, was eminently sound. It is accepted today as a truism. At that time, however, it was a new note to be struck by a college president. It impressed even such a man as Emerson as 'chilling and melancholy.' The trouble was that Everett, in the month preceding his inauguration, had come to the conclusion that the University was 'in a condition bordering on complete disorganization; its discipline a mere shadow; of religious influence not even a pretence, and the whole state of morals frightful, beyond anything I could have believed possible; and perhaps the worst feature of the whole, that such a state of things has been long known to exist by my predecessor and the faculty, without exciting alarm, or in fact deemed serious. I am even told,' he could declare, 'that when I have been here two years, I shall not mind things that now fill me with anguish. But my nature must undergo a great change before that can be the case.'

It was a constant complaint with Everett at this time, and

one which he freely expressed to his friends years afterwards, that the real condition of the College had been concealed from him. Had he been told, he declared, as he ought to have been frankly told, what a sad state of moral confusion and degradation existed among the students, he would never have put his neck into such a noose. And yet, in spite of his absence abroad for the five previous years, he must have known, in a general way, the things that were going on in the College. His journal for February 6, 1838, contains this entry, for example: 'President Quincy passed half an hour with me explaining the case relative to the recent explosion in the chapel. He related also the circumstance of the providential discovery (probably after a lapse of four or five years) of a most dangerous attempt to blow off the roof of the library, and otherwise injure the buildings which fortunately did not take place.'

The explosion in the chapel referred to was undoubtedly the affair of which Thomas Wentworth Higginson, of the class of 1841, gave an account in his diary. He wrote as a Freshman: 'What a sight the chapel presented at prayers this morning! About two hundred panes of glass blown up, the hands of the clock taken off, and the dial stove in, the front panels of the lower part of the pulpit removed, and all the damask between the pillars torn away, and "a bone for old Quin to pick" written on the wall.' [1]

Again, somewhat later on, we find this comment in the Higginson diary: 'Many of the class having become slightly boozy made somewhat of a noise in prayers.'

That was the kind of thing that had been going on in Cambridge for a number of years. Everett knew well enough that in his own days most of the fires in Cambridge were attributed to the incendiary activities of the students. Moreover, it is easy to believe that Mr. Quincy's loose and easygoing methods of discipline had not tended to improve

[1] *Thomas Wentworth Higginson; The Story of his Life*, by Margaret Thacher Higginson, p. 30.

matters. President Quincy had a way of closing his eyes to what was unpleasant, and his ears became so accustomed to rowdyism at night that he complained on moving into Boston that he could not sleep because of the unearthly quiet of the streets. In Cambridge there had been a bonfire in the Yard nearly every night.

At any rate, the trouble began the day after Everett's removal to Cambridge, and it was trouble of a kind that a man of his sensitive nature simply could not endure with equanimity. At half-past four in the afternoon he heard 'the music and shouts of the Navy Club, a strange sort of association which under various names has subsisted forty years and more among the students, embracing principally those who failed to obtain honors, and who have been allowed to keep a kind of saturnalia once a year, forming a procession with music and some masquerading and going round to cheer (and hiss?) the members of the Faculty. It is thought, I believe, better to permit a saturnalia of this kind than to have a revel take place as formerly at a distance; — but query, whether either is necessary, or proper. One fourth of the year in equal portions is given to vacation. Ought not the part of year spent in Cambridge to be devoted exclusively to the objects of the institution?'

Thus began the regular routine of Presidential duties, which, as we look back now, seem sufficiently heavy to have broken down the strongest man who attended punctiliously to his tasks. In the first place there was no Dean in those days, and the affairs of discipline, the records of attendance, of rank, of absences from lectures, and all such petty matters, together with the detection of disorderly conduct and the infliction of punishment, rested with the President. He was given no assistance and was not even supplied with a secretary. The College day was a long one. Morning prayers were held at six o'clock, and Everett was up at five in order to be ready to attend, and with him it was to be no occasional or spasmodic attendance. He was to have a practically perfect record during his administration, and for a period of three years he was absent from the morning chapel service only once! This in itself was not so hard, for Everett was a uniformly early riser. A more serious trouble lay in the fact that the nights were nearly always riotous and noisy. It was no wonder that Mr. Quincy was acutely conscious of the difference between Cambridge and Boston. Everett's journal tells the story.

April 16, 1846. At midnight outrageous singing and uproar in some place of assembly. This is, I think, the fifth time that this has happened since I have been here, and indicates a state of things in the University which must be cured or I quit it, and that soon.

Three weeks after taking office he was sufficiently exasperated to pour out his grievances to the treasurer:

Called on Mr. Eliot and had a free conversation with him on the condition of the University, pointing out the various points of relaxation and disorganization. Told him, if I had accurately known the condition of the University, the civil list of England would not have induced me to assume the office. He said that in proportion to its present disorganization would be the honor of reforming it. I told him I was now enlisted, and if no better motive operated with me pride would lead me to do my best; but I felt discouraged. Loud singing till eleven o'clock both to-night and Friday night.

April 29. The business of the office goes on as usual amidst the anxiety and care of preparation for to-morrow [his inauguration]. While meditating high-sounding phrases about liberal education and the ingenuousness of youth, I am obliged to reprove a member of the Senior class for casting reflections with a looking-glass on the face of a lady and gentleman passing through the College Yard.

It must not be supposed, however, that boyish pranks like these were the only troubles that afflicted him. He was not long in finding out that more serious abuses were existent in the College. It may be interesting to consider what some of the student abuses were, putting them together without much reference to dates.

Mr. Francis, the superintendent of public buildings, brought me a small vial of gunpowder found in one of the privies with twine and cord wound about it; to increase the exploding, a small roll of paper was stuck in the cork by the way of match. . . . I instantly perceived the writing on this paper to be that of one of the parts for the exhibition of Tuesday next that then lay in my drawer, written, however, by a young gentleman hardly capable of this gunpowder plot.

Hateful duties in the morning to question three students about beckoning to loose women in the College Yard on Sunday afternoon; to two others about whistling in the passage; to another about smoking in the College Yard. Is this all I am fit for? . . . The life I am now leading must end, or it will end me. . . . I take my regular walk to Mount Auburn: the only walk I ever take now, and envy the peace of the sleepers. . . . Went to the library to examine the contents of the safe, where I found things in considerable confusion — the case with everything which my worthy predecessor put in order. . . . Dr. Ware commences his lectures to the Freshman class (two in number) on Wednesday. It is necessary I understand to send in a proctor to protect the Professor from being pelted with chestnuts. . . . At Prayers in the evening, owing to the jostling and crowding of the Sophomore class in going out, the stove was thrown over with a crash. . . . In the evening, at about twenty before nine, I was told by my servant that University Hall was on fire. Found the south door burned through at the bottom and cotton and spirits of turpentine. None of the Faculty were present, and no students: but a few of the townspeople, one of whom kindly went to call Mr. Francis. . . . My time a good deal occupied in enquiries relative to the fire last evening. I addressed the students on the subject in the chapel this morning and told them that I should take the advice of the Corporation as to laying the matter before the Grand Jury. Dr. Walker and Mr. Felton approve this course. . . . My time taken up all day with the most disgusting details of discipline, such as make the heart perfectly sick — fraud, deception, falsehood, unhandsome conduct, parents and friends harassing me all the time and foolishly believe the lies their children tell them. . . . I hear that incendiary outrages were much more frequent in Mr. Quincy's time than now. Every outhouse, shed, workshop, and wooden fence near the Yard was marked for destruction. When Professor Peirce's house was building, he was obliged to keep the roof wet at night to prevent its destruction. Stones were occasionally thrown into the President's office through the windows when the Faculty were in session. . . . The students who were concerned in the fire of the 31st of March, to the number of six, came to my office and confessed their participation in the offence, a painful and harassing affair. . . . It is quite time that the students of our colleges were taught that they are not to commit felonies and call it sport. . . . Judge White [chairman of the Committee of Intellectual Philosophy] says many obliging things about the improvement in the tone and moral of College which has recently taken place. . . . A meeting of the Corporation in the evening. I brought before them the subject of the thefts frequently committed in the College and the appearance of prostitutes in the College Yard, recommending the appointment of a patrol. . . .

Such were the troubles that Everett quickly encountered at the College, and which wore upon him daily — giving him no peace in the daytime and allowing him no rest at night. 'I am filled with grief and despondency at the state of the College,' he could write after being only three months in office. 'I find nearly all the statements given me of its good condition grossly exaggerated, and some absolutely false. . . . I have grown five years older since the 28th of March. This morning was almost wholly taken up in writing letters to the parents of students punished and other letters on college business. In the afternoon, Mrs. Willard, a respectable landlady, sends her daughter to inform me that her boarders to the number of nine had conspired to drive her from the head of her table by profanity and indecency, the sons of some of our best families, one the son of a member of the Corporation.'

But his difficulties were not confined to the students. He soon found himself ill at ease with the Faculty. Its weekly meetings came to be a weariness to the flesh and a mental nightmare. 'Faculty in the evening,' he could write, 'so called from being, I suppose, from organization and habit destitute of faculty.' Again he wrote as the term began: 'Issued the notice for a Faculty meeting to-morrow evening, and thus ends all comfort for the next twenty-one weeks.' Again: 'Faculty meeting in the evening; the usual amount of miserable, tasteless, spirit-breaking detail.' 'The usual Faculty meeting in the evening: *lucus a non*. Faculty from its torpifying effects on the vital powers. It leaves me dispirited and broken-hearted. Unable to sleep the better part of the night.' 'I find myself at the close of this week' (Saturday, June 12, 1847), 'without any assignable cause to produce this effect, more than ever disgusted and worn out: My mind filled with the most gloomy images: My body weary and full of pains. Nothing is more certain than that if I remain long subject to the confinement, the mortification, and the poisonous cares of this place, I shall fall a victim to them.'

An examination of the Faculty records reveals much the same condition of things. Great men and distinguished scholars were busily engaged in punishing minor misdemeanors. Faculty meetings were held generally once and sometimes twice a week. Those attending constantly were Professors Channing, Walker, Longfellow, Felton, Peirce, Lovering, Beck, Torrey, Child, and Sophocles, and they solemnly punished boys for whistling in corridors, for smoking in the Yard, which was prohibited under the regulations, and for not adhering to the order of the Faculty which required black clothes on Sundays and fête days. Here are a few samples of Faculty votes in 1846–47:

Voted: That Section First of the Orders and Regulations of the Faculty of Harvard College be altered by striking out the words 'or black-mixed' so that the Section shall read 'On Sabbath and Exhibition days, and on all public occasions each student, in public, shall wear a black coat with buttons of the same color.'

Voted: That Plympton, Junior, be privately admonished for whistling in the South Entry of U. Hall, on Wednesday A.M., May 13th.

Voted: That Webb, Senior, be privately admonished for tardiness at Chapel Service, Sunday A.M., May 17th.

Voted: That Stevens 2d, Sophomore, be privately admonished for constant and repeated whispering and uneasiness at Prayers.

Voted: That Hayes, Sophomore, for having a festive entertainment at his room, on the evening of December 31st, 1846, and Hathaway 1 and Shaw 2, of the same class, for being present at said entertainment till a late hour of the night, be publicly admonished and put on special probation.

Voted: That Gardner 1 and Whitcomb, Seniors, be privately admonished for wearing at the Chapel on Sunday, May 23d, coats not 'black' after admonition from the Parietal Board for a similar offence.

Voted: That Hodges 1, Senior, be privately admonished for smoking in the College Yard after admonition from the Parietal Board.

Voted: That Hayward, Sophomore, be publicly admonished and placed on special probation for riotous disorder and drinking in his room at a late hour of the night on Wednesday, the 19th instant.

Voted: That Bonaparte, Junior, be publicly admonished for having the game of cock-fighting at his room on Fast Day, and that Johnston 1, Junior, be told that he also would be publicly admonished for being present at said game, if he were not on probation.

Voted: That Porter, Junior, be dismissed from the College unless he shall, within a reasonable time, satisfy the President that he was not guilty of gross immorality in having two females in his room at midnight of the 20th instant.

For a time, the President kept his troubles to himself, but it was not long before he began to tell his friends of his disgust, and also to confide to them the failing condition of his health.

To the Honorable Daniel Webster

CAMBRIDGE, *July 6*, 1846

Yours of the 3d reached me on Saturday. I sincerely wish it were in my power to undertake the proposed review of the negotiations at Washington. So strong is my desire on every occasion to comply with your wishes, that nothing but a real and overruling necessity prevents my undertaking it. But the pressure of my duties here — great and severe beyond my expectation — makes it impossible for me to think even of anything else. Instead of two or three hours daily, in which I was told the routine of the work could be gone through, I find the whole day, from five in the morning till ten at night too short for it, and my vacation, instead of being a season of repose which I greatly need, is filled up in advance with reserved labors. Instead of time for literary pursuits, I have not had two hours' reading since I came here, and the quality of my work is worse than its amount, being that of an usher and police magistrate combined.

You may remember that you repeated to me (when I was balancing about accepting the office) what you had said to Judge Story relative to the Law School, that it would kill me. But instead of standing it as he did fifteen or twenty years, I feel already as if rottenness had entered into my bones.

But there is now no retreat. The step was false, but irreparable; at least till its nature and effect upon my health and spirits are too apparent to leave any ground of doubt as to my duty, and then it will be too late.

You must not mistake the purport of this querulous strain. It is in perfect good faith. I have not the slightest wish to return to public life and had made up my mind at all events to leave it. Nothing would induce me to encounter the coarse violence into which our party contests have degenerated. My wish was for strictly private life and leisure to carry out some literary plans. I allowed myself to be overpersuaded and I must abide the consequences.

But complaints in themselves were not enough. If conditions were bad, they must be altered, and the new President set to work at once to bring about reforms. Such a thing as 'Student Government' was not known, nor even dreamed of, in those days. There was not even such a thing as student sentiment to which an appeal could be made. Moreover, it became evident that mere surface changes and sterner discipline were not enough. It seemed necessary to go deeper and awaken in the student mind some sense of moral obligation and religious sensibility. There must be a change of heart. In other words, the clergyman suddenly came out again in Everett. He set himself to reform the chapel service, and to make it decorous and dignified, in the first place, and appealing, in the second. And there can be no doubt that conditions in connection with the chapel called out loudly for radical reform. The conduct of worship had fallen into a disgraceful condition of disorder, and general lethargy. The professors as a rule did not attend chapel. The congregation was made up solely of students with just enough of the teaching staff or tutors to act as 'markers,' whose duties consisted in finding out who were absent. A youth from Mississippi calmly dubbed these proctors 'drivers.' The services lasted only so long as was necessary for the 'markers' to do their work. In this connection, Mr. Everett's first concern was with the students. He made the chapel more comfortable

— had it heated in cold weather and supplied the seats with cushions.

In all of this, he received neither thanks nor encouragement, but quite the contrary! His efforts seemed to excite amusement; and to cause irritation rather than respect. It came to be said of him in after years, by those who little understood the abuses which he checked, that on one occasion he had gone so far as to rebuke a student for sneezing in chapel. Long years afterward also, gray-haired graduates used to relate how they were summoned to the College office and solemnly reproved for having failed to touch their hats to the President when they met him in the Yard. And there can be no doubt that the recklessness and disorder of the students tended to exaggerate in Everett a natural tendency to haughtiness and pride. His sense of personal dignity, which was always acute, became inflamed. If he possessed a sense of humor, he failed to use it.

In the main, however, he was fairly successful with the students. But with the Faculty he was soon to encounter considerable difficulty on the chapel question. The boys were required to attend prayers morning and evening and church on Sundays, and it seemed to him that Faculty members ought to consider it part of their duties to attend also, at least with reasonable regularity. He set to work to secure this. The journal contains these entries:

June 14, 1846. I took this morning a very important step in sending to Dr. Walker for his consideration a draft of a letter to each of the Faculty requesting for reasons stated therein punctual and constant attendance at morning and evening prayers and on Sundays in church. Dr. W. readily approved it, and the letters will be sent out as soon as they can be copied. This is the first step of a vital reform in the institution if it succeed; if it fail, I leave.

June 21, 1846. This morning I sent to each member of the Faculty a copy of a letter on attending the devotional exercises. Deeming it a matter of delicacy not to place such a paper in the hands of a copyist, I made ten copies of the original draft myself, each letter being a full folio sheet.

It would be interesting to read this letter, with which he took such pains. He paid as much attention to it as he gave to his correspondence with Lord Aberdeen when he wrote him on the subject of 'Rough Rice,' or the 'Northeastern Boundary.' Probably, however, because he considered the matter one of 'great delicacy,' the letter was not set down in his journal nor copied into his letter-book; and I have not been able to discover it among the many papers that were preserved with care. It is fairly safe to suspect, however, that the Faculty members did not receive this formal and somewhat stately missive with entire equanimity. They were men — some of them elderly men — and they had been connected with the College for many years. Prayers were held at six o'clock in the morning, and at five in the afternoon, and church service came twice on Sundays. Under the circumstances, it was not a welcome suggestion from a new President that the good of the College required their attendance. They would hardly have been human if they had not rather resented this interference with their liberty, to say nothing of their time.

None the less, the request met with more success than might have been expected. It was complied with by all the tutors and by Dr. Walker and Professor Felton. Mr. Lovering agreed to go in the afternoon. The others, 'for various reasons, and some without any reasons, declined.' Such a meagre measure of response was not enough to satisfy the new President, who was deeply troubled by student disorders and disobedience. He was firmly convinced that nothing would be so salutary for officers and students as to have the former all attend prayers. Failing, therefore, in his effort to procure the voluntary attendance of most of the professors, Mr. Everett's next effort was to have a *law passed requiring* the daily attendance of the professors. He asked for a revision of the Statutes, and proposed to the Corporation that the following paragraph should be inserted:

All the officers of instruction and government in the College residing at Cambridge shall attend the religious exercises of the Chapel, or some other regular place of Christian worship, on the Lord's Day morning and evening, and on the days of the annual fast and Thanksgiving and the Dudleian Lecture. . . . They shall also *attend the daily devotional exercises of the Chapel morning and evening*, unless exempted from this duty on application to the Corporation, on account of the distance of the Chapel from their accustomed place of residence, or some other satisfactory reason.

The members of the governing boards were sympathetic; but when it came to the point of a statutory change, any such rigid requirement as this hardly seemed wise. The Corporation were willing to require the attendance of all members of the Parietal Board, but hesitated to go further. Inasmuch, however, as the Parietal Board had all voluntarily agreed to attend in response to the President's written request, such legislation would have seemed ungracious, and there the entire matter was finally allowed to rest. In all this, Everett probably had in mind the custom prevailing at the English universities, where matins and vespers were prescribed events for all members of the university. But if the English custom was the thing he aimed at, he never prejudiced his cause by calling attention to it. His one claim was that a beautiful and impressive chapel service would 'do more than any other one thing to elevate the standard of character and conduct among the students.'

Moreover, it hardly can be doubted that a reform of some kind in this department was sorely needed. Professor Jared Sparks, who succeeded Everett as President, was apparently so ignorant of the chapel services that the outgoing President found it necessary to write and give him full particulars as to the hours of the services, when the bell began to ring, and just how early, in order to avoid being jostled by the students, it would be advisable for him to get there. 'I used to find it convenient,' he wrote to the new President, 'to be in my place in the chapel, when the bell began to toll. I avoided in this way coming into collision with students hurrying into the chapel (the fear of which was assigned by President Quincy as a reason for not attending evening prayers.)'

In the meantime there was no apparent diminution in the number or nature of the student disorders. Such things weighed upon Everett's mind, and the duties of the office were such as to wear upon his spirits. He disliked the disciplinary feature. The infliction of penalties was extremely distasteful. Far from being able to prepare and deliver a course of lectures on the subject of the Law of Nations, he found himself enforcing petty regulations in regard to behavior in the classroom, while it was not always easy to persuade parents that their boys deserved reprimand. Before a year was up, he was thoroughly disheartened, and when the anniversary came around, he made note of it sadly in his journal.

March 27, 1847. This day completes the year since I took up my residence in Cambridge: a year of greater anxiety and care and of less intellectual improvement than I remember to have spent. The usual meeting of the Corporation. After the routine of business was over, I made known to the Corporation the entire disappointment I had experienced in the office, its ruinous effect upon my health, and my firm persuasion that I should not be able to hold on. Much concern was expressed. Some encouraging opinions expressed.

A fortnight later he wrote to the Treasurer, Mr. Eliot:

I am sorry to be obliged to ask you to call a meeting of the Corporation at eleven o'clock to-morrow at which I shall submit my resignation. A state of things exists here which I cannot endure, and which, if I could, I ought not. A large bundle of straw was placed last evening within the doorway of my house and lighted there, producing for the moment the impression that the house was on fire, the alarm of fire being raised in the street.

The crisis passed, however, and the President was encouraged to continue. It was intimated to him that he must put off some of the burdens of the office, and not undertake to do so much himself.

But the things that disturbed the President, as we have seen, and caused continuous irritation were not alone his relations with the students. A chief trouble with the governing boards came from his desire to restore what he considered the true and historic seal of the College. When he took up the question, at the very outset of his administration, he little suspected what prejudices were to be aroused. But the matter was so close to heart and conscience that he would not let it go! Moreover, he felt the thing to be so intimately connected with his primary object — namely, to revive religious feeling in the College — that his mind reverted to it constantly. We owe it to the insistency and pertinacity as well as to the historical accuracy of President Everett, that the seal of Harvard College bears to-day the double mottoes which are so familiar, 'Veritas' and 'Christo et Ecclesiæ.' The following significant entry, which marks the beginning of the controversy, shows how much emphasis the new President put upon the matter:

Sunday, May 22, 1846. I passed the greater part of the day in writing the letter to Mr. Eliot, the object of which is to induce him to consent to the restoration of the ancient seal containing the words 'Christo et Ecclesiæ' which was laid aside three years ago to make way for the present most unhappy substitute.

It was an important letter that it took Mr. Everett the better part of a day to compose, for he was an extremely ready writer, and generally knew from the start precisely what he wished to say. Evidently in this case he felt that it was going to be a difficult task to induce the Treasurer to change his mind. And so it proved; for the matter was debated in the Corporation for many months, and was at last very grudgingly decided in Everett's favor. In order to make it clear what the whole dispute was about, we cannot perhaps do better than to state the case in Everett's own words, as set down in his journal at a later date:

In writing the history of the University, Mr. Quincy thought he had discovered the record of our original College seal: a shield with three books, two face toward you, and one back, and the letters V E R I T A S distributed so that the word was spelled out from the inside of the two books and the outside of the third. There is no proof that it was ever engraved and used, but much the other way. On the faith of this notable *discovery* (which every one who had ever read the College records had made before), Mr. Quincy and Mr. Eliot persuaded the Corporation to discard the College seal known to have been used since 1691, and probably since 1650, the well known seal which contains the words 'Christo et Ecclesiæ.' This was accordingly done in 1843. It was one of my first cares on coming to the Presidency to get the true seal restored: and this fantastical and anti-Christian Veritas seal removed to the forgotten corner of the records where it had slept undisturbed for two hundred [years]. The discarding of the seal which contained the name of Christ produced no excitement in any quarter.[1]

When it came to touching the seal, therefore, Everett was dealing with a very delicate matter. He was putting himself against his predecessor in office, and was also antagonizing the Treasurer, who was a man of very forceful character, and who wielded great influence in the Corporation. If Mr. Eliot were to yield to Everett in the matter, it meant confessing himself in the wrong when he championed the change that President Quincy had advocated. Altogether the situation was difficult. But Everett was not a diplomat for nothing. He was always gentle and courteous in his ways — persuasive, not pugnacious — and he had too sincere a respect for the Treasurer not to approach him with deference and consideration.

That the matter of the change was not a welcome one is evident from the fact that it did not come before the Corporation until several months went by, and also by the nature of the following entry in the journal:

February 27, 1847. The affair of the seal, after a manifestation of great reluctance on the part of the Corporation to approach it, was at length by my perseverance brought up and referred to a committee consisting of the Chief Justice [Mr. Shaw], Mr. Loring, and Dr. Walker to consider and report. I brought the subject up by a resolution that the vote of December, 1843, changing the seal should be reconsidered and the old one restored. Should the Cor-

[1] Journal, *October* 19, 1861.

poration decline adopting this resolution, I shall consider it as indicating a want of confidence in me of a very serious character.

The committee took their time in considering the matter. It was more than six months before they were heard from.

July 31, 1847. Went to town to attend the meeting of the Corporation. The Committee on the Seal reported in favor of returning to the old seal. The report was as little satisfactory as possible for a report with a right conclusion. It placed the return to the former device solely on the ground of my wish — no principle was involved; it was a mere matter of expediency in reference to the harmony of the Board. They would not even make the change if there was a prospect of my resigning speedily. . . . Should I do nothing else during my Presidency but restore the venerable seal of the University, I shall feel that I have deserved well at its hands.

There the matter rested. Everett had won his point. There was, however, still another flare-up to the controversy that had been so long protracted.

Saturday, August 21, 1847. To town at half-past nine to attend the meeting of the Corporation. . . . The Treasurer proposed a vote that the alteration made in the seal was 'in consequence of circumstances which had occurred since the passage of the vote of December, 1843, and not from any doubt of the propriety of that act.' I objected to this on the ground that the vote of December, 1843, contained two historical errors, one that the Veritas seal was actually adopted and used, of which there is no proof, and which I deem highly improbable: the other that no other seal has the authority of a record, whereas there is a record of a sum paid in 1695 for the engraving of a seal, which is unquestionably the Christo et Ecclesiæ seal. After some discussion, Mr. Eliot withdrew his motion. He stated his object in bringing it forward to have been to prevent the interpretation which might be put upon the conduct of the Corporation in 1843 in changing the seal, and in 1847 in changing back again. What these interpretations were he did not say: he doubtless meant an imputation of irreligion in removing the name of the Saviour. I certainly do not lay that to their charge, though I deem it a hasty, ill-considered act, dictated by the passion for change that then existed, and resting upon Mr. Quincy's *supposed* discovery, which is no discovery at all.

Mr. Everett's meticulous persistency in the matter is

somewhat difficult to understand: but it is highly indicative of his character. He had a consuming passion for historical accuracy, and he had a great wealth of historical knowledge, exceeding, perhaps, that of all of his contemporaries. He did himself faint justice, however, in suggesting that the restoration of the College seal was in any sense one of the signal accomplishments of his administration. He established many other grounds for being gratefully remembered. Whatever his failures were, his brief career as President brought several lasting benefits to the University. Conspicuous among his achievements must be counted the establishment of the Scientific School. This was due almost entirely to his unaided efforts, and he was not disposed to have others claim the credit which was his by right. It was in June, 1847, that Mr. Abbott Lawrence gave the University $50,000, of which sum $30,000 was to be used for building a laboratory and the balance to serve as the basis of a foundation for two professorships. This was the largest sum ever given to the University up to this time by a living benefactor. It was Mr. Everett who interested Mr. Lawrence in the subject and persuaded him to make the generous donation, and he took no little credit to himself in the matter. He was always a keen mathematician himself; he followed with great interest the astronomical researches at the Observatory; and now the establishment of a Scientific School saw a pet dream of his fulfilled. He and Mr. Lawrence were close friends of long standing, and on Commencement Day, 1847, his announcement at the dinner that the Corporation had decided that the school should henceforth bear the name of Mr. Lawrence was received with great applause. Moreover, it was in connection with this School that Everett did another benefit to the University. He secured the appointment of Louis Agassiz to a professorship. Mr. Agassiz had come to America to lecture, having been given leave of absence for a time from his Government at home. Everett at once became attracted to him: went eagerly to hear him speak, and becoming deeply impressed with his genius he persuaded the Corporation to give him an appointment, and on September 25, 1847, Agassiz was elected Professor of Zoölogy and Geology in the 'Lawrence Scientific School in the University of Cambridge.'

Another eminent teacher whom we owe to Mr. Everett was Professor Sophocles. This famous Greek was to remain a picturesque feature of Harvard life for many years, and it was characteristic of Everett, who was ever fond of dramatic situations, that he secured a native of Greece to occupy the chair of Greek Literature.

Moreover, President Everett was to work effectively against one of the most persistent abuses of college life in general. I refer to the drink-evil. Temperance reform which he resolutely introduced, and for which there was great and very evident need, meets with much greater approval in these days of national prohibition than it did in 1847. There can be no doubt that the drinking among the students was excessive. Little or nothing had been done to stop it. To be 'boozy,' as T. W. Higginson reported his classmates to have been at chapel service at six o'clock in the morning, indicates a rather sad condition of things. In this respect as in others Everett was not content to close his presidential eyes, and to let things slide. He adopted strict measures, punishing delinquents, and doing what he could to break up bacchanalian organizations. As usual, he was unwilling to ask or expect of others what he was not prepared to practise himself. From this time on, he gave up the use of wine, and he ceased to serve it at College functions for which he was responsible — such as receptions to the students. Indeed, he went further, and during his Presidency he 'procured the passage of a College law excluding wine from all entertainments provided by the Corporation.' The following entry in his journal indicates both the need and the value of his efforts:

June 21, 1850. The Class Day of the Senior Class. . . . In the evening we had a reception for the class, Faculty, and friends generally — beautiful moonlight, band of music on the lawn, and very large company, all apparently well pleased. I notice on this as on many former similar occasions that the hilarity of the evening seemed in no degree to suffer for the want of wine. Had champagne and the other wines been served in the old way, some of the young heads would have been seriously affected and many more unduly excited. It was not an uncommon thing to see clergymen coming home drunk from the Phi Beta Kappa dinner. Nothing that I did caused greater offence, or shook my influence more in the Corporation, than my carrying this reform. One of the body, and he the most influential, though what is called a Temperance man, is a stern wine-drinker.

Such reforms were far from popular, and parents felt anything but grateful for these efforts to safeguard their sons. Hence it was that even the good he did and the better practices that he advocated were decried as evil or mistakes. Theodore Parker, however, gave credit to Everett for this reform at Harvard, and said, 'For this, he deserves the hearty thanks of the whole community.' [1] No wonder that he could write his brother 'I am fighting wild beasts in this my new Ephesus; where, however, I shall stay till all are satisfied that I can stay no longer.' In much the same vein, also, he wrote feelingly to Sidney Brooks: 'I never had so little time for literary pursuits. I am like a *wolf whose leg is caught in a steel trap*. The position is uncomfortable, but the mode of extraction not less so. The animal not seldom makes up his mind to wait quietly till he is knocked on the head.'

And, indeed, the knock seemed not unlikely to be given. His health gave way. In fact, it was failing health, under a serious physical complaint, that caused him so much mental discomfort, and that finally incapacitated him for the position.

When Everett accepted the Presidency of the College, his brother Alexander was in Boston and very seriously ill. He had been appointed Minister to China by President Polk. He had set out for the responsible post, but was taken ill on the journey, and was sent home under physician's orders to

[1] See Parker's sermon, 'The Perishing Classes,' note.

recuperate. As soon as he felt well enough, he started again on the long journey; but died on June 28, 1847, soon after taking up his official duties at Canton. By the time the news reached Everett, he had become aware of the fact that he was himself afflicted with the same complaint that had caused Alexander's melancholy and untimely death. His physician, Dr. Warren, warned him of the serious consequences of anxiety, and assured him that the disease might remain stationary for years if he avoided cares and mental perturbation. He wrote to Winthrop: 'My case is precisely that which is described in the following remark of Goldsmith as I find it cited in Forster's Life: "The mind being continually harassed with the situation, it at length influences the constitution and unfits it for all its functions."'

From this time on there are constant references in nearly all his letters to his health. 'I worry along here as usual, but I shan't be able to stand it much longer,' he wrote to one friend. Again:

If I go on as I have done for a twelve months past it will be a matter of indifference to the College whether I stay, or go. . . . I find myself by unmistakable symptoms steadily going astern. I am in such a condition — in Dr. Warren's opinion — as to have, with proper attention, a reasonable prospect of a life of average duration; but the same disease in my brother's case reached its crisis when he was three years older than I am. I am still worrying along here, deploring my coming, but not knowing how to get away without giving a shock to the public confidence in the institution. It is not unlikely that while I am hesitating nature will settle the question. Dr. Kirkland, with perhaps the best constitution and the happiest temperament ever enjoyed by man, was struck with palsy at fifty-seven, and President Webber at fifty.

At last he could stand it no longer. As early as 1847, he had asked a meeting of the Corporation called to which he might submit his resignation. The journal says:

April 14, 1847. I stated that it was not possible for me to remain in the Presidency under the operation of the constant causes of disgust and annoyance. The Treasurer asked if I wished anything done then, and when Dr. Walker said he wished nothing would be said about it, the Treasurer replied, 'Coming events cast their shadows before.' It will considerably alleviate the painful process of breaking away that my doing so will find no opposition on his part. He has seen that I am not inclined to have the College where it has hitherto been under his absolute dictation.

Three months later, the matter again came up, and the Corporation offered to make some changes in organization by which the burden would be lightened, but he himself doubted whether this was possible, and expressed the opinion that the Presidency was an 'impossible office.' Efforts were made to cheer him up. The Chief Justice told him that there was great satisfaction with his work, but that it was felt he perplexed himself with matters of detail, which were of no great consequence, and which others could do as well. He was advised not to trouble himself with matters 'which were really insignificant.' But to a man of his temperament nothing in the line of duty was insignificant. Had there been a Dean when he first assumed office, had he never begun to administer discipline and to interview students, it would have been different. But as it was, he went on struggling, constantly losing strength and adding to worries. His office door stood open all day, and when the file of students had passed through, he felt himself immeasurably fatigued. That such careful and conscientious attention to details should be rewarded in one way or another was natural. In more than one line he succeeded in bringing order out of what in his estimation bordered upon chaos. People told him that Cambridge was coming to be a really quiet place in which to live, and that the atmosphere in general had become entirely changed. Dr. Walker's wife quoted her husband as saying that 'one would scarcely know the College for the same place, it has changed so much since Everett came.' Mr. Sibley, the assistant librarian, was heard to say that during all the time he had been connected with the College he had 'never known so much quiet, order, and attention to study.'

But if the condition of the College was distinctly better, the same could not be said of the President. The time came when he could endure it no longer. The irritation of disease increased, and the burden of the College with it. At a meeting of the Corporation on November 25, 1848, he told the members that he still persevered in the conviction that the state of his health required him to resign, but that he would keep on till a successor was chosen.

In the meantime, sorrows of another kind pursued him. It was at this period that his wife's health began to give way under a strange and subtle nervous malady which was to afflict her with increasing violence for a period of nearly twenty years, until her reason 'became entirely prostrated.'

July 25, 1847. This morning at ten minutes past four I was awakened by C. who appeared to be in violent convulsions. I thought her to be dying and under that impression sent for Dr. Wyman. She came to herself before he arrived and by losing blood was quite restored. The circumstance gave me the greatest shock I ever experienced.

On the first day of January, 1849, Mr. Brooks died. He had been failing for some time, just quietly losing strength beneath the burden of more than eighty years. 'My best friend,' Everett could say in recording the fact in his journal; adding, he was 'a man of uncommon strength of mind, soundness of judgment, and goodness of heart.' He left a very considerable fortune for those days, thought by many to be much larger than it really was. It was divided equally among his children, and was to put Everett henceforth beyond all anxiety of a financial nature.

The long-delayed letter of resignation was dated December 15, 1848. He made no claim in it of great and far-reaching accomplishments; but he did claim for himself that he had served his Alma Mater with unswerving devotion, and at the sacrifice of nearly all things that he held most dear. He wrote:

Sensibly feeling how little I shall leave behind me, by which my connection with the University will be favorably and permanently remembered, I may yet claim the credit of having for three years lived exclusively for its service, giving to it my whole time and thoughts unshared by any other engagements of business or pleasure, and with the sacrifice even of those literary pursuits, never before intermitted in the same degree in the most active scenes of my life. I mention this [he could add] not by way of complaint. My course in this respect has been dictated not more by a sense of duty than inclination. Daily called to enforce upon the young the hard lesson of self-denial, I have acted upon the principle that this lesson is better taught by example than by precept. Whatever inconvenience has resulted to me from this course is more than repaid in the satisfaction of being able, without using the language of compliment, to bear witness to the propriety of conduct, the manliness of deportment and attention to study now and for some time past prevailing at the University. During the whole period — not a short one — to which my personal acquaintance with the University extends, I remember no season of more profound tranquillity.

When the resignation took effect, the members of the Faculty wrote him in cordial and appreciative terms. They had hailed his coming to the College as calculated to promote the cause of scholarship, and they bore witness when he went to the impetus which he had given to study and research.

CAMBRIDGE, *January* 12, 1849

To PRESIDENT EVERETT,

SIR: We have heard with regret that the state of your health has made it necessary for you to resign the Presidency of the University.

We deem it proper at such a time to express to you our sense of the value of your services to the Institution during the three years of your administration. We have seen in your course an unsurpassed fidelity in discharging the duties of the office, always laborious and often painful; and we have appreciated the spirit of self-sacrifice with which you have consecrated your time, your thoughts, your energies, to the intellectual and moral progress of the young men.

You have presided over our deliberations with dignity and courtesy; you have listened with candid attention, as well to opinions from which you have differed, as to those in which you have concurred, and we thank you for the kindness and consideration which have at all times marked your intercourse with us.

We take this occasion, also, to acknowledge your services to education and to science in watching over the new departments which have recently been established here by the munificence of eminent citizens. The interests of liberal education are advanced, not only by enlarging the sphere of literary studies to meet the higher demands of the age, but by increasing the means of scientific culture for the practical objects of life, and by encouraging and facilitating the labours of able men in the career of original investigation. We should fail to do justice to your Presidency if we did not recognize the wisdom of your efforts and the weight of your influence in cherishing those institutions which carry out and complete the idea of a University in fact as well as in name.

Our best wishes for your happiness will accompany you in your retirement. We trust that the repose and freedom from anxiety which you are about to enjoy will repair your broken health, and enable you long to prosecute those congenial studies which have been among the brightest distinctions of your life.

> EDWARD T. CHANNING
> JAMES WALKER
> CHARLES BECK
> HENRY W. LONGFELLOW
> CORNELIUS C. FELTON
> BENJAMIN PEIRCE
> JOSEPH LOVERING
> E. A. SOPHOCLES
> SHATTUCK HARTWELL
> P. F. C. SEARS
> F. J. CHILD

More interesting, however, than these formal documents are the entries in the journal.

January 7, 1849. Attended church all day in the Chapel. Dr. Walker preached and administered the communion. This is the last time that I attend the Sabbath services in the Chapel, and there is always something saddening in the words 'last time.' During the time I have been President I have neither been absent from my seat in the Chapel on Sunday *nor slept in it!* I do not mention this as a matter of any credit, but I believe it is a novelty.

The actual close of his period of service is mentioned as follows:

Thursday, January 11. The examinations close to-day. My time taken up in receiving students who come to get their matriculation and for various calls of discipline. It is the last day I pass at College in the discharge of the duties of President and I cannot deny that the relief is both acceptable and seasonable, for my health has reached a point at which it not only occasions inability and infirmity, but great dejection.

A few months later he betook himself to Sharon Springs, New York, where he began 'drinking the waters at the rate of six half-pint tumblers per diem.'

Everett's Presidency was a short one. It lasted only three years. It was not much shorter, however, than several that followed. He lived to see four successors inducted into office — Jared Sparks, James Walker, Cornelius C. Felton, and Thomas Hill — and he attended the inaugural exercises of each. Of these, Professor Sparks served but four years, Dr. Walker seven, Professor Felton three, and Thomas Hill six. It was an era of short administrations, to be followed by the forty long and fruitful years of Charles W. Eliot.

It hardly can be claimed that Everett made a wholly successful college president. But neither was his administration such a signal failure as sometimes has been asserted. Ticknor wrote to Charles Lyell of London, 'I feel confident he has done much good since he has been here.' Perhaps the truth of the matter was best stated by a writer in the 'New York Tribune' after his death: 'His administration was not attended with any considerable success. He failed to win the sympathies of the students. His manners were too formal and reserved for the ingenuous youth under his charge: his sensitive temperament presented a perpetual bait to the spirit of juvenile mischief, his health declined under the annoyance of the situation.'

The fact of the matter is, however, that Everett's case was one of those which went to prove that 'the finest scholastic training and the highest gifts of genius are not necessarily the best equipment for the head of a college.' In addition to which it must be remembered that Everett had already occupied such high positions of dignity and public responsibility that he was not particularly impressed with the greatness or importance of the presidential post. He must have missed, too, the adulation that he awakened in his youth, when he first returned from Europe and was followed like an Apollo. Youth is proverbially fickle, and it is peculiarly sensitive and suspicious when it seems to detect a consciousness of power. Everett was older now than when his welcome to Lafayette had inspired the calling of a Young Man's Convention. His eloquence remained, but the radiancy of life was gone. He was brilliant still, but more stately.

There is one incident that should not be forgotten in connection with his Presidency. It was significant and memorable. A colored boy by the name of Beverly Williams was offered for the examinations of admission to the college. He had tutored one of Mr. Everett's sons, and was ranked as the best Latin scholar of his class. When it became known that he was ambitious to go to Harvard, it was openly hinted in various quarters that though he might pass the examinations he would never be admitted by the authorities. But President Everett was of a different opinion. And he was not only firm, he was outspoken in that opinion. He said, and said with all the authority his position gave him: 'The admission to Harvard College depends upon examinations: and if this boy passes the examinations, he will be admitted; and if the white students choose to withdraw, all the income of the College will be devoted to his education.' That was the word not so much of a diplomat as of a scholar and a gentleman, who was an American to the core, and knew the meaning of equality and liberty.

Perhaps as good an evidence as any of the sort of service that Everett rendered to the College is supplied by a Report which he made to the Corporation in 1847 in regard to the desirability of securing some degree of seclusion in the College Yard. On his first visit to Cambridge, England, in his youth he was deeply impressed with the quiet and academic calm of the famous quads — contrasting them with the noisy thoroughfare of the Harvard Yard. In his capacity as

President, he now showed how a beginning might easily be made toward enclosing the Yard and shutting it away from the traffic of the town. Nothing came of the matter at the time. For nearly a century the vision has been delayed. But at the present time a considerable portion of President Everett's constructive scheme has begun to be achieved. Mr. Everett's Report was as follows:

The President takes this opportunity to express the opinion that among the improvements hereafter to be made, that of an effectual enclosure of the College grounds is among the most needed. In connection with the discipline of the Institution the facility of entering and leaving the College grounds and buildings has ever been the source of great evil. The American colleges are probably the only institutions of the kind in the world, in which no restraint is attempted on the movement of the students after nightfall. The appearance of the grounds within would be greatly improved by a proper enclosure. But the establishment of thoroughfares for the public, in fact, if not in law, is the evil most to be apprehended. So long as the land northeast and southeast of the Colleges was comparatively unoccupied, there were few persons to whom it was of any convenience to pass through our grounds. Compact settlements are now growing up in both directions, and the time has already arrived when a numerous and rapidly increasing population passes habitually through the College Yard. It is unnecessary to dwell upon the consequences of such a state of things. They are felt to some extent already. The college grounds are destitute of that air of quiet and repose so congenial with a place of education, and which produces so agreeable an impression in the English universities. Servants with parcels and dogs, noisy school-boys at their sports, workmen crossing on their way to and from their places of labor, are very frequently seen within the enclosure. Vagrants, hand-organists, beggars, and characters still more objectionable are not as rare as could be wished. At no remote period the College Square will form the centre of the population of Old Cambridge and will be traversed by all the direct lines of communication on foot.

A complete wall of enclosure is perhaps beyond the reach of the University, in the present or any probable state of its finances. But the same result may, in the course of time, be partially brought about by connecting the buildings which already exist, by suitable towers or corridors; and by disposing future edifices in such a way as to form an enclosure. Harvard and Hollis could be connected with great ease. The space between Hollis and Stoughton could be built up with improvement to the architectural appearance of the entire structure. Some similar connection could be established between Stoughton and Holworthy. In this way, and by closing the western doors of Hollis and Stoughton, an effectual enclosure of a considerable part of the grounds would be created, and one or two objectionable thoroughfares shut up.

It is not proposed by the President that any work of this kind should at present be undertaken, but it is his wish that the existing evil and the danger of its increase should be understood and the remedy suggested, in order that no opportunity of applying it be passed over through inadvertence.

All of which is respectfully submitted by

(Signed)   EDWARD EVERETT

President

CAMBRIDGE, *14th August*, 1847

XI

AN INTERLUDE

MR. EVERETT'S withdrawal from Harvard College was a matter of immense relief to himself and of sincere congratulations to his friends. Dr. Frothingham expressed himself as thankful that he had had the resolution to shake off the weight of cares that should never have been laid upon him and assured him that his administration had been of 'inestimable benefit to the University.' Webster wrote in the same vein, and asked that he might 'have an hour or two's talk' with him. 'From the first,' he declared, 'I have been afraid of your health under the labors of that office as I was of Judge Story's when he went to Cambridge. He had not, and I think you have not, immobility, if I should not rather say hardihood of feeling enough to get through such incessant attention to duties, all of them requiring more or less effort and attended with more or less excitement. "Eating cares" devour such persons as he and you, while on others they only share the fate of the vipers with the file.'

Macaulay wrote him, March 8, 1849:

We hear that you are out of trammels, and that you are perfectly your own master: and we hope that we shall profit by your liberty. I assure you that there is not a breakfast party, assembled by any of your old friends, at which the probability of your paying England a visit is not discussed. I am quite sure that every American whom you have furnished with letters of recommendation will tell you that a line from you is the best passport into the best society of London. Even your patriotism ought to impel you to come over often, and to stay with us long. For I am sure that you can do more than any other man living to promote good feeling between New England and Old England, and we are both, I am confident, equally convinced that the concord of the two great branches of the English race, is of the highest importance to the happiness of both. . . .

A few months later, May 7, 1849, in the same year, when there was talk that Everett might be reappointed to his former post, Macaulay wrote again:

I should be glad to hear that you had been appointed Minister; but, on the whole, more glad if you would come as plain Edward Everett, and let your countrymen see how little the high office you once held had to do with your place in the esteem of Englishmen. Come, however, in any way, and I shall be well pleased.

It was natural that political pressure, once more and almost instantly, should be brought to bear upon him. His friends were eager that he should stand for reëlection to Congress from his old district. Winthrop urged the step, and so did others, with some persistency. But he was obdurate, and not to be moved.

He was pleased, also, but not tempted, in the summer of 1849 by an invitation to become the President of the new University of the State of Missouri. The position was offered to him in very flattering terms; but he answered, naturally enough, that his health would not permit him to undertake such a responsibility, and that, except for failing health, he would have continued to serve his Alma Mater.

A brief respite, however, from the college duties, together with a visit to Sharon Springs, began to restore in part both mind and body. Less than a year after resigning at Harvard he could write with positive exultation: 'Relief from the cares, labor, and confinement of the office have done wonders for me. I often enjoy now a hearty laugh as in old times, which has done me great good. On leaving Sharon Springs I felt as if I had taken a new lease of health and strength.' The change appears in the tone of the letters to members of his family. His old playfulness returned, and he began to sing again as he went upon his way. His successor, Professor Sparks, had his own house in Cambridge, and did not care to move. Everett continued, therefore, to live on for a few years in Wadsworth House, becoming the tenant of the College.

Cambridge, however, became a new place to him without the
burdens of office, as his letters show.

To his daughter Charlotte

CAMBRIDGE, *July* 8, 1849

I send you all of your music that I can find; but I am sorry to say
that a good portion of the pieces indicated by you escape my search.
Neither the Irish Quadrilles, the Zampa Quadrilles, the Newport
Redowa, nor the Newport Polka can I find. Everything else
abounds: Cavatinas, Notturnos, Fantasies, Rondinos, Duettinos;
Music German, Italian, French; Scottish songs, Rossini's and
Auber's Operas; everything in short from 'Napoleon's Coronation
March' down to 'Governor Everett's Quick Step': — all but these
unfortunate Quadrilles and Redowas. The search has thrown me
into a tumult of musical emotion. My bosom has swelled with
Beethoven; glowed with Mozart, and sunk into dream repose with
Bellini and Döhler. The sight of 'Una voce poco fa' and 'De' tanti
palpiti' has almost unmanned me.

Seriously, dear Charlie, I am vexed to think I cannot execute
your commission in a more satisfactory manner. But I assure you
the missing articles were not with the others under the piano, nor
in any other place of deposit, that has occurred to me. And so you
must make the most out of Elfin, Alma, and Paradise Vogel.

Mr. and Mrs. Russell Sturgis sent P.P.C.'s; would it be proper
for us to return our B.D.'s?

Miss Allen sung to-day; but only in the P.M. and only one tune —
viz. 'Wells.' This was one of the first tunes, I learned to sing of
Sim Put; — I could hardly help striking in.

· Adieu, my dear Charlie; drink a great deal of the water, and believe me ever Your

(Music) (scherzando ma affetuoso)

(A sharp)   OBEDIENT HUMBLE

PAPA

CAMBRIDGE, *February* 14, 1851

...I do not recollect whether I told you that your Valentine for
Willy was sent to the Boston Post-Office by me and came out to
Cambridge in form with a post-mark and stamp and gave great
satisfaction. Yesterday morning, Mamma expressed a wish that I
would write a Valentine for Mary Palfrey.[1] What a conception! —
but it occurred to me, while I was shaving, that I might be good
for this, if for nothing else; and the following was accordingly per-
petrated in readiness for Mamma, when she came into my office.

---

[1] Mary Gorham Palfrey, born 1838, died April 23, 1917. .

To the Fair Maiden of Hazelwood

1

The rose is sweet, and bright the star,
But you are sweeter, brighter far;
Then, maiden dear, to me incline,
And I will be your Valentine.

2

The lamb is gentle, brisk the bee,
But not to be compared to thee;
Then prithee, gentle maid, be mine,
And I will be thy Valentine.

3

What San Francisco is to some,
In search of yellow dross who roam,
Be that to me, — be more, — be mine,
And I will be thy Valentine.

4

Like any Robin on the spray,
I'll hop about thee all the day,
With thee I'll breakfast, sup, and dine,
And be thy faithful Valentine.

                                                    ALONZO

CONSTANCY GROVE, *February* 14, 1851

Lastly I was cautioned not to forget Willy, who relies very much on the abundance of his Valentines, and with the following touching madrigal my efforts in this way closed:

To the Sweet William

1

Of all the flowers that deck the plain,
The pride and joy of Flora's reign,
That crown the hill, or paint the lea,
Sweet William is the flower for me.

2

The jonquil's grace, the tulip's tint,
The jessamine, and peppermint,
By youths and maids preferred may be,
Sweet William is the flower for me.

3

Let smart bouquets bestow their pride
On radiant belle or blushing bride,
For nought on earth will I repine,
With Willy, for my Valentine.

ANNIE

MYRTLE GROVE, *February* 14, 1851

CAMBRIDGE, *April* 12, 1851

. . . Last Wednesday we had a family dinner at Aunt Anne's [1]
for the Sidney Brookses. The family did not muster very strong.
The Edward and Gorham Brookses and Aunt Susan were absent.
Mamma was invited to tea, but not to dine. I was invited to dine.
The dinner — upon the whole — was extremely hilarious. Aunt
Abby adverted to the fact that your Uncle Charles, acting on my
suggestion, had scraped off the paint from the whole interior of the
dining-room in the old house at Quincy, ceiling included, and thus
laid bare the original mahogany, which is of the blackest hue. The
job has proved more expensive than was expected, and otherwise
less satisfactory in the result; but served as a *pièce de résistance* by
way of pleasantry, during the whole dinner. The impolicy of getting
into *scrapes;* the liability of people who live in mahogany houses to
heavier taxation; the probability that the other rooms were pan-
elled in the same style, and might equally reward the operation,
were gaily discussed. A silver penny of George I having turned up
in the *scrape*, it was plausibly suggested that, as no one would
hoard a solitary penny, this had no doubt dropped out of some great
pot of coin concealed in the wainscot, and no doubt to be found by
taking out the whole interior of the house, which Uncle Charles was
seriously advised to think of. As Mr. Longfellow in new shingling
his house found the roof covered with one hundred and twenty
hundredweight of sheet lead, the probability of a similar coating to
the roof of the old house at Quincy was strongly urged, and Uncle
Charles was warmly counselled to strip off every shingle before he
was a day older. Uncle Chardon, having playfully affected a little
impatience at being asked to help to a dish of jelly which stood before him, Aunt Abby, by winks and nods, got every one at table to
send to him for *some of the same*, and Aunt Anne was importuned
(if she had another dish just like it) to have it produced. Such nonsense, helped on with a hearty laugh, was kept up for a couple of
hours. I told Talleyrand's mot of *Savez vous nager*, with appropriate dumb show. Upon the whole, I was sick the next day from having laughed too much. It is not often I am sick of this disease; nor
is it quite as bad as *Cynanche trachealis.*

[1] Mrs. N. L. Frothingham.

With a return of happiness and vigor, there came quite naturally the thought of future prospects and activities. The Mexican War had come on and been carried through while he was wearing the robes of academic office and wearying himself with suppressing college pranks. But when the Whigs came back into power, with General Taylor in the White House, he had some hopes of another diplomatic appointment. 'If my friends,' he wrote, 'are kind enough to give me proof of their confidence, I should prefer the place from which Mr. Polk recalled me to any other. I am well aware, however, that there will be many other candidates for it.' He was disappointed when President Taylor passed him by, and did not ask him to go back to London; and yet he had too little hope in the matter to feel in any sense aggrieved. He would be satisfied, he said, if the President would but resolutely appoint the best man without consideration of congressional cliques, but added that it was as true as it was in the days of Louis XIV that every appointment makes nine enemies and one ungrateful friend. He expressed himself as 'perfectly satisfied' with the way the office had been filled,[1] and confessed that he had no right to think even that he deserved another appointment, though he felt himself 'well equipped to fill the office.' Altogether he had no expectation at this time, as he wrote Webster, but to pass the rest of his life in the care of his family and in the cultivation of those literary tastes which at all times he had cherished, and 'which generally gain strength as the advance of years unfits us for more active pursuits.'

The time apparently had arrived at last when he could devote himself to some substantial literary achievement and gratify his scholarly ambitions. We have seen how his friends had urged something of the sort upon him, and how keenly also he had felt the need of turning from the platform to the study, and while not ceasing to be the orator to build for himself a monumental work of history. Macaulay had

[1] Mr. Abbott Lawrence was given the coveted post.

written him before he left London, showing how highly he estimated the American's intellectual grasp of things; 'Why should not you undertake to give us a history of the United States, such as might become classical and be in every English as well as in every American library? In some way or other you will, I hope, keep us mindful of you till we see you again, as surely we shall.'

In his office at Grosvenor Place, during the days of sadness and seclusion that followed his daughter Nanny's death, he made a feeble start, as we have seen, upon a life of Cæsar. Earlier than that, in 1838, while serving as Governor, he had vaguely planned something larger and more ambitious, somewhat in line with what Macaulay was to suggest.

November 20, 1838. In the evening I delivered my lecture on the Northmen. This I propose shall be my *last appearance*. I leave the business to younger men, and resolve to devote what time I can spare from business to some *permanent effort of a literary character*.

November 29, 1838. *Plan of a Natural and Civil History of America.*

Part I. A complete description of the geography, geology, mineralogy, botany, and zoölogy, in all their branches, of the American continent.

Part II. The aborigines in every aspect.

Part III. Discovery, colonization, and history to the present time.

That was the last we hear, however, of either a natural or civil history of America. Before long, his active mind, which was stocked with an enormous store of information, had leapt with a bound across to Greece.

December 24, 1846. Purchased Grote's History of Greece for myself. It has been one of my *day-dreams* to write a history of Greece; but, alas, I am destined to pass away and leave no permanent memorial.

But as the day-dream faded, a more substantial vision took its place.

October 8, 1849. Were my health better and my mind free from some of the heaviest sorrows and most cutting cares of life, I think

I should make a serious beginning on a general treatise upon the Law of Nations. I have been lately requested by Chief Justice Parker to accept a lectureship or professorship of International Law in the Law School, which was in fact one of the visions with which I came to the Presidency. It would furnish a respectable and congenial occupation for my declining years.

He wrote to Webster at about this time:

My *opus magnum* that is to be is the modern law of nations. For this I have read and collected a good deal, but my life is wearing away with little definitely brought to pass.

It would now seem, however, that the long-desired time and opportunity had come. A fresh beginning is recorded in the journal. He set to work again to collect and sift material for an exhaustive treatise on International Law. But man proposes, and God disposes. It was to be as true again as it was in the days of the Proverb maker, that 'a man's heart deviseth his way, but the Lord directeth his steps.'

The interruption this time was to come in a characteristic fashion. Mr. Everett had constantly been placing his scholarship at the service of his friends, and he was to do so still. He had searched the Paris archives for Motley, and the library in Florence for Prescott, and had sent home valuable material from England for his friend Bancroft; and now he was to devote his pen to the greatest, closest, and most constant of his friends. It was to be 'a labor of love,' but no less arduous for that. Moreover, the task was one that a lesser mind might have done almost as well, and without so great a sacrifice. But Everett was first of all a friend, and no scholar of high rank was ever more ready to be of literary service.

It was felt at this time by friends of Mr. Webster that 'a valuable service would be rendered to the community by bringing together his later speeches.' The period to be covered was a most important one. It included events of great significance such as 'the admission of Texas to the Union, the settlement of the Oregon Question, the Mexican War, the acquisition of California and other Mexican provinces, and the exciting questions which have grown out of the sudden extension of the territory of the United States.' It was calculated that the speeches made by Mr. Webster in the Senate, and on public occasions during the progress of these controversies, would more than fill two volumes. This suggested the advisability of bringing out a new edition in uniform style of *all* Webster's speeches and writings to which a Memoir should be attached. For such an editorial task no one was so well fitted as Mr. Everett. Webster himself could not possibly undertake it. He was burdened with cares, professional and political. Moreover, his own health had begun to fail. Everett was, therefore, called upon, and put his shoulder to the wheel. It was no light task. A large amount of correspondence was involved, and the two friends exchanged endless letters at this time, consulting one another in regard to the addresses to be included, passages to be omitted, newspaper versions to be corrected, expressions to be changed, dedications to be made, and a thousand other large and little matters which necessitated scrupulous care and literary taste. In addition to all else, the biographical memoir was no slight affair. It involved considerable careful research, and formed a small volume in itself. But the task was carried through without complaint, and it was to prove the last great act of friendship by one great man to another.

Meanwhile, there were interruptions of another kind — some that were pleasant, and some quite otherwise, but all of them engrossing. Webster was once described as a 'steam engine in trousers.' In a similar vein, Everett might be called a 'dynamo in evening dress.' Even when a semi-invalid he was carrying a steady burden of correspondence and of hospitality. All this time he was writing constantly and regularly to friends in England. His journal, for instance, contains this entry:

Much of my time to-day passed in writing letters to friends in Europe for to-morrow's steamer. I am not sure that I have not given and do not give too much time to this correspondence. . . .

But I enjoy a great deal of pleasure in this intercourse. It has been my only solace under the burden of my office. I think a friendly correspondence between Europe and America not without beneficial effects of a wider kind than personal qualifications. *If anything I can write is likely to be remembered and give pleasure hereafter, some of my letters are as deserving as anything I have written.*

Then, in addition to English letters, there were the English and European friends who suddenly appeared, or the persons who came with letters from his many and notable friends. Henceforth, he was to be host *par excellence* in Boston to all distinguished visitors, both foreign and native. They came in a long line, and they always received a courteous, and, generally, a cordial welcome. Frederic Peel, the son of Lord Robert; Sir Charles and Lady Lyell; the Honorable Thomas Baring; Mr. Mildmay, a grandson of Lord Ashburton; Mr. C. D. Morris, a Fellow of Oriel College; Sir Henry Holland, and many others, including M. Ampère who was to speak of him pleasantly in his 'Promenade en Amérique.' He referred kindly to nearly all of them, and it is only occasionally that the journal records gossip, or deals in criticism.

September 17, 1850. Went to town to call on J. S. Skinner and Edmond Lafayette, the latter not arrived. In the afternoon [G. P. R.] James the novellist [*sic*] called upon me: redolent of snuff and wine. He spoke of the Northeastern Boundary and of a 'withering speech' in which Sir R. P. denounced 'one Featherstonhaugh.' Mr. James was in the House of Commons and heard it. I was in the House of Commons and *did not hear it*, inasmuch as Featherstonhaugh defended the treaty (instead of attacking it as Mr. J. said).

November 17, 1850. Mr. James the English novellist [*sic*] at tea with Charles Sumner. In London I never met with Mr. J. in any society, nor ever heard him spoken of except with derision in reference to the number of his novels. His conversation would lead you to think that he was the intimate friend and associate of all the great men literary and political in the kingdom. I mentioned that in Prince Albert's late speech at York he spoke very kindly of Sir Robert Peel, 'of his devotion to the Queen and of his friendship to himself.' Mr. James was very glad to hear of that because for several years during his life there was a coldness between the Queen and Sir Robert. She did not like him, and used to call him 'the man in the blue coat,' and Sir R. P. (you know) was not the man to forgive that.

February 5, 1852. At about nine o'clock this morning Mrs. S. G. Ward left a note at my house requesting me to come to her at a quarter before twelve, the object of the invitation not stated. Arriving at the appointed time, I was told that it was to witness the nuptials of Jenny Lind and Mr. Otto Goldschmidt, and that I was the only person out of the family and not officially connected with the occasion, who was invited. The ceremony was performed by Rev. Dr. Wainwright of New York, assisted by Rev. Charles Mason of Boston to make it legal.

Mr. Otto Goldschmidt is a young German of Hamburg, by birth a Jew, aged twenty-four. He came to this country by permission of Jenny Lind, to pursue his musical studies under her direction and at her expense, for he was himself without fortune. Last year he became converted to Christianity and was baptized by Dr. Wainwright. Dr. W. entertains a very favorable opinion of him.

The certificate of the marriage was witnessed by Mr. Ward, myself, and one or two other gentlemen present. It was a complete surprise to the public.

At this time a significant and interesting event took place in his own family. His daughter Charlotte became engaged to Lieutenant Henry A. Wise, of the United States Navy. Mr. Wise was a member of the famous Virginia family of the name, although himself born north of Mason and Dixon's line. He was a cousin of the vigorous Governor Wise of Virginia. He was older by a number of years than Charlotte Everett: but the match was considered a very fitting one. In addition to his naval training and his standing as a gentleman, he was a man of letters, and this fact made him a congenial son-in-law to Everett. The two became fast friends, and they wrote each other not only constantly, but in the frankest way on matters of great importance. The journal refers briefly both to the engagement and the marriage.

April 16, 1850. Our daughter's engagement announced yesterday. I should have preferred a gentleman not of the Navy, and of ample fortune. . . . He bears a character above reproach, as far as I can learn . . . and his book 'Los Gringos' shows him a man of talent.

August 20, 1850. The wedding day of our dear daughter. The ceremony was performed by Dr. Frothingham (who baptized her), assisted by Dr. Newell, our parish minister, whom we called in for the sake of giving him the fee. Louisa Adams and Anne Frothingham, cousins, acted as bridesmaids. . . . A great event for parents and child. God grant it may be for the happiness of both.

As Mr. Wise was in the Navy, the young people established themselves in Washington, so that Everett was soon to have new ties that drew him to the Capital. The amusing letter to his daughter which follows, tells of the passage of the Wises, bag and baggage, dog and trousseau, from Boston to their new home.

CAMBRIDGE, *December* 2, 1850

. . . The last intelligence from you was from Uncle Charles, by whom (as I understand) you were seen passing through Philadelphia as Jack Downing used to say 'full chisel'; tourist with three servants — a dog — and trunks of size unknown and number uncounted. The letter (which I have not seen) added that Mr. Wise retained his equanimity — a great thing alike with those who travel and those who stay at home.

I hope Ben behaves himself discretly. This is his first session of Congress. I wish all the members had the discretion of the member from Barkshire. If, instead of being quite so *dog*matical and tenacious of their own opinions, they would learn of Benjamin to think other people as good puppies as themselves, the world in general and Congress in particular would get along better.

I enclose a note to Aunt Lucy. As it contains a check I will thank you not to do up your hair with it. . . .

, Family events, however, were not all of them cheerful, nor calculated to call forth pleasantry like this. His own life had been one of ease, prosperity, and honor. He had many reasons to be happy, and he did not hesitate to count himself among the eminently fortunate and prosperous. Such dark and heavy shadows as lay upon his life were cast by the troubles and misfortunes of others. Edward Everett was one of a large family, but among all the brothers and sisters he was the only one who was not constantly in want. None of them prospered except himself: and on him was laid the heavy financial burden of them all for many years. Even Alexander was a financial failure, borrowed money freely, and attended to many things more faithfully than to matters of business. He involved his brother in the failure that he made with the 'North American Review,' so that a very embarrassing situation would have resulted except for the financial assistance of Mr. Brooks. The lack of fraternal consideration on Alexander's part led to a temporary rift between the two brothers, which was deepened by political differences. All this explains the 'burden' referred to in the journal.

October 13, 1851. Thus this terrible burden pursues me through life. Of all my family not one has prospered but myself. All have been in a condition to need some assistance: several great assistance: some I have been obliged to support through life. A great mass of debt exists in the aggregate, of which portions are constantly coming to me to be paid.... I am thus making constant sacrifices for which I get no credit.... I find the cares incident to a little property fully equal to the satisfaction.

April 20, 1852. The correspondence I have been obliged to carry on with every member of my family for more than thirty years on money matters has been of the most painful description. I suppose there is more or less of it in all families: but when the 'indescribable sadness' of my habitual expression is mentioned in public papers, I may say that should this correspondence be preserved it will solve the mystery. I have in my own individual relations been uniformly prosperous and from the age of eighteen have supported myself, owing nothing to my family with the exception of about two hundred dollars worth of books which my mother gave me when I was about twenty years. My income, however, though ample, was never large till within the last three years, and for the whole of my life up to that time I have been kept in a state of embarrassment by the wants of others: without the satisfaction of being able by my sacrifices to put them at ease.

February 22, 1852. I fear I make little or no progress in spirituality of character — in humility, in unselfishness, and in preference of others to myself. When I reflect how little remains to me of life and of that little how large a part is likely to be taken away by disease, I am appalled at the imperfection of my character.

But other burdens soon were to be laid upon him, and burdens of a most perplexing public nature. Whether he wished it or not, he was soon to be drawn back into the vortex of political intrigue, passion, and contention. Wherever Webster was, he wished for Everett's counsel, encouragement, and assistance. And Webster was now to meet his bitterest opposition, his greatest disappointment, and finally was to grapple with the 'last enemy,' before which the strongest and most resolute must surrender in the end. Never had there been a time since the two first met in the little Short Street schoolhouse when Webster so much needed all that his friend could give him. And Everett for the first time in his life was to hold back, on conscientious grounds, and to find it impossible to give the full support that was craved, and even asked for.

It was in 1850 that Daniel Webster made the speech in the United States Senate that has ever since been known by the date on which it was delivered. The Seventh of March Speech created a turmoil at the North. It was like the bursting of a high-explosive shell. The feelings that broke forth were intense throughout Massachusetts, but particularly in Boston. The feature in the great utterance that gave particular offence was the speaker's attitude in regard to the Fugitive Slave Law, and his censure of the North for their opposition to it. He supported Clay's famous compromise measure, and for the sake of peace and harmony he was willing to sacrifice the Wilmot Proviso and to stiffen the requirements in regard to the return of escaped slaves to their masters.

The outcry was instantaneous. Webster was accused of playing false to the North, and was spoken of as 'a fallen star.' The Massachusetts Legislature was sitting at the time, and paused in the consideration of other matters to listen while one member on the floor of the House described him as 'a recreant son of Massachusetts who misrepresented her in the Senate,' while another declared that his speech was 'Southern altogether in its tone, argument, aim, and end.' As the generations have slipped away, we have come to judge the Seventh of March Speech more fairly. The years have brought wisdom. We see things more clearly. The wild ravings of Theodore Parker on the subject, and of others like him, have charitably come to be forgotten. After all, Webster knew much more about the dangers of secession in 1850 than Boston preachers did. He did not lack conscience, and he excelled in vision. Towering high above his contemporaries, he saw further than they did, and could judge more wisely. It is recognized now that his eloquent gesture on March 7th served to postpone secession for a decade. And in that period the North increased in population and efficiency so much more rapidly than the South that when the break came the free States, both in sentiment and material power, had strength to save the Union.

We are concerned with the speech here, however, only so far as relates to its reaction upon Everett. Webster had a host of friends and followers in New England, and more particularly in Boston, who could be counted on rather confidently to follow where he led. Perhaps the most conspicuous among them, and the one who occupied the most commanding position, both personally and from a political standpoint, was Everett. After the first excitement created by the speech was over, and when people had had time to recover their breath, many of these friends came together and proceeded to take action. Testimonials were prepared and sent to the great man approving the position he had taken. Among them, and far and away the most important, was 'one from eight hundred solid men of Boston,' telling him that he had pointed out the path of duty, convinced the understanding, and touched the conscience of the Nation, and commending him for 'recalling us to our duties under the Constitution.' [1] Among the signers were Rufus Choate, George Ticknor, George T. Curtis, Benjamin R. Curtis, Jared Sparks, and William H. Prescott. It would naturally be expected that

[1] Rhodes: *History of the United States*, I, 156. Theodore Parker said 987 men. See *Sermons*.

the name of Edward Everett would 'lead all the rest': but it did not even appear upon the paper. For the first time, the younger man and the devout disciple, who owed so much to the counsel and friendship of the great 'Defender of the Constitution,' found himself unable to follow where the lead was given. It would seem that his first disposition was as usual to agree with Mr. Webster. He wrote, indeed, to that effect.

CAMBRIDGE, *March* 12, 1850

DEAR SIR,

Yesterday we got your speech — the speech — *in extenso*. I need not tell you with what satisfaction I read it. A wretched telegraphic abstract had reached us last week. Every point likely to discontent the North had been prominently stated, without any of the qualifications and preliminaries with which it was conditioned by you. As disapproval is always more active than approval, a good deal of dissatisfaction was expressed at the ground you had taken. I have not conversed with any one since we have the speech itself: but I take it for granted that reasonable men will be satisfied. The very circumstance, however, that your speech has been to some extent satisfactory at the South will lead our ultraists to dislike it. They do not wish for an adjustment; and to confess the truth, I suspect there are those at the South who wish it as little. . . .

The more he thought upon the matter, however, the less sympathy he had with Webster's position. The full text, too, of the speech when it was received put things in a somewhat different light. He had an intense dislike for the Fugitive Slave Law and could not countenance its enforcement. He declared with emphasis in connection with it:

I asked myself this question when Mr. Webster's speech came out, '*Could you as a good citizen assist in carrying out such a law: if you heard the hue and cry after a runaway slave, would you run out of your house and help catch him?*' This question I answered to myself in the negative, and so, I fancy, would Mr. W. himself. This is a question which the North must treat as the South does the imprisonment of black cooks.[1]

The journal and his letters tell the story of the struggle he

[1] From a letter to R. C. Winthrop, May 29, 1850.

passed through, and of the way in which conscience finally prevailed with him.

Monday, March 11. To-day we have the whole of Mr. Webster's speech, an exposition of great ability, well calculated if moderate counsels prevail to pilot the country through the broken and stormy sea; but —

Wednesday 13. Mr. Webster wishes me to attend a meeting at Faneuil Hall to be called to sustain his speech.[1] I doubt whether in the present state of my health I could endure the necessary confinement.

March 19. Mr. George T. Curtis called to converse upon the subject of a complimentary address to Mr. Webster on the subject of his address, to be numerously signed, expressive of entire concurrence in his opinions. I told him that I was precluded, I thought, from signing it by the fact that I had in 1838 officially approved as Governor a resolution which passed the two houses of our Legislature respectively denouncing the project of annexing Texas as unconstitutional, and protesting against the validity of any compact entered into for that purpose. I also told Mr. Curtis that I thought Mr. Mason's bill relative to fugitives a great deal too stringent, and that I thought any new bill for that purpose would be odious and not to be executed. . . . This movement is made, as Mr. Curtis informed me, at the suggestion of Mr. W. himself, Mr. Peter Harvey being the confidential agent here by whom the first impulse was given. . . . It is hardly worth while to be great on these terms.

A few days later he wrote Mr. Webster on the subject, and we can well believe that it was one of the hardest letters that he ever had to write.

CAMBRIDGE, *March* 22, 1850

I read your speech with so much admiration of its power and so much sympathy in its great object — the rescue of the Union from the great impending danger — and I have been so long accustomed to say 'ditto to Mr. Burke,' that I did not stop to scrutinize details. It was not till I began to examine the separate propositions, in order to prepare myself for a public meeting in Faneuil Hall, if one should be called to respond to it, that I found on looking back to papers and documents that I was pretty strongly committed on the subject of Texas.

During the elections of 1837 and 1838 and 1839, when I was a

---

[1] A brief letter from Webster, dated March 10th reads, 'My dear Sir: — If you can conscientiously defend my speech, I beg of you to go to Faneuil Hall, and do so.'

candidate for Governor, questions were proposed by the Abolitionists to all the candidates for State offices. My answers were written on consultation with friends, and expressed the opinions by which they were willing to abide. The correspondence of 1839 I enclose you.

Among the resolves of 1838 was one relative to Texas, which, if I mistake not, was *unanimously* adopted by both houses of General Court, in the following terms:

'Resolved that we, the Senate and House of Representatives, in General Court assembled, do, in the name of the People of Massachusetts, earnestly and solemnly protest against the incorporation of Texas into the Union, and declare that no act done or compact made for such purpose by the Government of the United States will be binding on the United States or the People.'

In a letter afterwards published by me,[1] I said that these resolutions not only received my official signature, but my personal concurrence. Such a committal seems to me to put it out of my power, with any credit or to any good purpose, to hold an opposite language at this time. The only friend to whom I have named the matter — Mr. George T. Curtis — fully concurs with me in this opinion.

On the extradition of fugitives I had misgivings from the first, not at all of the constitutional right; every word you say on that point I agree with, and it is argued with much power in a very able article of this day, in the 'Daily Advertiser.' It is, however, the incident of slavery — itself an anomaly in a free government — which is most repugnant to the public sentiment of the free States. It was under this sentiment that the law of 1793 broke down. I much fear that legislation by Congress will inflame instead of subduing this feeling. Cannot the real patriotic men of the South be made to see this and to extend to the North, on this point, the same toleration which they require us to exercise toward them when they violate, as they do each day, the first clause of the very same section of the Constitution, which, in the third clause, gives the right of extradition? It strikes me that some provisions of Mr. Mason's bill are unnecessarily stringent and otherwise ill-advised; such as the creation of a board of commissioners expressly for the arrest of fugitives *in every county* of the free States. I think such a step would give a vast impulse to anti-slavery agitation.

Pardon the freedom with which I express my dissent from you on this point (Mr. Mason's bill), and believe me, as ever.

But Webster was too great a man to take offence at an act

[1] This was the famous Borden letter, which almost cost him the confirmation as Minister to England in 1841.

of independence. He had a full and high respect for the rights of private judgment. Moreover, he appeared to be entirely confident of his own position, and believed that he saw things more clearly than most of his contemporaries. The following extract from the journal is interesting. The dinner referred to was attended by Webster's fastest friends: among others the Curtises, Choate, Judge Warren, and Ticknor.

May 2, 1850. Dined with Mr. Frank Gray to meet Mr. Webster, who was in good spirits and looking better than when I last saw him. After he had gone, his late speech was discussed. Every one admitted that he had made a great mistake about the Fugitive Slave Bill. In fact, before he left the table, he said that he had never read Mr. Mason's bill when he made his speech. But he says in the speech, 'My friend at the head of the Judiciary Committee has a bill on the subject now before the Senate with some amendments to it, which I propose to support with all its provisions to the fullest extent.' Every one at the table agreed that it would be madness for Mr. W. to support the bill referred to, and yet every one but Mr. Gray and myself had signed the letter declaring a full concurrence with Mr. W.

These events quite inevitably had a depressing effect on Everett. He saw ever more and more clearly the tragic end to which they led. The readiness of one portion of the South to dissolve the Union, and the avowed willingness of another portion to remain only on condition that the Fugitive Slave Law was rigidly enforced, awakened constant alarm in a naturally apprehensive mind. He watched the gathering clouds, massing themselves ever denser and darker in the political sky, and no period of clear sunshine seemed at hand. The political 'bargain' between the Free Soilers and the Democrats in the Massachusetts Legislature by which Charles Sumner was elected to the Senate shocked his faith in personal honesty. He admired Sumner, and paid glad tribute to his remarkable abilities; but the coalition itself, and what he called Sumner's 'hypocritical letter of acceptance,' were almost too much for his charity. He suggested having a memorial presented to the Senate at the opening of the session, calling attention to the corrupt bargain, giving a list of the persons who secured office by means of the arrangement, all looking toward the probability that Sumner's election might be set aside. He did not always agree in politics with his brother-in-law, Charles F. Adams, but he was relieved that 'Mr. Adams and his statesmen friends would have nothing to do with the bargain, for such a coalition was in their eyes like jockeys selling a horse-race.' [1]

But brighter days were near at hand, and he was soon to become identified again with great events on the national stage. On July 9, 1850, Zachary Taylor died, and Millard Fillmore became President in his stead. The members of the Taylor Cabinet resigned and Mr. Fillmore, in selecting a Cabinet of his own, made Daniel Webster Secretary of State. This return of Mr. Webster to the State Department meant almost at once a new association of Mr. Everett with diplomatic affairs. In the autumn of 1850, the new Secretary of State turned to his friend for assistance in connection with a letter that he wished to send to the Austrian Chargé d'Affaires, a Mr. Hülsemann. A revolution had been going on in Hungary, under the leadership of Louis Kossuth, and President Taylor had sent a special agent to Europe with instructions to study and report upon events, with a view to a possible recognition of Hungary. The Austrian Government took offence when it learned of the step, and an interchange of letters between the two Governments resulted. The correspondence was still in process when Webster took office, and in September he received 'a haughty and dictatorial letter' from Hülsemann objecting to the interference of the United States. An opportunity was offered for a declaration of American sentiment which was always popular with the mass of the people. It was too good an opening not to be made the most of, and Webster sought the aid and advice of Everett. He wrote him, asking that he would draft a reply to Mr. Hülsemann, at the same time sending him a copy of the

[1] See *The Education of Henry Adams*, p. 40.

President's Message to the Senate relating to the mission of the special agent, Mr. Mann, to Hungary. Everett immediately set to work, and at the end of four days Mr. Webster received what he had requested.

Mr. Everett's account of the affair, as set down in his journal at the time, is significant. The Hülsemann letter came to be received with such vociferous American acclaim that Everett's part in the document is a matter of considerable importance. Moreover, the question of the authorship was to expose Everett to some little misunderstanding when he revealed the secret to a few of his intimate friends some time after Webster's death.

Curiously enough, so strangely do the wheels of fate move round, the Chevalier Hülsemann, Secretary of the Austrian Legation, had been a fellow-student of Everett's at Göttingen more than thirty years before. It must have been with strange sensations, therefore, that the task was taken up in Mr. Webster's name.

October 21, 1850. Received a packet of papers and a note from Mr. Webster requesting me to prepare for him the draft of an answer to the Austrian Chargé d'Affaires, whose note he encloses to me. His health (Mr. W.'s) requires him to go to New Hampshire for a week to escape the crowd of men and letters which are continually pressing upon him. The note of Mr. Hülsemann is a protest against the steps taken by the United States to ascertain the progress of the revolution in Hungary.

October 22, 1850. Passed the quarter part of the day in preparing the answer to Mr. Hülsemann's note as requested by Mr. Webster. It cannot, I think, be denied that General Taylor, acting under Mr. Clayton's advice, was rather too hasty in this matter.

October 24. Employed most of the morning in copying the note to Mr. Hülsemann. The step taken by President Taylor in sending an agent to Vienna to obtain information relative to the Hungarians was perfectly proper. The instructions written by Mr. Clayton would have formed a good leading article for a penny paper, and the communication of them to Congress a capital error. But no harm will probably come of it. Our politics in every department are poisoned by electioneering and demagogism. Mr. Clayton was seeking popularity, *per fas et nefas*, in every quarter.

November 12. Mr. Webster called in the evening to bring his draft of the letter to the Chevalier Hülsemann, which is mainly prepared from mine. He asks me to read it and make any remarks upon it which occur to me. It is quite curious to compare both the additions and the omissions. One of the latter is, I think, judicious: but with this exception the document in my humble opinion stood better as it was. But *judicent peritores*, Mr. Webster's additions are too fierce and bitter, addressed not *ad rem*, in any fair estimate of the occasion: but to the American appetite for highly spiced statements.

January 2, 1851. The letter to Mr. Hülsemann appears in the 'Intelligencer' to-day. Some of the changes made by Mr. W. in the draft prepared by me, in the way of additions, are improvements: others decidedly the reverse.

The letter received President Fillmore's approval, and was sent out on December 21st.

Mr. Rhodes calls it 'the most striking of any of Webster's state papers while he was connected with the Fillmore Administration.' [1] It was received with enormous enthusiasm by both parties in the Senate, and was acclaimed by the people generally. It was just the kind of appeal that touches the hearts of Americans, being a species of 'stump-speech under diplomatic guise.' The United States, the letter said, 'cannot fail to cherish always a lively interest in the fortunes of nations struggling for institutions like their own.' In proportion, therefore, as the events in Hungary 'appeared to have their origin in those great ideas of responsible and popular governments on which the American constitutions themselves are wholly founded, they could not but command the warm sympathy of the people of this country.... The power of this Republic at the present moment is spread over a region, one of the richest and most fertile on the globe, and of an extent in comparison with which the possessions of the House of Hapsburg are but as a patch on the earth's surface .... Nevertheless, the United States have abstained, at all times, from acts of interference with the political changes of Europe.'

[1] Rhodes: *History of the United States*, I, 205.

Webster himself felt obliged to confess that the letter seemed 'boastful and rough'; but he justified it on the ground that he thought it wise at just that time to 'touch the national pride and make a man feel sheepish and look silly who should speak of disunion.'

Such was the famous Hülsemann letter — popular in tone, boastful and a trifle bombastic in expression, ultra-patriotic, and appealing to what Lowell came to describe as that 'popular prejudice called our country.' To what extent it was the product of Everett's pen, to what degree the result of Webster's careful revisions, amendments, and additions, can now be definitely decided. Curtis says that Mr. Webster submitted it to three revisions, made considerable changes in Everett's draft, 'striking out entire paragraphs,' altering some phrases, and writing 'new paragraphs of his own.' He confesses none the less that he 'adopted Mr. Everett's draft as the basis of the official paper; a purpose which he expressed to Mr. Everett on his return to Boston toward Washington.' [1] That Everett, however, considered the letter as essentially his seems equally clear. He expressed the conviction that Mr. Webster always meant to explain the authorship of the despatch, and that had he lived he would have done so. [2]

But Webster by this time was far advanced among the gathering shadows that deepened toward the end. At the Whig National Convention, which was held in June, 1852, he failed of the nomination for the Presidency. The disappointment broke his spirit. He returned to Marshfield in early September stricken by a fell disease that was far advanced.

The last exchanges of friendly intercourse between the two great men have a melancholy interest and are worth preserving. It was at this period that Webster wrote the touching letter in which he spoke of their friendship as re-

[1] Curtis: *Life of Webster*, II, 536.
[2] In a letter to Henry A. Wise, Washington, April 10, 1854, he wrote: 'Mr. Webster always intended to take the first opportunity, after he retired from office, to mention my agency in that matter.'

sembling a belt of 'clear cerulean blue sky stretching across the heavens without cloud, or mist, or haze.'

May 25, 1852. Mr. Webster called upon me this morning. He said that he thought I ought to know his intentions. If he or Mr. Fillmore were nominated at the Whig Conventions, he should resign the office he now fills. If General Scott be nominated, he should resign it unless Mr. Fillmore should strongly urge him to stay and consent to his taking a vacation of two months in the warm season. *Should he resign, he should strongly advise the President to offer the place to me:* as he knew no one so able to fill it from his knowledge of the public men of Europe; of the history of our affairs and from capacity of application, which was what oppressed him. If my health would not allow me to take it, he should then advise the President to offer it to Mr. Crittenden and the Attorney-Generalship to Mr. Choate. I told Mr. W. I presumed when his resignation was spoken of that this last-named arrangement would take place.

When Webster met his cruel defeat at the Baltimore Convention, Everett wrote him as follows:

BOSTON, *June* 22, 1852

I hope you will not allow yourself to be greatly disturbed by the disappointment of our hopes at Baltimore. However desirable success may have been for the country at large or your friends, you are the individual who has least reason to regret it. Assuming that election would have followed nomination, what could the Presidency add to your happiness or fame? Even before the office had been let down by second-rate and wholly incompetent persons, the example of Mr. Madison shows that even repeated election to the office is of very little moment to a great constitutional statesman. . . .

Upon the whole, I hope you will bear in mind that if there is no one in the country (as your friends think) who could have filled the office so much to the public interest and honor, there is, and for that reason, no one who is so little dependent upon office, even the highest, for influence or reputation.

September 20, 1852. Dined at Mr. T. W. Ward's with the Barings and a large party. Sat next to Mrs. S. G. Ward. She spoke with enthusiasm and intelligence of Dante, which she and her husband had thoroughly studied together. How many bankers and their wives in Europe can say as much? Mr. Webster came in at the dessert. This was the last time he came to Boston, and the last time I ever saw him alive.

Toward the middle of October, 1852, there began to be vague rumors, and then definite ones, about Mr. Webster's serious illness. They were circulated and then industriously denied. There seemed to be a conspiracy to keep back the news, and to give the impression that the great man was convalescent and indeed going about his work as usual. But Everett was soon in close touch with the Webster household.

On October 20th, Mr. Abbott, of the State Department, wrote from Marshfield giving Everett a frank statement regarding the serious nature of the illness. The next day he wrote again, and described Mr. Webster as 'sinking rapidly and very low.' On Sunday, the 24th, news came from Marshfield that the great man had died that morning at three o'clock. Minute guns were immediately fired and bells were tolled. Everett turned instinctively and at once to his desk, and between nine o'clock, when he got the news, and dinner time at two, he wrote a two-column obituary for the 'Advertiser,' going to church, of course, as usual in the meantime. 'I mention this,' he records in his journal, 'not as a feat, but as an apology for its imperfections, doing as it did not justice to the great theme.' Nevertheless, it was 'a feat,' and he knew it, and it gives us an idea of how rapidly he wrote.

On Monday morning, fifty or more of the leading men came together at the Revere House to plan for a public meeting in Webster's honor to be held in Faneuil Hall. Everett was appointed chairman of the committee on arrangements. He secured speakers, and drew up resolutions which were submitted to Mr. Ticknor and Colonel Heard, who was designated to read them.

At twelve o'clock noon on October 27th, Everett called the meeting to order and spoke for half an hour in honor of his lifelong friend. Just as he was leaving his house to go to the hall, he received a letter from President Fillmore offering him the State Department.

On the morning of the 29th, the Mayor stopped at his door and took him up to go to Marshfield for the funeral. He drove over from the Kingston Station in a carriage with the Mayor, Mr. Lawrence, who had just returned from his mission to London, and Alderman Rich. The coffin was placed in the open air under an immense tree in front of the house, and Everett joined the long procession that 'passed round to look upon the dreadfully changed features.' After a brief funeral service, the body was followed to the little graveyard on a beautiful eminence about a mile away from the house along a winding road. The procession was very long and passed almost the whole way through a double row of men and women. 'At the tomb the coffin was again laid upon the ground and a last look taken through the glass window.' Immense depredations in the meantime, so young Sidney Everett told his father, were practised on the farm, where shrubs, ears of corn, vegetables, and anything else which could serve as a relic, however incongruous in its nature, were carried away to be used for such a purpose. The Mayor's party dined at Plymouth, and returned from thence to Boston in the late afternoon.

For the past thirty-six hours, when Everett's mind had not been filled with memories of his dead friend and grief at his loss, he was endeavoring to decide whether or not he had better accede to the President's request that he should become Webster's successor in the State Department. There were many things to be considered — his own uncertain health, his wife's confirmed and distressing invalidism, the age of his youngest son William in whom he had great pride and who needed him at home to direct his studies. But Webster's dying wishes could not but weigh strongly with him. The next morning, which was Saturday, October 30th, Everett made up his mind, 'with much misgiving,' to go to Washington, and 'sent a telegraphic message to President Fillmore to that effect.' Preparations for departure were at once begun, the news of his appointment soon became known, and notes of congratulation immediately began to pour in. Charles Sumner called and expressed satisfaction, saying that the appointment would be agreeable to the Senate. 'Black Dalton, the waiter [at the Revere House], also offered his felicitations,' so that he felt himself 'obnoxious to the woe of having all men speak well' of him.

Tuesday, November 2d, was Presidential Election Day, and he deposited his vote for the Scott electoral ticket. It was a democratic sweep for Pierce, so that he knew, before leaving Boston, that there would be a change of administration in March and that his term of office would be brief. He took the cars for New York at eight o'clock in the morning on November 4th, passing the night with his brother-in-law, Sidney Brooks, who was having a large dinner-party that evening which was the occasion for new compliments and congratulations. The next day he pushed through to Washington, where he arrived at nine in the evening and went to Willard's Hotel, having borne the journey extremely well.

Saturday morning, the 6th, saw him in good season at the President's office, where a Cabinet Meeting was soon called to hear the instructions to Commodore Perry, Commandant of the Japanese Squadron. He passed the afternoon, at the President's request, drafting a letter to the Emperor of Japan. Thus, with dramatic suddenness he found himself again playing an important rôle on the stage of international affairs.

XII

SECRETARY OF STATE AND SENATOR

MR. EVERETT was given a warm welcome on his return to Washington. He had many friends there and a host of ardent admirers. To succeed Mr. Webster in the State Department was in itself a national and even an international distinction. He was soon, however, to establish a reputation on his own account as Secretary of State, and to attain a preëminence in the Cabinet that was in no sense less complete than that which had belonged to his predecessor. In Mr. Fillmore he was fortunate in finding a sympathetic Chief with whom it was easy as well as encouraging to work. The President was a man of solid, rather than brilliant, parts. He was safe and suave, and neither aggressive nor domineering. His large stature lent him the appearance of an autocrat or ruler; but his habitual attitude was one of courtesy and deference. He was conservative in much the same sense and along the same lines that Everett himself was conspicuous for conservatism. Like Everett, too, Mr. Fillmore believed in moderation as a principle, and disliked not only extreme positions, but extreme statements in supporting them. He had, however, none of Everett's genius nor brilliancy of intellectual attainments. He was not a man who shone so much as one who served and could be trusted. He and his new Secretary of State had known each other for several years, and, though both were old-fashioned Whigs, they were both of them adherents of the liberal or Unitarian position in religion.

Much the same might be said of the members of the Cabinet, who had been selected in large part by Mr. Webster because of their moderate views and their willingness to support the Compromise.[1] The ablest of them was perhaps

[1] Rhodes: *History of the United States*, I, 179.

John J. Crittenden, of Kentucky, who held the post of Attorney-General, and with whom Everett was to remain in close political touch for the rest of his life. This was also true of Joseph P. Kennedy, who was Secretary of the Navy.

Thus began a brief but very brilliant episode in the career of Mr. Everett. It is safe to say that in no other office that he held did he achieve so much, or cover himself with such well-deserved distinction, as during the four brief but crowded months when he was Secretary of State. Rhodes says that President Fillmore 'graced his administration by the appointment of Edward Everett.' [1] But he did that, and a great deal more besides! For strength as well as grace were contributed by Everett in a quite surprising way. His nomination was wholly acceptable to the Senate, and it was confirmed at once. Charles Sumner wrote him the same day from the Senate Chamber: 'Immediately on reading the message of the President containing your nomination as Secretary of State, Mr. [Jefferson] Davis rose to ask its consideration at once without reference. Mr. Cass said that he was about to make the same motion, remarking that there could be no objection to such a proceeding. Mr. Mason joined in this request, and Mr. Weller cried out "Question." It was at once put, and the nomination unanimously confirmed. With pleasure and pride I mention these things, though of little importance to you.'

As a matter of fact, however, it all was of great importance to Everett. No man ever responded more quickly and favorably to appreciation and success than he did, just as no man was ever more perceptibly pained and stung by censure and abuse.

He could write jubilantly to his wife: 'My health continues extremely good for me, better in many respects than it has been for a good while. I thought I knew what work was — but this is the beat-em. Owing to Mr. Webster's long absence and illness everything is in arrears, and all comes

[1] Rhodes: *History of the United States*, i, 291.

pouring in at once. But I continue to "worry" through. I take hold and do the things as they present themselves. I go to the Department at nine or half-past, and stay till three or four, and in that time a good deal can be done.'

And indeed a great deal was done, and done at once, and most efficiently. There were very important matters in the Department that had to be attended to quickly. The very day, for instance, after his arrival in Washington, and in his first Cabinet meeting, the Japanese Squadron matter came up. He was asked by the President as we have seen to draft a letter to the Emperor of Japan which should go with the expedition soon to sail under the command of Commodore Perry. The new Secretary had very scanty and no detailed information in regard to the expedition; but he heard the general instructions read over at the Cabinet meeting in the morning, took home such papers as were put into his hands, and that evening wrote the desired letter. Little did he real-ize — little did any one suspect at the time — the amazing results that were to follow from this expedition which led to the opening-up of Japan to the world.

This historic document, so its author took the pains to set down minutely in his journal, accompanied by Commodore Perry's 'letter of credence,' was 'beautifully engrossed on parchment, bound up in covers of blue velvet, the great seal in a box of solid gold with splendid tassels of silk and gold; deposited in rosewood boxes, the hinges and clasps of which are of gold, said rosewood box in an oaken one, all rich and in good taste.'

But other, less decorative and more delicate, matters than the Japanese Expedition pressed hard for Mr. Everett's at-tention. Mr. Webster, 'through haste and unsafe reliance on ill-informed and interested parties,' had blundered rather badly and taken a false step in connection with the Lobos Islands.[1] These islands, which lie off the coast of Peru, were

[1] Footnote in Everett's journal says: '*November* 15, 1852. The President gave me a history of the *Lobos affair*, which, through haste and unsafe reliance on ill-

rich in guano, and Mr. Webster, in reply to an inquiry from
some New York merchants, had expressed the opinion that
they did not belong to the Government of Peru. He asserted
that they were open to all the world, if they were not even
subject to the United States, in virtue of a supposed discovery of Mr. Morrell. Encouraged by this official assurance,
which exposed Mr. Webster to sinister suspicions, twenty or
thirty vessels were despatched from New York to bring back
guano, and the U.S.S. Raritan was ordered to protect them.
The expedition aroused the resentment of the Peruvians.
The islands lie only about a dozen miles off their coast, and
Peru laid claim to them as having been discovered by the
Spaniards as early as 1585. As the whole affair was a purely
commercial one, so far as the United States was concerned,
it put the Government in a most unfortunate position, and
naturally enough exposed Mr. Webster's reputation to possible misunderstanding. Mr. Everett had to steer a rather
careful course under these circumstances. He had to extricate
the country from the consequences of Mr. Webster's false
step, and he had to do this with tenderness and respect for
the memory of his dead friend. Moreover, it was necessary
that he should save the interests of those who had *bona fide*
engaged in the guano speculation on the faith of Webster's
promise of protection. In addition to all else, there was a
fourth difficulty to be overcome, which could not be publicly
referred to, but 'which required more address than all the
rest of the negotiation.' Altogether, when Everett took office
things were on the verge of an explosion from this direction,
due to the way in which the whole affair had been misman-
aged. It was quickly adjusted, however, and in a masterly
manner! Mr. Everett had not been at the Court of Saint
James' for nothing. He had learned important lessons from
Lord Aberdeen and other English statesmen. He imme-

informed and interested parties, was deplorably managed by Mr. Webster.... A
most embarrassing business which grew out of a false step of Mr. Webster. He had
the magnanimity toward the close of his life to take all the blame on himself.'

diately took the entire affair into his own hands. A few short notes were exchanged with the Peruvian Minister. A brief interview of half an hour followed, and the whole flare-up, which had wakened excitement in Europe as well as in this country, was 'promptly and quickly extinguished without even a call for papers by Congress.'

Mr. Everett took great satisfaction, as he had good cause to do, in the quiet and speedy way in which this difficulty was settled. But an even greater satisfaction and a more decided triumph were now to be his portion. The simple fact of the matter is that he was in his element again, as much so as he had been when representing his country at the Court of Saint James'. He wrote as follows to his ever-ready confidant, Mr. Winthrop, and the happy tone of the letter contrasts strongly with the wailing periods that went out so constantly from the College office.

WASHINGTON, *December* 6, 1852

Private.

... Politics truly are a game of chance, of which no stronger illustration is necessary than my being here. I can truly repeat the saying of the Doge of Genoa to Seignalary.[1]

I think we got very handsomely out of the Lobos affair considerin'. When I came, things were on the verge of a new explosion, owing to the warm southern temperament of my worthy predecessor, the acting Secretary; but I settled the affair with the Peruvian Minister in half an hour. ...

The portions of the message [2] referring to foreign affairs, with the exception of Mexico, Nicaragua, Venezuela, and Uruguay, are by me. ... I also furnished the paragraph on the Department of State, on Mr. Webster, and the two closing short paragraphs, and I had a kind of editorial charge of the whole.

P.S. I have in a very long, and (for me) bold letter to the English and French Ministers declined to join their Governments in a tripartite guaranty of Cuba, disclaiming, however, all purpose to ap-

[1] The Doge of Genoa was compelled by the imperious mandate of Louis XIV to come to Versailles, and 'after surveying and admiring its marvels exclaimed that he wondered at everything he saw, and most of all at finding himself there.' Everett, *Orations and Speeches* III, 383.

[2] The President's Message.

propriate it to ourselves. I have taken this occasion to glance at
the entire history of our territorial extension for the last century.
I have also addressed a pretty elaborate despatch to Mr. Ingersoll
on the fisheries trouble last summer, in reply to a letter of Lord
Malmesbury which I found on file. If my letter ever sees the light,
it will put Lord M. in a very tight place.

You must keep all this familiar and confidential chat to yourself.

That was a pretty large order for a man who had been only
four weeks in office, who was new to the Department, and
who had felt himself permanently broken in health by the
details of college administration. The reference in the postscript of the foregoing letter to a 'bold' communication to
the English and French Ministers upon the subject of Cuba
directs attention to Mr. Everett's greatest and most signal
triumph while Secretary of State.

It will be necessary for us to get the situation clearly before our minds, if we wish to understand what a wise and
resolute diplomacy accomplished. The South had for many
years cast longing eyes on the island of Cuba. It offered a
fertile field for the extension of slavery. In 1853, the normal
desire for this territory had been whetted and increased by
disappointment in regard to the outcome of the Mexican
conquests. Moreover, within a year or two, an expedition
under General Lopez, fitted out at New Orleans, had made
an attempt to coöperate with the Cuban insurgents and
seize the island. The very thing, however — the desire for
new slave-territory — that caused the South to covet Cuba
operated in the North to make the majority of people opposed to the idea. They wanted no extension of slavery, although a kind of manifest destiny appeared to indicate that
the island might eventually, but only by honorable arrangement, fall beneath our sway.

These circumstances, but more particularly the lawless and
adventurous expedition under Lopez, engaged the attention
of England first, and later of France. These two countries in
1852 proposed to the United States that she should unite with

them in a joint agreement guaranteeing to the Spanish Government the undisturbed possession of Cuba. The essential part of this so-called 'Tripartite Convention' was expressed as follows, in a single article:

The high contracting parties hereby severally and collectively disclaim, now and for hereafter, all intention to obtain possession of the island of Cuba, and they respectfully bind themselves to discountenance all attempts to that effect on the part of any Power or individuals whatever. The high contracting parties declare, severally and collectively, that they will not obtain or maintain for themselves, or for any one of themselves, any exclusive control over the said island, nor assume, nor exercise any dominion over the same.

On December 1, 1852, Mr. Everett addressed a communication to the Compte de Sartiges on the subject, which constituted his reply to the Governments of Great Britain and of France. The communication was a long one, and of marked importance. It became a great State document and passed into history, to be quoted and to guide our national policy at a later period when the Cuban question finally became acute. Yet we have Everett's own word for it that the composition of the document 'was the work of a single evening. It was written in pencil, standing at a sideboard at Willard's Hotel, for want of a standing desk.[1] The train of thought,' he added, in describing its preparation, 'had been long familiar to me.'[2]

The best and fullest account of the way the Cuban letter was prepared was given in a letter that he wrote to W. H. Trescot in which he outlined his work in general in the State Department. He said in the course of this letter:

Entering the Department as I did for a few months only, I intended to apply myself exclusively to the public business, especially to bringing up that portion of it which was in arrears, and had no thought of making political demonstrations on any subject. The Ministers of France and England called upon me on the 18th of November and pressed to have an early answer to their overture (made the preceding April) the reply to which had been a good deal

---

[1] Letter to Winthrop, January 20, 1853.
[2] His brother Alexander, when Minister to Spain, had written on this subject.

delayed. On the same day I got the decision of the Cabinet which was merely against going into the proposed convention. On the next day, the 19th (after a very hard day in the Department), I took up my lead pencil after seven o'clock in the evening, to sketch the *heads* of a letter on the subject. Instead of heads, I wrote the letter itself and read it to the President the next morning in the original pencil draft. I wrote it standing at the sideboard in my room at Willard's Hotel, between seven and eleven o'clock, without a book or a document of any kind to refer to. Very little alteration was afterwards made in it.

From President Fillmore the document went straight to the State Department. According to an account given by George J. Abbott; 'Mr. Everett came down to the Department with a large roll of manuscript in his hand, and said to me: "Mr. Abbott, please copy this, keep it close, and have it ready for to-morrow's mail." I called my swiftest copyist, gave him proper directions, and sent him to his desk, which he did not leave, except for a brief lunch, until ten o'clock at night, though that paper was written the night before.'[1] Perhaps it was for this reason that Mr. Abbott, at a later time, expressed it as his opinion that Mr. Everett was the ablest man who had been in the State Department during the several administrations that he knew about.

A careful study of this extraordinary document, which was written in this remarkable way, would be interesting and rewarding; but the vital points are all that call for comment. In brief: Mr. Everett gave the French and English Governments clearly to understand that, while the United States did not covet the acquisition of Cuba, it yet considered the condition of the island 'as mainly an American question.'

Cuba [he wrote] lies at our doors. It commands the approach to the Gulf of Mexico, which washes five of our States. It bars the entrance of that great river which drains half the North American continent, and with its tributaries forms the largest system of internal water-communication in the world. It keeps watch at the door-way of our intercourse with California by the isthmus route. If [he continued, using an illustration which presented the matter

[1] *Dorchester Centennial*, p. 50.

with graphic precision to French and English eyes] — if an island like Cuba, belonging to the Spanish Crown, guarded the entrance of the Thames and the Seine, and the United States should propose a convention like this to France and England, those Powers would assuredly feel that the disability assumed by ourselves was far less serious than that which we asked them to assume. . . . Still, for domestic reasons, on which, in a communication of this kind, it might not be proper to dwell, the President thinks that the incorporation of the island into the Union at the present time, although effected with the consent of Spain, would be a hazardous measure; and he would consider its acquisition by force, except in a just war with Spain (should an event so greatly to be deprecated take place), as a disgrace to the civilization of our age.

After these preliminary words, Mr. Everett went on to sketch the territorial development of the United States — the purchase of Louisiana, the incorporation of Texas in the Union, and the settlement of California by which 'the great circuit of intelligence round the globe was completed.'

Such [he could say] is the territorial development of the United States in the past century. Is it possible that Europe can contemplate it with an unfriendly or jealous eye? What would have been her condition in these trying years but for the outlet we have furnished for her starving millions? Every addition to the territory of the American Union has given homes to European destitution and gardens to European want. [In the meantime, he went on] Spain has retained of her extensive dominions in this hemisphere but the two islands of Cuba and Porto Rico. A respectful sympathy with the fortunes of an ancient ally and a gallant people, with whom the United States have ever maintained the most friendly relations, would, if no other reason existed, make it our duty to leave her in the undisturbed possession of this little remnant of her mighty trans-Atlantic empire. The President desires to do so; no word, or deed of his will ever question her title, or shake her possession. But can it be expected to last very long? Can it resist this mighty current in the fortunes of the world? Is it desirable that it should do so? Can it be for the interest of Spain to cling to a possession that can only be maintained by a garrison of twenty-five or thirty thousand troops, a powerful naval force, and an annual expenditure for both arms of the service of at least twelve millions of dollars? Cuba, at this moment, costs more to Spain than the entire naval and military establishment of the United States costs the Federal

Government! So far from being really injured by the loss of the island, there is no doubt that, were it peacefully transferred to the United States, a prosperous commerce between Cuba and Spain, resulting from ancient associations and common language and tastes, would be far more productive than the best contrived system of colonial taxation.

For these reasons, and because the Government of the United States from the days of Washington and Jefferson had disliked 'entangling alliances,' Mr. Everett informed the French and English Governments that the President felt constrained to 'decline respectfully the invitation of France and England to become parties to the proposed convention.'

This long and searching document, of mingled eloquence and insight, written, as we have seen, in a rush of rhetoric on the evening of November 19th, was copied the next day at the State Department; but it was not given to Congress and made public until January 5th. No sooner was it published, however, than the applause began. It was read not only with commendation, but with enthusiasm. N. L. Frothingham wrote:

Your brilliant State paper I read twice over as soon as it appeared, with my best care and highest admiration. This morning I have read it again. Such a truly American document will be the praise of the whole land. It seems to me the greatest Manifesto that has ever been made to the European nations from these shores. I hope you will pardon my saying thus much with my small knowledge upon such great matters. . . .

The approval was general; the national satisfaction spontaneous. Both parties united in their praises. In the Senate, General Cass said: 'It is marked by a lofty, patriotic, American feeling. I have seldom seen a document more conclusive in its argument, or more beautiful in its style or illustrations.' Stephen A. Douglas agreed, and declared that it was 'applauded by the almost unanimous voice of the American people.' Nearly fifty years later it was the judgment of James Ford Rhodes, the most impartial of American historians, that, 'Never had the success of a Secretary of State been more complete; and yet the Cuban question was an extremely delicate one to handle.' [1]

The reception of the letter abroad was naturally very different. It seems to have nettled Lord John Russell, who indulged 'in some sarcastic remarks' in presenting the correspondence to Parliament. He referred to the length of the document, and its unnecessary disquisition on well-known facts of history.

> It occurs to Her Majesty's Government [he said] to ask for what purpose are these arguments introduced with so much preparation, and urged with so much ability? It would appear that the purpose, not fully avowed, but hardly concealed, is to procure the admission of a doctrine that the United States have an interest in Cuba to which Great Britain and France cannot pretend.

To all this Lord Russell offered objection, and the objections were communicated to our State Department. Mr. Everett by this time was out of office; but his successor, Mr. Marcy, sent him the correspondence. The matter went no further; but Everett wrote Lord John a private letter, somewhat sharp as well as firm in tone, in which he took exception to his lordship's sarcastic comments.[2] There the matter ended till nearly half a century had gone by, and the Spanish War broke out. Then, in 1897, the whole correspondence was republished with an introduction by Edward Everett Hale, who included with Edward Everett's official letter as Secretary of State a letter by Alexander H. Everett written in 1825, when he was Minister to Spain, and addressed to the President of the United States.[3]

Taking account of this Cuban affair alone, it is no wonder that Everett could declare in his journal, a year or two after he had returned to private life: 'I am even now terrified at the thought of the amount of work done by me and of the necessary haste with which important documents were turned off.'

---

[1] Rhodes: *History of the United States*, I, 294.

[2] See *Correspondence on the Proposed Tripartite Convention relative to Cuba*. Little, Brown & Co., Boston, 1853.

[3] See *Cuba: The Everett Letters on Cuba*. Boston, George H. Ellis, 1897.

The Whigs went out of office and the Democrats came in on March 4th, Franklin Pierce having been elected President. Everett's term as Secretary of State automatically, therefore, came to an end. He had been in office for four months, and they were, as I have said, among the most memorable and fruitful months of his whole career. His life at Washington, however, was still to continue; for, earlier in the year, he had been elected to the United States Senate. He was at the peak of popularity at the time, having just gained public favor in the Cuban matter, and he was the choice of the House on the first ballot which was taken on February 2, 1853. The next day the Massachusetts Senate concurred, giving him twenty-eight out of a possible thirty-five votes, his two opponents, Caleb Cushing and Stephen C. Phillips, receiving but seven votes between them. He was naturally pleased with the election, and the evidence of public favor that went with it. And yet he had his misgivings from the first. He had an intense dislike for the strife of tongues. Contention was hostile to his whole nature. He enjoyed calm seas, and was not meant to 'ride the storm.' His place was in a diplomatic sphere and not where the baser passions of mankind were stirred. And yet, knowing himself as well as he did, he never seriously thought of putting by the honor. The only thing that seriously disturbed him was the fact that, in case he declined election, his friend Robert C. Winthrop would probably be the candidate. But there was no feeling in the matter so far as Winthrop was concerned. He frankly recognized the superior claims of his older and more distinguished friend. The fact of the matter was, too, that Everett was constantly mentioned at this time as the next Whig candidate for the Presidency. He appeared a natural choice. His State papers had given enormous satisfaction. His nomination three years hence seemed distinctly probable. Everett clubs at this time, to promote his candidacy, were formed in many of the chief cities. Under the circumstances, it seemed natural that he should desire to remain in public office. But therein lay danger quite as much as opportunity. The Senate at that time contained several Presidential aspirants, among them Stephen A. Douglas and William H. Seward. The Chamber was, therefore, rather unusually charged with plottings and plannings of a partisan character. And when it came to political schemes and wire-pulling campaigns, Everett was at a hopeless disadvantage. He was too guileless to play politics successfully — too high-minded to have anything to do with the making of bargains or the exchange of pledges. 'Politics,' according to Lord Morley, 'is not an art, but a dodge'; and in proportion as Edward Everett was good at the one, he was wholly disqualified for the other.

But no signs of trouble were apparent in the spring of 1853. The political sky was clear: a period of calm water apparently lay ahead of the Ship of State. And yet, Everett had distinct premonitions of approaching trouble, which he attributed, however, to his domestic anxieties, and to the uncertainty of his own health. He wrote his daughter immediately after hearing of his overwhelming election to the Senate.

DEAREST CHARLIE, — I was yesterday and the day before chosen a Senator of the United States for six years from 4th of March, 1853. This is another important and unexpected event in my life. I shall accept it, but whether my health will hold out (I might well add my life) for six years is a great question. . . .

Nor did misgivings cease as time went on. He took his seat on March 4th, and in due season became a member of the Committee on Foreign Relations, which was surely where he belonged. He was also, however, made a member of the Committee on Territories which was soon to become a storm centre.

In the main, however, he was in good spirits, and his hopes were high. He had desired the new position and was glad to obtain it. He told Winthrop that he thought the post ought to have been offered him in 1850, and he felt hurt on that occasion 'at being unceremoniously whistled down.'

Three weeks after the session opened, in the course of a debate, he said to the Senators that he considered his new position as perhaps the highest of his public life. Except for his own uncertain health and for the deplorable illness of his wife, a period of smooth sailing seemed to lie ahead. He had every reason to believe that 'the horrible question of slavery,' as he called it, had been settled by the Compromise of 1850 for at least a generation. There seemed ample ground for confidence and little cause for fear. In addition to all, his buoyancy of spirit was added to by the fact of his being so constantly spoken of for the Presidency. He wrote to his son-in-law, in the late autumn of 1853:

There has been a good deal said this summer about my being a candidate; but it is owing merely to the fact that Clay and Webster are gone and General Scott out of the question. Somebody must be talked about. If I were as young as Senator D.,[1] an old Democrat, and the owner of one hundred slaves, I should stand a chance. One other if, I must add; and that is, if I was willing to do the hard work required for a candidate; as I suppose I should be, though a great fool for my pains.

Nevertheless the talk naturally pleased him, and when the Senate met in December he found himself on friendly terms with nearly every one and occupying a conspicuous position. He anticipated a certain enjoyment in the Senate; and felt that he could exert an influence that would be helpful. His journal gives the following account of the success of his first speech:

March 21, 1853. Spoke for about two hours on Central America and with greater success than I expected. . . . After I had finished, I received warm congratulations from every side of the House. One of the Senators from Indiana came up and said, 'I never thought before that I wanted to be any one but John Pettit; but while you were speaking I felt as if I wished I were E. E.'

My speech had two objects, to allay the apprehensions that we were likely to have difficulty with England in consequence of the affair of Central America, and then to administer a gentle rebuke to Judge Douglas's bellicose and annexing propensities.

[1] Douglas.

The next day Democratic Senators told him that his 'compliment' to Douglas was hugely enjoyed; for many Democrats regarded him as 'the greatest demagogue in the country,' and Everett's 'remark would do him good.'

But he was not left long to enjoy his new position. There suddenly arose a little cloud out of the West, 'as small as a man's hand.' But the hand was the hand of Senator Douglas, and, to nearly every one's amazement, the political sky became quickly and ominously dark. There were sounds of thunder in the South. Flashes of sectional hatred became apparent; and all at once the storm-winds of partisan passion were let loose. On Monday, January 23d, Stephen A. Douglas introduced into the Senate the famous Kansas-Nebraska Bill.

The motives of Senator Douglas in framing this bill and then presenting it are not wholly clear. He was, however, like Everett, an aspirant for the Presidency, and it may safely be asserted that the move of the Illinois Senator was made for the purpose of securing Southern support in the next Democratic Convention. This is not the place for describing in detail the provisions of the momentous bill.[1] It is enough for our present purpose to remind ourselves that this bill 'divided the Territory covered by the previous Nebraska Bill into two Territories, one directly west of Missouri and between the parallels of 37° and 40°, to be called Kansas, and the other north of this and between the parallels of 40° and 43°, to be called Nebraska. According to the Compromise of 1820 both of these Territories were forever barred to slavery. But this bill distinctly declared that the Compromise of 1820 was inconsistent with the constitutional principle of non-interference with slavery by Congress, that it was therefore inoperative, void, and repealed by the Compromise of 1850, and that hereafter each Territory, whether north or south

---

[1] Rhodes calls it the most momentous measure in the history of Congress up to the time of the Civil War. (*History of the United States*, 1, 490.)

of the parallel of 36° 30', should admit or exclude slavery as its people should decide.'[1]

The bill was like the explosion of a bombshell. The Missouri Compromise had been in operation for more than thirty years. It had never been seriously questioned. It had come to seem almost a part of the Constitution itself. And now, it was suddenly to be done away, and territory which had been looked upon as forbidden to slavery was possibly to be opened to the ugly system. Free-Soilers, Abolitionists, and independent Democrats were up in arms at once. The North was deeply stirred, and rose with a great Remonstrance Address which was circulated freely.

Everett took quick and deep alarm. He foresaw with terrible clearness the trouble that lay ahead. In letters to his daughter and son-in-law there are constant references to this 'horrible Nebraska Bill,' this 'detested bill,' etc. The bill was reported by the Territorial Committee, of which he was a member, and he opposed it in committee. This is an important point to bear in mind, for in the tempest of charges and countercharges which soon were vehemently made, it was asserted of Everett that he was doubtful for a time whether to oppose the bill or not, and Pierce asserts in his 'Life of Sumner'[2] that Everett had not opposed it in committee. Everett's journal, however, gives direct evidence to the contrary. The passages should be quoted.

January 4, 1854. The Territorial Committee met this morning. Present, the Chairman, General Jones of Iowa, Mr. Johnson, and myself. Judge Douglas read the report which he proposed and which was adopted by the concurring vote of all present but myself. I dissented on the ground that by introducing into the bill the territorial compromise of 1850, and by reënacting the Fugitive Slave Law, the anti-slavery agitation of 1850 would be reopened and that it would be better to take the bill of last year without variation. I also expressed doubts whether there were sufficient inhabitants in the country to need a territorial government of the first class, and

---

[1] Johnston: *History of American Politics*, p. 159.
[2] See Pierce: *Memoir and Letters of Charles Sumner*, vol. III, for a full discussion of this whole episode.

also whether we could, without injustice to the Indians, proceed to organize a Territory.

January 18, 1854. Had a conversation with Judge Dawson of Georgia on the subject of the Nebraska Bill. I told him that I apprehended it would be impossible for me to vote for it. He intimated that one great object for which it was brought forward was '*to put me to the test.*'

January 23, 1854. A meeting of the Territorial Committee in the House to-day and a substitute for the Nebraska Bill brought forward, creating two Territories instead of one, rendering the provision relative to the Fugitive Slave Law more stringent, and repealing the eighth section of the Missouri Law commonly called the Compromise.

January 27. At the instance of Mr. Walley, and with the concurrence of Messrs. Appleton and Edmands, a letter was sent signed by us four and expressing the opinion that it was inexpedient to get up resolutions in the Legislature of Massachusetts against the repeal of the Missouri Compromise. I felt a little dubious of the policy of this step, which was taken on the suggestion of Mr. H. J. Gardner. They were fearful that if resolutions were passed they would contain matter which might embarrass us. A greater danger may be that if none are brought forward by conservatives, the business will fall into other hands.

The debate on the bill in the Senate was long and fierce. It began with an angry and intemperate speech by Douglas on January 30th, and it lasted until daybreak on March 4th. Scenes took place which were far from educational or edifying. Douglas lost his temper at the outset, and his language was described as 'violent and abusive — more becoming a pothouse than the Senate.' Chase spoke with great effect against the bill, and so did Seward and Charles Sumner. Everett took the floor on February 8th, after all three of them had made long and forceful speeches. It has been charged that he was doubtful at first which side to take upon the subject — that he hesitated, wavered, and took counsel of his political friends at home. But that is not an accurate description of his attitude of mind. It is true that he turned to his friends for advice. But he also sounded a warning. The following circular letter, dated January 19, 1854, is interesting. Everett was opposed to the bill, and stood firmly by the Missouri Compromise; but he was eager none the less not to formulate and proclaim his opposition in such a way as would needlessly injure his political prospects and promote disharmony.

I enclose you herewith a Senate document containing: 1st, Mr. Douglas's report on the territorial organization of Nebraska; 2d, a bill which passed the House of Representatives by a large majority last winter, and was lost in the Senate, probably for want of time; 3d, Mr. Douglas's bill reported in the Senate this winter. The material points of difference between the two bills are those which pertain to slavery. I have placed a mark against them in the margin.

The measure with these new features is of great importance, and likely to be not less interesting as a subject of controversy in and out of Congress than the admission of Missouri in 1820 or of the new Territories in 1850.

I take the liberty to request your attention to the contents of this document, and I should be grateful to you for the communication of your own views of the subject and those of such confidential friends as you may think proper to consult. I subjoin a list of gentlemen to whom I have sent a copy of this letter and of the Senate document, in case you should think it expedient to join with them in a united expression of opinion.

The discussion of the subject, it is intended, shall begin on Monday the 23d. Copies sent to the following gentlemen; it would have been sent to more could more copies of the document have been procured: Governor Washburn, President of the Senate, Speaker of the House, Hon. R. C. Winthrop, Hon. N. Appleton, Hon. N. Hale, Hon. A. Lawrence, Hon. R. Choate, Hon. G. S. Hillard, Hon. E. Kellogg, S. Lawrence, Esq.

By comparing Section 10th, page 16th, with the latter part of Section 14th, page 18th, it will appear that the reënactment of the Fugitive Slave Law is purely gratuitous.

Everett was not in the best of condition when he arose to speak, as the journal well explains:

February 7. Obliged to take the floor to-day on the Nebraska Bill, but Douglas having brought in a new amendment concocted with great care and skill, I asked a postponment of a day to consider it, which was very ungraciously yielded by Douglas, but handsomely granted by the House. My preparation is very inadequate, and it happens, unfortunately, that I am called to speak on the most important subject and the most critical occasion of my life, with less premeditation than almost ever before.

February 8. Sidney and Fanny arrived from New York yesterday at 9 P.M. to make me a visit. Right glad to see them, although it cost me a precious hour and a half of preparation. Obliged to sit up till one last night and to rise at four this morning after a restless night. I was, of course, in rather poor condition to speak. . . . Although the weather was adverse, the Senate was thronged, and hundreds, as I was told, had to go away. I spoke about an hour and a half, and never with greater success. After I had finished, I received the congratulations of the Senators from every part of the country and every shade of opinion from the most ultra free-soil to the most ultra pro-slavery. This, according to the Scripture, is dangerous. I dare say the *contre-coup* will come.

The last words were unfortunately only too prophetic. The '*contre-coup*,' however, did not come at once. There was a lull before the storm-winds were let loose. The speech itself was a good one, if not among his greatest. It produced an immediate effect, and secured a wide circulation, thirty thousand copies being needed to meet the demand. The galleries of the Senate Chamber were crowded, as the journal says. The House was deserted. The great orator was to deliver himself on a great question, and interest was increased for the reason that the report had gone around that he would favor the bill. But if there had been any serious doubt on that point it was quickly dispelled. Mr. Everett said:

I rise to speak for myself, and without authority to speak for anybody else, as a friend and supporter of the Compromises of 1850, and to inquire whether it is my duty, and how far it is the duty of others who agree with me in that respect, out of fidelity to those compromises, to support the bill which is now awaiting the action of the Senate. [He then went on to say:] It was with great regret . . . that, as a member of the Committee on Territories, I found myself unable to support the bill which the majority of that Committee had prepared to bring forward for the organization of these Territories. I should have rejoiced had it been in my power to give my support to the measure. But the hasty examination which, while the subject was before the Committee, I was able to give to it, disclosed objections to the bill which I could not overcome, and more deliberate inquiry has increased the force of those objections.

He next referred to the position of Mr. Webster, which he could do with peculiar authority, having been his lifelong friend and literary executor. He was listened to at this point with the closest possible attention, and what he had to say constituted the chief value of his speech. Referring to the famous Seventh of March Speech, saying that on that occasion Mr. Webster rose to a strain of impassioned eloquence which had never been surpassed within the walls of the Senate, he directed the attention of his hearers to that great speech, by so great an authority, in which the principle was laid down 'that the condition of every foot of land in the country, for slavery or non-slavery, is fixed by some irrepealable law.'

I trust that nothing which I have now said will be taken in derogation of the Compromises of 1850. I adhere to them: I stand by them! I do so for many reasons. One is respect for the memory of the great men who were authors of them. . . . But besides this, I am one of those — I am not ashamed to avow it — who believed at that time, and who still believe, that at that period the Union of these States was in great danger, and that the adoption of the compromise measures of 1850 contributed materially to avert that danger.

And finally, as he drew to a close, he used these impressive words which sum up the faith and principles upon which, up to this time, he had conscientiously shaped his whole political career:

One word more, Sir, and I have done. With reference to the great question of slavery — that terrible question — the only one on which the North and South of this Republic differ irreconcilably — I have not on this occasion a word to say. My humble career is drawing near its close; and I shall end it as I began, with using no other words on that subject than those of moderation, conciliation, and harmony between the two great sections of the country. I blame no one who differs from me in this respect; I allow to others, what I claim for myself, the credit for honesty and purity of motive. But for my own part, the rule of my life, as far as circumstances have enabled me to act up to it, has been to say nothing that would tend to unkind feeling on this subject. I have never known men on this, or on any other subject, to be convinced by hard epithets or denunciation.

I believe the Union of these States is the greatest possible blessing — that it comprises within itself all other blessings political, natural, and social; and I trust that my own eyes may close long before the day shall come — if it ever shall come — when that Union shall be at an end. Sir, I share the opinions and the sentiments of that part of the country where I was born and educated, where my ashes will be laid, and where my children will succeed me! But in relation to my fellow-citizens in other parts of the country, I will treat their constitutional and their legal rights with respect, and their feelings with tenderness. I believe them to be as good Christians, as good patriots, as good men as we are. And I claim that we, in our turn, are as good as they. I rejoiced to hear my friend from Kentucky utter the opinion that a wise and gracious Providence, in His own good time, will find the ways and the channels to remove from the land what I consider this great evil, and I do not expect that what has been done in three centuries and a half is to be undone in a day, or a year, or a few years; and I believe that in the meantime the desired end will be retarded rather than promoted by passionate, sectional agitation. . . . And finally, I doubt not that in His own good time the Ruler of all will vindicate the most glorious of His prerogatives,

From seeming evil, still educing good.

The speech, especially in its closing clauses, must have sounded strangely in that chamber which had listened to so much rancor and personal abuse. But, compressed into that final paragraph we have Everett's whole creed as a statesman. He was a clergyman in politics. He endeavored from first to last to employ the principles of the pulpit and to practice the gentle virtues of the Ministry of Religion amid all the heat and dust of the political arena. It was his constant endeavor to be a true disciple of the Master. But whether on principle, or because of temperament, it may be that in living out and giving expression to the *gentle* precepts of the Nazarene, he forgot about the sterner ones! He called to mind the Beatitudes, but he put aside the 'Woes' that were pronounced upon the Pharisees. He was mindful of the

Master's attitude of forgiveness toward 'publicans and sinners,' and he failed to see the significance of the fact that the money-changers were driven from the Temple precincts.

Nevertheless, as I have said, the speech was received with favor, and made an instant impression which almost equalled anything that he had done in recent years. Charles Sumner, as soon as he sat down, crossed the Senate Chamber, thanked and congratulated him, and said: 'You have dealt the monster a blow between the eyes.' It was referred to as a 'great speech,' and when first made it seemed to give exceptional satisfaction North and South, and he said himself that for 'immediate effect' he had seldom done better. The Abolitionists complained of it as 'tame,' and 'weak,' and yet they were forced to acknowledge that it accomplished more than many of their violent diatribes. Even the ardent biographer of Sumner had to confess that the 'speech, wanting in spirit as it was, was nevertheless effective with a large body of conservatives at the North, who were by habit braced against any arguments or appeals which savored of anti-slavery sentiment.'[1]

It is well to take note of and remember all of this, for trouble lay ahead when invective and abuse were heaped on Everett as they had never been before in the course of his long and dignified political career. The outburst and the occasion of it were as sudden and as unexpected as the introduction of the bill itself, and with quite as little solid ground on which to rest. The debate had lasted for somewhat more than a month. On March 3d, the Senate having met at the usual hour, a lively discussion took place which continued through the afternoon and evening. The Chamber was crowded. Douglas then arose to close the debate. It was just before midnight. He spoke until the day was breaking; and then the vote was taken. It had been fully understood that the bill would pass, and the vote stood 38 in favor, and 14 in opposition. But when the 'roll of honor,' with the names of

[1] Pierce's *Sumner*, III, 355.

those fourteen men, was published, the name of Everett was not among them. What had happened? Why had he failed when the crucial moment came? It seemed like a dodging of the issue — an attempt to hedge! But the explanation was very simple. Mr. Everett was in the Senate during the final debate and he remained in his seat until three-thirty in the morning. He then went home, *ill* — feeling it impossible to stay any longer, and believing that the vote would not be taken for another day. There was an instant outcry. The Press was venomous. It was said of him that he had spoken only, and had failed to act. Many of his friends even seemed to suspect his motives. The accusation cut him to the quick. When the Senate met again on March 7th, he stood up in his place and asked the privilege of having his vote recorded; but it was refused; a single objection prevented.

A description of what happened may not be amiss. On Tuesday, March 7th, standing in his place, Mr. Everett said:

Mr. President: I am desirous of making a brief explanation to the Senate in regard to myself. I was absent from my place, necessarily, when the vote on the passage of the Nebraska Bill was taken on Monday morning. I was severely indisposed at the time: and, as is well known to my friends, my general state of health for the last two or three weeks has not been good. I was over-fatigued by the lateness of the hour, and having remained in the Senate till half-past three o'clock, was utterly unable to remain any longer. I suppose it cannot be a matter of doubt with any of my brother Senators how I should have voted. Having non-concurred in the Committee on Territories, before the bill was brought into the Senate, on the question of reporting it; having expressed my opinions in full in opposition to the policy of the bill in the remarks which I had submitted to the Senate, and having voted in the negative on the last amendment of the Senator for Illinois (Mr. Douglas) proposing to declare the Missouri restriction 'inoperative and void,' it is hardly necessary to say that, if I had been here, my vote would have been recorded in the negative on the passage of the bill. Nevertheless, Sir, as it is a matter of very great consequence and interest, I am desirous, with the permission of the Senate, which the Presiding Officer informs me can be given by unanimous consent, of having my vote entered on the Journal as against the bill.

I will, therefore, venture to ask the favor of the Senators to allow my vote to be thüs recorded.

Mr. Clayton thereupon stated that he also was absent because of illness and asked that *his* vote likewise should be recorded against the bill.

There was some discussion. Senators asked what the precedent was, and whether a precedent had better be established. It appeared that only once in the history of the Senate, and that very recently, had such action been taken, and a vote recorded afterwards. Thereupon Mr. *Dodge* of Iowa objected to having the thing done. 'If this request is granted,' he said, 'there will be no end to the thing. It is with great respect to the two Senators that I object.' Mr. Everett and Mr. Clayton thereupon waived the request.[1]

The whole episode is so important and proved so disastrous to Everett's career that it is best to let him tell his own story. The account in the journal is as follows:

Friday, March 3. I went to dine with the Secretary of the Treasury. Ten Senators who were expected sent excuses at five o'clock. Went back to the Senate at nine. . . . Douglas made his general reply. He spoke with great vehemence and personality toward all whom he supposed to be non-combatants. It must be admitted that Chase, Sumner, and Wade had given him great provocation. But his replies were coarse and ungentlemanlike. There was on the part of many members evident excess in liquor, among others —— who kept continually rising to explain. Douglas spoke I think at least four hours. He was followed by Houston. I could not stay later than half-past three and came home exhausted and ill. The vote was taken at five, and stood 37 to 14. Had all been present the vote would have stood 40 to 20.

Saturday, March 4. Very much exhausted to-day. Found that the Senate had adjourned over till Tuesday. Few things within my knowledge have happened more discreditable to our legislation than the passage of the Nebraska Bill. It is wholly uncalled for . . . and is a wanton breaking-up of the settlement of the slavery question which took place thirty-four years ago. At the beginning of the session, Douglas said to me in committee that the provisions of the bill as at first reported were well calculated to make a Northern man hesitate, and that no man was so wild as to think of repealing the Missouri Compromise. When, however, a motion to repeal it was made by a Southern Whig (Mr. Dixon of Kentucky), it was eagerly adopted by him. Houston of Texas and Bell of Tennessee, members of the Committee on Territories, both voted against the bill. Had they done so in committee, it would not have passed, but Bell took care to be absent at his mines, and Houston (so Douglas told me) neglected to attend the committee, but told Douglas he might report anything if he would only put in the Compromise of 1850.

March 5. The New York 'Herald' extremely abusive of the Senators who did not vote on the Nebraska Bill, accusing them of 'dodging.'

March 7. The New York 'Tribune' contains a savage attack on me for not voting on the Nebraska Bill. I asked Seward why he allowed his organ to abuse me at that rate? A short time afterwards he brought me the draft of a letter addressed to the 'Intelligencer' and signed by himself and Truman Smith, stating that they knew I left the Senate from ill-health. It was afterwards signed by Foot, Wade, and Fish. Seward and Wade carried it to the 'Intelligencer' office. Seaton thought its insertion of doubtful expediency, and Gale came up to tell me so. I fully concurred with him and requested its omission. Mr. Edmands (who happened to be in the office of the 'Intelligencer') came up on the same errand. I sent to Seward to inform him.

It is always difficult, however, to call back anything of the kind when once it has been put into a reporter's hand. It may even be that Seward was not very eager to suppress the statement. He was astute enough to know that it could do Everett no possible good, and might do him positive harm; and Everett was a dangerous rival in the race for the Presidential nomination. At any rate, the statement was published in the New York 'Tribune' and the injury proved almost irreparable. A great battle had been fought, and 'Crillon was not there.' His vote would have made no difference in the result. The bill was destined to pass by a large majority whether with or without his vote. But that was not the point. The fact that he had been suspected of vacillation beforehand gave ground for suspicions of weakness and timidity. Charles Eliot Norton voiced the general opinion when he wrote to

Arthur Hugh Clough: 'Everett's course has been pitiably timid and time-serving, and his political career may be considered finished — he wanted the Presidency, and misses it by trying too hard for it. "He hasn't got backbone enough to be sexton of a church," was a judgment pronounced on him by one of the "people" in an omnibus the other day.' In somewhat the same vein Charles F. Adams wrote to Sumner: 'Your colleague has not bettered himself here by his last movement. He has entirely verified what I predicted of him to you the year of his election — stuff not good enough to wear in rainy weather, though bright enough in sunshine.' [1]

Much of this censure, however, was distinctly unjust. Of Everett's illness, there can be no doubt. Moreover, his position in regard to the burning question of slavery was entirely tenable. It was the position of all moderate men, and of those who had wisdom enough to count the cost. Much as he hated slavery, he loved the Union more. The Union with him was what liberty was with Gibbon. 'Liberty,' we are told of Gibbon, 'was in fact his ultimate standard. Perhaps there was no deeper feeling in his breast than jealousy of personal freedom and independence which he described as the first of earthly blessings.'

And thus it was with Everett in regard to the Union. All his hopes and his entire confidence in the future progress of the world were centred around the preservation of the Federal Union. If that failed and became broken up by secession, so that a United States South and a United States North were the result, he saw nothing but border warfare and endless causes for friction in the days to come. 'The Union,' therefore, was his criterion and cry from first to last. If Daniel Webster was rightly called the great Defender of the Constitution, Edward Everett was in his way the great Defender of the Union.

With this passionate devotion to the Union, he also cherished a positive hatred of slavery. This latter fact is one that

[1] Pierce's *Sumner*, III, 369.

must not be ignored. Over and over again, after his one rhetorical blunder in 1825, he was strong and constant in affirming it. He wrote to Fillmore on March 7, 1849:

I am opposed to the extension of slavery where it does not exist and earnestly desire its cessation where it does. But I greatly doubt whether these objects are to be promoted by popular agitation, and as far as it is right and proper that they should be drawn into the vortex of party, I look to the great Whig Party of the country, South as well as North, as the party by whose united counsels, moderation, and patriotism, this object is to be effected.

In 1848, when he was wanted as Vice-Presidential nominee of the Free Soil Party — an honor which Charles F. Adams later accepted — he wrote to Charles Sumner:

With the avowed object of the Buffalo Convention, viz. to prevent the extension of slavery, I deeply sympathize. If I thought my accepting a nomination from them would promote that object, I would not hesitate a moment. Such, however, is not my opinion, and this without any reference to the probable success or failure of the nomination. . . . I have derived from my political experiences an extreme dislike of third parties. . . . I pray God that I may live to see the day when all good citizens North and South will unite in wiping out this dreadful blot upon the fair name of our country.

A year or two later, he expressed himself still more strongly. He could write to *Sumner* in *1850*, after acknowledging the receipt of a volume of orations that Sumner had sent him:

I think I do not yield to any man in my abhorrence of slavery. Could I emancipate the slaves in America by one act of my will, and with the assurance of bettering their condition, I feel that for that purpose I could cheerfully sacrifice ease, property, and life itself. It is because I believe that the agitation of the slavery question, as it is carried on among us, and especially in connection with party politics, tends rather to retard than promote this end, that I cannot sympathize with you in reference to it. As this is perhaps the only thing of importance on which we differ, and there is otherwise, if you will allow me to say so, so much which is congenial in our tastes and pursuits, I am not at times without misgivings that you, and your friends who act with you, may be in the right, and I in the wrong. But so often as I reconsider the subject, I find new reasons to think that the anti-slavery agitation as conducted in the

North tends directly to disunion, civil war, and a murderous struggle between the races, and that it must in the same degree obstruct and postpone the mild influences which, under divine Providence, are at work to effect the eventual abolition of slavery.

The consciousness of being right, however, and of holding firmly to a carefully thought-out and tenable position did not save Mr. Everett from much mental suffering. He was very sensitive to hostile criticism, and he was reported by his friends in Washington at this time as looking sad and melancholy. Seward referred to him in his diary as 'worried about his mishaps and the uncharitableness of the press.' On the very day, March 12th, that Seward made this entry, Everett wrote to Winthrop:

I fear it will be long before we hear the last of Nebraska. I have been a good deal wounded at the readiness manifested to suspect me of 'dodging'; a suspicion — after the ground I had taken against the bill — as absurd as it was gratuitous. You may depend upon it — notwithstanding all mean insinuations to the contrary — that my vote against the bill was regarded by every Senator as just as certain as that of Douglas for it.

What seemed like an opportunity for Everett to redeem himself came a few days after his failure to vote upon the Kansas-Nebraska Bill. He was handed a Remonstrance against the passage of the bill and asked to present it to the Senate. It was a petition couched in very emphatic language, and was signed by more than three thousand clergymen of various sects and denominations in New England. The petition read:

The undersigned, clergymen of different denominations in New England, hereby, in the name of Almighty God, and in His presence, do solemnly protest against the passage of what is known as the Nebraska Bill. . . . We protest against it as a great moral wrong, as a breach of faith eminently unjust to the moral principles of the community, and subversive of all confidence in national engagements; as a measure full of danger to the peace, and even the existence of our beloved Union, and exposing us to the righteous judgments of the Almighty.

The Remonstrance was signed by many great and eminent men, among them being Mark Hopkins, President of Williams College; T. D. Woolsey, President of Yale; Edward Hitchcock, President of Amherst; and Lyman Beecher, Horace Bushnell, Theodore Parker, and Cyrus A. Bartol. The petition would have counted for little if presented by Sumner, whose views on the matter were well known and extreme. So Everett was entrusted with the document. It was the purpose of the signers to have it reach Washington before the vote on the bill was taken. Owing to delay, however, it arrived too late, and of course was robbed of any influence it might have had. Nevertheless, Everett presented it on March 14th, having an opportunity to do no more than glance at it hastily before he did so. He explained to the Senate that it was signed by three thousand and fifty New England ministers, there being in that section only thirty-eight hundred clergymen of all denominations, so that it represented an overwhelming majority of all the ministers of the New England States. Everett then read the Remonstrance and a sensational and angry outburst was the result. Senators on the Nebraska side sprang to their feet, and one by one protested against the preaching of political sermons; the 'desecration of the pulpit'; 'prostituting the sacred desk'; and the mistake of the clergy when they 'plunged into the turbid pool of politics.' Douglas himself bitterly denounced 'political preachers,' and said it was understood that on one day in New England fifteen hundred to two thousand sermons had been preached against the bill. On the opposite side, Senators and others complained afterwards that Everett had been lukewarm in his presentation of the petition, and had spoken for it in a weak and half-apologetic way. And there probably was ground for this complaint. The whole business was distasteful to Everett. As he wrote to Winthrop: 'My position is extremely difficult here, as I am thrown, in spite of myself, into coöperation with men whose general course on this subject I greatly disapprove; while the ultraism of the

South leaves no middle ground to stand upon.' That expressed his dilemma precisely. He was opposed to slavery — bitterly opposed to it, as we have seen; but he was also, and quite as bitterly, opposed to the methods that were being used to get rid of slavery. He was a disciple of Erasmus, not of Luther! It was his belief that in getting rid of the evil by violent means, a greater evil would befall the country and the Union be destroyed! The 'operation' might be 'successful,' as modern surgery so often says; but he did not wish to have the patient — that is, the Union — die! A few of his letters addressed to members of his family tell the somewhat pathetic story of his feelings and his physical condition at this time.

To Mrs. Henry Augustus Wise

WASHINGTON, *March* 30, 1854

... My health has rapidly fallen off, as it did the second year at Cambridge, and for the same cause, too much worry, and in the present instance both on account of public and private cares. I had a long talk with Dr. Warren while I was at home, the result of which was — if I found this to continue — that I had better give up at once, and before what little there is left of vitality in my constitution is subdued. I begin to think it impossible to get through dog-days, and the protracted daily sessions which take place at that stage of the Congressional Session. Besides this, the state of things at home is a constant burden to my spirits. I know if I were at home I could do your mother no substantial good; but my absence is a standing source of painful reflection to her — her wasted, death-like face follows me in my dreams — and, though some of her complaints are imaginary, what she says of Will's suffering in my absence is well founded. He really needs my supervision, and is not safe without it. The last month he was down as low as the 9th (!), although unquestionably able to be the head of his class. It would be a subject of lasting remorse with me if so fine a mind should make shipwreck through my neglect. Then, finally, the aspect of things in the political world is wholly changed since I agreed to come to the Senate; in fact the change has taken place within three months. There was then a fine field of usefulness, if not of distinction, open to me. Now the National Whig Party has ceased to exist — its conservative portion in the non-slaveholding States is annihilated — and we have nothing in prospect, for the next three years, but anti-slavery agitation. This I cannot conscientiously join, for it leads inevitably toward the dissolution of the Union; but I cannot oppose it, for it is justly provoked by the attempt to repeal the Missouri Compromise; nor resist it — for it is sweeping all before it. Discouraging as the state of things is, I will stand my ground as long as my health permits; but if I find that is really giving way — as I have too much reason to apprehend — I shall beat a retreat....

To Henry Augustus Wise

WASHINGTON, *April* 10, 1854

... You speak of not having yet got my 'great speech.' When it was first made it gave great satisfaction North and South, and for immediate effect I never did better. Over thirty thousand copies were subscribed for for distribution. But with the progress of anti-slavery excitement at the North, my speech was found to be below the war-fever....

Just as these things were blowing over a little, an old affair — quietly disposed of last summer — relative to my having furnished the original draft of the Hülsemann letter to Mr. Webster — has been dragged before the public by the New York 'Evening Post,' with highly invidious comments and charges of breach of confidence toward Mr. Webster, though he always intended to take the first opportunity, after he retired from office, to mention my agency in that matter. An attempt is making to get up a clamor against me on this ground, although I think it will not succeed. All these things, however, in my feeble state of health worry me. I am not *pachydermatous* enough. You will think at my age — I am sixty to-morrow — I ought to be callous, but I am not so, and the very suspicion of having done wrong makes me uneasy — especially as we New-Englanders have the amiable habit of being the first to lacerate the characters of our public men. Then with all these political troubles, my letters from home come filled with the most perplexing details of domestic care. Under all these troubles, I really think I shall have to quit public life and live at home:— a strange idea you will think after the preparations made to establish myself here, but everything has changed within a twelvemonth. The revival of slavery agitation has put an entirely new face on public affairs — and the failure of my health, and the state of the family have done the same to all that concerns me personally. I dwell a little more on this, because the increasing probability that I shall resign takes away all motive for your hastening your return on my account. I really doubt whether another winter will find me here; indeed, I doubt if I could live through dog-days.

The reference in this letter to the fact that he had prepared
the original draft of the Hülsemann document calls attention
to another matter which was adding to his worries at this
time. Just after leaving the State Department, where he had
covered himself with glory, it seemed to Mr. Everett that he
might fairly and properly enough take the public into his
confidence in regard to his share in the preparation of one
of Mr. Webster's most popular State papers. The general
similarity in tone between the Cuban letter and the one to
Hülsemann might well have struck the careful observer.
Moreover, when Fletcher Webster was going through his
father's papers, and came upon the proof of Everett's authorship of the document, he said very naturally, 'This ought to be
made known,' without having any fixed or definite intention,
however, of giving the facts to the general public. Everett,
therefore, had his draft of the letter, and the document as
given out, showing Webster's amendments and additions,
printed in a little pamphlet. He did not do so, however,
without first consulting George T. Curtis and Fletcher
Webster, neither of whom saw any objection to the step.
Nathan Hale, however, strongly disapproved of the proceeding and urged that nothing should be made public.
'It would look,' he wrote to Everett, 'like a robbing of the
dead.' In the meantime, too, the printer had been cautioned
that he must consider the matter as wholly confidential.
Everett himself gave away only one copy of the pamphlet.

Nevertheless, there was a leak somewhere. The newspapers
learned the facts, and Everett was accused of betraying
a trust and playing false to a dead friend who could not
defend his reputation! Everett was deeply hurt. He felt
aggrieved that a man could not lay claim to what was his
own, and asserted that, except for his illness and untimely
death, Webster would himself have made the facts public.
Altogether, the newspaper attacks that were somewhat
bitter caused him to realize that he had been playing with
two-edged tools. His authorship of a famous State paper,

instead of adding to his reputation and helping his Presidential candidacy, worked directly the other way. He recognized too late that he had been precipitate. A fuller knowledge of the world would have warned him that what another might do for him, he could not do for himself. Here, therefore, he had added reason for worry and self-searching. Altogether, his troubles were becoming greater than he could bear. His equanimity was wholly lost. The joy and success of his four months in the State Department were all destroyed by the pain and discomfort of his position as Senator. The whole wretched business became more and more distasteful. A great longing laid hold upon him to resign from the Senate and secure a little peace. Unlike Browning's hero, he was *never* a fighter, and now his physical condition made continued struggle out of the question. He had always been easily wounded by adverse opinion and criticism. He was extremely sensitive. In this respect he was the very opposite of his friend Macaulay, of whom Trevelyan wrote at a later day, 'He kept his happiness in his own hands, and never would permit it to depend upon the good-will or the forbearance of others. His biographer has no occasion to indite those woeful passages in which the sufferings of misunderstood genius are commended to the indignant commiseration of posterity.' With Everett it was absolutely different. He was much too self-reflecting, and, while he was grieving over what was past, his happiness slipped out of his grasp and he became poignantly sorry for himself.

At last, after another interview with Dr. Warren, he took the decisive step. He announced the fact to Mr. Winthrop in the following letter, May 12, 1854:

I have this day sent a private letter to the Governor acquainting him that I felt obliged by Dr. Warren's advice to resign my seat in the Senate. The deciding cause is my health, although the state of my family would justify my doing so. Were my symptoms of an equivocal nature, I would have made a longer trial; but my experience in Cambridge taught me the danger of delay in escaping the causes of disease at my time of life.

Winthrop wrote at once in reply and endeavored to dissuade him, alleging that his action would put him in a false light, and cause him to be still more severely criticized. He consulted others. Abbott Lawrence and George Ticknor urged delay. Rufus Choate cautioned him to say nothing about *finality*. The Whig Committee besought him strongly *not* to resign. George Hillard was the only one who was sympathetic and declared that he could not blame him for withdrawing. A second letter to Mr. Winthrop, immediately following the first one, made it evident that the die was definitely cast.

I am aware to how much invidious comment my resignation at this time will give rise; but it will come mainly from those who, let me do or say what I will, will make the same comments. There is no course left for men of moderate counsels between extremists at both ends of the scale.

I would not have quitted the field had it been physically possible for me to keep it; but if you will converse with Dr. Warren you will find that this is not the case. I of course consider my resignation as the end of my political career. I am quite content that it should close at this time, and though the *finale* is not particularly brilliant, I hope that the candid who survey the whole will allow me the praise of having tried to do my duty.

It must have been hard for Everett to write those closing words; but it cannot be doubted that he meant them. He fully considered that an end had come to all political activity, and indeed to further activity of any kind. This final period of service in Washington had lasted over eighteen months. He had begun it, as Secretary of State, by rising to his highest pitch of popularity. He now resigned as Senator baffled and defeated.

It had been his intention to return to Washington for the rest of the session, but 'Dr. Warren strenuously advised against it,' and the consequence was that he did not occupy his seat again in the Senate after the gruelling experiences in connection with the fatal and detested Kansas-Nebraska Bill. Perhaps it was well that it should have been so! At least it was appropriate: for that, after all, was the direct cause for his definite withdrawal from public life. I do not mean that his health was not an actuating reason, for it was. His health was definitely impaired; but it would not have become so painfully broken except for the worry that the bill had caused. The terrible and fatal problem of slavery had stepped suddenly across his path, and once again he had tried to find some middle ground on which to stand. His aim and object and ideal was to harmonize; and he was roughly thrust aside by the extremists of both North and South. The time had come for heroism, not for harmonizers: for duty, not decorum. The need of the hour was for conscience, not for compromise. And yet, the seeming failure was a prelude only to new and unexpected service. Everett was destined to withdraw from posts of statesmanship; but henceforth as an 'unofficial statesman' he was to render unexpected service, and to reach a pinnacle of influence in what was after all his truer sphere of action. For the moment, however, he retired, sad of heart and broken in body and spirit, to the seclusion of his library and the companionship of his books. After withdrawing from Cambridge, he had built for himself a spacious room extending back of his house on Summer Street which, large as it was, but barely sufficed to contain his books and works of art. It had become quite the talk of the town, and for a time visitors came almost daily to ask if they might see it.

Moreover, in his retirement, Mr. Everett had interests enough to occupy all his time and to engage such strength as his failing health had left him. The Boston Public Library, for example, at that time a very young but rapidly growing institution, claimed a great deal of his careful thought and assiduous attention. It was an institution very close to his heart, and it was he, in 1849, who really gave the impetus which led to the Library being established. In that year, while still living in Cambridge, he sent word to the Honorable J. P. Bigelow, the Mayor of Boston, saying that he should be glad to give the city his collection of public documents if the city would provide a suitable place for them. The offer having been ignored, he again wrote the Mayor on the subject early in the year of 1850, saying: 'I hope you will be able to do something this year toward the establishment of a city library. I shall be happy to offer to the acceptance of the city my collection of public documents, whenever you think it will be convenient to the city to receive them. It will contain near a thousand volumes when some chasms, which I hope to fill this winter, are supplied.'

No attention was paid to the matter for another six months and more, and then action was taken which gave the appearance of robbing Everett of any distinction which might attach itself to a possible claim of being the founder of the Library. An extract from the journal is pertinent in this connection.

October 30, 1854. My time much occupied to-day in preparing the second annual report of the Public Library. The first important step toward the establishment of this library was the donation of my collection of public documents and State papers. More than a year before the donation took place, I had requested Mr. Bigelow, the Mayor, to inform the City Council that I would make the donation if they would make any provision for the reception of the books. I am not aware that Mr. B. took any notice of this suggestion. Being led to think that this omission was not accidental, I addressed a note to him in January, 1850 (I think), making the same tender in writing. Even this, I believe was not communicated to the City Government. In August of that year, it was announced that Mayor Bigelow intended to appropriate to founding a city library the sum of $1000 which had been subscribed to procure some testimonial of gratitude to him for his services in suppressing the cholera: and paragraphs appeared in the public papers to the effect that in consideration of the *munificent* donation the library was to be called the Bigelow Library.

It is evident from this, and from other passages in the journal which might be quoted, that Mr. Everett considered himself the real founder of the Library. It was he who supplied the initiative and followed up the suggestion with a substantial gift. And his interest in the institution as it grew was constant, his service unremitting. He and his friend George Ticknor gave it of their very best, and bestowed upon it parental attention as Trustees for many years, Everett himself being President of the Board from 1852 to 1864. They did not always agree upon matters of detail, but they were a unit in their devotion to the cause and to all that a Public Library stood for in a Republic.

The Library was only one of many interests, however, to engage the attention and to claim the time of the retired statesman. There were literary enterprises, clubs, societies, public movements of all kinds which occupied as many hours as he could spare to them. There was no good cause in which his assistance was not asked — no unfortunate one that he was not quick to offset if he could. His doorbell rang constantly with all sorts of public and private demands. Everett from this time on was the most conspicuous private citizen of Boston. Dr. Holmes called him 'the yardstick by which men are measured in Boston.' In his leisure he found time to take up with renewed activity his correspondence with friends abroad. They congratulated him on having retired from the turmoil of public life; but their congratulations on that score were not as welcome as the evidences of their constant friendship. Lord John Russell wrote that he was sorry to learn of his impaired health, and that it must be counted a misfortune for such an eminent and respected body as the Senate to lose at this time a member of his 'cultivated understanding and high character.'

A more interesting letter was one that came to him at this time from Carlyle. The rugged gloom of the rough Scotchman was just the sort of message to cheer him and call back his courage. Everett was so impressed with the letter that he sent it on to Emerson to read. But such an epistle was not much of a novelty to the Concord Sage, although he returned it with words of gracious thanks.

At this time, too, there was a very charming little interchange of literary courtesies between Mr. Everett and Emerson on their own account. A careful reading of Mr. Everett's journal and letters makes it very evident that, while Everett cordially disapproved of Emerson's theological position, he never wavered in his love of the man, nor in a cordial recognition of his radiant nature. He could call his writings 'egotistical nonsense,' but after doing so he would invariably add that his grace as a speaker was unsurpassed and that in his early years his genius was unclouded by transcendental theories. Thus he wrote to his friend the Duchess of Argyle:

Emerson is as hard to fathom as his own philosophy. I like him much better than I do his writings. How I should relish them if I understood them, I cannot say. I imagine, however, that if they were reduced to common sense they would verify anew the old antithesis, 'that what is new in them is not true, and what is true is not new.' He is, however, an amiable man — of pure life, simple manners, and most brilliant powers. Before he stepped forward as an original theorist, I thought him one of the most gifted and fascinating speakers I ever heard.[1]

In the autumn of 1855, Everett set to work putting together material for a third volume of his orations and speeches. In going through his files he came upon the notes of an address that he had made at the Harvard Phi Beta Kappa celebration in 1837. Emerson was the orator that year and gave his famous oration on 'The American Scholar.' At the dinner which followed the oration, Everett made a brief but noteworthy and very touching address, in which he referred, not only to Emerson himself, but more especially to his two brothers who had died so prematurely. He now thought of printing the address in his new volume, but thought it wise to ask Emerson's consent before doing so. As a matter of fact, the great mass of material was such that the little piece was crowded out which makes it all the more interesting that it should have been preserved and can be

[1] From a letter to the Duchess of Argyle, May 7, 1849. Emerson was then in England.

printed now. Lovers of Emerson who remember the poet's devotion to his brothers and his blighting sorrow when they died will be able to appreciate how deeply he was touched by receiving the following, which nearly twenty years before he had listened to with tears in his eyes.

At the dinner of the Phi Beta Kappa Society on the 31st of August, 1837, an oration having been pronounced in the morning before the society by Mr. Ralph Waldo Emerson, in reply to a complimentary toast by the President of the society, Mr. Justice Story, Mr. Everett made the following remarks, after some response to the toast:

It was my intention, Sir, if any opportunity of addressing you was afforded me, to express the feelings, which I am sure I share with you, and all our brethren, in reference to the entertainment which we have enjoyed in another place, when we have listened with delight to a train of original remark and ingenious speculation, clothed in language the most exquisite, and uttered with a natural grace beyond the reach of art. You, Sir, however, have already done justice to this topic; and I am unfitted for enlarging upon it, by a rush of tender emotions, which I will not endeavor to repress. You will the rather allow me to indulge their expression, as it has ever been one of the cherished duties of our association, to consecrate our academic gatherings to the recollection of the brethren we have lost, and to strengthen the bond of kindness toward survivors, by common tributes of affection to the departed.

I cannot, Sir, while the music of the orator's voice still vibrates in my ears, forget that, in times not long past and within the classic precincts of Harvard, I listened on more than one occasion to the voice of two young men — connected with him by the closest ties of kindred — but scarcely less dear to such of us as had the happiness to know them well — each a most valued member of our fraternity, and, young as they both were, already recognized among the rising lights and hopes of our American republic of letters. Our Alma Mater — considering their age — never boasted nor deplored two gentler or brighter spirits than Edward Bliss Emerson, and his brother Charles Chauncy Emerson.

My relation with the former was of the largest standing and somewhat more intimate. It was one of the kindliest relations, that can subsist between man and man, that of a pupil grown up to be a friend. He was of a very superior nature intellectually and had extended his reading far beyond ordinary professional limits. He had already laid a deep foundation for further eminence. Too soon, alas, the bright prospect was clouded. The fervid action of a spirit touched to the firmest issues proved an overmatch for a sensitive physical organization, and we were compelled to witness

> — that noble and most sovereign reason
> Like sweet bells jangled out of tune and harsh;
> That unmatched form and feature of blown youth
> Blasted with ecstasy.

He left his native land for a foreign country in search of health; but found a shorter path to that higher and purer sphere, for which he was already mature.

Charles Chauncy, by four years the junior, after an interval of four years followed his brother to the grave. He, too, was a young man of most distinguished talent, of the most amiable disposition, and of a character in all respects as nearly faultless as belongs to the lot of humanity. He had completed his legal education in the Law School and was engaging in the practice of his profession, patient of delay and modestly confident of success. Life was opening upon him, radiant with its brightest promises, when suddenly and without the melancholy alleviation of a slow decline, he was cut down in the bloom of youth and hope:

> Purpureus veluti cum flos succisus aratro
> Languescit moriens, lassove papavera collo
> Demisere caput, pluvia cum forte gravantur.

It is superfluous to say that I took the deepest and most affectionate interest in these young men, beholding them, as I did, in the pure and unsophisticated morning of life, rapidly unfolding every mental quality and every trait of character which can inspire confidence or win attachment. But I forbear: I feel that I ought not, on this festive occasion, to pursue farther a subject of this kind. I trust, however, that I shall not be thought to overstep the limits of delicacy if I complete this humble tribute to our departed brethren, and fulfil the more immediate purpose for which I rose, by asking you to join me in saying:

'The orator of the day; — the beauty of living excellence recalls to us the memory, but alleviates the loss of that which we deplore.'

An address like that is in itself the best answer one can offer to the common charge which used to be made so constantly that Everett was a block of ice, that he had no heart, that he was lacking in emotion. It is an attribute of culture to control emotion; and that Everett did so with success is no proof that deep sentiment was unknown to him. It is no wonder that Emerson's own feelings were deeply stirred. Edward, his 'brother of the brief but blazing star,' had died as long ago as 1834, and Charles in 1836, but one can feel the throb of living grief in the letter with which Emerson acknowledged the great orator's courtesy.

CONCORD, *November* 24, 1855

MY DEAR SIR,

I was interrupted yesterday just as I went to acknowledge your kind note. I certainly can have no objection to this generous bestowal of your praise on friends so dear to me, and must thankfully accept it, passing the all-unmerited compliment to myself, with which it is inextricably connected. I well remember the joy and pride of heart with which, so long ago, I drew from each of those youths in turn the account of your marked notice and growing kindness — believing that they could not then win a surer certificate of literary merit than your approving regards; and they well knew how warmly I shared their admiration of their friend. You will forgive me, if I add, that when I recall the zeal of praise and delight which your eloquence in those days kindled in many and many a household of educated young men and women — what a literature, glory, and hope it was — I doubt, could you have seen those interiors, whether any or all your manifold tasks and triumphs since could yield so deep a pleasure; — so rare, costly, and not to be divided with any other, is that influence of the muse. I once attempted in a lecture at Philadelphia some sketch of the influences working on us from your quarter of the heavens, say from 1820 to 1825, and if I should have an hour of leisure and of courage presently, I may venture to extract something from it that may amuse you. Your genius, like all genius, has done many benefits when it meant them, and many which it knew not of.

Another evidence of Everett's capacity for feeling and affection is afforded by the memoir of Peter C. Brooks which he prepared at this time. It was written for the Genealogical Register; but he included it in the third volume of his 'Orations and Speeches,' 'from a wish,' as he said, 'to extend as widely and permanently as I could this tribute to the memory of one of the most honorable and upright of men.' We have seen that when Mr. Brooks died, his son-in-law could speak of him as 'my best friend.' And when he finished the memoir, he could make an entry in his journal to the effect that he had written it 'as much *con amore* as anything that he ever wrote in his life. Deprived,' he could say, 'of my own father, I found in Mr. Brooks from my first acquaintance with him everything which I could have found in a natural parent; the kindest interest in my welfare, the wisest counsel, and the most effectual assistance. In looking back upon the past, I cannot think of a single thing which could have been done to promote my happiness by Mr. Brooks which was neglected. There were certain circumstances in our relations to each other which caused a more than ordinary sympathy and fellow-feeling.'

Withal, however, he could not keep his mind off the burning political question of the day. He wrote an article on the reception of Douglas at Chicago, disclaiming all political sympathy with him, but censuring the manner in which he was silenced by the mob of Free-Soilers. This party, which had made a great deal of its sufferings from persecution, now appeared to him preëminently the intolerant, persecuting, and abusive party. He could declare that 'the most violent journals of both the political parties taken together do not in virulence and personality equal the abuse contained in a few Free-Soil papers.'

Altogether, the period was a distinctly unhappy one. There was loneliness and darkness in his home: there was confusion and turmoil in the Nation. It is at this time that the journal records almost the only evidences to be found in it of bitterness and uncharitable judgment. He was lonely: and solitude and cynicism generally go together. A few examples will suffice.

January 12, 1857. In my younger days I lived much alone while on my travels in Europe: now it depresses me. I wrote to a friend the other day that if I added another petition to the Litany it would be, '*From solitude at the fireside, Good Lord deliver us.*'

He heard of some one — a clergyman — who was accused of giving so much time to reforms that he neglected a good deal his duties. In that remark he found a compendium of the Philosophy of Agitation: '*You neglect your duty to attend to your neighbors' faults.*'

March 7, 1857. A long, querulous, and uncomfortable letter from Mr. Ticknor about the library, throwing vaguely on us here at home the blame of miscarriage abroad, for which nobody perhaps is to blame, but he as much as anybody. *I come more and more to the conclusion that the most thankless thing a man can do is to give his time and thought to any public business. They only can expect peace who shut themselves up in their shells; and then they are trampled on.*

He could refer to Brook Farm as a 'nauseous humbug,' and passed judgment on 'The Marble Faun' as 'a very extraordinary and it seems to me a silly book, as far as the story goes.' Dr. Frothingham, whose literary judgment was sounder and more catholic than his, had brought him a copy of 'Walt Whitman's "Grass Leaves"' (*sic*) which contained Mr. Emerson's letter greeting the author 'at the beginning of a great career.' But he can see in the volume only a 'most unimaginable compound of nonsense, mysticism, the lowest materialism, and the most vulgar bestiality. They are written in the flattest prose . . . fit to be read in the brothel and there alone.'

July 23, 1858. The article on Mr. Choate's oration in the 'Atlantic Monthly' is written by Mr. James Russell Lowell, Professor of Modern Languages and Belles-Lettres at Cambridge. He thinks a lawyer not well qualified to write a 4th of July oration: but he thinks a young Free-Soil Professor is well qualified to sneer at and deprecate Mr. Choate. . . . Perhaps it would be as well, at least while he is asking for indulgence in reference to the full performance of his duties, if Mr. J. R. Lowell would mind his own business.

But these judgments were not characteristic of the man at his best. They were the moods of a moment when he was not sufficiently employed; but they were also an evidence of his distress at the increasing signs of secession. The probable break-up of the Union preyed upon him like a nightmare. He tried to forget, plunging into Grotius and accumulating material for his study of International Law. But he could not find a sufficient or satisfactory outlet through his pen. There was a suppressed vehemence in the man's nature, a high pressure of impulse, that seemed to unfit him for a purely literary life. He was constantly thinking that he wanted leisure to write, and yet discontented when the leisure came. Once again he was to make it evident that the voice, and not the pen alone, was his natural medium of self-expression.

XIII
THE ORATOR

WHEN Mr. Everett resigned his seat in the Senate
and beat a full retreat from Washington in 1854,
he was, as we have seen, broken in spirits and in
health — a disappointed and defeated man! His resignation
was an evidence of failure, and he seemed to make public confession of his inability to cope any longer with the storm that
was sweeping the country into civil war. He was mournfully
convinced that his work was done, that his public career had
come to an end, and that except for such limited activities
as were possible for a semi-invalid he would have to live
henceforth in scholarly seclusion. But never was an expectation so completely nullified nor fears so entirely proved base-
less. A sphere of usefulness was to open out before him
which was most congenial in its nature. He was to come at
last to the work for which natural endowment, temperament,
and talents fitted him, and where exertion was to prove a
tonic and activity a healthy stimulant. This man was pre-
eminently an orator, and now at last he was to exercise his
gift of speech in a sphere above the discordant and disturb-
ing notes of party passion and sectional dispute. It happened
this way.

Soon after settling down in his comfortable home on
Summer Street, with his books around him, making his
spacious library a temple of peace, he prepared a lecture or
oration on the character of Washington. He had been asked
by the Mercantile Library Association of Boston to give the
introductory lecture in their course for the season of 1855–56.
He had declined, as he was now in the habit of declining
nearly all invitations of the kind. Some weeks after doing
so, however, it occurred to him that the year 1856 would
mark the hundredth anniversary of Washington's first visit

to Boston, and that the anniversary might well be celebrated. He wrote, therefore, to the Library Association that if they cared to have him speak on February 22d, making the meeting a patriotic affair in honor of Washington, he would be glad to accept their invitation, it being understood that the proceeds of the lecture would be applied to some commemorative object. The happy suggestion was readily accepted, and Everett set to work to prepare what proved to be the most famous, though it hardly was the greatest, of all his orations.

Announcement of these facts having appeared in the newspapers, invitations at once came pouring in from various cities asking for a repetition of the address. With a good deal of hesitation he agreed to repeat it in New Haven, New York, and Baltimore — declining, among others, an invitation to go to Richmond. Soon afterward, however, he read in a New York paper an account of the Ladies' Mount Vernon Association, which had been organized for the purpose of buying and preserving the historic home of Washington. Another idea suddenly struck Mr. Everett. He wrote to the Richmond people and said that he would repeat his Washington oration there provided the proceeds should be devoted to the Mount Vernon Association. This offer was made entirely on his own initiative, and not in response to any appeal from the Ladies' Association.

February 22, 1856, marked the one hundred and twenty-fourth anniversary of Washington's birth. The celebration in Boston was a huge success. Everett's oration formed the climax of an interesting programme, which included an ode by Oliver Wendell Holmes. The orator spoke for about an hour and forty minutes with great effect. The only inharmonious note in the whole affair was a caustic communication from Charles Sumner, censuring Everett for not making his eulogy an abolition lecture. It is referred to in the diary as follows: 'A letter was written by Mr. C. Sumner, Senator, in answer to the invitation of the committee, which is equally mean and malicious, intended to set the whole pack of Free-Soil papers upon me for not making my eulogy an abolition lecture.'

But others were not of Sumner's mind. The eulogy was a marked triumph, and the following letters tell of its repetition in various places as he began what was destined to prove one of the most dramatic labors of his life. The letter to his daughter is particularly interesting because it describes the first of his visits to the Everett House in New York, at that time a new hotel built on Union Square and named in his honor. His portrait hung upon the wall, and, as the letter says, the Everett coat of arms appeared on all the china and the glass. From this time on, whenever he went to New York, he made headquarters at the Everett House, being as pleased as a child apparently with the compliment that had been paid him.

NEW YORK, *February* 28, 1856

DEAR CHARLIE,— I found yours of the 27th waiting me here where I arrived at one. I delivered my 'Washington' at New Haven last evening, to an immense audience in the largest church in the city, which was completely filled as soon as the doors were opened. I got through pretty well, though some local matters of interest in Boston (such as the portrait of Washington and some historical specialties) were wanting at New Haven. Then, too, I wanted the hearty applause; for the managers at New Haven, as it was an Orthodox Church, expressed the wish that there should be none. This produced some effect, though three or four times they broke through, and at the close gave me a hearty token of their satisfaction. It is a pretty tedious thing to lay out all your breath and all your brains upon an idea or an image; and encounter a dead silence at the end. On Tuesday March 3, I am to give it here in the new Music Hall, which Bancroft says will hold six or seven thousand; but this I think impossible. The 11th is the day fixed for Baltimore. I do not think I shall give it at Washington. Professor Henry asked me to repeat it before the Smithsonian some months ago, but I declined.

The sort of itinerancy into which I have been drawn is not at all to my taste. Sid,[1] I suppose, will join me here on Saturday the 8th and proceed with me to the South. By the way, they have engaged

[1] His son, Sidney.

lodgings for me at the 'Gilmore House' in Baltimore, which I mention that you may come to the same. . . .

I am staying here at the Everett house. On arriving at 26th Street, I found the proprietor of the house waiting for me with a carriage and I am installed in very elegant apartments; though the particular room which bears my name was occupied in such a way that it could not be vacated. Every piece of china in the house, as far as I have seen, bears our coat of arms [1] like that service we had from Paris; the glasses have it cut in the glass. A good deal overdone. . . . I am very full of engagements, but shall probably get away on Sunday evening the 9th.

To Henry Augustus Wise

NEW YORK, *March 5*, 1856

I have not been able to make up my mind about repeating my 'Washington' at the seat of Government. The application came without any letter, and I hardly know to whom to send my acknowledgement.

I am overwhelmed with applications to repeat it. It went off on Monday night here extremely well. I never addressed — never saw assembled — such an audience. Every square inch of the vast opera house crowded: gentlemen and ladies standing in the aisles; the stage filled; and hundreds turned away who had tickets, owing to the fact probably that many went in without; for the doorkeepers were overpowered. Once in, however, the attention was breathless and sustained to the last. To-day I am to 'exchange salutations with my fellow-citizens,' from two to four.

This exchange of 'salutations' referred to consisted in a public reception which was tendered him in the New York City Hall, where he shook hands steadily for two hours with a rapid succession of people, mostly men.

This whole experience of hotel, lecture, and public reception proved another turning-point in his career. The success of the oration was positively overpowering. Washington Irving spoke of it to him 'with the greatest emotion,' and succeeded in making the orator feel that the address was successful beyond anything he had ever delivered.

---

[1] When Mr. Everett adopted for himself one of the Everett coats of arms for use as a bookplate, he *added as a motto of his own*, the characteristic words, *Patria, Veritas, Fides*.

With feelings of elation such as these, Mr. Everett left New York *en route* for Baltimore and Richmond. He stopped over at Philadelphia to visit friends, and there he went to see — thus meeting for the first time — 'the Southern Matron,' Miss A. P. Cunningham, the founder of the Mount Vernon Association. The journal contains these references to the interview:

March 10, 1856. I called very early on Miss Cunningham, the Southern Matron, who has been principally active in getting up the Ladies' Mount Vernon Association. She is a confirmed invalid and confined to her chamber; but by great mental energy has contrived with infinite embarassment and disgusts to collect subscriptions to a large amount. Promised that I would repeat the address in Philadelphia for the benefit of the fund. . . .

An invalid maiden lady seems the last person to manage a difficult business affair, but I believe this poor little woman, dropping into the grave with a spinal complaint, has done all that has been done for the purchase of Mount Vernon.

The saving of Mount Vernon as a national monument was brought about in so large a part by the efforts of Mr. Everett, and for several years he devoted to the cause so large a measure of his time and strength, that it will be wise for us to refresh our memories in regard to the way in which the whole thing came about.

In 1853, the mother of Miss Ann Pamela Cunningham, passing Mount Vernon in a steamer at night, was struck by the signs of dilapidation in the place, which were visible even in the moonlight. As the steamship bell, when the tomb was passed, tolled out the customary requiem to the Father of his Country, she thought to herself that it was a disgrace to the South that the historic place should thus be suffered to fall into ruin. She wrote to her daughter Ann upon the subject, who was then an invalid living quietly at home in Rosemont, South Carolina. It seemed, so the mother wrote, as though the women of the South ought to get together and do something to preserve the place. The daughter's imagination was kindled. She decided that the thing should be done and that she would do it. Her friends, when she asked them to help, ridiculed the idea, and did their best to dissuade her. But she was not to be deterred. She went to work on the matter with the idea of having the State of Virginia buy and preserve the property. But serious obstacles met her, many of them of an unexpected kind. First of all, the proprietor of the historic place, John Augustine Washington, had to be persuaded — which was no easy task. Little by little the scheme became more inclusive as one by one the difficulties were surmounted. From being a purely Southern movement it came gradually to be a national movement whose centre only was the South. From first to last, however, it remained a women's movement pure and simple; and it was the first among the many public movements that American women have started and successfully carried through. It involved, at the outset, raising the sum of two hundred thousand dollars, which was the purchase price of the property.

In 1856, Miss Cunningham, then a good deal discouraged in her efforts, went to Richmond to use her influence with the Virginia Legislature. There, a few days after Mr. Everett had called upon her in Philadelphia, she heard him deliver his oration on 'The Character of Washington,' and she was thrilled and uplifted by the great experience. It has been generally represented that she then and there persuaded the orator to take up the cause in which she was enlisted. But such was not the case. Everett was already interested, and had himself suggested to the people of Richmond, as we have seen, that he would lecture there on behalf of Mount Vernon. It is a truer statement of the facts to say that the two enthusiasts, having met, became partners in a common undertaking, and that henceforth the ultimate success of the cause became assured. Everett gave the movement a national prestige, and solemnly dedicated his oration to the saving of Mount Vernon.

In the course of the next few years he went from State to State in the Union, delivering his 'Washington' in all the

large and many of the unimportant centres, asking no pay
for himself, not even deducting his travelling expenses from
the receipts of the lecture, until, at the end, he turned over
to the Mount Vernon Association the sum of nearly seventy
thousand dollars. It was a unique and quite remarkable
undertaking — national in scope, patriotic in character, and
with a noble motive behind it all which did not appear upon
the surface. For there can be no doubt that Everett was
interested in a good deal more than merely saving Mount
Vernon. The saving of the Union was the greater end he had
in view! In speaking of the Father of his Country, Everett
put himself above all sectional differences and rivalries.
The great orator had a great subject, and what was more
important still, he had the great incentive of trying to calm
the angry passions of Northerners and Southerners by re-
minding them of their common interests and their common
allegiance to the great man of their past. He never failed, in
delivering the lecture, to recall to his hearers the words of
Jefferson when he set himself to dissuade Washington from
declining a renomination. 'North and South,' said Jefferson
in 1792, 'will hang together while they have you to hang to.'
And that was the great end and aim of Everett from first to
last — to persuade the discordant sections of the country
to hang to the sacred memory of Washington, and thus to
compose their differences.

It was a big piece of work for a man of Mr. Everett's age
to undertake. For one whose health was broken, it involved
great sacrifices. The long journeys, the constant absences
from home, the nights that were passed on railways and
steamships, and in hotels that were none too good, and in
private houses that frequently lacked many comforts — it
was all of it fatiguing and much of it distasteful! But Everett
never complained. His letters throughout the whole campaign were cheerful, and even playful; and the miracle of
it was that his health in the process came to be partially
restored! The burden and the strain were lost sight of in the

joy of public speech and the sense of public service rendered with success.

In the course of these oratorical tours Mr. Everett wrote almost daily to his wife or daughter or son-in-law, and his letters give a graphic picture of places, people, crowded halls and churches, while they also indicate how wide was the circuit of his travels. The first of these letters to his daughter, is interesting because it tells, in connection with his journal, a somewhat unusual difficulty that he encountered.

BOSTON, *April* 18, 1856

DEAR CHARLIE,— I am just returned from Providence, rather tired. I delivered my address there, for the fourteenth time, to a very large audience, which was sufficiently demonstrative; the grandees on the stage, for the most part, as cold as ice. The gentleman at whose house I staid, and who entertained me in the most hospitable manner, did not even say to me 'that's nae so bad.' But it will not do for me — proverbially a block of ice — to blame others for being chilly: though I really think I could not sit upon a platform and hear a poor creature strain his lungs for an hour and three quarters, and then go home with him, and not say one civil word. . . .

April 16, 1856. Took the cars to Providence at ten minutes after four and arrived there at ten minutes after six. Found Mr. R. H. Ives waiting for me at the station and went to his house. . . . On my way from the station to Mr. Ives's house, he stated to my dismay that in consequence of the appearance of Mr. Washington's letter saying that Mount Vernon was not on sale, he (Mr. Ives) had agreed with the young men of the Association before whom I was to deliver my address that the proceeds should be applied to *their* benefit. I remonstrated firmly but gently against this unauthorized departure from our agreement, which I must say inspired me with considerable disgust.

April 17. Rose early and took a walk in Mr. Ives's pleasant grounds. Professor Gammell, Mr. Ives's son-in-law, joined me and renewed the disagreeable subject of the appropriation of the proceeds. I stood my ground firmly, a little annoyed at the pertinacity with which I was pressed to this violation of the condition on which I agreed to deliver the address at Providence. Finding me inflexible on the main point, Mr. Ives proposed that I should let the young men have two hundred dollars and take the rest, perhaps five hundred dollars for the fund. This I waived. He then proposed that I should leave the young men in the possession of the proceeds of this lecture and come again for the benefit of the fund! Mr. Ives appears to think it a trifling matter to travel forty miles, pass a whole day, and speak an hour and three quarters to two thousand people. Mr. Ives is worth a million and a half dollars, and his brother as much more. It would not hurt them to draw a check for the amount of seven hundred dollars and hand it to the young men as compensation for the disappointment induced by the mismanagement of Mr. R. H. Ives.

The spring of 1857 found Mr. Everett in the West, delivering the 'Washington' in St. Louis, Detroit, Michigan City, Chicago, and other places. He was a born traveller; took things easily; seldom fretted; and rejoiced in every new evidence he gained of the country's greatness. 'The journey is made with great comfort,' he wrote to Mr. Winthrop from St. Louis. 'As far as I can judge, the trains are about as well conducted as at the East and North; the company rather more "promiscuous." The cars are sometimes superior to those on the Massachusetts roads. . . . I wish you would come and see this wonderful country. It is impossible to form an adequate idea of it in any other way. The people here are intelligent, conservative, liberal, and hospitable.'

His family letters are intimate and personal, giving details, and recording impressions which are interesting.

To Mrs. Henry Augustus Wise

ST. LOUIS, *April 23, 1857*

. . . I delivered my Washington on the 20th with success. The tickets were a half a dollar, and it was said nearly as many went away as got in; about seventeen hundred tickets were sold, and a large number of persons attended by invitation. I am to repeat it by special request on the 25th. Yesterday was the occasion which brought me to St. Louis, the inauguration of the Washington University of the State of Missouri. I delivered an address prepared for the occasion; and — if I may be permitted to say it of myself — worried through as well as could be expected. I took occasion toward the close of the address to recommend the building of an observatory, as St. Louis stands on the ninetieth meridian west of Greenwich, which would be a convenient circumstance in comparing observations. After it was over, Mr. Lucas, a very wealthy man here, in fact the richest man in St. Louis, told a gentleman that he believed he (Mr. L.) must build that observatory, though he added, 'I suppose it would cost me from $30,000 to $100,000.' 'It would,' answered the gentleman, 'but you can afford it.' 'I can,' said Mr. Lucas; and they say he will be as good as his word.[1] ... ·

MICHIGAN CITY, *May* 3, 1857

Here I am in a very quiet, out-of-the-way place, lying under the lee of the sand hills blown up from the southern shore of Lake Michigan, passing Sunday in repose, the first day since I left home that I have been at rest and alone. I wrote you twice from Detroit. I dined there on Friday with Mr. Ledyard; she was not well enough to be at table. In the course of the day Miss Cass arrived; but I was not aware of it till I saw that she was at my Oration in the evening. I went off so early the next morning that I had no time to pay my respects to her, which you can mention on proper occasion if one presents itself.

I delivered my 'Washington' successfully in a large church, which was crowded. The present Governor (Republican) came seventy miles to Detroit to hear me, and in company with the new Senator Chandler called upon me. Governor McClelland, late Secretary of the Interior, introduced me to the audience, which I was told contained the *élite* of the intelligence of Detroit. It was certainly an attentive and apparently an appreciative audience; though as it was delivered in a church, applause was interdicted. My visit to Detroit was highly satisfactory, though the weather was bad.

The next day — yesterday — I had, in some measure, to retrace my steps, coming back as far as this place on the Michigan Central Road. Here I take a midnight train to Indianapolis to-night. There was no other way of getting there with certainty in season to speak to-morrow evening. On Tuesday I go to Cincinnati, though I do not speak there till the Thursday and Saturday. My movements for the following week are not definitely arranged. The week after I go up to Buffalo, and speak my way down to New York City, pretty much as Mr. Coolidge's terrier bit his way through the Continent of Europe.

This certainly is a funny concern (?) for a man of my age. But we are the creatures of circumstances. I do not give up the hope of seeing you at Washington before I go home, though I cannot fix a time.

[1] He was.

LOUISVILLE, *May* 11, 1857

Having completed my engagements in the Northwestern States, by delivering my 'Washington' a second time in Cincinnati on Saturday evening, I came down the river to this place yesterday. My visit to Cincinnati was eminently successful. There was an attempt there — as at Chicago — on the part of some of the 'Republican' newspapers to throw cold water on me and my errand, but it was more signally unsuccessful at Cincinnati than at Chicago, where, however, it wholly failed. I had immense audiences at Cincinnati, though Thalberg was giving concerts alternate nights. I had my portrait painted three-fourths length at Cincinnati, to be presented by the President of the last year to the Young Men's Association, by whose invitation I came. They might well do it, for they made about one thousand dollars by my visit; for only one of the evenings was for the Mount Vernon fund.

One of the most agreeable incidents of my visit to Cincinnati was meeting Aunt Ellen and Mr. Shepherd. They were on their way to Virginia and had arrived at Cincinnati from New Orleans the day I got there. Aunt Ellen seems quite well. They both went to hear me and I saw a good deal of them.

Here I am the guest of the Louisville Bar, who invited me by a committee of which Mr. Guthrie is chairman. The William Prestons invited me to stay at their house, but I had previously accepted the invitation of the Bar. I dine with the Prestons to-morrow. Mr. and Mrs. Stanard are here, on their way home from New Orleans, where they have been for his health, which is very poor. They came up the river with Aunt Ellen. I have not yet seen them, but hope to do so in the course of the day. I give this week to Kentucky. Next week I go to Buffalo, where I am to speak on the 19th or 20th.

BUFFALO, *May* 20, 1857

... I had a very agreeable tour in Kentucky, though I had to hurry amazingly. I spoke four times in the course of the week; but I believe I wrote you this from Maysville. On Sunday evening, I went aboard a little steamer bound down the river, laden to the very water's edge from the Great Kanawha. I felt a little nervous at the thought of a night voyage in such a craft, especially when I saw some beds made up on the floor and a life-preserver carefully put under every pillow. But we got to Cincinnati at the seasonable hour of half past one in the morning; got our trunks carried up by a porter to the hotel, and enjoyed a comfortable night's rest of two hours; being called at half-past four in the morning. At a quarter before six I took the cars for this place; and did the whole without stopping — about six hundred and twenty-six miles. On the way a poor young mother, travelling with two children and six canary birds, while tending her birds was robbed of her purse, containing eighty dollars — all she had, and she six hundred miles from home. The agony for a while was infinite, mother and children wept in chorus. But we raised a subscription in the cars, and made good her loss.

Yesterday I gave to Niagara, and found it looking as it did thirty-six years, probably as it did thirty-six centuries ago, and will to the end of time. Unhappily I left my cane in the car, and I have failed thus far to recover it. I speak here to-night; at Utica to-morrow night; at Troy Friday, and on Sunday morning next or Monday hope to be with you. But it is so uncertain which day I come that I would not have you send for me to the station.

ERIE, PENNSYLVANIA, *October 15, 1857*

. . . I started from home on the 6th; stopped that night at Albany, and the next reached Buffalo, where I was hospitably entertained by Dr. Foote, who, under Mr. Fillmore, was Chargé d'Affaires to Bogota and Vienna; a man of great talent and highly cultivated mind; but unfortunately afflicted by Saint Vitus's dance — which makes it painful to look at him — and quite deaf, so that it is not easy to talk with him. But I was so hospitably treated by him and his amiable family that I soon forgot these drawbacks. The next day in the afternoon, I went to Fredonia to repeat my 'Washington,' a very pretty, thriving country in Chautauqua County, the southwesternmost county, I believe, in New York. I was to have been the guest of a Mr. Stiles, the president of a bank, but Mrs. S. being ill, I was transferred to Judge Edwards. I was hospitably and comfortably entertained; but found out, to my dismay, the next morning, that my obliging host was the member of Congress of the name of Edwards implicated with Mattheson, &c. at the last Session! *Par exemple.*

Went back to Buffalo the next morning, where I arrived at eleven A.M. and delivered my new address at one, under a tent, most of the audience standing in the open air roundabout. It was two hours long, but had the good luck to hold the attention of the audience — miscellaneous as it was — to the last. I believe I did as well as on any former occasion. Mr. Moseley told me that one lady — a very interesting one — was so pleased at one passage that she reached out her hand and pressed *his*. I told Moseley that this circumstance was highly gratifying to *me*. After the address we had a State dinner at Dr. Foote's; President Fillmore, Governor King, &c., of the company. The next day, in the forenoon I went down to the Falls alone, and enjoyed it highly. Among other fine views, I got a noble one in the little row ferryboat, in which you cross the river directly under the American Falls. It looks rather scarey; but is, I believe, perfectly safe.

Saturday evening I left the Footes, and took passage in the noble steamer Mississippi for Detroit. She is of twenty-two hundred tons and superbly fitted up. I was put into what is absurdly called the 'bridal chamber.' It was eleven feet by twenty in size, as I ascertained by actually pacing it. I had a bureau and dressing-glass, card table, sofa, four chairs, a washing apparatus supplied by a pipe, and a water-closet. The night was superb; the stars shone with steely lustre which I have never seen before. But before morning the wind shifted, and it blew pretty hard. I was rather qualmish at breakfast time, though able to sit at table. At ten, it was pleasant again and I read and wrote. Captain Langley would take nothing. Reached Detroit in safety in the afternoon and went on to Ann Arbor, the seat of the University of Michigan. Here I was entertained by President Tappan. The next day I was introduced to the students in the chapel and made a short speech, and in the evening gave my 'Washington' to a good audience, about half students and half townsfolk. The college is well conducted and prosperous.

Rose at four o'clock the next day (the 13th), took the train to Detroit, and thence by Toledo to Cleveland. In the *depot* at Toledo, my pocket was picked of my precious watch! I could have cried when I found it out; but what good would that do? The superintendent of the road said the pickpockets had just appeared at Toledo; that they had their eye on them; and that he thought they could recover it. Recover the lost Pleiad! I shall never see it again, my invaluable, much-loved white face; the faithful companion of so many scenes and sorrows. At Cleveland I went to Angier's Hotel and delivered my 'Washington' in the evening to an immense crowd. Every inch of sitting or standing room was filled. Yesterday morning I came here. I am staying at General Reed's; in a house larger and more expensively furnished than any in Boston! I gave my discourse in the evening to a smallish but intensely appreciative audience.

All this was in 1857; but in 1858 there came another trip, and we find him going through the South as well as through the West, always with the same results — admiring throngs, crowded halls, great applause! It was invariably Washington; but sometimes another subject also, as when he pre-

pared and delivered an oration on Franklin which was asked
for in Philadelphia.

PHILADELPHIA, *January* 28, 1859

I delivered my 'Franklin' last night to the largest and finest
audience, with one or two exceptions, that I ever addressed. It was
in the new Opera House, an immense building. It rained like guns,
and the carriages formed an immense queue. Every seat on the
stage, in the parterre, the circles and galleries, up to the very ceiling,
was filled. When a man is naturally oppressed with diffidence, it is
no small job to face such an audience. Tell Charlie that Mrs.
Gillespie and all the other Franklinians were on the stage. I spoke
to Mrs. G., while we were on the stage, and she accompanied me
into the Green Room, when she examined the record of Franklin's
baptism, which I had brought with me. Altogether, the people
seemed pleesed [*sic*] and expect to get about two thousand dollars
for the Pennsylvania Institute, by whose invitation I delivered the
address. I sometimes think it would not be a bad thing to divide
the profits on these occasions; but this would take away the *sweet
satisfaction* of laboring without a selfish motive.

MIDDLETOWN, *January* 25, 1859

I have but a moment to scratch you a line, but I suppose that
will not be unacceptable. We had a fine day for travelling yesterday, bright and snapping, but the cars warm enough.

From Berlin (not in Prussia, but in Middlesex County, Connecticut) I went to Middletown, twelve miles off, where I was met at
the station by the Mayor and other gentlemen and conducted to
the house — the palace, rather — of Mr. S. Russell, the famous
China merchant who belonged to that set of Americans who went
to China some years ago and made money so fast that they had to
provide themselves a barrel and shovel to shovel in the guineas,
they came so fast.

Nothing could exceed the comfort — the luxury — of my
quarters. A whole wing of the house comprising rooms for myself
and a charming little room for Willy, who (they had heard) was to
come with me. After a magnificent lunch, which thanks to the
sandwiches I did not need, we went to the church where I delivered
my 'Washington' for the one hundred and ninth time. Excepting
a slight diffidence, which I believe belongs to the family, I got
through as well as might be expected from my youth and inexperi-
ence. After getting home we had dinner; after dinner a brief nap;
after the nap a reception of the ladies and gentlemen of Middletown, and I assure you as polite and well-bred a circle as you often

meet; and after that a little family *cause*, and then to bed, and oh! how I did sleep! I might be said really to have sunk into the arms of Morpheus, and he grabbed me so tight that I thought he would never let me go. But this morning no button fresh from the factory ever looked brighter than I feel.

I am to go to New Britain (not Great) at eleven; give my 'Washington' at two-thirty, and in the evening proceed to New York. I shall not arrive there till midnight and as I start at eight in the morning, I shall not probably be able to write you to-morrow. From Philadelphia the next day you shall have a line.

NEW YORK, *March* 6, 1859

... Yesterday I had a great treat in a visit to Mr. Lenox's gallery and library. He is very chary in admitting visitors. Scarce any one has ever been permitted to see his treasures; but he was good enough to send Uncle Sidney a note, inviting him to come. The immediate object was to see a beautiful statue just received from Powers, which he calls Penserosa. The subject was originally suggested to him by me, with reference to Milton's description; but he has not followed Milton closely. There is nothing 'sad,' in the air or expression of the figure; and the costume is not imitated from that of Milton's 'Nun.' It is extremely beautiful. Mr. Lenox has many other works of art of great beauty; and some of the most valuable and costly books; among them the first edition of the entire Bible in two volumes, for which he paid five hundred pounds sterling; and the original manuscript of the Farewell Address of Washington, for which he paid twenty-five hundred dollars; or very nearly a hundred dollars a page. . . .

It was at this time that Mr. Everett took upon himself another burden in connection with Mount Vernon. It was not enough that voice should be employed, his hand was needed also. In the autumn of 1858, Robert Bonner, the proprietor of the New York 'Ledger,' made him what was in those days a most unusual offer. Mr. Bonner suggested that if Mr. Everett would pledge himself to contribute a weekly article for one year to the 'Ledger,' he, Mr. Bonner, would thereupon send a check of ten thousand dollars for the benefit of the Mount Vernon Association. It was a tempting offer; but one to stagger a man who was already very busily employed. Mr. Everett took a month to think the matter over, and then accepted it. The 'Ledger' at that time had a circulation of three hundred thousand. A great many copies of the periodical went into families and clubs, and it was estimated that the paper was read each week by at least a million people. That was a big audience. The check for ten thousand dollars went to the Mount Vernon Association, and Everett went to work. His first article was published in November, 1858, and the last one — fifty-three in all — in the autumn of 1859. The weekly articles were immediately brought together and published in book form under the title of 'Mount Vernon Papers.'

Before we leave this Mount Vernon campaign and the famous oration on Washington which he repeated so many times, it may be well to give some account of Everett as an orator and to get a clear idea of the methods that he used. 'The Character of Washington' was the greatest of his orations — so far as popularity was concerned. More people, that is to say, knew him by that one oration than by any other, and it was thoroughly typical both of his art and of his manner. In the first place, the very subject gave scope to his patriotism, and Everett was of all men in his generation the most exuberant of patriots. His appeal — the note he struck that caused his hearers to be thrilled and stirred — was the note of love and pride of country. His speeches and addresses make it clear that here was a man to whom 'Bunker Hill was a more magic word than the Marathon,' and one whose central aim was to inspire the youth of his generation with the thought that 'Lives better than Plutarch's were lying at their feet.'

The subject of Washington, therefore, was just the kind of subject to suit him best. It allowed him to give free play to his most characteristic gifts. Moreover, with his wide and intimate knowledge of the Old World it was natural for him to compare Washington with the great men of other countries in the past. Thus he described the Duke of Marlborough; paid full tribute to his military genius, but pictured him as of doubtful moral character comparing many of his meaner qualities with Washington's integrity and sense of honor. He had visited Blenheim several times, and he contrasted that enormous and pretentious pile with the simplicity and dignity of Washington's home on the Potomac. Then there was Frederick the Great of Prussia — another military genius. The orator compared Washington to him, contrasting Frederick's materialism, brutality, and lack of religious faith with Washington's chivalry, and courtesy, and simple Christian confidence in a guiding Providence.

Nowhere [said the eulogistic speaker] can you find another leader and Father of a people to compare with the greatness of Washington! There was none in America, there was none in Europe, there was none in the modern world, there was none in the ancient world. I cast my eyes along the far-stretching galleries of history, still echoing to the footsteps of the mighty dead; I behold with admiration the images and the statues of the great and good men with which they are adorned; I see many who deserved well of their country in civil and military life, on the throne, in the council-chamber, on the battle-field; while they lived, wreathed with well-won laurels and scarred with honest wounds — Hampden and William of Orange, William Tell and Robert Bruce and King Alfred, and in the olden times Cato and Tully and Demosthenes and Timoleon and Epaminondas; but I behold in the long line no other Washington. I return from the search, up and down the pathways of time, grateful to the Providence which, at the solemn moment when the destinies of the continent were suspended in the balance of a doubtful future — doubtful to human apprehension — raised up a chieftain endowed with every quality of mind and heart to guide the fortunes of a nascent state.

The speaker then went on, having outlined the greatness of Washington, to enforce a lesson and to make clear the duties of American citizenship in times of danger. Here was the orator's opportunity to call his hearers to the higher ground that lay above the range of sectional disputes. It was for the men and women who had love of country, and who pretended to reverence the memory of the Father of the Country — it was for them to follow where he led and remember the lessons that he taught, the example that he gave, the exhortations that he uttered! Washington taught the virtue of American citizenship in his life and character, and it was for those of succeeding generations to learn of him to hold the Union sacred!

But to us citizens of America, it belongs above all others to show respect to the memory of Washington, by the practical deference which we pay to those sober maxims of public policy which he has left us — a last testament of affection in his Farewell Address. Of all the exhortations which it contains, I scarce need say to you that none are so emphatically uttered, none so anxiously repeated, as those which enjoin the preservation of the Union of these States. On this, under Providence, it depends in the judgment of Washington whether the people of America shall follow the Old World example, and be broken up into a group of independent military powers, wasted by eternal border wars, feeding the ambition of petty sovereigns on the life-blood of wasted principalities — a custom-house on the bank of every river, a fortress on every frontier hill, a pirate lurking in the recesses of every bay — or whether they shall continue to constitute a confederate republic, the most extensive, the most powerful, the most prosperous in the long line of ages. No one can read the Farewell Address without feeling that this was the thought and this the care which lay nearest and heaviest upon that noble heart; and if — which Heaven forbid — the day shall ever arrive when his parting counsels on that head shall be forgotten, on that day, come it soon or come it late, it may as mournfully as truly be said, that Washington has lived in vain. Then the vessels as they ascend and descend the Potomac may toll their bells with new significance as they pass Mount Vernon; they will strike the requiem of constitutional liberty for us — for all nations.

But it cannot, shall not be; this great woe to our beloved country, this catastrophe for the cause of national freedom, this grievous calamity for the whole civilized world, it cannot, shall not be. No, by the glorious 19th of April, 1775; no, by the precious blood of Bunker Hill, of Princeton, of Saratoga, of King's Mountain, of Yorktown; no, by the undying spirit of '76; no, by the sacred dust enshrined at Mount Vernon; no, by the dear immortal memory of Washington — that sorrow and shame shall never be. Sooner let the days of colonial vassalage return; rather let the Frenchman and savage again run the boundary with the firebrand and scalping-knife, from the St. Lawrence to the Mississippi, than that sister States should be arrayed against each other, or brother's hands be imbrued in brother's blood.

A great and venerated character like that of Washington, which commands the respect of an entire population, however divided on other questions, is not an isolated fact in History to be regarded with barren admiration — it is a dispensation of Providence for good. It was well said by Mr. Jefferson in 1792, writing to Washington to dissuade him from declining a renomination: 'North and South will hang together while they have you to hang to.' Washington in the flesh is taken from us; we shall never behold him as our fathers did; but his memory remains, and I say, let us hang to his memory. Let us make a national festival and holiday of his birthday; and ever, as the twenty-second of February returns, let us remember, that while with these solemn and joyous rites of observance we celebrate the great anniversary, our fellow-citizens on the Hudson, on the Potomac, from the Southern plains to the Western lakes, are engaged in the same offices of gratitude and love. Nor we, nor they alone — beyond the Ohio, beyond the Mississippi, along that stupendous trail of immigration from East to West, which, bursting into States as it moves westward, is already threading the Western prairies, swarming through the portals of the Rocky Mountains and winding down their slopes, the name and the memory of Washington on that gracious night will travel with the silver queen of heaven through sixty degrees of longitude, nor part company with her till she walks in her brightness through the golden gate of California, and passes serenely on to hold midnight court with her Australian stars. There and there only, in barbarous archipelagos, as yet untrodden by civilized man, the name of Washington is unknown; and there, too, when they swarm with enlightened millions, new honors shall be paid with ours to his memory.

No one can read even these brief extracts from the famous oration without perceiving certain things in regard to Mr. Everett's method as an orator.

In the first place, he left nothing to chance — nothing to what is often foolishly described as 'the inspiration of the moment.' Everything with this man was carefully worked out, studied, and perfected, sometimes even to the minutest details. In this, as in so much else, Everett was essentially Greek. For among the ancient Greeks an oration was something to be planned and developed and constructed as carefully as a play, or a statue, and any piece of architecture. Oratory in ancient Athens was one of the arts. It was a fine art. Public speakers did not delude themselves into thinking that it would be given them what to say when the time came; but they prepared their addresses with persistent and attentive thoroughness. And that was Mr. Everett's careful and conscientious method. His orations were all written out beforehand with as much precision and verbal accuracy as though the manuscript were to be placed in the hands of a printer. He then read over what he had written, or carefully rewrote it, and his memory was so remarkable that the whole thing was thus imprinted on his mind. In a letter to Mr. Allibone of Philadelphia he gave this account of the method he pursued in 'getting up' his speeches: 'With respect to speaking *memoriter*, I write out all my elaborate passages beforehand, some passages two or three times over. These imprint themselves on my memory by writing them. For the body of the discourse, I find a little study sufficient, and the written text is not accurately followed except in a few passages.'

In all this his extraordinary memory, combined with unusual alertness and power of concentration, formed a great asset. This was strikingly shown on several occasions. A remarkable instance was when he gave one of his Phi Beta Kappa orations at Cambridge — a task which he accepted at short notice, some other speaker having given out toward the last moment. Longfellow was the poet of the day, and his part on the programme preceded the oration. What was the poet's surprise, after reading his verses, to hear Everett, a few minutes later, repeat with exquisite cadence and expression several of the lines of the unprinted poem which had impressed him, and which he memorized as they fell from Longfellow's lips — introduced, too, into the oration as though they belonged there, and had been carefully prepared beforehand. On another occasion, speaking, we are told, at a Commencement Dinner, his address was interrupted by a sudden flash of lightning and a peal of thunder. Quick as the lightning itself, Everett quoted the lines from Virgil where the Cyclops forge the thunderbolts of Jove beneath Mount Etna, beginning:

> Ac veluti, lentis Cyclopes fulmina massis
> cum properant.[1]

Now it was not unnatural — Everett's method being what it was — that he was often criticized for being artificial and affected. His was the grand manner. He was over-ornate, and too perfect. The art on more than one occasion became unpleasantly apparent. Some of the orations would have been better if they had not been so good. Thus there are people who find fault with the scenery at Lake Louise. It is so exquisite, they say, that it seems artificial — like something on the stage! The lake is too round, the mountains too regular, and the glacier would be more impressive if it did not descend to the precise centre of the circle of blue water.

That appears to have been the contemporary opinion regarding Everett's oratory. He was sometimes described as the Raphael among orators while Webster was called the Michaelangelo. The latter was more rugged, forceful, natural, while Everett was always graceful and delicate — with an excess, however, of sweeping line and brilliant color. In his early days he was given to ornamental writing, and was super-rhetorical. We have noticed this tendency in his pulpit days, when Henry Clay complained of him that he was too dramatic. This was a tendency that he corrected in large part, and yet always had to fight against. It appears, for example, in the closing passage of the eulogy of Washington that we quoted, where he speaks about the name of Washington travelling 'with the silver queen of heaven till she walks in her brightness through the golden gate of California and passes serenely on to hold midnight court with her Australian stars.' When he was preparing his speeches for publication in 1849 he wrote in the preface: 'In revising the

[1] For this, and the preceding incident, see Tribute, New England Historic-Genealogical Society, January, 1865.

earlier compositions in this collection for the present edition,
I have applied the pruning-knife freely to the style. This
operation might have been carried still farther with advantage; for I feel them to be still deficient in that simplicity
which is the first merit.' He wrote his friend and classmate,
Dr. Gilman, on the subject, saying: 'I have diligently applied the file to some of the orations, mostly the earlier ones,
and more than all to the first in the volumes, of which the
identity is seriously impaired. That oration, at the time of
its delivery, had greater success than any of its successors —
and its leading principles are, I believe, sound. But it exhibited the faults of my manner in their most exaggerated
form and I have been struggling with it ever since.'

Even at his simplest, therefore, he was still very far from
Wendell Phillips's ideal, who described oratory as 'animated
conversation.' Everett's standard was quite different. He
was seldom animated, and seldom wholly conversational.
He never wished to give the impression of unpremeditated
speech. When he came upon the platform to deliver his
'Washington' for the fiftieth, or the hundredth time, he had
his manuscript with him, and placed it carefully upon a desk
or table. He never by any chance referred to it. But there
it was, in plain view of the audience, as though to say to them:
'This is no casual, unprepared address to which I ask your
attention. It is something that has been carefully studied,
and worked over at great length.' At times, too, he took
small pains to hide the means by which he worked things up
for effect. This led Emerson to complain of his Lexington
oration in 1835. 'He is all art, and I find in him nowadays,
maugre all his gifts and great merits, more to blame than
praise. He is not content to be Edward Everett, but would
be Daniel Webster. This is his mortal distemper.'[1] Andrew
D. White, in somewhat the same vein, many years later,
says that he happened to sit beside him at a public dinner
in Boston where he was to be the chief speaker. Mr. White

[1] Emerson's *Journal*, April 22, 1835.

says that when the table was being cleared, he noticed that Everett motioned to the waiter not to remove a bouquet of flowers that stood before his plate which contained two small American flags. Later in the evening, in the course of his speech and at just the right point, he caught up the flags as if without premeditation, and waved them. 'Everything with Everett as with Choate,' added Mr. White, 'seemed to be cut and dried, so that even the interruptions seemed prepared beforehand.' [1]

Curiously enough, this episode is explained in his journal, and shows that the degree of preparation was much exaggerated by Mr. White.

January 18, 1856. It was ten minutes before eight before I rose. My speech occupied an hour and twenty minutes, and appeared to give great satisfaction. Some little flags were among the decorations of the table. *It occurred to me just before I rose* that I would wave one of them in a passage of my speech where the American flag was alluded to. They were, however, not attached to the little sticks on which they were displayed and I saw that they would fly off. I accordingly got James Anderson (the head waiter at the Revere House who came with me from England) to get me a couple of pins, with which I nailed my colors to the mast in a somewhat novel manner. Dr. Holmes read a very pretty poem. All went off in a pleasing, satisfactory manner.

That he went to the trouble to record this somewhat trivial episode shows that he thought particularly well of the very thing for which he was criticized. And yet the little artifice did not occur to him until just before he rose to speak. It was very far from having been 'prepared beforehand.'

In this connection, therefore, a good deal of injustice has been done to Everett's memory. We forget, for instance, and his contemporaries forgot, that it was just as natural for this man to be graceful and finished and exquisite in diction and manner as it is for other people to be awkward and stammering and involved. Hand, voice, and eye acted in harmony. He was an exquisitely adjusted machine. Part fitted into

[1] Andrew D. White: *Autobiography.*

part, and made the man a unit. That was what Carlyle meant when he spoke of him as 'a dignified, *compact* kind of man.' There was nothing either loose or awkward about him. His self-command was perfect. Emerson saw in him precisely what impressed Carlyle. He said of him, 'Nature finished this man. He seems perfectly built, perfectly sound and whole; his eye, voice, hand exactly obey his thought.'

To complain of such a man on the ground that he was too finished and graceful was a good deal like objecting because his eyes were too bright or his hands too delicately formed. These things were parts of himself, and only to be changed by an artificial cultivation of hesitancy or seeming forgetfulness.

Moreover, much the same may be said in regard to the degree of thoroughness of his preparation. In spite of the fact that he spoke in large degree *memoriter*, it is likewise a fact that he left himself a large measure of freedom. He seldom followed word for word what he had written, but introduced changes as he went along. He had such complete mastery of his subject that he often let go at pleasure parts separated from each other, and took up others without destroying the continuity or connection. We find occasional entries in the journal in which he describes and justifies his method, and which may be interesting. Thus, in connection with his Dorchester Oration in 1855, he wrote:

July 4, 1855. My detractors say I cannot speak save what I have committed to memory. It is true that this oration was carefully prepared and thoroughly studied. Who but a maniac would undertake to address such an audience without? But a very few only of the sentences were spoken exactly as written; one third left out; not by whole omissions entirely, but in some parts by an extemporized abridgment. Which of the creatures daily picking at me could do that before an audience of four thousand to save his neck from the gallows?

A still more illuminating entry occurred after the delivery of his address at Barnstable when the second centennial anniversary of the settlement of the town was celebrated.

Mr. Everett was Governor at the time, and perhaps because of the pressure of public duties he did not write out his speech beforehand. He spoke from a few notes and then afterwards made a full copy of the address for publication. The journal says:

September 7, 1839. Passed the morning in writing off the Barnstable speech. I find by the various newspaper notices that the passage most noticed (as was evident at the time) was the descending of the mountains into the deep to encircle the Mayflower. That passage was the least premeditated of any in the speech. I had in my notes that 'the Cape seems to stretch itself further out to meet and encircle the Mayflower'; and I then apostrophized the Cape in the words of Waller to a girdle, altered to the occasion

> 'What monarch would not give his throne,
> His arms might do what thou hast done.'

But though the imagery which occurred to me at the moment was infinitely to be preferred, yet I by no means draw the conclusion that careful preparation is not desirable. Such preparation secures method, coherency, and appropriateness (great merits in themselves), and furnishes a basis on which any happy thought which presents itself at the moment can be exhibited. But perfect self-possession acquired by long practice is necessary to enable you to pass from what is premeditated to what is extempore, and back from what is extempore to that which is premeditated.

From this word of explanation it is interesting to turn to the Barnstable oration as it appears in the third volume of his 'Orations and Speeches,' and there we find this dramatic passage as it framed itself so suddenly in his mind: 'I see the mountains of New England rising from their rocky thrones. They rush forward into the ocean, settling down as they advance, and there they range themselves, a mighty bulwark around the heaven-directed vessel.'

Such a magnificent image, full of dramatic force, and so much to be preferred to the picture of the girdle, might well have persuaded Everett to trust more fully to unpremeditated speech. But it never did. It added to his self-possession, that was all. Twenty years after this Barnstable experience he tells us of his preparation for the St. Louis Address at the inauguration of Washington University: 'I passed most of the time this morning in studying my oration for St. Louis, and mastered, I think, twenty-one pages of it, or what it will take forty minutes to speak. This was the work of about three and a half hours with many interruptions by the doorbell and a severe headache caused by the unhappy use of ether last evening.'

Thus he kept up to the end his patient method of preparation, and yet he was careful as time went on to give himself more and more freedom, and to develop spontaneity of expression. He confessed to himself after returning from England, and in connection with a speech at Plymouth, 'I am afraid my manner is too stately; not sufficiently flowing and natural.' He had to confess also, 'It is continually happening to me to find those efforts most successful on which I have bestowed least labor. I constantly find those efforts which cost me least preparation most applauded. I believe that I pursued a mistaken course in the labored preparation of some of my early speeches.' There is something rather pathetic, too, in this entry which occurs in his journal only a few months before his death: 'Willy thought my little, nearly impromptu speech the best he ever heard from me.' None the less, it is probable that his method was rooted deep in his temperament, and was the one best suited to his nature. It gave him a degree of confidence that he needed. For Everett, although many people never guessed it, was naturally a very shy man. He referred on occasions and with his intimates to the 'confounded diffidence that had hung like a millstone around his neck all through.' Acute observers noticed this attribute. The only person, so far as I know, who ventured to make face-to-face suggestions to Everett in regard to his way of public speech was Sydney Smith, who was extraordinarily discerning. Mr. Smith, after complimenting his oratory, called Everett's attention to two minor faults. He told him that he gestured from the elbow, instead of from the shoulder, and added that in rising to speak, he ought to guard against 'a shy and somewhat distrustful countenance.'

None the less, whatever the minor defects, due in large part to the taste of the time, nothing can seriously detract from the reputation of Everett as an orator. His fame was world-wide! Charles Eliot Norton, as a young man travelling in India, noticed a volume of the 'Orations and Addresses' on the Raja's table in Calcutta. It is impossible to read those orations to-day without an awakening sense of their wide scope, their sweep of history, their thorough mastery of the subject in hand. They cover a broad field, and are compact with accurate scholarship, dealing with such varied subjects as 'The Importance of Knowledge, the Necessity of Popular Education, the Value of Public Improvements, Invention in the Arts, the Practical Application of Science, the Obligations of Charity, the Duties of Enlarged Love of Country, and more than all, and above all the indispensable necessity of Enlightened Christian Faith.' It was said of Demosthenes that 'the history of Athens during a critical period is summed in his orations,' and the same might be said of Everett. He wrote on one occasion to Robert C. Winthrop, 'Much of my life has run to waste (as Dr. Watts says) in every way, but particularly in writing orations and lectures.' And yet, that hardly was the case, for the orations were repositories of learning, and can be referred to with as much confidence in regard to facts as exhaustive histories or elaborate essays.

Moreover, whatever may be the soundness of the charge in regard to artificiality of manner and the lack of simplicity in speech, the fact cannot be disputed that as an orator for special occasions 'he had no rival near the throne with the single exception of Daniel Webster.' In the opinion of Edwin P. Whipple he was 'the last great master of persuasive elo-quence.' It could truly be said of him, as Ben Jonson said of Bacon, that 'the fear of every man that heard him was that he should make an end.' A factor contributing in large part to this result was the orator's voice. It not only had great carrying power, so that he could make himself heard by enormous audiences, but it must have had truly magical qualities of melody and richness. The best description that I know of to be preserved for us is that of Andrew P. Peabody. Dr. Peabody says in his 'Harvard Reminiscences,' 'The timbre of Mr. Everett's voice resembled very closely that of the bells which have in their metal the largest proportion of silver. Several years ago, in listening to the bells of Moscow, which have the maximum of silver, and are kept ringing a large part of the time, I was perpetually reminded of Mr. Everett's oratory.' But whatever it was — whether voice, or manner, or material, or much more probably, all of them combined and fused into a magic whole — the effect cannot be doubted or disputed. Judge Story, though a prejudiced friend, was hardly one to flatter, and he wrote after the famous Pilgrim Oration at Plymouth, 'One hour and fifty-five minutes is a long time to hold an audience in delighted silence. That triumph belongs to you in connection with very few.' But the testimony of John Quincy Adams is more important still, because it was set down in his diary, and people do not ordinarily flatter in the pages of a private journal. Here is what Mr. Adams wrote under the date of August 8, 1836:

Mr. E. E., now Governor of the Commonwealth, and Mrs. E. paid us a morning visit; and he gave me a volume of his orations and speeches recently published. They are among the best ever delivered in this country, and, I think, will stand the test of time. ... Of the thousands and tens of thousands of these orations, which teem in every part of this country, there are, perhaps, not one hundred that will be remembered 'Alteri seculo,' and of them, at least one half have been, or will be, furnished by E. E. He has largely contributed to raise the standard of this class of compositions, and his eloquence has been the basement story of his political fortune — as yet, one of the most brilliant ever made in this Union.[1]

Such was the man who lifted up his voice in all parts of the country between 1856 and 1860 in the interests of national

[1] *Memoirs*, comprising portions of his diary, IX, 305.

harmony and peace. He never spared himself,— weary journeys, poor hotels, uncomfortable private hospitalities as well as lavish entertainments — all these were endured without complaint if only he could be of service to the country. The labor of the whole thing was enormous. He had no manager, as is common with public lecturers nowadays, to arrange dates and tours, look up railway connections, and all the rest. It was all done by himself, with requests coming from various sections of the country, and literally hundreds of invitations that it was simply impossible for him to accept. The conditions of travel, too, were not as luxurious as they are to-day. There were no Pullman cars, and nothing else that we now look upon as indispensable. As for the hotels — the less said regarding most of them the better. A few extracts from the journal will give us some idea of conditions, and they are rather amusing, especially when we remember that Everett was of all men of his day perhaps the most fastidious.

Slept badly last night (at Lowell, Massachusetts) owing to fatigue and the wretched bed. I habitually sleep with very light bed clothing. I found on my bed an immense wadded comforter (so called from being the most uncomfortable thing ever contrived), a double-blanket, fresh cotton sheets — I never sleep in anything but linen — a feather bed resting on a husk mattress. Such an uncouth accumulation of horrors I have rarely encountered.

Took the express train at half-past eight to Springfield, where we arrived punctually at twelve. The person who sat before me in the car opened his window about once in three minutes the whole way to eject a mouthful of tobacco juice.

Rather a poor night, but up at five A.M. I hoped to see the sun rise, but the hotel faces the south. Mr. Gill accompanied me to the station (Portland). A cold northwest wind. A woman near me in the car would have the window open. She needed fresh air. Presently another woman, a Quakeress, got in — elderly person afflicted with asthma, also required fresh air. She sat on the other side of the car, and there was consequently a clean sweep of cold air through it. I felt my neck stiffening and represented my forlorn case to the conductor. He provided me a seat directly against the *stove:* but that was too hot!

The air absolutely poisonous in the train from Erie to Dunkirk. The car overcrowded, very hot and filled with villainous smells of whiskey, cheese, and grease. . . . Before reaching Oran I began to feel symptoms of cholera morbus. . . . I could eat no breakfast and had to get my host to send for the doctor. He took me vigorously in hand and up to twelve м. it was very doubtful whether I should be able to speak. . . . At eight I walked to the hall and found a crowded house. I began with a brief apology and then went on about as usual. I had taken no food all day.

Quite weary on my arrival (home) and pursued by a terrible thirst; the result, I suppose of the morphia taken on Friday. Went to bed early and slept ill. The life I lead is hard, but would an easier life make me happier?

Reached Hartford a quarter after ten, and had to wait two hours for the New York train. I sat in the public room at the depot, trying to occupy the time and my thoughts with a newspaper, an attempt in which I was not aided by a boy who occupied his time and want of thought by whistling.

At four-fifty took the train for Cleveland. The ticket agent very grand. Refused, with immense airs, a Kentucky bill which a poor bewildered French woman offered him. I changed the bill for her: this humbled him a little, and he said he was not allowed to take any bills not marketable in Toledo. This was probably true, but he might have been civil. The poor woman was then starting without having her baggage checked. I put her in the way of doing it. She was still more helpless when we arrived in Cleveland. How these poor friendless creatures, ignorant of our language and ways — especially the women — get along is inconceivable. She was bound to the Catholic Asylum at Cleveland, apparently as a servant, and had but barely money enough to reach her destination. Her expressions of gratitude were touching. The surly neglect of almost all who came in her way revolting in the extreme.

But there were likewise amusing episodes — as for instance, when the barkeeper on one of the Great Lake steamers expressed such delight with an address, and especially with the exordium in which the praises of the Mississippi were sounded, that he offered him the freedom of the bar, and wanted to set him up to a 'Catawba Cobbler.'

Of a less amusing experience, he writes:

I occupied the double lower berth, and there were two persons above me in the second and third tier of the same compartment.

My friend in the upper story and myself got up early in the morning and we wanted the occupant of the middle berth to do the same
that the day seats might be made. Seemingly for the purpose of
disobliging us he doggedly remained in his berth, though wide
awake and reading.

Up at *half-past two:* brought trunks downstairs myself in order
not to trouble the servants. Governor Graham's carriage came at
half-past three, and he took me at that hour to Hillsboro' where
we endeavored in vain to get breakfast. The train came along a few
minutes after seven: stopped to change at Raleigh and met Mr.
Mordecai at the station. . . . Reached Mr. Stannard's (Richmond)
at half-past seven.

That was a sufficiently hard day from half-past 2 A.M. till
7.30 in the evening. Yet he went out to dine that evening,
and the next day, Sunday, saw him at church for the morning service. The preacher was a former professor of William
and Mary College — a learned man of German birth. He
had been in the United States for fifteen years, and yet
spoke, though correctly, with a strong accent. This fact dissuaded Everett from carrying out a plan which he had had in
mind for some time, namely, to translate his 'Washington'
into German and deliver it in Cincinnati, Pittsburgh, and
other cities where there were large German populations. He
feared, however, that after forty-two years his pronunciation
would not be good, especially as his residence in Germany
had lasted only two and a quarter years. As one looks back
now, however, it seems a pity that the plan had not been put
into effect. A little imperfection in accent would have been
easily offset by the dramatic exhibition of this thorough-
going American speaking of Washington to foreign-born
Germans in their native tongue. Mr. Everett, however,
always shrank from anything that failed to approach a
flawless performance.

But there was little opportunity at Richmond to plan for
additional work. Two days after his arrival, there came another early start:

April 20. Rose at a quarter before five and dressed in haste.
At half-past five the carriage came to take me to the landing-place

of the steamer Glencove, Captain Gifford.... A very pleasant sail down the James. Took in President Tyler on the way going to Hampton. Arrived at Lower Brandon about half-past ten. I got a little nap before luncheon, and passed the greater part of the time after luncheon in writing the twenty-second Mount Vernon Paper.... Sat up till half-past twelve writing.

April 21. At about ten this morning we went on board a small steamer to visit the ruins of Jamestown. The day was fine. The ruins consist of a considerable part of the church and several ancient tombs and grave-stones. We dug a trench on the north side of the tower and planted a row of ivy-roots, each of the company planting one. This was done in consequence of an agreement to that effect between Miss Belle Harrison and myself on occasion of my visit to Brandon last year.

April 25. Rose before five and got a cup of tea before starting for Stanton.... At Charlottesville the committee got into the train and went up with me to the University Station.... A bad headache and very weary. The audience very impossible. Almost discouraged at the thought of getting but five hours' sleep.

April 26. Rose at a quarter before five, much refreshed by a short night's sleep, and feeling equal to the duties of the day. Strange as it sounds I continually encourage myself to support these unseasonable hours and fatiguing journeys by the reflection of what naval and military officers are obliged to go through. I think, for instance, of Napoleon's retreat from Russia! My power of physical endurance is probably as great as his and I have only to add the will. The oration went off well. Unceremonious reception in the evening, and so end my engagements for this tour. Laus Deo!

Reached Boston at about a quarter after four, being eight and a quarter hours on the road.... Absent four weeks and two days: during which I spoke eight times; got about thirty-three hundred dollars for the Mount Vernon fund, and about fifteen hundred dollars by the repetition of my 'Franklin.'

The weariness of the journeys would have been little, however, had it not been for the weariness of heart that came from political disturbances and the anxiety of spirit which increased as the secession movement gathered strength and vehemence. He deplored, of course, the attitude of the South and condemned it; but he also deplored and condemned the attitude of the North in being willing to sacrifice if necessary the Union. At this time he was particularly distressed by the casual way in which disunion was talked about as though it

were the lesser of two evils only, and much to be preferred
to continuing a covenant with crime. Governor Banks stated
that 'in a certain contingency he would *let* the *Union slide*,'
and the Reverend Dr. Bellows of New York took the ground
in a sermon 'that opposition to slavery was a question of
right and humanity, while the preservation of the Union is
only one of policy and expediency, and that, if the two could
not coexist, the Union must give way.'

Things reached a pre-war climax at this time with the
brutal assault on Mr. Sumner in the Senate Chamber. Mr.
Everett deplored the dastardly act as deeply as any one, but
he could not but confess that Sumner's speech which led up
to it was unwarrantably bitter and abusive — just the kind
of speech that was uncalled for at the time. He was engaged
to deliver his 'Washington' at Taunton, Massachusetts,
a few days after the assault, and he referred to the calamitous
event, using words of condemnation that he hoped would
calm and chasten the public mind. 'Lawless violence,' he
said, 'of which I know no example in the annals of constitutional government, has at length stained the floor of the
Senate Chamber with the blood of a defenceless man, and
he a Senator from Massachusetts. O my friends! these are
events which, for the good name, the peace, the safety of
the country, it were well worth all the gold of California
to blot from the records of the past week.'

Like all men who pursue moderate counsels, as Thucydides
pointed out two thousand years ago, he had the misfortune
to be attacked from both sides. The Abolitionists were continually hounding him, and the ultra-conservatives blamed
him for holding so firmly to the necessity of preserving the
Union.

John Brown's abortive attack at Harper's Ferry gave
added agony, and again involved him in controversy. He
wrote to Mr. Winthrop, who was in Europe at the time:
'The affair of Harper's Ferry is of very painful interest. It
has produced unmeasured irritation at the South. The

extremists at the North have already canonized Brown.
Emerson calls him "a sweet saint."' These were the contentions that stirred Everett to his depths, and that gave
him positive anguish. For a time he seemed to lose heart,
and hesitated to go on with his lecture campaign.

November 17, 1856. I am very much urged to go to St. Louis to
deliver an inaugural address on the opening of the University there.
But for these detestable sectional feuds which have convulsed the
country, I should like much to speak on the subject of Education to
a Western audience. But as likely as not while I was at St. Louis
some detestable outrage would be committed in Kansas. If I
allude to it in terms of just reprobation, I disgust my audience: if
I ignore it, I draw a hornet's nest about myself at home. There is
nothing which zealots on both sides detest like a man who will not
enlist in either troop.

None the less, the old call gradually appealed to him
again, and he soon took the field once more to go to St. Louis,
and to many other places on a Western pilgrimage. But so
far as any large results were concerned, the case was hopeless.
The tide of secession moved steadily on.

October 20, 1858. At six o'clock I took carriage for Waltham
where I repeated my 'Washington.' The attention profound, but
the *demonstration* cold. I extorted, however, considerable applause.
The 'Union' sentiment met with no response. This never happened
before. Waltham is Governor Banks's home, and he is willing in a
certain contingency to 'let the Union slide.'

He still kept on, however, undaunted, though with fading
hopes and increasing apprehensions. He wrote to his old
friend Dr. Holland:

BOSTON, *June* 13, 1859

MY DEAR SIR HENRY, . . . I have passed the interval since I last
wrote you, principally in repeating my 'Washington,' for the benefit of the Mount Vernon Fund, and for that purpose have again
made several excursions to the more Southern cities, as far south
as Wilmington, in North Carolina. When I wrote you last I had
given it ninety times. I have now given it one hundred and twenty-
nine times, and the total aggregate receipt has been about fifty-five
thousand dollars. To this I have been able to add ten thousand

dollars for a series of weekly papers written for the New York 'Ledger,' a weekly journal which has attained the astonishing circulation of four hundred thousand copies, and about three thousand dollars contributed by readers of that journal on my invitation, to the fund for the purchase of Mount Vernon, to which I have altogether added about sixty-eight thousand dollars in the ways mentioned. In addition to this, I have in the course of the last eighteen months contributed about twenty-two thousand dollars to various charitable and other public institutions, by the repetition of two or three discourses — altogether about ninety thousand dollars. . . .

In the meantime, he saw his old party, the Whig Party, definitely disintegrating. Its doom, he knew, was sealed, and had been sealed ever since, in 1854, the Missouri Compromise had been repealed by the Kansas-Nebraska Bill. In 1856, the Republican, or Free-Soil Party cast 105,000 votes in the State, the whole Whig vote being less than 6000. And yet he could not, or would not, desert the old camp, and enter the new. He thought better of Buchanan than most of his friends did, and altogether better than Buchanan himself deserved. He had corresponded with him, in a rather intimate way, ever since that statesman had succeeded him in London. In the meantime his wife died after a distressing invalidism of many years' duration, his oldest son married, and soon after died, his youngest son William, after graduating with high rank at Harvard, left him to continue his studies at Cambridge, England.

In more than one sense he was left very much alone. Under these depressing circumstances the time drew near in 1860 for the Presidential nomination. The Democratic Convention met at Charleston, South Carolina, in April. The proceedings were stormy and a split took place. The delegates from the Southern States withdrew. The other delegates, after balloting for candidates many times without a choice, adjourned to meet again in Baltimore, where Senator Douglas was nominated for President. The seceding delegates, at an adjourned convention held in Charleston, finally

put John C. Breckinridge in the field. The Republican
National Convention came together in Chicago on May 16th.
William H. Seward was the leading candidate; but his hopes
were blighted and the nomination went to Abraham Lincoln.
The result was a surprise to Everett, but no cause for grief.
He had never cared for Seward, nor trusted his judgment.
The journal says:

Telegraphic news of the nomination of Mr. Lincoln at Chicago,
as the candidate of the Republican Party for President. This is the
result of Western local feeling. It is a righteous retribution on Mr.
Seward, who has for twenty years been laboring to build up a party
on anti-slavery agitation and who has done as much as any other
person to bring about the present critical state of things, and who
is now for the second time thrown overboard by the party which he
has himself mainly contributed to build up, and that, too, in favor
of a man every way his inferior.

The belief in Lincoln's inferiority to Seward was general at
that time. Everett had no reason not to share it; but he was
soon to have the distinction, which was lost by many of his
friends, of recognizing his mistake, and of giving glad support to President Lincoln.

But other events, which very closely concerned Mr. Everett,
were now absorbing his attention.

A few days before the Republican Convention met in
Chicago, the fragments of the old-line Whigs, calling themselves the Constitutional Union Party, came together in
Baltimore. They were eminently respectable as a group.
There could be no question of their ability, public spirit,
and earnest purpose. Their standing in the country was of
the highest. Many of them had held important public positions. Their controlling quality was conservatism. For the
most part they were old men. Youth was conspicuous by its
absence. For many years they had watched with alarm the
rising tide of sectional wrath, and they wished if possible to
check it. They hoped to save the Union from going on the
rocks; for they were painfully conscious of the breakers that
were close ahead. They lacked boldness, however, and,

instead of steering fearlessly toward the deep, they believed in clinging to the shore. They adopted a vague and somewhat evasive platform which declared for 'The Constitution of the country, the Union of the States, and the enforcement of the laws.' Those were principles which every one could accept; but the practical question before the country was how to have them enforced. The candidates nominated were John Bell of Tennessee and Edward Everett of Massachusetts. The two men had been friends for many years. They had served together in Congress. Their points of view were similar. They both were eminently upright and honest men, of wide experience, tried ability, and conservative principles. They were admirable representatives of a large body of conservative voters who had confided in this convention to furnish them with a safe middle road to follow.

Thus, at the momentous election of 1860, four Presidential candidates were in the field. The Breckinridge platform expressed the determination to carry slavery into the Territories, at whatever cost. The Lincoln platform proclaimed as its purpose the exclusion of slavery from the Territories, at whatever cost. The Douglas platform expressed the conviction that the whole matter should be left to the Supreme Court and to the people who were living in the Territories. The Bell-Everett platform endeavored to leave the whole question alone. The people who accepted it, and stood by it, appeared to think that it was still possible to settle the question of slavery by ignoring it. Because they could not decide what to do, they recommended doing nothing! The one thing of importance was to avoid war, prevent secession, and save the Union!

Before the convention met, it was thought highly probable that Mr. Everett might receive the Presidential nomination. His interests were in the hands of his old friend George S. Hillard. The Massachusetts delegates were instructed for Crittenden first, and then for Everett. The thought of being the Vice-Presidential candidate had never occurred to Mr.

Everett. Indeed, he had little hope or interest in the entire matter. He had done nothing directly to further his candidacy or to stimulate support. Ever since resigning from the Senate he had consistently spoken of himself as out of politics. On the morning of May 9th, when the convention met, he telegraphed and also wrote to have his name withdrawn. This was done after the second ballot, the voting at that time being strong for Houston and Bell as the ticket. Unfortunately, Mr. Hillard neglected to state that Everett's name was withdrawn at his own request. After Mr. Bell was nominated for President, no ballots were taken for the second place on the ticket. Everett's name was suggested, and he was nominated by acclamation, with a rush and without opposition! It put him in an awkward position. He did not want the nomination. He was anxious to decline it. Any *second* place, and naturally enough, was never to his liking! And yet, it would cause considerable confusion and embarrassment were he to decline. He expressed his doubts and perplexity to his daughter and her husband, writing also to others in a confidential vein.

BOSTON, *May* 14, 1860

... This horrible Baltimore nomination has already doubled my correspondence. I thought I had taken effectual measures to prevent my name being brought forward; not merely by abstaining from all measures to procure a nomination, as well as by uniformly and most sincerely professing a wish not to return to public life, but by requesting, both by telegraph and by letter, that my name, if brought forward, might be withdrawn. The Massachusetts delegation acted in entire conformity with my wishes, in dropping my name on the second ballot; but I am very sorry they did not state that it was done at my request. Had it been so stated, I cannot think the nomination for V.-P. would have been tendered me. It looks like favoring an officer with the command of a sloop-of-war, after he had magnanimously waived his claim to the flag of the Mediterranean Squadron, in favor of a junior officer. When the nomination of Vice-President came, it was done with a kind of *furore* which precluded explanations: otherwise Mr. Hillard would then no doubt have stated that, having declined being a candidate for the first office, he could not think the second ought to be offered me. I am much perplexed and distressed at the present state of affairs. I wish most earnestly to decline: I am pressed most vehemently to accept. I have not yet answered Governor Hunt's letter, communicating the nomination, but I have written him a private letter, intimating my wish to decline it. It would be as well, at present, not to mention out of doors the circumstances stated in this letter. . . .

He was perfectly well aware, of course, that there was no chance of election, and he yielded only to the earnest appeals of his friends in letting his name stand.

On May 25th he had a long and 'painful interview, of an hour's duration,' with Leverett Saltonstall and W. G. Bates, of the Massachusetts State Central Committee. They were quite insistent that he should accept the nomination. They agreed that he should not have to make anything in the way of an active campaign, and they offered to relieve him of all the burden of correspondence. Every possible weight would be lifted from his shoulders, and it was understood that he would be consulted only on really important matters. On May 29th he wrote Governor Hunt accepting the nomination, but expressing regret that it should have been forced upon him. He called attention, in a long letter, to the work that he had been doing for the Mount Vernon Association in which connection he had stood apart from and above all party disputes. Such a position was what appealed to him and he felt that it was one in which he could be of greatest service to the country. Altogether, he regretted that the convention had not put in nomination some other man whom he could cordially endorse and heartily support. He repeated the assertion which he had made so often since 1854 that he considered himself entirely withdrawn from political life, and wrote: 'In yielding at length to the earnest solicitations which have been addressed to me, from the most respectable sources in almost every part of the Union, I make a painful sacrifice of inclination to what I am led to believe a public duty.'

The whole performance was half-hearted. He yielded because he could not well refuse, in much the same spirit that he had accepted the Presidency of Harvard. Charles Eliot Norton wrote to Lowell on June 3: 'Are you pleased that Mr. Everett has consented to take the nomination of the Vice-Presidency? His letter reminds me of the advertisement of "the retired Doctor whose sands of life have nearly run out." We have patriots left. In the view of the Union Party it would seem that the Union itself were in a similar condition to the English gunboats, planks rotted, sham copper bolts not driven half through, and a general condition of unsoundness making them wholly unsafe in a sea.' [1] According to Lowell, 'Mr. Everett in his letter accepting the nomination gave only a string of reasons why he should not have accepted it at all.' And that was the way he felt. Yet acceptance was the wiser course, although success was clearly out of the question. There was no prospect of election, and none knew it better than he. But the very fact of having been a party leader, with a following that was respectable, at least, was to give him in the days that followed a certain position of command and influence that was destined to be of considerable political importance when he gave himself with ardor to the support and reëlection of Lincoln. The ballots being cast and counted in November, the Republicans were overwhelmingly successful, and the Whigs, or Unionists, were far down the line. Lincoln and Hamlin carried States enough to give them 180 electoral votes; Douglas received 12; Breckinridge 72; Bell and Everett 39. Every free State but New Jersey was for Lincoln, and there the electoral vote was divided. So far as the popular vote was concerned, Bell and Everett were at the bottom of the list with 646,124 votes to their credit, while Lincoln and Hamlin had 1,857,610.

The meaning of the election was clear. The North had found its voice, and spoke with conviction. There was to be no more temporizing, no further attempts at compromise.

[1] *Letters of Charles Eliot Norton.*

Slavery was an evil, and it should not be extended! It remained to be seen what the answer of the South would be. That question was uppermost in everybody's mind at the North. Mr. Everett waited with the rest to see what would happen. The personal disappointment was nothing; for where there had been no hope of success, there could be no bitterness in the hour of defeat. His one thought as well as fear was for the country he had loved so long and served so well! He was convinced that the apprehensions of a lifetime were now to be realized. His policy of harmony had failed. What the Fathers had established and perfected, the children were to overthrow and trample in the dust. There seemed nothing further for him to do. He had prophesied, and the prophecy was coming true; he had warned, and the warning went unheeded! His energies seemed almost spent, and apparently they had been wholly wasted. He waited and brooded, as the clouds massed ominously on the southern horizon. The night would soon descend! But — little as he dreamed it — at evening, so far as he was concerned, there was destined to be light. His greatest public service remained to be done. The apostle of peace and harmony was to become a stern, unyielding advocate of war. The Union was still the one thing to be thought of, and defended. As the Fathers had fought for glorious independence, so the Children must be taught through strife the glory of interdependent action.

XIV

WITH THE GOD OF BATTLES

THE march of events was rapid after the election of
Lincoln in November, 1860. In the South, preparations to secede were made secretly as well as openly;
in the North, propositions for conciliation and compromise —
all of them equally futile — followed one another quickly.
In February, 1861, a convention of delegates from the seceding States met at Montgomery, Alabama, and formed a government called the Confederate States of America. In the
meantime the Crittenden Resolutions, looking toward compromise, were voted down in Congress. 'My good friend,'
Mr. Everett wrote to Crittenden, 'we are in a bad way.
Cannot our Southern friends be persuaded to proceed more
deliberately? They give us no time for healing counsels to
take effect, nor do they consider in what a position they place
their friends here.' But the time had gone for healing counsels and deliberation. The programme of Everett and his
friends was proved at last to be utterly and hopelessly vain.

The country was in desperate straits. A few extracts from
the journal tell in brief, tense terms the story of the next few
weeks which has been so often and minutely told in biography
and history. Lincoln at this time was an unknown force to
most people — to Everett as well as others. But Everett was
destined much sooner than many people to wake up to the
character and genius of the 'Man of Destiny' and to give him
full allegiance.

February 15, 1861. The President-elect is making a zigzag progress to Washington, called out to make short speeches at every important point. These speeches thus far have been of the most ordinary kind, destitute of everything, not merely of felicity and grace,
but of common pertinence. He is evidently a person of very inferior cast of character, wholly unequal to the crisis.

March 4. The inaugural address received in the evening by telegraph. The tone is as conciliatory as possible, but the intention is intimated of holding the forts and collecting the duties in the ports of the seceded States. Either measure will result in Civil War which I am impelled to look upon as almost certain.

April 3. The last arrivals from Europe bring the comments of the English Press on the President's inaugural. It is almost universally spoken of as feeble, equivocal, and temporizing. It has evidently disappointed public expectation. The truth is the President's situation is impossible. He cannot do his duty in any one point. It is his duty to preserve the Union; he cannot. It is his duty to hold, or regain the Southern forts; he cannot. It is his duty to conciliate the Southern States; he cannot. This impossibility arises from the fact that he represents a party organized on a principle destructive of the Constitution. That principle is compromise. The Republican Party long since proclaimed that the day of compromise was past.

A few days after this, Mr. Everett set forth on the last lecture tour that he was destined to make in times of peace. The next entry in the journal finds him at Washington, and tells of his first meeting with Lincoln.

April 7. To church at Saint John's. The President and Mr. Seward were present. After the service I met them on the portico and Mr. Seward introduced me to the President. His manner and appearance were better than I expected to find them, and particularly courteous toward me.

Leaving Washington, Mr. Everett moved rapidly off to the West by way of Wheeling and Columbus to Cincinnati, Indianapolis, Buffalo, and other places. At Cleveland he heard the news of the firing on Fort Sumter. He was on his way home at the time, travelling as rapidly as possible, and the following entry is significant:

April 17. The New York papers at Springfield filled with warlike intelligence. An immense excitement pervades the country and a resolute purpose to sustain the Government in the prosecution of the great struggle. This result has been produced by the assault and capture of Fort Sumter. Disapproving as I did conscientiously the course of policy pursued by the Republican Party, I disapprove much more that of the Secessionists; and inasmuch as it is now an alternative between supporting the Government and allowing the country to fall into a state of anarchy and general confusion, I cannot hesitate as to the path of duty.

Nor did he hesitate from that time on. He was destined before long to find his friends in many instances cooling off and becoming faint-hearted. But not so he! There was no wavering any longer; nor did he ever get faint-hearted. He might disapprove of certain acts on the part of the Administration, but so far as his letters and his journals show he never really doubted the final issue. He was as confident as men ever can be, when face to face with a great issue, that right would win, and that the Union would be saved. Week by week, too, it became more clear to him that Abraham Lincoln was the man of the hour. The time was to come when some of his most intimate friends would fall by the wayside and utterly disapprove of his course upon the Union side. Ticknor and Winthrop were to come at last to decline his invitations to dinner because they did not like his Republican company, incurring for themselves the sobriquet of 'Copperheads.' His brother-in-law, Sidney Brooks, with whom he had always been in most cordial sympathy on public matters, failed him, and believed in compromise.

But all of this was to develop at a later period. For the moment, the North awoke with a start, and awoke completely. There was clamor everywhere for arms, for leaders, for the exercise of force! Edward Everett awoke with the rest. The attack on Sumter was like an attack on some dear and precious possession. It was as though his mother, or wife, or a member of his family had been struck! Whatever there was of resentment in his nature, and all that there was of passionate resistance, became suddenly aroused. In proportion as he had urged moderation before, lest the Union should be endangered, so now he was the outspoken and undaunted champion of force — and of force to the utmost, and of persistency in attack, that the Union should be maintained.

He reached home on April 18th. His first concern was to arrange for a flag to be flown on the Boston Public Library. That same day he heard Governor Andrew address the troops on the steps of the State House, and he could not but recall 'that the Governor, in the first speech made by him after his inauguration, had ridiculed the motto of the Union men, "The enforcement of the Laws."' He thought, too, of the way the Abolitionists — Theodore Parker, Wendell Phillips, and others — had mocked at what they called this 'Union-Saving Business,' declaring that the threats of secession on the part of the South were 'the barkings of a dog that would not bite.' He had been the truer prophet, and the catastrophe that he had dreaded and foretold for more than thirty years had finally come to pass.

It was no time, however, to be thinking thoughts of 'I told you so.' The word of the hour was for action — and evermore for action! Lincoln's first call for troops had come on April 15th. Twelve days later there was a flag-raising in Chester Square. Everett eagerly consented to speak. And then and there he sounded the forceful note that he was to sound, and sound persistently, until at last the trumpet-call was given by which he was finally mustered out to join the shining ranks of the Immortals. He said that day in Chester Square of the flag of his country as it was thrown to the breezes:

Its mute eloquence needs no aid from my lips to interpret its significance. Fidelity to the Union blazes from its stars — allegiance to the Government beneath which we live is wrapped in its folds. ... Upon an issue in which the life of the country is involved, we rally as one man to its defence. All former differences of opinion are swept away; we forget that we have ever been partisans; we remember only that we are Americans, and that our country is in peril. ... When on this day fortnight, the 13th of April (a day forever to be held in inauspicious remembrance, like the Dies Allienses in the annals of Rome), the tidings spread through the land that the standard of United America had been, for a day and a half, the target of eleven fratricidal batteries, one deep, unanimous, spontaneous feeling shot, with the tidings, through the bosoms of twenty millions of freemen, that its outraged honor must be vindicated. ... All hail to the flag of the Union! Courage to the heart and strength to the hand to which in all times it shall be entrusted! May it ever wave in unsullied honor over the dome of the Capitol, from the country's strongholds, on the tented field, upon the wave-rocked topmast. . . . As it was first given to the breeze within the limits of our beloved State, so may the last spot where it shall cease to float, in honor and triumph, be the soil of our own Massachusetts.

In the meantime, members of his own family gave him great although needless concern. His son-in-law, Henry Augustus Wise, a Lieutenant in the Navy, was, as we have seen, a Southerner by descent, a member of a distinguished Virginia family. He was a man of conspicuous position, bound by the strongest possible ties to his native State, and what was he to do? Lee and others had made 'the Great Refusal,' renounced allegiance, and gone over! Word reached Everett that his son-in-law was inclined to resign his commission. Hence this letter, written on the day of his return from the West.

BOSTON, *April* 18, 1861

. . . I can easily conceive that it must be painful to you to be exposed to the risk of meeting in arms old associates and friends. But this happens to all men — whether in service or not — in times like these. It will not be your fault.

If in 1775 our patriotic fathers had refused to serve, on account of unwillingness to come in conflict with old brother officers, our independence would not have been achieved. Washington, in the old French war, had been the comrade of many of the British officers, with whom he fought in the Revolution. General Gage, whom he held besieged in Boston, was his comrade at Braddock's defeat.

Southern officers who have taken service in the Confederate forces do not scruple to fight against their Northern brethren.

If you resign, you will be supposed to act in some degree under my influence, in consequence of my known defence of Southern rights.

But earnest as I have always been in that cause, I honestly think that the extremists of the South have forced this crisis upon us, and that the Administration must be sustained, as the only means of preserving the country from general anarchy and confusion.

A week later he wrote to his daughter on the same subject. It is clear that he was very apprehensive on the matter, and felt that he must exert all the influence he had.

... I am sensible that, considering his [Mr. Wise's] Virginia connections, his first wish must be to avoid the risk of being brought in collision with her. But I would have him reflect, first, that, as he himself told Commodore Paulding, an officer's first duty is to obey orders; second, as I said before, the Southern officers who resign will not scruple to serve against their Northern brethren. You reply to this, they fight for their rights. But this, dearest daughter, is only saying they are right and we are wrong. We can say, with equal truth, we are right and they are wrong. There has been wrong on both sides. You know my views of the more recent controversies between South and North, but, in all the Southern manifestoes it is ostentatiously maintained that it is not the anti-slavery excitement which has led the South to take up arms; but the old State-Rights quarrel, in which most assuredly we are right and they are wrong. The 'right of secession' is an absurdity.

But these are abstractions. Pray ask your husband to look ahead. If he resigns, he must do one of two things — live in the South or in the North. If in the South (besides separating you and the children from us here), he will have to serve in *their* navy; that is, fight the North. He could not live in peace in the North after resigning his commission in the present crisis. . . .

But the tension and anxiety were of short duration. Malevolent gossips had been busy, and Mr. Everett was unspeakably relieved to learn from Lieutenant Wise, in answer to his letters, that all his fears were groundless; that the Lieutenant recognized the allegiance due to Federal authority. The following letter tells of his feelings, and also of Wise's brave and patriotic action:

To Miss M. M. Hamilton [1]

... The reports about the Wises are gossip, tinged with a little malice. Mrs. D. was my daughter's most intimate friend, and it is possible they have kept up a little correspondence since they parted. Wise returned to Washington from Japan on the 14th of this month. Being of a Virginia family, second cousin to Governor Wise, and in childhood brought up in his family, and some of his most intimate brother officers having resigned, it would not have been very strange if he had experienced some struggles of feeling.

[1] A daughter of Alexander Hamilton.

Four days after his return from Japan, he was sent for by Commodore Paulding, who said, 'Harry, I am sorry to order you off so soon, but I hope you will obey.' 'I always obey,' was Wise's reply. The sequel appears in the following extract of a letter, which I received from him last evening, written since his return from Norfolk: 'I went down to Norfolk with Commodore Paulding, and last Sunday morning at about three o'clock I laid the trains and applied the torch to the entire fleet of ships at the Navy Yard. It was a grand scene of flame and roar and by a very narrow chance I escaped destruction. I did the work, however, effectually, and was publicly thanked on my return to the Pawnee. The flag officer has since spoken of me in very handsome terms in the report to the Navy Department. The only damage I received was a broken thumb and a few bruises. I have as yet no other orders, but I presume I shall be sent to defend the Navy Yard, as second to Dahlgren. I have not the slightest intention of resigning, and in case anybody fires at me, I shall fire back.'

It is a little annoying that, while a brave young man, with nothing but his good name to depend upon, is thus risking his life, in the performance of his duty, people who are comfortably and safely at home, and whose patriotism consists in sentiment, find a pleasure in inventing and propagating the poisonous gossip, to which you allude, and which had already reached me from other sources.

At the same time he wrote to Lieutenant Wise as follows:

BOSTON, *April* 29, 1861

... Your assurance that you have not the slightest thought of resigning fills me with joy unspeakable. To have done so would have been wrong in principle, ruinous to your family, and would have blighted forever your prospects, at a moment when Providence is just opening a way to your rapid advancement. I trust you will not take in ill part the frequency and the earnestness with which I have written on the subject. It has weighed heavily on my mind. I could fully appreciate the conflict of your feelings toward your brother officers of the South, especially in considering your Virginia connections. But you have decided virtuously and honorably. The seceders of the South — I mean the Yanceys, Rhetts, and Toombs — are not a whit better than the Greeleys, Phillips, and Giddings; and it is not to be endured that they should break up the Union. Nor will they be allowed to do it. I was in favor of letting them go peaceably, because I thought in two years they would come back on their knees, and that in the meantime we should hold the border States. But Fort

Sumter is a little too much for me. You have no conception of the feeling at the North. If the President should ask for two hundred and fifty thousand men, he can have them just as easily as he has had the fifteen thousand now at Washington, and money as plenty as men. I hope Commodore Paulding will be considerate with you; but whatever the orders may be, you will never regret obeying them.

But other events were not so cheering. Inevitable breaks came with his many friends at the South. These friends had always thought of him as sympathetic and understanding to an unusual degree for a Northern man. They were taken aback, therefore, by his determined stand for the Union, and by his outspoken eagerness to see the Government supported. He received a painful letter from his friend 'The Southern Matron,' with whom he had toiled so ardently and long to save Mount Vernon. He answered her as follows:

BOSTON, *May* 30, 1861

I received a few days ago, by a circuitous route, your kind letter of 26th April–2d May. I regard, with greater pain than I can express, the difference of opinion and feeling which exists between us, in reference to the present unhappy contest. I receive in the most perfect good part your intimations of the propriety of my remaining neutral. Such a course would have been much more congenial with my general disposition, with my years, and especially with my deep interest in the Mount Vernon cause, in which you and I have so happily coöperated. But I felt that my relations with the community in which I live — perhaps I may venture to say with the country — forbade my standing neutral. My convictions were strong, and I could not doubt that it was my duty to make them publicly known. I regard the war as entirely defensive on the part of the North. The enclosed speech contains in brief my general views of the contest.

I perceive, both from the newspapers and letters from friends, that surprise is felt at my having contributed to the expense of Mr. Webster's Regiment, as if my doing so was inconsistent with the kind feelings I have ever cherished and still feel toward the South. But this contribution was not made till the Secretary of War of the Southern Confederacy had announced that its flag should float over the Capitol at Washington by the 1st of May, and in due time over Faneuil Hall. I have asked the friends who have written to me on this subject whether General Beauregard's shells and red-hot cannon balls would have spared the roof which shelters my daughter and four little ones at Washington, and my own roof in Boston, and whether it was my duty, because I am a friend of the South, to sit quiet while her house and mine are reduced to ashes? It is certain that nothing has saved Washington but the alacrity with which troops have been hurried from the North to its defence.

Do not doubt, my dear friend, the sincerity with which I deplore the present state of things. I struggled against it to the last moment at the cost of favor and influence at home, and would at any time have sacrificed fortune and even life to avert it. My daily prayer to our Heavenly Father now is that He would, in His own good time, heal these cruel wounds, and again make us a united and happy people.

As soon as the firm position he had taken became known, he was at once in demand again for addresses. An official invitation soon came from New York to speak there on the Fourth of July on the subject of 'The Present State of the Country.' He accepted readily. When the time came, he found the Academy of Music full, and the stage even thronged to capacity. He spoke for two hours, being listened to with rapt attention, and he could note in his journal, 'there was a greater press around me than ever before after speaking. Siddy came from Washington to hear me; nothing pleased me more in the whole affair.'

The address itself was clear and powerful — that, and little else! It was a masterpiece of direct statement, forceful argument, and historical development; and it was prepared and delivered without the usual Everett embroidery. Indeed, it was wholly devoid of 'fine writing,' and moved steadily, forcibly on from point to point with irresistible logic. It was the first great speech of Everett's after the outbreak of the war, and it deserves careful study, for it shows with vividness the significant change that had taken place in him. He was as simple now as truth itself: as direct and forcible as fate. He was terribly in earnest. At last he was swept off his feet, and carried away by a great emotion. For the first time in his life he was a Michelangelo as well as a Raphael of speech.

The scholar come to be the advocate, reformer, agitator! The man who had been accused of 'dodging,' and who had fled before the storm, now stood out as a Luther, and proclaimed himself as unable to do otherwise. The oration in question was called 'The Great Issues now before the Country.' After being delivered before an immense throng in New York, the address was added to and published in Putnam's 'Rebellion Record,' and widely circulated in pamphlet form.

He began the address by a careful, searching study of the 'Rights of Secession.' Reviewing the steps by which the Federal Constitution grew, he declared that even 'the old Confederation, distinctly as it allowed for the sovereignty of the separate States, recognized in them no right to withdraw at their pleasure from the Union. On the contrary, it was specially provided that the Articles of Confederation should be inviolably preserved by every State, and that the Union should be perpetual.' But the 'Confederation,' when it sickened and died, poisoned by the heresy of State Sovereignty, gave place to the Federal Constitution which was ordained and established 'in order to form a *more perfect Union*' — more durable than the old Union which yet was to be 'perpetual.'

The cause of Secession [he said] gained nothing by magnifying the doctrine of the Sovereignty of the States, or calling the Constitution a compact between them! Calling it a 'compact' does not change a word of its text, and no theory of what is implied in the word 'sovereignty' is of any weight, in opposition to the actual provisions of the instrument itself. . . . In fact, to deduce from the Sovereignty of the States, the right of seceding from the Union is the most stupendous *non sequitur* that was ever advanced in grave affairs. The only legitimate inference to be drawn from that Sovereignty is precisely the reverse. . . . What would be thought in private affairs of a man who should seriously claim the right to revoke a grant, in consequence of having an unqualified right to make it? A right to break a contract, because he had a right to enter it?

Everett then went on to state and answer one by one the various claims and grievances of the South. Having done so briefly, he turned from the past to consider the present and survey the future, and said in closing:

Such, fellow-citizens, as I contemplate them, are the great issues before the country, nothing less, in a word, than whether the work of our noble Fathers of the Revolutionary and Constitutional age shall perish or endure; whether this great experiment in National polity, which binds a family of free Republics in one United Government — the most hopeful plan for combining the home-bred blessings of a small State with the stability and power of great empire — shall be treacherously and shamefully stricken down, in the moment of its most successful operation, or whether it shall be bravely, patriotically, triumphantly maintained. We wage no war of conquest and subjugation; we aim at nothing but to protect our loyal fellow-citizens, who, against fearful odds, are fighting the battles of the Union in the disaffected States, and to reëstablish, not for ourselves alone, but for our deluded fellow-citizens, the mild sway of the Constitution and the Laws. The result cannot be doubted. Twenty millions of freemen, forgetting their divisions, are rallying as one man in support of the righteous cause — their willing hearts and their strong hands, their fortunes and their lives, are laid upon the altar of the country. We contend for the great inheritance of constitutional freedom transmitted from our Revolutionary fathers. We engage in the struggle forced upon us, with sorrow, as against our misguided brethren, but with high heart and faith, as we war for that Union which our sainted Washington commended to our dearest affections. The sympathy of the civilized world is on our side, and will join us in prayers to Heaven for the success of our arms.

Such a speech, and from a man as guarded and conservative as Everett had always been, was calculated to exert great influence at home, and, when widely distributed, as it came to be among Everett's English friends, its influence abroad was equally considerable. Its most immediate result, however, was to draw down upon the orator insistent and almost innumerable demands to speak, and speak constantly in behalf of the cause. As he had given himself in time of peace to try to save Mount Vernon by his lecture upon Washington, so now he devoted time and strength to help restore the Union as he pleaded for the forceful prosecution of the war; — and again he did not spare himself. He soon found himself, as he expressed it, 'being worked like a dray-horse.' He could say in his journal: 'How rapidly the time flies when you wish it to go slowly. I am now in want of a little more time than I can command, and the moments fly with inconceivable rapidity. It is ten, eleven, twelve in the forenoon before I can turn round'; but 'what is life worth when we cease to be useful?'

He prepared at this time a new address, called 'The Causes and Conduct of the War,' which he delivered sixty times in all, beginning at Boston in 1861, and reaching as far west as Dubuque in 1862, stopping on the way at Cleveland, Madison, St. Paul, Chicago, and other places. It was a good deal for a man approaching seventy to do, who was contending all the time with a serious physical ailment; but his ardor was undimmed and his courage high. We need not consider in detail the arguments and contentions of this new address. It was forcible and persuasive, graphic and dramatic. It followed the lines that he was constantly calling attention to in private letters and in printed articles. The war was a war of aggression on the part of the South; the right to secede was not contained in the Constitution, which was much more than a mere 'compact,' to be dissolved at will: the Federal Union was the greatest achievement in human history, and at all costs it must be preserved!

And then he closed with these fervent and ringing words:

This glorious fabric shall not be allowed to crumble into dishonorable fragments. This seamless garment of Union, which enfolds the States like a holy Providence, shall not be permitted to be torn in tatters by traitorous hands. No; a thousand times no! Rise, loyal millions of the country! hasten to the defence of the menaced Union! Come, old men and children! come young men and maidens!

> 'Come as the winds come,
> When forests are rended:
> Come as the waves come
> When navies are stranded.'

Come with your strong hands, come with your cunning hands: come with your swords, come with your knitting-needles: come

with your purses, your voices, your pens, your types, your prayers:
— come one, come all, to the rescue of the country.

Letters that he wrote to his daughter and to Mr. Charles
Francis Adams may be interesting.

DETROIT, *May* 29, 1862

I wrote to you last from St. Louis. While I was there I saw a good
deal of Captain Wise. He was very attentive to me. He seemed
rather feeble, and said he had been in poor health at Cairo, but
was improving. His wife was with him. She also had been ill. I
was not much prepossessed with her appearance, but I dare say she
is a very good woman. I had a very pleasant time at St. Louis, and
a most splendid audience to hear my address, which was more enthusiastically applauded than in any other place. On the 21st I
went to Peoria: arrived after a long day's journey at seven-fifteen
in the evening and spoke at eight. The next morning I passed in
driving round the town with a very amiable family, husband, wife,
and daughter, as refined and well-bred people as you would find in
Boston or New York. Peoria stands nobly on the bank of the Illinois River. The cemetery is of extreme beauty and even grandeur
of scenery. From Peoria to Galesburg, fifty miles farther west,
where there is an excellent college — learned and sensible professors — and a very intelligent society. Here, too, I was most
kindly and hospitably received, as indeed I am everywhere. On
Saturday, 24th, I went back to Chicago, and passed a quiet Sunday: went to church both parts of the day, and found myself much
at home with the friends there. The next day I went up to Milwaukee and spoke in the evening. This is one of the new creations
of the West: fifty thousand inhabitants — all the work of twenty
years: the houses some of them equal to any on the Fifth Avenue.
The next day back to Chicago, and then in the evening I took the
night train to this place; had a tolerable rest in the sleeping-car;
found about thirty letters forwarded from Boston, and had to pass
most of the morning in answering them, and spoke in the evening
to an overflowing audience in one of the finest halls in the country.
Among others I had letters from Sid and Will. Will had returned
from Paris; passed his examination with success; and gained a University scholarship. This, besides the honor, gives him about seventy pounds sterling a year.

I have determined, after completing my engagements in this
region, to turn back to the North-West and visit St. Paul on the
Upper Mississippi. I shall probably never be so near it again, and

the scenery is well worth eight or ten days added to my tour. This will bring me to Washington a little later than I expected.

I suppose you had another 'scare,' in consequence of Banks' retreat from the Valley of the Shenandoah. It has an ugly look at this distance; but we cannot expect an unvarying tide of success.

STEAMER MILWAUKEE
UPPER MISSISSIPPI, *June* 13, 1862

...You have, I believe, seen something of this wonderful Northwest. Yesterday I was at St. Paul. I believe I voted as a Senator in 1853 for the treaty by which the Indian title was extinguished in the State of Minnesota, and now it contains two hundred thousand inhabitants. The climate has a great repute for salubrity, and pulmonary patients are now sent by the doctors to pass the winter here. With the glass going down sometimes to forty degrees below zero. If this is wise practice, it must be confessed that the opposite one of sending to Saint Augustine and Cuba is a species of scientific murder.

I note what you say of the Red Line Map affair. When I get back to the coast, I will send you my articles on that subject. It is no matter of surprise that journalists, ignorant and self-sufficient, should dash off flippant articles on these questions; or that professional libellers, like Grattan, should elaborate their deliberate misstatements. But I own I am surprised that writers like the 'Edinburgh' and 'Quarterly' reviewers should accept their one-sided assertions as authentic statements; and I am even simple enough to wonder that there is not old-fashioned English (pretended) love of fair play enough to lead even a man like Lord Palmerston, who knows how groundless their clamor is, to say one word to stop it. But I own my once rather exalted opinion of English *droiture* has been of late grievously shaken.

WASHINGTON, *June* 28, 1862

...The general tone of the public, outside of the Cabinet, as far as I can gather it, is one of anxiety and distrust, for which I do not find sufficient cause. Mr. Sumner appeared to me to contemplate the last advices from Europe with alarm. The menacing spirit in which Butler's proclamation was discussed and the threat of mediation appeared to him to forebode mischief. I think, however, he is disposed to look upon the dark side of our foreign relations in consequence of not confiding fully to the Department of State.... Mr. Seward told Wise that you had got the impression that I was in favor of a war with England. His remark, I believe, was jestingly made. I certainly am as far as possible from desiring

a war with England, but I wish I felt sure that Lord Palmerston
does not desire one with America. I infer from what Stoeckel repeated to me of Lord Lyons' conversation that England is afraid,
if the war is protracted, it will bring about a general emancipation,
and consequently a permanent failure in the supply of cotton.
What a spectacle it would be to see England not only sympathizing
with the slave-holding South, as she has from the first, but actually
interfering with the prosecution of the war, for fear it should lead to
the emancipation — of the slave!!

The foregoing letters to Mr. Adams call attention to the
fact that Mr. Everett's influence during the Civil War was
far from being confined to America alone. He had numerous
friends in England, France, and elsewhere with whom he had
kept up a constant correspondence since 1846, and he took
particular pains at this time to keep in touch with them and
to get them to see straight in regard to America. Moreover,
his natural facilities for doing so were increased by the official
presence in London of his brother-in-law.

One of the best and wisest of President Lincoln's foreign
appointments was the naming of Charles Francis Adams to
represent the United States at the Court of Saint James'.
No choice could have been better. In the critical and trying
times that ensued, it needed a man like Mr. Adams with his
firmness, his wisdom, his family prestige, his absolute fear-
lessness, his persistent readiness to speak the truth, and to
speak it plainly in genuine British fashion — it needed a man
with sterling qualities like these to represent us in a country
that had already become unfriendly, and even hostile, before
Mr. Adams arrived upon the scene.

The appointment naturally interested Mr. Everett deeply.
Of all the public positions that he had held, none ever appealed to him so strongly as that of Minister to England. It
was a post to which he had hoped sometime to return, and
which he looked back upon with positive longing. He and
Mr. Adams were utterly unlike in temperament, and they
had occupied different camps politically. But Everett saw at
once Mr. Adams's fitness for the important post at a most

critical time, and he proceeded to give him the full benefit of his own experience. He wrote him constantly during the war, kept him posted in regard to affairs at home, told him of important events, commended him to his many London friends, and warned him of possible pitfalls. That Mr. Adams valued and appreciated all this is evident from his letters in return, in which he spoke of his indebtedness. A considerable correspondence grew up between the two, and they came together, helping and advising one another, much more closely with the ocean between them than they ever had been while living as neighbors in Boston.

They addressed each other in the course of this intimate correspondence, as 'My dear Sir,' or 'My dear Mr. Adams,' or 'Mr. Everett': but that was the custom of the time and indicates no coldness nor unusual formality. Mr. Everett never became sufficiently informal — not in his letters, at least — to address his son-in-law as 'Henry.' To the end of their relationship, which was close and intimate, it was always 'My dear Wise,' or 'Dear Sir.' The time had not arrived when Christian names were to be bandied about freely. In the sixties, more especially in Boston, formality reigned supreme, and dignity was an essential part of duty. With this explanation, let us look at some of these intimate family letters.

To Charles Francis Adams

BOSTON, *August* 4, 1861

I have to thank you for your letter of the 12th of July.

The disaster of Bull Run, which happened a fortnight ago to-day, has not, I think, disheartened the country. In fact the Confederates appear to have suffered as much in the *field* as we did. In other words, the disorderly retreat was the result of a real panic, not of defeat. The causes of the panic are not well made out, which is not to be wondered at, as it is of the nature of a panic to have no sufficient cause.

The new regiments move to the South with alacrity.

I have received a letter from Lord John Russell, in reply to one which I wrote to him, and of which he read you a part. He does not attempt to answer the only complaint I made, which was of the *haste* shown in recognizing the Confederates as belligerents before your arrival. I will, by the next steamer, send you a copy of the letter. It is at present in the hands of a friend.

I send the third copy of the 'Rebellion Record': the fourth has not reached Boston.

BOSTON, *September* 17, 1861

I send you by this steamer a newspaper containing an Agricultural Address delivered by me last week. I introduced the topic of the reopening of the African slave-trade by the Southern Confederacy, in the event of its establishing its independence, under the impression that, on that point, if on no other, the British Government, out of decent respect for their antecedents, would be compelled to show some sensibility to the moral complexion of the struggle. Mr. Motley informed me, as he probably has informed you, that the first question put by Lord John to the Confederate envoys, in their unofficial interview, was how the Confederate Government stood affected toward the opening of that trade, and that their answer was not very satisfactory.

I also venture to enclose you an article from the New York 'Ledger,' written for the purpose of lessening a little the discouraging influence of the deplorable reverse of the 21st of July.

I do not think that event has had much effect on the public mind. The new regiments are rapidly filling up, and the defences of Washington are considered altogether adequate for its protection. The state of things in Kentucky is much better than we feared. In Maryland the government is acting with firmness and vigor. Missouri is in a chaotic state: but I saw a letter full of courage from a business man in St. Louis, a day or two since, and I received yesterday an invitation to deliver 'one or more lectures' there, the ensuing winter!...

That Everett's labors were helpful in England, and that his correspondence with Mr. Adams was of influence cannot be doubted. Mr. Adams wrote him:

LONDON, *July* 12, 1861

I am much obliged to you for your note of the 25th and for the extracts from the letters of Lieutenant Wise.... These letters are doing a great deal here to correct opinions as to the nature of the struggle. But I cannot help feeling every day that the secret wish of almost all classes is to see us permanently divided....

I have also to thank you for the hint in regard to the Legation.

I have been very careful to impress upon all the members the importance of obeying the injunctions of the Department which prohibit all communication with the press.

LONDON, *July 26, 1861*

I am greatly obliged to you for the copies of your clear and powerful address. I cannot doubt that it will do great good at home as well as in Europe. This country is full of wrong impressions of the nature of our government. Even intelligent Americans are quoted here as talking about the right to dissolve the partnership, just as if we were a mere trading firm.

LONDON, *September 6, 1861*

. . . I write these speculations to you in confidence, as what I hear, and what I believe. One safeguard will be success in our undertakings. The blockading force must be effective. That is the *sine qua non,* so far as our exterior relations are concerned.

LONDON, *October 5, 1861*

. . . I am much obliged to you for your note of the 7th of last month, and for the copies of the excellent address, which I have distributed where I thought it would be useful. . . .

There is no doubt in my mind that the general conviction here is that the disruption is final: and that, among the higher classes at least, the wish is father to the thought. . . .

To Charles Francis Adams

BOSTON, *October 29, 1861*

I had much pleasure in receiving yours of the 5th of October by the last steamer. The fair prospect, to which you allude, as produced by the prosperous turn of things here, is a little clouded by the news which this steamer will carry to you of another reverse to our arms near Leesburg. It seems to have been a sad blundering piece of business. There is a general willingness to lay the blame on poor Colonel Baker. *Les morts, aussi bien que les absens, ont toujours tort.* The great naval expedition has sailed from Fortress Monroe. Its success, if it fully succeeds, will be all-important, — and its failure proportionably disastrous.

Mr. de Stoeckel sat half an hour with me to-day. He talked in the sense of Prince Gortschakoff's letter; but rather gloomily of our cause. He distrusts the ability of McClellan to handle the large army under his command, and thinks General Scott, though his faculties are unimpaired, pretty nearly 'used up': — I am sorry to use that cant phrase of the noble old chief. Stoeckel says that

France and England have intimated to our Government that the domestic interests of their subjects absolutely require that the supply of cotton should not be much longer obstructed, and that, if the present state of things continues, they shall be compelled — with great reluctance — to take measures for the relief of their subjects, who, according to Stoeckel, will otherwise starve or rebel; and of course the latter. He says *he knows* these intimations have been made.

I read to Stoeckel a part of your letter — not, of course, that which you wrote in confidence. He said, *à propos* of the European complications, that Prince Gortschakoff wrote him that they were numerous and grave; that Russia could not prevent their existence, but thus far had been able to prevent their leading to war; and that as this season had passed, without a rupture, and winter was at hand, peace was sure to be preserved, at least till next year. Baron Brunnow writes to Stoeckel that John Bull affects to weep from sympathy, when Brother Jonathan cries with the toothache, but chuckles in his sleeve, as poor Jonathan's teeth, with which he is accustomed to bite so hard, are pulled out by his own doctors. Mr. Seward has requested me to come to Washington to confer on some public business (he does not say what), and I shall start on Wednesday.

The summons 'to Washington on some public business,' referred to above, was the first of many that Mr. Everett was to receive from the Administration. He was destined as time went on to come more and more closely into touch with Mr. Lincoln and his Cabinet, until, on one occasion, he found himself present when important letters were discussed, and was told by Lincoln that he was looked upon 'as one of the Cabinet Council.'

The immediate business on hand in 1861, however, related to a proposition from Seward that he should go abroad for the Government as one of a group of men who should act to influence public opinion in England and on the Continent. This proposition was to be renewed several times in the course of the war, and each time in very flattering terms. The journal tells of this diplomatic offer — and of other things as well.

Friday, August 23, 1861. Called on Mr. Sumner and had a long conversation on foreign affairs. He is evidently very hostile to Mr.

Seward. He says that when Mr. Lincoln came to Washington, he consulted him — Mr. S. — on the formation of his Cabinet, telling him that Seward and Welles were the only names on which he had decided. S. replied that he thought Seward was designated by public opinion for the Department of State; but added, 'You must watch him and overrule him.' When S. reached Washington on the 21st of May he found the President and every one else under the apprehension of an immediate rupture with England and France proceeding from suggestions of Mr. Seward. It turned out that Seward had determined to direct our Ministers at London and Paris to quit their missions if the envoys of the Confederates were officially or unofficially received — as Dallas and Sandford had written him they had been. Seward's despatch to this effect had already been drafted. S. afterwards saw this original draft, with the President's corrections, which completely emasculated it. Two whole pages were ordered to be omitted at the end; and instead of being directed to leave a copy of it with Lord John — as in the first draft — he was told that it was for his own eye alone.

When S. called on the English and French Ministers at the time referred to, to confer with them, he found that they had both been so repelled by Seward's lofty tone with them that they went to him as little as possible. Seward himself, when S. called upon him, actually raved about England and France. His language was, 'God damn them, I'll give them hell. I'm no more afraid of them than I am of Robert Toombs.'

I should judge from the tone and substance of Mr. S.'s remarks that he was planning to supplant Seward, and if his representations of his own relations with the President can be relied upon, he is not unlikely to succeed.

Monday, November 4, 1861. Mr. Kennedy came to confer with me on the subject of Mr. Seward's proposal. He said that in addition to ourselves, Winthrop, Bishop McIlvaine, Archbishop Hughes, of New York, Catholic Archbishop, had been applied to. He said that Bishop McIlvaine had asked him (K.) what sum he — the Bishop — should name to the Secretary of the Treasury as a suitable allowance for expenses and that he (K.) had answered one thousand dollars per month, but such part only to be paid as might be actually expended; and he requested me, if I saw Seward, to propose this amount.

Friday, November 1, 1861. Breakfasted with Mr. Seward at eight. No one present but ourselves, his son, and a fourth gentleman whom I think he also called Seward. Some birds on the table he said were sent by Mr. Russell — a kind of peace offering, after some unpleasant passages between them. After breakfast Mr. Seward explained the object for which he had sent for me. Considering the activity of the Confederates in prepossessing the public mind of Europe against us, he asked some gentlemen of independent position, patriotism, and fortune to consent to go as volunteers to Europe, for the purpose, as far as possible through social channels, of contradicting the Confederate influence. The Government would pay their expenses, but wished their mission to be unofficial and as far as possible confidential. He named Mr. J. P. Kennedy, of Baltimore, and Bishop McIlvaine, of Ohio, as the persons to whom he had made the same overture as to myself. I think he did not name Mr. Winthrop, who, however, I learn by letter from him in the course of the morning, had just returned from Washington on the same errand as mine. I told Mr. Seward I would take the subject into consideration. I then went with him to the President's, where I was introduced to him, to the Secretaries of the Navy and the Interior; Judge Bates (Attorney-General) I have long known. The President came up and shook hands with great cordiality, saying that he had been shown a letter of mine in the summer (meaning my letter to Lord J. Russell in reply to one to me) 'which did honor even to Mr. Everett.' Speaking of his 'leisure,' he misquoted the line of Pope, "'Tis nowhere to be found or everywhere,' transposing the two clauses; but he immediately corrected the error. At two o'clock I left a card for Mr. L. At half past six went to Mr. Seward's to meet the French Princes — Prince de Joinville, Count de Paris, and Duc de Chartres — at dinner. No one else but the two Mr. Sewards. Prince de J. tall, dark, deaf, and dressed in deep black; speaks English slowly, but pretty well. The Count de Paris and his brother tallish young men, rather slim; in their uniform as aides to General McClellan. Speaks English pretty well. Conversation not particularly interesting. Mr. Seward gave a long account from 'Modern Chivalry' of the contest between the two preachers. I told the beautiful anecdote of Archbishop Asher's 11th Commandment. I was able to repeat to the Prince portions of his father's conversation with me at Saint-Cloud, relative to the comparative facilities for traveling in America then and when he (Louis-Philippe) was in the country.

To Charles Francis Adams

BOSTON, *November 9, 1861*

I have to thank you for your two very valuable letters of the 5th and 25th of October. I write a little in advance of the sailing of the steamer, as I shall be much engaged next week.

You and Abby will be sorry to hear of the death of my oldest son,[1] which took place here on the 5th inst. He had long been a great invalid, but his death, when it took place, was very sudden and unexpected. I was unfortunately absent from home.

I do not attempt to send you any intelligence, as the steamer will bring you four days' later dates, and especially will probably bring some important information about the great naval expedition. It was the impression at Washington that it had escaped the fury of the gale of the 2d, and what little information we have is to that effect.

We have had another atrocious military blunder at Ball's Bluff. As usual nobody is to blame, and nobody is responsible. The fault is generally ascribed to Colonel Baker, he being dead. Our Massachusetts young men appear to have behaved nobly; but it is almost maddening to see these precious young lives thrown away, and the great Cause endangered, by these constantly recurring blunders.

What I said of Mr. Seward's too belligerent propensities was founded a good deal on Mr. Sumner's statements. I made allowance for the evidently unfriendly tone in which they were made, but I could not have supposed them so exaggerated, as I now incline to think them. They were in part confirmed by a Captain Taylor, late of the British army — who brought me two or three days ago a letter from his uncle the late Archbishop of York — who told me that Mr. Seward had said to Russell, the correspondent of the 'Times,' that he was willing to go to war with England and France to-morrow, and that on his (Taylor's) repeating this to Lord Lyons, Lord L. replied, 'I can believe it; he has said much the same to me,' adding, 'he treats me so I can't go to the department.' All this, however, cannot be true, if any of it is. Mr. Seward told me his personal relations with Lord L. were perfectly friendly. I saw a letter of the Duke of Argyll to Mr. Sumner, expressing lively fears that Mr. Seward was driving the country into a war — this was some three months ago; and Dean Milman, in a letter to me of the 16th October, speaks of Mr. Seward's having threatened an invasion of Canada. . . .

Mr. Seward has requested me, as he has Thurlow Weed, Archbishop Hughes, J. P. Kennedy, Bishop McIlvaine, and R. C. Winthrop, to go to England and France for two or three months unofficially and as volunteers, to endeavor, through social channels, to counteract the influence of the Secessionists, who are said to be swarming at London and Paris and producing an effect on public opinion. I see many objections to going — the vagueness of the errand — the strangeness of the grouping (which, however, is of less consequence, as there is no official character to be kept up and

[1] Edward Brooks Everett, M.D., died at Boston, November 5, 1861.

consequently no joint action necessary, nor probably expedient), the wintry voyage, some twenty-five or thirty engagements to speak, and now the attention, which it may be necessary to give to my son's affairs, which may, indeed, prove to me an insuperable barrier. I will add also, in entire sincerity, that I believe, from all I know and all I hear, not only that the official duties of the American Minister are performed by you in a manner which leaves nothing to desire, but that whatever can be effected through social influences is accomplished with equal skill and success. I am not quite sure that it would be wise to send out half a dozen *volunteers* when the *regular* service is so efficient.

I wish you would, with entire unreserve, give me your opinion of the matter, by which, if I am able to come (which is quite doubtful), I should be much governed.[1]

You will not suppose for a moment that I imagine Mr. Seward to labor under the impression that your hands need strengthening. But he seems to think something can be done by purely unofficial influences, in social intercourse by private travellers, in which capacity only the persons named are to go abroad. The whole movement was to be confidential, but it is already in the papers, I know not through what means.

I have written too long a letter already, but having half a page left, I will add, that, while in Washington the other day, I had a long and interesting conversation with M. Mercier, the purport of which was that France suffered so much by the present state of things in this country that she would be compelled, in self-defence, *to take measures of relief.* I asked him what measures, and he answered, 'Recognition of the Confederacy.' I told him that of itself, though it would give great moral aid to the South, would not help France. He admitted this, and said in substance they must break the blockade. I replied, 'This would be war with the United States.' He did not deny this, but seemed to think, on the near and certain approach of such a result, we should give way. I told him he could not be in earnest in thinking his Government would go to war with a friendly power merely to promote domestic interests. He said necessity knew no law. I believe substantially the same language is held by him officially. I think it is intended to frighten us into yielding, and told him so. But that he disclaimed. Stoeckel told me Louis Napoleon was thoroughly frightened at the fear of a general *émeute.* You will put your own interpretation on all this. *Valeat quantum.*

[1] [Written in margin:] I learn to-day from Washington, much to my satisfaction, that Mr. Seward consents to postpone for some time — perhaps indefinitely — further action in this matter.

P.S. The New York 'Herald' says, 'Mr. Adams is the right man in the right place.' If the 'Herald' commends you, you will begin to read the first clause of Luke VI. 26, with some authority.[1]

Almost immediately after this came the excitement of the Mason and Slidell affair. Everett was entirely convinced that the action of our Government in removing the two Southern representatives was justified by historical precedent and the Law of Nations. He took this stand instantly, and held to it very tenaciously, and it did more almost than anything else during the war to wean him from his love for England.

Sunday, November 17, 1861. The mail brings us the account of a very striking incident — the detention of the British mail-steamer Trent in the Bahama Channel and the taking from her of Messrs. Slidell and Mason, the ministers of the Confederates, and Messrs. Eustis and Macfarland, their secretaries, by the San Jacinto, steam frigate, Captain Wilkes; their families were allowed to proceed.

This very important step was probably taken without any instructions, but there is not the slightest doubt of its legality. The right of search by a national vessel is undoubted. It is a belligerent right and the British Government has recognized the Confederate States as belligerents. The best writers affirm the right of a belligerent to arrest the ambassadors of the enemy and Lord Stowell asserts it distinctly in the case of the Caroline, 6 Robinson, 468.

To William Everett

BOSTON, *November* 23, 1861

... The capture of Messrs. Mason and Slidell is also a very important event. It was authorized by the most undoubted principles of International Law, as laid down by English text-writers, and administered by English Courts of Admiralty. The case of Mr. Laurens in the Revolutionary War is precisely parallel. He was on his way as Minister to Holland, then a neutral power. Being on board a Dutch packet, the vessel was captured by a British frigate, and carried into St. John's, Newfoundland; Mr. Laurens sent to England, and confined two years in the tower *as a traitor.* After the capitulation of Yorktown, he was considered as a prisoner of war and exchanged for Cornwallis. ...

The attitude of the English Press and the English Government in the crisis saddened as well as angered him. He could

[1] 'Woe unto you, when all men shall speak well of you.'

declare, 'If England avails herself at this moment of our weakness to make such a demand [the surrender of Mason and Slidell] it will be an act of national cowardice, bullying, and meanness not often paralleled.'

None the less, he was glad, when the time came, to have the matter adjusted without a clash, and he congratulated Mr. Seward on the forbearance he had used and the dexterity he had displayed. His feelings, however, in regard to England and to the course she was pursuing underwent no change. The attitude of the governing class toward America was a cause for great grief. He had, he could say, in writing to his friends, 'brought from England the warmest feelings of attachment and admiration, but she has exhibited so much political and commercial selfishness and so much hypocrisy as a great anti-slavery power, that those feelings have undergone a change which will sadden the few remaining years of my life. . . . The malignity and hypocrisy of a considerable portion of the English Press have so disgusted me since the war broke out that I have ceased to read their spiteful comments.'

None the less, he faithfully kept in touch with his English friends, doing all that lay in his power to correct their point of view and expose malicious falsehood. He was given a happy opportunity to do this by reason of the fact that his youngest son William was at this time a student at the English Cambridge, having gone there after completing his undergraduate course at Harvard. This called for letters to his old friends, commending the youth to their kindness, and telling them at the same time of the Civil War and what the whole thing meant. The following letter, for instance, to Sir John Coleridge is a sample of his correspondence of this kind, and serves to show that he aimed at those who were moulders of opinion in England:

BOSTON, *March* 3, 1862

I have been inexcusably tardy in acknowledging the receipt of your letter of the 15th of August. I had intended to thank you for it

about the close of the year when the unpleasant affair of the Trent
came on, and the danger of an immediate collision between the two
countries seemed to divest every other topic of interest, and about
that it was painful to write.

With respect to the civil war now raging, it is certainly unavail-
ing to discuss the right of secession. Every people, numerous or
not, has a right to revolt if oppressed, and they must, of course, be
their own judges of that fact. But, on the other hand, every people
has a right to maintain its political integrity, and is bound as a
moral person to contend for its existence. This war has been forced
upon the North by a small circle of disappointed political aspirants
at the South (so it was publicly affirmed, in substance, by Mr.
Stephens, the Vice-President of the Confederacy, after South
Carolina had seceded), and the Government and loyal people of
the United States are under all the obligation that can rest on a
government and people to put down an insurrection that strikes at
the life of the body politic. It certainly adds to the weight of the
obligation, in this case, that the great lever, by which these ambitious leaders of the revolt have been able to move the masses of
the South, is slavery and the desire to extend and perpetuate it.

The clamor about the tariff is merely to enlist British sympathy.
There never was a greater and more general prosperity than that
which has prevailed at the South for thirty years. I did not intend
what I said on that subject, in the discourse I sent you, merely as
an *argumentum ad hominem*, justifying retaliation on the part of
the North; but as an authority by way of answering the Southern
doctrine that protective duties are unconstitutional. This I
thought I did, by showing that the leading statesmen of the South
had, from the foundation of the Government, sought, by the enact-
ment of these duties, to foster Southern interests.

I had hoped to visit England again, before my son leaves it, but
in these times one does not like to leave his country. My boy continues to be much gratified with his residence, both as to society
and study. He is at Trinity, where his maternal ancestor in the
seventh generation (John Cotton, famous in our ecclesiastical
annals and even in our civil history, for our Boston was named in
honor of him, as Vicar of Boston in Lincolnshire), was a student at
the close of the sixteenth century. Dr. Whewell writes me the best
accounts of him, and all my old friends are exceedingly kind to him.
The Prince of Wales has honored him with the most condescending
attentions. . . .

His efforts of this kind were not confined, however, to

England alone. There was danger lest France and England should come together in their opposition to America. Such a combination would be formidable, indeed; and at this particular time the United States had only one real friend in Europe, and that was the Emperor of Russia. The Prince Napoleon had visited America in 1861. A public dinner was tendered the Prince in Boston at which Everett made a speech, which found its way to Paris. The French Emperor having written Mr. Everett thanking him for his words, an opportunity was given, which Everett seized, for writing the following explicit letter, which did no beating about the bush, but went direct to the matter in hand.

BOSTON, *January* 4, 1862

SIRE,

I have had the honor to receive the letter of the 24th of November which your Imperial Majesty has had the condescension to address to me, and I pray you to believe me duly sensible of your kindness.

It emboldens me to take the great liberty — I hope your Imperial Majesty will pardon me if I pass the limits of the *convenances* — of praying you not to support England in her intentions to force a war on this country. Your Imperial Majesty knows that there *cannot* be any foundation for her pretence, as ridiculous as it is insincere, that the Government of the United States desires a war with England. Neither is it the wants of her manufacturers, though urgent, nor yet the eagerness of parties to keep or to gain place; nor the old Tory prejudice against the country. These causes no doubt have their influence; but the main cause, for which the Government of England is willing to go to war with us, in this hour of our trial — I am sure your Imperial Majesty penetrates it — is the traditionary apprehension of the growth of a great naval power in the West, destined one day to become a very important counterpoise to her own maritime strength. Your Imperial Majesty's gracious approval of my little speech at Prince Napoleon's dinner confirms me in the views there expressed of the high motives of policy, which originally led France to contribute her all-powerful aid toward the establishment of our Independence; which induced the great chief of Your Imperial Majesty's dynasty, as one of the first acts of his accession to power in 1800, to close up the breach between the two countries, which had arisen under the Directory; and which, above all, decided him to make that magnificent cession of Louisiana. I am aware that France suffers from the temporary interruption of commercial relations with the United States. This, although a serious, is not a permanent evil. The sacrifice of our navy — both as a material force and a growing influence in the world — would be an irreparable injury to France. We can never be anything but the natural allies of France; never anything but the natural rivals of England; whose friendship, in the long run, and for the same reasons, can no more be depended upon by France than by the United States.

I pray Your Imperial Majesty to forgive my presumption in writing this letter (to which of course, I expect no reply), and believe me, with profound respect, of Your Imperial Majesty the obliged, faithful servant.

In the meantime, in addition to these private letters, Mr. Everett was writing again in a public way for the New York 'Ledger.' Mr. Bonner's offer in connection with the Mount Vernon affair had worked so well that he renewed it when the question of saving the Union came to the front. Instead of a weekly letter, however, Everett wrote once a month, and he wrote on a great variety of subjects — all of them connected, however, with the great issue that absorbed all thoughts. These are the 'writings' referred to in the following letter to Mr. Adams.

BOSTON, *August* 3, 1862

The month which will have elapsed when this reaches you, since the date of yours of the 18th, will not have brightened the skies much for you. It is true the Confederates at Richmond have not been able to follow up their advantage. Considering the very heavy loss on our side and the discouragement which always attends a reverse, the fact that the rebels have made no attempt to harass McClellan shows that they also have suffered severely, which we know from other sources to be the case. The appointment of Halleck as Commander-in-Chief gives very general satisfaction. McClellan's friends take no offence, and Stanton's, I think, are glad to have him relieved from the responsibility of the immediate control of military operations. It cannot be denied that the division of opinion in the Cabinet, in Congress, and in the country is a very dangerous element of weakness. In truth it is paralyzing us. And yet I do not see the remedy. Men differ honestly as to the confiscation of the property and especially the slaves of the rebels, and they cannot be prevented from speaking and acting accordingly. But all this is a familiar subject of reflection with you.

The speech of Lord Palmerston and the withdrawal of Mr. Lindsay's motion give us a little respite, but unless the year closes with signal advantages to the arms of the Union, I suppose it is but a respite, as far as 'Recognition' goes. That does not necessarily imply war, but it would be very likely to furnish occasions of collision. If England and France are determined on a rupture, they will find a pretence for it. I cannot, however, yet persuade myself that England thus far (as she tries to make us think) has been holding France back; but the reverse. Of this, however, you know much more than I do. Lord Russell does me injustice if he thinks I am actuated by any unfriendly feelings toward England. I think her diplomacy toward us and her treatment of us have almost always been unfriendly, and when occasion called for it, I have said so; but not I think with bitterness. I have, since the war began, written or spoken upon every topic that has come up, and notwithstanding the virulence of the British Press (not excepting the Quarterlies) on the same topics, I do not remember having used one harsh expression. I left England with a really affectionate attachment to Lord Aberdeen and the utmost regard to many individuals including Lord Russell, and these feelings I still retain. But they are not inconsistent with the opinion that the course of England has been unfriendly, on the part of her Press eminently so, since the war began. I rather think Lord R.'s impressions of my 'speeches and writings,' is formed less on what they really contain than on the false representations of one or two of the venal correspondents of the London Press, who seem to be stationed in this country to do the devil's work of promoting 'war on earth; ill-will toward men.'

Naturally enough these patriotic, painstaking efforts were fully appreciated at Washington. It was not long before the suggestion was renewed that he should go abroad to influence public opinion. This time, however, the offer was one of greater distinction, and eventually he came to be wanted as a kind of envoy or plenipotentiary-at-large, commissioned to all the European Governments. It was a signal testimony to his capacity and tact, to his personal influence and social charm. No one, it was felt, could do so much as he to counteract the propaganda that was being carried on by the representatives of the Southern Confederacy. The story of this offer, and how he met it, will best be told by a few of his letters, and by some extracts from his journal.

To F. P. Blair, Esq.

I have your important letter of the 27th August. The very flattering character of that part of it which is personal to myself makes it difficult for me to say anything by way of reply, beyond expressing my thanks. I hope you took care to let the President know, if not I beg you to do so at the first opportunity, that you had never, either in writing or conversation with me, alluded to the step which it seems you have recommended to him.

Mr. Seward must, of course, have much better means than anybody else of judging of the intentions of foreign powers; and I agree with him that there is no danger of intervention *at present*. But how long will it be before the present in this respect becomes *the past?* Lord Russell's letter of the 28th of July is decidedly offensive in its tone, and the circumstances mentioned by him as inducements to intervention hitherto resisted by them are all such as can hereafter be made use of, whenever they choose. I own I think Lord Palmerston is eager for a cause of quarrel. The Press almost unanimously backs him; the cotton manufacturers do the same; the old monarchical and Tory leaven is fermenting at the thought of the 'model Republic' going to pieces; the writers and publishers — a very influential class — are against us because we will not allow them copyright (which I, when Secretary of State, tried to do and which, as I learned last week from an English nobleman, fresh from Richmond, the Confederates have offered to do), and the Anti-Slavery Party, for reasons well known to you, are not strongly with us. I enclose a translation of a part of a letter from Prince Napoleon of the 30th January last, from which you can gather his opinion of the feelings of the English Government and aristocracy toward this country. I received by the last steamer a letter from my particular and confidential friend Sir Henry Holland, one of the Queen's physicians and physician to Lord Palmerston, which gives me much pain, as showing that a person, on whose friendly feelings toward us I had ever relied, was fast drifting in the opposite direction.

You are quite right, in my judgment, in thinking that on the part of all the great monarchies of Europe, there is a vague feeling of uneasiness in reference to the growth of a prosperous Republican power on this side of the Atlantic. This feeling, however, does not influence the political conduct of any power but England. In fact they don't like her parliamentary government better than they do our republican system. England has an old grudge against us from the times of the Revolution; she fears our growing maritime strength and our manufacturing competition, and dreads the contagion of republican principles through the channel of a common language. She endeavors to carry the Continental Powers with her, and to make us and the world at large think she is doing so, but with little reason. Louis Napoleon is sorely pressed by his manufacturers, and he is possibly willing that we should be kept busy with our own troubles at home, in order to prevent our interfering with his operations in Mexico. But I have no belief that he will depart from the traditionary policy of his country and eminently of his uncle — that of strengthening the United States as a counterbalance to England; which is still more the hereditary policy of Russia than of France. Both of these Powers have been and are assailed with all the arts of England's diplomacy to make common cause with her against us.

This brings me to the topic discussed in your letter, viz. the means of counteraction, which I have a very strong conviction is not only expedient, but absolutely necessary. Though there may be no danger at present, it is equally true that when the evil is upon us it will be too late to ward it off. Napoleon's guide at Waterloo kept ducking his head as the cannon balls went singing over the hollow road where they were posted. Napoleon said to him goodnaturedly, 'There's no use in that, Costa, when you hear them they don't hit.' This I was told by the guide. So, too, when England lets us know she is about to intervene, it will be too late for countervailing measures. She will amuse us with professions of neutral intentions to the last.

With respect to the *personal* part of your suggestions, I am the last man to express, perhaps I should say to form, an opinion. I cannot, however, deny, that I think the individual employed should be not only acquainted with French and German, but should have had considerable experience of European society and official life. I believe the gentleman [1] named by you, and who has lately gone a second time, has much tact in managing our domestic politics and he has been kindly received in England. I have been under the impression (derived mainly from Sir Henry Holland's letters) that he had accomplished much in the way of removing prejudices against the North. But Sir Henry's last letter, of which I enclose you an extract, leads me to fear that, in his anxiety to gain the credit of 'candor' and impartiality, he has gone too far. At any rate, it is quite evident that his representations and suggestions have not been such as to produce a desirable effect — but the reverse — on a person like Sir Henry and the class he represents; who, from being a decided friend of the North, has evidently

[1] Thurlow Weed.

of late undergone an unfavorable change. That a person not familiar with the two diplomatic languages of the Continent, and without any experience of public life abroad, should be able to exert an important influence, official or unofficial, is contrary to all my own observation and experience of affairs. But on this topic I cannot enlarge. I will only enclose a translation of a French note addressed by Prince Gortschakoff last summer to Mr. Cassius Clay, and one of a German letter to myself from Baron Brunnow, the Russian Ambassador in London.

I can easily conceive that, at present, the President might not feel it in his power to appoint any person to high civil office who was not in 1860 a member of the Republican Party. He would, I dare say, as far as his own feelings are concerned, willingly do it; and men who, like yourself and Judge Blair, are patriotic enough to rise above that consideration, would sustain him in it. But the mass of his nominal supporters (among whom are some of his most dangerous opponents) would not. There are too many hungry and clamorous mouths yet to be filled. For myself, having long since abandoned all thought of further political service, satiated with the honors of office, and standing in no need of its emoluments, nothing but your obliging opinion, that, in the evening of my days, and in a threatening crisis of the country, I could still render an important service, has induced me to write this letter. These are not times for an over-fastidious personal delicacy.

Sunday, September 21, 1862. Reached Wise's house about seven last evening, and found a nice dinner, prepared by the servants, waiting. Sent to Mr. Seward that I would call upon him whenever he would appoint a time. He named after church to-day. I attended Mr. Pyne's church and afterwards called on Mr. S., who requested me to go to Europe unofficially, but to exercise a salutary influence to discourage hostile intervention. Captain Fox, the Assistant Secretary of Navy, drove me out to 'Silver Spring' to dine with Mr. Blair. Passed a picket within his grounds. After dinner a long conversation with Mr. Blair, Senior, about the proposed visit to Europe, which he urges with great earnestness, requesting me particularly to talk with the President about it. Horse quite lame; nearly two hours on the way home.

Monday, September 22, 1862. Wrote a note to the President, requesting him to give me an interview. He appointed to-morrow morning at nine. Made a few calls: read a good deal in Grammont. The transition of the morals and manners of London from the state of things under the Commonwealth to that of the Court of Charles II is frightful and would be incredible if it were not history.

Tuesday, September 23, 1862. Called upon the President by appointment. I stated to him very plainly the view I took of Mr. Seward's proposal; that I did not feel inclined to go abroad as a mere agent of the Secretary of State, but that, if I was authorized to say I was, however, unofficially *his* agent, it would alter the matter. He said no one would suspect me of seeking an office — that if the state of things now existing had existed when the Administration was framed, I should no doubt have been one of those entrusted with foreign missions. That there was some difficulty in an authorized agency on account of the jealousy with which it would be viewed by our Ministers abroad, and if he should undertake himself to authorize an unofficial agency, the Secretary of State might be annoyed. He would, however, draft a letter, if I would come the next morning and read it with him.

Wednesday, September 24, 1862. While I was with the President yesterday, Mr. S. brought a portfolio full of letters principally to our foreign Ministers and would not let me go away till he read them, saying he considered me as of their Cabinet Council. After leaving the President yesterday, I went to the Secretary of State's office: went over the ground fully with him; told him I did not think he cared much about my going, that he had said as much to Mr. Blair a month ago. He said he had since altered his mind, in consequence of a communication of an alarming character from the French Minister, which led him to think my services abroad would be very important. He then read me a despatch to Mr. Dayton detailing that conversation, which ended by saying that Mr. Everett and Mr. Weed would probably go abroad. This was yesterday.

Called at the President's to-day. He read me the draft of a paper which he had written as a kind of unofficial letter of credence; excessively non-committal and curiously characteristic. He asked me if I wished anything added, to which I replied in the negative.

Thursday, September 25, 1862. Went to the President's the third time and he gave me the paper signed. He then conversed freely about our armies, generals, etc. Said that nothing could have been better fought than the battle of Antietam; but that he did not know why McClellan did not follow up his advantage. That McClellan was strongly recommended by General Scott as his successor and this, too, after General S. had withdrawn his personal friendship from McClellan, in consequence of his not reporting to him after the latter was placed in command at Washington. The President said he tried to cultivate 'good temper'; 'not to let any of them get mad with him, nor gain much by getting mad with each other.'

To the Honorable W. H. Seward

225 H. STREET, *September* 23, 1862

As I may not have an opportunity of conversing with you in private again, I have thought it might be well to state, in this way, my understanding of your proposal. It is that I should go to Europe for the sake of imparting correct information and removing unfavorable impressions, relative to our affairs, especially with a view to prevent hostile intervention. The mission, if it deserves that name, is entirely unofficial, but it is undertaken at your request and with the sanction of the President. You will furnish me with private letters to the Ministers of Foreign Affairs in London, Paris, and St. Petersburg. It may be as well to add Berlin, which I may pass through on my way to the North. I should like also a similar letter to Brussels. I am personally acquainted with King Leopold, who is one of the wisest sovereigns in Europe, and who, if he is not impaired by age, has great influence with the other Governments, especially that of England.

You have not indicated what length of time I am expected to devote to this errand, except that it is to be longer than was proposed last winter, which was about three or four months, afterwards extended to six or seven. Events may occur in a much shorter time which will make it manifestly useless for me to remain, and, on the other hand, the reverse may take place and is more probable. I suppose you would wish me to stay as long as I seem to be rendering any service to the country.

I expect nothing in the shape of salary or compensation, but I think it reasonable that my expenses incidental to going abroad and travelling and living there, including a moderate allowance for my son, whose aid I shall require as a private secretary, should be paid by the Department. I include among reasonable expenses that of returning the hospitalities I may receive abroad — a very important element of social influence in Europe. If I am able to make the domestic arrangement, which I mentioned in my last interview, this item of expense would be reduced one half.

You will be so obliging as to let me know whether the foregoing is a correct understanding of your proposal, and I will, as soon as possible after I get home, return you a definitive answer. I am drawn by powerful considerations both ways. It is in more than one respect a great sacrifice, but if I can persuade myself that it is a matter of duty, I shall make it.

The suggestion fell through, however, and for much the same reason that its predecessor had come to nothing. Mr.

Everett could not persuade himself that such a mission would not interfere with the work that was being done, and well done, by the regularly accredited Ministers and Ambassadors. He referred to the matter in writing Mr. Adams:

BOSTON, *September 30,* 1862

I have to thank you for your letter of the 5th. It seems a little perverse on the part of our European friends that the desire to interfere in our affairs should be in inverse ratio to our success. They are willing to remain neutral, if we will be so obliging as to go to perdition ourselves; but, in proportion as we are able to sustain ourselves, they are determined to do all they can to prevent it. There have been no important movements since the great battles three weeks ago, which, resulting as they did in the retreat of the Confederates into Virginia, are beginning to be understood in their true light at Richmond.

I mention, because you will probably hear it in other ways, that Mr. Seward has lately renewed to me the proposal, which you are aware he made to me last November (in common with five or six other gentlemen), to go to Europe in an unofficial capacity. My son's death and the condition in which he left his affairs would have prevented me then, had no other difficulty stood in the way. But I should not probably have gone, at any rate. I have been much urged to yield to the renewed proposal, but have finally determined to decline it. In England, nothing is wanted that I could do. The interests of the United States could not possibly be looked after and protected better than they now are by you. Pardon me for repeating to you what I have invariably said to others. The case, I think, is different at the important posts on the Continent, but the deficiency, if any exist, cannot be made up by private and unauthorized agencies. They carry no weight with foreign Governments — are justly distasteful to the accredited Minister (such, at least, was my own feeling when Mr. Tyler sent General Duff Green to London while I was Minister), and, in my case, are not in sufficient harmony with my years and antecedents to require my acceptance.

The President's proclamation for prospective emancipation is the great topic of the day. It gives satisfaction to the radical wing of the Republican Party, though not fully up to their standard. It is, I think, regretted by the conservative wing of the same party, but will, on the whole, be sustained by them as an Administration war measure. When my own opinion on the subject was asked, in advance by a member of the Cabinet, I answered that I thought the matter stood better without any proclamation. Where our armies are in force, emancipation already exists; where they are not, the proclamation will not liberate the slaves; while it raises many troublesome theoretical questions and augments the difficulties under which Union men already labor in the Border States.

To the Honorable F. P. Blair

BOSTON, *October* 18, 1862

... I was willing, though very far from being desirous, to go on such an errand, and on the best reflection I can give the subject, aided by the advice of disinterested personal friends, I do not think I ought to go on any other. Either the position of affairs warrants and requires the distinct and positive strengthening of our representation on the Continent of Europe or it does not. On the last supposition, there is no occasion for my going; on the first there is a regular way of effecting the object, and in no other way can much success be hoped for. In 1776, we had an accredited Commissioner — Silas Deane — at Paris. Afterwards Dr. Franklin and Arthur Lee were joined with him. If, instead of that, Dr. Franklin had been invited to go abroad, in an unofficial capacity, to strengthen Mr. Deane's hands by personal and unofficial conferences, I think he would have declined. I am not guilty of the egregious vanity of comparing myself in any other respect with Dr. Franklin, but I am within two years as old as he was in 1776, and I have filled more and higher offices at home and abroad than he had then. The Doctor, in his Autobiography, thinks it worth while to mention, with reference to the text in the Proverbs, 'Seest thou a man diligent in his calling, he shall stand before kings,' that he had 'stood before five kings, and even had the honor of sitting down with one (the King of Denmark) to dinner.' I have stood before fifteen or sixteen Kings, Queens, Emperors, Sultans, Popes, reigning Archdukes, and Turkish Pashas governing vast provinces with despotic authority. I have sat down to dinner with eight of them and found them no better nor worse company than uncrowned mortals. I may add that I have enjoyed a distinction, which I prize quite as much, which, of course, was not within Dr. Franklin's reach, that of the personal acquaintance or friendly correspondence — in one or two cases confidential — of every President of the United States, except the first. I can add, with truth, that as a class of men they have been superior to their royal contemporaries beyond the water.

But whether in the Government, or out of it, Everett's influence was constantly being felt. He stood out firmly against the disposition of timid men to call the war a failure so far as restoring the Union was concerned. He was vehemently opposed to any cessation of hostilities, and as the men who favored this timid course found their way into the Democratic Party, Everett became more and more firm in the support of President Lincoln. At this time the sentiment for the Union showed itself in the formation of social clubs among Union men in different parts of the country. 'The Union League Club' was formed in New York with the purpose of fostering the Union spirit, and the well known 'Union Club' was organized in Boston. Mr. Everett was elected President of the Boston club, and, much to the chagrin of his conservative friends like Robert C. Winthrop, he accepted the position. At the opening meeting of the club, he made a stirring address, unfolding, much as he did in his New York oration on 'The Great Issues before the Country,' the Union cause, and the great need of pushing the war to a successful issue. The manuscript of this address, carefully and fully written out in Mr. Everett's own hand, has been handsomely bound and is still kept, locked away in a case by itself, in the club library. He referred to this Union Club election and to other kindred matters in a rather interesting way in his journal, as well as in letters to his friends.

February 17, 1863. A meeting of the Library Trustees in the evening. On the way home, Mr. Ticknor expressed great anxiety on the subject of the 'Union Club.' He said it was regarded by conservative men as an Abolition concern, and stigmatized as a 'Jacobin Association.' The truth is that the conservatives here and elsewhere are about as far gone in one extreme as the radicals in the other.

February 28, 1863. At the new Union Club last evening I was elected President. I have been told that the first impulse toward its formation was given by the rude and insulting language addressed to the Governor's aides (who are very gentlemenly men, Harrison Ritchie is one) by some violent 'Conservatives' at the 'Somerset Club.' This, however, I cannot vouch for.

March 24, 1863. Mr. Winthrop called to invite me to his Wednesday Night Club. We conversed on the Union Club, which he has not joined. He thinks the pledge given by those who join the Union Leagues of 'unconditional' support of the Government, in efforts to put down the rebellion, is rather a dangerous one. The word in our Articles is '*unwavering.*' He apprehends some repugnance on the part of moral and religious people to billiards and card tables, and that the organization of clubs is *mali exempli;*—an expensive club in Park Street of little value in influencing public opinion, etc., etc.

April 30, 1863. If the war is necessary and just, why grieve and perplex us with eloquent commonplaces on the evils and sorrows of war in general?

We now approach, however, one of the last great triumphs of Mr. Everett's life, and what may be called his last conspicuous appearance on the National Stage. In November, 1863, he was invited to give the oration at Gettysburg, and there upon the field of battle he spoke his crowning word on the war and the Union. He had been the orator on many a memorable occasion. With polished periods and paragraphs of graceful prose he had held great audiences enthralled. But no occasion quite equalled this in solemnity or impressiveness of scene. His rhetorical career had begun at Cambridge, where in early manhood he had welcomed back to America, in the person of Lafayette, a veteran of the Revolutionary War. And now, when he had almost reached the Psalmist's limit, he was to speak for those young men who had died heroic deaths on the bloodiest battle-field of the Rebellion.

When the tide of the Rebellion rolled back from the town of Gettysburg there were left upon the field the human débris of that awful struggle between North and South. Lee's forces having retreated, and Meade having gone in pursuit, the solemn duty of caring for the wounded and burying the dead was left to the State of Pennsylvania. The Governor of the State undertook the sacred task. It occurred to him, while carefully discharging it, that a portion of the field might fittingly be dedicated as a permanent cemetery for the hero-dead. Soldiers from seventeen loyal States had taken part in the battle, and the Governors of those States, being appealed to, entered heartily into the pious plan of Pennsylvania's Chief Executive.

The work proceeded in due order. The dead were removed and properly buried in a prominent part of the field of battle, and elaborate exercises were planned for Thursday, November 19th. Mr. Everett was the unanimous choice of the seventeen Governors to serve as orator. President Lincoln was invited to be present and 'set apart' the grounds 'to their sacred use by a few appropriate remarks.' The selection of Mr. Everett for so important a function was natural, and almost inevitable. There was no more stanch supporter of the Union cause than he, and in the realm of oratory he still reigned supreme. The words of Nicolay and Hay in this connection may well be quoted: 'If there was an American who was qualified by moral training, by literary culture, by political study, by official experience, by party affiliation, by long practice in historical criticism, and ripe experience in public utterances, to sit in calm judicial inquiry on the causes, theories, and possible results of the Civil War, that man was Edward Everett.' And, in the opinion of the famous biographers of Lincoln, the orator did not fall short of what was expected of him. They could add, 'It is not too much to say that for the space of two hours he held his listeners spell-bound by the rare power of his art.' [1]

The date for the exercises had originally been set for October. Everett, however, was extremely busy when the invitation of the committee reached him, and he accepted it on condition that the ceremonies were postponed until November, in order that he might have time for adequate preparation. This was agreed to, and the 'adequate preparation' was duly made. It included, among other things, getting to Gettysburg a day or two before the appointed date in order that he might have time to go over the battle-field, and get the geography of it clearly in his mind. The night

[1] John G. Nicolay and John Hay: *Abraham Lincoln: A History*, VIII, 192.

before the celebration there was a dinner at the house o David Wills, Esq., which was attended by President Lincoln and other such notables as the French Ambassador, the Admiral of the French Fleet, members of the Cabinet, diplomats, representatives of the Army and Navy, and others.[1] It was the first and only time that Everett saw Mr. Lincoln on a social occasion, and he made good use of it. For he was able to say at a future time, when his Boston friends were emphasizing Lincoln's uncouthness, lack of culture, and absence of good manners, that the President, as he appeared at Mr. Wills's table, 'was the peer of any person present so far as manners, appearance, and conversation were concerned.'

But brilliant as was the gathering the night before, it was nothing in comparison with the impressive scene the next day! Forney, in his 'Anecdotes of Public Men,' says that it was the last time he ever saw Edward Everett, and that if he lived for a thousand years the scene, with all its incidents, would remain vivid in his memory:

> Mr. Lincoln was seated between Edward Everett and William H. Seward on the main stand, and around them were the other members of the Cabinet, and the great War Governors — Curtin of Pennsylvania, Morton of Indiana, Parker of New Jersey, Todd of Ohio, John Brough the Governor-elect, and ex-Governor Dennison of the same State. General Meade could not attend because he was detained at the headquarters of the Army of the Potomac, and the Secretary of the Treasury, Mr. Chase, was kept in Washington by official duties. The procession and crowd were immense, and included men of all parties and conditions. It was a cold, gloomy day, in sympathy, perhaps, with the mournful occasion, and with the hearts of the living mass throbbing for the thousands of heroes who slept beneath the sod. On all sides stretched the battlefields, and from Cemetery Hill the eloquent words of Everett were spoken.

[1] The journal says: At Mr. Wills's. Governor Curtin did not arrive till eleven on the evening of the 18th, and at first it was proposed to put the Governor into my bed with me. He kindly went out and found a lodging elsewhere. Two ladies were put into bed with Charlie; the bed broke down, and she betook herself to the floor. . . . I mention these facts only to show the prodigious resort to the little town.

ιt was played by the orator on this memorable
been cast into the shadow of oblivion by reason
,ummate words that were spoken by Lincoln.
e sometimes declared in derision that Lincoln said
two minutes than Everett did in two hours. But
they ι get that such was Everett's own opinion, magnanimously expressed afterwards to Mr. Lincoln, and that
Everett's was much the harder and the more exacting task.
Posterity has forgotten, too, that Everett in this Gettysburg
Oration was the first to sound the note of reconciliation and
eventual harmony between North and South. Long before
Lincoln recommended acting 'with malice toward none and
charity for all' while binding up the Nation's wounds,
Edward Everett had confidently foretold the time as not
far distant when the bonds of union would again be recognized as having perennial force, while old wrongs were for-
given and forgotten. He could declare that there was no
bitterness on the part of the masses, that the heart of the
people North and South was for union, and that in time
the familiar and beloved flag would float above a reunited
country.

But let us look for a moment at the Gettysburg Oration,
which occupied two hours in delivery, — the customary thing
in those days — and held a throng of people literally enthralled while it was being spoken.

The orator began by quietly assuming without argument
that the battle of Gettysburg was one of the greatest battles
of all history. He classed it with Marathon and other classic
events in Greece by referring briefly at the outset to an
apposite and sacred custom of the Athenians.

It was appointed by law in Athens that the obsequies of the
citizens who fell in battle should be performed at the public expense
and in the most honorable manner. Their bones were carefully
gathered up for the funeral pyre, where their bodies were consumed,
and brought home to the city. . . . In that famous Ceramicus, the
most beautiful suburb of Athens . . . whose pathways gleamed with

the monuments of the illustrious dead, the work of the most consummate masters that ever gave life to marble — there, beneath
the overarching plane-trees, upon a lofty stage erected for the purpose, it was ordained that a funeral oration should be pronounced
by some citizen of Athens, in the presence of the assembled multitude. Such were the tokens of respect required to be paid at Athens
to the memory of those who had fallen in the cause of their country. [So, the orator went on to say, he could not stand] unmoved
over the graves of the dear brethren who so lately on three of those
all-important days which decided a nation's history rolled back the
tide of an invasion, not less unprovoked, not less ruthless, than that
which came to plant the dark banner of Asiatic despotism and
slavery on the free soil of Greece.

What would have been the consequences to the country, to
yourselves, and to all you hold dear, if those who sleep beneath our
feet, and their comrades who survive to serve their country on
other fields of danger, had failed in their duty on those memorable
days? . . . Let a nation's fervent thanks make some amends for
the toils and sufferings of those who survive. Would that the
heartfelt tribute could penetrate these honored graves!

Everett then proceeded to trace the steps in the great
conspiracy which led up to the war. He gave a brief but
graphic description of the battle itself, making the manœuvres clear, and praising with deft words the skill of the generals, the valor of the soldiers, which threw back the invad-
ing tide. Continuing further, he placed the blame for the
Rebellion where it belonged,— on those, 'the disappointed
great men of the cotton-growing States, who had rebelled
"against the most beneficent government of which history
gives us an account."'

I call the war which the Confederates are waging against the
Union a rebellion, because it is one, and in grave matters it is best
to call things by their right names. I speak of it as a crime, because
the Constitution of the United States so regards it, and puts rebellion on a par with invasion. The litanies of every church in Christendom, whose litanies embrace that office, . . . concur with the
Church of England in imploring the Sovereign of the Universe . . .
to deliver us from 'Sedition, privy conspiracy, and rebellion'! And
reason good; for while a rebellion against tyranny . . . is an enterprise on which good men and angels may look with complacency,

an unprovoked rebellion of ambitious men against a beneficent government, for the purpose — the avowed purpose — of establishing, extending, and perpetuating any form of injustice and wrong, is an imitation on earth of that first foul revolt of the 'Internal Serpent' against which the supreme majesty of Heaven sent forth the armed myriads of his angels. Lord Bacon [he continued] 'in the true marshalling of the sovereign degrees of honor,' assigns the first place to the *conditores imperiorum*, founders of states and commonwealths. And truly to contribute in some notable degree to this, the greatest work of man, by wise and patriotic counsel in peace, and heroism in war, is as high as human merit can rise. . . . But if to achieve, or help to achieve, this greatest work of man's wisdom and virtue gives title to a place among the chief benefactors and rightful heirs of the benediction of mankind, by equal reason shall the bold, bad men who seek to undo the noble work, *eversores imperiorium*, destroyers of states, who for base and selfish ends rebel against beneficent governments, seek to overturn wise constitutions by equal reason, I say, Yes, a thousandfold stronger, shall they inherit the execrations of the ages.

The speaker then proceeded to tell how a sad foreboding of what would happen if a war should ensue had haunted him through life, and led him to tread, perhaps too long, the path of hopeless compromise. He went on to speak of the *reconciliation* that must and would ensue.

The gracious Providence, which overrules things for the best, has so constituted our natures that the violent excitement of the passions in one direction is generally followed by a reaction in an opposite direction, and the sooner for the violence. . . . If it were not so — if injuries inflicted and retaliated led to new retaliation . . . then the world, thousands of years ago, would have been turned into an earthly hell, and the nations of the earth would have been resolved into clans of furies and demons, each forever warring with his neighbors! But it is not so: all history teaches a different lesson.

He then reminded his hearers how, after the Wars of the Roses and the great civil war in England, people had speedily come together again. He recalled how the same thing had happened in Germany after the Thirty Years' War and the Seven Years' War, and how, too, in France, after the Revolution, 'Jacobins whose hands were scarcely cleansed from the best blood of France met in the imperial antechambers the returning emigrants whose estates they had confiscated and whose kindred they had dragged to the guillotine. And when, after another turn in the wheel of fortune, Louis XVIII was restored to his throne, he took the regicide Fouché, who had voted for his brother's death, to his Cabinet and confidence.'

The hour is coming and now is [he continued] when the power of the leaders of the Rebellion to delude and inflame must cease. There is no bitterness on the part of the masses. The people of the South are not going to wage an eternal war, for the wretched pretext by which this rebellion is sought to be justified. The bonds that unite us as one people — a substantial community of origin, language, belief, and law — these bonds of union are of perennial force and energy, while the causes of alienation are imaginary, factitious, and transient. The heart of people North and South is for Union. . . . The weary masses of the people are yearning to see the dear old flag again floating upon their Capitols, and they sigh for the return of peace, prosperity, and happiness which they enjoyed under a government whose power was felt only in its blessings.

It was a great oration, nobly conceived, and upholding high public standards and Christian ideals! Indeed, it was worthy of Everett at his best, although he was now upon the verge of seventy, and wearing many of the marks of age.[1]

Forney, who was an attentive listener and excellent critic, said that when Everett spoke and prophesied a time to come when the old wounds would be forgotten and the Union restored, 'he looked like a Prophet of old, and every heart palpitated Amen.'

That he was able, after so great an exertion, to feel the penetrating force and beauty of Mr. Lincoln's brief utterance is a tribute to his sound and accurate judgment, and likewise to his generous nature. Lincoln's famous Gettysburg Address did not impress the Nation at once, but Everett was quick to perceive its power. He wrote to the President the next day from Washington:

---

[1] The journal says: 'I omitted a good deal of what I had written, but was nevertheless two hours long. Parts of the address were poorly memorized, several long paragraphs condensed, several thoughts occurred at the moment, as happens generally.'

MY DEAR SIR:

Not wishing to intrude upon your privacy, when you must be much engaged, I beg leave in this way to thank you very sincerely for your great thoughtfulness for my daughter's accommodation on the platform yesterday, and much kindness otherwise to me and mine at Gettysburg. Permit me also to express my great admiration of the thoughts expressed by you, with such eloquent simplicity and appropriateness, at the consecration of the Cemetery. I should be glad if I could flatter myself that I came as near the central idea of the occasion in two hours as you did in two minutes. My son, who parted from me at Baltimore, and my daughter, concur in this sentiment.

To this courteous and discerning letter, Mr. Lincoln replied as follows:

Your kind note of to-day is received. In our respective parts yesterday you could not have been excused to make a short address, nor I a long one. I am pleased to know that, in your judgment, the little I did say was not entirely a failure. Of course, I knew Mr. Everett would not fail; and yet, while the whole discourse was eminently satisfactory, and will be of great value, there were passages in it which transcended my expectations. The point made against the theory of the General Government being only an agency, whose principals are the States, was new to me, and, as I think, is one of the best arguments for the National supremacy. The tribute to our noble women for their angel-ministering to the suffering soldiers surpasses in its way, as do the subjects of it, whatever has gone before.

The Gettysburg Oration, like all of Everett's utterances at this time, found its way to England, where Mr. Adams saw that it was read by those in power who needed most to hear what the great conservative had said. That Everett himself thought well of his effort, and placed particular value on what he said about the forces of reconciliation, appears from the word he sent to Mr. Adams. In a letter dated Boston, January 5, 1864, he wrote:

. . . I was in hopes of being able to send you by this steamer a pamphlet copy of the Gettysburg Address, but some accidental delays have attended its publication in this form. . . . The address was listened to with rapt attention, by an immense throng, most of whom had been standing for hours before I began.

There is one portion of the address in which I took greater pleasure than in any other part, both on account of the hopeful view which it authorized for the future, and because I have not elsewhere seen a similar train of remark. I refer to the historical parallels by which I endeavored to show that the feuds generated by civil wars are as transient as they are bitter while they last.[1] If this is sound, it furnishes an answer to an objection much urged against the war, viz. (as it was stated to me eighteen months ago by the French Minister) that the success of our arms, instead of leading to the restoration of the Union, would have the direct contrary effect, by still further embittering the minds of the Confederates.

When the Presidential campaign came on, there was a great deal of question in the public mind as to what Mr. Everett's position would be. Many of his old-time Whig friends were making common cause with the Democratic Party and coming out for McClellan. Among them were Robert C. Winthrop and George S. Hillard. These men — conservative, cautious, often captious — were ready to declare the war a failure. They said derisively of Lincoln that he neither knew 'how to make war, nor to make peace.' They expressed the weak opinion that it would be impossible to restore the Union by force. It would be better and wiser, they said, to make terms with the rebels, and let them go their way. With men of this type Everett had all his life been in sympathy. He had stood with them, thought with them, acted with them in the past! And there were many reasons for assuming that he would do so still — among them the fact that he had always thought well of McClellan's capacities as a general, and had disapproved when he was removed from the command of the Army of the Potomac.

And yet, from another point of view, Everett's support of Lincoln was a foregone conclusion. The two statesmen were absolutely of one mind in regard to the Union. When Lin-

---

[1] He was more or less criticized in the public Press of the day for these sentiments. Hundreds of congratulatory letters poured in upon him, but there were literally *only two* which alluded to this particular part of the oration, which to his mind formed 'by far the most original and the most valuable portion of the address.'

coln in 1862 made his famous and memorable statement in
regard to slavery and the Union, he was only taking the position that Everett had firmly held for a score and more of
troubled years. Lincoln wrote Horace Greeley:[1]

My paramount object in this struggle is to save the Union. . . .
If I could save the Union without freeing any slave, I would do it;
and if I could save it by freeing all the slaves, I would do it; and if
I could save it by freeing some and leaving others alone, I would
also do that. What I do about slavery and the colored race I do
because it helps to save the Union; and what I forbear, I forbear
because I do not believe it would help to save the Union. I shall
do less whenever I shall believe what I am doing hurts the cause;
and I shall do more whenever I shall believe doing more will help
the cause.

As Everett never from the first lost his faith in the ultimate success of the Northern arms, so almost from the first
he became convinced that stanch support of the President
was the surest way to secure such success. There was no
charge of 'dodging' now, and his trumpet gave forth no
uncertain sound. He came to have implicit confidence in
Lincoln. He said in his journal:

December 9, 1863. The President's message appeared yesterday
afternoon. A very remarkable document: better written than usual
and calculated to produce a great effect abroad.

While the complacent residents of Beacon Hill, on the one
hand, and the professional malcontents like Wendell Phillips,
on the other, were abusing him, speaking of his uncouth appearance and ill-fitting clothes, and referring to him as 'the
missing link,' Everett stood to his guns and defended both
the man and his measures.[2] He said at this time in the course
of an address:

1 Nicolay and Hay, VI, 153.
2 Wendell Phillips said: 'The President . . . has no mind whatever. . . . He may
be honest — nobody cares whether a tortoise is honest or not: he has neither insight,
nor prevision, nor decision. . . . He is not a genius. I will tell you what he is. He is
a first-rate, second-rate man. He is one of the best specimens of a second-rate man.
. . . The President is an honest man; that is, he is Kentucky honest, and that is
necessarily a very different thing from Massachusetts or New York honesty. A man
cannot get above the atmosphere in which he is born.' (See *Speeches and Lectures,*
by Wendell Phillips, pp. 454–57; 554.)

The President gave ample proof of his intellectual capacity, when he contested a seat in the Senate of the United States with Judge Douglas. When I sat in the Senate with Judge Douglas, I thought him, for business and debate, the equal of the ablest in that body; but his speeches in the senatorial canvass were in no respect superior to Mr. Lincoln's. I believe the President to be entirely conscientious in the discharge of his high trust; and that, under circumstances of unparalleled difficulty, he has administered the Government with the deepest sense of responsibility to his country and his God. He is eminently kind-hearted. I am sure he spoke the truth, the other day, when he said that he never willingly planted a thorn in any man's bosom. He is one of the most laborious and indefatigable men in the country; and that he has been able to sustain himself under as great a load of care as was ever laid upon the head or the heart of a living man is in no small degree owing to the fact that the vindictive and angry passions form no part of his nature, and that a kindly and playful spirit mingles its sweetness with the austere cup of public duty.

The most important objection urged against Mr. Lincoln is that personally he lacks fixedness of purpose, and that his Cabinet and Administration have wanted unity of counsel. I think I shall offend no candid opponent (I certainly am no partisan myself) if I remind you, that precisely the same charge, on the same grounds, might be brought against General Washington and his Administration.

In connection with the Congressional election of 1862 he wrote to a group of political grumblers in New York:

... It is my purpose to continue to support the President, to the best of my ability, in the conduct of the unprovoked and cruel war which had been forced upon the loyal people of the country. A severely contested election in New York at this time will cost the country a hundred millions of treasure and thousands of precious lives; while the union of her intelligent and patriotic citizens on one list of candidates would be worth a well-appointed army of a hundred thousand men. .... We have more to fear from our own dissensions than from the utmost efforts of the enemy.

As election time drew near he held more and more firmly to this position. Many of his most intimate friends, as we have seen, went over to the Democratic Party and championed the cause of McClellan; but there was nothing of the Copperhead about Everett.

May 31. After dinner we had pretty warm discussions, Hillard and Ticknor supporting the 'Copper-head' (I use that term of necessity) and Dr. Lothrop and I the other side of the question.

August 31, 1864. The nomination of General McClellan as the candidate for President at the Chicago Convention is an event of great importance. Although pledged to a vigorous prosecution of the war till the military force of the rebellion is crushed, he is nominated by a convention led by men who are for 'Peace à tout prix.'

He had a great personal regard for McClellan and believed firmly in his generalship.[1] Under these circumstances, it required a great and determined effort to withhold his support. But the times, as he wrote the Honorable Charles G. Loring, 'are too serious to allow us to govern our conduct by personal particularities. The course I have pursued since the war began has cost me some friends, and this last step will, I fear, cost me more; but the path of duty has seemed to me plain.'

He wrote at this time to an ardent supporter of McClellan:

... I fully share your anxiety for the future of our beloved country, in which we have a common interest, and I regret we do not agree as to the best course to be pursued at the approaching election. I cannot but think, under the circumstances of the case, that a change of administration in November would paralyze military operations and compel a cessation of hostilities on such conditions as Mr. Davis might dictate, with the inevitable result of the disintegration of the Union. For this reason, though my personal relations with General McClellan are most friendly, I cannot support him as a candidate. ...

He was naturally pleased to be asked, quite unexpectedly, to serve as one of the Presidential Electors at large on the Republican ticket, and he was still more pleased when he was nominated by acclamation and amid great enthusiasm. That was on September 15th. But other things soon took place that were not so pleasant.

---

[1] He wrote to his son William, September 22, 1862: 'He seems very much like Turenne, as described by Voltaire. "He never made great and celebrated conquests, nor even gained those great and important victories by which nations are subjected: but having always repaired his defeats, and done a great deal with a little, he was regarded as the first General in Europe."'

September 22, 1864. A large dinner party. General Burnside was to have been one of the guests, but sent me a telegraphic message the evening before that he could not come. Mr. William Gray, on account of ill-health, declined about two hours before the time. I asked Professor Lowell, but he was preëngaged; also Messrs. Ticknor and Winthrop, who declined probably from not wanting to meet some of the company. Mr. Ticknor even intimates that it was on account of my own political 'condition,' which, considering that he was greatly troubled at the organization of the Union Club, because it threatened 'social ostracism,' is rather cool.

October 26. Abused as a 'rhetorical orationist' at a Democratic meeting on Saturday night at which my lifelong friend Hillard presided! *Tu quoque, Brute!*

November 15. Some of the first persons I encountered were Hillard and Peter Harvey. Friendly greeting: but both soon moved off. My speech was in response to a toast complimentary to Mr. Lincoln.

There was, however, one more thing that he could do. It was not enough, in the apostolic sense, that he should '*stand*,' he must fight the good fight also; and he did it with a will. He had claimed for many years that he had withdrawn from political life, and stood aside from all party strife; but the call was too insistent to be resisted, and he 'took the stump' for Lincoln at Faneuil Hall.

October 18, 1864. Remained at home all day preparing for tomorrow's labor. The spirit indeed is willing, but the flesh is weak. The burden of seventy years does not fit a man for these great physical efforts.

October 19. Willy went with me to the Hall. The attendance was immense. I spoke an hour and three quarters. Mr. Loring made a short introductory speech. No one spoke but myself. When I alluded to the shipbuilders in England who furnished the rebel rams and called them '*wretches*,' Mr. Goldwin Smith clapped and cried, 'Hear, Hear.'

October 28. Mr. Waters of the 'Daily Advertiser' called. He proposes to reprint my speech in a pamphlet form in a larger type for extensive campaign circulation. He said that a contract has been made with one printing house in this town, to the extent of fifteen thousand dollars for campaign documents to circulate in New Hampshire, a copy to be sent to every household. A. Belmont to pay the bill. What a scandal that an election should be carried by the money of a German Jew (his name is Schönberg), the agent of the Rothschilds!

But the situation had its painful side as well as all the furor and acclaim. While he was speaking for Lincoln and the Union at Faneuil Hall, his lifelong and devoted friend Robert C. Winthrop was speaking for McClellan and concession to the South at New London. Mr. Winthrop wrote almost apologetically for the course he had taken. But Everett was so convinced that his own position was right that he took no offence and wrote forbearingly in reply:

SUMMER STREET, *October* 20, 1864

I am much obliged to you for your kind note. I have not seen the 'Post' of this morning, and shall not unless some 'good-natured' friend sends it to me.

I am sure I have no right to complain of anything on your part, in the visit to New London and speaking there, which you had as good a right to do as I to stay at home and speak at Faneuil Hall.

I am not afraid that we shall give each other cause of offence, and we will not let others put us at variance.

Thus the last Presidential election of Everett's lifetime came and went. It was the most momentous with which he had ever been connected, and he was not only on the winning side, but he was on the side at last of progress, development, enlightenment, justice, freedom, and reform. He had brought forth fruit in old age, and had done much to redeem the somewhat cautious choices of his youth and middle-manhood.

Tuesday, November 8. A rainy day for the election; but the vote was the largest ever given. It was truly disgusting to see the vote distributors of the Democratic Party in our ward — the very dregs of the Irish population. The most unexpected and unexampled majorities for all the Republican candidates. In the evening Mr. Hooper and two other gentlemen came as a deputation to invite me to Faneuil Hall. Mr. George Sennott was making a rambling speech as I came in. When he had finished, and Mr. Hooper reported that I was present, on my ascending the platform there was a scene such as I never witnessed before. The Hall was crowded to its utmost capacity and every individual in it seemed to cheer for some minutes. I was quite overcome and attempted to utter only a few congratulatory sentences. Messrs. Hooper and Rice drove me home. The streets alive with the crowds about the printing offices.

It took a good deal to make a man of Everett's long experience and steady self-possession confess himself 'overcome.' But the occasion and the scene must have been remarkable. The 'Evening Gazette' of the next day confirms the account that has been quoted from the diary. The scene at Faneuil Hall on the night of election was described as 'exciting beyond precedent. When Mr. Rice and Mr. Hooper spoke, they were received as faithful representatives should be, and when Edward Everett, who was called from his quiet library to come and hear the result of the day's work, toward which he had done so much — stood upon the old rostrum, there was an exhibition of enthusiasm which surpassed the wildest demonstrations of delight we ever witnessed. Hats were thrown up regardless of ever seeing them again, and he must be more than human who could fail to appreciate an ovation so justly deserved and so spontaneously accorded.'

The result of the election was satisfactory in more than one sense to Mr. Everett. He not only rejoiced in having Mr. Lincoln continued in office — thus giving assurance of the successful prosecution of the war; but he was also gratified to have it felt that his own efforts had counted for much. This was generally and openly recognized. Many of the Bell-Everett Party, who had been undecided, followed his lead. Charles F. Adams, Jr., wrote to his brother Henry:

... We exult very much over Massachusetts and her verdict. She has not left treason a hiding-place in her limits. I cannot but attribute the unanimity of that result to Mr. Everett's manly and decided course. For the influences which led to it do not seem to have gone beyond the State, and the most surprising changes are to be found in the strongholds of the old Bell-Everett Party. He seems to have carried with him the bulk of his party, and left the opposition only its stock leaders and organ. I delight and triumph over some of the dead in this struggle, e.g., R. C. Winthrop. During the last fifteen years our old Commonwealth has been not infrequently sorely tried. Few of her children were silent when Sumner was assailed and fewer still when Sumter surrendered. One of these few was Winthrop. In our moments of anger and sorrow and exultation, he could not find his voice, or even make a sign: but at last, when the traitors within struck hands with the traitors without — then at last Winthrop found his voice and his strength. . . . He made haste to affiliate himself with traitors and verily he has his reward.[1]

Mr. Everett wrote in an exultant strain on the matter to the Minister at the Court of Saint James'; but he was modest in regard to the value of his own services.

BOSTON, *December* 18, 1864

I received your letter of the 22d November by the last steamer. Chatsworth is a place to see. I visited it twice, once going up with the late Duke from Derby, and once in his absence, but with a card of a privileged color, which procured for me and my family the same attentions from the housekeeper as if the Duke had been present. I am glad to hear that one of his sons takes an enlightened view of affairs on this side of the water. Lord Hartington, I am told, sympathizes with the South, though, when he was here, he told me the North was compelled to go into the war.

The election was carried magnificently, and by a far greater majority than was anticipated. Greeley conceded six States to General McClellan, of which one was to have been New York. Had the soldiers of Massachusetts and several other States been allowed to vote, there would probably have been from 75,000 to 100,000 added to the majority. One of the most agreeable incidents has been the good-humored acquiescence of a large number of Democrats in the result. I lament, with you, that Mr. Winthrop parted from me, for the first time in his life. I have reason to think that he laments it too.

The news which this steamer will bring you from the seat of war is of the utmost importance, but, as it will be three days later than this letter, I will not enlarge upon it.

A malicious paragraph was set on foot by a New York paper, to the effect that my son William was an applicant for the office of Secretary of Legation in London or some other office. There is not a word of truth in it. In fact, it was a falsehood concocted to strike me over Will's shoulders, the object being to trace the part I have taken, since the war began, to interested motives.

[1] *A Cycle of Adams Letters,* II, 222.

I am much gratified with what you say of my address of the 19th of October. I cannot deny that I think myself it did some good. The Bell-Everett men of 1860 were hesitating what course to take. The influence of Messrs. Fillmore and Washington Hunt in New York, and of Winthrop and Hillard here, was brought to bear upon them. The National Democratic Committee (Belmont's) scattered Winthrop's speeches by the hundred thousands. And if that party had gone pretty generally for McClellan, they would have turned the balance in several States, New York and Pennsylvania among them. I suppose my course and my speech may have had something to do in keeping them straight, at least I am constantly told so. For this, however, I claim no merit. I only did what I thought my duty to the country, in a very critical juncture of affairs.

Mr. Everett's support and influential assistance were duly appreciated by the Administration at Washington. Valuable and notable as his help had been, however, it was felt that there were yet other ways in which his coöperation would be particularly serviceable. There still was need for work abroad in England and on the Continent, where the aims of the North were not yet clearly understood. Everett's fitness for service in such a connection was generally recognized, and Mr. Lincoln and his Cabinet were desirous of rendering honor where honor was so manifestly due. It was again suggested, therefore, that he should be given some foreign mission.

December 30, 1864. The 'World' says I am the person best qualified for the French Mission; but that Seward will not appoint me because he will have no one in the diplomatic service superior to himself. Mr. S. has, so far as I know, no jealousy of me: he certainly has no reason to have any, but it is somewhat edifying to hear language like this from a paper which, on the eve of the election, described me as a dreamer and a bookworm.

A letter to Mr. Wise makes it clear, however, that he no longer felt the lure of worldly honor.

BOSTON, *January* 5, 1865
I have your letter of the 3d. I am much obliged to my friends at Washington, who think so favorably of my appointment. I do not myself think it very likely. The geographical argument is

pretty strong against it; although, if the foreign Ministers are generally to return or be recalled, its force will be much weakened. The idea of a special mission also admits of some disregard of the principle of geographical distribution.

The occasion will serve as a test of Mr. Seward's sincerity, in wishing me to go abroad, which I do not doubt. He offered me, you know, a confidential mission to all the great Powers; full Secretary of Legation and Envoy's pay of the first class for myself; to stay as long as I thought fit in any Capital and keep house; an accredited circular from the President, and a letter from himself to the respective Ministers of Foreign Affairs; and when I told him I thought he did not care much about my going, but only yielded to the urging of Mr. Blair, he owned that was the case, at first, but things had changed abroad, and now he wished it, and thought it my duty to go. I thought that, having been a conspicuous public minister, I could not accept what was, after all, a mere agency of the Department.

You will perhaps be incredulous when I say that, even if a special mission to all the Powers were offered me, which would be the highest diplomatic honor ever paid a man, I am by no means sure that I would accept it. If I consulted my own ease and comfort, most assuredly I should not. The appointment would be in the highest degree honorable, but it is by no means certain that I should add to what reputation I may have by the mission. I do not want the salary, and indeed I should spend it all abroad. I do not want to see Europe, where I have passed ten years of my life; I do not want the place as a stepping-stone to future honors, which at seventy-one are out of the question. Nothing but a distinct prospect of doing some good to the country in a critical state of affairs could outweigh these considerations. But I do not think I shall be put to the test.

Tell me what is really thought of Wilmington. I kept your counsel about the powder-ship, even after I saw it all in the New York papers.

If Mr. Sumner has made any overture toward a friendly *rapprochement*, I hope you will not stand aloof.

Everett's days were now rapidly drawing to an end. Political troubles were over. The war was well in hand and approaching a successful close; but he was worried toward the last by some rather trivial private matters. He had bought, some years before, as a residence for his oldest son, a house in Winchester. It was charmingly situated on the shore of Mystic Lake. The house still stands on a little tongue of land that is almost wholly surrounded by water and sheltered by great trees. Just opposite, in Medford, were the Brookses, while Dr. Frothingham and family were not far away in rural Burlington. When the City of Charlestown, however, took possession of the ponds at Winchester, the level of the water was considerably raised and the Everett property was injured. This led to a friendly lawsuit, and the matter dragged along in court much to Mr. Everett's discomfiture. He felt that he was not being fairly dealt with, and he resented the injustice of the situation as well as its inconvenience.

In regard to troubles of the kind — and the right spirit in which to look upon and meet them — he had written once to his nephew and namesake, Edward Everett Hale:

I once read of Saint Bernard that he used to say, if Providence did not send us troubles, we ought to pray for them, to prevent our hearts hardening, and for some time, in our family, we used to call any little annoyance, by way of playful resignation, 'a good Saint Bernard.' I once, in a half-querulous mood, repeated to Sydney Smith this saying of Saint Bernard, accompanied with some remark on the cares and troubles of life. He replied, 'Saint Bernard was an old fool; come and breakfast here next Wednesday, and we'll have some other pleasant fellows, and a good hearty laugh; that's the true Philosophy.'

I do not mean wholly to concur with Sydney, but merely to tell you a pleasant anecdote.

But in this connection Saint Bernard and Sydney Smith both failed him. He was as busy as usual aiding war causes, and then to be called into court and kept waiting till his testimony could be given proved a heavy strain upon his failing strength. His last public appearance was at Faneuil Hall, where he made a speech in behalf of the Savannah sufferers. From there he went to the court-room, and then home to bed. That was on Monday, January 9th. For two days there was no entry in the journal — the first break in a period of forty years. After that occur these characteristic words:

Wednesday, 11th, and *Thursday*, 12 *January*, 1865. A hard struggle against disease and the remedy. The doctor says I have escaped a severe attack of pneumonia. I had a very poor night last night, and Wednesday night I sat up most of the time in the armchair, finding that more comfortable than the bed. Mr. Durant came in the afternoon and prepared some papers. *What a waste of time is not illness!* ...

Those were fitting words with which to close the record of a life of ceaseless activity! Illness 'a waste of time'! The next day he gathered strength to write his daughter:

BOSTON, *January* 13, 1865

On Monday morning I was at the court-room two and a half hours, testifying. I then went to Faneuil Hall, which was cold, and until my turn came I sat in a draft of air. When I had got through — though I spoke but half an hour — my hands and feet were as ice, and my lungs on fire.

In this disagreeable condition I had to go and pass three hours in the court-room. This finished me. I came home, sent for Hayward,[1] and went regularly to work. I hardly left my bed next day. I have barely weathered an attack of pneumonia. Hayward comes twice a day. I have turned the corner, and as soon as I can get a little appetite, shake off my carking cough, and get the kidneys to resume their action, and subdue the numbness of my limbs, and get the better of my neuralgic pain in the left shoulder, I hope to do nicely.

But the 'corner' he had turned was the corner to Eternity. At 3.45 o'clock on Sunday morning, January 15th, the faithful Ruah, an old family servant, who had been an institution in the household for many years, looked into his room and saw him sleeping peacefully. In less than half an hour afterwards she was wakened by a heavy fall, and found him lying on the floor, breathing heavily. Dr. Hayward was quickly sent for, but all was over in a quarter of an hour.

As the news spread, the tributes rapidly poured in from all parts of the country and abroad. The grief was general, the sense of loss was national. It was universally recognized that a Prince had fallen in Israel. Gideon Welles wrote in

[1] Dr. George Hayward.

his diary under date of January 16th: 'Edward Everett died suddenly yesterday morning. It seems a national loss, although he has reached a ripe age. . . . At no moment of his life did he stand better with his countrymen than when stricken down.'

Mr. Seward, as Secretary of State, made the following official announcement:

The President directs the undersigned to perform the painful duty of informing the people of the United States that Edward Everett, distinguished not more by learning and eloquence than by unsurpassed and disinterested labors of patriotism at a period of political disorder, departed this life at four o'clock this morning. The several executive departments of the Government will cause appropriate honors to be rendered to the memory of the deceased, at home and abroad, wherever the national name and authority are acknowledged.

The Mayor of Boston on hearing the news immediately summoned a special meeting of the Board of Aldermen and the Common Council. A call was issued to the citizens of Boston inviting them to attend a meeting to be held in Faneuil Hall on Wednesday, January 18th, at noon. Mayor Lincoln presided. The Reverend Dr. Lothrop, of the Brattle Street Church, offered prayer. Robert C. Winthrop spoke with deep feeling and affection. Others added words of tribute and appreciation. The funeral was held on Thursday, January 19th, from the First Church on Chauncy Street.

It had been expected that President Lincoln would attend; but official duties made it impracticable for him to do so. All public buildings, and many places of business in the city were closed. It was said at the time that 'since the death of Mr. Webster no such general and profound manifestations of sorrow had been exhibited.' Edward Everett Hale conducted simple services for the family at the house on Summer Street. The First Corps of Cadets were stationed in the street outside and escorted the body to the church. Dr. James

Walker, an ex-President of Harvard, offered prayer. The Reverend Rufus Ellis, minister of the church, made a brief address. A special funeral march, written by Benjamin A. Burdett, was rendered at the service by the Brigade Band. As the funeral procession formed and wound its way out to Mount Auburn, the bells on all the churches were tolled, and minute guns were fired on the Common. The college in Cambridge was slowly passed where the great man in his radiant youth had scored so signal a success, and where, in the prime of later life, and wearing many honors, he had encountered troubles and disappointment. The grave at last was reached which had been dug on a sloping hillside in the highest part of the famous cemetery. As friends and relatives turned away, there were those, no doubt, who called to mind the last stanza of the poem on Santa Croce, written five and twenty years before.

> 'Yet not for me, when I shall fall asleep,
> Shall Santa Croce's lamps their vigils keep.
> Beyond the main, in Auburn's quiet shade,
> With those I loved and love my couch be made.
> Spring's pendent branches o'er the hillock wave
> And Morning dewdrops glisten on my grave;
> While Heaven's great arch shall rise above my bed,
> When Santa Croce's crumbles on her dead;
> Unknown to erring, or to suffering fame,
> So may I leave a pure, though humble name.'

THE END

INDEX

INDEX

Abbot, J. L., E.'s funeral oration, 27.

Abbotsford, E. at, 55.

Abbott, G. J., and Webster, 326; on E.'s Cuban despatch, 335.

Aberdeen, Earl of, and E., 188, 196, 199, 205, 210, 261, 263; E. on, 188, 205, 256; at Windsor, 192, 257; and E. and Chinese mission, 232; and slave trade, 236; Queen's Birthday dinner, 246; Bay of Fundy fisheries, 251; letter from E., 263.

Adair, ——, bequest to Ashburton, 249.

Adams, Abigail (Brooks), 96.

Adams, C. F. [1], voyage with E., 36; relations with E., 62; engagement, 96; E. on lecture, 140; and Sumner's election to Senate, 321; on E. and Kansas-Nebraska Bill, 354; letters from E., 427, 429, 430, 431, 434, 441, 448, 458, 466; E. and, as minister, 428–31, 436, 448; letters to E., 430, 431.

Adams, C. F. [2], on campaign of 1864, 465.

Adams, Henry, letter from brother, 465.

Adams, John, letter introducing E. to Jefferson, 31; and Stewart, 54.

Adams, John Q., and E. and Greek commission, 77, 79–81; relations with E., 77, 96; E. and candidacy, 87; public office and professorship, 89; E. as champion in House, 96, 110, 112–15; and E.'s candidacy for Senate, correspondence, 111; and defeat, letter from E., 116; and E.'s gubernatorial candidacy, 127, 129; Anti-Mason, 128; letter from E. on State banks, 140; and E. and Chinese mission, letter, 230–32, 233 n.; on E. as orator, 400.

Adams, Mrs. John Q., E. and party, 80; on E.'s speech, 103.

Adams, Louisa, bridesmaid, 313.

Adelaide, Madame, 162, 163.

Agassiz, Louis, E. and professorship, 290.

Albert, Prince, and E., E. on, 193, 194, 258–60; Literary Fund Society, 197; levée, 198; at state dinner, 215; at review, 246.

Ali Pasha, and E., 37, 59.

Allston, Washington, and painting for Capitol, 113.

Amelia, Queen, E. on, 163, 164.

Amory, Thomas, house, 83.

Ampère, J. J., E. entertains, 311.

Andrew, J. A., E. on, 416.

Angoulême, Duchess d', E. on, 43.

Ann Arbor, E.'s lecture at, 385.

Anti-Masonic Party, and E., 127, 128, 135; rise, 127.

Antietam, battle, 446, 448.

Antiquities, E.'s lecture, 66.

Appleton, Nathan, E.'s circular letter, 346.

Appleton, William, and Kansas-Nebraska Bill, 345.

Archdall-Gratwicke, George, and E., 240.

Arder, Col. ——, 243.

Argyll, Duchess of, letter from E., 366.

Argyll, Duke of, on Seward, 435.

Armagh, Archbishop of. See Beresford.

Armstrong, S. E., and governorship, 129.

Aroostook War, 147.

Ashburton, Lord, Northeastern boundary, 238; Adair bequest, 249.

Avignon, E. at, flood, 166–68.

Babbage, Charles, calculator, 197; and E., 210.

Baker, E. D., Ball's Bluff, 431, 435.

Baltimore, Unitarian Church, 65.

Bancroft, George, letter from Hamilton, 99; and Roger Williams correspondence, 244; and E. and presidency of Harvard, 266; E.'s research for, 309.

Bank of United States, E.'s support, 120.

Banks, N. P., and secession, 405, 406; Shenandoah Valley, 427.

Banks, E. and crisis (1837), 139, 141.

Baring, Bingham, and E., 197, 248.

Baring, Lady Harriet, and Carlyle, 248, 249.

Baring, Thomas, E. entertains, 311.

Barnstable, Mass., E.'s oration at, 396, 397.

Barnum, P. T., at London, 241.

Barre, Mass., normal school, 139.

Bartol, C. A., Kansas-Nebraska Remonstrance, 357.

Bates, Joshua, and Americans at London, 197, 198, 200.
Bates, W. G., and E.'s nomination, 411.
Bay of Fundy, fishing rights, 251, 261.
Beaumont, ——, 160.
Beck, Charles, at Faculty meetings, 280; letter on E.'s services, 296, 297.
Bedford, Earl of, E's visit at seat, 209.
Beecher, Lyman, Kansas-Nebraska Remonstrance, 357.
Bell, John, and E. at Nashville, 119; and Kansas-Nebraska Bill, 353; presidential campaign, 409, 412.
Bellows, H. W., and secession, 405.
Belmont, August, and E.'s speech, 463; E. on, 464.
Belsham, Thomas, and E., 50.
Belvoir Castle, 206.
Bent, Rev. Josiah, 145.
Bentley, William, on E.'s dismissal, 35.
Beresford, Archb. J. G. de la P., and E.'s degree, 199.
Bernard, Saint, on troubles, 469.
Berri, Duc de, 44.
Berry, Mary, circle, and E., 214, 242, 261.
Bethune, George, book, E.'s reply, 28–30.
Beverley, Earl of, 200.
Bigelow, J. P., and E.'s defeat, 151, 154; and Boston Public Library, 363, 364.
Bingham, K. S., and E. 382.
Binney, Horace, on E.'s slavery speech, 106.
Birmingham, Eng., oratorio, 211.
Blair, F. P., Sr., letters from E. on unofficial mission, 443–45, 449.
Blair, Montgomery, and E., 445.
Blenheim Castle, E. on, 204.
Blockade, effective, 431; France and, 436.
Blomfield, Bishop C. J., and E., 199, 200.
Blumenbach, J. F., and E., 38.
Board of Education, first Massachusetts, 138.
Bonaparte, Jerome N., disciplined, 281.
Bonaparte, Joseph, at Florence, 178.
Bonaparte, Lætitia, at Rome, 58.
Bonaparte, Louis, at Rome, 57; at Florence, 178.
Bonaparte, Lucien, at Rome, evenings, 57, 58.
Bonner, Robert, E.'s Ledger articles, 387, 441.
Books, American reprint of English, 50; English reprint of E.'s, 61; international copyright, 443.

Booth, Dr. ——, 198.
Borden, N. B., slavery questions, 149, 150.
Border States, in war-time, 430.
Borghese, Pauline, at Rome, 58.
Borrow, George, as lion, 210.
Boston, E.'s return from England, 263, 265; E. as first citizen, 365; flag-raising, 417; E. and Union Club, 450, 451; in campaign of 1864, 463–65, 467.
Boston and Albany Railroad, building, 141.
Boston Latin School, E. and, 8.
Boston Public Library, E. and, 363–65, 371.
Boulogne, Napoleon's camp, 45.
Bowditch, Nathaniel, and E. and presidency of Harvard, 266.
Bowdoin, ——, and E. at Naushon, 144–46.
Bowen, Francis, on schools, 136.
Brattle Square Church, call to E., 20–24; position, 21, 22; E.'s ministry, 24–28; dismissal of E., 34, 35.
Breckinridge, J. C., nomination, 408; electoral vote, 412.
Brevoort, Henry, Campbell on, 49.
Brewster, Sir David, 217.
Bridgewater, Mass., normal school, 139.
Bridgman, Laura, English interest, 210.
Briggs, G. N., at E.'s inauguration, 271.
Britannia, steamer, 262.
British Association for the Promotion of Science, meetings, 216, 217, 255.
Brook Farm, E. on, 371.
Brooks, Abigail, Mrs. C. F. Adams, 96.
Brooks, Ann G., Mrs. N. L. Frothingham, 75, 76.
Brooks, C. T., and normal schools, 137.
Brooks, Charlotte G., Mrs. Edward Everett, 75.
Brooks, Edward, at Rome, 57.
Brooks, Peter C., and E., 75, 76, 295; and E.'s inaugural, 134; letters from E., 161, 167, 170, 191, 196, 199, 200, 205, 206, 224, 229, 243, 245, 256, 267; and house for President of Harvard, 270; death, 295; and A. H. Everett, 314; E.'s memoir, 369.
Brooks, Preston, Sumner assault, 405.
Brooks, Sidney, letters from E., 165, 292; dinner for, 306; dinner for E., 328; and Lenox, 387; and E.'s war attitude, 416.

Brough, John, at Gettysburg dedication, 453.
Brown, John, E. on raid, 405.
Buccleugh, Duchess of, 214, 216, 257.
Buccleugh, Duke of, 257, 259.
Buckland, William, and E., 203; house, 204; Dean of York's assault, 217.
Buckminster, J. S., death, E. on, 20.
Buffalo, E.'s lectures at, 382, 384, 415.
Bull Run, E. on, 429, 430.
Buller, Charles, 242.
Bulwer, Lady, E. on, 173.
Bunbury, Lady, 216.
Bunker Hill, E. and monument, 88, 143.
Bunsen, Baron von, and E., 57, 199.
Burdett, B. A., at E.'s funeral, 472.
Burdett-Coutts, Baroness, and E., 197, 249.
Burdett-Coutts, Sir Francis, 197.
Burnside, A. E., and E., 463.
Bushnell, Horace, Kansas-Nebraska Remonstrance, 357.
Bust, E.'s, 169, 182.
Buttmann, Philipp, E.'s translation of grammar, 61.
Byron, Lord, and Waterloo, 37, 38.

Cæsar, Julius, E.'s projected biography, 239, 308.
Calhoun, J. C., and Greeks, 77, 78; and E., 125; Anti-Mason, 128.
Cambreling, C. C., in House, 97; on E.'s slavery speech, 107.
Cambridge, Mass., in 1807, 10. See also Harvard University.
Cambridge University, E.'s visits, 51, 240, 244; installation of Chancellor, E.'s degree, 199; dining customs, 244; William Everett at, 439.
Campbell, Thomas, E. on visit, 47–49; Stewart on, 54; letter from E., 68; and E.'s poem, 69; decline, 197, 247; and Wordsworth, 218; funeral, 247.
Canning, Lady, 196.
Canterbury, Archbishop of. See Howley.
Capisthorne, Davenport seat, 262.
Carlyle, Thomas, 190; and Emerson, 212; and E., 247–49, 365; on lynch law, 248, 249; on E., 396.
Carpenter, Lant, E. on, as Liberal, 50.
Carroll, Charles, and E., 32.
Carroll, John, and E., 32.
Carter, J. G., Board of Education, 138.

Cass, Miss ——, and E., 382.
Cass, Lewis, and E., 160, 179, 186; dinner at court, 162, 163; and retirement as minister, 228; and E. and Cabinet, 330; on E.'s Cuban despatch, 338.
Castelcicala, Prince, at Windsor, 192–94.
Castlereagh, Viscount, Byron on, 37.
Catlin, George, Indian prints, 258.
Cavendish, Miss ——, 193, 195.
Central America, E.'s speech, 342.
Chabaunes, Col. —— de, 163.
Chandler, Zachariah, and E., 382.
Channing, E. T., at Faculty meetings, 280; letter on E.'s services, 296, 297.
Channing, W. E., influence, 19; and Brattle Square Church, 21; and E.'s book, 29; Sydney Smith on, 241.
Charles X of France, E. on, 44.
Charles I of Württemberg, at Windsor, 214.
Chartres, Duc de, at Washington, 434.
Chase, S. P., and Gettysburg dedication, 453.
Chatsworth, E. on, 466.
Cherokee Indians, E. and removal, 109.
Chester Square, flag-raising, 417.
Chicago, E.'s lectures at, 381, 383, 425.
Child, F. J., at Faculty meetings, 280; letter on E.'s services, 296, 297.
China, E. and mission, 226–34; A. H. Everett's mission, 292.
Choate, Rufus, as orator, 129; and E.'s appointment, 184, 185; Webster testimonial, 316, 320; and Cabinet, 325; E.'s circular letter, 346; and E.'s resignation from Senate, 362; E. on Lowell on, 371.
Church, R. W., and E.'s degree, 223.
Church Missionary Society, meeting, 49.
Cincinnati, E.'s lectures at, 382, 383, 415; E.'s portrait, 383.
Civil service, E.'s appointments, 134.
Civil War, E. on Lincoln's position before outbreak, 415; E. on outbreak, 415; E.'s attitude, 416–22, 460; E.'s addresses and tours, 422–27; E. and foreign relations, 427–32, 436, 438–44; Bull Run, 429, 430; South and slave trade, 430; Border States, 430; Ball's Bluff, 431, 435; E.'s proposed unofficial missions, 432–36, 442, 444–49, 467, 468; Seward and foreign war, 433, 435;

Port Royal expedition, 435; *Trent* affair, 437; E. on causes, 439; E.'s articles in *New York Ledger*, 441; Peninsular campaign, 441; Halleck, 441; confiscation question, 441; Antietam, 446, 448; Emancipation Proclamation, 448; Union Club, 450, 451; Gettysburg dedication, 451–59; E. and reconciliation, 454, 456, 457; as rebellion, 455; presidential campaign, 459–67.

Clanwilliam, Lord, 196.

Clark, John, letter from E., 87.

Clarke, James F., and E.'s inauguration, 273.

Clay, Henry, on E.'s sermon, 28; and the House, 93; and E. at Lexington, 118; relations with E., 125; and E.'s appointment, 184, 185.

Clayton, J. M., and Kansas-Nebraska Bill, 352.

Clementine, Princess, 163, 214.

Cleveland, E.'s lectures at, 385, 425.

Clifford, J. H., and E., 142, 143.

Clive, ——, E. visits, 211.

Clive, Lady Harriet, 211.

Clough, A. H., 354.

Coat of arms, E.'s, 213, 376 *n.*

Cockburn, Dean William, on modern science, 217.

Codman, John, and E. and presidency of Harvard, 270.

Codrington, Sir Edward, and E., 216.

Coesvelt, Dane. *See* Mazares.

Coffin, Isaac, school at Nantucket, 144.

Cogswell, J. G., at Rome, 57.

Coke, Sir Edward, daughter, 243, 244; and Roger Williams, 243.

Coleman, O. M., and E., 248; piano improvement, 258.

Coleridge, Sir John, letter from E., 438.

Colonization Society, E.'s advocacy, 120.

Columbus, E.'s lecture at, 415.

Compromise, E. and effort (1861), 414.

Compromise of 1850, E. and Webster's speech, 315–20, 348.

Confiscation question, 441.

Congress, E. and chaplaincy, 66. *See also* House of Representatives; Senate.

Conservatism, E.'s, 102.

Constant, Benjamin, and E., 42.

Constantinople, E. at, 59.

Constitutional Union Party, E. and nomination, 408–12.

Cook, C. E., E.'s circular letter, 346.

Copyright, E. and international, 443.

Cotton, John, at Trinity College, 439.

Courtenay, C. L., 259.

Craigie, Miriam, boarding-house, 76.

Craigie House, boarding-house, 76; lead roof, 306.

Creek Indians, E. and removal, 109.

Creole case, 236, 237.

Crittenden, J. J., in Cabinet, 325, 330; and presidential candidacy (1860), 409; and compromise, 414.

Crocker, Capt. (?) John, E. on, 143.

Cromwell, Oliver, Carlyle on, 249.

Cuba, E.'s despatch on Tripartite Convention, 333–39.

Cunningham, Ann P., and E., 377, 378; Mount Vernon Association, 377, 378; letter from E. on war, 421.

Curtin, A. G. and Gettysburg Cemetery, 451; at dedication, 453.

Curtis, B. R., Webster testimonial, 316, 318, 320.

Curtis, C. P., E.'s roommate, 11.

Curtis, G. T., on E. and Northeastern boundary, 189; Webster testimonial, 316, 320; on Hülsemann Letter, 323, 360.

Curtis, G. W., on E.'s slavery statement, 134.

Cushing, Caleb, candidacy for Senate, 340.

Custine, Marquis de, Lockhart's criticism, 245.

Dacre, Lady, 216.

Dalkeith, Lord, at Eton, 259.

Dalton, Mrs. Henry, and E., 143.

Dana, Martha, 146.

Dana, R. H., Sr., and E.'s inauguration, 273.

Davenport, ——, and E., 262.

Davis, Jefferson, and E. and Cabinet, 330.

Davis, John, election to Senate, 126, 128; and vice-presidential candidacy, 250.

Davys, Bishop George, on Victoria, 260.

Dawson, W. C., and Kansas-Nebraska Bill, 345.

Dearborn, H. A. S., and E.'s defeat, 151.

Death, mystery, 239.

Dedham, Mass., Everett house, 1, 2.

Defence of Christianity, E.'s book, 28–30.

Dennison, William, at Gettysburg dedication, 453.

Detroit, E.'s lectures at, 381, 382, 385, 426.
Devonshire, Duke of, and E., 466.
Dexter, Samuel, and E., 21, 23.
Dickens, Charles, *American Notes*, 210.
Diplomatic office, E. and, 172, 176, 179–85.
'Dirge of Alaric,' 69–71.
Disraeli, Benjamin, 190.
Dissen, G. L., and E., 38.
District of Columbia, E. and slavery in, 150.
Dixon, Archibald, and Kansas-Nebraska Bill, 353.
Dodge, A. C., and E., 352.
Dolomieu, Marchioness de, 163.
Dorchester, Mass., Everett house, 4; E.'s oration, 396.
Douglas, S. A., on E.'s Cuban despatch, 338; presidential aspirations, 341, 342; E. on, 342, 343, 461; motive in Kansas-Nebraska Bill, 343; bill in committee, 344, 352; bill in Senate, 345, 350, 352; on Remonstrance, 357; E. on mobbing, 369; nomination, 407; electoral vote, 412.
Dover, Eng., tavern runners, 46.
Drawing, E.'s essay, 170.
Drawing-Room, 246.
Drayton Manor, 205.
Dress, court, 43, 161, 170, 192; diplomatic, 198, 221, 222; Sabbath, at Harvard, 280.
Drink, at Harvard, reform, 275, 291.
Dubuque, E.'s lecture at, 425.
Duckinfield, Sir H., and E., 253.
Dudgate,——, and E., 47.
Dundas, Sir David, 253.
Dwight, Edmund, Board of Education, 138; and normal schools, 139.
Dwight, Timothy, and E., 32; 'triple hat,' 32.

Ealing Park, 254.
East Bridgewater, Mass., E.'s school, 13.
Edgeworth, Maria, E. on, 210.
Edinburgh, E. at, 52, 53.
Edmands, J. W., and Kansas-Nebraska Bill, 345, 353.
Education, moral side, 274. *See also* Normal schools.
Edward VII of England, as a child, 259; and William Everett, 439.
Edwards, F. S., and E., 384.

Egerton, Lord Francis, and E., 197; and Hiram Powers, 252.
Eichhorn, J. G., and E., 38.
Eliot, Capt. ——, 197.
Eliot, Samuel, endowment of Harvard, 34.
Eliot, Samuel A., letters from E., 148, 268; Harvard, and E. and presidency of 265, 269, 270, 277, 286, 288, 293, 294; and college seal, 287–89.
Ellis, Rufus, at E.'s funeral, 472.
Elphinstone, Emily, 197.
Emancipation Proclamation, E. on, 448.
Emerson, C. C., E.'s tribute, 367, 368.
Emerson, E. B., and E., 25; E.'s tribute, 367.
Emerson, R. W., early admiration for E., 25, 62; on E. as professor, 63, 64; on E. as lecturer, 66, 67; and Carlyle, 212, 249; E. on Essays, 212; on E.'s inauguration, 271–73, and E.'s tribute to brothers, 366–69; letter to E., 369; on E. as orator, 394, 396.
England, E.'s first visits, 37, 38, 44–52; E.'s appointment as minister, 179–85; Webster and supplanting E. as minister, 227–30, 233; E.'s attitude, 242, 255; Tripartite Convention on Cuba, 333–39; and Civil War, 427–31, 433, 435, 438–44; Adams as minister to, 428, 448; *Trent* affair, 437. *See also* Northeastern boundary; Search.
English Channel, crossing (1818), 45, 46.
Erie, E.'s lecture at, 385.
Erskine, Lord, E. on, 47.
Essex, Countess of, dowager, 198.
Eternity, E. on, 131.
Eton College, E. at, 201.
Eustis, George, *Trent* affair, 437.
Eustis, William, and Lafayette, 83.
Evans, George, and E.'s recall, 250.
Everett, Aaron, E.'s uncle, 2.
Everett, Alexander H., college, 7; teacher at Exeter, 9; and E. in Holland, 41; and presidency of Harvard, 115; J. Q. Adams on, 127; opposes E. politically, 154; Chinese mission and death, 292; finances, 314.
Everett, Anne G., E.'s daughter, at Florence, 170; illness and death, E.'s grief, 232, 238–41.
Everett, Charlotte G. (Brooks), E.'s wife, marriage, 75; letters to E., 79, 126; on E.'s speech, 103; letters from

E., 123, 124, 142; health and trip abroad, 155; decline, 295, 358: death, 407.

Everett, Ebenezer, E.'s grandfather, 2, 3.

Everett, Edward, *unofficial life at home:* ancestry, 1; father, 2–6; mother, 4; birth, 4; and memory of father, 5; schooling, 6–9; first connections with Webster, friendship, 8, 60, 77, 315, 324; early declamation, 9; enters college, mates, 9, 10; and Kirkland and Ware, 11; rooms at college, 11, 12; Boston visits, 12; as scholar, 12, 13; as college editor, 13; as teacher, 13; Commencement, part, song, 14; and law, 15, 71; study for ministry, 15; poetry, 15–18, 69–71, 174, 175; Latin tutor, 18; Master part, 18; call to Brattle Square Church, 20–24; ordination and installation, 24; ministry, 24–28; Abbot funeral oration, 27; *Defence of Christianity*, 28–30; breakdown, excursions, 30; Washington trip (1814), 30–33; appointment as Professor of Greek, inauguration, 34; dismissal by church, 34, 35; as professor, influence, 61–64, 71, 81, 91; translation of Buttmann's Greek grammar, 61; and Winthrop, 62, 150; occasional sermons, 64; sermon at Washington (1820), 65, 66; lecture on Antiquities, 66; as editor of *North American Review*, 67–69; and residency at Cambridge, 72–75; marriage, and father-in-law, 75, 76, 295; at Craigie House, 76; and Greek Revolt, 76–81; ΦBK oration, and Lafayette, 82–87; and Bunker Hill Monument, 88, 143; vacating professorship, 89–91; Winter Hill house, 115; Harvard Overseer, 115; and presidency of Harvard (1828), 115; trip through West (1829), 117–19; coat of arms, 213, 376 n.; proposed life of Cæsar, 239, 308; and accepting presidency of Harvard (1845), 251, 260–62, 265–70; hospitality to foreign visitors, 263, 269, 311, 312; and international law, 269, 270, 309, 371; health, 270, 292–95, 298, 303, 358, 361, 362, 373, 379; and Wadsworth House, 271, 303; inauguration as President of Harvard, 271–73; and disorganization of college, 273–79, 286; and routine as President, 276, 281, 294; and Faculty meetings, 279–

81; disgust with position, 281, 282, 286, 292; Chapel reform, 282–86, 297; resignation, relief, 286, 292–98, 302; college seal controversy, 287–90; Scientific School, 290; and Sophocles, 291; temperance reform, 291; results of presidency, 294, 296–98; and wife's decline, 295; finances, 295, 313; Faculty letter on services, 296, 297; and colored student, 299; and enclosure of Yard, 299–301; and presidency of University of Missouri, 303; valentines, 304–06; proposed history, 307; research for friends, 309; edition of Webster's speeches, 309; correspondence, 310, 365; and son-in-law, 312; and dependent relatives, 313, 314; and Webster's Seventh of March Speech, 315–20, 348; and Fugitive Slave Law, 317, 319, 320; and Sumner's election to Senate, 317, 319, 320; share in Hülsemann Letter, 321–24, 359–61; and Webster's death and funeral, 326, 327; and Union and slavery, 348, 349, 354–56, 358, 359, 363; library, 363; and Boston Public Library, 363–65, 371; as first citizen, 365: and Emerson, 366; tribute to Emerson's brothers, 366–69; memoir of father-in-law, 369; and Free-Soil mob, 370; period of discouragement, 370–73; final sphere of great influence, 373, 413; lecture on Washington, 373–75; origin of Mount Vernon aid project, 374, 377, 378; tours with lecture, 375–87, 415; public reception at New York, 376; lecture tours and Unionism, 379, 390, 400; portrait, 383; experiences of travel on tours, 383, 385, 401–04; Franklin lecture, 386; *New York Ledger* articles, 387, 404, 441; character of Washington lecture, 388–91; and German translation of lecture, 403; at Jamestown, 404; and secession, 404–06, 413, 415, 419, 420, 423; and assault on Sumner, 405; clings to Whiggism, 407; attitude toward Lincoln, 408, 414–16, 434, 450, 460; later effects of candidacy, 412; and compromise (1861), 414; war attitude, 416–22, 449, 450, 460; political estrangement of friends, 416, 463, 464, 466; and war attitude of son-in-law, 418–21; war-time addresses and tours, 422–27; and war-time foreign relations,

427–32, 438–41; and C. F. Adams as minister at London, 428–31, 436, 437, 448; relations with war administration, 432, 446; and Trent affair, 437; Union Club, 450, 451; Gettysburg oration, 451–59; in campaign of 1864, 459–67; and McClellan, 462; and suit over estate, 468; last public appearance, 469; last illness, 469, 470; death, 470; tributes, 470, 471; funeral, 471, 472.

Unofficial life abroad: and study in Europe, 22; permission to travel abroad, 34, 41; voyage (1815), 35, 36; and Hundred Days, 37, 38; at Göttingen, 38, 39; excursions, and Goethe, 39–41; and Mineralogical Society, 40; with brother in Holland, 41; Ph.D., 41; at Paris, presentation at court, 41–44; journey to London, 44–47; at London (1818), 47–51; at Cambridge and Oxford, 51; Oxford degree row, 51, 222–26; in Lake Region, 51; in Scotland, and Scott, 51–56; journey to Rome, 56, 57; at Rome, and Bonapartes, 57, 58, 178, 186; in Balkans, 58, 59; return home (1819), 60; takes family to Europe (1840), voyage, 155–58; travel experiences, 158, 165–68, 186; at Paris, 158–65, 186; with Lafayette family, 159; dinner with Louis Philippe, 161–64; quarters at Florence, 168; and Greenough and Powers, bust, 169, 182; and Grand Duke of Tuscany, 169, 170; research at Florence, 169, 171: tries drawing, 170; social life at Florence, 170–74: 'Santa Croce,' 174, 175; villa near Florence, 177; at Naples, 182, 183; and English literary circle, 190, 195, 212, 217, 218, 241, 242, 247–49, 365; and Rogers, 190, 262, 264; in London society, 195–203, 210, 213–16, 241–47, 253, 254; Trinity and Cambridge degrees, 199; in English country society, 200–12, 216, 262; and loss of daughter, 238–41; British Association, 216, 217, 255; farewells in England, 261–64; return to America (1845), 262, 265.

In public office: candidacy for Congress (1824), 81, 86–89; lack of preparation, 94, 188; journey to Washington, 94; in Washington life, 95, 123; and Adams, his champion in House, 96, 110, 112–
15; expectation and position, 96, 97; committees, 97, 112, 113, 120; informal maiden speech, 97–99; first set speech, constitutional amendment, 99–103; on right of slavery, effect on career, 103–08; and removal of Indians, 109; and pensions for veterans, 110; and candidacy for Senate (1827), 111, 112; reëlections to House, 112; and paintings for Capitol, 113; occasional orations, 113; and defeat of Adams, 116; and rise of West, 116, 141; and Jackson, 120; in opposition, 120; dissatisfaction with life as congressman, 120–22, 124, 125; and French Spoliation Claims, 125; results of years in House, 125; first election as Governor, 126–30; and Anti-Masons, 128, 135; inaugural, remarks on anti-slavery, 131–34; appointments, 135; and normal schools, 135–39; and banks, 139–41; and railroads, 141; travel as Governor, 142–46; and Northeastern boundary, 146–49, 189, 237, 238; reëlections as Governor, 149; and extension of slavery, 150; defeat for governorship, 149–55; and diplomatic appointment, 172, 176, 179–85; quarters at London, 187, 191; reception as minister, at Windsor, 188, 189, 191–95, 201, 256–60; and Aberdeen, 188, 196, 199, 205, 261, 263; right of search and slave trade, Creole case, 189, 235–38; accused of neglecting duties, 220, 221; and of undue display, 221, 222; and mission to China and Webster, 226–34; success as diplomat, attitude, 238, 241, 255, 256; and vice-presidential nomination (1844), 249, 250; (1848), 355; recall, 250–54; Bay of Fundy fishing, 251, 261; Webster's influence, 272; and return to House, 303; and return to diplomatic service, 307; and Texas, 318, 319; appointment as Secretary of State (1852), 325–30; Perry's Japanese expedition, 328, 331: business as Secretary, 330, 333, 339; Lobos Islands, 331: Tripartite Convention on Cuba, 333–39; election as Senator (1853), 340–42; and presidential candidacy for 1856, 340–42, 353; Senate committees, 341; Central America, 342; and Kansas-Nebraska Bill in committee, 344; and in debate, 345–50, 359; failure to

vote on it, 350–56; and Remonstrance against Bill, 356–58; resignation from Senate, 358, 359, 361–63; Constitutional Union candidacy, 408–12; proposed unofficial war-time missions, 432–36, 442–49, 467, 468; presidential elector, 462.

Views: on father, 5; on schooling, 6, 7; on the Yard, 10; on fellow scholars, 12; on memorizing, 13; poetry: Commencement song, 14; ΦBK verses, 16, 17, 20; 'Dirge of Alaric,' 70; 'Santa Croce,' 175; game, 208; death of daughter, 240, 241; valentines, 305, 306; on Buckingham, 20; accepting call to Brattle Square Church, 23; funeral oration, 27; on Byron, 37; on meeting Goethe, 40; on going to Paris, 41; on journey to London, 44–47; on London experiences, 46, 47, 49; on Poet's Corner, 47; on Campbell, 47–49, 247; on Wilberforce, 49, 50; on Cambridge University, 51, 199, 244; on visits to Scott, 52, 53, 55; on reading aloud, 54; on political prejudice, 55; on preaching and Unitarianism, 65, 66; on *North American Review*, 67, 68; on discontent with teaching and on studying law, 71, 72; on future greatness of Nation, 84, 85; on Lafayette, 85; on candidacy for Congress, 87; on vacating professorship, 90; on first speech in Congress, 98, 100; on constitutional amendment, 101, 102; on slavery, 104–08, 132, 150; on slavery speech, 108; on Cherokee Indians, 109; on pensions for veterans, 110; on candidacy for Senate, 111, 112; on Adams and reëlection, 116; on nationalism, 119; on woes as congressman, 121, 122; family letters, 122; on death of daughters, 130, 238–41; on Eternity, 131; on schools, 136–39; on banks, 140; on burdens of governorship, 142; on travel in State, 142–46; on Northeastern boundary, 148, 427; on gubernatorial defeat, 150–53; toast to Story, 156; on shopping in Paris, 159; on visit to Lafayette's family, 159, 160; on getting court dress, 161; on Paris rioting, 161, 162; on dinner with Louis Philippe, 162–64; on Rachel, 164, 165, 209; on travel troubles, 165–68; on Grand Duke of Tuscany, 169; on Florentine society, 170–72; on aspects

of Florence, 172; on diplomatic office, 172, 176, 177, 179–82; on opera, 173; on Villa Careggi, 177; on Powers's 'Greek Slave,' 182, 252; on Lord Aberdeen, 188; on court at Windsor, 191–95, 201, 256–60; on London society, 195–200, 210, 214, 241–43, 253, 254; on missing clothes, 198, 211; on English society in country, 200–10, 216, 248, 249; on Eton, 201; on seat of Penn family, 202; on Gray's church, 203; on Oxford, 203–05; on Blenheim Castle, 204; on shooting experience, 206; on literary games, 207, 208; on son's precocity, 212, 243; on Emerson, 212, 366; on English Everetts, 213; on state dinner, 214–16; on British Association, 216, 217, 255; on Wordsworth, 218; on accusation of display, 221; on row over Oxford degree, 223–26; on Webster and English mission, 228; on Chinese mission, 232, 233; on position as diplomat, 241; on knighthood, 242; on Sydney Smith, 242; on social burdens, 243, 247, 253; on Williams-Sadler correspondence, 243, 244; on Tom Thumb, 244, 253; on Macaulay, 245; on Queen's Birthday observances, 245–47; on Carlyle, 248, 249; on recall, 250–54; on candidacy for presidency of Harvard, 251, 267, 268; on McLane as successor, 254; on fishing rights, 261; to Aberdeen on returning home, 263; to Rogers on friendship, 264; on moral side of education, 274; on college disorganization, 276–79; on Chapel reform, 283–85; on seal controversy, 287–89; on wineless Class Day, 291; on health and resignation, 293, 297; on wife's decline, 295; on services to college, 295–97; on colored student, 299; on enclosure of Yard, 300, 301; on correspondence, 310; on foreign visitors, 311; on marriage of Jenny Lind, 312; on marriage of daughter, 312, 313; on daughter's baggage, 313; on dependent relatives, 314; on Webster's Seventh of March Speech, 317–20, 348; on Hülsemann Letter, 322, 323; on State portfolio, 325, 330; on Webster's defeat for presidential nomination, 325; on culture of business men, 325; on activities as Secretary of State, 330, 333, 339; on Cuba, 335–38; on election to Senate,

341; on presidential candidacy for 1856, 342; on Central American speech, 342; on Kansas-Nebraska Bill, 344–49, 352, 359; on Union as paramount over slavery question, 349, 355, 359, 390, 391; on failure to vote on Bill, 351–53, 356; on third parties, 355; on resignation from Senate, 358, 359, 361, 362; on Public Library, 364, 371; tribute to Emerson's brothers, 367, 368; on father-in-law, 370; on Walt Whitman, 371; on Lowell, 371; on oration on Washington, 375; on Everett House, 376; on lecture tours, 375, 376, 380–87; on observatory for Washington University, 381; on incidents of American travel, 383, 385, 401–04; on losing watch, 385; on Franklin lecture, 386; on Lenox's treasures, 387; on Powers's 'Penserosa,' 387; on Washington, 389; on his orations, 392, 394–98; on assault on Sumner, 405; on John Brown's raid, 405; on sectionalism, 406; on financial results of lectures, 406; on Republican Convention (1860), 408; on Constitutional Union nomination, 410, 411; on compromise (1861), 414; on Lincoln, 414, 415, 434, 453, 460, 461; on outbreak of Civil War, 415; on war-time fidelity to Union, 417, 425; on son-in-law and war, 419–21; on secession, 419–21, 423, 439; on justification of war, 421, 422, 424, 439, 451; on war-time address tours, 426; on English and French attitude during Civil War, 427–30, 432, 436, 438, 442–44; on Bull Run, 429, 430; on Border States, 430; on Ball's Bluff, 431, 435; on proposed unofficial missions, 433–36, 444–49, 467, 468; on Seward and foreign war, 433, 435; on French princes at Washington, 434; on Port Royal expedition, 435; on *Trent* affair, 437; on causes of Civil War, 439; on son in England, 439; to Napoleon III on war, 440, 441; on Peninsular campaign, 441; on Halleck, 441; on confiscation, 441; on international copyright, 443; on Weed's mission, 444; on Adams as minister, 448; on Emancipation Proclamation, 448; on royalty and presidents, 449; on Union Club, 450, 451; Gettysburg oration: on Greek funeral orations, 454; on rebellion, 455; on reconciliation,

456, 457, 459; on Lincoln's Gettysburg address, 458; on the oration, 458, 459; on campaign of 1864, 462–67; on Belmont, 463; on relations with Winthrop, 464; on troubles, 469; on last illness, 470.

Traits: memory, 13, 392; industry, 14, 38; patriotism, 17, 101, 119, 388; poetic instinct, 17; public oratory, 25–28, 64; 'Ever-at-it,' 30; as minister, 35; as professor, 62–64; as Unitarian, 64, 66; restlessness, 71, 81, 120; as speaker in Congress, 99, 100; conservatism, 102; and controversy, sensitiveness, 121, 267, 359, 361; and family, 122–25, 130; as Governor, 129; and travel, 142; in defeat, 154; family prayers, 158; and discipline, 286; and detail, 294; playfulness, 303–06, 313; emotion, 368; cynicism, 370; as orator, 388–400, 422; shyness, 398; accuracy, 403; formality, 429.

Everett, Edward B., E.'s son, death, 407, 434; house, 468.

Everett, Grace F., E.'s daughter, death, 130.

Everett, John, 2.

Everett, Lucy (Hill), E.'s mother, 4; Boston home, 6.

Everett, Moses, E.'s uncle, 2, 3.

Everett, Oliver, E.'s father, training, 2, 3; ministry, 3, 4; family, 4; later activities, 5; oration on Washington, 5, 6; death, 5; E. and memory, 5.

Everett, Richard, immigrant, 1.

Everett, Sarah, Mrs. Nathan Hale, 65.

Everett, Sidney, E.'s son, and father's tours, 375, 422.

Everett, William, E.'s son, 157; precocity, 212, 243; valentine, 305, 306; and E.'s absence, 358; in England, 407, 426, 438, 439; letters from E., 437, 462; and E.'s proposed mission, 447; and E.'s campaign speech, 463; and foreign service, 466.

Everett, William, of London, 213.

Everett family in England, 213.

Everett House in New York City, 375, 376.

Faber, F. A., and E.'s degree, 223.

Falmouth, Mass., E. at, 145.

Featherstonhaugh, G. W., and Northeastern boundary, 311.

Felton, C. C., and E., 62; and E. as President of Harvard, letter, 271, 278, 296, 297; and Chapel reform, 284.
Fillmore, Millard, character, and E., 329; E. and message, 333; at dinner to E., 384; supports McClellan, 467.
First Corps of Cadets, at E.'s funeral, 471.
Fish, Hamilton, and E., 353.
Fisheries, Bay of Fundy, 251, 261; E.'s despatch (1852), 334.
Flahant, Madame de, 197.
Florence, E.'s first visit, 57; quarters of E.'s family (1840), 168; Greenough and Powers, 169; Grand Duke, 169, 170; social life, 170–74; aspects, 172; E.'s villa near, 177; Bonapartes at, 178.
Foot, Solomon, and E., 353.
Foote, T. M., and E., 384.
Forcolo, Hugo, and E., 49.
Forney, J. W., on Gettysburg dedication, 453, 457.
Forsyth, John, in House, 97.
Fox, G. V., and E., 445.
Framingham, Mass., normal school, 139.
France, E. in, 41–45, 158–68, 186; Tripartite Convention, 333–39; and Civil War, 432, 433, 435, 436, 440, 441, 444.
Francis, ——, and college pranks, 277.
Franklin, Benjamin, and Stewart, 54; E.'s lecture, 386; in France, 449.
Frederick the Great, compared with Washington, 389.
Fredonia, N.Y., E.'s lecture at, 384.
Free-Soil Party, E. and, 355, 369, 371.
Freeman, James, and Oliver Everett, 4.
French Spoliation Claims, E.'s report, 125.
Frothingham, Ann G. (Brooks), 75; dinner, 306.
Frothingham, Anne, bridesmaid, 313.
Frothingham, N. L., E.'s classmate, 10; as student, 12; Commencement oration and hymn, 14; Master part, 18; and E., 75; and Carlyle, 248; and E.'s inauguration, 273; on E.'s resignation, 302; marries his niece, 313; on E.'s Cuban despatch, 338; and Whitman, 371.
Fugitive Slave Law, E.'s attitude, 317, 319, 320; Webster's ignorance, 320.
Fulham Palace, 200.
Fuller, H. H., as student, 12.
Furness, W. H., and E., 62.

Gainsborough, Countess of, 193, 195, 258.
Gaisford, Thomas, and E., 42.
Gales, Joseph, and E., 353.
Galesburg, Ill., E.'s lecture at, 426.
Gallatin, Albert, and E. at Paris, 42.
Games, E. and literary, 207, 208.
Gammell, William, and E.'s lecture, 380.
Gannett, E. S., and E., 62.
Gardner, H. J., and Kansas-Nebraska Bill, 345.
Gardner, J. F., disciplined, 280.
Gaston, William, and E., 33.
Georgetown, D.C., Crawford's Hotel, 33.
Germans, and E.'s Washington lecture, 403.
Gettysburg Cemetery dedication, E.'s oration as crowning career, 451, 452; origin of cemetery, 451, 452; E.'s preparation, 452; dinner before, 453; scene, 453; scant accommodations, 453 n.; E. and Lincoln's address, 454; E.'s note of reconciliation, 454, 456, 457, 459; E.'s oration, 454–59; E.'s correspondence with Lincoln on, 458.
Gifford, Capt. ——, 404.
Gillespie, Mrs. ——, and E.'s Franklin lecture, 386.
Gillies, John, and American edition, 50.
Gilman, Samuel, E.'s classmate, 10; as student, 12; E.'s roommate, college paper, 13.
Glencove, river steamer, 404.
Gloucester, Bishop of. See Monk.
Gloucester, Duchess of, 197.
Goethe, J. W. von, and E., 40; on teaching, 62.
Göttingen University, E. at, 38, 39.
Goldschmidt, Otto, marriage, 312.
Gore, Christopher, and E., 33; Executive Mansion, 83.
Gortschakoff, Prince, and Civil War, 431, 432.
Goulburn, Henry, 199.
Governor of Massachusetts, E.'s first election, 126–29; E.'s inaugural, remarks on anti-slavery, 131–34; E.'s appointments, 135; E. and normal schools, 135–39; E. and banks, 139, 141; E. and railroads, 141; E. on burden, 142; and Northeastern boundary, 147–49; E.'s defeat, 149–55.
Graham, W. A., and E., 403.
Granby, Lord, E. and shootings with, 206.

Grattan, T. C., on Red Line Map, 427.
Gray, F. C., on E.'s appointment, 185; dinner to Webster, 320.
Gray, J. C., E.'s collegemate, 10; as student, 12; and Morehead, 52; and E.'s inauguration, 131; and E. and presidency of Harvard, 267, 270.
Gray, Thomas, and Stoke Church, 203.
Gray, William, and E., 463.
Great Lakes, steamer on, 385.
Greece, E.'s oration, 18; E.'s journey, 58, 59; revolt, E.'s interest, 76; E. and Webster's speech, 77, 78; E. and proposed commission, 77–81.
Green, Duff, unofficial mission, 448.
Greenough, Horatio, and E. at Florence, 169.
Grenville, (?) Thomas, and E., 242, 249.
Grinnell, Joseph, and E., 143.
Guthrie, James, and E., 383.

Hale, E. E., E. on, and ministry, 212; and E.'s return, 262; and E.'s Cuban correspondence, 339; letter from E., 469; at E.'s funeral, 471.
Hale, Nathan, E.'s brother-in-law, 65 n.; and E.'s slavery speech, 108; letter from E., 216; E.'s circular letter, 346.
Hale, Sarah (Everett), letters from E., 65, 98, 100, 108, 124, 125, 172, 177, 203, 212, 213, 214, 216, 218, 244, 248, 251, 252, 253.
Hall, Joseph, and E., 21, 23.
Hall, Prescott, at London, 200.
Hallam, Henry, and E., 38, 190, 195, 242; loquacity, 196, 242.
Halleck, H. W., E. on, 441.
Hamilton, James, Jr., on E.'s speech, 99; and Jackson, 113.
Hamilton, Miss M. M., letter from E., 419.
Hamilton, Sir William, and E., 54.
Harcourt, Archb. Edward, and E., 197, 217, 240, 249, 254.
Harper, R. S., and E., 31.
Harper's Ferry Raid, E. on, 405.
Harrison, Belle, and Jamestown, 404.
Hartington, Lord, and Civil War, 466.
Hartwell, Shattuck, letter on E.'s services, 296, 297.
Harvard Lyceum, 13.
Harvard University, E.'s class, 9; conditions then, 10; Kirkland and Ware, 11; The Den, 11; E. as student, 12, 13;

students' paper, 13; E.'s Commencement, 14; E.'s ΦBK poem, 15–17; E. as Latin tutor, 18; Master parts, 18; E.'s appointment as professor, inauguration, 34; contrast with Cambridge, 51; E. as professor, 61–64, 71; E. and residency of professors, 72–75; E.'s ΦBK orations, and Lafayette, 82–86, 392; vacating E.'s professorship, 89–91; E. as Overseer, 115; E. and presidency (1828), 115; Southern students, 243; E. and accepting presidency (1845), 251, 260–62, 265–70; and religious controversy, 267; E. and lectures on international law, 269, 270; President's house, 270, 271; E.'s inauguration as President, 271; E. and demoralization, 273–79, 286; E. and routine, 276, 294; character of Faculty meetings, 279–81; Sabbath dress, 280; E.'s disgust, 281, 282, 292; Chapel reform, 282–86, 297; E.'s health and resignation, 286, 292–95, 302; seal controversy, 287–90; Scientific School, 290; Prof. Sophocles, 291; temperance reform, 291; results of E.'s presidency, Faculty letter to E., 294, 296–98; E.'s reforms, 294; E. and colored applicant, 299; E. and enclosure of Yard, 299–301.
Harvey, Peter, and Webster testimonial, 318; supports McClellan, 463.
Hathaway, Francis, disciplined, 280.
Haven, ——, voyage with E., 36.
Hawthorne, Nathaniel, E. on *Marble Faun*, 371.
Hawtrey, E. C., and E., 201.
Hayes, A. L., disciplined, 280.
Hayward, (?) Abraham, and E., 241.
Hayward, George, attends E., 470.
Hayward, Nathan, disciplined, 281.
Heard, J. T., and death of Webster, 326.
Hedge, F. H., and E., 62; and E.'s inauguration, 273.
Heeren, Arnold, and E., 38.
Henry, Joseph, and E., 375.
Herschell, Sir John, E.'s speech, 255.
Hewell, E. at, 211.
Higginson, T. W., on demoralization of Harvard, 275.
Hill, Alexander [1], 6.
Hill, Alexander [2], E.'s grandfather, 4.
Hill, Lucy, E.'s mother, 4.
Hillard, G. S., and E., 62; E.'s circular letter, 346; Constitutional Union Con-

vention, 409; supports McClellan, 459, 462, 463, 467.

Hitchcock, Edward, Kansas-Nebraska Remonstrance, 357.

Hixon, J. S., E.'s roommate, 12.

Hoar, Samuel (or E. R.), and E. and presidency of Harvard, 270.

Hobhouse, J. C., and E., 49.

Hodges, C. E., disciplined, 281.

Hoffman, Michael, on E.'s slavery speech, 107.

Holland, Lady, and E., 197.

Holland, Sir Edward, and E., 190, 197, 210, 242; at Boston, 263, 269, 311; letter from E., 406; and Civil War, 443, 444.

Holley, Mrs. ——, and E., 157.

Holmes, Abiel, and ordination of E., 24.

Holmes, O. W., poem at E.'s inauguration, 271, 273; ode, 374.

Homes, E.'s ancestral, 2; E.'s birthplace, 4; E.'s own, 115, 363.

Hooper,(?) Samuel, and E. at Republican celebration, 464, 465.

Hopkins, Mark, Kansas-Nebraska Remonstrance, 357.

Horticultural Festival, 263.

Hotels, E. on experiences, 46, 47, 158, 375, 376, 401.

House of Representatives, E.'s election, 81, 86–89; as more important chamber, 93; E. as Adams's champion in, 96, 110, 112–15; E.'s position, 96, 97; his committees, 97, 112, 113, 120; members, 97; E's maiden speech, 97–99; constitutional amendment on presidential election, E.'s speech, 99–103; slavery remarks in speech, 103–08; E. and Indians, 109; E. and military pensions, 110; E.'s dissatisfaction, 120–22, 124, 125; French Spoliation Claims, 125; E. and return, 303.

Houston, Sam, and Kansas-Nebraska Bill, 353.

Howard, Lady Mary, 253.

Howard, W. A., and E., 143.

Howe, Julia Ward, and Sydney Smith, 210.

Howe, S. G., at London, 210.

Howley, Archb. William, and E., 200.

Hülsemann Letter, E. and drafting, 321–24, 359–61.

Hughes, John, and proposed unofficial mission, 433, 435.

Humboldt, Alexander von, and E., 42, 44.

Humboldt, William von, and E., 44.

Hunt, Col. ——, at Washington, 123.

Hunt, Moses, as student, 12.

Hunt, Samuel, Latin School, 8.

Hunt, Washington, and E.'s nomination, 411; supports McClellan, 467.

Huntington, Joshua, and ordination of E., 24.

Hyslop, Lady, 242.

Ice, American, in India, 200.

India, American ice, 200.

Indianapolis, E.'s lectures at, 382, 415.

Indians, E. and removal, 109; in England, 258.

Ingersoll, J. R., and fisheries, 334.

Inman, Henry, portrait of Macaulay, 242.

International law, E. and exposition, 269, 270, 309, 372.

Inverness, Duchess of, 209.

Iowa, packet, 156.

Irving, Washington, Campbell on, 49; Scott on, 52; E. on, 69; at London, 196–98; English opinion, 212; on E.'s Washington oration, 376.

Ives, R. H., and E.'s lecture, 380, 381.

Jackson, Andrew, E.'s joke, 80; and anti-Adams movement in House, 113; and E., 120; Carlyle on, 249.

Jackson, Charles, and E.'s non-residency, 74.

James, G. P. R., E. on, 311.

Jamestown, Va., ruins, ivy, 404.

Japan, E. and Perry's expedition, 328, 331.

Jay, John, and Stewart, 54.

Jefferson, Thomas, Adams's letter introducing E., 31; and Stewart, 54; and E., 126.

Jena Mineralogical Society, and E., 40.

Jersey, Countess of, and E., 198.

Johnson, R. W., and Kansas-Nebraska Bill, 344.

Johnston, ——, at Washington, 123.

Johnston, J. L., disciplined, 281.

Joinville, Prince de, and Rachel, 209; at Washington, 434.

Jones, G. W., and Kansas-Nebraska Bill, 344.

Judd, Sylvester, and E.'s inauguration, 273.

Julius, N. H., in America, 137.

Kansas-Nebraska Bill, motive, 343; opposition, 344; in committee, 344, 352, 353; debate, E.'s speech, 345–50, 352, 359; E.'s failure to vote, 350–56; Remonstrance, 356–58.
Kant, Immanuel, exploded philosophy, 54.
Kellogg, E., E.'s circular letter, 346.
Kennedy, J. P., in Cabinet, 325; proposed unofficial mission, 433–35.
Kent, Duchess of, E. on, 193, 194, 215, 259, 260; on Victoria and succession, 260.
Kent, James, at London, 253.
Kentucky, E.'s lecture tour, 383; and war, 430.
Keyes, John, candidacy, 89.
King, J. A., at dinner to E., 384.
King, Rufus, and E., 33.
King, W. R., and E.'s appointment, 184.
Kirkland, J. T., President of Harvard, and E., 11, 15, 29, 266; and ordination of E., 24; and E.'s professorship, 34; and vacating E.'s professorship, letter from E., 89, 90; resigns, 115.
Knighthood, E. on, 242.
Knox College, E. on, 426.

Lafayette, Marquis de, and E. at Paris, 42; at New York and Boston, 82, 83; at Harvard, E.'s oration, 83–86; E.'s visit to family, 159, 160.
Lafayette, Edmond, and E., 311.
Lagersnärd, Baroness, 169.
Lake Region, E. in, 51.
Lambeth Palace, 200.
Lane, G. M., Latin oration, 271.
Langley, Capt. ——, 385.
Lansdowne, Marquis of, and E., 197.
Lathrop, John, and ordination of E., 24.
Laurens, Henry, parallel in Trent affair, 437.
Law, E. and study, 15, 71.
Lawrence, Abbott, and railroads, 141; and Scientific School, 290; English mission, 307 n.; at Webster's funeral, 327; E.'s circular letter, 346; and E.'s resignation from Senate, 362.
Lawrence, S., E.'s circular letter, 346.
Lawrence, Sir William, and E., 254.
Lawrence Scientific School, origin, 290.
Ledyard, (?) Henry, and E., 382.
Lehzen, Baroness, 195.
Lenox, James, E. and treasures, 387.

Leopold I of Belgium, at London, 246; and E., 447.
Leopold II of Tuscany, and E., 169–71.
Leveson, ——, on Rachel, 209.
Lexington, Ky., E. at, 118, 119.
Lexington, Mass., normal school, 139.
Liberalism, hide-bound, 50.
Liebig, Justus von, 217.
Lincoln, Lord, 257.
Lincoln, Abraham, E.'s attitude, 408, 414–16, 434, 450, 453, 460, 461; position before outbreak of war, 414, 415; relations with E., 432, 446; and unofficial missions for E., 432, 434, 445; and Seward's bellicose attitude, 433; on McClellan, 446; at dinner before Gettysburg dedication, 453; at dedication, E. and address, letters, 454, 458; E.'s support for reëlection, 457–63, 467; and Union, 460; Phillips on, 460 n.; tribute to E., 471; and E.'s funeral, 471.
Lincoln, F. W., memorial to E., 471.
Lincoln, Levi, and candidacy for Senate, 112.
Lind, Jenny, marriage, 312.
Lindsay, W. S., and Civil War, 442.
Literary Fund Society, 197, 247.
Little, Ezekiel, as teacher, 7.
Lobos Islands controversy, 331.
Lockhart, J. G., criticism of Custine's book, 245.
London, Bishop of. See Blomfield.
London, E. at (1818), 47–51; Petersburg Hotel, 47; E.'s quarters as minister, 187, 191; society, 195–200, 210, 214, 216, 241–43, 247, 253, 254; end of season, 200, 247; literary circle, 212.
Longfellow, H. W., and E. as President of Harvard, letter, 271, 273, 296, 297; at Faculty meetings, 280; and lead roof, 306; and E.'s memory, 392.
López, Narcisso, filibuster, 334.
Loraine, Lord, 200.
Lord, O. P., E.'s circular letter, 346.
Loring, C. G., and college seal, 288, 289.
Lothrop, S. K., supports Lincoln, 462; memorial to E., 471.
Louis XVIII of France, E.'s presentation, appearance, 42, 43.
Louis Philippe, and Paris rioting (1840), 161, 162; E. on dinner with, 162–64; appearance, 164; visit to Victoria, painting, 242, 259.

Louisville, E.'s lecture at, 383.
Lovering, Joseph, and E. as President of Harvard, letter, 271, 296, 297; and Chapel reform, 284.
Lowell, J. R., on ministry, 19; on slavery agitation, 133; E. on, 371; on E.'s nomination, 412; and E., 463.
Lucas, J. H., observatory for university, 382.
Lunt, W. P., and E., 62.
Lyell, Sir Charles, and E., 241; letter from Ticknor, 298; E. entertains, 311.
Lyman, Theodore, and E. at Paris, 42; and Morehead, 52; journey to Greece, 59.
Lynch law, Carlyle on, 248, 249.
Lyons, Lord, and Civil War, 428, 435.

Macaulay, Lord, and E., 190, 195, 212, 241, 242, 262; loquacity, 195, 196, 242; on Irving, 212; memory, 242; E. on, 245; letter to E. on return to England, 302, 303; on E. and historical writing, letters, 307; and criticism, 361.
Macaulay, Zachary, and E., 38, 49.
McClellan, G. B., as commander, 431, 446, 462; Peninsular campaign, 441; and Halleck, 441; candidacy, 459, 462.
McClelland, Robert, and E., 382.
McDuffie, George, in House, 97; presidential election amendment, 99, 100.
Macfarland, James, Trent affair, 437.
McIlvaine, C. P., and proposed unofficial mission, 433–35.
Mackintosh, ——, on Carlyle and Emerson, 212.
McLane, Louis, and Northeastern boundary, 147; succeeds E., E. on, 253.
McLean, John, and E. in Congress, correspondence, 120, 121.
McLeod affair, 188.
McNab, Sir A. N., 200.
Macready, Catherine F. (Atkins), and E., 253.
Madison, E.'s address at, 425.
Madison, James, and E., 33, 125.
Mahon, Lady, 196.
Mahon, Lord, and E., 195, 242.
Maise, Miss ——, 103.
Maitland, Sir Thomas, and E., 59.
Malmesbury, Lord, 196; fisheries troubles, 334.
Mann, A. D., mission, 322.

Mann, Horace, and schools, 138.
Manning, ——, and E.'s defeat, 153.
Mansfield, ——, and E. at London, 253.
Marcy, W. L., and E., 339.
Marlborough, Duke of, compared with Washington, 388.
Marshall, John, Anti-Mason, 128.
Marshall, John, of England, and E., 196.
Martens, Count, and E., 39.
Maryland, and war, 430.
Mason, Charles, 312.
Mason, James M., and E. and Cabinet, 330; Trent affair, 437.
Mason, Jeremiah, and E., 33.
Massachusetts, General Court and Kansas-Nebraska Bill, 345. See also Governor.
Matteson, O. B., 384.
Mazares, Marquis de, at Florence, 171.
Meade, G. G., and Gettysburg dedication, 453.
Melbourne, Lord, and Northeastern boundary, 147.
Memory, E.'s, 13; Macaulay's, 242.
Mercantile Library Association, E.'s oration on Washington, 373, 374.
Mercier, Henri, and Civil War, 436.
Messes, congressional, 95.
Michigan City, E.'s lectures at, 381, 382.
Middletown, Conn., E.'s lecture at, 386.
Mildmay, ——, E. entertains, 311.
Mills, E. H., retires, 111.
Milman, H. H., E. on, 49; and E., 241; on Seward, 435.
Milnes, Monckton, and E., 190, 196, 242; jest at Macaulay, 242.
Milwaukee, E.'s lecture at, 426.
Ministry, E.'s study, 15; status (1813), 19; E's attitude, 24–28, 66.
Mississippi, Lake steamer, 385.
Mississippi River, travel, 118.
Missouri, and war, 430.
Monk, Bishop J. H., and E., 197, 201.
Monroe Doctrine, and Greek Revolt, 78.
Montgomery, ——, and E. at New Orleans, 117.
Moore, Thomas, E. on, 49; at Literary Fund Society, 197.
Morehead, ——, and E., 52.
Morgan, Lady, 197.
Morgan, William, disappears, 127.
Morpeth, Lord, and Kent, 253.
Morris, C. D., E. entertains, 311.
Morris, Gouverneur, and E., 31, 32.

Morton, Marcus, defeats E., 149–55.

Morton, O. P., at Gettysburg dedication, 453.

Moseley, ——, and E. at Buffalo, 384.

Motley, J. L., E.'s research for, 309; on England and Civil War, 430.

Mount Vernon, E.'s oration on Washington, 373; origin of E.'s project, 374, 377, 378; origin of Association, 377, 378; E.'s lecture tours, 378–87, 415; E.'s fund, 379, 406; E.'s *Ledger* articles, 387, 404; character of lecture, 388–91; E. on experiences of tours, 401–04.

Mount Vernon Papers, 388.

Mozeley, J. B., and E.'s degree, 223.

Münster, Count, and E., 39.

Murchison, Charlotte (Hugonin), 249.

Murchison, Sir R. I., and E., 197, 217, 255.

Murray, John, and E., 47, 49.

Murray, C. A., Master of the Household, and E., 193, 194, 202, 241.

Nantucket, E. at, 144.

Napoleon I, Byron and Waterloo, 37, 38; Boulogne camp, 45; popular French sentiment (1818), 45.

Napoleon III, and Civil War, E.'s letter to, 436, 440, 441, 444.

Napoleon, Prince, and E., 440, 443.

Nashville, E. at, 118, 119.

Nationalism, E. on, 119. *See also* Union.

Naushon, E. at, 144–46.

Navy Club at Harvard, 276.

Nemours, Duc de, 163.

New Bedford, E. at, 142, 143.

New Britain, Conn., E.'s lecture at, 387.

New Monthly Magazine, 68, 69; E.'s poem, 69–71.

New Haven, E.'s lecture at, 375.

New Orleans, painting on battle, 113; E. at, 117.

New South Church, Oliver Everett as minister, 3.

New York, E. and Unitarian Church, 64; E.'s lectures at, 375, 376, 422; Everett House, 375, 376; public reception for E., 376.

New York Herald, on C. F. Adams, 437.

New York Ledger, E.'s articles, 387, 404, 430, 441.

New York Tribune, abuse of E., 353.

Newell, William, marries E.'s daughter, 313.

Niagara Falls, E. on, 384.

Niebuhr, B. G., and E., 57.

Norfolk Navy Yard, destruction, 420.

Normal schools, E. and establishment, 135–39.

North American Review, E. as editor, 67–69; A. H. Everett and, 314.

Northampton, Marquis of, and E., 197, 199, 217, 242.

Northeastern boundary controversy, rise, 146; Aroostook War, 147; E.'s interest as Governor, 147–49; Palmerston's plan, 148; E. and negotiations, 189, 237; Featherstonhaugh and, 311; Red Line Map, 427.

Northumberland, Duke of, installation as Chancellor, 199; grand breakfast, 200, 201.

Norton, C. E., on E. and Kansas-Nebraska Bill, 353; on E.'s fame as orator, 398; on E.'s nomination, 412.

Ogden, ——, at Washington, 123.

Oliver, Robert, house, 4.

Opera, E. and, 170, 173.

Oratory, E. and early declamation, 9; E.'s pulpit, 25; E.'s traits, 99, 388–400, 422.

Orleans, Duc de, and wife, 163.

Osgood, David, and ordination of E., 24.

Otis, H. G. [1], and E., 31.

Otis, H. G., [2], E.'s college mate, 10.

Oxford University, E. at (1818), 51; degree for E., row, 51, 199, 222–26; E.'s visit (1842), 203–05.

Palfrey, Mary G., valentine, 304, 305.

Palmerston, Lord, and Northeastern boundary, 148, 427; and Civil War, 428, 442, 443.

Panama Congress, E.'s speech, 98.

Paris, Comte de, at Washington, 434.

Paris, ——, and E., 253.

Paris, E. at (1817), 41–44; (1840), 158–65; (1841), 186; shopping at, 159; labor riots, 161, 162.

Parke, Baron, 253.

Parker, Gov. Joel, at Gettysburg dedication, 453.

Parker, Judge Joel, and E., 309.

Parker, Theodore, and E.'s inauguration, 273; on E.'s temperance reform, 292; and Webster's speech, 316; and Union, 416.

Patriotism, E.'s trait, 17, 101, 119. *See also* Union.
Paulding, Hiram, and Wise, 419–21.
Peabody, A. P., and E., 62; on E. as orator, 400.
Peacock, George, and E., 217, 240.
Peel, Frederic, E. entertains, 311.
Peel, Sir Robert, and Northeastern boundary, 147, 311; and E., 189, 197, 200, 201, 261; E.'s visit at seat, 205; at Windsor, 257; and Victoria, 311.
Peirce, Benjamin, and E. as President of Harvard, letter, 271, 296, 297; at Faculty meetings, 280.
Pell, Capt. ——, 156.
Peninsular campaign, 441.
Penn, Granville, 202.
Penn, Granville J., 202.
Penn, John, 202.
Penn, William, papers, 202.
Penn family, seat, 202.
Pennsylvania Institute, E.'s lecture for, 386.
'Penserosa,' Powers's statue, 387.
Pensions, E.'s advocacy, 110.
Peoria, E.'s address at, 426.
Perier, Madame ——, 160.
Perkins, S. G., voyage with E., 36, 38.
Perkins, T. H., excursion with E., 56.
Perry, M. C., Japanese expedition, 328, 331.
Peru, Lobos Islands, 331.
Peterboro, Bishop of. *See* Davys.
Pettit, John, on E., 342.
Phi Beta Kappa, E.'s poem, 15; E.'s orations, 82–86, 392; E.'s dinner address, 366–68.
Philadelphia, E.'s lectures at, 377, 386.
Phillips, S. C., candidacy for Senate, 340.
Phillips, Wendell, on E.'s slavery speech, 106; and Union, 416; on Lincoln, 460 *n.*
Phillips Exeter Academy, E. at, 9; E.'s sermon, 26.
Pickering, John, and E.'s non-residency, 74.
Plymouth, Mass., E.'s oration, 400.
Plympton, C. H. P., disciplined, 280.
Poetry, E.'s, Commencement song, 14; ΦBK. poem, 15–17; instinct, 17; 'Dirge of Alaric,' 69–71; 'Santa Croce,' 174, 175; game, 208; verses on dead daughter, 240, 241; valentines, 305, 306.
Poland, and Duke of Sussex, 209.

Politics, prejudice, 55.
Poniatoffsky, Prince, at Florence, 172.
Popkin, J. S., Greek professorship, 91.
Port Royal expedition, 435.
Porter, Anna M., and American edition, 50.
Porter, J. A., disciplined, 281.
Portrait, E.'s, 383.
Powers, Hiram, and E. at Florence, bust, 169, 182; 'Greek Slave,' conception, London sensation, 182, 252; E. and 'Penserosa,' 387.
Prescott, W. H., Commencement part, 18 *n.*; on E.'s appointment, 185; and E.'s inauguration, 273; E.'s research for, 309; Webster testimonial, 316.
Presidential elections, E. and proposed amendment, 99; E. and vice-presidential nomination (1844), 249, 250; (1848), 355; E. and candidacy for 1856, 340, 353; (1860), Democratic Convention, 407; E. on Republican Convention, 408; E. and Constitutional Union nomination, 408–12; meaning of result, 412, 413; (1864), E.'s support of Lincoln, 459–64, 467; E. and victory, 464–67.
Preston, William, of Louisville, and E., 383.
Preston, William C., and E.'s appointment, 185.
Prince of Wales. *See* Edward VII.
Princeton disaster, 244.
Providence, E.'s lecture at, 380.
Pusey, ——, 160.
Puseyites, and E.'s Oxford degree, 223–26.
Putnam, George, Board of Education, 138.

Quincy, Josiah, and Lafayette, 83; President of Harvard, 115; resigns, 260; Emerson on, 272, 273; and discipline, E. on, 275, 286; and college seal, 287.

Rachel, E. on, 164, 165; and Joinville, 209.
Railroads, E. and extension, 141.
Randolph, John, and E.'s slavery speech, 108; attack on Adams, 115.
Rantoul, Robert, Jr., Board of Education, 138.
Raritan, U.S.S., and Lobos Islands, 331.
Reading, Scottish manner, 54.

Rebellion, E. on, 455.
Reconciliation, E. on, 454, 456, 457.
Red Line Map, 427.
Reed, C. M., and E., 385.
Reed, W. B., letter from E., 256.
Rees, Abraham, and Wilberforce, 50.
Republican Party, and E.'s lecture on Washington, 374, 383; E.'s attitude, 415.
Repudiation, Sydney Smith on American, 220.
Reynolds, Edward, E.'s college mate, 10.
Rhett, R. B., at London, 243.
Rhodes, J. F., on Hülsemann Letter, 323; on E. in Cabinet, 330; on E.'s Cuban despatch, 338.
Rhododendron, culture, 254.
Rice, A. H., and E., 465.
Rich, T. P., at Webster's funeral, 327.
Richardson, Jeffrey, and E.'s defeat, 153.
Richmond, E.'s lecture at, 375.
Riemer, F. W., and E., 40.
Ripon, Earl of, and E., 201.
Ritchie, Harrison, and Somerset Club, 450.
Rives, W. C., at London, 212.
Rodman, William, and E., 142, 143.
Rogers, Samuel, and E., letters, 190, 196, 198, 242, 249, 253, 262, 264; on Irving, 212.
Roman Catholicism, E. and, 32.
Rome, E. at (1818), 57; (1841), 186; foreign colonies, 57; Bonapartists, 57, 58.
Rothschild, Baron Leonil de, and E., 196.
Ruah, E.'s servant, 157; and E.'s death, 470.
Rush, Richard, Anti-Mason, 128.
Russell, Lord John, and Northeastern boundary, 147; on E.'s Cuban despatch, 339; on E.'s retirement, 365; E. and Civil War attitude, 429, 430, 434, 442, 443.
Russell, S., of Middletown, and E., 386.
Russell, W. H., and Seward, 433, 435.
Russell, Lord Wriothesley, 259.
Russia, and Civil War, 432, 444.
Rutland, Duke of, E. visits at seat, 206.
Ryan, Michael, and E., 252.

Sadlier, Anne, Williams correspondence, 243, 244; father, 244.
St. Louis, E.'s lectures at, 381, 406, 426;

inauguration of Washington University, 381, 398.
St. Paul, E.'s lecture at, 425–27.
Sainte-Aulaire, Count de, dinner, 198.
Saltonstall, Leverett, and E.'s nomination, 411.
'Santa Croce,' E.'s poem, 174, 175.
Sardinia, American relations, 176.
Sartiges, Comte de, and Cuba, 335.
Sartorius, ——, and E., 40.
Savage, James, and E.'s defeat, 153.
Schadow, Rudolph, and E., 57.
School, E.'s instruction, 6–9; E. as teacher, 13.
Scott, Charles, 53, 56.
Scott, Sophia, E. on, 53, 55.
Scott, Sir Walter, Campbell on, 49; E.'s account of visits, 52, 53, 55; and his novels, 52, 55; popularity in West, 118.
Scott, Winfield, and recall of E., 250; and McClellan, 431, 446.
Search, right of, E. and English controversy, 189, 235–38.
Sears, P. F. C., letter on E.'s services, 297.
Seaton, W. W., and E., 353.
Seaver, Benjamin, at Webster's funeral, 327.
Secession, E.'s attitude, 404–06, 413, 415, 423; E. and compromise, 414. See also Union.
Secretary of State, E.'s appointment, 325–30; his activities, 330, 333, 339; Perry's Japanese expedition, 331; Lobos Islands, 331–33; Cuba, 333–39.
Sectionalism, E. on, 406. See also Union.
Sedgwick, Adam, on modern science, 217.
Senate, E. and candidacy (1827), 111; and E.'s nomination as minister, 179, 181, 183–85; and E.'s nomination as Secretary of State, 330; E.'s election, 340–43; his committees, 341; Kansas-Nebraska Bill, 343–56; Remonstrance on Bill, 356–58; E.'s resignation, 358, 359, 361–63.
Senior, N. W., and E., 241.
Seniors, congress of, 249.
Sennott, George, at Republican celebration, 465.
Sergeant, John, and attack on Adams, 114; and diplomatic office, 176.
Seward, W. H., presidential aspirations, 341, 353; and E. and Kansas-Nebraska Bill, 353; E. on defeat for nomination,

408; and unofficial missions for E., 432, 433, 434–36, 445–48, 467, 468; and Sumner, 433; and foreign war, 433, 435; and Russell, 433, 435; *Trent* affair, 438; letter from E., 447; at Gettysburg dedication, 453; tribute to E., 471.

Seymour, Lady, 214.

Sharon Springs, E. at, 298, 303.

Shaw, Lemuel [1], and E. and presidency of Harvard, 262, 270, 294; and college seal, 288, 289.

Shaw, Lemuel [2] (or G. S.), disciplined, 280.

Shenandoah Valley, Jackson's campaign, 427.

Shepherd, Ellen, 383.

Shooting, E. on experience, 206.

Sibley, J. L., on E.'s presidency, 294.

Silliman, Benjamin, and E., 32.

'Sir,' English use of term, 215.

Skinner, J. S., and E., 311.

Slave trade, Confederacy and, 430. *See also* Search.

Slavery, E.'s speech on rights, effect on his career, 103–08; E.'s remarks in inaugural on agitation, 132–34; E. and, in District of Columbia, 150; E. and extension, 150; and E.'s diplomatic appointment, 181, 183; E.'s later attitude, 348, 349, 354–56, 358, 359, 363; in campaign of 1860, 409, 413; as cause of war, 439. *See also* Compromise of 1850; Kansas-Nebraska Bill.

Slidell, John, *Trent* affair, 437.

Smith, Mrs. ——, dinner at Washington, 123.

Smith, Goldwin, and E.'s campaign speech, 463.

Smith, Sydney, and E., 190, 197, 198, 216; on Macaulay's loquacity, 196; on American pronunciation, 210; E.'s visit, 220; on E., 220; on Channing, 241; death, 242; E. on, 242; on E. as orator, 398; on Saint Bernard's philosophy, 469.

Smith, Truman, and E., 353.

Society, Court of Louis XVIII, 42–44; Washington, 95, 96, 103, 123; court of Louis Philippe, 163, 164; Florence, 169–74; court at Windsor, 191–95, 256–60; London, 195–200, 210, 214, 216, 241–43, 247, 253, 254; English, in country, 200–10; state dinner, 214; Queen's birthday, Drawing-Room, 245–47.

Somerset Club, conservatism, 450.

Sophocles, E. A., at Faculty meetings, 280; E. and professorship, 291; letter on E.'s services, 296, 297.

Sorelli, Guido, translates E.'s poem, 174.

Sparks, Jared, Baltimore church, 65; on normal schools, 137; Board of Education, 138; and chapel, 285; house as President, 303; Webster testimonial, 316.

Speech, English unrestrained, 47, 49; Sydney Smith on American, 210.

Spring, M. B., letter from E., 87.

Staël, Madame de, and E., 42.

Stanard, ——, at New Orleans, 383.

Stanley, Lord, and E., 196; Bay of Fundy fishing, 251.

Stannard, ——, of Richmond, and E., 403.

Stanton, E. M., and Halleck, 441.

Starkweather, J. C., and E.'s defeat, 153.

State dinner, 214.

Stephen, James, and E., 49.

Stephens, A. H., on secession, 439.

Stetson, C., letter from E., 87.

Stevens, W. O., disciplined, 280.

Stevenson, Andrew, and E.'s succession, 180, 181, 188; and right of search, 189.

Stewart, Dugald, E.'s visit, 54.

Stiles, ——, of Fredonia, and E., 384.

Stoeckel, Edward de, and Civil War, 428, 431, 432, 436.

Stoke Pogis, Penn seat, 202; church, 203.

Story, H. C., as student, 12.

Story, Joseph, letters from E., 71, 73, 74; and E.'s non-residency, 73; on E.'s defense of Adams, 115; Anti-Mason, 128; and E.'s defeat, 155; toast, 156; E.'s toast, 156; and presidency of Harvard, 252; and E. and presidency, 265; on E. as orator, 400.

Sullivan, Richard, clerk of Brattle Square Church, 21.

Sumner, Charles, and James, 311; E. and election to Senate, 320; and E. and Cabinet, 327, 330; letter to E., 330; on E.'s Kansas-Nebraska speech, 350; letters from E., 355; on E.'s Washington oration, 374; assault on, 405; and wartime foreign affairs, 427; and Seward, 432, 433, 435; and Wise, 468.

Surplus revenue, use in Massachusetts, 136.

Sussex, Duke of, and Poland, 209.

Sutherland, Duchess of, and E., 210, 214.
Sutherland, Duke of, and E., 198, 214; E.'s visit at seat, 208, 209.
Swain, W. W., and E., summer home, 144–46.
Swift, Capt.(?) Elijah, 145.
Switzerland, E. in, 57.
Syon House, Northumberland's seat, 200, 201.

Tagore, Dwarkananth, 200.
Talbot, Fox, 217.
Talfourd, Sir T. N., 197.
Tappan, H. P., and E., 385.
Tariff, E.'s support, 120; and secession, 439.
Taunton, Mass., E.'s lecture at, 405.
Taylor, Capt. ——, on Seward, 435.
Taylor, Henry, and E., 197, 198.
Taylor, Zachary, and E., 307; Mann's mission, 321.
Texas, E. and annexation, 318, 319.
Theater, Campbell on American, 49; E. on Rachel, 165.
Third parties, E. on, 355.
Thorndike, ——, and E. at Paris, 186.
Thorwaldsen, Bertel, and E., 57.
Ticknor, George, voyage with E., 36; at Göttingen, 38, 39, 41; at Rome, 57; and visit to Greece, 58; letter from Story, 115; on E. and presidency of Harvard, 267, 298; Webster testimonial, 316, 320; and death of Webster, 326; and E.'s resignation from Senate, 362; and Public Library, 365, 371; and E.'s war attitude, 416; and Union Club, 450; supports McClellan, 462, 463.
Tilestone, John, as teacher, 7.
Tod, David, at Gettysburg dedication, 453.
Tom Thumb, General, at London, 241, 244, 253, 258.
Torrey, H. W., at Faculty meetings, 280.
Transcendentalists, Carlisle and, 249; E. and Emerson, 366.
Travel, stage-coach, 31; French diligences, 44, 56; across the Channel, 45, 186; English coaches, 47, 56; Boston to Washington (1825), 94; western river, 118, 383; experiences of European (1840), 158, 165–68; Great Lakes, 385; E. on experiences in the fifties, 401–04.
Trent affair, 437.

Trentham Hall, 208, 209.
Trescot, W. H., letter from E., 335.
Trevelyan, C. E., and E., 195.
Trevelyan, Sir G. O., on Macaulay and criticism, 361.
Trinity College, Cambridge, Master of. See Whewell.
Trinity College, Dublin, E.'s degree, 199.
Trollope, Frances, and E., 173, 174.
Troy, E.'s lecture at, 384.
Trubetskoi, Prince, at Florence, 169.
Tuscany, Grand Duke of. See Leopold II.
Tuscany, American relations, 176.
Tyler, John, and diplomatic appointments, 180; and E. and Chinese mission, 226, 232; and Webster, 227–29, 234 n.; and slave trade, 235; travel with E., 404.

Union, E. and paramount condition, 119, 349, 354, 358; and E.'s lecture tours, 379, 390, 400; Constitutional Union Party, 408, 409; vindication of E.'s attitude, 416; E. and war-time fidelity, 417, 425; agency theory, 458; Lincoln on, as paramount, 460. See also Secession.
Union Club, E. and organization, 450, 451.
Unitarianism, early stage, 19, 24; E. and, 64, 66; Baltimore church, 65; and Harvard, 267.
United States, E.'s proposed history, 308.
University of Michigan, E. on, 385.
University of Missouri, E. and presidency, 303.
University of Virginia, E.'s lecture at, 404.
Upham, C. W., and E., 143.
Upshur, A. P., letter from E., 235; killed, 244.
Upton, ——, and E., 144.
Urquhart, ——, at Florence, 168.
Utica, E.'s lecture at, 384.

Valentines, E.'s, 304–06.
Van Buren, Martin, and E., 120, 125; and Northeastern boundary, 147, 148.
Van Rensselaer, Mrs. Stephen, on E.'s speech, 103.
Vaughan, Sir Charles, and Northeastern boundary, 147.
Venice, E. at, 57.

Victoria of England, receives E., 191, 193; court at Windsor, 191–95, 256–60; state dinner, 214; and Tom Thumb, 241, 244, 258; birthday observance, Drawing-Room, 245–47; and knowledge of succession, 260; and Peel, 311.
Villa Careggi, E.'s quarters, 177.
Villiers, Lady Clementina, 198.

Wade, B. F., and E., 353.
Wadsworth House, E. at, 271, 303.
Wainwright, J. M., officiates at marriage of Jenny Lind, 312.
Walker, James, Commencement part, 18 n.; and E. as President of Harvard, letter, 270, 271, 278, 294, 296, 297; at Faculty meetings, 280; and Chapel reform, 284; and college seal, 288, 289; at E.'s funeral, 472.
Walley, S. H., and Kansas-Nebraska Bill, 345.
Waltham, Mass., E. lecture at, 406.
Ward, ——, and E.'s inauguration, 273.
Ward, Mrs. S. G., and Jenny Lind, 312; culture, 325.
Ward, T. W., dinner, 325.
Ward, William G., and E.'s degree, 223.
Ward, William J., letter from E., 87.
Ware, Henry [1], influence on E., sermon system, 11.
Ware, Henry [2], on E. as minister, 26; on Bethune's book, 28, 29; ΦBK poem, 84.
Ware, John, and students, 278.
Warren, C. H., and E., 143; and Webster, 320.
Warren, J. C., as E.'s physician, 270, 293, 358, 361.
Washburn, Emory, E.'s circular letter, 346.
Washington, George, Oliver Everett's oration, 5, 6; manuscript of Farewell Address, 387. See also Mount Vernon.
Washington, J. A., and Mount Vernon Association, 378.
Washington, D.C., E.'s trip (1814), 32, 33; E.'s sermon at Capitol, 65, 66; in 1825, 95; social life, 103, 123; paintings for Capitol, 113; and E.'s lecture on Washington, 375.
Washington University, E.'s address, 381, 398; observatory, 381, 382.
Waterloo, Byron on, 37, 38; treachery, 45.

Waters, E. F., and E.'s campaign speech, 463.
Wayne, Mrs. J. M., E. on, 123.
Webb, Nathan, disciplined, 280.
Webber, Samuel, President of Harvard, 11.
Webster, Daniel, teaches E., 8; E.'s friendship, 8, 60, 77, 315, 324; and E. and Greeks, speech, 77–81; and interest in topics, 78; letters to E., 78, 81, 130, 179, 230, 237, 318 n.; and E.'s candidacy for House, 81; own candidacy, 88; in House, 97; candidacy for Senate, 111, 112; McLean's belittlement, 121; in Washington society, 123; on death of E.'s daughter, 130; on E.'s inaugural, 134; dinner (1836), 142; letters from E., 176, 180, 228, 281, 309, 317, 318, 325; and E.'s diplomatic appointment, 176, 177, 179, 180, 184; finances and office, 180; Northeastern boundary, 189, 237; and Tyler, 227–29, 234 n.; Chinese mission and supplanting E., 227–30, 233; and E.'s return home, 263; and E. and presidency of Harvard, 269, 271–73, 302; Emerson on E. and, 272; and E.'s return to House, 303; E.'s edition of speeches, 309; Seventh of March Speech, inspired testimonial, E.'s attitude, 315–20, 348; and Fugitive Slave Bill, 320; and E. as successor in Cabinet, 325; E. and Hülsemann Letter, 321–24, 359–61; defeat for presidential nomination, E. on, 325; death and funeral, 326, 327; Lobos Islands, 331, 332.
Webster, Edward, in Europe, 166.
Webster, Ezekiel, school, 8.
Webster, Fletcher, father's clerk, 181; and E. and Hülsemann Letter, 360; E. and regiment, 421.
Webster, J. W., E.'s classmate, 10.
Weed, Thurlow, on E.'s display, 221, 222; unofficial mission, 435, 444.
Weller, J. B., and E. and Cabinet, 330.
Welles, Gideon, tribute to E., 470.
Wellington, Duke of, Waterloo, 37, 38; and Northeastern boundary, 147; and E., 190, 199, 262; at review, 246.
West, E. and development, 116, 141; E.'s trip (1829), 117–19; E. on, 381, 426, 429.
West Newton, Mass., normal school, 139.
Western Railroad Corporation, 141.

Westfield, Mass., normal school, 139; and E.'s defeat, 153.
Westminster Abby, E. on Poet's Corner, 47.
Whateley, Richard, E. on, 210.
Wheaton, Henry, and official duties, 254.
Wheeling, E.'s lecture at, 415.
Whewell, William, and E., 190, 196, 244, 254; and William Everett, 439.
Whig Party, victory (1840), E. and office, 172, 176; dissensions, 180; E. and disintegration, 407.
Whipple, E. P., on E. as orator, 399.
Whipple, Thomas, on E.'s slavery speech, 106.
Whist, E. and, 194, 215.
Whitcomb, A. C., disciplined, 280.
White, A. D., on E. as orator, 394.
White, D. A., and E. as President of Harvard, 279.
Whitman, Walt, E. on, 371.
Whittemore, J. M., letter from E., 87.
Whittier, J. G., on E. on slavery, 134.
Wilberforce, William, E. on, 49, 50.
Wilkes, John, Trent affair, 437.
Williams, Miss ——, and E., 47.
Williams, Beverly, and Harvard, 299.
Williams, Roger, Sadlier correspondence, 243, 244; and Coke, 243.
Wills, David, and E., 453.
Wilmot, Barbarina, 216.
Windsor Castle, E. on court at, 191–95, 201, 256–60.
Winterhalter, F. X., royal painting, 259.
Winthrop, R. C., and E., 62, 150; letters from E., 150, 152, 160, 221, 223, 233, 236, 250, 317, 333, 356, 357, 361, 362,

405, 464; and E. and candidacy (1844), 249; and recall of E., 250; at E.'s inauguration, 271, 273; and Senate, 340; E.'s circular letter, 346; and E.'s resignation from Senate, 362; and E.'s war attitude, 416, 464; proposed unofficial mission, 433–35; and Union Club, 450; supports McClellan, 459, 463–67; memorial to E., 471.
Wise, Charlotte (Everett), E.'s daughter, illness abroad, 166, 167; at Florence, 172; letters from E., 304, 341, 358, 375, 380, 381–87, 410, 419, 426, 470; marriage, 312, 313; at Gettysburg dedication, 453 n., 458.
Wise, G. D., and E., 426.
Wise, H. A., marriage, and E., 312, 313; letters from E., 324 n., 342, 359, 376, 420, 467; E. and war attitude, 418–21; and destruction of Norfolk Navy Yard, 420; war letters in England, 430.
Wiswall's Den, 12.
Woburn Abbey, E. on, 209, 210.
Wolff, ——, and E., 40.
Woolsey, T. D., Kansas-Nebraska Remonstrance, 357.
Worcester, J. E., letter from E., 121.
Wordsworth, William, and E., 190, 196, 197, 217–19; at court, 218.
Wylde, Col. ——, 259.
Wyman, Morrill, attends Mrs. Everett, 295.

Yellow Springs, Ohio, E. at, 119.
York, Archbishop of. See Harcourt.
York, Dean of. See Cockburn.

Zetland, Lady, and E., 243.